HOW TO USE THIS GUIDE

■ How it Is Organized

This book is organized into the following geographical areas: Africa, Asia, Europe, Pacific Region, Canada, Caribbean, Latin America and United States. Each area is organized alphabetically by country and, within each country, alphabetically by state (or province) and city, or just by city.

SAMPLE LISTING

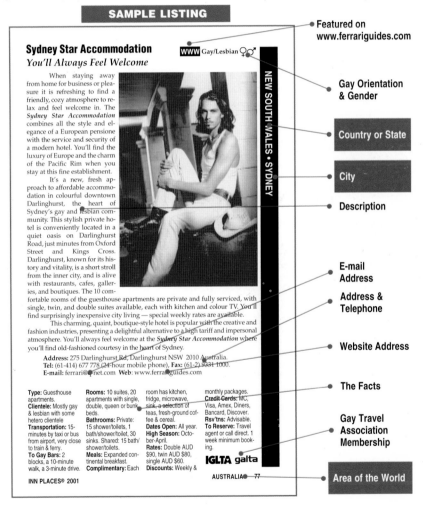

Featured on
www.ferrariguides.com

Gay Orientation
& Gender

Country or State

City

Description

E-mail
Address

Address &
Telephone

Website Address

The Facts

Gay Travel
Association
Membership

Area of the World

Sydney Star Accommodation
You'll Always Feel Welcome

WWW Gay/Lesbian

NEW SOUTH WALES • SYDNEY

When staying away from home for business or pleasure it is refreshing to find a friendly, cozy atmosphere to relax and feel welcome in. The *Sydney Star Accommodation* combines all the style and elegance of a European pensione with the service and security of a modern hotel. You'll find the luxury of Europe and the charm of the Pacific Rim when you stay at this fine establishment.

It's a new, fresh approach to affordable accommodation in colourful downtown Darlinghurst, the heart of Sydney's gay and lesbian community. This stylish private hotel is conveniently located in a quiet oasis on Darlinghurst Road, just minutes from Oxford Street and Kings Cross. Darlinghurst, known for its history and vitality, is a short stroll from the inner city, and is alive with restaurants, cafes, galleries, and boutiques. The 10 comfortable rooms of the guesthouse apartments are private and fully serviced, with single, twin, and double suites available, each with kitchen and colour TV. You'll find surprisingly inexpensive city living — special weekly rates are available.

This charming, quaint, boutique-style hotel is popular with the creative and fashion industries, presenting a delightful alternative to a high tariff and impersonal atmosphere. You'll always feel welcome at the *Sydney Star Accommodation* where you'll find old-fashioned courtesy in the heart of Sydney.

Address: 275 Darlinghurst Rd, Darlinghurst NSW 2010 Australia.
Tel: (61-414) 677 778 (24-hour mobile phone), **Fax:** (61-2) 9331 1000.
E-mail: ferrari@net.com **Web:** www.ferrariguides.com

Type: Guesthouse apartments.
Clientele: Mostly gay & lesbian with some hetero clientele
Transportation: 15-minutes by taxi or bus from airport, very close to train & ferry.
To Gay Bars: 2 blocks, a 10-minute walk, a 3-minute drive.

Rooms: 10 suites, 20 apartments with single, double, queen or bunk beds.
Bathrooms: Private: 15 shower/toilets, 1 bath/shower/toilet, 30 sinks. Shared: 15 bath/ shower/toilets.
Meals: Expanded continental breakfast.
Complimentary: Each

room has kitchen, fridge, microwave, sink, a selection of teas, fresh-ground coffee & cereal.
Dates Open: All year. **High Season:** October-April.
Rates: Double AUD $90, twin AUD $80, single AUD $60.
Discounts: Weekly &

monthly packages.
Credit Cards: MC, Visa, Amex, Diners, Bancard, Discover.
Rsv'tns: Advisable.
To Reserve: Travel agent or call direct. 1 week minimum booking.

IGLTA galta

INN PLACES® 2001

AUSTRALIA 77

Continued on Page 446

W9-CJE-166

Inn Places® 2001

13th Edition

Published by
Ferrari International Publishing, Inc.
PO Box 37887
Phoenix, AZ 85069 USA
Tel: (602) 863-2408
Fax: (602) 439-3952
E-mail: ferrari@q-net.com
Web: www.ferrariguides.com

Published
January 2001

Inn Places is a registered trademark of Ferrari International Publishing, Inc.

Ferrari, Marianne
Inn Places 2001

Includes index
ISBN 0-942586-71-9

Special Sales
Purchases of 10+ copies of any combination of Ferrari Guides can be made at special discounts by businesses and organizations.

Printed in the United States of America

FERRARI GUIDES™

CONTENTS

INTRODUCTION

COLOR SECTION

WORLDWIDE LISTINGS

INDICES

INDEX TO COLOR SECTION

Featured Inns

Manor House Boutique Hotel

The Ultimate in Gay Boutique Hotels

Experience the finest gay and lesbian accommodation Sydney has to offer at *The Manor House,* an historic heritage residence in the heart of the city's premier entertainment district. Mr. Edward Riley, the first Lord Mayor of Sydney, originally built the Manor House in 1850. The property was, and still is, one of the most prestigious houses of its time. The hotel is ideally situated less than two minutes' walk from Oxford Street, less than five minutes' walk from the new Fox Studios, and even the central business district is a short stroll through Hyde Park.

The Manor House is comprised of 24 elegantly appointed rooms, all with ensuites and some with spa baths. All rooms have TV and video, personal safes, irons and boards, and complimentary tea and coffee facilities. Most rooms contain reverse cycle air-conditioning and luxurious king- or queen-sized beds. "Lush" restaurant is located on the ground floor, along with our "Club" bar. A large glass atrium covers the courtyard restaurant and pool area, creating an intimate and relaxing atmosphere. "Lush" caters for dinners of up to 80, and cocktail functions for up to 150 guests. An ideal venue for that 21st birthday, anniversary, product launch, or commitment ceremony!

Address: 86 Flinders St, Darlinghurst, Sydney, NSW 2010, Australia
Tel: (61-2) 9380 6633, **Fax:** (61-2) 9380 5016.
E-mail: info@manorhouse.com.au **Web:** http://www.manorhouse.com.au

Type: Hotel with restaurant & bar.
Clientele: Mostly men with women welcome
Transportation: Taxi, car or bus.
To Gay Bars: 300 metres to Oxford St.
Rooms: 24 rooms, 6 serviced apartments.
Baths: All private.
Meals: Continental buffet breakfast.

Vegetarian: Nearby.
Complimentary: Tea & coffee.
High Season: Feb & Oct.
Rates: Standard AUD $120, deluxe AUD $160, superior AUD $210.
Credit Cards: MC, Visa, Amex, Diners, Bancard.
Rsv'tns: Usually required.
Reserve Thru: Travel agent or call direct.
Min. Stay: 1 week minimum

required during high season.
Parking: Limited off-street parking.
In-Room: Color TV, VCR, phone, coffee & tea makers, fridge, mini bar, electronic safe, hair dryers. Deluxe & superior rms: AC, king beds.
On-Premises: Video tape & CD libraries.
Exercise/Health: Nearby gym.
Swimming: Pool, ocean

nearby.
Sunbathing: Poolside & at beach.
Smoking: Permitted.
Pets: Not permitted.
Children: No.
Languages: English, Chinese.
Your Hosts: Mark Magennis & Collon Dearman.
galta **IGLTA**

See Our Listing Under Sydney, New South Wales, Australia

Cooper Island Beach Club

Gay-Friendly ⚥

A Casual Caribbean Beachfront Resort

Cooper Island Beach Club is a small resort on a 1 1/2-mile by 1/2-mile island. At our beachfront restaurant and bar, sheltered from the sun, you can enjoy a cool drink with the Caribbean Sea only a few feet away. We've built a reputation for serving quality meals in an informal setting, at a reasonable price. Our guestrooms are on the beach and have an open-plan bedroom/living room/kitchen, plus balcony, bathroom, a shower that is almost outdoors. Activities include sunbathing, swimming, hiking, enjoying meals in the restaurant and conversation in the bar. We can arrange day sails and boat trips.

Guest Comment: "There are not enough words to do justice to the immense beauty, tranquility and serenity to be found here."

Mail To: PO Box 512, Turners Falls, MA 01376
Tel: (413) 863-3162, (800) 542-4624 (USA office), **Fax:** (413) 863-3662.
E-mail: info@cooper-island.com **Web:** http://www.cooper-island.com

Type: Beach resort with restaurant, bar, & scuba dive shop.
Clientele: Mainly straight with gay & lesbian following
Transportation: Pick up from ferry dock, no charge on scheduled trips.
Rooms: 12 rooms with queen beds.
Baths: All private shower/toilets.

Vegetarian: Available for lunch & dinner with prior notice.
Dates Open: All year.
High Season: Dec 15-Apr 15.
Rates: Per night for 2: US $95 (Jun 1-Oct 30); US $175 (Dec 15-Apr 15); US $115 (Apr 15-May 31 & Nov 1-Dec 14). Meal and/or dive packages available.

Discounts: Weekly discounts available.
Credit Cards: MC, Visa, with 5% handling charge.
Rsv'tns: Required.
Reserve Thru: Travel agent or call direct.
Parking: Boat moorings available.
In-Room: Ceiling fans, kitchen, refrigerator & maid service.

Exercise/Health: Full scuba facilities & watersports.
Swimming: In the ocean.
Sunbathing: On the beach.
Pets: Not permitted.
Handicap Access: No.
Children: Permitted, preferably over 10 yrs old.
Languages: English.
Your Hosts: Chris.

See Our Listing Under Cooper Island, Virgin Islands - B V I

Sand Castle on the Beach Resort

WWW Gay/Lesbian ♀♂
Gay-Owned & -Operated

The Perfect Gay & Lesbian Paradise

Your Caribbean dream, **Sand Castle on the Beach Resort** is located on a beautiful white sandy beach on the quiet side of St. Croix... a special place for special people. This is the perfect oasis for gay and lesbian vacationers, where romance and relaxation go hand-in-hand. Our paradise location offers spectacular views, a swimming beach, snorkeling, two pools (one is clothing-optional), rooms and suites with kitchens and dining balconies with beach view, guaranteed warm weather, crystal-blue calm seas and lush landscapes. Proudly serving the gay and lesbian community since 1978. Ask about our commitment ceremony package.

Address: 127 Smithfield, Frederiksted, USVI 00840
Tel: (340) 772-1205, (800) 524-2018, **Fax:** (340) 772-1757.
E-mail: onthebeach@virginislands.net **Web:** http://www.gaytraveling.com/onthebeach

Type: Hotel with boutique.
Clientele: Gay & lesbian. Good mix of men & women
Transportation: Our limo driver will pick you up at airport ($10 1 or 2 people, $5 each addt'l person).
To Gay Bars: 1/2 mile.
Rooms: 12 rooms, 9 suites, 2 luxury villas with queen or king beds.
Baths: All private.
Meals: Expanded continental breakfast. Weekly BBQ or cocktail party.
Complimentary: 1 bottle of rum, 2 cokes.
High Season: Dec-Mar.
Rates: Low $65-$150, shoulder $75-$185, high $115-$250.
Discounts: 10% to returning guests. Inquire about other discounts.
Credit Cards: MC, Visa, Amex, Discover.
Rsv'tns: Required.
Reserve Thru: Travel agent or call direct.
Min. Stay: 3 nights.
Parking: Ample, free off-street parking.
In-Room: Phone, AC, ceiling fans, color cable TV, VCR, kitchen, fridge, coffee & tea makers, maid svc.
On-Premises: Laundry, free video tape library.
Exercise/Health: Masseuse available. Nearby gym & massage.
Swimming: Pool & ocean on premises.
Sunbathing: Poolside, on private & common sun decks, patio & at beach.
Nudity: Permitted, 1 of 2 pools is clothing-optional.
Smoking: Permitted anywhere, a few rooms are non-smoking.
Pets: Inquire.
Handicap Access: Yes.
Your Hosts: Ron, Irma, Tanya & Allen.
IGLTA

See Our Listing Under Saint Croix, Virgin Islands - U S

Cormorant Beach Club & Hotel

For Those Who Like to Honeymoon Every Time They Travel

Praised as "the best small hotel in the American Virgin Islands" by *Andrew Harper's Hideaway Report*. The **Cormorant Beach Club** boasts 34 large guestrooms and four penthouse suites, two tennis courts, an 88,000 gallon freshwater pool and an open-air seaview lounge and restaurant.

Address: 4126 La Grande Princesse, Saint Croix, USVI 00820-4441
Tel: (340) 778-8920, (800) 548-4460, **Fax:** (340) 778-9218.
E-mail: info@cormorant-stcroix.com **Web:** http://www.cormorant-stcroix.com **IGLTA**

See Our Listing Under Saint Croix, Virgin Islands - U S

Casa Palapa

Between the Mountains and the Moon

At *Casa Palapa* we have tried to create an exceptional Vallarta experience. Guests are immersed in a contemporary architectural masterpiece filled with original artwork. From our Grand Palapa living room, look across our secluded Infinity Pool to the tropical valley below as it disappears into the sea.

Address: #107 Paseo de Conchas Chinas, Col. Conchas Chinas, Puerto Vallarta, JAL 44380, Mexico
Tel: (52-3) 221 5561 (Tel/Fax).
E-mail: CasaPalapa@pvnet.com.mx **Web:** http://www.casapalapa.com

See Our Listing Under Puerto Vallarta, Mexico

Casa Dos Comales

WWW Gay/Lesbian ⚥
Gay-Owned & -Operated

Vacation Apartments in Puerto Vallarta

Casa Dos Comales offers centrally located vacation apartments, along with a guesthouse, on a hillside overlooking the town of Puerto Vallarta. The ocean is just a few blocks away. Cable TV, sun decks, maid service and a small pool are all available. On the ground floor is the display gallery of Hugh Holland, locally known for his dreamlike color photo scenes that reveal the magic of everyday life in Vallarta. José can help you, in English or Spanish, to have the best possible time with advice and directions for dining and other pleasures.

Address: Calle Aldama 274, Puerto Vallarta, JAL , Mexico **Mail To:** 2554 Lincoln Bl. #378, Marina del Rey, CA 90291, USA
Tel: (52-3) 223 2042 (Tel/Fax). Toll-free in USA: (888) 881-1822 (Tel/Fax).
E-mail: comales2@casadoscomales.com **Web:** http:// www.casadoscomales.com

Type: Apartments.
Clientele: Mostly gay & lesbian with some straight clientele
Transportation: Free pick up from airport.
To Gay Bars: 2 blocks, 1/2 mile, a 5 min walk, a 2 min drive.
Rooms: 8 rooms, 1 suite with double beds.
Baths: 9 private bath/ shower/toilets.
Meals: Continental

breakfast.
Dates Open: All year.
High Season: Nov 2-Apr 30.
Rates: May 1-Nov 1: US $35-US $75, Nov 2-Apr 30: US $70-US $125. Rates are per room + 15% tax.
Discounts: 15 days 10% off.
Credit Cards: MC, Visa, Discover.
Rsv'tns: Required with 50% deposit.

Reserve Thru: Travel agent or call direct.
Min. Stay: 2 nights.
Parking: Adequate on-street parking.
In-Room: AC, color cable TV, kitchen, refrigerator, coffee & tea-making facilities, maid & laundry service.
On-Premises: Laundry facilities.
Exercise/Health: Nearby gym.

Swimming: Pool on premises, ocean nearby.
Sunbathing: On roof, patio & at beach.
Smoking: Non-smoking rooms.
Pets: Permitted.
Handicap Access: No.
Children: Welcome.
Languages: Spanish, English.
Your Hosts: José.

See Our Listing Under Puerto Vallarta, Mexico

Casa Dos Comales

*Vacation Apartments in
Puerto Vallarta*

Casa De Mis Padres

 **Men** ♂
Gay-Owned & -Operated

Your Oasis in the Desert

A private and exclusive resort-like retreat, *Casa De Mis Padres* is an oasis in the Arizona Desert. This 8,000 square foot Santa Barbara-style home is surrounded by mature palm trees, fragrant citrus and lawn areas. The pool garden features an outdoor fireplace and shower, Mexican paver patios, and manicured lawn areas. The pool is heated in cooler months for evening swims by firelight.

The Pool Casita includes two king suites, full kitchen with separate dining and living rooms that open to the pool patio, barbeques and outside wet bar. The two-room Library Suite features a home theatre system, extensive video library (available to all guests), book and magazine collection. *Casa De Mis Padres* is just two miles from Old Town Scottsdale. The business traveler is provided all the services of a hotel resort, yet our relaxed atmosphere lets you be *who you are* as if you were at home.

Address: 5965 E Orange Blossom Lane, Phoenix, AZ 85018
Tel: (480) 675-0247, **Fax:** (480) 675-9476.
E-mail: info@casadmp.com **Web:** http://www.casadmp.com

Type: Bed & breakfast in a private home.
Clientele: Men only
Transportation: Car or a short taxi drive.
To Gay Bars: 2 miles.
Rooms: 2 suites, plus casita with king beds.
Baths: All private: 2 bath/shower/toilets, 2 shower/toilets.
Meals: Expanded continental breakfast.
Complimentary: In-room tea, coffees & cold beverages.
Dates Open: All year.
High Season: Late Oct-May.
Rates: $150-$300, double occupancy.
Discounts: 5+ nts 10% off, corp. rate.
Credit Cards: MC, Visa, Amex, Discover.
Rsv'tns: Preferred.
Reserve Thru: Travel agent or call direct.
Min. Stay: 2 nights. 3 nights on holiday weekends.
Parking: Ample free off-street parking.
In-Room: Private telephones, AC, ceiling fans, color cable TV, VCR, coffee & tea-making facilities, maid service. Casita has kitchen. Library suite has refrigerator/freezer.
On-Premises: Video tape library, pool shower.
Swimming: Pool on premises, heated in cooler months.
Sunbathing: Poolside & in garden patios.
Smoking: Permitted outside. All non-smoking rooms.
Pets: Not permitted.
Children: No.
Languages: English.
Your Hosts: Brian & Vic.

See Our Listing Under Phoenix, Arizona, United States

Tortuga Roja Bed & Breakfast

Come, Share Our Mountain Views

For men only, the *Tortuga Roja Bed & Breakfast* is a 4-acre cozy retreat at the base of the Santa Catalinas, whose windows look out on an open landscape of natural high-desert vegetation. Some accommodations have fireplaces and kitchens. A bicycle and running path along the Rillito River behind our house can be followed for four miles on either side.

Address: 2800 E River Rd, Tucson, AZ 85718
Tel: (520) 577-6822, (800) 467-6822.
E-mail: redtrtl@goodnet.com **Web:** http://www.goodnet.com/~redtrtl **IGLTA**

See Our Listing Under Tucson, Arizona, United States

Santiago Resort

Palm Springs' Most Spectacular Private Men's Resort

We're winner's of Out & About's 1997 Editor's Choice Award for "exceptionally notable & distinctive gay lodging...a men's guesthouse that reflects stylish sophistication," and *Genre Magazine* says we're "...one of Palm Spring's most refined gay resorts," voting us "the most elegant men's guesthouse." Exotically landscaped, secluded grounds provide a peaceful enclave for the discriminating traveller. Enjoy magnificent mountain views from our terrace level, while an oversized diving pool, a 12-man spa and an outdoor cooling mist system complete the setting.

Address: 650 San Lorenzo Rd, Palm Springs, CA 92264-8108
Tel: (760) 322-1300, (800) 710-7729, **Fax:** (760) 416-0347.
E-mail: santiagops@earthlink.net **Web:** http://www.santiagoresort.com

See Our Listing Under Palm Springs, California, United States

Applewood Inn & Restaurant

WWW Gay-Friendly ♂♂

Russian River's Preeminent B&B

Once a mission-style redwoods retreat, *Applewood* is now an elegant country inn and restaurant that has become the darling of food critics and editors steering their readers to romantic getaways. *Wine Spectator* calls *Applewood*, "intimate and refined," while *Condé Nast Traveler* suggests the meals at the Applewood Restaurant meet the "Burgundian ideal."

Address: 13555 Hwy 116, Guerneville, CA 95446
Tel: (707) 869-9093, (800) 555-8509, **Fax:** (707) 869-9170.
E-mail: stay@applewoodinn.com **Web:** http://www.applewoodinn.com

See Our Listing Under Russian River, California, United States

Eagle's Peak

WWW Gay/Lesbian ♂
Gay-Owned & -Operated

Luxurious Amenities, Glorious Seclusion

Soaring above the Russian River, *Eagle's Peak* is a private, 1500-square-foot vacation home on 26 secluded acres, commanding majestic views of the lovely rolling hills above Forestville. Escape the city and indulge yourself in total relaxation. Enjoy a gourmet meal served as the sun sets over wooded wilderness and vineyards.

Address: Forestville **Mail To:** PO Box 750, Forestville, CA 95436
Tel: (707) 887-9218, **Fax:** (707) 887-9219.
E-mail: info@lacount.com **Web:** http://www.eaglespeak.net

See Our Listing Under Russian River, California, United States

Fern Falls

Romance Amidst the Redwoods

Fern Falls is a hillside habitat in a captivating canyon of Cazadero, whose cascading creeks merge with the languid waters of the Russian River. The custom-designed curved deck of the main house looks over the creek and ravine, and an ozonator spa sits above the waterfall on a hill nestled below a giant boulder amidst beautiful gardens. Nearby you can try wine tasting at the Korbel Winery, horseback riding, or canoeing the languid waters of the Russian River.

Address: 5701 Austin Creek Rd, Cazadero **Mail To:** PO Box 228, Cazadero, CA 95421
Tel: (707) 632-6108, **Fax:** (707) 632-6216.

> **See Our Listing Under Russian River, California, United States**

King George Hotel

Charm, Warmth & Tradition in San Francisco

The King George Hotel, a charming English-style hotel, is very gay-friendly and well-informed about gay venues and events. Experience the pleasure of staying in any of our first-class rooms, all with baths, remote control TVs, phones with voice mail and dataports, safes, ironing equipment, hairdryers, and electronic door.

Address: 334 Mason St, San Francisco, CA 94102
Tel: (800) 288-6005, (415) 781-5050, **Fax:** (415) 391-6976.
E-mail: KingGeorge@KingGeorge.com **Web:** http://www.kinggeorge.com
IGLTA

> **See Our Listing Under San Francisco, California, United States**

Renoir Hotel

Classic European Style in the Center of Gay San Francisco

The *Renoir Hotel* is a gay-friendly and cosmopolitan boutique hotel located in the lively heart of downtown San Francisco. Originally built in 1909, the ornate interior of this triangle-shaped historical landmark building has been renovated to restore its classic European turn-of-the-century charm. Union Square and the Cable Cars are only a few steps away. The unique Civic Center Complex, and the largest collection of Beaux Arts architecture in the United States, is literally at our doorstep. Moscone Convention Center, the Museum of Modern Art and the Yerba Buena Center for the Arts are also within walking distance.

The hotel is centrally located between the popular downtown tourist sites and the Castro, and within walking distance to the clubs on Folsom and Polk Street. It is ideally situated with rooms facing Market Street for the annual Gay Pride Parade. Theaters, Chinatown, and the San Francisco Shopping Centre are also nearby.

Address: 45 McAllister St, San Francisco, CA 94102
Tel: (415) 626-5200, Reservations: (800) 576-3388, Sales **Fax:** (415) 626-0916, Main **Fax:** (415) 626-5581.
Web: http://www.renoirhotel.com

Type: Hotel with Brazilian restaurant.
Clientele: Mostly straight, gay/lesbian following
Transportation: BART, airport shuttle van. Near all Bay Area transport.
To Gay Bars: Folsom St: 3-5 blocks; Polk St: 7-10 blocks; Castro: 10 min by streetcar, subway.
Rooms: 135 rooms with 2 suites & 4 view rms.
Baths: All private.

Meals: Brazilian restaurant & café in hotel.
High Season: Apr 1-Nov 15.
Rates: Standard: $119-$139; View: $139-$169; Suites: $175-$250.
Discounts: Inn Places rate: $79-$99 (based on avail.).
Credit Cards: All major credit cards accepted.
Rsv'tns: Required.
Reserve Thru: Travel agent or book directly.

Min. Stay: 2 days Gay Pride Wknd, some sold out periods (Folsom St. Fair).
Parking: Valet $18/day.
In-Room: Color TV with remote, clock radio, in-room safe, hair dryer, ironing board, maid, room & laundry service.
On-Premises: Restaurant, lounge, cafe.
Exercise/Health: YMCA 1 block, $7 a day with Renoir Hotel Discount.

Swimming: YMCA.
Smoking: 3 smoking floors, 3 non-smoking floors.
Pets: Not permitted.
Handicap Access: Full wheelchair accessibility to public places, some rooms wheelchair accessible.
Children: 12 & under stay free with adult.
Languages: English, German, French, Spanish, Portuguese, Italian, Tagalog.
IGLTA

See Our Listing Under San Francisco. California. United States

SAN FRANCISCO • CALIFORNIA

Gaige House Inn

WWW Gay-Friendly ⚥

Sonoma's Most Luxurious Inn

The *Gaige House Inn* is a stylish luxury inn nestled just 20 minutes from Napa in the heart of Sonoma Wine Country. *Travel & Leisure* touted the inn, in 2000, as "the best Bed & Breakfast in America." Sophisticated décor reflects West Indian, Asian and Plantation influences. *Frommers* reports, "This is the finest Bed & Breakfast in the Wine Country. First Class."

Address: 13540 Arnold Dr, Glen Ellen, CA 95442
Tel: (707) 935-0237, (800) 935-0237, **Fax:** (707) 935-6411.
E-mail: gaige@sprynet.com **Web:** http://www.gaige.com

See Our Listing Under Sonoma, California, United States

CALIFORNIA • SONOMA

Morrison House

WWW Gay-Friendly ♂

The Romance of Old Europe, The Charm of Early America

Designed and staffed with the utmost care, *Morrison House* blends the romance of Old Europe with the charm of Early America. Elegantly decorated with authentic Federal Period reproductions, we offer gracious hospitality and uncompromising service. Designed after the grand manors of the Federal Period, our guestrooms evoke the traditional elegance of late-eighteenth century Alexandria with their four-poster mahogany beds, brass chandeliers and sconces, and decorative fireplaces. *The Morrison House* is centrally located in historic Old Town Alexandria, just minutes from Washington, DC and Ronald Reagan National Airport.

We're a Mobil four-star and AAA four-diamond hotel.

Address: 116 South Alfred Street, Alexandria, VA 22314
Tel: (703) 838-8000, (800) 367-0800, **Fax:** (703) 548-2489.
E-mail: mhresrv@morrisonhouse.com **Web:** http://www.morrisonhouse.com

Type: Inn & hotel with 4-diamond restaurant & bar.
Clientele: Mostly straight clientele with a gay male following
Transportation: Taxi from National Airport. 7 blocks from metro station.
To Gay Bars: 7 miles, a 15 min drive.
Rooms: 42 rooms, 3 suites with single, queen or king beds.
Baths: 45 private bath/shower/toilets.

Meals: Continental breakfast.
Vegetarian: Can be accommodated at all times.
Complimentary: Continental breakfast & newspaper in the parlor, turn-down "treat" (cookies).
Dates Open: All year.
High Season: Apr-Jun & Sept-Nov.
Rates: Jan-Feb & Jul-Aug: $150-$350/nt, Mar-Jun & Sept-Dec: $200-$350/nt.
Credit Cards: MC, Visa,

Amex, Diners.
Rsv'tns: Required.
Reserve Thru: Travel agent or call direct.
Parking: Ample, pay covered parking. Valet parking.
In-Room: Telephone, AC, color cable TV, maid & room service.
On-Premises: Meeting rooms, 2 award-winning restaurants.
Exercise/Health: Gym nearby.

Smoking: Permitted in the Grill & Library. Smoking & non-smoking rooms available.
Pets: Not permitted.
Handicap Access: Yes, elevator.
Children: Welcome.
Languages: English, Spanish, Japanese, Ethiopian, Arabic, Italian, French.

See Our Listing Under Washington, District of Columbia, United States

Deauville Inn, The

Steps to the Beach...

Fort Lauderdale Beach's *Deauville Inn* offers beautiful, affordable hotel accommodations — from cozy rooms to efficiency apartments with full kitchens. Vacation within a block of the Atlantic Ocean beach and enjoy swimming in the ocean, or relax by our courtyard swimming pool. We are located near dozens of favorite Florida vacation attractions, sports activities and Fort Lauderdale's night life.

Address: 2916 N. Ocean Blvd, Fort Lauderdale, FL 33308
Tel: (954) 568-5000, **Fax:** (954) 565-7797.
E-mail: info@ftlaud-deauville.com **Web:** http://www.ftlaud-deauville.com

See Our Listing Under Fort Lauderdale, Florida, United States

Heron House

Feel Free...Feel Relaxed...Feel Welcomed

Amidst orchids, bougainvillaea, jasmine and palms, a secluded tropical garden fantasy awaits you. This warm and friendly place is *Heron House* — meticulously designed by Key West's most gifted artists and craftsmen. Lacking pretense, this style has been inspired by the informality of the Florida Keys' natural environment, free of rigid architectural conformities,

lending itself to a casually elegant style in which you will feel totally free, welcome and relaxed. Thus, with generous private decks and balconies, your private room merges with private gardens. Luxurious tropical gardens, draped around our rich complex of luxurious tropical homes, seem to penetrate every room as if to share themselves with you.

Many rooms feature "signature walls" in teak, oak or cedar. Granite baths are elegantly understated. Tile floors are cool and tropical. Our shady Chicago brick patios are reminiscent of old English gardens. Stained-glass transoms above French doors capture the warmth of natural sunlight and filter it through sparkling colors. Interiors feature rich, original commissioned watercolors of the Keys created by local artisans. We even have our own Heron House vintage champagne ready to put on ice. In 1998 we were awarded the AAA 4-Diamond rating and 4-Crowns by the American Bed & Breakfast Association.

Address: 512 Simonton St, Key West, FL 33040
Tel: (305) 294-9227, (888) 676-8654, **Fax:** (305) 294-5692.
E-mail: HeronKYW@aol.com **Web:** http://www.heronhouse.com

Type: Guesthouse.
Clientele: Mostly straight with a gay & lesbian following
Transportation: Car or airport, then taxi.
To Gay Bars: 1 block.
Rooms: 21 rooms with double, queen or king beds.
Baths: All private.
Meals: Deluxe continental breakfast.

High Season: Dec 20-Apr 30.
Rates: Dec 20-Apr 30: $179-$349; May 1-30 & Oct 20-Dec 19: $139-$299; Jun 1-Oct 19: $109-$229.
Credit Cards: MC, Visa, Amex, Diners.
Rsv'tns: Recommended.
Reserve Thru: Travel agent or call direct.
Min. Stay: During holidays

and special events.
Parking: Ample on-street.
In-Room: Maid svc, ceiling fans, AC, color TV, fridges, phones, private entrances.
Exercise/Health: Some rooms have Jacuzzis.
Swimming: Pool, ocean beach.
Sunbathing: At poolside, on roof or on private or common sun decks.

Nudity: Permitted on sun deck.
Smoking: Restricted.
Pets: Not permitted.
Handicap Access: Yes. Ramps.
Children: Not permitted.
Languages: English.

See Our Listing Under Key West, Florida, United States

Cliff's Edge Oceanfront Estate, The

Private, Private, Private...

The Cliff's Edge Oceanfront Estate is just that. This two-acre estate, perched at the edge of a 300-foot cliff overlooking Waipio Bay, is situated in the middle of the Pacific Ocean; at the end of the road; at the edge of a cliff; at the end of the world. Accommodations offer spectacular views of the turquoise bay, surrounding lava cliffs and Maui's dormant volcano, Haleakala. Relax, read, romanticize and realize that you have found paradise. Let the waves crashing against the rocks below sing you to sleep at night. Visit the natural pools of Twin Falls, just minutes away, or watch the whales and dolphins from your private hot tub just feet from the cliff's edge. We are only 30 minutes from the airport, yet close to natural pools and waterfalls. Perfect for private getaways or secret rendezvous. Private, Private, Private...

Address: Maui's North Shore, Huelo, HI
Tel: (808) 572-4530.
E-mail: clifedge@maui.net **Web:** http://www.cliffsedge.com

Type: Bed & breakfast cottage.
Clientele: 50% gay & lesbian & 50% straight clientele
Transportation: Car is best.
To Gay Bars: 20 miles.
Rooms: 2 rooms, 1 cottage with double, queen or king beds.
Baths: Private: 3 bath/

shower/toilets, 3 shower/toilets.
Meals: Continental breakfast.
Dates Open: All year.
Rates: $125-$250.
Discounts: Weekly.
Rsv'tns: Required.
Reserve Thru: Travel agent or call direct.
Min. Stay: Required.
Parking: Ample, free

parking.
In-Room: Telephone, ceiling fans, color cable TV, VCR, kitchen, refrigerator, coffee & tea-making facilities, laundry service.
On-Premises: Laundry facilities.
Exercise/Health: Jacuzzi. Nearby massage.
Swimming: Pool. Nearby ocean, river & natural pools.

Sunbathing: Poolside, on private sun decks & patio.
Nudity: Permitted.
Smoking: All rooms & cottage are non-smoking. Permitted outside.
Pets: Not permitted.
Handicap Access: No.
Children: No.
Languages: English, German.

See Our Listing Under Maui, Hawaii, United States

Cabana at Waikiki, The

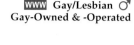

WWW Gay/Lesbian ♂
Gay-Owned & -Operated

Waikiki's Hot Gay Getaway

Sun-drenched beaches... towering palm trees... blue skies and beautiful bronzed bodies as far as the eye can see... welcome to *The Cabana at Waikiki!* Friendly and exclusively gay, this is "the gay place to stay" in Waikiki. Located off the beaten path yet close to it all, this four-story, fifteen-unit upscale property is perfectly situated on Cartwright Street (a quiet respite off Kapahulu Avenue), one block from world-famous Waikiki Beach. Suites feature custom furniture, queen-sized bed and pull-out sofa, entertainment center with TV, VCR, stereo with CD player, equipped kitchen, and individual private lanai.

Bathed in sun and drenched by Hawaii's clear, blue skies, we're just a short stroll from Queen's Surf Beach, Waikiki's gay beach. Other local and tantalizing treats include Kapiolani Park, Hula's Bar, a gym, unique shops and the best restaurants in Waikiki. Such tropical delights make this the ideal choice for your next vacation. Honolulu's proximity to the neighbor islands of Maui, Kaua'i, Moloka'i, and The Big Island make us part of the perfect island-hopping vacation. And since Waikiki is the "gay crossroads of the Pacific," we're an ideal stop-over for the Asia-bound traveller, or for a long weekend in the sun with the "in" crowd.

Address: 2551 Cartwright Rd, Honolulu, HI 96815
Tel: (808) 926-5555, toll-free: (877) 902-2121, **Fax:** (808) 926-5566.
E-mail: infocabana@cabana-waikiki.com **Web:** http://www.cabana-waikiki.com

Type: Guesthouse.
Clientele: Mostly men with women welcome
Transportation: Rental car or taxi from airport.
To Gay Bars: 1 block.
Rooms: 15 suites with queen & queen sofa beds.
Baths: All private.
Meals: Expanded continental breakfast.

Complimentary: Bi-weekly Mai Tai parties.
Dates Open: All year.
Rates: $99-$175 per night.
Credit Cards: MC, Visa, Amex.
Rsv'tns: Recommended.
Reserve Thru: Travel agent or call direct.
Parking: Adequate covered off-street pay parking.

In-Room: Phone, AC, ceiling fans, color cable TV, VCR, stereo w/ CD, kitchen, fridge, coffee & tea makers, maid svc.
On-Premises: Laundry facilities.
Exercise/Health: Jacuzzi. Nearby gym, weights, sauna, steam, massage.
Swimming: Ocean nearby.

Sunbathing: At beach.
Smoking: Permitted on each private lanai.
Pets: Not permitted.
Children: No.
Languages: English, Chinese.
IGLTA

See Our Listing Under Oahu, Hawaii, United States

Old Town Bed & Breakfast

WWW Gay/Lesbian ⚥

Old Town Bed & Breakfast rests in an Art Deco mansion in a leafy Lincoln Park neighborhood adjacent to the Gold Coast, North Michigan Avenue shopping, restaurants, museums, theaters, art galleries, coffeehouses and world-famous boutiques. The neighborhood is a mixture of the hip and the chic. It is highly diverse, relaxed, vibrant and always lively.

There are four suites in the main house. A separate and private guesthouse has three bedrooms, private gardens, roof decks and a playroom. It is just steps away from the main house. The main house has a fifty-foot drawing room with a grand piano and black marble fireplace, a dining room, a chef's kitchen, a gymnasium, a conference room, and a penthouse sitting area. Both the main house and the guesthouse have laundry facilities available to guests. Public transportation is a half block away. Both airports and all five train stations are short rides from us.

Guests can sun and relax in the rooftop gardens whose city views take in a dramatic part of Chicago's skyline, including the Sears Tower and the John Hancock Building.

Address: 1442 N North Park Ave, Chicago, IL 60610
Tel: (312) 440-9268, **Fax:** (312) 440-2378.
Web: htto://www.oldtownbandbchicago.com

Type: Bed & breakfast.
Clientele: Mixed
Transportation: 1/2 block to bus.
To Gay Bars: A short walk.
Rooms: 4 suites, 1 private guesthouse.
Baths: All private.
Meals: Continental

breakfast and snacks at all times.
Vegetarian: Always available.
Complimentary: Coffee, teas, juices, yogurt, popcorn, cookies.
Dates Open: All year.
Rates: $139 to $189.

Discounts: Negotiated.
Credit Cards: MC, Visa, Amex.
Rsv'tns: Required.
Reserve Thru: Call direct.
Parking: Ample.
In-Room: TV, phone.
On-Premises: Sitting rooms, private gardens.

Exercise/Health: Gym.
Sunbathing: Roof, gardens, decks, and walled garden.
Smoking: Not permitted.
Pets: Not permitted.
Handicap Access: No.
Your Hosts: Michael & Elizabeth.

See Our Listing Under Chicago, Illinois, United States

Bed & Breakfast at Sills Inn

Southern Hospitality ~ 10 Minutes from Lexington

Enjoy the ambiance of Southern Hospitality as you step into **Bed & Breakfast at Sills Inn**, a 1911, three-storied restored Victorian inn. The nearly 9000 square feet are highly decorated and filled with Kentucky antiques. The B&B is located in historic downtown Versailles and the hub of activity in the Bluegrass Horse farm region.

Address: 270 Montgomery Ave, Versailles, Lexington, KY 40383
Tel: (606) 873-4478, (800) 526-9801, **Fax:** (606) 873-7099.
E-mail: sillsinn@aol.com **Web:** http://www.SillsInn.com **IGLTA**

Lafitte Guest House

The French Quarter's Premier Guest House For Over 40 Years

This elegant French manor house, meticulously restored to its original splendor and furnished in fine antiques and reproductions, has all the comforts of home, including air conditioning and cable TV. Located in the quiet, residential section of famous Bourbon St., **Lafitte Guest House** is just steps from the French

Rob Ambelang, Photographer

Quarter's attractions. Continental breakfast is served in your room or in our tropical courtyard. Wine and hors d'oeuvres are served each evening at cocktail hour.

Address: 1003 Bourbon St, New Orleans, LA 70116
Tel: (504) 581-2678, (800) 331-7971, **Fax:** (504) 581-2677.
E-mail: lafitte@travelbase.com **Web:** http://www.lafitteguesthouse.com

Admiral's Inn & Guesthouse & Hotel

Unique in Ogunquit...

The Admiral's Inn is located 65 miles north of Boston in Ogunquit, Maine. Our spacious grounds are within walking distance of the beach and all other village pleasures, and the privacy of our backyard pool is perfect for enjoying a morning or late-night swim, or a quiet afternoon retreat. Guests are also invited to enjoy our six-man hot tub, enclosed deck and clothing-optional area.

Address: #79 US Rte. 1 South **Mail To:** PO Box 2241, Ogunquit, ME 03907
Tel: (207) 646-7093, **Toll-free:** (888) 263-6318, **Fax:** (207) 646-5341.
E-mail: Office@theadmiralsinn.com **Web:** http://www.theadmiralsinn.com

See Our Listing Under Ogunquit, Maine, United States

Inn at Two Village Square, The

Ogunquit, Maine —The Quiet Alternative

Overlooking Ogunquit Square and the Atlantic Ocean, **THE INN** is an 1886 Victorian home perched on a hillside amidst towering trees. Our heated pool, hot tub and extensive decks provide views far to sea. Our atmosphere is congenial and relaxed. Deluxe continental breakfast is served in our wicker-filled dining room, and guest rooms have color TV, ceiling fans and air conditioning.

Address: 135 US Rte 1 **Mail To:** PO Box 864, Ogunquit, ME 03907
Tel: (207) 646-5779, **Fax:** (207) 646-6797.
E-mail: reservations@theinn.tv **Web:** http://www.theinn.tv

See Our Listing Under Ogunquit, Maine, United States

White Wind Inn

WWW Gay/Lesbian ⚥
Gay-Owned & -Operated

"A Provincetown Landmark —
Come Make Your Own History..."

The *White Wind Inn*, "A Provincetown Landmark," is a gracious New England mansion built in the mid 1800s. Today, guests enjoy its well-appointed accommodations that feature high ceilings, antiques, chandeliers, four-poster and brass beds. Several rooms have private decks, some with water views, so that you can enjoy your own unique perspective on Provincetown from the comfort of your room. Fireplace rooms provide that extra romantic touch for visits throughout the year.

The *White Wind's* veranda that overlooks Commercial Street, across from Provincetown Bay, is a favorite — whether it's starting the day with breakfast, catching some afternoon rays, enjoying a drink in the evening while watching "The Tea Dance parade" or relaxing with friends, old and new. There is no better place to take in the sights that give Provincetown so much character.

Address: 174 Commercial St, Provincetown, MA 02657
Tel: (508) 487-1526, (888) 449-WIND (9463), **Fax:** (508) 487-4792.
E-mail: wwinn@capecod.net

Type: Bed & breakfast.
Clientele: Gay & lesbian. More men in season, good mix of men & women other times
Transportation: Car, plane, bus & ferry. Free pick up from airport & ferry dock.
To Gay Bars: 1/2 block, a 2 min walk.
Rooms: 11 rooms, 1 suite with double or queen beds.
Baths: All private bath/shower/toilets.
Meals: Expanded continental breakfast.

Complimentary: Weekly social on porch - cocktails, snacks.
Dates Open: All year.
High Season: Memorial Day weekend thru 2nd weekend in Sept.
Rates: Off season $75-$145, season $120-$225.
Credit Cards: MC, Visa, Amex, Discover.
Rsv'tns: Required.
Reserve Thru: Travel agent or call direct.
Min. Stay: Required in season & on certain holiday/events.

Parking: Ample, free off-street parking.
In-Room: Color cable TV, VCR, refrigerator, maid service. AC (most rooms) or ceiling fans, phones, voicemail, data ports.
On-Premises: Video tape library.
Exercise/Health: Nearby gym, weights, massage.
Swimming: Nearby pool, ocean.
Sunbathing: On private sun decks, common front porch

sun deck, or at beach.
Smoking: All rooms & inside common areas are non-smoking. Smoking on outdoor decks/patio areas only.
Pets: Permitted. Limited rooms, with prior approval, additional charge.
Handicap Access: No.
Children: No.
Your Hosts: Michael & Rob.

See Our Listing Under Provincetown, Massachusetts, United States

Beaconlight Guest House, The

 WWW Gay/Lesbian ♀♂

"The Kind of House We Wished We Lived In"

Beaconlight's exceptional reputation for comfort and service has grown by the word of mouth of our many returning guests. Awaken to the aroma of freshly brewed coffee and home-baked cakes and breads. Relax in the English country house charm of elegant bedrooms and spacious drawing rooms.

Address: 12 Winthrop St, Provincetown, MA 02657
Tel: (508) 487-9603 (Tel/Fax), (800) 696-9603.
E-mail: beaconlite@capecod.net **Web:** http://www.capecod.net/beaconlight/
IGLTA

See Our Listing Under Provincetown, Massachusetts, United States

Viva Las Vegas Villas

A Stone's Throw from the Bustle of the Las Vegas Strip!

Imagine spending a night in the Elvis and Priscilla Suite with decor that's been all shook up in gold lamé and splashes of hot pink, surrounded by memorabilia from the King's early career. You're sure to love the one-of-a-kind pink Cadillac bed. And the wrought-iron headboard is a replica of the gates of Graceland, with an incredible painting of the mansion in the distance behind it. Sure, it will be hard to check out in the morning, but you'll hardly be able to wait to tell your friends about your night with Elvis and Priscilla. Want something a bit more laid-back? We think newlyweds who've just thrilled to our most popular Elvis Blue Hawaii wedding will go coconuts over the tropical Blue Hawaii Room, complete with tiki hut bath, island scenery and palm-tree bed posts. You'll feel like you're sleeping right on the beach, but no sand in your shoes the next morning.

Our Camelot Room features a drawbridge bed across a painted moat, a dragon-slaying knight on horseback, and lots of medieval touches. Only Merlin knows where the magical television screen will be found. You'll revel in the storybook atmosphere of an English castle during the days of the Knights of the Round Table. Maybe you'd prefer our Austin Powers Suite, complete with beaded doorways, lava lamps and "groovy, baby" green shag carpet! Or an exotically different Egyptian Room gilded with decorative artifacts? A night in any of the rooms at *Viva Las Vegas Villas* will be one long-remembered and one never duplicated elsewhere!

Address: 1205 Las Vegas Blvd South, Las Vegas, NV 89104
Tel: (702) 384-0771, (800) 574-4450, **Fax:** (702) 384-0190.
E-mail: info@vivalasvegasvillas.com **Web:** http://
www.vivalasvegasvillas.com

Type: B&B themed rooms.
Clientele: Straight, gay & lesbian clientele
Transportation: Cab or limo.
To Gay Bars: 1 mile or less.
Rooms: 36 with doubles, queens, kings, suites.

Baths: All private, some with Jacuzzi.
Meals: Continental breakfast.
Dates Open: All year.
High Season: Feb-Oct.
Rates: $75-$175.
Discounts: 3+ nites.
Rsv'tns: Preferred.

Reserve Thru: Phone or website.
Parking: Ample, free.
In-Room: VCR, AC, heat, some fridges.
On-Premises: Diner, florist, chapel, disco, private parties, reception & catering facilities.

Exercise/Health: Gym, free weights, massage therapy.
Smoking: On balcony or outside rooms.
Pets: No.
Handicap Access: Limited.
Languages: English, German, Spanish.

See Our Listing Under Las Vegas, Nevada, United States

Notchland Inn, The

A Magical Location...Naturally Secluded

Get away from it all, relax and rejuvenate at our comfortable 1862 granite mansion located on 100 acres in the midst of beautiful mountain vistas. *The Notchland Inn* rests atop a knoll at the base of Mount Bemis and looks out upon Mounts Hope and Crawford. Experience the comforts and pleasures of attentive and friendly hospitality! Settle in to one of our seven guest rooms or five spacious suites, each individually appointed and all with woodburning fireplaces and private baths, several with Jacuzzis. The front parlor is a perfect place to sit by the fire and read or to visit with other guests. The music room draws guests to the piano, or to the stereo to listen to music they personally select. The sun room offers a great place to sip your coffee and read a novel or just enjoy the great views.

In the evening, a wonderful 5-course dinner is served in a romantic, fireplaced dining room looking out to the gazebo by our pond. Our Chef creates a new menu daily, his elegant flair respecting the traditional while exploring the excitement of international cuisines. Morning brings a bountiful country breakfast to fuel you for the adventures of the day. Nature's wonders include 8,000 feet of Saco River frontage, two swimming holes, and the Davis Path hiking trail. Other activities to enjoy are mountain biking, cross-country skiing, snowshoeing, or soaking in the wood-fired hot tub. For animal lovers there are two Bernese Mountain dogs, a Belgian draft horse, miniature horses and two llamas. Nearby attractions include: Crawford Notch, ski areas and factory outlet stores.

Address: Harts Location, NH 03812-9999
Tel: Reservations: (800) 866-6131 or (603) 374-6131, **Fax:** (603) 374-6168.
E-mail: notchland@aol.com **Web:** http://www.notchland.com

Type: Inn with restaurant with full liquor license.
Clientele: Mostly straight clientele with a gay & lesbian following
Transportation: Car is best. Free pick up from bus.
To Gay Bars: 2 hours.
Rooms: 7 rooms, 5 suites, single, queen, king beds.
Baths: All private.
Meals: Full breakfast & dinner.
Vegetarian: Inquire.

Complimentary: Various treats at various times.
High Season: Foliage (Sep 15-Oct 20) & Christmas to New Year (Dec 23-Jan 1).
Rates: Per person per night MAP double occupancy: $112.50-$142.50, Holiday & foliage $137.50-$167.50. B&B rates on request.
Discounts: Inquire.
Credit Cards: MC, Visa, Amex, Discover.
Rsv'tns: Subject to prior booking.

Reserve Thru: Travel agent or call direct.
Min. Stay: Required at times.
Parking: Ample free off-street parking.
In-Room: Maid service, ceiling fans, some rooms have AC.
On-Premises: Meeting rooms.
Exercise/Health: Spa, massage by appointment.

Nearby gym, weights, Jacuzzi, steam, massage, skiing, sleigh & carriage rides.
Swimming: River. Nearby pool, river & lake.
Sunbathing: On patio, lawns or at the beach.
Smoking: No smoking.
Pets: Not permitted.
Children: Mature children over 12.
Languages: English.
Your Hosts: Les & Ed.

See Our Listing Under Harts Location, New Hampshire, United States

Inn of the Turquoise Bear B & B

`WWW` Gay/Lesbian ⚥
Gay-Operated

Where the Action Is... Stay Gay in Santa Fe!

This rambling adobe villa, built in Spanish-Pueblo Revival style, is one of Santa Fe's most important historic estates. With its signature portico, tall pines, magnificent rock terraces, meandering paths, and flower gardens, the *Inn of the Turquoise Bear* offers guests a romantic retreat near the center of Santa Fe.

The inn occupies the home of Witter Bynner (1881-1968), a prominent gay citizen of Santa Fe, staunch advocate of human rights and a vocal opponent of censorship. Bynner and Robert Hunt, his lover of over 30 years, were famous for the riotous parties they hosted, referred to by Ansel Adams, a frequent visitor, as "Bynner's Bashes." Their home was the gathering place for the elite of Santa Fe and guests from around the world, including D.H. & Frieda Lawrence, Igor Stravinsky, Willa Cather, Errol Flynn, Martha Graham, Christopher Isherwood, Georgia O'Keeffe, Rita Hayworth, Thornton Wilder, Robert Frost — and many others.

The only gay-oriented B&B in downtown Santa Fe, it's the perfect choice for couples or those traveling alone. Owners, Ralph and Robert, reside on the property providing their guests a unique setting that captures the essence of traditional Santa Fe. Out & About Editor's Choice Award, Santa Fe Heritage Preservation Award.

Address: 342 E Buena Vista Street, Santa Fe, NM 87501
Tel: (505) 983-0798, (800) 396-4104, **Fax:** (505) 988-4225.
E-mail: bluebear@newmexico.com **Web:** http://www.turquoisebear.net

Type: Bed & breakfast inn.
Clientele: 70% gay & lesbian and 30% straight
Transportation: Car is best, shuttle bus from Albuquerque airport.
To Gay Bars: 8 blocks.
Rooms: 9 rooms, 2 suites with queen or king beds.
Baths: Private & shared.
Meals: Expanded continental breakfast.
Vegetarian: Nearby.
Complimentary: Tea, coffee & fruit all day. Wine & cheese in afternoon. Sherry & brandy in common room.

High Season: Apr-Oct & Thanksgiving to New Year.
Rates: Per room, dbl occ: high $95-$195, low $95-$175.
Discounts: 10% AAA, AARP. Wkly rate: 10% off (low season).
Credit Cards: MC, Visa, Amex, Discover.
Rsv'tns: Required, but we accept late inquiries.
Reserve Thru: Travel agent or call direct.
Min. Stay: Required during certain holidays.

Parking: Ample free, walled off-street parking.
In-Room: Color cable TV, VCR, fans, phone, maid svc. Some rooms have fridges.
On-Premises: Meeting rooms, video tape & book libraries, fax.
Exercise/Health: Jacuzzi planned. Nearby gym, weights, Jacuzzi, sauna, steam, massage.
Swimming: Pool nearby.
Sunbathing: On patios.
Nudity: Permitted in various patio areas.

Smoking: Permitted on patios, not in rooms or public rooms.
Pets: Small pets OK in some rooms.
Handicap Access: One guest room accessible.
Children: Inquire.
Languages: English, Spanish, French, Norwegian, German.
Your Hosts: Ralph & Robert.
IGLTA

See Our Listing Under Santa Fe, New Mexico, United States

Chelsea Pines Inn

The Cozy Bed & Breakfast in the Heart of Gay New York

Fodor's Gay Guide USA calls us "The best-known gay accommodation in the city... equidistant from the Village and Chelsea attractions... this 1850 town house is run by a helpful staff... pleasantly furnished rooms... it's a great deal!" Bordering Greenwich Village and Chelsea, *Chelsea Pines Inn* is a short walk to restaurants, shops, clubs, bars and the famous Christopher Street area. Out & About Editor's Choice Award for Excellence in Gay Travel.

Address: 317 W 14th St, New York, NY 10014
Tel: (212) 929-1023, **Fax:** (212) 620-5646.
E-mail: cpiny@aol.com **IGLTA**

See Our Listing Under New York, New York, United States

Inn at Highview, The

Vermont the Way You Always Dreamed It Would Be...

Everyone who arrives at *The Inn at HighView* has the same breathless reaction to the serenity of the surrounding hills. Our hilltop location offers incredible peace, tranquility and seclusion, yet is convenient to skiing, golf, tennis and antiquing. Enjoy our gourmet dinner, relax by a blazing fire, snuggle under a down comforter in a canopy bed, or gaze 50 miles over pristine mountains.

Address: 753 East Hill Road, Andover, VT 05143
Tel: (802) 875-2724, **Fax:** (802) 875-4021.
E-mail: hiview@aol.com **Web:** http://www.innathighview.com

See Our Listing Under Andover, Vermont, United States

Gaslight Inn

WWW Gay/Lesbian ⚥

Welcome to *Gaslight Inn,* a Seattle four-square house built in 1906. In restoring the inn, we have brought out the home's original turn-of-the-century ambiance and warmth, while keeping in mind the additional conveniences and contemporary style needed by travelers in the nineties. The interior is appointed in exacting detail, with strikingly rich, dark colors, oak paneling, and an enormous entryway and staircase.

Our comfortable and unique rooms and suites are furnished with quality double or queen-sized beds, refrigerator and television. Additional features, such as private bath and phone service, are available in some rooms. Some rooms also have decks with fabulous views or fireplaces. The living room, with its large oak fireplace, is always inviting, as is the library. Through the late spring and summer, we encourage you to unwind with a glass of wine beside our private, in-ground, heated pool with several decks and interesting plant arrangements. We're convenient to central Seattle's attractions and to a plethora of gay and lesbian bars, restaurants and shops in the Broadway district.

Address: 1727 15th Ave, Seattle, WA 98122
Tel: (206) 325-3654, **Fax:** (206) 328-4803.
E-mail: innkeepr@gaslight-inn.com **Web:** http://www.gaslight-inn.com

Type: Guesthouse.
Clientele: Mostly gay/lesbian, some straight
Transportation: Airport Shuttle Express $15, (206) 286-4800 to reserve.
To Gay Bars: 2-3 blocks.
Rooms: 9 dbls, 7 suites.
Baths: 14 private, 2 shared.
Meals: Expanded continental breakfast.

Complimentary: Coffee, tea & juices, fresh fruit, pastries.
Dates Open: All year.
High Season: Summer.
Rates: $88-$178.
Credit Cards: MC, Visa, Amex.
Rsv'tns: Recommended at least 2 weeks in advance.
Reserve Thru: Call direct.

Min. Stay: 2 days wknds, 3 days holidays.
Parking: Ample on-street & off-street parking.
In-Room: Color TV, cable, telephones, maid service.
On-Premises: Meeting rooms, living room, library.
Swimming: Seasonal heated pool.
Sunbathing: On private or

common sun decks or at poolside.
Smoking: Permitted on decks & porches only.
Pets: Not permitted.
Children: Not permitted.
Languages: English.
Your Hosts: Trevor, Stephen & John.
IGLTA

See Our Listing Under Seattle, Washington, United States

Malindi Beach House

Kenya's Best-Kept Secret and... a Way of Life

This private home is one of the few remaining colonial-style houses, situated directly on Silversand Beach in Malindi. Do not expect a Malibu-style villa, but a cosy, friendly house. *Malindi Beach House,* built in the Kenyan tradition of spacious rooms, is decorated in the relaxed low-key settler style on a four-acre beachplot. Included for your comfort are a houseboy, gar-

dener, watchman and a cook. A swimming pool and floodlit tennis court are on the estate. The main house has a living/diningroom with connecting big terrace facing the sea. The two bedrooms with ensuite shower and toilet are air-conditioned. The separate guestroom/cottage facing the pool also has two bedrooms with shower/toilet and air conditioning. **V. I. P. Treatment** (at extra cost, on request): Let us take care of your shopping, meals, parties; Just relax and enjoy personalized hospitality. Activities include: Road safaris to Tsavo East or Amboseli National Park; Air safaris to Masai Mara or Samburu Game Reserves; Deep-sea fishing, diving, goggling, surfing, golf, horse riding, mountain biking. Excursions to: Lamu — the magical island, Mombasa, Che-Shale, Camel safaris, bird watching Dhow trips, or just meet the friendly people.

Address: Malindi **Mail To:** PO Box 849, Malindi, Kenya
Tel: (254 123) 31951, **Fax:** (254 123) 31952.
E-mail: promote@africaonline.co.ke **Web:** http://www.kenya-travel.com

Type: Private house.
Clientele: Mostly men
Transportation: Taxi or car. Free pick up from Malindi airport, $50/pp from Mombasa airport.
Rooms: 4 rooms with single or double beds.
Baths: 4 private shower/ toilets.
Meals: Full breakfast. Dinner on arrival 1st day.

Vegetarian: Available.
Complimentary: Coffee, tea, water, soft drinks.
Dates Open: All year.
High Season: Dec-Feb.
Rates: US $100-US $150 per person, per day.
Discounts: By 4 pay 25% & by 6 pay 50% discount.
Credit Cards: MC, Visa.
Rsv'tns: Required.
Reserve Thru: Travel agent

or call direct.
Min. Stay: 6 days.
Parking: Ample free parking.
In-Room: AC, ceiling fans.
On-Premises: Laundry facilities.
Exercise/Health: Nearby gym, weights, massage, reflexology.
Swimming: Pool, ocean.
Sunbathing: Poolside,

patio, at beach & in garden.
Smoking: Permitted. Non-smoking rooms available.
Pets: Not permitted.
Handicap Access: Yes, wide doors.
Children: No.
Languages: English, Swaheli, German, Dutch.
Your Hosts: Hans.

Sixty-Five Kloof Guest House

WWW Gay/Lesbian ♂
Gay-Owned & -Operated

Experience Cape Town in Comfort & Style

Situated in one of the city's most convenient locations, *65 Kloof Guest House* welcomes you to Cape Town. Accessibility is the key with shops, restaurants and beaches just a five-minute walk from us. And a 10- to 15-minute drive takes you to Sandy Bay, our beautiful gay nudist beach. Relax by our private pool or sunbathe on the deck or in the gardens. Afterwards, unwind in your colonial-style en-suite bedroom. Your hosts reside on the property and will help make your stay the first of many. Experience our hospitality.

Address: 65 Kloof Road, Seapoint, Cape Town, South Africa
Tel: (27-21) 434 0815 (Tel/Fax).
E-mail: 65kloof@netactive.co.za **Web:** http://www.web.netactive.co.za/ ~65kloof/

Type: Guesthouse with bar.
Clientele: Mostly men with women welcome
Transportation: Pick up from airport (free on stays of over 1 wk, $15 on stays of under 1 wk). Car rental arranged.
To Gay Bars: 5 kms.
Rooms: 5 rooms & 2 cottages w/ twin or double beds.
Baths: All ensuite.

Meals: Continental full buffet breakfast.
Vegetarian: Vegetarian breakfast always available.
Complimentary: Tea & coffee in rooms.
High Season: Dec-Feb.
Rates: ZAR 160-250 pp.
Discounts: Inquire.
Credit Cards: Not to pay, but may use to guarantee reservation.
Rsv'tns: Required.

Reserve Thru: Call, fax, e-mail direct.
Parking: Ample off-street parking.
In-Room: Ceiling fans, color TV, coffee & tea-making facilities.
On-Premises: TV lounge.
Exercise/Health: Nearby gym, weights, Jacuzzi, sauna, steam, massage.
Swimming: Pool. Nearby pool & ocean.

Sunbathing: Poolside & on common sun decks.
Nudity: 15 min drive to gay nude beach.
Smoking: Permitted. Non-smoking rooms available.
Pets: Not permitted.
Children: No.
Languages: English, French, Greek.
Your Hosts: Kos & John.
IGLTA

Bliss Flatlits

Gay-Friendly 50/50 ♀♂
Lesbian-Owned

Privacy is key at *Bliss Flatlits*, comfortable, well-appointed units on the premises of our home — near all amenities and with stunning lagoon views. Your hostesses have lived in this area for many years and can advise and guide you during your stay. Knysna, located in the heart of the Garden Route (an area extending from Cape Town to Port Elizabeth), has beautiful beaches, scenic drives, the largest indigenous forest in South Africa, an elephant park and art galleries. Enjoy eateries such as Mike's Can-De-Light Bistro and Brigit's The Old Jail, or visit John-Mark's shop "Wild At Heart."

Address: 12 Faure Street, West Hill, Knysna, 6570, South Africa
Tel: (27-44) 382 4569, **Cell:** (083) 265 2188.
E-mail: bliss@knysna.lia.net

Type: 2 self-catering cottages.
Clientele: 50% gay & lesbian & 50% hetero
Transportation: Car. Free pick up from bus. Pick up from George Airport R160 per person (40 min drive).
Rooms: 2 cottages with twin or double beds.
Baths: Private shower/ toilets.
Meals: Full, continental or expanded breakfast. Basket

provided at extra cost.
Vegetarian: At most food outlets.
Complimentary: Tea & coffee.
Dates Open: All year.
High Season: Dec-Mar.
Rates: Per person: low R100, high R200.
Credit Cards: Visa, MC.
Rsv'tns: Highly recommended in high season.
Reserve Thru: Call direct.

Min. Stay: 2 nights.
Parking: Off-street parking.
In-Room: Color TV, sitting areas, fully equipped kitchen, fridge, coffee & tea facilities, linen, towels, maid service. Private & separate entrances. Laundry service by arrangement.
On-Premises: Braai facilities, scenic tours.
Exercise/Health: Nearby gym, weights, sauna, massage.

Swimming: Pool. Nearby ocean, lake.
Sunbathing: At beach.
Nudity: We don't mind.
Smoking: No limits.
Pets: Not permitted.
Children: Only 18+ yrs.
Languages: English, Afrikaans.
Your Hosts: Noreen & Grace.

Shangri-La Country Lodge

Gay-Friendly ⚣

Luxury Rondavels in the Waterberg Mtn. Foothills

Shangri-La Country Lodge, near Nylstroom in the Northern Province, is an idyllic retreat offering the comfort, style and intimacy of days gone by. Nestling cosily in dense bushveld in the foothills of the Waterberg mountain range, *Shangri-La's* mild winters and sub-tropical summers invite you to relax and unwind all the year round in a true haven of peace and tranquility. Guests are accommodated in luxury thatched rondavels, each with en suite bathroom, antique decor, country-style handmade quilts and festoon blinds.

Address: Eersbewoond Rd **Mail To:** PO Box 262, Nylstroom, 0510, South Africa
Tel: (27-14) 717 53 81, **Fax:** (27-14) 717 31 88.

Type: Country lodge with restaurant & bar, 1 hour north of Pretoria.
Clientele: Mostly hetero clientele with a 40% gay/lesbian following
Transportation: Pick up from airport.
To Gay Bars: 1-hr drive.
Rooms: 34 rooms with single or double beds.
Baths: All private bath/toilets.
Meals: Buffet breakfast, dinner included
Vegetarian: Available on request.
Complimentary: Tea & coffee.
Dates Open: All year.
High Season: Apr, Jul, Oct, Dec.
Rates: R360-R490 per person sharing, including dinner bed & breakfast.
Credit Cards: Diners, Visa, MC, Amex.
Rsv'tns: Required.
Reserve Thru: Travel agent or call direct.
Parking: Adequate free parking.
In-Room: Color TV, telephone, coffee/tea-making facilities, maid, room & laundry service.
On-Premises: Meeting rooms, laundry facilities.
Exercise/Health: Tennis court. Nearby gym, weights, Jacuzzi, sauna, steam, massage.
Swimming: Pool on premises. Nearby pool, river, lake, hydro health hot water spa.
Sunbathing: At poolside.
Smoking: Permitted.
Pets: Not permitted.
Handicap Access: Yes.
Children: Welcome.
Languages: Afrikaans, English.
Your Hosts: Lieben.

Elephant Springs Hotel

Gay-Friendly ⚣

The days of the old African hunters and explorers live again in Warmbaths, the recreational and fun capital of the Northern Province, less than 90 minutes' drive from Johannesburg. The *Elephant Springs Hotel* commemorates the discovery over a century ago of a veritable graveyard of animal bones and elephant tusks in the marshland surrounding the famous Hetbad Mineral Spring. Forty large bedrooms, all with en suite bathrooms, TV, telephone and ceiling fans, surround a lawn courtyard with its sparkling swimming pool. Some rooms have air conditioning. A delicious range of South African traditional dishes is served in our restaurant. The wine list is excellent, and the atmosphere is warm and friendly.

Address: 31 Sutter St, Warmbaths, 0480, South Africa
Tel: (27-14) 736 21 01, **Fax:** (27-14) 736 35 86.
Web: http://www.satis.co.za/elephant/index.htm

Type: Bed & breakfast with restaurant & bar.
Clientele: Mostly hetero clientele with a 30% gay/lesbian following
Transportation: Car is best. Pick up from airport.
To Gay Bars: 1-hr drive.
Rooms: 40 rooms & 20 apartments with single or double beds.
Baths: All private bath/toilets.
Meals: Full breakfast.
Vegetarian: On request.
Complimentary: Tea & coffee available in rooms.
Dates Open: All year.
High Season: Apr, Jul, Oct, Dec.
Rates: R144-R200 per person, sharing.
Credit Cards: Diners, Visa, Amex, MC.
Rsv'tns: Required.
Reserve Thru: Travel agent or call direct.
Parking: Adequate free parking.
In-Room: AC, ceiling fans, color TV, telephone, coffee/tea-making facilities, room, maid & laundry service.
On-Premises: Meeting rooms, laundry facilities. Discount tickets to Aventura Resort & Hot Springs.
Exercise/Health: Nearby gym, weights, Jacuzzi, sauna, steam, massage.
Swimming: Pool. Nearby pool, river, lake, health hydro hot water spa & hot springs.
Sunbathing: At poolside.
Smoking: Permitted. No non-smoking rooms available.
Pets: Not permitted.
Handicap Access: Yes.
Children: Welcome.
Languages: Afrikaans, English.
Your Hosts: George & Johan.

Naari Women's Guesthouse

India's First Women's Guesthouse

Independant women travellers to Asia now have the opportunity to stay in the first women's guesthouse in India. *Naari* is a small, friendly women-owned company offering a unique private guesthouse. Located in an upmarket area of South Delhi, it's situated in pleasant surroundings, within easy access of the airport and near the city centre. Rooms are tastefully decorated in simple, ethnic design and furnished to give a special character. Guests can lounge outside in a private sunny garden, or relax in the evening in the spacious sitting room. We offer personalised tours of the city and can accompany you to local market places. Contact us about our new guesthouse in Goa, opening in December 2000!

Tel: (91-11) 613 8316 or 618 3163, **Fax:** (91-11) 618 7401.
E-mail: naari@del3.vsnl.net.in **Web:** http://www.astroatlas.com/naari

Type: Women's guesthouse.
Clientele: Women only
Transportation: Pre-paid government taxi (black & yellow) from airport, or airport pick up by prior arrangement with Naari.
Baths: Ensuite, hot & cold showers.
Meals: Extra charge for breakfast, dinner, lunch.
Vegetarian: Catered for.
Dates Open: All year.
High Season: Oct-Mar.
Rates: Per person, per night: Oct-Mar Rs 800; Apr-Sept RS 800 (AC), Rs 650 (non-AC).
Rsv'tns: Tel, fax or email booking office or guesthouse for reservation & address.
In-Room: Air coolers, ACs, ceiling fans.
On-Premises: Local travel info, lounge w/ colour TV, email, pure spring water, BBQ on request, sunny balconies. Dining facility, laundry service on request. ISD/STD phone.
Exercise/Health: Holistic massage on request. Near yoga centre.
Sunbathing: On balconies.
Smoking: Permitted.
Pets: Not permitted.
Handicap Access: Ground floor only.
Children: Permitted.
Languages: Hindi, English.
Your Hosts: Betu, Cath & Archana.

Dusun Jogja Village Inn

Gay-Friendly ⚥
Partly Gay-Owned & -Operated

Relaxed, Distinctive, Unique

We welcome you into our extended family where *Jogja's* charms embrace you. This is a tranquil guesthouse where intimacy, luxury, comfort and style come together to create a peaceful respite. Guests enjoy a gardened environment, individually designed rooms with private terraces, an open-air dining pavilion and an inviting swimming pool. Relaxed, distinctive and unique, a visit here with create a unique personal experience and many memories.

Address: Menukan St. #5, (south of Prawirotaman), Yogyakarta, Central Java 55153, Indonesia
Tel: (62-274) 373031, **Fax:** (62-274) 382202.
E-mail: jvigecko@indo.net.id **Web:** http://www.jvidusun.co.id

Type: Boutique hotel with restaurant, pool bar & gift shop.
Clientele: Mostly straight clientele with a gay & lesbian following
Transportation: Taxi: 20 min from airport, 15 min from train, 10 min from bus. Free pick up from airport upon reservation.
Rooms: 20 rooms, 1 suite, 3 semi-cottages with single, double.
Baths: All private bath/ shower/toilets.
Meals: Full breakfast.
Vegetarian: We have an extensive vegetarian menu.
Complimentary: Welcome drink upon checking in.
Dates Open: All year.
High Season: May-Aug & Dec-Feb.
Rates: US $70-US $160 (US $1 = approx 8000 Rp).
Credit Cards: MC, Visa, Amex, Diners, JBC.
Rsv'tns: Very advisable.
Reserve Thru: Travel agent or call direct.
Min. Stay: 1 day/night.
Parking: Adequate, free on- & off-street parking.
In-Room: Telephone, AC, ceiling fans, maid, room & laundry service.
On-Premises: Meeting room, TV lounge, laser disc library, phone, fax, game pavilion, movie room, tour & travel info, restaurant & pool bar.
Exercise/Health: Nearby gym, weights, massage.
Swimming: Pool on premises & nearby.
Sunbathing: Poolside, in garden & on patio. 30 min drive to nearby beach.
Smoking: Permitted in open-air areas.
Pets: Permitted.
Handicap Access: No.
Children: Welcome, but limited.
Languages: Indonesian, English.
Your Hosts: Paul (Amron), Adam, Ruby.

Tarntawan Place Hotel

Gay-Friendly 50/50 ♀♂
Gay-Owned & -Operated

The *Tarntawan Place Hotel* takes great pleasure in welcoming you to an experience of truly friendly service and vibrant surroundings. Situated in a quiet courtyard in the heart of Bangkok's business and entertainment district, the we're within walking distance of international banks, major companies, shopping centres and airline offices. The city's best nightlife venues are just around the corner, including the famous Patpong Night Bazaar and Thaniya Plaza. Rooms in our boutique-style hotel are nicely appointed, spacious and light, creating a friendly and intimate atmosphere. Our personalised service and attention to detail ensure a special comfort and charm. We look forward to welcoming you with us!

Address: 119/5-10 Surawong Rd, Bangkok, 10500, Thailand
Tel: (66-2) 238 2620, **Fax:** (66-2) 238 3228.
E-mail: tarntawan@tarntawan.com **Web:** http://www.tarntawan.com

Type: Boutique-style hotel.
Clientele: 50% gay & lesbian & 50% hetero
Transportation: Taxi, hotel limo. Airport pickup THB 550, train THB 200, bus THB 70.
To Gay Bars: 1 min walk.
Rooms: 63 rms, 7 suites w/ single, queen or king beds.
Baths: Private bath/shower/ toilets.
Meals: Full breakfast 24 hrs.
Vegetarian: 24 hours.
Complimentary: Welcome drink, in-room tea & coffee, weekly guest cocktail party.
Dates Open: All year.
High Season: Oct-Mar.
Rates: THB 1,900-2,500.
Credit Cards: MC, Visa, Diners, Amex, Eurocard.
Rsv'tns: Required.
Reserve Thru: Call direct.
Parking: Adequate free off-street parking.
In-Room: Phone, AC, color satellite TV, fridge, coffee & tea-making facilities, maid, room & laundry service.
On-Premises: Meeting rooms, business services.
Exercise/Health: Massage. Nearby gym, weights, steam, massage.
Swimming: Nearby pool.
Sunbathing: Nearby pool.
Smoking: Permitted. Non-smoking rooms available.
Pets: Not permitted.
Handicap Access: Yes, rails in bathroom.
Children: Free if stay w/ parents. Babysitting & baby cribs available.
Languages: Thai, English, French, German, Spanish, Italian.
Your Hosts: Lukas.

Lotus Hotel

The Center of Gay Chiang Mai

Nightly, the street in front of the *Lotus Hotel* becomes the lively center of gay Chiang Mai. Across from the hotel is the largest and most popular gay club in town — The Adams Apple Club. Four floors of gay entertainment include a restaurant serving Western and Thai dishes, a gift shop, private rooms with traditional Thai massage, a showplace with 40 go-go dancers swaying to the latest pop music, and a karaoke facility. The gay *Lotus Hotel* in Chaing Mai is perfectly located in the busiest district with easy access to local Thai markets, shopping centers, movie theaters, banks, and post office. A popular feature of the hotel is a tropical garden with its very busy Garden Bar that sells inexpensive drinks.

All the rooms have en suite bathrooms and are equipped with air conditioning, mini bar, stereo, cable TV, and VCR. Amenities are of top quality: therapeutic mattresses, soft pillows, and cotton linens. The hotel also: serves meals at any time to your room or the terrace, has laundry service, rents cars, offers guided tours around Chiang Mai, confirms tickets and reservations, has a video and book library, and, best of all, has a very friendly staff.

Address: 2/25 Soi Viangbua, Tambol Chang-Phuk, Amphur Muang, Chiang Mai, 50300, Thailand
Tel: (66-53) 215 376, 215 462, **Fax:** (66-53) 221 340.
E-mail: mohamad@loxinfo.co.th **Web:** http://www.angelfire.com/biz/lotushotel

Type: Gay-owned hotel with bar, restaurant, kiosk shops, drag & boys show, karaoke, massage.
Clientele: Mostly men with women welcome & some gay-friendly hetero clientele
Transportation: Pick up from airport, bus, train station. Taxi 150 baht. VIP 250 baht
To Gay Bars: Opposite hotel.
Rooms: 6 rooms with king & queen beds & 3 suites.
Baths: All private.
Vegetarian: Available on restaurant menu.
Complimentary: Fruit, flowers & free airport transfer for regular customers.
Dates Open: All year.
High Season: Nov-Apr 15 & Aug.
Rates: High season 880-1850 Baht.
Discounts: 20% in low season or for stays over one month.
Credit Cards: MC, Visa.
Rsv'tns: Required.
Reserve Thru: Travel agent or call direct.
Parking: Limited free parking.
In-Room: Color TV, video tape library, AC, phone, refrigerator, maid, room & laundry service. VCR in suite, cable TV.
On-Premises: Bar, terrace & garden.
Exercise/Health: Outdoor gym.
Sunbathing: Private sun decks in the garden.
Smoking: Permitted without restrictions.
Pets: Not permitted.
Handicap Access: No.
Children: Not permitted.
Languages: Thai, English, French & Arabic.

Villa Maria

WWW Gay/Lesbian ⚥
Gay-Owned & -Operated

Home from Home in the Heart of Europe

Villa Maria is situated in a luxury villa on the south side of Brussels' city centre. Each room has tea- and coffee-making facilities, as well as phone, fax and e-mail. Two bathrooms and two toilets serve three very comfortable guest bedrooms. Guests are invited to use the large lounge area, where we have a large collection of music CDs — or watch television, we have TV channels in most European languages. Continental breakfast is served in the lounge throughout the morning and guests may choose what time they would like breakfast. Dinner (table d'hote) is also available most evenings at about 8 p.m. Guests arriving late may reserve meals for their arrival.

Discounts are available for seven nights or more, and long-stay and group prices are available on request. Laundry service is also available to guests. Brussels is an ideal base for your European holiday. Situated right in the center of Europe, by train we are only 80 minutes from Paris and 150 minutes from London. And by car, we're only 120 minutes from Koln and 120 minutes from Amsterdam. It is also possible to find inexpensive flights from Brussels to other European cities.

Address: Brussels, Belgium
Tel: (32-2) 375 9792, **Fax:** (32-2) 375 4673.
E-mail: credence@hebel.net **Web:** http://www.hebel.net/~credence/gay

Type: Bed & breakfast with restuarant & bar.
Clientele: Mostly gay & lesbian with some hetero clientele
Transportation: Airport train to city station, then direct tram.
To Gay Bars: 10 min drive, 15 min by tram.
Rooms: 3 rooms with single, double or queen beds. 1 group room sleeps 6.
Baths: Shared: 2 bath/shower/toilets, 2 WCs only.
Meals: Continental breakfast. Dinner on request.
Vegetarian: On request.
Complimentary: Free welcome drink. Drinks & snacks available.
Dates Open: All year.
Rates: Single BEF 1700, double BEF 2500. Group room BEF 1,250/nt.
Discounts: Inquire about +7 nights 10% discount.
Rsv'tns: Required.
Reserve Thru: Call direct.
Parking: Ample free on-street parking.
In-Room: Tea & coffee-making facilites, maid, room & laundry service.
On-Premises: TV lounge, CD & videotape libraries, phone, fax, e-mail.
Exercise/Health: Nearby gym, sauna, park.
Swimming: Nearby pool.
Smoking: No restrictions.
Pets: Not permitted.
Handicap Access: No.
Children: No.
Languages: French, English, German.
Your Hosts: Richard & Cyril.

Finns Hotel Pension

Gay-Friendly ⚥
Gay-Owned & -Operated

Finns Hotel Pension is a beautiful old wood house decorated in the old style. It's a great place to stay for a holiday in this very special corner of Denmark, the most famous holiday place in the country. Enjoy the sun drenched beaches, lovely scenery, and outstanding local museums. The owner and hotel staff are gay and promote a relaxed atmosphere for gay people.

Address: Ostre Strandvej 63, Skagen, 9990, Denmark
Tel: (45) 98 45 01 55.
Web: http://www.skaw.dk/finnshotelpension

Type: Hotel with restaurant for guests.
Clientele: Mostly hetero with some gay & lesbian clientele
Transportation: Car or train is best. Free pick up from train.
Rooms: 6 rooms with single or double beds.
Baths: Sinks in rooms. 2 rooms with private full baths, 1 room with private WC. Shared: 2 full baths & 1 WC.
Meals: Expanded continental breakfast.

Optional lunch & dinner.
Vegetarian: Available if ordered before arrival.
Dates Open: All year. If visiting in winter, call first, could be closed during some part of winter months.
High Season: May 15-Aug 31.
Rates: High season: single Dkr 350-475, double Dkr 600-875. Low season: single Dkr 325-450, double Dkr 550-800.
Discounts: 10% for stays of 3+ days, 15% for stays of

7+ days.
Credit Cards: MC, Visa, JCB, Eurocard, Dan-kort.
Rsv'tns: Required.
Reserve Thru: Call direct.
Parking: Limited free off-street parking.
In-Room: Radio & room service.
On-Premises: Garden, library, lounge, telephone, & laundry facilities.
Exercise/Health: Small weights.
Swimming: Public pool 1 km. Ocean beach nearby.

Sunbathing: At the beach or in the garden.
Nudity: Permitted at the beach.
Smoking: Permitted. No non-smoking rooms available.
Pets: Permitted.
Handicap Access: No. Stairs to rooms.
Children: Permitted, but maximum of 2.
Languages: Danish, English, German & Swedish.
Your Hosts: Finn.
IGLTA

Fosse Farmhouse

WWW Gay-Friendly ⚥

English Country Living with Style and Flair

Fosse Farmhouse, a romantic country retreat constructed of honey coloured stone under a clay tiled roof, was built over 300 years ago by the Duke of Beaufort for his estate manager. Situated beside the historic Roman Fosseway, the farmhouse sits on the edge of the picturesque Cotswolds. Caron Cooper, has created a romantic hideaway with canopied beds and stylish interiors that have been featured in interior design magazines worldwide. Rooms are exquisitely decorated with a blend of decorative French antiques and traditional fine English linens and lace. Delicious afternoon cream teas and dinner by request.

Address: Nettleton Shrub, Nr. Chippenham, Nettleton, Wiltshire SN14 7NJ, England
Tel: (44-1249) 782 286, **Fax:** (44-1249) 783 066.
E-mail: caroncooper@compuserve.com **Web:** http://www.fossefarmhouse.co.uk

Type: B&B with cottage, restaurant, bar, tea room, antique decorators shop.
Clientele: Mostly hetero, gay/lesbian following
Transportation: Car, train, taxi. Ask re train pick up.
To Gay Bars: 12 miles.
Rooms: 2 doubles, 1 twin, 1 triple, 1 cottage, 1 loft (sngl or dbl beds).

Baths: All private.
Meals: Full English breakfast. Dinner optional.
Vegetarian: On request in advance.
Complimentary: Tea, coffee, biscuits, mineral water.
Dates Open: All year.
Rates: £55-£165.
Discounts: 10% 3+ nights.

Credit Cards: MC, Visa, Amex.
Rsv'tns: Required.
Reserve Thru: Call, fax, email direct.
Parking: Ample free off-street parking.
In-Room: Colour TV, coffee & tea makers, maid & laundry service.
Exercise/Health: Nearby

gym, golf, horse riding, ballooning.
Sunbathing: In garden.
Smoking: OK in guest lounge & some rooms.
Children: Welcome.
Languages: English, French.
Your Hosts: Caron.

Kennard Hotel, The

A Georgian Town House of Charm and Character

Staying at *The Kennard Hotel* gives you a chance to discover and enjoy a true Georgian Town House. Now restored to a charming small hotel with its own special character, it was originally built in 1794 during Bath's grand era of elegance and prosperity. Each of its 13 bedrooms are thoughtfully and individually furnished for your comfort. The original Georgian kitchen, now a delightful garden-style bistro, is the setting for a full choice of English or continental breakfasts.

Quietly situated in Henrietta Street, its city centre location is ideal — just over Pulteney Bridge, only minutes from the Abbey and Roman Baths and with easy access from London or the Station. We're also a wonderful touring base for the South and West of England.

Travel north to the picturesque villages of the Cotswolds; south to Glastonbury Abbey and the beautiful cathedral city of Wells; east to the most awe-inspiring sight in Europe, Iron Age Stonehenge, and west to Bristol. Your hosts, Richard and Malcolm.

Address: 11 Henrietta Street, Bath, Avon BA2 6LL, England
Tel: (44-1225) 310 472, **Fax:** (44-1225) 460 054.
E-mail: kennard@dircon.co.uk **Web:** http://www.kennard.co.uk

Type: Bed & breakfast hotel.
Clientele: Mostly hetero with a gay & lesbian following
To Gay Bars: 5-minute walk.
Rooms: 10 doubles & 2 singles.

Baths: 10 private, others share.
Meals: Full English breakfast.
Vegetarian: Available upon request.
Complimentary: Coffee & tea-making facilities in room.
Dates Open: All year.

Rates: £78-£95.
Credit Cards: MC, Visa, Amex, Diners.
Rsv'tns: Required.
Reserve Thru: Call, fax or e-mail direct.
Parking: On-street parking.
In-Room: Colour satelite TV, direct-dial phone with

modem, hair dryers, tea & coffee.
Smoking: Non smoking.
Children: Not permitted.
Languages: English.
Your Hosts: Richard & Malcolm.

Leigh House

WWW Gay/Lesbian ⚢
Gay-Owned & -Operated

Log Fires, History & Home Cooking... England at its Best

Deep in the heart of the West Country lies the beautiful historic town of Bradford-on-Avon, set on a hillside with a winding river at its base and terraces of weavers' cottages and grand merchants' houses. The town dates from its 7th-century Saxon church, 14th-century tithe barn, and medieval bridge with pilgrims' chapel (later used as a lock-up cell), to the woollen trade of the 18th century. It is here, in this town rich in tradition, that you will find the beautiful 16th-century farmhouse called *Leigh House*. It was one of four farms granted by Queen Elizabeth I to the only man she cared to marry, Robert Dudley, Earl of Leicester, in 1574 and sits in six acres.

Each room has individual, tasteful style with views to the hills or overlooking the walled garden. There is a converted 16th-century bakehouse available for bed and breakfast or self catering up to seven people. In the sitting room, with its beamed ceiling and old tiled floor, are an open-hearth fireplace, bread oven, and a separate smoking oven. Fresh home-cooked meals are served at a long chestnut table on a flagstone floor, glowing with dark woods and candles, complimented by rustic country furniture and low beams. Enjoy surrounding rivers, canals and countryside, with walks, cycle rides, canoes and narrowboats, or visit nearby Bath City with its grand Georgian buildings, museums, attractive shops and famous Roman Baths. There is a main railway link for Bath, London, Plymouth and the Midlands.

Address: Leigh Road West, Bradford-on-Avon, Wiltshire BA15 2RB, England
Tel: (44-1225) 867835. For urgent reservations, please telephone. We answer e-mails in 3-4 days.
E-mail: leigh.house@virgin.net **Web:** http://business.virgin.net/leigh.house/

Type: Bed & breakfast guesthouse with restaurant & self-catering cottage.
Clientele: Mostly gay & lesbian with some hetero clientele
Transportation: Car is best. Free pick up from train.
To Gay Bars: 8 miles to gay bars.
Rooms: 5 rooms, 1 cottage with single, double or king beds.
Baths: 2 private bath/shower/toilets, 1 private bath/toilet.
Meals: Full breakfast. Evening meals available (confirm when booking).
Vegetarian: Special diets catered for, please inform when booking.
Complimentary: Tea & coffee any time, wine with meals.
Dates Open: All year.
High Season: Jun-Aug & Christmas.
Rates: £26-£35 per person.
Discounts: 15% for 3 or more nights B&B & reduction for self-catering & groups/house parties.
Rsv'tns: Required.
Reserve Thru: Call direct.
Parking: Ample free off-street parking.
On-Premises: TV lounge, video tape and laser library.
Swimming: Pool nearby.
Sunbathing: On patio.
Smoking: Permitted in guest lounge. All bedrooms are non-smoking.
Pets: Permitted with advance notice when booking.
Handicap Access: Yes. Cottage has ground-floor bedroom & bath.
Children: Not heavily encouraged.
Languages: English.
Your Hosts: Alan & Peter.

Fountain Inn, The

Gay/Lesbian ♂

Built as a traditional Victorian public house, *The Fountain Inn* retains much of its original character. With guest accommodations refurbished to the highest standards, we offer a warm and welcoming stay. All rooms are en suite or have separate, private toilet, and have telephone, central heating, colour TV with satellite movie channel and in-house video channel, and guest keys. Our very popular, ground-floor gay bar is only a 5- to 10-minute walk from the other gay bars and clubs, the main railway station and Birmingham's shopping and entertainment areas. Birmingham is known as the "Second City" (London being the first!), and is at the heart of the motorway network, with London about 1-1/2-hour's drive away and "Shakespeare country" only a half-hour's drive. Birmingham boasts one of the largest conference centers, exhibition centers and international airports in Europe.

Address: 102 Wrentham St, Birmingham, West Midlands B5 6QL, England
Tel: (44-121) 622 1452, **Fax:** (44-121) 622 5387. In USA call (407) 994-3558, **Fax:** (407) 994-3634.

Type: Guesthouse inn. Our bar has pub food & is open evenings & Sat & Sun days.
Clientele: Mostly men with women welcome
Transportation: Car, 5-min taxi from train stn (£2), taxi from Birmingham Int'l Airport about £12.
To Gay Bars: 5 min walk.
Rooms: 5 rooms with single or double beds.

Baths: All private.
Meals: Full English breakfast. Continental breakfast served in bedroom.
Vegetarian: Available on request before arrival.
Complimentary: Tea/coffee making facilities & biscuits.
Dates Open: All year.
Rates: £30-£50 per night.
Discounts: 10% for 3

nights & over.
Credit Cards: All major except not Amex.
Rsv'tns: Required.
Reserve Thru: Call direct.
Parking: Free off-street parking for 5 cars, on-street pay parking, free weekends.
In-Room: Color TV with in-house, non-porn video channel, movie channel via satellite, telephone, coffee/

tea-making facilities & maid service.
On-Premises: Meeting rooms.
Smoking: Permitted.
Pets: Not permitted.
Children: Not permitted.
Languages: English.
Your Hosts: Erick.

Alandene Licensed Hotel, The

WWW Gay-Friendly 50/50 ⚥
Gay-Owned & -Operated

Large Enough To Cope, Small Enough To Care

The Alandene Hotel is a detached residence that caters to a more discerning clientele. Situated in the centre of Blackpool, we are easily accessible to the gay scene, theatres, town centre and pleasure beach. We have private parking facilities and, once parked, everything is within walking distance. Families, couples and singles are all warmly welcomed. We accommodate guests in double and family rooms — en-suite and standard. Should you wish to stay in and relax after a hectic day, we have a licensed bar lounge for your comfort. We're ideally situated for visiting the Lake District, Morecambe, Liverpool and Preston. **Directions:** M55 — Junction 4 — turn right onto A583 Blackpool — landmarks to see on left — Windmill, McDonalds, CS Lounge Suites. We're 1000 yards further on, on the left-hand side. We welcome you to visit our website.

Address: 131 Park Road, Blackpool, FY1 4ET, England
Tel: (44-1253) 623 356 (Tel/Fax), Toll-free: (0800) 783 9489.
E-mail: alandene@aol.com **Web:** http://members.aol.com/markymarke/alandene.htm

Type: Hotel with bar.
Clientele: 50% gay & lesbian & 50% hetero
Transportation: Car, rail, coach all easily accessible.
To Gay Bars: A 5 min walk.
Rooms: 10 rooms with double beds.
Baths: Private: 5 shower/toilets, 10 sink/washbasin only. Shared: 1 bath/shower/toilet, 1 shower only, 1 WC only.

Meals: Full or continental breakfast. Dinner optional.
Vegetarian: Available on site & in town.
Complimentary: Mints on pillows. Tea/coffee & biscuits on arrival.
Dates Open: All year.
High Season: Sept.-Nov.
Rates: £12-£20.
Discounts: Mention Inn Places for 10% off.
Credit Cards: All major

credit cards accpeted.
Rsv'tns: Recommended during high season.
Parking: Adequate free parking.
In-Room: Colour TV, coffee & tea-making facilities, maid service.
On-Premises: Laundry facilities.
Exercise/Health: Nearby gym, weights, Jacuzzi, sauna, steam, massage.

Swimming: Nearby pool & ocean.
Sunbathing: At beach.
Smoking: No smoking in dining room.
Pets: Permitted. Separate room with run for animals.
Handicap Access: Yes, ground-floor bedrooms.
Children: Welcome.
Languages: English.
Your Hosts: Mark & Keith.

Creffield, The

WWW Gay/Lesbian ♂

Exclusively Gay Hotel With the Air of a Country Home

A well-appointed red-brick, late Edwardian house, *The Creffield* was originally built as a rich man's family summer home. It stands on its own grounds with a car park to the fore and a large private garden to the rear. All of the bedrooms are en-suite and the single rooms are actually small doubles. Our two largest bedrooms have four-poster beds. Breakfast is served either in the conservatory or outside on the patio. It is an easy walk from *The Creffield* to all of Bournemouth's main venues. If you have a car, like a drink, but don't relish the thought of walking your feet off, then park your car in the free car park and five licensed venues are a hop, skip and a jump away (no taxis necessary).

Address: 7 Cambridge Road, Bournemouth, BH2 6AE, England
Tel: (44-1202) 317 900.
E-mail: roger@thecreffield.freeserve.co.uk

Type: Bed & breakfast guesthouse with bar for residents on premises.
Clientele: Mostly men with women welcome
Transportation: Car, train from London, taxi.
To Gay Bars: 2 min walk.
Rooms: 9 rooms with singles or doubles. 2 rooms have 4-poster beds.
Baths: All private shower/ toilets.

Meals: Full English breakfast.
Vegetarian: Always available.
Complimentary: Tea & coffee. Courtesy trays in each room.
Dates Open: All year.
High Season: Jun-Sept.
Rates: Single £35; Double £50-£55; 4-poster £60-£70.
Discounts: 10% on stays of 7 or more nights.

Reserve Thru: Call direct.
Min. Stay: Two nights during high season.
Parking: Adequate free, well-lit off-street parking.
In-Room: Color TV, coffee & tea-making facilities, maid service.
On-Premises: Meeting room, TV lounge, full central heating, large private garden.
Exercise/Health: Nearby

gym, sauna, steam.
Swimming: Pool & ocean nearby.
Sunbathing: On patio.
Smoking: Permitted only in rooms.
Pets: Permitted. Must be kept on a lead.
Children: Absolutely not.
Languages: English.
Your Hosts: Roger.

Alpha Lodge Private Hotel

Gay/Lesbian ♂

THE Gay Hotel for Single People

Brighton's longest established exclusively gay hotel, *Alpha Lodge* overlooks the Victorian Palace Pier, a few yards from the beach and most gay clubs. The Steine Room Suite consists of Turkish Bath, rest area with open fire and colour TV, shower area, hair dryer, toilet and lockers. Towels and wraps are provided, and the facility is free to residents Wednesday, Friday and Saturday for 1-1/2 hours in early evening. Guests have front door keys, and friends may be brought in at all times. A map of Gay Brighton, privilege card for entry to gay clubs, and a welcoming drink on arrival are provided.

Address: 19 New Steine, Brighton, E Sussex BN2 1PD, England
Tel: (44-1273) 609 632, **Fax:** (44-1273) 690 264.

Type: Guesthouse.
Clientele: Mostly men with women welcome
Transportation: Taxi or bus.
To Gay Bars: 2-min walk.
Rooms: 10 rooms with single & double beds.
Baths: Shared.
Meals: Full English breakfast.
Vegetarian: Available with overnight notice.
Complimentary: Coffee,

tea, soft drink on arrival.
High Season: July, Aug & Bank Holidays, mid-season May/June & Sept/Oct.
Rates: Per room: low £22-£44; mid: £25-£50; high: £26-£52. Bank holidays £29-£58.
Discounts: Stay 6 nights & get 1 night free to all & 10% to members of gay groups.
Credit Cards: MC, Visa, Amex, Eurocard, JCB, Switch, Electron.

Rsv'tns: Recommended in summer 10 days in advance.
Reserve Thru: Travel agent or call direct.
Min. Stay: Longer stays on bank holidays.
Parking: Free & pay parking on street at or near hotel.
In-Room: Color TV, beverage-making facilities, radio/alarm clock & intercom. Room service for continental breakfast.

On-Premises: TV lounge, public phone, meeting rooms, fridge.
Exercise/Health: Steam room suite.
Swimming: Pool, ocean beach nearby.
Sunbathing: At beach.
Nudity: 10-min walk to public nudist beach.
Smoking: Permitted.
Pets: Not permitted.
Languages: English.
Your Hosts: Derrick.

Avalon Guest House

The Friendly Place to Stay in Brighton

From the minute you step through the door, *The Avalon* offers a warm, friendly and comfortable stay. The guesthouse occupies an 1820's terraced house in a tree-lined road, only a few minutes' stroll to the sea. Our location is superb, within minutes of Brighton town centre, the pubs and clubs, theatres and, of course, the beaches and marina.

We run our guesthouse ourselves and offer a high standard of cleanliness and service. The eight rooms are all full en-suites, having toilets and baths/showers, tea and coffee facilities and TV. We have single, double, twin and triple rooms, with three deluxe rooms (one with a wrought-iron four-poster, one with bed and sofa, and the other with a king-sized bed). All three have CD players and fridges. If you are interested in booking, please call or e-mail Gary or John.

Address: 7 Upper Rock Gardens, Brighton, East Sussex , England
Tel: (44-1273) 692 344 (Tel/Fax).
E-mail: avalongh1@aol.com

Type: Guesthouse.
Clientele: Mostly gay & lesbian, some hetero
Transportation: Car or taxi from Brighton Station, Gatwick airport.
To Gay Bars: 1 block.
Rooms: 8 rooms with single, double or king beds.
Baths: 8 private bath/shower/toilets.
Meals: Full breakfast.
Vegetarian: Vegetarian

breakfast available.
Complimentary: Tea, coffee.
Dates Open: All year.
High Season: May-Sept.
Rates: Summer: dbl £40-£60, sngl £22.50; winter: dbl £35-£55, sngl £20.
Discounts: On mid-week & multiple day stays.
Credit Cards: MC, Visa.
Rsv'tns: Required.
Reserve Thru: Call direct.

Min. Stay: Wknds 2 nts, Bank Holidays 3 nts.
Parking: Adequate on-street parking.
In-Room: Ceiling fans, color TV, refrigerator, coffee & tea-making facilities, maid service.
On-Premises: Video tape library.
Exercise/Health: Nearby gym, weights, Jacuzzi, sauna, steam.

Swimming: Nearby pool & ocean.
Sunbathing: At beach.
Smoking: Permitted in designated smoking bedrooms. Non-smoking rooms available.
Pets: Not permitted.
Children: No.
Languages: English, German.
Your Hosts: Gary & John.

Barrington's Hotel Ltd.

Gay-Friendly 50/50 ♀♂

Right in the Center of Brighton's Gay Scene

Luxury rooms, all with direct-dial telephones, and a full English breakfast enhance your stay at *Barrington's Hotel Ltd.* Most rooms in this Regency Building overlook the Royal Pavilion and Pavilion Gardens. Our fully licensed bar and lounge are open to the public, and an enclosed patio garden is just off the bar. Brighton's gay scene is one of the busiest in England. We are located above the Brighton Oasis Sauna, the largest on England's South Coast, and we are only two minutes from Revenge nightclub.

Address: 76 Grand Parade, Brighton, BN2 2JA, England
Tel: (44-1273) 604 182 (Tel/Fax).

Type: Hotel with licensed lounge bar & conservatory.
Clientele: 50% gay & lesbian & 50% hetero clientele
Rooms: Luxury rooms with double & twin beds.

Baths: Private showers, shared bath, 1 private bath.
Meals: Full English or vegetarian breakfast.
High Season: June-Sept.
Rates: £25-£30 per person.
Reserve Thru: Call direct.

Parking: Free parking behind hotel
In-Room: Remote control colour TV, radios & intercom, direct-dial telephone.
Swimming: 2-minute walk to ocean.

Smoking: Permitted.
Pets: Small pets permitted.
Handicap Access: No.
Children: Permitted over 5 years of age.
Languages: English.
Your Hosts: Barry.

Beynon House

Gay-Friendly 50/50 ♀♂
Gay-Owned & -Operated

Call Us For a Holiday to Remember

Beynon House is situated in a quiet terrace in the heart of Kemptown Village, yet is just a couple of minutes walk from Brighton's seafront, the nudist beach, gay bars and clubs. This location make us very well-placed to discover and explore Brighton's historic Lanes and Royal Pavilion. Our guests praise our excellent breakfasts, cleanliness and warm, welcoming atmosphere. We offer a good range of facilities and original artwork is displayed in the rooms. We are a non-smoking guest house. Call us for a holiday to remember — we're English Tourist Board "Commended."

Address: 24 St George's Terrace, Brighton, BN2 1JJ, England
Tel: (44-1273) 681 014 (Tel/Fax).

Type: Bed & breakfast.
Clientele: 50% gay & lesbian & 50% hetero clientele
Transportation: Walking distance from centre of Brighton. Few minutes by taxi from Brighton station.
To Gay Bars: A 5 min walk, a 1 min drive.
Rooms: 7 rooms with single, double or king beds.
Baths: All rooms have

showers. Private: 1 shower/toilet, 6 sink/washbasin only. Shared: 2 WC/toilets only.
Meals: Full breakfast.
Vegetarian: Full vegetarian breakfast options available. Excellent vegetarian restaurants within walking distance.
Dates Open: All year.
High Season: Jul-Aug.
Rates: Per person, summer & winter: £20-£35.

Discounts: Telephone for special rates & discounts.
Credit Cards: MC, Visa, Eurocard.
Reserve Thru: Call direct.
Parking: Adequate, free on-street parking outside guesthouse.
In-Room: Colour TV, coffee & tea-making facilities.
Exercise/Health: Nearby gym, weights, Jacuzzi, sauna, steam, massage.

Swimming: Pool & ocean nearby.
Sunbathing: At beach. Closest gay guesthouse to nudist beach.
Smoking: Non-smoking guesthouse.
Pets: Not permitted.
Handicap Access: No.
Children: No.
Languages: English.
Your Hosts: Phil & Karl.

Coward's Guest House

Coward's Guest House is a Regency-style guesthouse in the heart of Brighton's gay area, five minutes' walk from gay bars and clubs. Brighton is a very gay town with a lively gay nightlife. The town is known for its Regency architecture and for The Pavilion, a winter palace which was built by the Prince Regent. The train from London takes only 50 minutes, making Brighton an easy commute to London's tourist attractions.

Address: 12 Upper Rock Gardens, Brighton, BN2 1QE, England
Tel: (44-1273) 692677.

Type: Guesthouse.
Clientele: Men only
Transportation: Brighton Station, then taxi.
To Gay Bars: Many gay pubs & clubs within 5 min walk.
Rooms: 2 singles, 4 doubles & 2 triples with single & double beds.

Baths: Nearly all ensuite.
Meals: Full English or vegetarian breakfast.
Vegetarian: Tell us when you arrive.
Complimentary: Tea & coffee in all rooms.
Dates Open: All year.
High Season: Apr-Oct.
Rates: Double £50-£60,
single £27.
Credit Cards: Visa, Access.
Rsv'ns: Required.
Reserve Thru: Call direct.
Parking: On-street parking.
In-Room: Color TV, tea & coffee.
Swimming: At nearby sea, a 3 min walk.
Sunbathing: On the beach.

Nudity: Permitted on nude beach 10 min walk.
Smoking: Permitted in rooms.
Pets: Not permitted.
Handicap Access: No.
Children: Not permitted.
Languages: English.
Your Hosts: Gerry & Cyril.

Hudsons Guest House

Exclusively Gay & Centrally Located

Designer converted, *Hudsons'* guestrooms offer clean, comfortable accommodation. Breakfast is included and has prompted such press reviews as "The best we had in Britain," "Hudsons' breakfast is first-class," and "It's fab". Britain's *Pink Paper* said "I was lucky enough to snap up the last room at Hudsons — the ace of the pack". Our welcome gives you a cup of tea (or glass of sherry) and a map and guide to Brighton. The only exclusively gay hotel inspected and approved by the Tourist Office, we're classified with three diamonds by the English Tourism Council, and are in the UK's prestigious *Which? Hotel Guide.*

Address: 22 Devonshire Place, Brighton, E Sussex BN2 1QA, England
Tel: (44-1273) 683 642, **Fax:** (44-1273) 696 088.
E-mail: hudsons@brighton.co.uk **Web:** http://www.brighton.co.uk/hotels/hudsons

Type: Guesthouse.
Clientele: Good mix of gay men & women
Transportation: Train to Brighton then taxi or #7 bus.
To Gay Bars: 2 min walk.
Rooms: 9 rooms w/ single, queen or king beds & 1-BR central seafront apt.
Baths: All private.
Meals: English breakfast.
Complimentary: Tea,
coffee, sherry, juice, biscuits.
Rates: £24-£60.
Discounts: Mid-week, extended stay.
Credit Cards: MC, Visa, Amex.
Rsv'ns: Recommended.
Reserve Thru: Travel agent or call direct.
Min. Stay: Bank holidays, wknds.
Parking: On-street parking
nearby.
In-Room: Washbasins, tea-making facilities, colour TV, phone, central heating, laundry & maid service.
On-Premises: Guests lounge, garden.
Exercise/Health: Nearby gym, weights, Jacuzzi, sauna, steam, massage.
Swimming: At nearby ocean beach & pool.

Sunbathing: Patio & nearby beach.
Nudity: At nearby beach.
Smoking: Not in dining room or some bedrooms.
Pets: Not permitted.
Children: Not permitted.
Languages: English, some French, German.
Your Hosts: Frank & Graham.

Pear Tree House

WWW Gay/Lesbian ♀♂
Gay-Owned & -Operated

240-Year-Old Former Village Inn

Pear Tree House is centrally located for exploring the historic counties of Cambridge, with its colleges dating back to 1294. A short drive away are Ely with one of the most magnificent cathedrals in England, dating from 1081, Bury St. Edmunds with its architecture and Abbey ruins, and Newmarket, the centre of world horseracing and bloodstock. Further afield are historic country houses, and picturesque villages which take you back hundreds of years. We have a local gay pub and are very near USAF Mildenhall which has direct charter flights from the US. **1999 English Tourist Board Award. 4-Diamond Rating & Silver Award.**

Address: Chapel Road, West Row, Mildenhall, Suffolk 1P28 8PA, England
Tel: (44-1638) 711 112 (Tel/Fax).
E-mail: peartree@hello.to **Web:** http://www.peartree.hello.to

Type: Guesthouse, 20 min from Cambridge.
Clientele: Gay & lesbian. Good mix of men & women
Transportation: Car is best. To London airports: Stansted 30 min; Heathrow 1 hr 40 mins.
To Gay Bars: 3 miles.
Rooms: 4 rooms with single, double or king beds.
Baths: 2 private bath/shower/toilets, 1 shared shower/toilet.
Meals: Full English breakfast.
Vegetarian: Vegetarian breakfast available.
Complimentary: Tea & coffee.
Dates Open: All year.
High Season: May-Oct.
Rates: £19-£29 per person.
Discounts: Negotiable midweek discounts on stays over 3 nights.
Credit Cards: Visa, MC, debit cards.
Rsv'tns: Required.
Reserve Thru: Travel agent or call direct.
Parking: Adequate free off-street parking.
In-Room: Color TV, coffee & tea-making facilities, hair dryer, maid service.
On-Premises: TV lounge.
Swimming: Nearby pool, ocean & river.
Sunbathing: On patio, at beach.
Smoking: Permitted in lounge only.
Pets: Inquire.
Handicap Access: No.
Children: No.
Languages: English.
Your Hosts: Mike & Michael.

Foxden

Gay-Friendly ♀♂
Gay-Owned & -Operated

Herne Bay, a peaceful residential area on the coast, is only seven miles from Canterbury. Our spacious, 1920's home, *Foxden*, offers elegant bedrooms with fine furnishings, television, fresh flowers and a large selection of books. Mornings, enjoy substantial breakfasts with eggs from our own hens. A delightful garden with fish ponds is yours to explore; walk through the aviary or play croquet. The town centre, the sea and cliff walks are just a short walk away.

Address: 5 Landon Rd, off Beltinge, Herne Bay, Kent CT6 6HP, England
Tel: (44-1227) 363 514.

Type: Bed & breakfast.
Clientele: Mostly hetero clientele with a gay/lesbian following
Transportation: Train from Victoria to Herne Bay, or car.
Rooms: 4 rooms with single or double beds.
Baths: Private: 2 shower/toilets (doubles). Shared: 2 bath/shower/toilets (singles).
Meals: Full breakfast.
Vegetarian: Vegetarian breakfast on request. Vegetarian meals at nearby pub/restaurant.
Dates Open: All year.
High Season: Apr-Oct.
Rates: £20 per person, per night.
Discounts: On stays of 3 or more nights.
Rsv'tns: Required.
Reserve Thru: Call direct.
Parking: Ample free off-street parking.
In-Room: Color TV, coffee & tea-making facilities.
Exercise/Health: Nearby gym, weights.
Swimming: Nearby pool, ocean.
Sunbathing: On patio & in beautiful garden.
Smoking: Permitted in garden. No smoking indoors.
Pets: Permitted.
Handicap Access: No.
Children: Welcome over 12 years.
Languages: English.
Your Hosts: Michael & Tony.

Woodbine Villa

Gay/Lesbian ♂
Gay-Owned

Woodbine Villa is a grade II listed 18th century former farmhouse in the centre of the pretty Georgian village of Grampound. The house is furnished with antiques. Your spacious bedroom may have a Victorian brass bed, mahogany half-tester, or even a genuine regency four-poster. Our substantial British breakfast includes Cornish hogs pudding, even Kedgeree, if you fancy it! Quality fresh-cooked evening meals can be provided. I'll even throw in a complimentary decanter of wine (not literally). The sauna is open some nights for both guests and non-residents. All in all, spectacular scenery, fine beaches, pleasant weather, verdant countryside, pleasant walks and masses of historic houses, gardens and interesting places to visit make a trip to Cornwall a must. I hope to welcome you as a house guest, offering true Cornish hospitality and wishing to make your stay with me both pleasant and memorable.

Address: Fore St, Grampound, Truro, Cornwall TR2 4QP, England
Tel: (44-1726) 882 005.

Type: Bed & breakfast & sauna in a private home.
Clientele: Mostly men with women welcome
Transportation: Coaches from Victoria Stn. & Heathrow, but car is best.
To Gay Bars: 8-15 miles.
Rooms: 4 rooms with double beds.
Baths: Shared: 1 shower, 1 bath/shower/toilet , 1 toilet.

Meals: Full English bkfst.
Vegetarian: 24 hr notice for evening meal. Restaurants & pub in village.
Complimentary: Choice of teas & coffees.
Dates Open: All year.
High Season: May-Oct.
Rates: £23-£30 singles, £42-£50 doubles.
Discounts: 10% to Bears Club members, return

guests, PWA.
Rsv'tns: Advisable.
Reserve Thru: Call direct.
Min. Stay: Additional charge for 1-night stays.
Parking: Free on- & limited off-street parking.
In-Room: Maid service.
On-Premises: TV, VCR, log fireplace in drawing room.
Exercise/Health: Sauna.
Swimming: A few miles to

sea beaches.
Sunbathing: On beach or in garden.
Nudity: Nude beach 7 mi.
Smoking: Permitted outdoors only.
Pets: Not permitted.
Children: Not permitted.
Languages: English, limited French.
Your Hosts: Mike.

Crestow House

English Victorian Stone Country House in a Picturesque Cotswold Village

Crestow House was built in 1870 out of Cotswold sandstone by a local wool merchant. The generously-sized rooms and 12 foot ceilings speak of the affluence this region once knew. Stow is on the old wool route built during the Roman occupation. The town still preserves its Mediaeval stocks and has one of the oldest pubs in Britain. The wool trade has since given way to the antiques business, with Stow having about 64 antique dealers. The area, filled with castles and stately homes, is also known for its high quality food. We are glad to recommend our fine local restaurants or cook for you if you let us know in the morning that you would like to eat with us that evening. Stow is about a 2-hour drive from London (1-1/4-hour train ride from Paddington Station), 20 minutes north of Oxford and 15 minutes south of Stratford-on-Avon, home of the Royal Shakespeare Company.

Crestow House boasts a large conservatory, living room, dining room, large country breakfast room and back veranda, with some of the best views and sunsets in Britain. The house has a large walled back garden with heated swimming pool. The four double bedrooms have en suite baths, antique furnishings, English country decor, modern queen beds and floor-to-ceiling windows. The owners live on the upper floor.

Address: Stow-on-the-Wold, Gloucestershire GL54 1JX, England
Tel: (44-1451) 830 969, **Fax:** (44-1451) 832 129.
E-mail: fjsimon@compuserve.com

Type: Bed & breakfast country manor house.
Clientele: 50% gay & lesbian & 50% straight
Transportation: Car. Train: London's Paddington Stn to Moreton In Marsh.
To Gay Bars: 15 miles.
Rooms: 4 rooms with queen beds.
Baths: All en suite.

Meals: Full English breakfast.
Vegetarian: Available upon prior request. 5-minute walk to restaurant.
Complimentary: Tea or coffee on arrival, pre-dinner sherry.
Dates Open: Feb-Dec.
High Season: June-Sept.
Rates: £34 per person.

Single suppplement add £10 per person.
Discounts: 2+ nts.
Credit Cards: MC, Visa.
Rsv'tns: Preferred.
Reserve Thru: Call direct.
Parking: Free off-street.
In-Room: Color TV, laundry service.
On-Premises: Laundry facilities. Send/rcv fax.

Exercise/Health: Gym & sauna on premises.
Swimming: 38'x18' in-ground pool on premises.
Sunbathing: At poolside.
Smoking: Not permitted.
Pets: Not permitted.
Children: Not especially welcome.
Languages: English, Spanish, Italian & German.
Your Hosts: Frank & Jorge.

Holly Park House

In the Heart of the English Lake District

Holly Park House is an elegant Lakeland stonebuilt house which has been tastefully modernised and furnished to a high standard to provide our guests with a comfortable base from which to explore the beautiful Lake District countryside. Situated in a quiet area only five minutes' walk from the railway station and bus terminus in Windermere, it is convenient for tours to famous beautiful spots such as the Langdales, Tarn Hows, Grasmere or Hawkshead, and is just one mile from bustling Bowness and the Lake, itself.

Each of the six spacious bedrooms has its own private bath or shower room, tea and coffee making facilities and colour television. Five are double or twin and one is a family room with cot available on request. A full English breakfast is served from 8:30 to 9:00 a.m. Evening meals are available if required, and the premises has a licensed bar.

The Lake District is justly renowned for the beauty of its scenery and for many people this alone is sufficient to call them again and again to its fells. Walks can be graded to suit all, from gentle strolls by the lakes and through the woods to strenuous, exhilarating hikes over its peaks. There is also a wide variety of attractions to appeal to all tastes: exploring the many pretty villages, each with its own charm, touring stately homes, or investigating the craft centres and museums.

Address: 1 Park Rd, Windermere, Cumbria LA23 2AW, England
Tel: (44-15394) 42107, **Fax:** (44-15394) 48997.

Type: Guesthouse with bar.
Clientele: Mostly hetero clientele with a gay/lesbian following
Transportation: Car or train. Free pick up from train or bus.
Rooms: 6 rooms with single or double beds.
Baths: Private: 1 bath/shower/toilet, 5 shower/toilets.

Meals: Full breakfast.
Vegetarian: Available, if ordered.
Complimentary: Tea, coffee. Sweets in room.
Dates Open: All year.
High Season: Easter to end of Oct.
Rates: Summer £25-£34; winter £20-£33.
Credit Cards: MC, Visa, Amex, Diners.

Rsv'tns: Not always.
Reserve Thru: Call direct.
Parking: Adequate, free off-street parking.
In-Room: Color TV, coffee & tea-making facilities, maid service.
On-Premises: TV lounge.
Exercise/Health: Nearby walking, climbing, fishing, boating, golf.
Swimming: Nearby pool &

lake.
Smoking: Permitted in lounge.
Pets: Permitted by arrangement.
Handicap Access: No.
Children: Not especially welcome, but we do sometimes have them.
Languages: English.
Your Hosts: Roger & James.

Central London Apartments

WWW Gay/Lesbian ⚣
Gay-Owned & -Operated

Deluxe Accommodations Uniquely Located in London's West End, Theatreland, Shopping District & Gay Village

Your host, Simon, welcomes you to an extraordinary stay in the very heart of London. Accommodations overlook Soho and Covent Garden, with panoramic views, within walking distance of everything... Nearby are the great sights — Buckingham Palace, Big Ben, Houses of Parliament. The famous thoroughfares — Oxford Street, Bond Street, Regent Street. The amazing stores — Harrods, Harvey Nicholls, Selfridges, Heals, and a wide choice of excursions, museums, art galleries, theatres, parks, cafes, restaurants, bars and nightclubs.

Central London Apartments are fully-furnished/ equipped, self-catering flats with kitchen, sitting/dining room, balcony and double bedroom(s). Ideal for singles, couples or groups, and weekly, monthly, or longer stays at rates most central hotels cannot match. *Guestrooms* are bright, spacious and inviting double rooms with modern decor and quality furnishings, plus free kitchen and laundry access — perfect for those on a budget! Maid service is weekly — extra cleaning/provisions on request. We're regularly the chosen base for travellers to England, Scotland, Wales and Europe. For a wonderful time on your next trip to London, be sure you stay in the most central apartments!

Tel: Outside UK: (44-20) 7497 7000; Inside UK: 020 7497 7000.
E-mail: londonapts@yahoo.com **Web:** http://www.go.to/londonapts

Type: Rooms & apartments, self-catering or serviced.
Clientele: Gay/Lesbian
Transportation: Excellent connections via main line train, tube, bus, car, taxi.
To Gay Bars: Astoria & others nearby.
Rooms: 5 apartments for 1-6 persons; 6 double rooms.
Baths: Private & shared. Some apts with Jacuzzi & powershowers.

Meals: Continental buffet breakfast.
Complimentary: Maps, magazines, travel guide/ planners. Tea, coffee, ice.
High Season: All year.
Rates: Rooms £65-£80pn; Apartments £142-£185pn.
Discounts: Inquire.
Credit Cards: MC, Visa, Amex.
Rsv'tns: Recommended.
Reserve Thru: Call direct.

Min. Stay: 1 week (less if we've gaps between bookings, gaps only released 10 days before check-in).
Parking: Free & paid on-street parking.
In-Room: Colour TV, VCR, clock radio, mirrored wardrobes, desk, hair dryer, cool fans & heaters. Apts: kitchen (fridge, dishwasher, m'wave), lounge/dining room, balcony.
On-Premises: 2 fast lifts, tel, fax, copier, laundry rooms, steam iron/board, maid service.
Exercise/Health: 1 min to gyms & saunas.
Swimming: 1 min to pools.
Smoking: Limited.
Pets: Not permitted.
Languages: English.
Your Hosts: Simon James.

London Holiday Accommodation

WWW Gay/Lesbian ♂♂
Gay-Owned & -Operated

A Hotel Alternative, Without Sacrificing Quality

Make your stay in London truly memorable. For those looking for an alternative to hotels, but not wanting to sacrifice quality, *London Holiday Accommodation* offers the perfect answer. Stay in your own apartment and have the freedom to do what you want, with whom you want, and when you want. We have penthouses, studios, one- and two-bedroom apartments at rates that you will find very hard to beat. Or, you could always stay with a host in one of our shared apartments. This offers a great deal of freedom for a more personal experience allowing you to instantly make new friends in London. All hosts are either gay men or women.

We'll collect you at the airport in our own car, for a reasonable rate, or meet you when you get off the tube, and escort you to the property, where a representative will show you around the apartment. You also have the peace of mind that our apartments have been approved by the London Tourist Board quality control, and we are indeed a member of The London Tourist Board and uphold the standards expected by them. For people who are new to London, we are also happy to show you, free of charge, around Soho, and The Gay Village — we even buy a round!

Address: 16 Chalk Farm Road, Camden Town, London, NW1 8AJ, England
Tel: (44-20) 7485 0117 (Tel/Fax).
E-mail: sales@londonholiday.co.uk **Web:** http://www.londonholiday.co.uk

Type: Self-catering apartments & hosted gay homes.
Clientele: Mostly gay & lesbian, some hetero
Transportation: By tube or overground Heathrow Express. Airport pick up in private car (small fee).
To Gay Bars: Walking distance.
Rooms: 4 rooms in 4 shared apts w/ gay owner, 8 apts, double or queen beds.

Baths: Private & shared.
Complimentary: Tea, coffee, milk, basic foods, fresh flowers, guide books, maps.
High Season: All year.
Rates: Hosted homes from: £30/nt, £120/wk. Self-contained from: £45/nt, £300/wk.
Discounts: Most apts: book 1 wk, get 1 nt free.
Credit Cards: Inquire.
Rsv'tns: Required.

Reserve Thru: Travel agent or call direct.
Parking: Some free parking, inquire.
In-Room: Phone, TV (color cable, BW), VCR, stereo w/ CD, kitchen, fridge, coffee & tea makers, micros, iron, ironing board, washing machine, dishwasher. Some balconies, maid svc on request.
On-Premises: Laundry facilities. Email in some

apts, owners allow reasonable usage.
Exercise/Health: Gay gym in Soho, most very mixed.
Swimming: Pools in Covent Garden.
Smoking: Inquire.
Pets: Not permitted.
Children: Inquire.
Languages: English, Spanish.
Your Hosts: Karen.

Number Seven Guesthouse

Voted Best UK Gay Hotel

A warm welcome awaits you at *Number Seven*, voted Best UK Gay Hotel, where we're setting the standard for others to follow. This elegant Victorian townhouse, with private parking, is situated in a quiet tree-lined avenue in Brixton, a lively cosmopolitan neighborhood, just south of the centre. Just a short walk from The Fridge (voted Best London Gay Club) and Sub-Station South, one of London's favourite gay dance clubs, we're within easy reach of a variety of gay bars and clubs. We have good connections with all London airports and rail termini.

The guesthouse is tastefully decorated with striking colours and antique pine furnishings and maintains many original features. Our variety of rooms cater for most travellers, from the single person on a budget to our larger deluxe rooms for those who require something more special, and our air-conditioned suites. The Honeymoon Suite with a king-sized bed and large bathroom with corner-bath is very popular. Breakfast is served in the conservatory overlooking our enchanting private, walled garden; with a background of classical music we offer freshly-pressed coffee and a selection of teas served in the pot, to accompany our expanded continental breakfast. Your gay hosts, John and Paul, will provide good orientation and information on London's gay scene, theaters and major attractions. You'll have your own keys, and check-in is by prior arrangement.

Address: 7 Josephine Ave, London, SW2 2JU, England
Tel: (44-20) 8674 1880, **Fax:** (44-20) 8671 6032, in US (707) 885-2959.
E-mail: hotel@no7.com **Web:** http://www.no7.com

Type: B&B guesthouse.
Clientele: Gay & lesbian. Good mix of men & women
Transportation: Main line train, tube, bus, car, or taxi from London airports, intercity train stns; pick ups cost petrol plus time.
To Gay Bars: 4 min walk or tube.
Rooms: 8 rooms with single, twin, double, triple or queen beds.
Baths: All ensuite.
Meals: Full, buffet, continental or expanded continental breakfast.
Vegetarian: Vegetarian breakfast always available. Local restaurants.
Complimentary: Tea & coffee in rooms.
Dates Open: All year.
Rates: £59-£99.
Discounts: On application.
Credit Cards: MC, Visa, Amex.
Rsv'tns: Required. Credit card booking essential.
Reserve Thru: Call direct, or reserve on-line.
Min. Stay: 2 nights.
Parking: Ample easy off-street free parking.
In-Room: Clock/radio, remote CTV w/ satellite, direct-dial phone, ceiling fans, tea/coffee makers, Bahama fans, hair dryer, maid & laundry svc. Iron & ironing board on request. AC in some rooms.
On-Premises: Pay phone, dining room with maps & guides, conservatory, private walled garden, photo copier, fax machine, message srvc.
Exercise/Health: Weights, rowing machine, situp bench on request. Rec. centre & park nearby.
Swimming: 2 pools 1/2 mile away.
Sunbathing: In gardens.
Smoking: Permitted without restrictions in bedrooms.
Pets: Not permitted.
Children: Not permitted.
Languages: English, British Sign Language.
Your Hosts: Paul & John.

A Jolly Good Place

Gay/Lesbian ⚥
Gay-Owned & -Operated

Wing and Chris welcome gay and lesbian friends from all over the world to their comfortable and friendly home. We live in a Victorian terraced house in a quiet residential area of south London, but within easy and quick access to central London and all the main tourist and gay locations. We are not only convenient to public transport but also to the shops, restaurants, bars and cinema of Clapham's thriving High Street. We are also within walking distance of the gay scene in Clapham and Brixton, and of the green spaces of Clapham Common. We think that you, too, will join our many guests who believe that this is truly *A Jolly Good Place* to stay in London.

Address: 31 Tremadoc Rd, London, SW4 7NF, England
Tel: (44-20) 7622 6018.
E-mail: jollygoodplace@compuserve.com **Web:** http://www.geocities.com/WestHollywood/Village/9220

Type: Bed & breakfast.
Clientele: Gay & lesbian. Good mix of men & women
Transportation: Tube to Clapham North (5 min walk), buses 24hrs.
To Gay Bars: 1 block, a 2 min walk.
Rooms: 4 rooms with twin or double beds.
Baths: Private: 4 sinks only.

Shared: 1 shower/toilet.
Meals: Full breakfast.
Vegetarian: Available on request.
Complimentary: Tea & coffee.
Dates Open: All year.
High Season: Apr-Oct.
Rates: £35-£55.
Discounts: 10% for stays of 1 week or above.

Rsv'tns: Required.
Reserve Thru: Call direct or e-mail.
Parking: Limited, pay on-street parking (free at weekends).
In-Room: Color TV, coffee & tea-making facilities, maid service.
Swimming: Pool nearby.
Sunbathing: At Clapham

Common (a 5 min walk).
Smoking: No smoking.
Pets: Not permitted.
Handicap Access: No.
Children: Not actively encouraged.
Languages: English, Mandarin, Cantonese, German, French, some Spanish, Malay, Japanese.
Your Hosts: Wing & Chris

New York Hotel, The

Gay/Lesbian ♂

The New York Hotel is London's newest and most luxurious gay hotel, situated in the heart of London's gay scene, ideally located for the many local gay bars, clubs, shops and activities in the Earl's Court area. The hotel offers a luxury lounge, beautiful private rear garden and licensed bar facilities. Guests have 24-hour access to our Jacuzzi and sauna. Our 14 spacious and well-decorated single, double, or twin rooms all have 24-hour room service, en suite bathrooms equipped with high-powered showers and hairdryers, colour TV, direct dial telephones, coffee-making facilities, trouser press and iron. If you are looking for a wonderful time in London, then *The New York Hotel* is for you!

Address: 32 Philbeach Gardens, Earls Court, London, SW5 9EB, England
Tel: (44-20) 7244 6884, **Fax:** (44-20) 7370 4961.

Type: Hotel.
Clientele: 90% gay men & 10% women
Transportation: Tube or taxi.
To Gay Bars: 2 blocks or 3-5 min walk to several.
Rooms: 4 singles, 10 doubles.
Baths: 12 private, 2 shared.
Meals: Expanded continental breakfast.

Complimentary: Tea & coffee in room.
Dates Open: All year, except 3 days during Christmas.
High Season: May-Dec.
Rates: £50-£90.
Credit Cards: MC, Visa, Amex, Access, Eurocard.
Rsv'tns: Required.
Reserve Thru: Call direct.
Min. Stay: Required on

holiday weekends.
Parking: Paid parking up the street for £12 a day (24-hr access).
In-Room: Color cable TV with remote, telephone, maid & room service.
On-Premises: TV lounge.
Exercise/Health: Jacuzzi & sauna with shower area.
Swimming: At nearby pool.
Sunbathing: Hotel garden

or 1 hr on train to beach at Brighton.
Nudity: 1 hour to Brighton Beach.
Smoking: Permitted.
Pets: Not permitted.
Handicap Access: No.
Children: Not permitted.
Languages: English, Spanish.
Your Hosts: Barrie.

Interludes

Gay-Friendly 50/50 ⚥

Little "Scene," But Great Scenery

Interludes is an elegant Georgian townhouse with sea views, peacefully situated in a conservation area, yet close to beach, town centre, theatres, castle, etc. The hotel is licensed, and, because of our connections with the Stephen Joseph Theatre, has a theatrical theme. Bedrooms are well equipped for guests' comfort and, as befits rooms over 200 years old, have sloping, creaking floors and south-facing sash windows. Scarborough is an ideal centre for exploring nearby North Yorkshire Moors Nat'l Park and the towns of York and Whitby.

Address: 32 Princess St, Old Town, Scarborough, North Yorkshire Y011 1QR, England
Tel: (44-1723) 360 513, **Fax:** (44-1723) 368 597.
E-mail: interludes@cwcom.net **Web:** http://www.interludes.mcmail.com/family.htm

Type: Hotel.
Clientele: 50% gay & lesbian & 50% hetero
Transportation: Car, bus or train (rail link to Manchester Airport).
Rooms: 5 rooms with twin, king & four poster beds.
Baths: 4 en suite, 1 with sink & adjacent shower & toilet.
Meals: Full breakfast. 3 course dinner at extra cost.

Vegetarian: Available with prior notification.
Complimentary: Tea, coffee, chocolate, juice, etc.
Dates Open: All year.
High Season: Jul-Sept.
Rates: Standard: single £27, double £47. Superior: single £32, double £55.
Discounts: Special pkg w/ SJ Theatre. For 3-6 nts & major discount for 7+ nts.
Credit Cards: MC, Visa.

Rsv'tns: Recommended.
Reserve Thru: Call direct.
Min. Stay: 2 nights public holiday weekends.
Parking: Adequate free on-street parking, limited during high season.
In-Room: Color TV, coffee & tea-making facilities, maid service.
On-Premises: Laundry facilities.
Swimming: Nearby pool &

ocean beach.
Sunbathing: On the patio, at the beach.
Smoking: Strictly forbidden in bedrooms, hall & dining room. Not encouraged in lounge.
Pets: Not permitted.
Handicap Access: No.
Children: Not permitted.
Languages: English.
Your Hosts: Bob & Ian.

Brockett House

Elegant City Hideaway in the Heart of England

Brockett House, an 1873 Victorian, is situated five minutes from Sheffield's city centre and the train station, 10 minutes to gay Sheffield, and 15 minutes to the beautiful Peak National Park. Kheng and Ian warmly welcome you to an exclusively gay and elegant environment that is friendly, comfortable and relaxed. All beautiful rooms are spacious and individually designed with a mix of modern and antique Colonial furniture. Nearby, is an abundance of eating and drinking places, and antique shops.

Sheffield is in the middle of England, a 2-1/2 hour drive from London, 1-1/4 hours from York and Harrogate, and 1 hour from Nottingham, Derby, Leeds and Manchester. Our thriving gay scene includes gay bars, sauna, a regular club, and several very popular monthly clubs, including Poptastic, Trade and Climax. Major attractions include the Castleton limestone caves, picturesque Bakewell village, Chatsworth House, Haddon Hall, and many other country houses.

Address: 1 Montgomery Road, Sheffield, S. Yorks S7 1LN, England
Tel: (44-114) 258 8952 (Tel/Fax).
E-mail: bracketthouse@yahoo.com **Web:** http://www.bracketthouse.com

Type: Guesthouse.
Clientele: Mostly gay men, women welcome
Transportation: Near train station. Bus stop outside.
To Gay Bars: 10 min.
Rooms: 4 rooms with double, twin or king beds.
Baths: Private & shared.
Meals: Full English or continental breakfast.
Vegetarian: Vegetarian breakfast available.
Complimentary: Beverage tray, in-room video/TV, free movies.
Rates: £30-£50 per night.
Discounts: On 4+ nights.
Rsv'tns: Essential.
Reserve Thru: Phone, fax or e-mail direct.
Parking: 1 private space, ample on-street parking.
In-Room: TV/video, drinks tray, fan, hair dryer.
On-Premises: Video tape library, fax, copier, iron/board, TV lounge.
Swimming: Pool nearby.
Nudity: Permitted in the house.
Smoking: No smoking in house.
Pets: Not permitted.
Children: No.
Languages: English, Mandarin, Cantonese, Malay.
Your Hosts: Ian & Kheng.

Cliff House Hotel at the Beach

WWW Gay/Lesbian ♀♂

England's First and Foremost Gay Hotel

Originally a millionaire's home, *Cliff House*, celebrating its 27th year, is an exclusive, luxury hotel with a secluded garden at sea's edge. Here one can view the sea from the terrace that fronts the comfortable bar lounge. All bedrooms have a bathroom en suite, and full central heating warms us in cooler months, which are so delightful in this beautiful part of the country. There are ample parking facilities. Old friends meet, and newfound friends are made, and no one ever wants to leave.

Address: St. Marks Rd, Meadfoot Beach, Torquay, TQ1 2EH, England
Tel: (44-1803) 294 656, **Fax:** (44-1803) 211 983.
E-mail: alan@cliffhouse.co.uk **Web:** http://www.cliffhouse.co.uk

Type: Hotel with restaurant & bar.
Clientele: Good mix of gay men & women
Transportation: Train or bus from London. Pick up from train.
To Gay Bars: A 5-minute walk or 2-minute drive.
Rooms: 16 rooms with single or double beds.
Baths: All private bath/ toilets.
Meals: Full English breakfast.

Vegetarian: With prior arrangement.
Complimentary: Tea & coffee in room.
Dates Open: All year.
High Season: Easter, Jun-Oct & Christmas.
Rates: Double £25 pp per day, single £29 pp per day, plus VAT.
Discounts: Party discounts. Oct-Mar 3rd night free.
Credit Cards: MC, Visa, Access, Switch.
Rsv'tns: Required during

high season.
Reserve Thru: Call direct.
Parking: Ample on- and off-street parking.
In-Room: Color TV, coffee & tea-making facilities & room service.
On-Premises: TV lounge, bar & public telephone.
Exercise/Health: Steam room, Jacuzzi, massage and gym.
Swimming: Ocean beach.
Sunbathing: On the beach, sun deck or in the secluded

garden.
Nudity: Permitted in the secluded garden.
Smoking: Permitted without restrictions.
Pets: Dogs are permitted, but not in public rooms.
Handicap Access: Yes, 2 rooms.
Children: Not permitted.
Languages: English.
Your Hosts: Alan & Robbie.

Rainbow Villa

Gay/Lesbian ♂
Gay-Owned & -Operated

An Elegant, Comfortable & Relaxing Sojourn is Assured

Built in the 1870s, *Rainbow Villa* stands on a tree-lined road near the church where Agatha Christie worshipped. We're only a few minutes' walk (depending, of course, on your disposition — and the scenery) of central Torquay, the harbourside, clubs and bars. Recently updated, renovated and redecorated, our guestrooms each have private bathroom, tea and coffee courtesy tray, hairdryer and television. Dinner "a deux" or "en famille" is a tantalising additional option. Trained at London's Inn on the Park, Tony's cuisine is inventive and international. We're near scenic Dartmoor and historic Plymouth. Visit Drake's home at Buckfastleigh, take a picnic to the Moor, or simply enjoy our local beaches.

Address: 24 Bridge Road, Torquay, Devon TQ2 5BA, England
Tel: (44-1803) 212 886 (Tel/Fax).
E-mail: rainbows@globalnet.co.uk

Type: Guesthouse.
Clientele: Mostly men with women welcome
Transportation: Train from London. Free pick up from local train or bus.
To Gay Bars: 10 min walk, 2 min drive.
Rooms: 3 rooms w/ king beds.
Baths: All private.

Meals: Full or continental breakfast.
Vegetarian: Available.
Complimentary: Tea & coffee in rooms.
High Season: July-Oct.
Rates: £22.50-£27.50, per person per night.
Discounts: 10% on stays of 7 nights.
Credit Cards: MC, Visa.

Reserve Thru: Call direct.
Parking: Ample on-street parking.
In-Room: Colour TV, tea & coffee-making facilities, maid & laundry service.
On-Premises: TV lounge.
Exercise/Health: Nearby gym, weights, Jacuzzi, sauna, steam, massage.
Swimming: Nearby pool &

ocean.
Sunbathing: On patio & at beach.
Smoking: Not in house. Permitted in gardens only.
Pets: Not permitted.
Children: No.
Languages: English, Spanish, French.

Ellesmere House

A Friendly Welcome to the Heart of England

Ellesmere House is an elegant, early Victorian town residence with spacious rooms furnished in antiques. It has been modernized by the friendly resident owners to a high standard of comfortable accommodation and is situated in a quiet, tree-lined avenue within walking distance of all the facilities of this attractive regency town. Shakespeare's Stratford, The Castles at Warwick and Kenilworth are all within easy reach, as are Birmingham (England's "second city") and the beautiful Cotswolds countryside.

Address: 36 Binswood Ave, Royal Leamington Spa, Warwickshire CV32 5SQ, England
Tel: (44-1926) 424 618.
E-mail: ellesmere@36bins.freeserve.co.uk

Type: Bed & breakfast homestay.
Clientele: Mostly men with women welcome
Transportation: Own vehicle is best, but train, bus OK.
To Gay Bars: Coventry gay bar 10 miles.
Rooms: 3 rooms with single or double beds.
Baths: 2 private bath/toilets & 1 private shower/toilet.
Meals: Full English breakfast.
Dates Open: All year.
Rates: £25-£50.
Rsv'tns: Required.
Reserve Thru: Call direct.
Parking: Adequate, free on-street parking.
In-Room: Color TV.
Sunbathing: In garden.
Smoking: Not encouraged.
Pets: Not permitted.
Handicap Access: No.
Children: Not permitted.
Languages: English, Spanish, limited French, Italian.
Your Hosts: Francisco & Colin.

Bull Lodge

"The History of York is the History of England"

Bull Lodge is a modern, detached residence on a quiet side street, three quarters of a mile from the city centre and close to the University and Barbican Leisure Centre. We're on a bus route and have private, enclosed parking. Single, twin, or double bedrooms are available. Twins and doubles can be with or without private shower and toilet. A full-choice English breakfast is served, evening meals can be ordered, and snacks and drinks are available. York is an excellent base to explore the surrounding countryside, the moors and the dales, to visit Castle Howard of "Brideshead Revisited" fame, or nearby Bronte country.

Address: 37 Bull Lane, Lawrence St, York, YO10 3EN, England
Tel: (44-1904) 415522 (Tel/Fax).

Type: Guesthouse.
Clientele: Mostly straight clientele with a gay/lesbian following
Transportation: Convenient direct bus from train/bus stns. Pick up by prior arrangement if min. 2 night advance booking.
To Gay Bars: 1 mile.
Rooms: 1 single, 6 doubles, 1 twin.
Baths: 3 private, 2 shared.
Meals: Full English breakfast. Evening meal extra charge (low season only).
Complimentary: Tea & coffee.
Dates Open: End Jan to mid-Dec.
High Season: Jun-Oct.
Rates: 2000: summer £17-£22; winter £16-£19.
Discounts: £1 pp pn for over 3 nights. Off-season breaks.
Rsv'tns: Recommended weekends & summer.
Reserve Thru: Travel agent or call direct.
Parking: Private enclosed parking. Garage for motorbikes, bikes.
In-Room: Color TV, tea/coffee makers, radio alarm clocks, hot & cold water, maid service, phone, hair dryer.
On-Premises: Non-smoking TV lounge with books & games.
Swimming: 10-min walk to Barbican pool & leisure centre.
Smoking: Permitted except in lounge & dining room.
Pets: Permitted.
Handicap Access: Yes, ground floor en suite double room.
Children: Permitted, min. age 3 years.
Languages: English.
Your Hosts: Roy & Dennis.

Mas La Bonoty Hotel & Restaurant

A 17th-Century Farmhouse in the Heart of Provence

In the heart Provence, 20 kilometres from Avignon, in a region rich in history and scenic beauty is *Mas La Bonoty*, an elegantly restored Provençal farmhouse dating from the 17th century. The bedrooms have ensuite bath or shower rooms with WC, television and tea- and coffee-making facilities. The hotel is situated on over two acres of private landscaped gardens featuring lavender and olive trees, and has its own pool, as well. The comfort, tranquility, sophisticated Provençal cuisine and the carefully selected wine list found here will ensure a memorable stay. Lunch can be served under the shade of pine trees and dinner on the terraces surrounding the pool.

Pernes Les Fontaines, not far from Mont Ventoux, is a medieval town with 36 fountains and numerous ramparts, monuments and churches. Within easy reach of *Mas La Bonoty* are the famous vineyards of Côtes du Rhône, Châteauneuf du Pape and Tavel, as well as the excellent "vins du pays" such as Côtes de Ventoux and Côtes de Luberon. Many vinyards are pleased to arrange wine tastings. Day excursions can include Aix en Provence, the Mediterranean coast and many other well-known attractions throughout Provence. The area is also internationally renowned for its diverse cultural activities, among which are the celebrated Avignon Festival and opera in the magnificent Roman arenas at Orange and Nîmes. Sporting activities such as golf, tennis and horseriding are also available nearby.

Address: Chemin de la Bonioty, Pernes Les Fontaines, 84210, France
Tel: (33) 04 90 61 61 09, **Fax:** (33) 04 90 61 35 14.
E-mail: bonoty@aol.com **Web:** http://www.bonoty.com

Type: Hotel with restaurant, 20 km from Avignon.
Clientele: Mostly hetero clientele with a gay/lesbian following
Transportation: Car is best. Nearest airports in Avignon or Marseille.
To Gay Bars: 14 miles, a 30 min drive.
Rooms: 8 rooms with single or double beds.
Baths: 8 private bath/shower/toilets.
Meals: Expanded continental breakfast 45FF.
Vegetarian: Available, please advise in advance.
Complimentary: Welcome cocktail. Tea & coffee in rooms.
Dates Open: Closed Jan 14-Feb 12, 2000 & Nov 12-Dec 8, 2000.
High Season: June-Sept.
Rates: 300FF-400FF per night for 2 persons. Half board 360FF per person, per day for 2 people sharing a double room.
Credit Cards: MC, Visa, Amex, Eurocard.
Rsv'tns: Required.
Reserve Thru: Travel agent or call direct.
Parking: Ample free, private off-street parking.
In-Room: Telephone, color TV, coffee & tea-making facilities, maid service.
On-Premises: TV lounge, fax.
Exercise/Health: Nearby gym, weights.
Swimming: Pool on premises. Ocean nearby.
Sunbathing: Poolside.
Smoking: Permitted, no restrictions.
Pets: Small dogs permitted by arrangement.
Handicap Access: No.
Children: No.
Languages: French, English.
Your Hosts: Peter & Richard.

Chez Jacqueline

A Women's B&B in Brittany

Jaqueline Boudillet offers her quiet, rural home as a bed and breakfast for women only. Here, in this quiet village three hours from Paris, you can enjoy the peaceful countryside, visit many nearby touristic areas or simply stay at home. The home has a women's library with books in French and English, a lovely garden and musical instruments which guests are free to play. Guests are encouraged to take advantage of activities including swimming, riding, walking through forests (3 kms away), by the lakes or the sea-side (15 kms away, a 20-minute drive).

Address: Saint Donan **Mail To:** Jacqueline Boudillet, La Croix Cadio, Saint Donan, Brittany 22800, France
Tel: (33) 02 96 73 81 22.

Type: Bed & breakfast in a big country house in Brittany.
Clientele: Women only
Transportation: Car is best.
Rooms: 3 doubles.
Baths: 2 shared.

Meals: FF 20 for continental breakfast.
Dates Open: All year.
Rates: Room FF 200.00.
Rsv'tns: Required, call ahead.
Reserve Thru: Call or write direct.

Parking: Ample free off-street parking.
On-Premises: TV room.
Swimming: Ocean beach 20 minutes by car.
Sunbathing: In the garden.
Smoking: Permitted.
Pets: Only dogs who love cats are permitted.
Handicap Access: 1 bedroom is on ground floor.
Children: Not permitted.
Languages: French, English & some German.

Chateau des Ormeaux

WWW Gay/Lesbian ♂
Gay-Owned & -Operated

In the Heart of the Loire Valley...

Situated in the heart of the prestigious Chateaux de La Loire, *Chateau des Ormeaux* is a romantic château that, from its Italian terrace looks out over the Loire Valley. The bedrooms, with their painted panelings and antique furniture, also feature private baths, direct phones and beautiful views. Guests will enjoy relaxing in the livingroom with fireplace, books, and TV with satellite channels. There is a swimming pool on premises, as well as a 67-acre park. Enjoy antique shops, walks through the woods and vineyards. We're in the middle of the Vouvray and Touraine-Amboise vineyards, and are close to the Chinon, Bourgueil and Saumur vineyards.

Address: Route de Noizay, Nazelles, Amboise, 37530, France
Tel: (33) 02 47 23 26 51, **Fax:** (33) 02 47 23 19 31.
E-mail: chateaudesormeaux@wanadoo.fr **Web:** http://pro.wanadoo.fr/
chateaudesormeaux

Type: Guesthouse.
Clientele: Mostly men with women welcome
Transportation: Car is best.
Rooms: 6 rooms wtih single, double or king beds.
Baths: Private: 3 shower/toilets, 3 bath/toilets.
Meals: Expanded continental breakfast.

Inquire about dinner at the chateau.
Vegetarian: On reservation.
Complimentary: Food & drinks available on request.
Dates Open: All year.
High Season: Summer season.
Rates: 550 FF-650 FF for 2 people, including breakfast.
Rsv'tns: Recommended.

Reserve Thru: Travel agent or call direct.
Parking: Adequate free parking.
In-Room: Telephone, laundry service.
On-Premises: TV lounge.
Exercise/Health: Nearby sauna.
Swimming: Pool on premises.

Sunbathing: Poolside.
Smoking: Permitted everywhere, non-smoking rooms available.
Pets: Not permitted.
Handicap Access: No.
Children: No.
Languages: French, English, Italian, German.
Your Hosts: Philippe, Eric, Emmanuel.

Saint Ferréol's Hotel

A 3-Star Hotel Unlike Any Other

Come and discover *Saint Ferréol's Hotel*, 200 meters from the Vieux Port and the Canebière, on the most beautiful pedestrian street in Marseille — as lively during the day as it is calm at night. The hotel's cozy and elegant ambience features stylish room decor, inspired by famous painters (Van Gogh, Gauguin, Cezanne, Picasso...), with flock wall covering, English carpeting, marble bathroom, whirlpool bath and many other refinements. Amenities also include air conditioning, double-glazed windows, direct telephone, satellite TV and VCR. And at the Saint Ferréol's Bar, decorated with "Orezza Green" granite (one of the loveliest granites on earth), we will do our utmost to make you feel welcome. The hotel is close to local gay venues.

Address: 19 rue Pisançon, at Rue St. Ferreol, Marseille, 13001, France
Tel: (33) 04 91 33 12 21, **Fax:** (33) 04 91 54 29 97.
E-mail: St.Ferreol@wanadoo.fr **Web:** http://www.hotel-stferreol.com

Type: Hotel with bar.
Clientele: Mostly hetero clientele with a gay/lesbian following.
Transportation: Airport bus to Saint Charles' station, then taxi or metro.
To Gay Bars: 5 min walk.
Rooms: 20 rooms with single or double beds.
Baths: 20 private bath/ shower/toilets.
Vegetarian: Nearby.
Dates Open: All year.
Rates: Single 320 FF-530 FF, double 370 FF-580 FF.
Discounts: 10% off room rate for bookings from Ferrari Guides.
Credit Cards: MC, Visa, Amex, Diners, Eurocard.
Rsv'tns: Required.
Reserve Thru: Travel agent or call direct.
Parking: Ample off-street, public, covered pay parking.
In-Room: Telephone, AC, color cable TV, VCR, maid & room service.
On-Premises: Safe.
Exercise/Health: Jacuzzi. Nearby gym, weights, sauna, steam, massage.
Swimming: Nearby sea.
Sunbathing: At beach.
Smoking: Permitted. No non-smoking rooms.
Pets: Permitted.
Handicap Access: No.
Children: Welcome.
Languages: French, English, Arabic, Spanish, Italian.
Your Hosts: Bernard.

Hotel Place Clichy

Five Minutes from the Moulin Rouge & Pigalle

Hotel Place Clichy is ideally situated, with the hottest Parisian nightlife and major tourist attractions at your fingertips. Always bustling with activity and full of people, this is an area that Henry Miller once compared to New York's Broadway. This comfortable two-star hotel is situated between Montmartre and the business district with its famous restaurants. It is quite close to Montmartre, the Moulin Rouge, and is not far from major department stores, Pigale, the Champs Elysées and the Opera. For your convenience, the hotel offers satellite cable television, direct-dial phones, baths with shower, and a pleasant breakfast room overlooking Place Clichy.

Address: 71, rue de Douai, Paris, 75009, France
Tel: (33) 01 48 74 76 41, **Fax:** (33) 01 48 74 00 42.
E-mail: hotelclich@aol.com **Web:** http://hotelclich.com

Type: Bed & breakfast, hotel.
Clientele: 50% gay & lesbian & 50% hetero clientele
Transportation: Subway, bus, taxi.
To Gay Bars: 4 blocks, 1/2 mile, 10 min walk.
Rooms: 31 rooms with single or double beds.
Baths: Private: 15 bath/ shower/toilets, 16 shower/ toilets.
Meals: Continental breakfast FF 30.
Dates Open: All year.
Rates: Single: FF 300/320, double: FF 350/380, twin: FF 390/430.
Credit Cards: MC, Visa, Amex, Diners, Eurocard.
Rsv'tns: Required.
Reserve Thru: Travel agent or call direct.
Parking: Ample pay parking.
In-Room: Telephone, AC, color satellite TV, maid service.
On-Premises: Meeting rooms, TV lounge.
Exercise/Health: 5 min to gym, sauna, steam, massage.
Smoking: Permitted.
Pets: Permitted.
Handicap Access: No.
Children: No.
Languages: French, English, German, Spanish, Arabic.

FRANCE • MARSEILLE

FRANCE • PARIS

Brandon's

 WWW Gay/Lesbian ⚥

Private Luxury & Exquisite Surroundings in the Center of Paris

Brandon's, a XVIIth-century townhouse built on XVth-century vaulted cellars that have been excavated and renovated, is situated on the same street and a few steps away from the oldest house in Paris (1407). At the intersection of the Marais-Beaubourg and les Halles, this is the most central and desirable location in Paris. This townhouse is entirely furnished in XVIth-, XVIIth- and XVIIIth-century furniture with some IXXth-century decorative pieces.

Each guest room has its own bath, is furnished in period pieces and has its own kitchenette with refrigerator, microwave and hot plate. The rooms are upholstered in fabric and are non-smoking. The house was entirely refurbished between 1999 and early 2000, and was fitted with all-new English baths, air conditioning, and elevator. A sauna and basic exercise room is available in the XVth-century stone cellars.

This, indeed, is most probably the only "hotel particulier" in Paris still occupied by the owners and open to the public. One certainly has no idea that they are paying guests in this luxurious home situated in the centre of Paris. Private chateau accommodations can also be booked through the house.

Tel: From USA: (800) 353-3727, in New York (212) 977-3512, in Paris (011) 33 6 20 97 10 29. From Europe: 06 20 97 10 29.
E-mail: smartsleep@aol.com **Web:** http://www.worldaccommodations.com

Hotel Central Marais
In the Middle of Everything

Gay/Lesbian ♂

Hotel Central Marais is a small, exclusively gay hotel in the Marais, the old, aristocratic, historic quarter of central Paris. Surrounded by the principal gay bars and restaurants, it is a 5-minute walk from Notre Dame, La Bastille and Les Halles. The 17th-century hotel has been carefully restored to enhance the charm of its old-world character, while providing modern conveniences. Accommodations consist of two double-bedded rooms per floor, with a bathroom off the short lobby between. A small, communal salon is available to guests on the first floor. Guests are substantially on their own, with limited guest services. On the ground floor is the famous Belle Epoque bar, *Bar Hotel Central*, a popular gay rendezvous. Available in the building opposite is a 2-room apartment with kitchenette, bath and small balcony. We speak English and French. A bientôt — Maurice

NOTE: *Hotel entry with intercom at 2, rue Ste. Croix de la Bretonnerie (corner building).*

Address: 2, rue Sainte Croix de la Bretonnerie, Paris, 75004, France
Tel: (33) (0) 48 87 56 08, **Fax:** (33) (0) 42 77 06 27.
E-mail: hotelcentralmarais@wanadoo.fr

Type: Hotel above a popular men's bar & 2-room apartment across street.
Clientele: Mostly men with women welcome
Transportation: From: CDG airport Bus Train (RER); Orly airport ORLY VAL (RER) to Chatelet Les Halles Sta, exit Centre Georges Pompidou.

To Gay Bars: On premises & 10 min walk.
Rooms: 7 rooms with double beds.
Baths: 1 shared bath per floor, private bath 5th fl. (no lift).
Meals: Continental breakfast 35 FF per day.
Rates: Hotel: FF 540. Apt: FF 650-FF 795.

Credit Cards: MC, Visa, Eurocard.
Rsv'tns: Required.
Reserve Thru: Call direct.
Min. Stay: Apt: 3 days.
Parking: Garage under Hotel de Ville
In-Room: Phone, maid svc.
On-Premises: TV lounge, meeting room & gay bar.
Exercise/Health: Nearby

gym, weights, Jacuzzi, sauna, steam, massage.
Swimming: At nearby pool.
Sunbathing: By the river.
Smoking: Permitted.
Pets: Not permitted.
Children: Not permitted.
Languages: French & English.
IGLTA

Paris Marais Studio Guesthouse

Gay/Lesbian ♂♂
Gay-Owned & -Operated

A Romantic & Charming Studio in the Heart of Paris

Tastefully furnished and decorated, this lovely 3-star studio in a newly renovated 18th-century house is situated in Le Marais, both an historical and gay district of Paris. Better and less expensive than a three-star hotel, the charm, silence, comfort and privacy of **Paris Marais Studios Guesthouse** make this the perfect place for romance, culture, fun and history. Among the studio's amenities are two high-quality single beds, television, video, hifi, safe and kitchenette The refrigerator is always filled with everything you need for breakfast.

Address: Paris - Le Marais, Metro: Republique/Temple

E-mail: parismarais@hotmail.com **Web:** http://www.perso.cybercable.fr/ parima/

Type: Private studio.
Clientele: Gay & lesbian. Good mix of men & women
Transportation: Metro: Republique/Temple.
To Gay Bars: 1 min walk.
Rooms: 1 apartment with twin or king beds.
Baths: Private shower/ toilet.
Meals: Expanded continental breakfast items

left at your disposal.
Complimentary: 1 free bottle of champagne on stay over 10 days.
Dates Open: All year.
High Season: Summer, Christmas & New Years.
Rates: 400 FF-700 FF per day, 2 persons.
Discounts: 10% for single use & students.
Rsv'tns: Required, plus

deposit check. Cancellation policy: 1 week in advance.
Reserve Thru: Travel agent or call direct.
Min. Stay: 3 days.
Parking: Covered pay parking 100 FF/day.
In-Room: Phone, color cable TV, VCR, selection of free tapes, HiFi system, hair dryer, iron, ironing board, kitchen, microwave, coffee &

tea-making facilities, toaster, fridge.
Exercise/Health: Nearby gym, weights, Jacuzzi, sauna.
Swimming: Nearby pool.
Smoking: Permitted.
Children: Welcome.
Languages: French, English, German.

Villa Bonheur

WWW Women ♀
Lesbian-Owned & -Operated

Savor the Enchanting Pleasures of Southern Provence

Women, savor the enchantments of Provence with its picturesque villages and marketplaces. Unwind while wandering through fragrant vineyards and romantic lavender fields, or indulge in a tranquil day lounging around our swimming pool and sauna. Sunbathe on our sheltered balcony, even in winter. If you prefer a more active vacation, you can swim, surf, hike, bike and play tennis. We also offer tennis or surf lessons. Relax in our comfortable guesthouse called *Villa Bonheur*. In a big sunny kitchen, you can cook your own meals or have them cooked for you. Day trips to Aix-en-Provence, Avignon, Marseille, and Côte d'Azur are easy.

Address: Quartier Sous St. Michel, Quinson, 04500, France
Tel: (33) (0) 49 27 40 285 (Tel/Fax).
E-mail: Villabonheur@aol.com

Type: Guesthouse.
Clientele: Women only.
Transportation: Car is best. Pick up: Marseille/Nice airport, Aix en Provence train, minimum FF300.
To Gay Bars: 62 miles, a 2 hr drive.
Rooms: 3 rooms, 1 apartment witih double beds.
Baths: 2 private shower/

toilets, 1 shared bath/ shower/toilet.
Vegetarian: Available.
Dates Open: All year.
Rates: Per room/night: FF260-FF450.
Discounts: For groups - duration over 2 weeks.
Rsv'tns: Required.
Reserve Thru: Call direct.
Parking: Ample, free,

shaded off-street parking.
On-Premises: Hi Fi stereo, TV lounge, video tape library, fully equipped kitchen. Ask about renting one of our cars.
Exercise/Health: Gym, sauna.
Swimming: Pool. Nearby pool, river & lake.
Sunbathing: Poolside, at

beach & on patio.
Smoking: Permitted in lounge with prior approval. Non-smoking rooms available.
Pets: Permitted with prior approval.
Handicap Access: No.
Children: No.
Languages: French, German, Italian, English.

Domaine de l' Amérique

An Unexpected Paradise in the Heart of Provence

Come stay in a XVIIIth-century *Mas*, in the heart of the *Domaine de l'Amérique*, next to the mythical Grand Rhône river and near the most beautiful saltern in Europe. We are only ten kilometers from the sea (a 10-minute drive), where you will find 15 kilometers of fine, unspoilt sandy beach. Patrolled during the summer, part of the beach area is available to naturists and gays. Other activities include horseback riding, brisk walks, wind-surfing, swimming, cycling, and photography.

Discover the landscapes and the fabulous light made famous in the paintings of Van Gogh and Cézanne. The guesthouse is situated about one hour by car from the Cévennes or the Lubéron, Arles, Saint-Rémy, Les Baux de Provence, Nîmes, Avignon, Montpellier, Aix-en-Provence, and Marseille.

For your comfort, rooms have a kitchenette. You are welcome to relax in our very large garden, pick fresh vegetables in season, and enjoy fresh products from our poultry. If you wish to keep in touch with your business, our "cyber home" provides you with a study and access to the internet.

Address: Salin de Giraud, Camargue 13129, France
Tel: (33) 4 42 86 87 88, **Fax:** (33) 4 42 86 86 24.
E-mail: domaine.amerique@free.fr **Web:** http://www.provenceweb.fr/13/domaine-amerique

Type: Guesthouse.
Clientele: Mostly hetero clientele with a gay/lesbian following
Transportation: Car is best. 3 hours by TGV train from Paris.
To Gay Bars: 70 km, a 45 min drive.
Rooms: 2 suites, 2 apartments with single or double beds.
Baths: Private: 4 shower/ toilets. Shared: 4 bath/ shower/toilets.
Meals: Continental breakfast 30FF per person.
Vegetarian: Available on request.
Dates Open: All year.
High Season: Jul-Aug.
Rates: 300 FF-3500 FF (depending on season & type of accommodation).
Rsv'tns: Required.
Reserve Thru: Call direct.
Min. Stay: 2 days in high season.
Parking: Ample free parking in the Domaine.
In-Room: Telephone, color TV, kitchen, refrigerator, coffee & tea-making facilities.
On-Premises: Personal library, laundry facilities.
Exercise/Health: Nearby gym.
Swimming: Pool. 10km to beach with gay & naturist area.
Sunbathing: Poolside.
Smoking: Inquire.
Pets: Small pets permitted.
Handicap Access: No.
Children: No.
Languages: French, English, Italian, Spanish, German.
Your Hosts: Claude & François.

Arco Hotel

Gay-Friendly 50/50 ♀♂
Gay-Owned

The New ARCO Hotel

In January, 1996, the *ARCO* reopened on a quiet sidestreet two blocks from the central Wittenbergplatz. The pleasant, safe neighbourhood, right in the gay area, offers a wide range of restaurants, bars, shops and cafés. The 21 renovated rooms (most on the ground and first floors) all have telephones, safes, TV, radio, alarm clock and private bath or shower. The helpful *ARCO* staff is especially proud of the terrace and the quiet, shady garden and is looking forward to welcoming you in its new environment.

Address: Geisbergstr. 30, Berlin, 10777, Germany
Tel: (49-30) 23 51 48 0, **Fax:** (49-30) 21 47 51 78.
E-mail: arco-hotel@t-online.de **Web:** http://www.arco-hotel.de

Type: Hotel/pension.
Clientele: 50% gay & lesbian & 50% hetero clientele
Transportation: 5-minute walk from Wittenbergplatz U-bahn station: 3 U-bahn lines & several bus stops.
To Gay Bars: 2-8 minute walk.
Rooms: 14 double rooms, 7 single rooms.

Baths: All rooms have private toilet & shower or bath.
Meals: Breakfast buffet.
Dates Open: All year.
Rates: Singles DM 110-DM 145, doubles DM 145-DM 180.
Credit Cards: MC, Visa, Amex, Diners.
Rsv'tns: Preferred.
Reserve Thru: Call direct.

Parking: On the street or in nearby garage.
In-Room: Maid service, phone, safe, TV, radio, alarm clock.
On-Premises: Small lounge, terrace, garden.
Exercise/Health: Gym nearby.
Swimming: Lake nearby.
Sunbathing: At the lake or in the park.

Nudity: Permitted in park or at the lake.
Smoking: Permitted.
Pets: Permitted.
Handicap Access: Yes. Please inquire.
Children: Permitted.
Languages: German, English, French, Spanish, Portuguese.
Your Hosts: Jacques & Rolf.

Artemisia, Women-Only Hotel

[WWW] Women ♀

Relax in Our Women-Identified Atmosphere

Artemisia, the hotel for women only, is located minutes from the Kurfürstendamm, Berlin's most exciting avenue. Renovated and redecorated in soothing pastels, our hotel offers rooms with modern furniture, telephones and spacious, private bathrooms. *Artemisia's* special features include a sun deck with an impressive view of Berlin. Here, travelling women find complete comfort and convenience. If you come to Berlin, for business or pleasure, our personal, woman-identified atmosphere will make your stay a memorable experience.

Address: Brandenburgischestrasse 18, Berlin, 10707, Germany
Tel: (49-30) 873 8905, or (49-30) 860 9320, **Fax:** (49-30) 861 8653.
E-mail: Frauenhotel-Berlin@t-online.de **Web:** http://www.frauenhotel-berlin.de

Type: Hotel with gallery & breakfast cafe.
Clientele: Women only
Transportation: Taxi or U-bahn: Konstanzerstrasse, airport bus to Adenauerplatz.
To Gay Bars: 10-minute drive to women's bars.
Rooms: 7 rooms & 1 suite with single or double beds.
Baths: 1 private bath/toilet & 7 private shower/toilets.
Meals: Lavish buffet-style

breakfast with eggs, cereal, fruits, vegetables, yogurt, cheeses & meats, jams, etc.
Vegetarian: Buffet breakfast has a variety of items.
Complimentary: Room service till 22:00. Self-service drinks available after 22:00.
Dates Open: All year.
Rates: Single 109-148 DM, double 170-220 DM.

Discounts: On stays exceeding 1 week (7 nights).
Credit Cards: MC, Visa, Amex, Eurocard & Diners.
Rsv'tns: Recommended!
Reserve Thru: Call direct.
Parking: Adequate free on-street parking.
In-Room: Maid & laundry service, telephone, TV, heat. In suite only: color cable TV.
On-Premises: Meeting rooms, TV lounge, women's

art displays.
Sunbathing: On common sun deck.
Smoking: Permitted without restriction except during breakfast (no smoking).
Pets: Not permitted.
Handicap Access: No.
Children: Permitted, but males only up to 14 yrs.
Languages: German, English, Italian & French.

Hotel Königshof

We're More Than Different... Gay AND Comfortable

Hotel Königshof, which opened in June of 1998, is already regarded as Europe's most modern and comfortable gay hotel. Located in the middle of the St. Georg gay district, we are situated across the street from two dance bars and Hamburg's oldest leather bar. Next door to the hotel is Germany's most famous cabaret bar, as well as Hamburg's most popular sauna. The city center is just a few minutes' walk away, as are the central train station and several of Hamburg's finest museums.

Although the building itself dates back to 1875, the hotel is distinctive, modern and comfortable. Each of the hotel's 21 rooms is different in character and layout, featuring specially designed furniture — definitely rooms you will want to come back to after a day of sightseeing, or a night out on the town. You will find plush bedding and plush towels in all of the rooms, and most rooms have private baths. Wake up every morning to a complete continental buffet breakfast, available until noon in the comfortable breakfast area which overlooks the garden. We are also proud to sponsor local artists with regularly changing exhibits.

Services available from the hotel include telephones with ISDN computer connections, e-mail, fax, cable color television, wakeup calls, vending machines, and a very friendly staff who can assist you with any questions you may have. Room rates begin at DM 80 per night, including tax and breakfast.

Address: Pulverteich 16-18, Hamburg, 20099, Germany
Tel: (49-40) 284 074 0, **Fax:** (49-40) 284 074 74.
E-mail: hotelkhh@aol.com **Web:** http://members.aol.com/hotelkhh

Type: Hotel with apartment for rent.
Clientele: Mostly gay & lesbian with some hetero
Transportation: Airport bus to central station, then on foot or by taxi.
To Gay Bars: 1/2 min walk.
Rooms: 21 rooms, 1 apartment with single, double, queen or king beds.
Baths: Private: 16 shower/ toilets, 3 sinks only. Shared: 3 showers only.
Meals: Buffet breakfast.
Vegetarian: Nearby.
Complimentary: Tea & coffee.
Dates Open: All year.
Rates: DM 80-DM 150.
Credit Cards: Visa, Amex, Eurocard.
Rsv'tns: Requested.
Reserve Thru: Travel agent or call direct.
Parking: Adequate covered garage parking.
In-Room: Telephone, color cable TV, E-mail, fax, computer connections.
On-Premises: E-mail, fax, computer connections.
Exercise/Health: Nearby gym, sauna, steam, massage.
Swimming: Pool nearby.
Sunbathing: In garden.
Smoking: In most rooms. Non-smoking rooms avail.
Pets: Small pets permitted, DM 10 surcharge.
Handicap Access: No.
Children: No.
Languages: German, English, Dutch, Italian, French.
Your Hosts: Erik & Klaus-Werner.

Berkhöfel

Women ♀
Lesbian-Owned & -Operated

Along the Lower Rhine in Beautiful Westphalia

In the midst of pastures, orchards and fields, near the lower Rhine and the border between Germany and The Netherlands is *Berkhöfel*. Restored in 1994, our farmhouse offers bright, clean and welcoming guestrooms, meeting rooms, a livingroom and a dining hall where all-vegetarian meals are served. From the dining room, doors open out onto the sun-terrace and patio with deck chairs. The area has many manors and beautiful little museums and the wide, flat landscape is ideal for bicycle trips. *Berkhöfel* is a one hour's drive from Düsseldorf, 30 minutes from Nijmegen in The Netherlands and 1-1/2 hours from Amsterdam.

Address: Uedemer Str. 196, Bedburg-Hau, 47551, Germany
Tel: (49-2823) 29749.

Type: Guesthouse.
Clientele: Mostly women (with men welcome)
Transportation: Car is best, or train to Goch or Emmerich. Free pick up from train & Düsseldorf airport.
To Gay Bars: 10 min drive to "Le Journal" bar in Kleve, 30 min drive to Nijmegen, Netherlands gay bars.
Rooms: 12 rooms with single beds.

Baths: Shared: 5 showers only, 6 WCs only.
Meals: Full breakfast, supper, dinner.
Vegetarian: All meals are vegetarian.
Complimentary: Tea & coffee.
Dates Open: All year.
Rates: DM 40-DM 103.
Rsv'tns: Appreciated, if possible. Guests without reservations welcome if

rooms are available.
Reserve Thru: Call direct.
Parking: Adequate free off-street parking in our court.
In-Room: Maid service.
On-Premises: Meeting rooms, CD player, tape library.
Exercise/Health: Nearby gym, sauna, massage, golf.
Swimming: Nearby pool & lake.
Sunbathing: On patio.

Nudity: Permitted on patio.
Smoking: Permitted only in smoking room.
Pets: Not permitted.
Handicap Access: No.
Children: Please inquire. Playground, child's chair & bed.
Languages: German, English & Dutch.
Your Hosts: Brigitte.

K. M. — Saga Guest Residence

WWW Gay/Lesbian ♂♀
Gay-Owned & -Operated

Exclusive Guest Residence in Central Budapest

If you like antiques, romanticism, flavorful cuisine, classical music, opera, and strolling along the Danube, you'll enjoy Budapest. Buda and Pest are actually two cities occupying opposite sides of the Danube River. The *K. M. — Saga Guest Residence* is an 1890's home tucked away in a quiet, residential street on the Pest side of the river, within an eight to ten-minute walk of all gay bars and the city center. Our central location is also near the National Museum. The five double and single rooms in this exclusive guest residence are spacious — from 110 to 350 square feet — and have linens and towels from the United States.

Address: Lónyay u. 17. III. 1, Budapest, 1093, Hungary
Tel: (36-1) 217 1934, **Fax:** (36-1) 215 6883.

Type: Guest residence.
Clientele: Mostly gay & lesbian with some hetero clientele
Transportation: Airport mini bus. Airport pick up $6.
To Gay Bars: 4 blocks, 1/2 mi, a 5 min walk.
Rooms: 5 rooms, 1 suite with queen or king beds.
Baths: Private: 1 bath/ shower/toilet, 3 shower/ toilets. Shared: 1 bathtub only, 1 sink only.

Meals: Inquire.
Vegetarian: At in-house paid breakfast or a 5 min walk.
Dates Open: All year.
Rates: $35-$60.
Discounts: 10% on stays of 5+ nights.
Rsv'tns: Required.
Reserve Thru: Travel agent or call direct.
Min. Stay: 2 nights.
Parking: On- & off-street parking. 2 min to paid,

covered garage.
In-Room: Telephone, ceiling fans, color cable TV, refrigerator, coffee & tea-making facilities, maid & room service. Self service laundry.
On-Premises: Laundry facilities.
Exercise/Health: Nearby gym, Jacuzzi, sauna, steam, massage, pedicure.
Swimming: Nearby pool & spas.

Sunbathing: Poolside.
Smoking: Permitted in room. Non-smoking rooms available.
Pets: Not permitted.
Handicap Access: Limited wide doors & rails in bathroom.
Children: 12 years & older.
Languages: Hungarian, English, German, French, Russian.

Amazonia

An Unforgettable Vacation

From the hilltop windows of *Amazonia* you can look upon the beautiful, rolling, green hills of Ireland and the Atlantic Ocean. The beach is at the bottom of the hill and is very safe for swimming and sports. The walks to the nearby pubs afford marvelous views of the ocean rolling in along the rocky coastline. We have bikes, canoes, body boards, tennis racquets and golf clubs free for the guests' use and we can arrange horseback riding for you. Breakfast is served until 12:00 and there is free tea and coffee all day. We want you to feel at home and enjoy our Irish hospitality.

Address: Coast Road, Fountainstown, Myrtleville, Cork , Ireland
Tel: (353-21) 831 115.
E-mail: amazonia@indigo.ie **Web:** http://www.q-net.com/amazonia

Type: Bed & breakfast guesthouse with campsites.
Clientele: Women only
Transportation: Car or bus. Pick up from Cork city (airport, ferry dock) £8.
To Gay Bars: 10 miles.
Rooms: 2 log cabins & 3 rooms in house, twin & queen beds.
Baths: Private & shared.
Camping: 3 tent sites with breakfast in the main house.
Meals: Full breakfast.

Complimentary: Tea or coffee all day.
Dates Open: All year except Christmas.
High Season: May-Sept.
Rates: Cabins & rooms £17-£22/woman. Camping £4/tent + £6/woman (includes breakfast & use of house).
Discounts: 50% for children under 10 years.
Rsv'tns: Required in high season.

Reserve Thru: Call direct.
Parking: Ample off-street free parking.
Exercise/Health: Kayaks, bicycles, wind surfers, snorkeling equipment, wet suits, table tennis, body boards. Nearby tennis club, horse riding arranged.
Swimming: Nearby ocean, river.
Sunbathing: On patio, in garden.
Nudity: Permitted in

garden.
Smoking: Limited to garden.
Pets: Permitted. We have dogs & cats.
Handicap Access: Yes. Partial wheelchair access in bungalow.
Children: Welcome.
Languages: English, French.
Your Hosts: Penny & Aine.

Frankies Guesthouse

WWW Gay/Lesbian ♂

Your Private Guesthouse in Dublin's Center

Established in 1989 in a mews-style building over 100 years old, *Frankies* offers year-round accommodations exclusively for gays. Dublin has an expanding gay scene, which offers a variety of venues. We've recently added a sauna and bar on premises, and we're located near other bars, clubs and saunas. Our beautiful south-facing roof terrace & sun deck is surrounded with tropical potted plants and is a good place to relax after a day of sightseeing. Dublin is a capital city of many charms and delights, from magnificent Dublin Castle and the supreme architecture of the city's cathedrals, to Phoenix Park (Europe's largest enclosed park), the choice is endless. Travellers wishing to tour outside Dublin will find breathtaking scenery along the coast road which leads to sandy beaches and sand dunes. You'll be glad you visited Ireland, a country renowned for its hospitality.

Address: 8 Camden Place, (off Camden St / off Harcourt St), Dublin, 2, Ireland
Tel: Reservations: (353-1) 478 3087 (guestline) or (353-1) 475 2182, **Fax:** (353-1) 478 3087.
E-mail: frankiesguesthouse@ireland.com **Web:** http:// www.frankiesguesthouse.com

Type: Guesthouse with private bar.
Clientele: Mostly men with women welcome
Transportation: Airport bus to Camden St or taxi.
To Gay Bars: 8 min walk.
Rooms: 12 rooms with single or double beds.
Baths: 5 en suite.
Meals: Full Irish breakfast.
Vegetarian: On request.

Complimentary: Tea & coffee.
Dates Open: All year.
High Season: Jul-Sept.
Rates: Singles £25-£35, doubles £57-£70.
Discounts: On extended stays.
Credit Cards: MC, Visa, Amex, Eurocard.
Rsv'tns: Required.
Reserve Thru: Call direct.

Min. Stay: On weekends: singles 3 nights, doubles 2 nights.
Parking: Ample, free on-street parking.
In-Room: Color TV & maid service.
On-Premises: TV lounge.
Exercise/Health: Sauna opened on request.
Sunbathing: On the roof terrace.

Smoking: Permitted without restrictions.
Pets: Not permitted. We have our own dogs.
Handicap Access: Yes, some ground floor rooms.
Children: Not permitted.
Languages: English, Chinese & Malay.
Your Hosts: Joe & Frankie.

La Filanda Guesthouse

A Woman's Cultural Center and Guesthouse

This romantic Italian villa, surrounded by a huge wild garden, imposing old trees, and the lovely hills of the Piemonte region, was created by female artists. The ancient city of Acqui Terme, famous for its thermal baths and traffic-free center, is within walking distance, while Genova, Milan and the Mediterranean Sea are 40 miles away (a one-hour drive). Piemonte is well-known for its superb cuisine and high-class wines, such as Barolo and Barbaresco — a gourmet's delight! At *La Filanda* we organize a yearly workshop program along diverse cultural lines. We hope to see you soon.

Address: Reg. Montagnola No. 4, Acqui Terme, 15011, Italy
Tel: (39-0144) 32 39 56 (Tel/Fax). If call does not go through, try dropping the "0".

Type: Guesthouse & cultural center with music room & workshops.
Clientele: Women only
Transportation: Train from Genova to Acqui Terme (1 hour), then taxi. Pick up from train 10,000 lire.
To Gay Bars: 40 miles, 1-hour drive to Genova, Milan or Turin gay bars.
Rooms: 7 rooms with single or double beds.
Baths: Shared: 2 bath/shower/toilets, 2 showers only, 2 WCs only.
Vegetarian: Restaurants in town have vegetarian dishes.
Dates Open: Mar-Oct. Open in winter during special periods, on request.
High Season: June-Sept.
Rates: Double 45,000 LI, single 60,000 LI (35 Sfr-55 Sfr).
Discounts: Special group rates.
Rsv'tns: Required.
Reserve Thru: Call direct.
Parking: Free parking.
On-Premises: 2 fully equipped kitchens, living rooms, video library, books, music/cassettes.
Exercise/Health: Health center nearby with fango & massage.
Swimming: Pool & river nearby.
Sunbathing: In garden & on terrace.
Nudity: Permitted in garden.
Smoking: Permitted, but preferably outside.
Pets: Permitted if well-behaved.
Handicap Access: No.
Children: Welcome. Boy children welcome up to 10 years of age.
Languages: Italian, German, English, French.
Your Hosts: Regula.

Casa Scala

An Italian Home on a Picturesque Island

Picture Elba Island, covered with lush vegetation such as wild rosemary, anise, blackberries, grapes (small, family-owned vineyards), cactus, and trees as varied as apricot, lemon, almond, pine, fir, eucalyptus, cypress, and palm. Amidst this splendor is *Casa Scala.* This small, Italian house with four apartments and two sun terraces is surrounded by a garden with trees and flowers and has a view of some of the many tree-covered hills. The nearby hills are a brilliant red, due to iron-rich land. Abandoned mine sites are cluttered with stones and rocks waiting to be scooped up by hand. *Casa Scala* is just a few minutes by bike (available for the duration of your stay for a small fee) from one of the sandy beaches. Boating excursions to some of the caverns (accessible only by sea) are also available.

Address: Loc. Filetto No 9, Marina di Campo, Isola d'Elba 57034, Italy
Tel: (39-0565) 977 777, **Fax:** (39-0565) 977 770.
E-mail: fluxus@elbalink.it

Type: Cottage with workshops available.
Clientele: Women only
Transportation: Car is best or train from Florence to Elba, pick up from bus station Marina di Campo.
Rooms: 4 apartments with single beds.
Baths: Each apartment has its own bath.
Meals: Continental breakfast with workshop.
Dates Open: Mar-Oct.
High Season: Jul-Aug.
Rates: DM 35-DM 40 per night (35,000-40,000 Lire).
Credit Cards: Eurocheck.
Rsv'tns: Required.
Reserve Thru: Call direct.
Min. Stay: One week in general. Single days for women from overseas.
Parking: Adequate free off-street parking.
In-Room: VCR, video tape library, kitchen, refrigerator, coffee/tea facilities.
On-Premises: Meeting rooms, garden.
Swimming: Nearby ocean beach.
Sunbathing: In the garden, on the beach.
Nudity: Permitted in the garden.
Smoking: Permitted.
Pets: Not permitted.
Children: No boys over 10 yrs old.
Languages: German, Italian, English.
Your Hosts: Marianne & Elvira.

B & B

A Room with a View?

B&B is an exclusive bed and breakfast **for women only,** located at the top floor of an historical palace in the center of Florence, Italy. With a stunning view of Brunelleschi's cupola of the Duomo, it overlooks a quiet inner garden and is only minutes away from the Uffizi, Ponte Vecchio, Santa Croce, the Accademia, the main train station and air terminal. *B&B* has four double rooms all overlooking the garden, three with a view of the Duomo. The apartment has just been nicely renovated, with parquet floors, all wood beds, and some antique furniture.

Address: Borgo Pinti 31, Florence, 50121, Italy
Tel: (39-55) 248 0056.
E-mail: beb@mail.cosmos.it **Web:** http://www.bnb.it

Type: Bed & breakfast.
Clientele: Women only
Transportation: Airport bus to central station, then bus or taxi.
To Gay Bars: A 10 min walk.
Rooms: 4 rooms with single, double or queen beds.
Baths: 2 shared bath/shower/toilets. 2 rooms have sinks.

Meals: Expanded continental breakfast.
Vegetarian: Upon request. 5 min walk to vegetarian restaurant, vegetarian shop on same street.
Complimentary: Tea & coffee, fruit.
Dates Open: All year.
High Season: Easter, April thru mid-July, Sept-Oct, Christmas.
Rates: LIT 80,000/90,000

single, LIT 120,000/130,000 double.
Discounts: Weekly stay in low season.
Credit Cards: MC, Visa, Eurocard.
Rsv'tns: Required.
Reserve Thru: Travel agent or call direct.
Min. Stay: Required.
Parking: Off-street pay parking.
In-Room: Maid service.

On-Premises: Library.
Exercise/Health: Nearby gym, weights, massage.
Smoking: Smoking not allowed.
Pets: Not permitted.
Handicap Access: No.
Children: Welcome. Boys maximum 10 years old.
Languages: Italian, English, French.
Your Hosts: Paola.

Mini Hotel

The completely restored *Mini Hotel* is located in Genoa's historical city center, across the street from Giuseppe Mazzini's home (the Museum of Risorgimento), 150 metres from the Aquarium, and 200 metres from the Principe railway station. Our two-star hotel has 15 rooms — 12 with private bathrooms, one with a private bathroom outside the room, and two rooms which share a bathroom in common. All rooms have a television set and a telephone. We also offer bar service, a night concierge and fax service. There is a parking garage 80 metres from the hotel.

Address: Via Lomellini 6-1, Genoa, 16124, Italy
Tel: (39-10) 246 5803 (Tel/Fax).

Type: Hotel.
Clientele: Mostly hetero clientele with a gay/lesbian following
Transportation: Airport bus to Principe Station, then taxi or walking.
To Gay Bars: A 15 min drive.
Rooms: 15 rooms with single or double beds.
Baths: Private: 13 shower/

toilets, 15 sink/washbasins only; Shared: 2 bath/shower/ toilets.
Complimentary: Tea, coffee, milk & soft drinks.
Dates Open: All year.
Rates: Single: LIT 55,000-LIT 75,000, double LIT 80,000-LIT 110,000 (LIT 30,000 for any bed added).
Discounts: Inquire about discounts from Jan 2-Mar 31

& for stays over 7 days.
Credit Cards: Visa, Eurocard.
Rsv'tns: Required (preferred in summer).
Reserve Thru: Travel agent or call direct.
Parking: Adequate, covered pay parking.
In-Room: Telephone, color TV, maid & room service.
On-Premises: Fax service.

Swimming: Ocean nearby.
Smoking: Permitted everywhere.
Pets: Permitted.
Handicap Access: No.
Children: Welcome.
Languages: Italian, English, French, Spanish.
Your Hosts: Renato & Anna.

Miravalle

Gay-Friendly ⚥

Situated on top of a marvelous Umbrian hill, surrounded by panoramic scenery is *Miravalle*... We're just at the boundary separating Umbria from Tuscany, only two miles from the beautiful medieval town of Monteleone di Orvieto, one hour by car or train from Rome or Florence. We practice organic farming on 30 hectares of land, producing wine, olive oil, honey, vegetables, fruit and grains by using ecologically sound methods and no pesticides. We're pleased to offer our products directly to our guests.

Our large, comfortable apartments accommodate up to four persons and consist of a kitchen, bathroom, bedroom and living room with optional sofa bed. Each has its own entrance and separate exit to the garden, and a private picnic table. We also offer studios for up to three people. The property features a large outdoor swimming pool, huge meadow, fruit orchard, a sun-roofed picnic area with BBQ, and astounding views.

Address: Loc. Cornieto 2 Fraz. S. Lorenzo, Monteleone D'Orvieto, 05017, Italy
Tel: (39-0763) 835309
E-mail: miravalle@tiscalinet.it **Web:** http://www.phenix.it/miravalle

Type: Umbrian country house.
Clientele: Mostly hetero, gay/lesbian following
Rooms: Apartments & studios.
Baths: Private.
Dates Open: Mar 15-Oct

31, Easter, Christmas, New Year.
Rates: LI100,000-198,000 per day (final cleaning & heating not included).
Min. Stay: 7 nts July & Aug.
In-Room: Apartments: kitchen, bedroom, bathroom,

living room, optional sofa bed, private entrance, private picnic table.
On-Premises: Garden, fruit orchard, meadow, picnic area with BBQ. Can arrange guided tours of area.
Exercise/Health: Table

tennis, mountain bike rentals. Nearby hiking.
Swimming: Pool.
Smoking: Not indoors.
Pets: Not permitted. 3 loving dogs on premises.

Gayopen Bed & Breakfast

Gay/Lesbian ⚥
Gay-Owned & -Operated

Gay Holidays in Rome @ Vacanze Allegre a Roma

Welcome to *Gayopen Bed & Breakfast* in lovely downtown Rome. We're located in an 19th-century building, not far from S. Maria Maggiore Basilica. The apartment is well-furnished and comfortable and has two double rooms with shared bath solely for guests. The flat is on the 3rd floor, with elevator, satellite television, and is surrounded by lovely shops, cafés, bakeries, and reasonably priced restaurants. Gay bars, pubs, discos and saunas are also nearby. We are twelve minutes by subway from the Vatican, and a ten-minute walk from the Roman Forum. Reservations must be made in advance.

Address: Via Statuo 44, Apt 18, Rome, 00185, Italy
Tel: (39-064) 820 013 or 847 07, **Fax:** (39-064) 880 196.
E-mail: orsogrigio@hotmail.com **Web:** http://www.angelfire.com/mo/ RICLAUDIOHOLYDAYS/

Type: Bed & breakfast.
Clientele: Mostly gay & lesbian with some hetero clientele
Transportation: Shuttle train from Fiumicino Airport to Termini station. Inquire about airport & train pickup.
To Gay Bars: 4 blocks.
Rooms: 2 rooms with single or double beds.
Baths: Shared.

Meals: Expanded continental breakfast.
Complimentary: Tea, coffee, beer & other beverages.
Rates: US $32 pp/pn, breakfast & tax included.
Discounts: US $2 for 3+ nights.
Rsv'tns: Required.
Reserve Thru: Travel agent or call direct.

Parking: Adequate pay garage or street parking
In-Room: AC, color TV.
On-Premises: Meeting rooms, connection to internet.
Exercise/Health: Nearby gym, sauna.
Swimming: Nearby pool, ocean.
Sunbathing: At beach.
Nudity: Permitted.

Smoking: Permitted in a room. Nonsmoking rooms available.
Pets: Permitted.
Handicap Access: Yes, ramps, wide doors.
Children: Welcome.
Languages: Italian, English, French, Spanish, German.
Your Hosts: Claudio & Alba.

Il Piccolo di Piazza di Spagna

Gay-Friendly ♂♂

In the historical center of Rome, close to the Spanish Steps, the hotel *Il Piccolo di Piazza di Spagna* offers you the comforts of a big hotel in this little corner of art and culture. Completely restored, all the rooms are fully equipped with private baths, air conditioning, satellite TV, room safe, direct-dial telephone, and refrigerator/bar on request. A room with balcony and Jacuzzi is also available on request. We offer fax service and airport taxi service, can arrange your meal reservations at restaurants, and will help organize sightseeing tours.

Address: Via dei due Macelli 47, Rome, 00187, Italy
Tel: (39-06) 69 200 560 (Tel/Fax).

Type: Bed & breakfast hotel with bar.
Clientele: Mostly hetero clientele with a gay/lesbian following
Transportation: Taxi, train or subway. Airport pickup LIT 90,000 per cab.
To Gay Bars: 3-4 miles. Most bars in Trastevere, accessible by bus or taxi.
Rooms: 11 rooms with single or double beds.
Baths: All private: 9

Meals: Continental breakfast.
Dates Open: All year.
Rates: Single LIT 324,000, double LIT 380,000, triple LIT 513,000.
Discounts: 20% high season (Mar 15-Nov 2 & Dec 8-Jan 7). 30% low season (other periods). Also offer last minute.
Rsv'tns: Required.
Reserve Thru: Call direct.

Min. Stay: Weekends: 3 nights (Fri-Sun) or 2 nights (Sat-Sun).
Parking: Adequate covered pay parking.
In-Room: Telephone, AC, color TV, refrigerator, room & laundry service.
On-Premises: Meeting rooms.
Exercise/Health: Jacuzzi. Nearby gym, weights, Jacuzzi, sauna, massage.
Swimming: Nearby pool,

sea.
Smoking: Permitted in rooms. Non-smoking rooms available.
Pets: Yes, very small pets permitted.
Handicap Access: Yes, elevator. 2 rooms don't have steps.
Children: Welcome.
Languages: Italian, English, French, German, Spanish.

Rainbow Penthouse Bed & Breakfast

Gay-Friendly ♂♂
Gay-Owned & -Operated

If You Want to Live Like a Roman, This is the Place to Stay

Rainbow Penthouse Bed & Breakfast is a large penthouse apartment divided into two sections, connected by a winding staircase on the terrace. The B&B is on the uper level and offers a cozy bedroom with double bed. The living room also includes a sofa-bed and a soft leather sofa which can accommodate two more persons. A fully equipped kitchen, and a bathroom with tub, shower and bidet completes the interior. The panoramic terrace is ideal for sun bathing or a romantic candle-light dinner. All items necessary for a continental breakfast are in the kitchen, and if you have a special wish just knock on the door downstairs. The Colosseum is only a 15-minute drive away.

Address: Via Accademia Ambrosiana 41, Rome, Italy
Tel: (39) 0654 05484.
E-mail: aimone@hotmail.com **Web:** http://www.aimone1.com

Type: Bed & breakfast.
Clientele: 75% hetero & 25% gay & lesbian clientele
Transportation: Airport train, then bus 702 or taxi.
Rooms: 2 rooms, 1 apt.
Baths: Bath/shower/toilet: 1 private, 1 shared.
Meals: Continental bkfst.
Vegetarian: Yes.
Complimentary: Coffee & tea.

Dates Open: All year.
High Season: Easter, Christmas, New Years.
Rates: Low: Lire 120,000 (60,000/day for extra person); High: Lire 200,000. Rates per day, 2 persons.
Discounts: Weekly rate of Lire 750,000 for 2 persons, 7th night free for extra person.
Rsv'tns: Required with

20% deposit.
Reserve Thru: Call direct.
Min. Stay: 4 nights.
Parking: 300 meters to ample covered parking, Lire 20,000 per day.
In-Room: AC, color satellite TV, kitchen, refrigerator, coffee & tea-making facilities, private entrance.
Exercise/Health: Nearby gym.

Swimming: Nearby pool, ocean.
Sunbathing: On private sun decks.
Pets: Permitted with small supplement.
Children: No, not under 12 due to terrace.
Languages: Italian, English, German, French.
Your Hosts: Francesco.

Hotel Villa Schuler

History & Tradition, Comfort & Romance

Family-owned *Villa Schuler* was converted from a Sicilian villa to a hotel in 1905. The hotel has been extensively refurbished emphasizing its original elegance, charm and atmosphere. Superbly situated high above the Ionian Sea, its unique position offers stupendous views of snow-capped Mount Etna and the Bay of Naxos. Centrally located next to the delightful Botanical Gardens and just 2 minutes from Taormina's famous traffic free "Corso Umberto". The ancient Greek-Roman theatre and the cable-car to the beaches are just a 10-minute walk away.

Surrounded by extensive, shady terraced gardens, the fragrance of jasmine and bougainvillaea blend soothingly, enhancing the comfortable, romantic surroundings. Rooms are spacious, each with full bathroom, orthopaedic beds, radio, satellite TV, direct-dial telephone and electronic safe. Most have a seaview, furnished balcony, terrace or loggia. Other amenities include a palm-terrace pavillion, a winter garden, TV room, small library, piano, 24-hour bar and room service, laundry service, parking, garages and central heating. Have expanded "à la carte" breakfast served in the dining room, on the terrace overlooking the entire coastline, in the palm-terrace pavillion, or in your room. Courtesy mountain bikes on premises, tennis courts nearby. Shuttle-service to the hotel beach.

Address: Via Roma 17, Taormina, Sicily 98039, Italy
Tel: (39-0942) 23481, **Fax:** (39-0942) 23522.
E-mail: schuler@tao.it **Web:** http://www.villaschuler.com

Type: B&B hotel & bar.
Clientele: Mainly hetero; gay & lesbian following
Transportation: Airport bus, taxi. Airport pick up by arrangement LIT 120,000.
To Gay Bars: 5 min walk.
Rooms: 26 rooms, 2 suites & 4 apartments all with single or double beds.
Baths: All private.
Meals: Expanded continental breakfast à la carte.
Dates Open: Mar 10-Nov 18.
High Season: Easter, August.
Rates: LIT 90,000-LIT 115,000 per person for B&B.
Discounts: 20%: Mar 11-Apr 8, Jul 2-29, Nov 2-12.
Credit Cards: MC, Visa, Amex, Eurocard, Diners.
Rsv'tns: Recommended, by FAX or e-mail if possible.
Reserve Thru: Travel agent or call direct.
Parking: Free private parking, garage LIT 18,000 per day (reservable).
In-Room: Phone, safe, satellite TV, room, maid, laundry svc.
On-Premises: Lounge w/ color satellite TV, meeting rms, laundry facilities, solarium, exotic garden, furnished terraces.
Exercise/Health: Complimentary mountainbikes. Nearby gym, weights, sauna & massage.
Swimming: Nearby beach, shuttle avail.
Sunbathing: On the roof terrace or at nearby beach.
Smoking: Permitted.
Pets: Not permitted.
Children: Welcomed.
Languages: Italian, English, German, French, Spanish & Belgian.

Tuscan House

From Villas to Rooms-With-A-View in Romantic Tuscany

TuscanHouse Properties
Would you like to stay in a charming country inn with warm hospitality and delicious food, or rent an affordable apartment, private house or villa in the very heart of Tuscany? Whether you are traveling with a loved one or a group of friends, we can find you the right accommodations for your vacation. Looking for a place in Rome? Visit our website for more information.

A Fine Example of TuscanHouse Quality: Il Palazzotto Country Inn

Il Palazzotto is set in the classic Sienese landscape of cypress-lined avenues, castles, villas, vineyards and olive groves and dates back to the 18th century, when it was the manor house of the village. This country inn has six guest rooms, private baths, a library, a kitchen, spacious and fireplaced living and dining rooms, and a cottage with a private suite across the garden, all restored to the highest standards.

Guests can enjoy dining al fresco in the terrace garden with views of mountain sunsets. A few steps away, the pool has hydro massage, a sunbathing area and a shaded pergola.

Well-marked hiking and bike paths and country lanes lead away from the village. Thermal baths dating from the Roman era invite you to soak in their healing waters. But food and wine are what have really made this area famous. Yes, you can sample fine Brunellos while touring the vineyards, have lunch at a trattoria and come home to enjoy a four-course dinner at our inn. Tuscan food is fresh and seasonal, the local pasta is hand-rolled spaghetti, the "pici".

From Il Palazzotto's central location, you can easily tour ancient cities and monasteries. We're minutes from the Via Cassia and a 20 km drive from the gothic city of Siena. You can take daytrips to Florence, Assisi, San Gimingano and even Rome.

Tel: (39-577) 707 068; in USA: (801) 640-5012 (fax/voice mail).
E-mail: zak@tuscanhouse.com **Web:** http://www.tuscanhouse.com

Black Tulip Guesthouse

Europe's Only 3-Star Hotel Specifically Designed for Leathermen

Black Tulip Guesthouse is Europe's classiest hotel catering to leather guys. Newly opened in a 16th-century building on a central Amsterdam canal, this three-star hotel is minutes from the railway station, the leather district, restaurants and shops. Rooms share a high standard of comfort, equipped with a floor-heated bathroom, large, two-seater bathtubs and high-pressure showers. Some rooms have a wonderful canal view and all have typical Dutch wooden-beamed ceilings. One room has a period mantelpiece, two contain a bathtub spa system. Facilities include a breakfast/lounge area with a small patio with newspapers, books, magazines, and local tourist information.

Particular attention has been paid to noise insulation between rooms. Some rooms contain a metal cage, and the largest has a built-in play area with various fun pieces of equipment. Each room has strategically located bondage hooks, a sling and hygenically sealed douche hoses/nozzles. VCR tapes are available, in addition to the adult channel. Boots can be rented. Guests carry their own house key, and there is no charge, other than for breakfast, for someone you bring home for the night. Prior reservations are essential, as there are many gay events in Amsterdam throughout the year, including monthly leather parties, which attract many from outside the local community.

Address: Geldersekade 16, Amsterdam, 1012 BH, Netherlands
Tel: (31-20) 427 0933, **Fax:** (31-20) 624 4281.
Web: http://www.blacktulip.nl

Type: Guesthouse.
Clientele: Gay men only
Transportation: Direct airport train to central Amsterdam, then 3 min walk.
To Gay Bars: 2 blocks.
Rooms: 9 rooms with single or double beds.
Baths: Private: 8 bath/shower/toilets, 1 shower/toilet.
Meals: Buffet breakfast.
Vegetarian: Vegetarian breakfast available, many vegetarian restaurants in neighborhood.
Complimentary: Tea & coffee-making facilities, welcome drinks.
Dates Open: All year.
Rates: Hfl 195-Hfl 350 per night, inclusive of breakfast & sales tax.
Credit Cards: MC, Visa, Amex, Diners, Eurocard.
Rsv'tns: Required.
Min. Stay: 3 days wknds & special events.
Parking: Adequate on-street pay parking. Parking garages in neighborhood.
In-Room: Direct-dial phone, voice mail, color cable TV, radio, VCR, refrigerator minibar, coffee & tea-making facilities, safe deposit box, computer connections, maid service.
On-Premises: Meeting room, fax, voice mail, computer connections, video tape library, boot rental service.
Exercise/Health: Jacuzzi in some rooms, massage on premises. Nearby gym.
Swimming: Nearby pool, ocean, lake.
Sunbathing: 30 min train ride to beach.
Nudity: Permitted throughout building.
Smoking: Permitted everywhere. Non-smoking rooms available on request.
Pets: Not permitted.
Children: No.
Languages: Dutch, English, German, French, Spanish.
Your Hosts: Eelco & Frank.

Hotel Kap

WWW Gay-Friendly 50/50 ♀♂
Gay-Owned & -Operated

A (Gay-) Friendly 2-Star Hotel in the Centre of Amsterdam

Located in one of Amsterdam's many charming houses is *Hotel Kap,* a (gay-) friendly place providing bright, clean and functional rooms. Situated in a quiet residential area in the city centre, the hotel has been a popular family-style hotel since 1923. Run by various families over the years, the hotel has become known for its unconstrained atmosphere and friendly service. Early in 1998, the new (gay-) management began renovations in order to convert the hotel into a two-star establishment, thus increasing the comfort and service to their guests even more. All rooms were redone to include private showers and television. Our breakfast buffet is served in the reception area, a spacious and attractive reception and lounge area overlooking a charming patio.

It's just a ten-minute stroll to major museums, the floating flowermarket, trendy shopping centres and Amsterdam's swinging gay life. Famous Rembrandsquare, Reguliersdwarsstraat and Halve Maansteeg with their bars and discotheques are a few blocks away.

Address: Den Texstraat 5b, Amsterdam, 1017 XW, Netherlands
Tel: (31-20) 624 59 08, **Fax:** (31-20) 627 12 89.
E-mail: h.kap@worldonline.net **Web:** http://www.kaphotel.nl

Type: Hotel.
Clientele: 50% gay/lesbian & 50% hetero
Transportation: Train to Central Stn, then tram 24 to Wetering Circuit. We're behind Carousel restaurant.
To Gay Bars: 3 blocks.
Rooms: 13 rooms with single or double beds.

Baths: Private & shared.
Meals: Buffet breakfast.
Vegetarian: On buffet.
High Season: Apr 1-Oct 31.
Rates: Hfl 70-Hfl 280.
Credit Cards: MC, Visa, Amex, Diners.
Rsv'tns: Required.
Reserve Thru: Call direct.
Min. Stay: 2 nights.

Parking: Adequate on-street pay parking (Hfl 33/day). Hotel sells day parking tickets (saves up to 50%).
In-Room: Color cable TV, maid service.
On-Premises: TV lounge, garden patio.
Exercise/Health: Nearby gym, weights, sauna.

Sunbathing: At beach, 20 kms away.
Smoking: Yes. No non-smoking rooms.
Pets: Small pets only.
Children: Not encouraged.
Languages: Dutch, English, German, French, Spanish.
Your Hosts: Harry.

Maes B & B

Cozy Home Ambiance...

Maes B&B's recently renovated 18th-century home has quaint, comfortable guestrooms decorated in the style of that period, with the accent on cozy homelike ambiance. Awaken to fresh croissants, just part of the extended continental breakfast served. Complimentary coffee and tea are available throughout the day in the guest kitchen on the first floor.

In the city centre, our quiet residential area is minutes from museums and walking distance from all major sights, nightlife, restaurants and cafes. Our small shopping street is located between two canals (the Herengracht and Keizersgracht), near the Anne Frank house, Homomonument, open-air markets, and all public transport.

Address: Herenstraat 26, Amsterdam, 1015 CB, Netherlands
Tel: (31-20) 427 5165, **Fax:** (31-20) 427 5166. Mobile phone: 31-6 5472 1002.
E-mail: maesbb94@xs4all.nl **Web:** http://www.xs4all.nl/~maesbb94/

Type: Bed & breakfast.
Clientele: Mostly gay & lesbian with some hetero clientele
Transportation: Taxi from airport or train station. Or from central station, take trams #1, 2, 5, 13, or 17 to 1st stop. From there, turn into Korte Lijnbaanssteeg & continue over 2 bridges to Herenstraat.
To Gay Bars: 5-10 minute walk at most.
Rooms: 2 rooms with single, twin or king beds.

Baths: 2 ensuite.
Meals: Expanded continental breakfast.
Complimentary: Tea & coffee available from guest pantry all day.
Dates Open: All year.
High Season: Apr-Oct.
Rates: From NLG 125-NLG 275.
Discounts: On stays of 7 or more nights.
Credit Cards: MC, Eurocard, Amex, Visa, Diners.
Rsv'tns: Required.

Reserve Thru: Call or e-mail direct.
Min. Stay: 2 nights on weekends.
Parking: Paid parking (parking meters).
On-Premises: Laundry facilities & guest pantry with refrigerator & coffee/tea-making facilities. Telephone & fax services.
Exercise/Health: Nearby gym, weights, Jacuzzi, sauna, steam & massage.
Swimming: In nearby North Sea & city swimming pools.

Sunbathing: On the beach or in the parks.
Nudity: Permitted at the beach & in some parks.
Smoking: Non-smoking.
Pets: Not permitted.
Handicap Access: No.
Children: Welcome.
Languages: Dutch, English, Russian, some French & German.
Your Hosts: Ken & Vladimir.

Anco Hotel Bar

WWW Men ♂

Welcoming Leathermen from all over the World

The *ANCO* is a gay-owned and -operated hotel-bar that welcomes leathermen from all over the world. It is located in a historic canal building which dates from 1640, and is situated between the leather district (Warmoesstraat) and Amsterdam's famous red light district. The Central Railway Station is just a short walk from the hotel.

Address: Oudezijds Voorburgwal 55, Amsterdam, 1012 EJ, Netherlands
Tel: (31-20) 624 11 26, **Fax:** (31-20) 620 52 75.
E-mail: info@ancohotel.nl **Web:** http://www.ancohotel.nl

Type: Hotel & bar for leathermen.
Clientele: Men only
Transportation: Train from airport to central station, then taxi or 5-minute walk.
To Gay Bars: On premises, open from 9am-10pm. 2-min walk to other gay bars.
Rooms: 11 rooms, 2 dormitories & 1 suite with private bath.
Baths: Private: 14 sinks. Shared bath/shower/toilet on each floor.
Meals: Expanded continental breakfast.
Dates Open: All year.
High Season: July 1-Sept 30.
Rates: Dormitory: Hfl 70, single: Hfl 105, double: Hfl 150. With private bath: Hfl 195.
Credit Cards: All major cards accepted.
Rsv'tns: Required at least 4 weeks in advance in high season.
Reserve Thru: Call or fax direct.
Min. Stay: 3 nights during high season.
In-Room: Maid service, color cable TV, 24hr gay video.
On-Premises: Meeting room, gay bar.
Swimming: 20 miles to nude beach & lakeside Amsterdam.
Sunbathing: At the beach.
Nudity: Permitted. 30-minute train ride to nude beach.
Smoking: Permitted without restrictions.
Pets: Not permitted.
Handicap Access: No.
Children: Not permitted.
Languages: Dutch, English, German, Italian & French.
Your Hosts: Kees.

Chico Guest House

Gay/Lesbian ♂

Experience the home-like atmosphere of the *Chico Guest House.* Furnished in a contemporary style, our three rooms and two apartments are spacious compared to many other accommodations you will find in Amsterdam. Rooms offer single or double beds and share baths on the landing. Apartments have private baths. We're a 15-minute walk to gay bars. The Albert Cuyp Market, with both open-air and indoor areas, is also nearby.

Address: Sint Willibrordusstraat 77, Amsterdam, 1073 VA, Netherlands
Tel: (31-20) 675 4241 (Tel/Fax).

Type: Guesthouse.
Clientele: Mostly men with women welcome
To Gay Bars: 15 minutes walking, 3 minutes by tram.
Rooms: 3 rooms & 2 apartments with single & double beds.
Baths: Rooms share baths on landing. Apartments have private baths.
Complimentary: Coffee & tea.
Dates Open: All year.
Rates: Double Hfl 120 with shared bath, Hfl 150 with private shower/toilet.
Rsv'tns: Required.
Reserve Thru: Call direct.
Parking: Limited on-street parking.
In-Room: Clean towels daily, bed linen every 3-4 days.
Smoking: Permitted without restrictions.
Pets: Not permitted.
Handicap Access: No.
Children: We prefer not.
Languages: Dutch, German, English, a little French.
Your Hosts: Herman.

Riverside Apartments

Gay-Friendly 50/50 ⚥

Accommodations in Central Amsterdam and Beyond

Riverside Apartments offers short- and long-term rentals, with most short-term accommodations walking distance to most gay bars and discos. For those staying for six months or longer, apartments and houses are available along the canals, in the suburbs and in surrounding towns. Rates vary from Fl. 2,000 to Fl. 2,750 per week for single or double occupancy. Daily rates are available on request and require a minimum stay of four days. Rates for a stay of six months or more depend on the type of accommodation, as well as its location. Monthly rates vary from Fl. 3,000 to Fl. 9,000 and, in most cases, a deposit of one or two month's rent is required.

Singles, doubles and larger parties can also be accommodated in hotels, apartments and houses. All accommodations have private facilities, cable TV, fridge and coffee- and tea-makers. Some have fax, answering machines, minibars, and most have private kitchens, phones and VCRs. In some cases breakfast is included. As a rule, all major credit cards are accepted. Parking is difficult and expensive in the city center. Maid service is available, varying with accommodation. In most cases, pets aren't allowed and smoking is permitted. Although most places aren't handicap-accessible, some are and do allow pets. Children aren't especially welcome in most short-term rentals. The owner, Jerry, speaks Dutch, English, German and French. Please call direct.

Address: Weteringschans 187 E, Amsterdam, 1017 XE, Netherlands
Tel: (31-20) 627 9797, **Fax:** (31-20) 627 9858.
E-mail: geuje@worldonline.nl

Bordine Bed & Breakfast Studiorent

Gay-Friendly 50/50 ⚥
Gay-Owned & -Operated

Discover the Real Holland

Off the beaten track, 80 miles north of Amsterdam in the province of Friesland, you'll find the old city of Leeuwarden, with its canals and gay bars. The entire area is filled with lakes and wooded islands and is popular with Dutch tourists. *Bordine* features nicely decorated rooms with kitchenette and shower, TV, VCR (with gay videos), private phone, minibar, etc. A value for the money, it's near a canal and parks, and its friendly neighborhood is safe and quiet.

Address: Bordineweg 113, Leeuwarden, Friesland 8931 AN, Netherlands
Tel: (31-58) 280 2540, Toll-free (888) TELEBOT, ext (31-58) 280 2540, **Fax:** (31-58) 280 2518.
E-mail: bordine@telebot.net **Web:** http://gaybordine.mypage.org

Type: Bed & breakfast guesthouse.
Clientele: 50% gay & lesbian & 50% hetero
Transportation: Car, train, bus or bike.
To Gay Bars: 1-2 miles.
Rooms: 2 rooms, each w/ 2 single hotel beds.
Baths: 2 private bath/shower, 1 shared WC.
Meals: Buffet breakfast in room.
Vegetarian: Dinner express service on request.
Complimentary: Wine on arrival in room.
High Season: Jul-Aug.
Rates: HFL 45 pp/pn.
Discounts: 10% on stays of over 1 week.
Credit Cards: Visa, MC.
Rsv'tns: Required. 1 night deposit required, cancellation made if no deposit within 14 days. Deposits forfeited if cancellation made within 14 days of arrival.
Reserve Thru: Call, fax, e-mail, website.
Parking: On-street parking.
In-Room: Phone, color cable TV, VCR, kitchen, refrigerator, coffee & tea-making facilities, mini bar, room & laundry service.
On-Premises: Laundry facilities, video tape library, free internet LAN access, notebook rent service.
Exercise/Health: Free bikes. Nearby gym, sauna, Jacuzzi, steam. 45 min to gay sauna.
Swimming: Nearby pool, ocean.
Sunbathing: Poolside, at beach, on patio.
Nudity: Nearby beach, or at part of Terschelling Island.
Smoking: On patio. Non-smoking rooms available.
Languages: Dutch, English, German, Frisian.
Your Hosts: Wiebren.

Women's Country House

Women ♀
Lesbian-Owned & -Operated

Relaxation & Peace in Northern Netherlands

Women's Country House (Vrouwen Buiten Verblijf) is a small-scale guesthouse for women situated in northern Netherlands, between the towns of Assen and Groningen. Here, women come to meet other women, participate in weekend classes, enjoy a vacation, or to work and study. The beautiful countryside is ideal for hiking or cycling, canoeing and other water sports. The house accommodates a maximum of 14 guests in eight bedrooms. One room and a bathroom on the ground floor are available to women who can't easily climb the stairs. Outside, there are two gardens: one peaceful, the other more noisy. The lively town of Groningen in only 28 kilometers away and can be easily reached by bus.

Address: Tolweg 38, Oud Annerveen, 9655 PG, Netherlands
Tel: (31-598) 491578.
E-mail: vbv@xs4all.nl **Web:** http://www.xs4all.nl/~vbv

Type: Guesthouse.
Clientele: Women only
Transportation: Train to Assen, then taxi; or train to Groningen, then bus 57 to Annen, then 4 km walk.
To Gay Bars: 17.5 miles.
Rooms: 7 rooms with single or double beds.
Baths: 2 shared bath/shower/toilets.
Meals: Continental

breakfast, lunch, dinner.
Vegetarian: Always available. Meat only on request.
Complimentary: Tea, coffee, milk, fruit.
Dates Open: All year.
High Season: Jul-Aug.
Rates: 1999: Hfl 62.00-86.50.
Discounts: No dinner Hfl 15.00.

Rsv'tns: Recommended.
Reserve Thru: Call direct or email.
Min. Stay: 2 nts in Jul-Aug.
Parking: Limited free off-street parking.
On-Premises: 2 gardens, laundry facilities.
Swimming: Pool & lake nearby.
Sunbathing: At lake.
Nudity: Permitted in "quiet"

garden.
Smoking: Permitted in hall. Non-smoking rooms avail.
Pets: Permitted w/ advance owner consent. Resident cat.
Handicap Access: Yes, ramps.
Children: Yes.
Languages: Dutch, German, English.
Your Hosts: Tine.

Casa Marhaba

Gay/Lesbian ♂

"Marhaba" Means "Welcome" — We'll Make You Just That

Casa Marhaba is set on one acre in a pleasant rural area, 1 km from the nearest beach, 5 km from Carvoeiro and Lagoa, and 50 km west of Faro Int'l. Airport. Our double rooms have en suite bathrooms with showers. We serve a substantial continental breakfast on the poolside terrace and picnic lunches and pub-style snacks are available to order. Barbecue by the pool or enjoy the TV lounge with satellite TV and video facilities. The Algarve region's unspoiled countryside has miles of beaches, quaint and historical villages, lively towns and resorts, deep sea fishing, coastal boat trips, and great restaurants.

Address: Rua de Benagil, Alfanzina, Lagoa, 8400-427, Portugal
Tel: (351-282) 358720 (Tel/Fax).
E-mail: casamarhaba@hotmail.com

Type: Bed & breakfast guesthouse with bar.
Clientele: Mostly men with women welcome
Transportation: Faro Airport, then rental car. Pick up can be arranged for a fee.
To Gay Bars: 10 miles or a 15-minute drive.
Rooms: 5 rooms with single or double beds.
Baths: 5 private shower/toilets.

Meals: Expanded continental breakfast.
Vegetarian: Available upon advanced request. Vegetarian food nearby.
Complimentary: Welcome cocktail.
Dates Open: Apr-Oct.
High Season: Apr-Oct.
Rates: Single: 49,000 $00/wk, 8,250 $00/nt high season. Double: 59,500 $00/wk, 10,000 $00/nt high season.

Credit Cards: No.
Rsv'tns: Required.
Reserve Thru: Call direct.
Min. Stay: 3 nights.
Parking: Ample free off-street.
In-Room: Maid & laundry service.
On-Premises: TV lounge with satellite TV & video.
Swimming: Pool on premises, ocean nearby.
Sunbathing: At poolside, on patio & private sun

decks.
Nudity: Permitted on special sun deck poolside.
Smoking: Permitted throughout.
Pets: Not permitted.
Handicap Access: No.
Children: Not especially welcome.
Languages: English & French.
Your Hosts: Tony & Sam.

Quinta Santo Phunurius

Holiday on Portugal's Spectacular Western Algarve

Set in 21,000 square metres of lush gardens, fish ponds and orchard, with views to the ocean, *Quinta Santo Phunurius* offers a choice of self-catering accommodation to suit all tastes. The grand colonial-style villa features a spectacular marble staircase and huge balconies overlooking the gardens and open countryside to the ocean beyond. It has three large double bedrooms (all en-suite) with an enormous lounge and dining room, and fully equipped kitchen. The villa sleeps six to nine guests. A few metres away, the guest studio is a beautiful, large open-plan studio with picture window overlooking the gardens. The studio, which sleeps two, has a kitchen, bath/shower room and a private patio. At the bottom of the garden, with stunning views over the orchard and countryside, are three private cottages with three, two and one bedrooms. All cottages have kitchens, bath/shower rooms and their own patios. All the units have satellite TV and share the use of the large swimming pool and gardens.

The location is tranquil, yet within minutes' walk of the nearest supermarket and the tourist facilities of Old Lagos. The nearest beach is a 20-minute walk across the open countryside and there are gay beaches a few minutes' drive away. It is only a 15-minute walk to the nearest gay bar. Other local attractions can be reached after a short drive. These include the Monchique Mountains, the ancient town of Silves, and Cape St. Vincent (the most southwesterly point in Europe), where you can watch the sun set over the Atlantic Ocean.

Address: Lagos **Mail To:** Apartado 730, Lagos, 8601 900, Portugal
Tel: (351) 282 762397 (Tel/Fax).
E-mail: leightoncrook@hotmail.com

Type: Cottages, villa rental.
Clientele: 50% hetero & 50% gay & lesbian clientele
Transportation: Car is best. Pick up from airport in A/C Volvo 9,000 ESC. Free pick up from train or bus.
To Gay Bars: 1 mile.
Rooms: 1 villa, 1 studio, 1 apartment with single, double, king or bunk beds.
Baths: All private
Complimentary: Welcome pack on arrival: coffee, tea, sugar, milk, biscuits, etc.
Dates Open: All year.
High Season: Jul-Aug.
Rates: Per unit: winter £150-£390, summer £320-£990.
Discounts: Long stay (2+ wks) off-season. 5% for multiple unit bookings. 10% whole estate.
Rsv'tns: Required.
Reserve Thru: Call direct.
Min. Stay: 1 week (negotiable out of season).
Parking: Ample free off-street parking adjacent to units.
In-Room: Color satellite TV, kitchen, refrigerator, coffee & tea-making facilities.
On-Premises: Laundry facilities.
Exercise/Health: Nearby gym, weights, tennis, sailing, sea sports, diving, horse riding.
Swimming: Pool. 20 min walk to ocean.
Sunbathing: Poolside, on private sun decks, patio & at beach.
Smoking: Permitted. No non-smoking rooms.
Pets: Not permitted.
Children: Welcome.
Languages: Portuguese (sometimes), English, some French & Arabic.
Your Hosts: Leighton & Greg.

Casa Pequena

WWW Gay/Lesbian ♂

All the Comforts of Home... in our Pink House

Situated in 1100 square metres of gardens on a hillside overlooking the village and beach of Praia da Luz, *Casa Pequena* is, first and foremost, a home. You will find it comfortable and well-furnished with the usual amenities, including TV, video, audio equipment and a good library of books, all available to our guests. There are two guest rooms, each with adjacent bath/shower and we provide all linens, towels and beach towels. There is a swimming pool, hot tub, extensive terraces, sun-beds, and guests have their own keys. We can advise you where to visit and explain the eccentricities of gay nightlife in Portugal.

Address: Apartado 133, Praia da Luz, Lagos, Algarve 8600, Portugal
Tel: (351-282) 789 068 (24-hr tel/fax), mobile: (351-91) 982 0378.

Type: Guesthouse with honour bar.
Clientele: Mostly gay men with women welcome
Transportation: Car is best. Pick up from airport, train, bus. 6,000 escudos from Faro. Free from Lagos.
To Gay Bars: 5 km.
Rooms: 2 rooms with single or double bed.
Baths: Private, adjacent to room.
Meals: Expanded

continental breakfast. Other meals at reasonable fee.
Vegetarian: On request & at most restaurants.
Complimentary: Tea & coffee.
Dates Open: All year.
High Season: Apr/May-end of Oct.
Rates: 8,000 esc/night sngl; 11,000 esc/night dbl.
Discounts: 10% if both rooms booked by same party (4 persons).

Rsv'tns: Required.
Reserve Thru: Call direct.
Min. Stay: 3 nights minimum charge though you can stay for fewer nights.
Parking: Ample free off-street parking.
On-Premises: TV lounge. Entire house avail. to guests.
Exercise/Health: Jacuzzi. Nearby gym, weights, Jacuzzi, sauna, steam, massage.

Swimming: Swimming pool. Ocean nearby.
Sunbathing: Poolside, on common sun decks, nearby beaches.
Nudity: Permitted.
Smoking: Permitted. Non-smoking bedrooms.
Pets: No. 3 resident cats.
Languages: Portuguese, English, French.
Your Hosts: James.

Residencial Rubi-Mar

Gay-Friendly ♀♂
Gay-Owned

A Home Away From Home

In the old quarter of town, in the very heart of historic Lagos is *Residencial Rubi-Mar.* Varied restaurants, cafés and bars are at our doorstep, and the nearest beach is two minutes from our door (a 10-min. drive takes you to the nudist beach of Meia Praia). Stroll the cobbled streets to find local art and craft shops, visit the Golden Church and Museum, and Europe's first African slave market dating back to 1441. After a heavy night on the town, we don't make you struggle out of bed for breakfast — we serve it to you *in bed*. Guests have front door keys (no restrictions apply).

Address: Rua da Barroca 70-1o, Lagos, Algarve 8600-688, Portugal
Tel: (351-282) 763165, **Fax:** (351-282) 767749.
E-mail: rubimarlagos@yahoo.com **Web:** http://www.freeyellow.com/members7/rubimar

Type: Bed & breakfast.
Clientele: Mostly hetero w/ a gay/lesbian following
Transportation: Car or train. Airport pick up 8000$.
To Gay Bars: 5 min walk.
Rooms: 8 rooms with single, double or quad beds.
Baths: Private: 4 shower/ toilets, 4 sinks only. Shared: 2 bath/shower/toilet.
Meals: Continental

breakfast.
Dates Open: All year.
High Season: Apr - end of Oct.
Rates: High 8500-7000, low 6500-5500.
Credit Cards: MC, Visa.
Rsv'tns: Highly recommended, credit card details required.
Reserve Thru: Call direct.
Min. Stay: 3 nights in

summer.
Parking: Ample pay parking.
In-Room: Color TV, coffee & tea-making facilities, maid service.
Exercise/Health: Nearby gym, weights, Jacuzzi, sauna, steam, massage.
Swimming: Nearby pool, ocean.
Sunbathing: At beach, on

private balcony.
Nudity: Permitted at nearby gay nudist beach.
Smoking: Permitted.
Pets: Not permitted.
Children: Welcome.
Languages: Portuguese, English.
Your Hosts: David & Tony.

Auchendean Lodge Hotel

Gay-Friendly ⚥

Exceptional Dining in Sensational Highland Scenery

Come relax in the Scottish Highlands in our Edwardian hunting lodge. *Auchendean Lodge Hotel* is an elegant, comfortable country hotel furnished with antiques and fine paintings. While here, enjoy award-winning food, our own vegetables, good wines and malt whiskies, spectacular views of Spey and the Cairngorm Mountains, walking, fishing, golfing and skiing. Our hotel is set in a magnificent garden on the edge of 200 acres of mature forest. Call Ian or Eric for a brochure. Although our clientele is not exclusively gay, you will be warmly welcomed. **Reader's Comment:** "The Scottish dinners were superb. The hosts were very friendly and welcomed us warmly. The other guests, while not gay, were friendly and very nice. I would recommend this hotel without reservation, but plan on TWO nights. One night will make you want another." — *Richard H., St. Louis, MO*

Address: Dulnain Bridge, near Grantown-on-Spey, Inverness Shire, PH26 3LU, Scotland
Tel: (44-1479) 851 347 (Tel/Fax).
E-mail: auchendean@btinternet.com **Web:** http://www.btinternet.com/~auchendean/

Type: Inn with restaurant.
Clientele: Mostly hetero with gays & lesbians
Transportation: Car.
To Gay Bars: 2 hrs by car.
Rooms: 7 rooms, sngl, dbl, queen beds.
Baths: All private.
Meals: Full breakfast. Dinner opt'l £26 (book ahead).

Vegetarian: Available with advance notice.
Complimentary: Tea, coffee, biscuits.
High Season: Easter thru Oct, Xmas & New Year.
Rates: £25-£57.
Discounts: Inquire.
Credit Cards: MC, Visa, Amex, Diners.
Rsv'tns: Recommended.

Essential for dinner.
Reserve Thru: Call direct.
Parking: Ample free off-street parking.
In-Room: Color TV, coffee & tea-making facilities, room & laundry service.
Exercise/Health: Walk, fish, golf, ski, jog.
Swimming: Nearby pool, river, lake.

Sunbathing: In woods.
Nudity: In woods.
Smoking: Permitted in bedrooms & 1 lounge.
Pets: Permitted.
Handicap Access: Yes, restaurant. Steps to rooms.
Children: Permitted.
Languages: English, French.
Your Hosts: Ian & Eric.

SCOTLAND • AVIEMORE

Garlands Guest House

WWW Gay/Lesbian ⚥
Gay-Owned & -Operated

A Splendid Georgian House

Now that you've chosen the Georgian elegance of Edinburgh for your visit, why not add to your enjoyment by staying with us in our splendid Georgian house? We're now in our fourth year of welcoming guests and have had nothing but compliments from them. Many return to *Garlands* on a regular basis and confidently recommend us to their friends.

Relax in comfortable, smoke-free surroundings during your stay and enjoy a cooked breakfast in our elegant spacious dining room; you'll be well looked after. The house is fully centrally heated and you can control the temperature to suit your own requirements. There is always an ample supply of hot water. *Garlands* is only a 10-minute walk to the gay bars, and there is a gay sauna just around the corner. We look forward to welcoming you to share our home for a while. Why not visit our website for a virtual tour?

Address: 48 Pilrig Street, Edinburgh, EH6 5AL, Scotland
Tel: (44-131) 554 4205 (Tel/Fax).
E-mail: bill@garlands.demon.co.uk **Web:** http://www.garlands.demon.co.uk

Type: Guesthouse.
Clientele: Mostly gay & lesbian with some hetero clientele
Transportation: Airport bus to town, then taxi. Short taxi ride from train & bus stations.
To Gay Bars: A 10 min walk.
Rooms: 6 rooms with single or double beds.
Baths: 6 private shower/toilets.
Meals: Full or continental breakfast.
Vegetarian: Veggie breakfast available, veggie restaurants in town.
Complimentary: Tea, coffee & biscuits in room.
Dates Open: All year.
High Season: Aug-Sept.
Rates: £25.00-£40.00.
Discounts: By arrangement.
Credit Cards: MC, Visa.
Rsv'tns: Required.
Reserve Thru: Call direct.
Parking: Ample on-street (no restrictions) parking.
In-Room: Colour TV, tea & coffee-making facilities, maid service.
On-Premises: Pay phone.
Exercise/Health: Nearby sauna.
Smoking: Not permitted.
Pets: Permitted.
Handicap Access: No.
Children: No.
Languages: English.
Your Hosts: Bill & Ian.

Ardmor House

A Relaxing Retreat in Historic Edinburgh

Newly refurbished and lovingly restored, **Ardmor House** is situated in Edinburgh's historic city center, close to gay bars, cafes, etc. This stylish Victorian stone house combines many original features with a contemporary ambience to create the ideal base from which to explore the city. All of our rooms are fully ensuite with televisions and hospitality tray. We also provide a full Scottish breakfast with vegetarian options, and operate a non-smoking policy. Free and safe on-street parking and a regular bus service are conveniently found just across the city. Robin and Colin will be glad to welcome you and give lots of friendly advice on the best way to make the most of your trip to Edinburgh.

Address: 74 Pilrig Street, Edinburgh, EH6 5AS, Scotland
Tel: (44-131) 554 4944 (Tel/Fax).
E-mail: robin@ardmorhouse.freeserve.co.uk **Web:** http://
www.ardmorhouse.freeserve.co.uk

Type: Guesthouse with breakfast restaurant.
Clientele: 50% gay & lesbian & 50% hetero
Transportation: Car is best. Local bus or 15 min walk from city centre.
To Gay Bars: 5-7 min walk.
Rooms: 5 rooms with single, double or king beds.
Baths: All private.

Meals: Full breakfast.
Complimentary: Hospitality tray in rooms (tea, coffee, etc).
Dates Open: All year.
High Season: June-Sept.
Rates: £25-£40 per person. Double/twin room £50-£80.
Credit Cards: MC, Visa.
Rsv'tns: Required.
Reserve Thru: Travel agent

or call direct.
Parking: Ample free on-street parking.
In-Room: Color TV, coffee & tea-making facilities, maid & room service.
Exercise/Health: Nearby gym, weights, Jacuzzi, sauna.
Swimming: Nearby pool.
Smoking: Fully non-

smoking house.
Pets: Please check when booking.
Handicap Access: Yes. Ground-floor bedroom.
Languages: English, French.
Your Hosts: Robin & Colin.

Armadillo Guest House, The

Gay/Lesbian ♂♂

Rated 3 Stars by the Scottish Tourist Board

The Armadillo Guest House, highly commended by the Tourist Board of Scotland, is newly refurbished throughout to an excellent standard and provides a friendly, warm atmosphere. We have maps and full information on gay and happy life here in Scotland. Come and join in the fun of "Tartan Kilt" country, only at *The Armadillo.* Rated 3 stars by the Scottish Tourist Board.

Address: 12 Gilmore Place, Edinburgh, EH3 9NQ, Scotland
Tel: (44-131) 229 6457 (Tel/Fax).

Type: Guesthouse.
Clientele: Mostly gay & lesbian with some hetero clientele
Transportation: Bus, taxi.
To Gay Bars: A 20-minute walk or 5-minute drive.
Rooms: 6 rooms with single or double beds.

Baths: 2 private ensuite, others share.
Meals: Full breakfast. Late breakfast also available.
Vegetarian: Always available to guests.
Complimentary: Tea, coffee & set-up service.
Dates Open: All year.

High Season: Jul-Oct.
Rates: £18-£30.
Discounts: For longer stays.
Rsv'tns: Required.
Reserve Thru: Call direct.
Parking: Limited off-street & on-street parking.
In-Room: Color TV,

telephone, coffee/tea-making facilities, room, maid & laundry service.
On-Premises: Laundry facilities.
Pets: Permitted.
Handicap Access: No.
Languages: English.

Knowes, The

Gay-Friendly 50/50 ♀♂
Gay-Owned & -Operated

"Ca' the Yowes to the Knowes" — Robert Burns

Our 1920s home, *The Knowes* offers discretion, comfort and stylish accommodation. Traditional furnishings mix well with modern art and sculpture, and our expanded continental breakfast happily contrasts with the British breakfast you will get elsewhere. Stay two to five nights to fully enjoy all of the sights Glasgow has to offer — this is also a convenient point from which to easily tour the surrounding area. Young or old, you will feel welcomed here. If you need an early start, we will be helpful. If you come in late, that presents no problem. You arrive as guests, and many stay in touch as friends.

Address: 32 Riddrie Knowes, Glasgow, G33 2QH, Scotland
Tel: (44-141) 770 5213, **Fax:** (44-141) 770 0955.
E-mail: Stay@TheKnowes.sol.co.uk **Web:** http://www.sol.co.uk/t/theknowes

Type: Bed & breakfast & self-catering apartment.
Clientele: 50% gay & lesbian & 50% hetero clientele
Transportation: Airport bus to Buchanan bus station, then taxi.
To Gay Bars: 3 miles, a 12 min drive.
Rooms: 1 room, 1 apt with single or double beds.
Baths: Private: 1 bath/ shower/toilet, 1 shower/ toilet.
Meals: Expanded continental breakfast.
Vegetarian: Available on request & nearby.
Complimentary: Tea, coffee, juice.
Dates Open: All year.
Rates: £17-£22 each. Apt: £39/nt, 2-3 persons; £210/ wk.
Discounts: B&B £2 off daily charge on stays of 3+ nights. Apt: 15% 3 weeks, 20% 4 weeks.
Credit Cards: Eurocard, Visa.
Rsv'tns: Required.
Reserve Thru: Travel agent or call direct.
Min. Stay: Apt: 2 nights.
Parking: Adequate off-street parking.
In-Room: Coffee & tea-making facilities. Apt: phone, color TV, kitchen, fridge.
On-Premises: TV lounge.
Smoking: Non-smokers preferred. Restricted smoking allowed.
Pets: 1 pet permitted by previous arrangement.
Handicap Access: Yes, ramps, wide doors.
Children: No.
Languages: English.
Your Hosts: Hugh & Alan.

Ardmory House Hotel

WWW Gay-Friendly ♂
Gay-Owned

Fall in Love With This Restful Scottish Hotel

Golf, fishing, birdwatching, and walking are restful and relaxing pastimes for guests on the Isle of Bute, approximately 60 minutes from Glasgow and 30 minutes on the ferry from Wemyss Bay. *Ardmory House Hotel* sits in its own grounds on a hill overlooking Rothesay Bay, commanding an outstanding view over the Bay, Firth of Clyde, and Loch Striven. Although the hotel's clientele is not exclusively gay, gays are warmly welcomed. Contact Donald or Bill for a brochure.

Address: Ardmory Road, Ardbeg, Isle of Bute PA20 0PG, Scotland
Tel: (44-1700) 502 346, **Fax:** (44-1700) 505 596.
E-mail: Ardmory.House.Hotel@DIAL.PIPEX.COM

Type: Hotel with restaurant & bar.
Clientele: Mostly hetero with a gay male following
Transportation: Car is best, or rail from Glasgow, ferry, taxi.
To Gay Bars: 1-1/2 hours to gay bars.
Rooms: 5 rooms with single or double beds.
Baths: All private: 3 shower/toilets, 2 bath/ shower/toilets.
Meals: Full breakfast. Bar lunches & dinner optional.
Vegetarian: Available at breakfast, dinner or bar meal.
Complimentary: Tea, coffee, fruit basket & quarter bottle of wine in all rooms.
Dates Open: All year.
High Season: Jul-Aug.
Rates: B&B: single £47.50, double/twin £75. Dinner & B&B: single £65, double/twin £110.
Discounts: Dinner B&B: 10% on stays of 3 or more days.
Credit Cards: MC, Visa, Amex, Diners.
Rsv'tns: Required.
Reserve Thru: Travel agent or call direct.
Parking: Ample free off-street parking.
In-Room: Colour TV, telephone, coffee/tea-making facilities, maid & room service, limited laundry service.
On-Premises: Laundry facilities.
Swimming: Nearby pool & ocean.
Sunbathing: In garden.
Smoking: Not permitted in bedrooms, restaurant or conservatory.
Pets: Permitted.
Handicap Access: Please inquire.
Children: No.
Languages: English.
Your Hosts: Donald & Bill.

Casa Alexio

WWW Men ♂

A Mediterranean Paradise

On top of a rise above the bay of Talamanca is placed the very private gayhouse called *Casa Alexio,* far away from any road noise, but only 3 minutes by car to town.

From the breakfast terrace, one has a wonderful view over Ibiza Town, the harbor and the sea reaching to the neighboring island of Formentera. A pool with bar, terraces and a comfortable living room with cable TV add to your comfort. The beach is a five-minute walk.

Address: Barrio Ses Torres 16, Jesús, Ibiza, 07819, Spain
Tel: (34) 971 31 42 49, **Fax:** (34) 971 31 26 19.
E-mail: alexio@alexio.com **Web:** http://www.alexio.com

Type: Gayhouse with 24 hr self-service poolside bar.
Clientele: Men only
Transportation: Taxi from airport is best.
To Gay Bars: 1.7 miles or 3 minutes by car.
Rooms: 15 rooms with queen & king beds.
Baths: All private bathrooms.
Meals: Full breakfast.

Dates Open: All year.
High Season: April through October.
Discounts: Special off-season rates.
Credit Cards: Visa, MC, Amex, Eurocard.
Rsv'tns: Required.
Reserve Thru: Travel agent or call direct.
Parking: Free off-street parking.

In-Room: Satellite TV, AC, maid and laundry service.
On-Premises: TV lounge, meeting rooms.
Exercise/Health: Whirlpool. Workout possibilities in pool area.
Swimming: Pool, ocean beach next door.
Sunbathing: Poolside or on beach.
Nudity: Permitted at pool.

Beach nearby, gay beach 10-15 min. drive.
Smoking: Permitted without restrictions.
Pets: Not permitted.
Children: Not permitted.
Languages: Spanish, English, German, French, Italian, Portuguese.

Villa Maspalmeras

WWW Gay/Lesbian ⚥
Gay-Owned & -Operated

Escape to Freedom

A stylish, small guesthouse, surrounded by beautiful gardens, *Villa Maspalmeras* overlooks the ocean and the town of Puerto de la Cruz, Tenerife. With only five bedrooms, one apartment and a cottage, the villa focuses on a simple, stylish and friendly atmosphere. The Villa has been refurbished, adding a mini-gym, as well as a swimming pool and sun deck to the magnificent mature gardens. Breakfast is provided buffet style, daily snacks can be organised, and drinks are available each evening at the bar at sunset.

About ten minutes by car is the bustling, picturesque seaside town and working port of Puerto de la Cruz with its gay bars, discos and sauna. Also nearby is one of the most spectacular beaches on the island, with the double benefit of being both beautiful, as well as very gay-friendly and clothing-optional. Welcome to this truly relaxing escape destination, where guests are treated as guests, and where the freedom to be yourself is paramount.

Address: Vista Panoramica 20, Santa Ursula, Tenerife, 38398, Spain
Tel: (34-922) 302 607.

Type: Guesthouse with bar.
Clientele: Gay/Lesbian. Good mix of men & women
Transportation: Car is best. Airport pickup (inquire about charge).
To Gay Bars: A 10 min drive.
Rooms: 5 rooms, 1 apartment, 1 cottage with single or double beds.

Baths: 6 private shower/ toilets.
Meals: Buffet breakfast. Occasional supper/BBQ.
Complimentary: Tea, coffee in room.
Dates Open: All year.
Rates: Please inquire.
Discounts: Reduction for long duration of stay.
Credit Cards: MC, Visa.

Rsv'tns: Required.
Parking: Adequate, free on- & off-street parking.
In-Room: Telephone, coffee & tea-making facilities, maid & laundry service.
On-Premises: TV lounge.
Exercise/Health: Gym, weights.
Swimming: Pool. Ocean nearby.

Sunbathing: Poolside, on patio, common sun decks & at beach.
Nudity: Permitted poolside.
Smoking: Permitted in garden only. Non-smoking rooms available.
Pets: Not permitted.
Children: No.
Languages: Spanish, English, Italian.

Madrid Gay Guesthouse

The Best Value for Your Money in Madrid

Madrid Gay Guesthouse, a small and friendly gay-owned apartment, is situated in the classy Salamanca district in the center of Madrid. Within walking distance of the airport bus terminal in the Plaza de Colón, you'll find our location very central, yet very quiet. We're close to shops, museums, restaurants, and tourist landmarks such as the Puerta del Sol, Prado Museum, Thyssen Foundation, the Plaza Mayor, Rastro (Flea Market), and the Retiro Park. Your hosts will show you the way to the gay district of Chueca, only 15 minutes away walking (or five minutes by car), and provide you all the useful information on where to go and what's on! **Reservations by e-mail only.**

E-mail: cleston@lander.es **Web:** http://come.to/gaymadrid

Type: Bed & breakfast guesthouse.
Clientele: Mostly men with women welcome
Transportation: Walk from airport bus stn. (pickup available). Buses & metro nearby.
To Gay Bars: 6 blocks, 12 min walk, 5 min drive.
Rooms: 1 room w/ double bed. Extra single bed on request.
Baths: 1 private bath/ shower/toilet (ensuite).
Meals: Expanded continental breakfast.
Complimentary: Welcome drink on arrival. Complimentary coffee or similar drink throughout stay.
Dates Open: All year.
Rates: 5500 Esp-7500 Esp.
Discounts: 20% on stays of 7+ consecutive nights.
Credit Cards: Cash only.
Rsv'tns: Required.
Reserve Thru: Call direct.
Min. Stay: Required. Must stay Fri & Sat nights on weekend stays.
Parking: On-street pay parking. Several pay parkings nearby.
In-Room: AC.
On-Premises: Meeting rooms, TV lounge, laundry facilities, Hi-fi set. If required, use of computer & internet connection.
Exercise/Health: Fully equipped gym in nearby gay district.
Nudity: Permitted anywhere in guesthouse.
Smoking: Permitted anywhere but in the room, which is positively non-smoking.
Pets: Not permitted.
Children: No.
Languages: Spanish, English, French, German, Italian, some Dutch.
Your Hosts: José & César.

Antonio's

A Home in the Sun, Full of Rustic Temptations

Set within this idyllic location in Sitges, only 30 minutes from Barcelona, *Antonio's* offers the discerning traveller the chance to sample style, luxury and elegance in this five-bedroom house. Mornings, an expanded continental breakfast is served in the conservatory overlooking the garden. All rooms are en-suite, and laundry service is available. Perfect for sunlovers, we're only a few minutes walk from the famous Sitges beaches — a two-minute walk (3 blocks) to the gay beach, and a 15-minute walk to the nude beach. For the more adventurous and energetic, bicycles may be hired. At night the exciting nightlife of Sitges is yours to explore, as we are just a short walk from the bars and the town's many restaurants. We also operate a reservation service for rooms and apartments all over Sitges. We can put you in touch with a real estate agent who specializes in working with gays wanting to buy property in Sitges.

Address: Passeig Vilanova 58, Sitges, 08870, Spain
Tel: (34-93) 894 9207, **Fax:** (34-93) 894 6443.

Type: Guesthouse.
Clientele: Mostly gay & lesbian with some hetero clientele
Transportation: From Barcelona airport, train to El Prat de Llobregat, train to Sitges, then taxi.
To Gay Bars: 3 blocks, 4 min walk, 2 min drive.
Rooms: 4 rooms, 1 suite with single or double beds.
Baths: Private: 1 bath/shower/toilet, 4 shower/toilets.
Meals: Expanded continental breakfast.
Vegetarian: Upon request.
Complimentary: Tea & coffee, chocolates.
Dates Open: All year.
High Season: May-Oct.
Rates: High: 10,000-16,000 Pts, Low: 8,000-10,000 Pts
Credit Cards: MC, Visa, Eurocard.
Rsv'tns: Required.
Reserve Thru: Call direct.

Parking: Ample covered, free on- & off-street parking.
In-Room: Ceiling fans, color TV, refrigerator, coffee & tea-making facilities, maid, room & laundry svc.
On-Premises: Meeting rooms, TV lounge, fax.
Exercise/Health: Weights. Nearby gym, weights, Jacuzzi, sauna, steam, massage.
Swimming: Nearby pool, ocean.

Sunbathing: Garden, terrace, solarium.
Nudity: 15 min walk to nudist beach.
Smoking: Permitted everywhere.
Pets: Permitted.
Handicap Access: 1 rm wheelchair accessible summer 2001.
Children: No.
Languages: Spanish, English, Italian, French.
Your Hosts: Antonio.

Tybesta Tolfrue

In the Heart of Brecon Beacons National Park

Hosts Richard and Steve warmly welcome travellers to their listed 18th-century townhouse. Ideally situated in the town of Brecon, 45 miles north of Cardiff, *Tybesta Tolfrue's* location offers ample opportunity for guests to go walking, pony trekking, cycling, sailing, exploring the Brecon Beacons mountain range, or to simply relax. The attractive bedrooms are standard to full en suite, and offer amenities such as a full breakfast, in-room tea- and coffee-making facilities and colour TV. Convenient for travellers, Brecon is a good stopping point as it is situated two-thirds of the way from London to Ireland.

Address: Brecon, Wales
Tel: (44-1874) 611 115.
Web: http://www.tybesta.demon.co.uk

Type: Bed & breakfast.
Clientele: Gay & lesbian. Good mix of men & women
Transportation: Car is best. Nat'l Express Coach Network or rail to Merthyr Tydfil, then local bus service.
To Gay Bars: 45 miles to Cardiff, a 45-60 minute drive.
Rooms: 4 rooms with single or double beds.

Baths: 2 ensuite, 1 shared.
Meals: Full English or vegetarian breakfast.
Vegetarian: Vegetarian breakfast on request. Available locally for lunch & dinner.
Complimentary: Tea, coffee in rooms.
Dates Open: All year.
High Season: July-Aug.
Rates: £20.00 per person per night.

Rsv'tns: Required when possible. Deposit preferred.
Reserve Thru: Call direct.
Min. Stay: Required over bank holiday periods.
Parking: Ample free off- & on-street parking.
In-Room: Colour TV, coffee/tea-making facilities, maid service.
On-Premises: TV lounge.
Exercise/Health: 1 mile to in-town gym with weights,

Jacuzzi, sauna & steam.
Swimming: 1 mile to pool.
Smoking: Permitted in the lounge & conservatory.
Pets: Permitted by prior arrangement.
Handicap Access: No.
Children: No.
Languages: English.
Your Hosts: Richard & Steve.

WALES • BRECON BEACONS

Courtfield Hotel

WWW Gay-Friendly ♂♂
Gay-Owned & -Operated

The *Courtfield Hotel* is a tastefully-decorated hotel close to Cardiff Castle and the city centre, set in a wide and tree-lined avenue with stately homes and buildings. The hotel is over 100 years old and retains its original features. Relax in our comfortable spacious reception lounge or have a drink with friends in our bar which is always well stocked with wines, spirits and ales. Mornings, a freshly prepared full traditional breakfast is served. All centrally heated bedrooms include: direct-dial telephone, alarm call, colour television, hospitality tray and Corby trouser press.

Our Victorian townhouse hotel is ideally situated for a truly memorable visit to this lively cosmopolitan city which offers a wealth of fascinating places for you to enjoy. In addition to Cardiff Castle, local sights include the Millenium Stadium, Cardiff Bay, the New Theatre, St. David's Centre, and St. Fagan's Folk Museum. Our hotel and bar have a mixed clientele, and gay bars are just 10 minutes away. Ensuite rooms are available, and guests have their own keys.

Address: 101 Cathedral Rd, Cardiff, CF1 9PH, Wales
Tel: (44-029) 2022 7701 (Tel/Fax).
E-mail: courtfield@ntlworld.com **Web:** http://www.courtfieldhotel.co.uk

Type: Hotel with bar.
Clientele: Mostly gay Thurs-Mon
Transportation: Cardiff (Wales) airport, then taxi to city.
To Gay Bars: 10 minutes to gay bars.
Rooms: 12 rooms with single & double beds.
Baths: 6 with private bath ensuite, 6 share.

Meals: Full traditional breakfast.
Vegetarian: Vegetarians catered for.
Complimentary: Tea & coffee facilities in rooms.
Dates Open: All year.
Rates: Single £25, double £55.
Credit Cards: MC, Visa, Amex, Access, Diners, Eurocard, JCB.

Rsv'tns: Required 48hrs.
Reserve Thru: Travel agent or call direct.
Parking: On-street parking.
In-Room: Maid & room service, color TV, telephone, tea making facilities, clock radio, hospitality tray.
On-Premises: Meeting rooms.
Swimming: Pool nearby.
Smoking: Permitted without

restrictions.
Pets: Permitted by prior arrangement.
Handicap Access: No.
Children: Permitted.
Languages: English, Dutch, German & French.
Your Hosts: Norman & Keith.

Brickfield Hill Bed & Breakfast Inn

WWW Gay/Lesbian ♀♂
Gay-Owned & -Operated

Sydney's Warm & Inviting Guesthouse

When Mrs. Lydia King opened a boarding house here in 1885, she doubtless welcomed visitors from Europe, the Americas and the Australian Colonies. Today, our guests come from every continent and the inn is noted for its peace and tranquility in the middle of the continent's most exciting and spectacular city. Located in a residential part of Sydney's gay district, *Brickfield Hill Bed & Breakfast Inn* has been restored and reflects its 1880's character. The rooms are very comfortable and inviting with large four-poster beds, antiques, rugs, damask cotton sheets, pure new Australian wool blankets, cotton waffle dressing gowns, and other modern conveniences. You'll enjoy our complimentary full breakfasts and afternoon teas, with homemade jams, cakes and biscuits.

A few minutes' walk away is Oxford Street, Sydney's famous "Golden Mile," with its incredible choice of restaurants, bars, cafes, nightclubs, bookshops and cinemas. All of Sydney's famous sights are within easy reach: the beaches, the Opera House, the parks and the city. With rail and bus stations nearby, it's easy to get to other places like the Blue Mountains, too. I think you'll agree, that when you stay with us, you'll enjoy a memorable experience in an amazing city.

Address: 403 Riley St, Surry Hills, Sydney, NSW 2010, Australia
Tel: (61-2) 9211 4886, **Fax:** (61-2) 9212 2556.
E-mail: fields@zip.com.au **Web:** http://www.zip.com.au/~fields

Type: Bed & breakfast inn.
Clientele: Mostly gay & lesbian with some hetero clientele
Transportation: Taxi or city shuttle direct from Sydney Airport, or airport bus to Central Station, then taxi or walk. Good public transport.
To Gay Bars: 3 blocks to Oxford St, an 8 min walk.
Rooms: 5 rooms with double, queen or king beds.
Baths: Private: 1 bath/toilet, Shared: 2 bath/shower/ toilets.
Meals: Expanded continental breakfast.
Vegetarian: Vegetarians catered for here & at good local restaurants.
Complimentary: Tea & coffee, afternoon tea.
Dates Open: All year.
High Season: Jan-Mar.
Rates: AUD $95-AUD $220.
Credit Cards: MC, Visa.
Rsv'tns: Required.
Reserve Thru: Travel agent or call direct.
Parking: On- & off-street parking. Please reserve parking space when booking room.
In-Room: Colour TV, maid service.
On-Premises: Meeting rooms, fax & limited word processing service, refreshments, piano, telephone, library.
Exercise/Health: Nearby gym, weights, Jacuzzi, sauna, steam, massage.
Swimming: Pool, ocean & harbour nearby.
Sunbathing: Some rooms have private verandahs.
Smoking: Permitted on balconies, outside areas.
Pets: Not permitted.
Handicap Access: No.
Children: No.
Languages: English, Japanese, French, German, Italian.
Your Hosts: Ivano & David.
IGLTA

Governors on Fitzroy B & B

WWW Gay/Lesbian ⚥

An Australian B&B in the Heart of Sydney

Whether traveling for pleasure or business, *Governors on Fitzroy B&B Guesthouse* will be your home in Sydney. Our quiet location is a sanctuary from the busy city of Sydney, yet conveniently just half a mile from the city centre. The B&B was established in 1987, with refurbishment of an 1863 terrace-style house. Six guest rooms provide comfortable, private accommodation, and a full American-style breakfast is served each morning. Our private garden, lounge and TV rooms are available for guest use.

There are many restaurants of every ethnic variety and price range within walking distance of the guest house. We're 3 blocks from Oxford St, convenient to all bars and venues, shopping and coffee bars. World-famous Bondi Beach is only 20 minutes away, and Lady Jane Beach (our official nude beach) is easily reached by public transport. Your hosts live on the property and are available for travel information and tips on making your stay in Sydney the best!

Address: 64 Fitzroy St, Surry Hills, NSW 2010, Australia
Tel: (61-2) 9331 4652, **Fax:** (61-2) 9361-5094.
E-mail: governor@zip.com.au **Web:** http://www.governor.zip.com.au

Type: Bed & breakfast.
Clientele: Good mix of gays & lesbians
Transportation: Taxi from airport approximately AUD $20.
To Gay Bars: 2 blocks to men's/women's bars.
Rooms: 6 rooms with double & queen beds.
Baths: 5 private sinks, 2 shared bath/shower/toilets & 2 shared toilets.
Meals: Full American-style

breakfast.
Vegetarian: Upon request.
Complimentary: Coffee, tea available 24 hours.
Dates Open: All year.
High Season: Feb-Mar, during Gay & Lesbian Mardi Gras.
Rates: Single AUD $80, double AUD $100.
Discounts: 7 nights for price of 6 nights.
Credit Cards: MC, Visa, Amex, Diners Club.

Rsv'tns: Recommended.
Reserve Thru: Call direct.
Min. Stay: 5 nights during Mardi Gras.
Parking: Limited on-street parking.
In-Room: Maid service.
On-Premises: Meeting rooms, telephone, fax, piano, library, TV lounge, private garden.
Exercise/Health: Spa on premises. Nearby gym, sauna & massage.

Swimming: 20-min drive to ocean.
Sunbathing: On common sun decks or ocean beach.
Nudity: Permitted in spa area.
Smoking: Permitted, but not in bedrooms.
Pets: Not permitted.
Handicap Access: No.
Children: Not permitted.
Languages: English.
Your Hosts: Tom & Phillip.
IGLTA

Manor House Boutique Hotel

WWW Gay/Lesbian ♂

The Ultimate in Gay Boutique Hotels

Experience the finest gay and lesbian accommodation Sydney has to offer at *The Manor House,* an historic heritage residence in the heart of the city's premier entertainment district. Mr. Edward Riley, the first Lord Mayor of Sydney, originally built the Manor House in 1850. The property was, and still is, one of the most prestigious houses of its time. The hotel is ideally situated less than two minutes' walk from Oxford Street, less than five minutes' walk from the new Fox Studios, and even the central business district is a short stroll through Hyde Park.

The Manor House is comprised of 24 elegantly appointed rooms, all with ensuites and some with spa baths. All rooms have TV and video, personal safes, irons and boards, and complimentary tea and coffee facilities. Most rooms contain reverse cycle air-conditioning and luxurious king- or queen-sized beds. "Lush" restaurant is located on the ground floor, along with our "Club" bar. A large glass atrium covers the courtyard restaurant and pool area, creating an intimate and relaxing atmosphere. "Lush" caters for dinners of up to 80, and cocktail functions for up to 150 guests. An ideal venue for that 21st birthday, anniversary, product launch, or commitment ceremony!

Address: 86 Flinders St, Darlinghurst, Sydney, NSW 2010, Australia
Tel: (61-2) 9380 6633, **Fax:** (61-2) 9380 5016.
E-mail: info@manorhouse.com.au **Web:** http://www.manorhouse.com.au

Type: Hotel with restaurant & bar.
Clientele: Mostly men with women welcome
Transportation: Taxi, car or bus.
To Gay Bars: 300 metres to Oxford St.
Rooms: 24 rooms, 6 serviced apartments.
Baths: All private.
Meals: Continental buffet breakfast.

Vegetarian: Nearby.
Complimentary: Tea & coffee.
High Season: Feb & Oct.
Rates: Standard AUD $120, deluxe AUD $160, superior AUD $210.
Credit Cards: MC, Visa, Amex, Diners, Bancard.
Rsv'tns: Usually required.
Reserve Thru: Travel agent or call direct.
Min. Stay: 1 week minimum

required during high season.
Parking: Limited off-street parking.
In-Room: Color TV, VCR, phone, coffee & tea makers, fridge, mini bar, electronic safe, hair dryers. Deluxe & superior rms: AC, king beds.
On-Premises: Video tape & CD libraries.
Exercise/Health: Nearby gym.
Swimming: Pool, ocean

nearby.
Sunbathing: Poolside & at beach.
Smoking: Permitted.
Pets: Not permitted.
Children: No.
Languages: English, Chinese.
Your Hosts: Mark Magennis & Collon Dearman.
galta **IGLTA**

Color Photo on Page 6

Stellar Suites on Wentworth

Your Sydney Home Away from Home

Stellar Suites on Wentworth is situated just off Oxford Street, near Hyde Park and all that Sydney has to offer. The hotel features spacious, award-winning rooms and has a friendly, helpful staff who will assist you with any requirements you may have — from booking a tour to helping you purchase some party tickets. Let us help you make your stay in Sydney an enjoyable one. Surrounded by restaurants, cafés and bars, the hotel is the perfect spot to stop for your holiday.

Address: 4 Wentworth Avenue, Sydney, NSW 2000, Australia
Tel: (61-2) 9264 9754, (1-800) 025 575, **Fax:** (61-2) 9261 8006.
E-mail: reservations@stellarsuites.com.au **Web:** http://www.stellarsuites.com.au

Type: Hotel.
Clientele: 50% gay & lesbian & 50% hetero clienteˡe
Transportation: Airport bus, pick up $7 per person.
To Gay Bars: 1 block, a 4 min walk, 300 meters.
Rooms: 36 suites, 2 apartments with single, double, queen or king beds.
Baths: All private bath/shower/toilets.
Vegetarian: Available

nearby.
Complimentary: Tea & coffee.
Dates Open: All year.
High Season: Feb, Mar, Nov.
Rates: From $125-$190 per night, all year.
Discounts: Pensioner discount.
Credit Cards: MC, Visa, Amex, Diners.
Rsv'tns: Inquire.
Reserve Thru: Travel agent

or call direct.
Parking: Limited off-street covered pay parking.
In-Room: Telephone, AC, color TV, VCR, kitchen, refrigerator, coffee & tea-making facilities, maid & laundry service.
On-Premises: Meeting rooms, laundry facilities, business services.
Exercise/Health: Nearby gym, weights, Jacuzzi, sauna, steam, massage.

Swimming: Nearby pool, ocean.
Sunbathing: At beach.
Smoking: Some non-smoking rooms.
Pets: Not permitted.
Handicap Access: No.
Children: Welcome.
Languages: English, Chinese, Russian, Vietnamese, Thai, Fijian.
Your Hosts: Rod, Hien.

Witchencroft

Welcome to *Witchencroft,* two very private and comfortable self-contained apartments for women only. Relax and enjoy a nature-based holiday in five acres of gardens on the Atherton Tablelands. We specialise in 4WD and bushwalking tours to suit your individual interests. This is an ideal base from which to escape the tourism of Cairns and explore a great diversity of nature, including the World Heritage tropical rainforest. There is all-year-round fine weather within an hour of *Witchencroft!* Your host is a fourth generation north Queenslander, and a great source of local information.

Address: Atherton **Mail To:** Jenny Maclean, PO Box 685, Atherton, QLD 4883, Australia
Tel: (61-740) 912 683 (Tel/Fax).
E-mail: jenny.maclean@iig.com.au

Type: Guesthouse on a 5-acre organic farm.
Clientele: Women only
Transportation: Free pickup from Atherton, bus from Cairns daily.
To Gay Bars: 90 kms to Cairns.
Rooms: 2 apartments with double beds.
Baths: All private shower/toilets.
Camping: Tent sites,

powered sites.
Meals: Self-cater or enjoy our vegetarian cuisine.
Vegetarian: Vegetarian, vegan.
Complimentary: Tea, coffee & milk.
Dates Open: All year.
High Season: Jul-Aug.
Rates: Single US $50, double US $70.
Discounts: Garden work exchange.

Rsv'tns: Required.
Reserve Thru: Call direct.
Min. Stay: Two nights.
Parking: Ample parking.
In-Room: Color TV, ceiling fans, kitchen, refrigerator, coffee & tea-making facilities.
Exercise/Health: Bushwalks.
Swimming: 10 minutes to rivers & lakes.
Sunbathing: In the garden.

Nudity: Permitted.
Smoking: Permitted outdoors.
Pets: Permitted with restrictions because of resident livestock.
Handicap Access: Yes.
Children: Permitted.
Languages: English, some French & German.

Eighteen Twenty-Four James

WWW Gay/Lesbian ♂
Gay-Operated

Bring Your Body to where Summer Never Ends...

Gay-owned and -operated *18-24 James* in Cairns, Australia, has been designed by gay people, exclusively for gay people. This plantation-style hotel, set in tropical rainforest gardens, is located five minutes from Cairns International Airport and is a 20-minute walk along the Esplanade to the city centre.

18-24 James consists of 26 rooms on two levels, with facilities which have been architecturally designed around the central pool and spa for a completely private, clothing-optional area. Bring your body to where summer never ends...peel off around our pool, or pump it up in our gym and sweat it out in our sauna. All guestrooms have ensuite baths, king-sized beds, television with free, in-house movies, clock radio, direct-dial telephone, refrigerator and tea- and coffee-making facilities. As a further convenience, the hotel also provides guest laundry facilities and free airport transfers. Mornings, luxuriate while a complimentary tropical breakfast is served to you poolside. There is a licensed, indoor/outdoor restaurant and bar on premises with outdoor poolside dining available.

Our tour desk can arrange your gay-only tours to the Great Barrier Reef, World Heritage-listed rainforests and, for the more adventurous, white water rafting trips. A local bus which runs every 20 minutes will take visitors to the unofficial gay/nude beach, Buchan Point, and offers a good opportunity to see the beach suburbs of Cairns. Guests wanting an exciting and varied nightlife will not be disappointed by the city's many restaurants, nightclubs and casino. But then, you may never want to leave the hotel...

Address: 18-24 James St, Cairns, QLD 4870, Australia
Tel: (61-7) 405 14644, **Fax:** (61-7) 405 10103.
E-mail: 18_24james@internetnorth.com.au **Web:** http://www.eagles.com.au/james

Type: Plantation-style hotel with restaurant & bar.
Clientele: Mostly men with women welcome
Transportation: Free pickup from airport, bus & train. Complimentary airport transfers.
To Gay Bars: 1 mile.
Rooms: 26 rooms with king & single beds.
Baths: All private.
Meals: Poolside tropical breakfast.
Vegetarian: Please inquire.
Complimentary: Tea & coffee in room.
Dates Open: All year.
Rates: AUD $55-AUD $120.
Credit Cards: MC, Visa, Amex, Diners, Bancard.
Rsv'tns: Preferred.
Reserve Thru: Travel agent or call direct.
Parking: Ample off-street parking.

In-Room: AC, ceiling fans, color TV with free in-house movies, direct-dial phone, clock radio, fridge, coffee/tea makers, maid svc.
On-Premises: Laundry facilities, meeting rooms, tour booking desk, hire cars.
Exercise/Health: Gym, weights, Jacuzzi, sauna, massage. Nearby gym, weights, Jacuzzi, sauna, massage.

Swimming: Pool on premises. Nearby pool, ocean, river, lake.
Sunbathing: Poolside.
Nudity: Permitted poolside.
Smoking: Permitted.
Pets: Not permitted.
Handicap Access: Yes.
Languages: English, Dutch.
Your Hosts: Keith & Peter.
galta IGLTA

Turtle Cove Resort Cairns

WWW Gay/Lesbian ♂♂

Turtle Cove is Gay Heaven

Once you get to *Turtle Cove* you'll soon know why it's one of the world's most popular gay resorts. Just 30 minutes from Cairns Int'l Airport, your choice of accommodation is a garden cabin, one of our brand new elevated oceanview terraces, or beachfront room with only lawn, sand and the odd palm tree between you and the Coral Sea. Rooms feature queen and single beds, en suite bathrooms, AC, ceiling fans, TV with in-house video, radio, phones with modem points, and refrigerator. The resort features a fully stocked cocktail bar open from early to late, and a licensed restaurant serving great tropical food. Complimentary breakfasts are served on the terrace, and lunch and dinner are available by the pool and under the stars.

With the backdrop of tropical rainforest, our exclusively gay, private beach is ideal for sunning, relaxing under an umbrella, swimming, or cruising. Our facilities include a large pool, Jacuzzi, extensive tropical gardens and lawns, rental cars, a resort shop, tour desk, billiards room, guest lounge, gym and trips to the Great Barrier Reef. Our location is private, but many restaurants, bars and clubs are within 30 minutes of the resort.

Address: Captain Cook Hwy, PO Box 158, Smithfield, Cairns, Far North QLD 4878, Australia
Tel: (61-7) 4059 1800, **Fax:** (61-7) 4059 1969.
E-mail: gay@turtlecove.com.au **Web:** http://www.turtlecove.com.au

Type: Beachfront resort with full-service restaurant, bar & resort shop.
Clientele: Good mix of men & women
Transportation: Airport bus. Pick up from airport, RR, bus stn, city hotel.
To Gay Bars: 35 minutes.
Rooms: 31 rooms with single, double or queen beds.
Baths: All private.
Meals: Tropical & continental buffet breakfast.

Vegetarian: Available.
Complimentary: Tea & coffee in rooms, welcome drink on arrival.
Dates Open: All year.
Rates: AUD $125-$240
Discounts: Inquire.
Credit Cards: MC, Visa, Amex, Diners, Bankcard.
Rsv'tns: Suggested.
Reserve Thru: Travel agent or call direct.
Parking: Ample free off-street covered parking.
In-Room: Colour TV, AC,

fridge, phone, ceiling fans, coffee/tea makers, room & daily maid service. In-house video, video tape library.
On-Premises: Meeting rooms, private dining rooms & laundry facilities.
Exercise/Health: Jacuzzi, massage, beach equipment, volleyball, gym & weights.
Swimming: Pool, beachfront & river swimming hole on premises.
Sunbathing: At poolside, on our patio, common sun

decks & on the beach.
Nudity: Permitted poolside & on the beach.
Smoking: Permitted without restrictions.
Pets: Not permitted.
Handicap Access: Yes. Mostly single story with minimal steps.
Children: Not permitted.
Languages: English, French.
Your Hosts: Michael.
galta IGLTA

Falcons at Peregian

Men ♂
Gay-Owned & -Operated

A Man's Place in the Sun

Make our home your beach house on the Sunshine Coast, 10 kms south of Noosa, and just 200 metres from the Pacific Ocean. *Falcons at Peregian* offers cool rooms, a comfortable TV lounge, video library, mini-gym and a clothing-optional secluded pool and sundeck. Rates include a continental breakfast, served al fresco, if you like. Noosa is the best-known centre on the Sunshine Coast which, along with the Gold Coast to the south, consitutes the "play and relax" zone for Brisbane. The Gold Coast is rather glitzy and brash, while the Noosa area is more into "understated elegance" (and expensive sophistication!).

Mail To: PO Box 254, Peregian Beach, QLD 4573, Australia
Tel: (61-7) 5448 3710, **Fax:** (61-7) 5448 3712.
E-mail: falcons@nbcnet.com.au **Web:** http://www.linstar.com.au/falcons

Type: Bed & breakfast.
Clientele: Men only
Transportation: Car is best. Free pick up from Sunshine Coast airport, Nambour train & South Peregian bus.
To Gay Bars: 10 min drive.
Rooms: 3 rooms with double or queen beds.
Baths: Private: 1 bath/shower/toilet; Shared: 2 shower only, 2 WC only.

Meals: Continental breakfast.
Vegetarian: Milk, but no meat, fish or eggs in continental breakfast.
Complimentary: 24-hr self-serve tea & coffee.
Dates Open: All year.
Rates: AUD $50-AUD $60.
Credit Cards: MC, Visa, Bankcard.
Rsv'tns: Preferred.
Reserve Thru: Travel agent

or call direct.
Parking: Limited, covered, free off-street parking.
In-Room: Ceiling fans, maid service.
On-Premises: Meeting rooms, TV lounge, laundry facilities, video tape library.
Exercise/Health: Gym, weights, massage on premises & nearby.
Swimming: Pool on premises. Ocean nearby.

Sunbathing: Poolside & at beach.
Nudity: Permitted poolside.
Smoking: Outside. Inside is non-smoking.
Pets: Not permitted.
Children: No.
Languages: English, French.
Your Hosts: John & Mark.

Horizons at Peregian

WWW Gay/Lesbian ⚥
Gay-Owned & -Operated

Australia's Most Popular Gay Beachside Holiday Resort

Recently opened, *Horizons at Peregian* is a 15-unit holiday apartment property situated on 14 kilometres of pristine ocean beach, near Noosa Heads on Queensland's Sunshine Coast. Noosa Heads is fast becoming Australia's most popular gay holiday destination. Penthouse apartments have ocean views, private rooftop patios and spas. Facilities include heated pool, spa, secure parking, tour desk and on-site manager. All apartments feature two bathrooms, master bedroom with ensuite, gourmet kitchens and computer/phone connections. We're 15 minutes from the Sunshine Coast airport, 10 minutes from Noosa Heads, and 90 minutes north of Brisbane.

Address: 45 Lorikeet Drive, Peregian Beach, QLD 4573, Australia
Tel: (61-7) 5448 3444, **Fax:** (61-7) 5448 3711.
E-mail: admin@horizons-peregian.com **Web:** http://www.horizons-peregian.com/gay

Type: Holiday apartments.
Clientele: Mostly gay & lesbian with some hetero
Transportation: Car is best. Free airport, bus, train pick up.
To Gay Bars: 6 miles.
Rooms: 15 apts with single, double or queen beds.
Baths: All private.
Complimentary: Tea &

coffee, mints on pillow.
High Season: Dec-Jan & Easter.
Rates: Low: $95-$170, holiday season: $130-$190.
Discounts: 10% to Mardi Gras members.
Credit Cards: MC, Visa, Amex.
Rsv'tns: Required.
Reserve Thru: Travel agent

or call direct.
Parking: Ample covered parking.
In-Room: Phone, AC, ceiling fans, color cable TV, VCR, kitchen, refrigerator, coffee & tea-makers.
On-Premises: Fax, e-mail, video tape library.
Exercise/Health: Jacuzzi, massage. Nearby gym,

weights, massage.
Swimming: Pool, ocean.
Sunbathing: Poolside, on private sun decks, at beach.
Nudity: Permitted on private penthouse patios.
Handicap Access: Yes, wide doors.
Your Hosts: Rod.
galta IGLTA

Sandy's on the Strand

Gay/Lesbian ⚤
Gay-Owned & -Operated

Townsville's Only Gay Bed & Breakfast

Sandy's, Townsville's only gay bed and breakfast, is situated on the beachfront, offering picturesque views across Cleveland Bay to Magnetic Island. Our accommodations include air-conditioned bedrooms with queen-sized beds, ensuite bathrooms and your own balcony. We are centrally located, within walking distance to the city centre, casino, rock pool, marine wonderland and many other attractions. If you wish to travel further afield, *Sandy's* can offer motor scooters for your exclusive use. Guests can swim at the safe beach across the road, the rock pool, or try the salt-water pool on premises. Hosts, Peter and Robert will go out of their way to make your stay enjoyable.

Mail To: PO Box 193, Townsville, QLD 4810, Australia
Tel: (61-7) 4772 1193 (Tel/Fax).

Type: Bed & breakfast.
Clientele: Gay & lesbian. Good mix of men & women
Transportation: Car is best. Free pick up from airport, train & bus.
To Gay Bars: 2 miles, a 20 min walk, a 5 min drive.
Rooms: 2 rooms with queen beds.
Baths: 1 private bath/

shower/toilet, 1 shared bath/ shower/toilet.
Meals: Continental breakfast.
Vegetarian: Available in nearby cafes & restaurants.
Complimentary: Hot or cold drinks & nibbles.
Dates Open: All year.
Rates: AUD $55-$65.
Rsv'tns: Required.

Bookings are essential.
Reserve Thru: Call direct.
Parking: Ample, free off-street parking.
In-Room: Telephone, AC, ceiling fans, color TV, VCR.
On-Premises: TV lounge, laundry facilities.
Exercise/Health: Nearby gym, weights, massage.
Swimming: Pool. Ocean

nearby.
Sunbathing: Poolside & on patio.
Smoking: Permitted outside & on patio.
Pets: Not permitted.
Handicap Access: No.
Children: No.
Languages: English.
Your Hosts: Peter & Robert.

Greenways Apartments

Gay/Lesbian ⚤

Adelaide, our state capital, features traditional stone architecture and wide encircling parklands. This elegant city is situated near one of the world's most famous winegrowing districts, and its residents are relaxed and friendly. These features, combined with the picturesque backdrop of the Adelaide Hills, give Adelaide an atmosphere found nowhere else in Australia. South Australia was the first Australian state to legalize homosexuality. *Greenways* provides excellent, comparatively cheap accommodations in fully furnished, self-contained private apartments. It is situated near city center and gay venues. Hosts are gay-friendly and are willing to assist with local information and they especially welcome international travelers.

Address: 45 King William Rd, North Adelaide, SA 5006, Australia
Tel: (61-8) 8267 5903, **Fax:** (61-8) 8267 1790.
E-mail: bpsgways@camtech.net.au

Type: Holiday apartments.
Clientele: Gay & lesbian, straight-friendly
Transportation: Taxi best from airport, bus or train station.
To Gay Bars: 1 mile to gay/ lesbian bars.
Rooms: 25 apartments with single or double beds.
Baths: All private.
Dates Open: All year.
Rates: 1-bdrm AUD $70, 2-

bdrm AUD $100 & up, 3-bdrm AUD $140 & up (cheaper for longer stays).
Discounts: AUD $5/night on stays of 4 nights or longer (private bookings only).
Credit Cards: MC, Visa, Bancard, Diners, Amex.
Rsv'tns: Required 1 month in advance, we're very popular.
Reserve Thru: Travel agent

or call direct.
Min. Stay: 3 days.
Parking: Ample free off-street parking.
In-Room: Telephone, kitchenette, refrigerator, weekly maid service, AC/ heat, color TV.
On-Premises: Coin-operated laundry facilities.
Exercise/Health: Public gym, spa & sauna 3/4 mi.
Swimming: Public pool 3/4

mile, ocean 15 miles.
Sunbathing: At public pool, on ocean beach (nude beach 1 hour).
Smoking: We prefer that you smoke outside only.
Pets: Not permitted.
Handicap Access: No.
Children: Permitted.
Languages: English.
Your Hosts: Brenton, Simon & Keith.
galta

Corinda's Cottages

Awaken to the Sound of Birdsong!

Overlooking a cobbled courtyard are the converted coach-house and servant's quarters of *Corinda,* an award-winning National Trust Classified property in the heart of Hobart. Its historic outbuildings are now delightful gay-owned, self-contained cottages. *Corinda's* gardens are a real delight. Lime trees and hedges of box and yew create formal enclosed areas, each with its own colour scheme. Though only a five-minute stroll from Sullivans Cove, the property has a real "country" feel as it adjoins the Queens Domain, a large park teaming with birdlife.

Address: 17 Glebe St, Glebe, Hobart, TAS 7000, Australia
Tel: (61-03) 62 34 1590, **Fax:** (61-03) 62 34 2744.

Type: Self-contained cottages.
Clientele: 50% gay & lesbian & 50% straight clientele
Transportation: Car is best.
To Gay Bars: 1 mile, a 15-min walk, a 5-min drive.
Rooms: 3 cottages with single, double or queen beds.
Baths: Private: 1 shower/toilet, 1 bath/shower/toilet, 1 spa/shower/toilet.
Meals: Expanded continental breakfast.
Vegetarian: Vegetarian restaurants nearby.
Complimentary: Tea, coffee, decaf, fruit juice, range of condiments, fudge.
Dates Open: All year.
High Season: Jan-Feb.
Rates: AUS $160 per cottage (2 persons), all year. Spa cottage AUS $175.
Discounts: 20% to readers of Ferrari Guides if booked directly with owners.
Credit Cards: Visa, Bancard, MC, Amex, Diners.
Rsv'tns: Required.
Reserve Thru: Travel agent or call direct.
Parking: Ample, free, on- & off-street parking.
In-Room: Color TV, refrigerator, kitchen, coffee & tea-making facilities, maid & laundry service.
On-Premises: Laundry facilities & use of phone/fax.
Exercise/Health: Nearby gym, weights, Jacuzzi, sauna, steam, massage.
Swimming: Nearby pool, ocean & river.
Sunbathing: At beach & in garden.
Smoking: Permitted anywhere. Non-smoking rooms available.
Pets: Not permitted.
Handicap Access: No.
Children: No children under 12.
Languages: English, Dutch.
Your Hosts: Wilmar & Matthew.
galta **IGLTA**

Edenholme Grange

An Elegant Experience of Times Past

This grand Victorian mansion is set amongst secluded grounds near magnificent Cataract Gorge. Rooms and suites at *Edenholme Grange* are superbly decorated, furnished with antiques, and some have spa baths. Take in the views of the city and Tamar Valley from our balconies. Enjoy the fine nearby restaurants (or be creative on the BBQ along with a fine Tasmanian wine from the cellar), after which we offer complimentary port and chocolates. Mornings, join other guests at the banquet table for a full Tasmanian breakfast cooked to your taste. If you prefer privacy, delight in the comfort of self-contained Settlers Cottage. *1998 Tourism Awards winner for hosted accommodation.*

Address: 14 St Andrews St, Launceston, TAS 7250, Australia
Tel: (61-3) 6334 6666, **Fax:** (61-3) 6334 3106.
E-mail: edenholme@microtech.com.au **Web:** http://www.vision.net.au/~webspace/edenholme

Type: B&B, cottage, boutique hotel with bar.
Clientele: Mostly hetero, gay/lesbian following
Transportation: Car.
To Gay Bars: 12 blocks.
Rooms: 4 rooms, 1 suite, 1 apartment, 1 cottage w/ single thru king beds.
Baths: All private.
Meals: Full breakfast.
Complimentary: Tea & coffee inroom, port & sherry in guest lounge.
High Season: Dec-Feb.
Rates: AUD $74-$170.
Discounts: Inquire.
Credit Cards: MC, Visa, Amex.
Rsv'tns: Usually necessary in high season.
Reserve Thru: Travel agent or call direct.
Parking: Ample free off-street parking.
In-Room: Phone, color TV, coffee & tea-makers, maid, room & laundry svc. Some fridges. Kitchen in cottage & apartment.
On-Premises: Guest lounge, books, games, etc.
Exercise/Health: Jacuzzi.
Nearby gym, weights, sauna, massage.
Smoking: All non-smoking house. Permitted outside.
Pets: Not permitted.
Children: Welcome in ground-floor room & cottage.
Languages: English, some French.
Your Hosts: Paul & Rosemary.

TASMANIA • HOBART

TASMANIA • LAUNCESTON

Laird O'Cockpen Hotel

WWW Men ♂

Where Men Meet Men

Enjoy top class accommodation in-house or at our annex, Norwood. Built in 1888, just 3km from the C.B.D. (city centre), *The Laird* reflects the charm of Melbourne. All our rooms are serviced daily and our friendly staff are here to make you feel at home. *The Laird* music/video bar is the most popular gay mens' bar, perfect for socializing. Nuggets bar is home to the leather scene, with two clubs meeting weekly. Included in our low tariff is free entry to Club 80, Australia's most famous gay mens' club, and Peel dance bar is just a short walk away. We're in the center of the gay Northside, near all public transport.

Address: 149 Gipps St, Collingwood, Melbourne, VIC 3067, Australia
Tel: (61-3) 9417 2832, **Fax:** (61-3) 9417 2109.
E-mail: hotel@laird.com.au

Type: Hotel & guesthouse, 2 bars, pool room, shop & beer garden.
Clientele: Men only
Transportation: Taxi from the airport.
To Gay Bars: Men's bar on premises. Others 1 block.
Rooms: 8 rooms with double or queen beds, one-bedroom apartments.

Baths: Shared.
Meals: Continental breakfast.
Vegetarian: Cafés & restaurants nearby.
Complimentary: Tea, coffee & juice.
Dates Open: All year.
Rates: Per night: from AUD $65 single, AUD $75 double.
Discounts: Weekly rate

(stay 7 nts, pay for 6).
Credit Cards: MC, Visa, Amex, Diners Club, Bankcard.
Rsv'tns: Required.
Reserve Thru: Call direct or e-mail.
Parking: Adequate on-street parking.
In-Room: Fans, heaters, electric blankets, clocks,

artwork, antiques.
On-Premises: TV lounge, laundry facilities, public telephone, 2 bars with pool table, pinball, video games, beer garden.
Smoking: Permitted without restrictions.
Pets: Not permitted.
Children: Not permitted.
Your Hosts: Ron & David.

Palm Court Bed & Breakfast

WWW Gay/Lesbian ⚥

Melbourne's Premier Bed & Breakfast

Palm Court B&B is a gracious boutique accommodation offering a friendly atmosphere in a non-smoking environment. The house has been restored to its former glory with relaxed living areas and large bedrooms, ensuring the most intimate and cosy environment for holiday guests. Bedrooms are spacious doubles with television, electric blankets and all of the comforts of home. The landscaped gardened courtyards provide a pleasant outdoor retreat. Facing the Melbourne cricket ground, *Palm Court* is surrounded by parks and gardens. It is a fifteen-minute walk to CBD.

Address: 22 Grattan Place, Richmond, Melbourne, VIC 3121, Australia
Tel: (61-3) 9427 7365 (Tel/Fax), **Mobile:** (0419) 777 850.

Type: Bed & breakfast.
Clientele: Gay & lesbian with straight friends welcomed
Transportation: Airport bus to city, then taxi. Taxi from airport about AUD $27
To Gay Bars: 1 km, a 10 min walk, a 3 min drive.
Rooms: 8 rooms with single or double beds.
Baths: Private & shared.
Camping: Within 1 hour of

Melbourne in the country.
Meals: Expanded continental breakfast.
Vegetarian: Vegetarian restaurants a short walk away.
Complimentary: Tea, coffee, biscuits, 24-hr coffee/tea facilities.
Dates Open: All year.
Rates: AUD $50-$60 single, AUD $80-$90 double. One rate all year.

Discounts: Weekly rate.
Credit Cards: Visa, MC.
Rsv'tns: Advised.
Reserve Thru: Call direct or travel agent.
Parking: Adequate unlimited on-street parking.
In-Room: Color TV, electric blankets, fans, mini bars.
On-Premises: TV lounge, video tape & CD libraries, laundry facilities.
Exercise/Health: Gyms

nearby.
Swimming: Pool & ocean nearby.
Sunbathing: On patio.
Nudity: Discreetly.
Smoking: Non-smoking accommodation. Permitted in gardens only.
Pets: Not permitted.
Handicap Access: No.
Children: Tolerated.
Languages: English, Thai.
Your Hosts: Trevor & Mac.

Aspen Lodge

Gay-Friendly ⚥
Gay-Operated

A Tranquil Little Oasis in the Heart of the City

Known as the "Pink Palace" this colourful landmark is not an exclusive gay residence, just a quiet, friendly house where gays, lesbians and other folks enjoy budget B&B hospitality in central Auckland. We keep the local gay & lesbian newspaper, as well as books on gay accommodation and travel in NZ. At *Aspen Lodge*, our gay manager and his partner will do their best to provide information on gay nightlife and activities. An "all you can eat" breakfast is included in the tariff, and beverage making facilities are provided free in the TV lounge.

Address: 62 Emily Place, Auckland, North Island , New Zealand
Tel: (64-9) 379 6698, **Fax:** (64-9) 377 7625.
E-mail: aspenlodge@xtra.co.nz **Web:** http://www.aspenlodge.co.nz

Type: Bed & breakfast. **Clientele:** Mostly hetero with 20% gay & lesbian clientele **Transportation:** Supershuttle from airport to door NZ $10-$15 per person. **To Gay Bars:** 5-min walk. **Rooms:** 14 singles, 6 doubles (1 dbl bed) & 6 twins (2 single beds). **Baths:** Shared: 5 showers, 6 toilets. **Meals:** Continental breakfast. **Vegetarian:** 5-min walk. **Complimentary:** Tea & coffee. **Dates Open:** All year. **High Season:** Nov-Apr. **Rates:** Single NZ $54, twin NZ $78. **Discounts:** Winter, May 1-Sept 30. Annual winter specials available. **Credit Cards:** MC, Visa, Amex, Diners, JBC. **Rsv'tns:** Required, especially in high season. **Reserve Thru:** Travel agent or call direct. **Parking:** Limited on-street pay parking. **In-Room:** Maid service. **On-Premises:** TV lounge, laundry facilities, public telephones. **Exercise/Health:** 5 min to nearby gym, weights, sauna, steam, massage. **Swimming:** 5 min to nearby pool, 20 min to city beach. **Sunbathing:** On the patio. **Smoking:** Entire hotel is non-smoking. **Pets:** Not permitted. **Children:** Permitted. **Languages:** English, Swedish, Spanish. **Your Hosts:** Paul & John.

Dorothy's Boutique Hotel

Gay-Friendly ⚥
Gay-Owned & -Operated

A Boutique Hotel of Exceptional Quality

Dorothy's Boutique Hotel has an established, excellent reputation for ambience, service and quality. Recognized with a New Zealand Historic Places classification, this large, fully restored Edwardian mansion houses museum-quality collections of Asian and European antiques. Our hotel restaurant is a market leader in Christchurch, and features local seasonal produce. The hotel is a two minute walk to the centre of the city, Cathedral Square, and is linked to a wide variety of tours and tourism operators. Featured in *Friars' Guide to New Zealand Accommodation for the Discerning Traveller,* this is a unique property where reservations are advised for both the restaurant and accommodation.

Address: 2 Latimer Square, Christchurch, New Zealand
Tel: (64-3) 365 6034, **Fax:** (64-3) 365 6035.
E-mail: dorothys@xtra.co.nz

Type: Boutique hotel. **Clientele:** Up-market domestic & foreign travelers **Transportation:** Excellent access to public trans. **To Gay Bars:** 2 min walk to all venues. **Rooms:** 5 rooms. **Baths:** All en suite. **Meals:** Continental breakfast. **Vegetarian:** On request. **Dates Open:** All year. **High Season:** Nov-May. **Rates:** NZ $120-NZ $150. **Credit Cards:** All major credit cards. **Rsv'tns:** Highly recommended. **Reserve Thru:** Direct or through travel agent. **Parking:** Off-street on-site parking. **In-Room:** Telephones, computer jacks, clock radios, room & maid service. **On-Premises:** Bar, restaurant, upstairs lounge for house guests w/ TV, VCR, balcony. Guest kitchen w/ tea, coffee, homemade shortbread, iron, ironing board, hair dryer, etc. **Exercise/Health:** Across from park & gymnasium. **Swimming:** 2 min walk to major pool complex. **Sunbathing:** In grounds outside. **Smoking:** Allowed on upstairs balcony & in bar. Prohibited elsewhere. **Pets:** Not permitted. **Handicap Access:** Available. **Children:** Acceptable. **Languages:** English. **Your Hosts:** Sam & Tony.

Residence Linareva

Just What you Need!

Linareva is located 2,5 km. from the village of Haapiti on the wild side of the island of Moorea: 10 minutes by air or 35 minutes by boat from the island of Tahiti. Impressive lodgings in a tropical garden, the inn is situated at the foot of lush, green hills, on the shores of a lagoon, providing seclusion and privacy. Each of our seven typical Tahitian grass "fare" has its own character, and special care has been taken in decorating them with traditional crafts. Our floating-restaurant, "Le Bateau," is considered by locals to be one of the finest eating establishments on Moorea. Moored directly off the "Résidence's" grounds, 100 meters from the beach, it offers the panoramic views of the reefs and the high peaks nearby. Charmingly converted from a former inter-island trading boat, this delightful floating-restaurant features fresh local seafood, with a European flair.

Address: Haapiti **Mail To:** BP 1 H, Haapiti, Moorea 98729, French Polynesia
Tel: (689) 561535 (Tel/Fax).
E-mail: linareva@mail.pf **Web:** http://www.tahiti-paradise.com/linareva

Type: Inn with floating restaurant.
Clientele: 50% gay & lesbian & 50% hetero
Transportation: Taxi, rental car.
Rooms: 3 rooms, 1 suite, 2 bungalows, 1 cottage.
Baths: All private.

Meals: Lunch, afternoon snack & dinners at floating restaurant.
Rates: 8500-19000 PF.
Discounts: Inquire.
Credit Cards: MC, Visa, Amex.
Rsv'tns: Required.
Reserve Thru: Call direct.

Min. Stay: 2 nights.
Parking: Free parking.
In-Room: Color TV, ceiling fans, kitchen, fridge, coffee & tea makers, maid svc.
Exercise/Health: Bicycles, outrigger canoes, kayaks, masks, snorkels.
Swimming: Directly on our

beach or at end of our pier.
Nudity: Permitted on our floating pontoon.
Pets: Permitted.
Children: Inquire.
Languages: French, English & Italian.

G. W. C. Rentals

Eleuthera means "freedom" in the language of the Greeks. Named such by the Loyalists who arrived after the American Revolution, it is the site of the first Parliament in the Bahamas. From Preacher's Cave in the north (first landfall) to Bannerman Town in the south, the island stretches 104' long and only 2 miles wide, with elevations of 150'. Settlements are few and far between and car rental is recommended if you wish to sightsee (average $60-$80 per day). The islands boast many historical sights and natural wonders: beaches of pink sand, coastal and underground caves, natural whirlpools carved out of the limestone by the pounding of the ocean and land covered with rich clay soil, vegetables, fruit trees, pineapples and lush tropical greenery. It is surrounded by the mostly tranquil turquoise waters of the Exuma Sound to the west, and to the east by the Atlantic Ocean. By ferry one can visit Spanish Wells, St. George's Island in the northwest (a community that leads the Bahamas in the fishing industry) and/or Harbour Island to the north (a friendly, lively, historical and picturesque area where one can ride a horse the length of the island along its magnificent three-mile stretch of beach).

For many of your gay-friendly travel needs within Nassau and the family islands, Marina can assist in arranging accommodation, transport and activities such as watersports, including fishing, diving and kayaking. A native who does property management and maintenance for a living, past owner of The Guest House in Nassau, and owner of Marlin Watersports, is now expanding *G. W. C. Rentals* to Eleuthera, with more properties becoming available for rent. Marlin Watersports has now joined Pierre Dive Shop in The Current, North Eleuthera.

"Somet de l'arc ciel" — "Top of the Rainbow" is the photo featured property with 3/4 panoramic views. It is a 2-bed, 2-bath house within 1-2 miles of beaches. It will be available for rent Dec. 1. Rates for this property are $800/week > 4 persons, $100/week additional persons (max. 6). All rooms are equipped with fans. Rates on other properties for > 6 persons $800-$1200/week, > 10 persons $1200-$1800/week. Most properties do not have housekeeping services in place. These and other services can be arranged (Housekeeping $40-$60/day, Cook $15-$20/hour, Guide $75-$125/day). **Please address all correspondence or information requests through our Nassau office (Thermotek AC). Responses may take up to one week if I am off on an island (available phones are few, if working, in many areas). So, plan ahead.**

Mail To: MWS, Attn: Marina, PO Box SS 6181, Nassau, NP , Bahamas
Tel: (242) 322-7822 (Tel/Fax), evenings: (242) 394-7460.
E-mail: MWS@coralwave.com

Atlantic Beach Hotel

The leading hotel where the world's most beautiful gay and lesbian people visit to enjoy our culture, relax, swim, party and fall in love with an enchanted tropical island.

The *Atlantic Beach Hotel* is an Art-deco hotel located in the heart of the Condado Tourist Zone on the Atlantic Coast beachfront. All rooms have been remodeled, with air con-

ditioning, color TV, phone, and most with private baths. Laundry facilities are available. The breezy ocean-view bar, restaurant decks, and the roof sun deck with large Jacuzzi are ideal for relaxing and socializing. Luxury penthouse suite, rate details available on request. Continental breakfast is included with all rooms. Value may apply towards any items on menu.

We're walking distance to popular restaurants, and the historic district and performing arts center are nearby. Twenty minutes from airport. All major credit cards accepted. Reasonable rates, free parking. Call us about our available accommodations, rates, guarantee reservation policy, or any other questions.

Address: Calle Vendig #1, Condado, San Juan, PR 00907
Tel: (787) 721-6900, (888) 721-6900, **Fax:** (787) 721-6917.

Type: Hotel with restaurant & bar.
Clientele: Mostly men with women welcome
Transportation: Taxi is best.
To Gay Bars: 3 or 4 blocks.
Rooms: 37 rooms with single or double beds. 1 luxury penthouse suite.
Baths: 27 private shower/ toilets, other share.
Meals: Free continental breakfast, regular breakfast & lunch.

Vegetarian: Available upon request & vegetarian restaurant within 3 min walking distance.
Complimentary: Coffee, tea, cocoa & muffins every morning on the roof sun deck.
Dates Open: All year.
High Season: Dec 23 to 1st Tues after Easter Sunday
Rates: Winter $85-$130, summer $70-$100. Add $15 on double.
Discounts: 20% to airline

employees.
Credit Cards: MC, Visa, Amex, Diners, Discover.
Rsv'tns: Required.
Reserve Thru: Travel agent or call direct.
Parking: Free off-street parking.
In-Room: Maid service, AC, color TV, telephone.
On-Premises: Laundry facilities.
Exercise/Health: Jacuzzi on roof sun deck.
Swimming: Hotel overlooks

ocean beach.
Sunbathing: On private roof sun deck, beach.
Smoking: Permitted.
Pets: Not permitted.
Handicap Access: Yes. Some areas have ramps, bathroom facilities.
Children: Not permitted.
Languages: Spanish, English, French.
IGLTA

Ocean Park Beach Inn

Gay/Lesbian ⚢
Gay-Operated

Tropical Gardens by the Ocean

Overlooking a palm tree-lined, turquoise sea, *Ocean Park Beach Inn* offers a tropical retreat for men and women. All rooms surround a lush courtyard with hundreds of plants and flowers, songbirds, ocean surf... A quiet oasis in San Juan, steps from restaurants, bars and shopping. Single and double rooms have private baths, AC, refrigerator or kitchenette. Sun and shade decks wrap the upper level and provide views of the beach. A rattan-furnished verandah, TV lounge and complete bar invite guests to relax. Tropical breakfast and beach equipment are complimentary. Year-round weekly rates.

Address: Calle Elena 3, Ocean Park, San Juan, PR 00911
Tel: (787) 728-7418 (Tel/Fax), reservations: (800) 292-9208.
E-mail: opbi@coqui.net **Web:** http://home.coqui.net/opbi

Type: Bed & breakfast inn with bar & cafe.
Clientele: Gay & lesbian
Transportation: Taxi $12 or rental car from airport.
To Gay Bars: 2 to 25-min walk.
Rooms: 10 rooms with queen or 2 double beds.
Baths: All private.
Meals: Tropical continental breakfast.
Vegetarian: At breakfast & lunch. Several restaurants nearby.

Complimentary: Tea, coffee, ice.
Dates Open: All year.
High Season: Dec 15-Apr 15.
Rates: Daily $55-$130; weekly $330-$780.
Discounts: Weekly rates, 7th night free.
Credit Cards: MC, Visa.
Rsv'tns: Required.
Reserve Thru: Travel agent or call direct.
Min. Stay: 6 nights high season, 4 nights low

season.
Parking: Adequate free on-street parking.
In-Room: AC, ceiling fans, refrigerator, radio, maid service. Some with kitchenette.
On-Premises: TV lounge & fax. Beach towels, chairs & equipment provided.
Exercise/Health: Water sports. Full service gym nearby, massage by appointment.
Swimming: Ocean on

premises. Gay beach at Ocean Park.
Sunbathing: Private & common sun decks, gay beach.
Smoking: Permitted in designated rooms & outdoor areas.
Pets: Permitted with special arrangements.
Handicap Access: Yes, with assistance.
Children: Permitted with special arrangements.
Languages: English, Spanish.

La Vista Caribeña

WWW Gay/Lesbian ♀♂
Gay-Owned & -Operated

A Peaceful Getaway on a Beautiful Little Island

La Vista Caribeña is a three-bedroom, Caribbean home located on the friendly Puerto Rican island of Vieques, in the village of Esperanza. If you're looking for a peaceful getaway on a beautiful little island, then this is the spot. Have a cocktail on the front veranda while gazing out over the nearby Caribbean. You can cook and eat-in or walk to several wonderful restaurants and bars. The weather is ideal and the beaches are beautiful and nearly deserted.

Address: 300 Calle Almendros, Vieques Island, PR 00765
Tel: USA reservation number: (607) 733-4171

Type: Vacation rental.
Clientele: Exclusively gay & lesbian
Transportation: We can arrange your transportation from San Juan & car rental.
Rooms: 3 rooms with double beds.
Baths: 1 bathroom.
Meals: Restaurants (walking distance to several) & markets on island.
Dates Open: All year.
High Season: Nov 1-May 1.
Rates: $600-$800 per week, $100-$125 per night.
Credit Cards: Visa, MC.
Rsv'tns: Necessary.
Reserve Thru: Call direct.
Min. Stay: 2 nights.
On-Premises: Ceiling fans, linens, towels, fully equipped kitchen, TV, iron & ironing board, beach chairs.
Swimming: 5 min walk to white beaches & crystal clear water.
Your Hosts: Bill & John.

Rainbow Realty

WWW Gay-Friendly 50/50 ♀♂
Lesbian-Owned & -Operated

A Gay Mecca in Paradise... Friendly & Accepting!

A small island paradise, Vieques Island, is located in turquoise Caribbean waters eight miles off the southeastern coast of Puerto Rico. It's a "laid back" getaway without clubs, casinos or glitz, no traffic lights and no fast food! We do have wild horses, gorgeous deserted beaches, dazzling sunsets, magical reefs, a bioluminescent bay, perfect weather and... affordability! *Rainbow Realty* offers 25 homes, villas, cottages and apartments — from small and inexpensive to spacious and spectacular. We also do vacation home sales!

Mail To: HC-01 Box 6307, Vieques, PR 00765-9019
Tel: (787) 741-4312 (Tel/Fax).
E-mail: rainbowrealty@hotmail.com **Web:** http://enchanted-isle.com/rainbow

Type: Vacation rental agency.
Clientele: 50% gay & lesbian & 50% straight
Transportation: Fly to San Juan, then small airline (20 min) or ferry (2 hrs). Free pick up from airport, ferry.
To Gay Bars: Inquire, most are gay-friendly.
Rooms: 25 suites, apartments, cottages or villas with single, double, queen, king or bunk beds.
Baths: At least 1 bath per house.
Dates Open: Year round.
Rates: High: $450-$2400, low: $200-$2000. Off season May 1-Nov 1.
Discounts: Inquire.
Credit Cards: MC, Visa.
Rsv'tns: Required.
Reserve Thru: Travel agent or call direct.
Min. Stay: In season: 1 wk (addt'l nights pro-rated). Off season: 4 nights.
Parking: Inquire.
In-Room: Ceiling fans, fully equipped kitchen, refrigerator, coffee & tea-making facilities. Most have phone & laundry service. Some have AC, color TV, VCR. Maid service can be arranged.
On-Premises: Inquire.
Exercise/Health: Nearby gym, weights.
Swimming: Some pools. All 1-5 mi from ocean. 1 gay beach.
Nudity: Limited.
Smoking: Permitted.
Pets: Inquire.
Handicap Access: Some wide doors.
Children: Inquire.
Languages: Spanish, English.
Your Hosts: Lin & Sandie.

Cooper Island Beach Club

Gay-Friendly ⚥

A Casual Caribbean Beachfront Resort

Cooper Island Beach Club is a small resort on a 1 1/2-mile by 1/2-mile island. At our beachfront restaurant and bar, sheltered from the sun, you can enjoy a cool drink with the Caribbean Sea only a few feet away. We've built a reputation for serving quality meals in an informal setting, at a reasonable price. Our guestrooms are on the beach and have an open-plan bedroom/living room/kitchen, plus balcony, bathroom, a shower that is almost outdoors. Activities include sunbathing, swimming, hiking, enjoying meals in the restaurant and conversation in the bar. We can arrange day sails and boat trips.

Guest Comment: "There are not enough words to do justice to the immense beauty, tranquility and serenity to be found here."

Mail To: PO Box 512, Turners Falls, MA 01376
Tel: (413) 863-3162, (800) 542-4624 (USA office), **Fax:** (413) 863-3662.
E-mail: info@cooper-island.com **Web:** http://www.cooper-island.com

Type: Beach resort with restaurant, bar, & scuba dive shop.
Clientele: Mainly straight with gay & lesbian following
Transportation: Pick up from ferry dock, no charge on scheduled trips.
Rooms: 12 rooms with queen beds.
Baths: All private shower/toilets.

Vegetarian: Available for lunch & dinner with prior notice.
Dates Open: All year.
High Season: Dec 15-Apr 15.
Rates: Per night for 2: US $95 (Jun 1-Oct 30); US $175 (Dec 15-Apr 15); US $115 (Apr 15-May 31 & Nov 1-Dec 14). Meal and/or dive packages available.

Discounts: Weekly discounts available.
Credit Cards: MC, Visa, with 5% handling charge.
Rsv'tns: Required.
Reserve Thru: Travel agent or call direct.
Parking: Boat moorings available.
In-Room: Ceiling fans, kitchen, refrigerator & maid service.

Exercise/Health: Full scuba facilities & watersports.
Swimming: In the ocean.
Sunbathing: On the beach.
Pets: Not permitted.
Handicap Access: No.
Children: Permitted, preferably over 10 yrs old.
Languages: English.
Your Hosts: Chris.

Color Photo on Page 7

Fort Recovery Estate

Gay-Friendly ♀♂

"A Bit of Britain in the Sun"

A great romantic getaway, **Fort Recovery Estate** boasts its own small private beach, fresh-water pool and 17th-century Dutch fort. The luxury three- to four-bedroom house on the beach and the one- and two-bedroom seaside and penthouse villas afford spectacular Caribbean views of six islands. All accommodations include daily continental breakfast, air-conditioning, cable TV, kitchen and housekeeping service. Each 7-night stay includes a dinner, served by waiter service in the privacy of your villa, and a half-day snorkeling trip, per guest. Massages and yoga classes on premises, by arrangement.

Address: Road Town **Mail To:** PO Box 239, Road Town, Tortola , BVI
Tel: (284) 495-4354, (800) 367-8455 (wait for ring), **Fax:** (284) 495-4036.
E-mail: villas@fortrecovery.com **Web:** http://www.fortrecovery.com

Type: B&B hotel & villa resort, chef on premises.
Clientele: Mostly straight clientele w/ a gay/lesbian following
Transportation: Taxi.
Rooms: 17 villas, king beds.
Baths: All private shower/toilets.
Meals: Continental breakfast.
Vegetarian: On menu.

Vegetarian food on island.
Complimentary: One welcome dinner per guest for each 7-night stay.
Dates Open: All year.
High Season: Nov-June.
Rates: Daily: $145-$710.
Credit Cards: MC, Visa, Amex.
Rsv'tns: Required.
Reserve Thru: Call direct or travel agent.
Parking: Adequate free

parking on premises.
In-Room: AC, ceiling fans, color cable TV, dataport phones & automated voicemail, kitchen, fridge, maid & room service.
On-Premises: Meeting rooms, E-mail, fax, phone, secretarial service.
Exercise/Health: Massage & yoga classes. Nearby gym, weights.
Swimming: Pool & the

Caribbean.
Sunbathing: Poolside, at beach, on private patio.
Pets: Not permitted.
Handicap Access: Yes.
Children: Welcome.
Languages: English, Spanish.
Your Hosts: Pamelah.
IGLTA

Cormorant Beach Club & Hotel

For Those Who Like to Honeymoon Every Time They Travel

Praised as "the best small hotel in the American Virgin Islands" by *Andrew Harper's Hideaway Report*. The **Cormorant Beach Club** boasts 34 large guestrooms and four penthouse suites, two tennis courts, an 88,000 gallon freshwater pool and an open-air seaview lounge and restaurant.

It is now under the ownership of Arthur Mayer (55) and Gregory Thomas (45), a committed couple of 19 years, whose love of hospitality and St. Croix inspired them to market it to gay and lesbian couples who like to honeymoon every time they travel. From the private balconies of all their guestrooms, enjoy a turquoise ocean view; step out the door and stroll onto six acres of palm-studded white sand beach or swim in the beachside freshwater pool. The hotel is part of an enclosed 12-acre compound directly on La Grand Princesse beach — three miles west of Christiansted. And with Long Reef directly in front of the hotel, the snorkeling is as good as it gets. It shares this unique location with the Cormorant Cove Condominiums, 10 of which are available through the hotel for larger house parties. In nearby Christiansted, duty free shopping and many fine restaurants abound. Scuba diving, sailing, deep-sea fishing and horseback riding are just minutes away. There are three golf courses, including the Carambola Golf Club, a Robert Trent-designed course.

Address: 4126 La Grande Princesse, Saint Croix, USVI 00820-4441
Tel: (340) 778-8920, (800) 548-4460, **Fax:** (340) 778-9218.
E-mail: info@cormorant-stcroix.com **Web:** http://www.cormorant-stcroix.com

Type: Hotel with bar & restaurant.
Clientele: 50% gay & lesbian & 50% straight
Transportation: Airport pickup on request ($15 per couple).
To Gay Bars: 15 miles.
Rooms: 34 rooms, 4 suites & 10 2-BR/2-BA condos with double, queen or king beds.
Baths: All private.
Meals: Meal plans available on request.
Vegetarian: Upon request.
Complimentary: Tea &
coffee machine in room, afternoon tea, coffee & homemade cookies in lobby, welcome cocktail upon check-in.
High Season: Dec 15-Apr 15.
Rates: Per couple: summer/fall $110-$225, winter/spring $150-$265.
Discounts: Inquire.
Credit Cards: MC, Visa, Amex, Diners, Bancard, Eurocard, Discover.
Rsv'tns: Required.
Reserve Thru: Travel agent
or call direct.
Min. Stay: Required.
Parking: Ample, free off-street parking.
In-Room: Telephone, AC, ceiling fans, color cable TV, refrigerator, coffee & tea-making facilities, maid service.
On-Premises: Meeting rooms.
Exercise/Health: 2 tennis courts, 1 beach volleyball net & professional massage therapist. Gym nearby.
Swimming: Pool & ocean.
Sunbathing: Poolside, on private sun decks, at beach.
Smoking: Permitted everywhere except in non-smoking sleeping rooms.
Pets: Permitted.
Handicap Access: Yes, ramps.
Children: Welcome.
Languages: English, Cruzian, German.
IGLTA

Color Photo on Page 9

Pink Fancy Hotel

WWW Gay-Friendly 50/50 ♀♂
Gay-Owned & -Operated
Pink Fancy Hotel is a quaint historic inn located in downtown Christiansted. The oldest part of the four-building complex dates from 1780. Many years ago the building was a private club for wealthy plantation owners. In 1948, Jane Gottlieb, a Ziegfield Follies star, opened the hotel and named it Pink Fancy. The hotel has always been a favorite of *Frommer's Travel Guides.*

Each room is charmingly decorated, and several of the deluxe rooms offer canopy or poster beds and antique furnishings. All rooms have AC, ceiling fans, cable TV, kitchenettes and phone. Our "Cottage on the Hill" can accommodate six comfortably. Deluxe room rates include continental breakfast. Duty-free shops and a large selection of fine restaurants are just a stroll away. Our nearby sandy beach, located on an island in Christiansted harbor, is a 5-10 minute walk and a 2-minute ferry ride from the hotel.

Christiansted, settled by the Danes in 1733, is considered by many to be one of the most beatiful towns in the Caribbean. The island of St. Croix, 23 miles long and 7 miles wide at most, is full of contrasts varying from arid desert to rolling hills to lush tropical vegetation. Exquisite beaches hug the shoreline, while ruins of old sugar cane estates with their mills dot the landscape.

Address: 27 Prince Street, Christiansted, USVI 00820
Tel: (340) 773-8460, (800) 524-2045, **Fax:** (340) 773-6448.
E-mail: info@pinkfancy.com **Web:** http://www.pinkfancy.com

Type: Hotel, inn.
Clientele: 50% gay & lesbian & 50% straight clientele
Transportation: Airport taxi.
To Gay Bars: 3 miles.
Rooms: 13 rooms with single, double, queen or king beds.
Baths: 13 private bath/shower/toilets.
Meals: Continental breakfast.
Vegetarian: Available

nearby.
Complimentary: Cocktail upon check-in.
Dates Open: All year.
High Season: Dec 15-Apr 15.
Rates: High: $85-$120. Low: $75-$105. Ask about Honeymoon, Fun, & Dive Pkgs.
Discounts: Weekly & pkg. rates.
Credit Cards: MC, Visa, Amex, Discover.
Rsv'tns: Required.

Reserve Thru: Travel agent or call direct.
Parking: Ample, on-street parking.
In-Room: Telephone, AC, ceiling fans, color cable TV, kitchen, refrigerator, maid & laundry service.
On-Premises: Fax, copier, e-mail.
Exercise/Health: Massage. Nearby gym, weights, sauna, massage.
Swimming: Pool. Ocean nearby.

Sunbathing: Poolside, on roof, private & common sun decks, patio, beach.
Smoking: Permitted poolside, garden & sun deck. All rooms non-smoking.
Pets: Not permitted.
Handicap Access: No.
Children: 12 & older.
Languages: English, Arabic, German.
Your Hosts: Motasem & David.

Sand Castle on the Beach Resort

The Perfect Gay & Lesbian Paradise

Your Caribbean dream, *Sand Castle on the Beach Resort* is located on a beautiful white sandy beach on the quiet side of St. Croix... a special place for special people. This is the perfect oasis for gay and lesbian vacationers, where romance and relaxation go hand-in-hand. Our paradise location offers spectacular views, a swimming beach, snorkeling, two pools (one is clothing-optional), rooms and suites with kitchens and dining balconies with beach view, guaranteed warm weather, crystal-blue calm seas and lush landscapes. Proudly serving the gay and lesbian community since 1978. Ask about our commitment ceremony package.

Address: 127 Smithfield, Frederiksted, USVI 00840
Tel: (340) 772-1205, (800) 524-2018, **Fax:** (340) 772-1757.
E-mail: onthebeach@virginislands.net **Web:** http://www.gaytraveling.com/onthebeach

Type: Hotel with boutique.
Clientele: Gay & lesbian. Good mix of men & women
Transportation: Our limo driver will pick you up at airport ($10 1 or 2 people, $5 each addt'l person).
To Gay Bars: 1/2 mile.
Rooms: 12 rooms, 9 suites, 2 luxury villas with queen or king beds.
Baths: All private.
Meals: Expanded continental breakfast. Weekly BBQ or cocktail party.

Complimentary: 1 bottle of rum, 2 cokes.
High Season: Dec-Mar.
Rates: Low $65-$150, shoulder $75-$185, high $115-$250.
Discounts: 10% to returning guests. Inquire about other discounts.
Credit Cards: MC, Visa, Amex, Discover.
Rsv'tns: Required.
Reserve Thru: Travel agent or call direct.

Min. Stay: 3 nights.
Parking: Ample, free off-street parking.
In-Room: Phone, AC, ceiling fans, color cable TV, VCR, kitchen, fridge, coffee & tea makers, maid svc.
On-Premises: Laundry, free video tape library.
Exercise/Health: Masseuse available. Nearby gym & massage.
Swimming: Pool & ocean on premises.
Sunbathing: Poolside, on

private & common sun decks, patio & at beach.
Nudity: Permitted, 1 of 2 pools is clothing-optional.
Smoking: Permitted anywhere, a few rooms are non-smoking.
Pets: Inquire.
Handicap Access: Yes.
Your Hosts: Ron, Irma, Tanya & Allen.
IGLTA

Color Photo on Page 8

Inn at Blackbeard's Castle, The

WWW Gay-Friendly 50/50 ♀♂

Built as a watchtower in 1679 when pirates ruled the Caribbean, *The Inn at Blackbeard's Castle* is now a national historical landmark commanding a spectacular view of the harbor. Newly renovated, guestrooms feature casually elegant appointments such as four-poster beds and crown moldings, and all rooms are steps away from one of the two luxurious swimming pools. Native and international cuisine, world-class entertainment and an unrivaled view, draws residents and tourists from other hotels to our restaurant. We're minutes from duty-free shops in downtown Charlotte Amalie, restaurants, a championship 18-hole golf course, and the island's many beautiful beaches. Accolades include: *VOGUE:* "...remarkable view...an excellent restaurant." *AMEX:* "A first-class hotel and restaurant." *PRACTICAL GOURMET:* "...best restaurant on St. Thomas."

Mail To: PO Box 6227, St Thomas, USVI 00804
Tel: (340) 776-1234, (800) 344-5771, **Fax:** (340) 776-4321.
E-mail: blackbeards@islands.vi **Web:** http://www.blackbeardscastle.vi

Type: Hotel with restaurant, bar & piano lounge.
Clientele: 50% gay & lesbian & 50% straight
Transportation: Taxi is best from airport.
To Gay Bars: 5-minute drive to gay/lesbian bars.
Rooms: 12 doubles, 4 junior suites.
Baths: All private.

Meals: Continental breakfast included. Lunch & dinner at restaurant.
Vegetarian: Yes.
Dates Open: All year.
High Season: Dec 15-Apr 30.
Rates: Summer $85-$145. Winter $110-$225.
Credit Cards: MC, Visa, Amex, Discover.

Rsv'tns: Required.
Reserve Thru: Travel agent or call direct.
Min. Stay: 3 days during high season.
Parking: Free adequate off-street parking.
In-Room: Cable color TV, AC, direct dial telephones, safes, daily maid service.
On-Premises: Gardens,

stunning water views.
Exercise/Health: Massage by appointment.
Swimming: 2 pools.
Sunbathing: At poolside.
Smoking: No restrictions.
Pets: Not permitted.
Children: Permitted, 16+.
Languages: English, Spanish & French.
Your Hosts: Craig.

Mata Rocks Resort

Gay-Friendly ♀♂

Where the Stress of Modern Life Disappears

Mata Rocks Resort is a small, intimate beachfront hotel providing personalized service and tropical elegance in a casual, relaxed atmosphere. Suites in native hardwood, all with ocean views, private baths, ceiling fans and daily maid service surround you in luxury. Large decks invite you to enjoy the Caribbean sunshine right on your front doorstep — or mingle with friends at the beachfront bar while enjoying a Mata Colada. Stroll the pristine white sand beach, lounge in a hammock, or explore the island on one of our courtesy bicycles. Diving, snorkeling, windsurfing, fishing and inland tours round out your stay.

Mail To: PO Box 47, San Pedro, Ambergris Caye, Belize
Tel: (501) 26 2336, (888) 628-2757, **Fax:** (501) 26 2349.
E-mail: matarocks@btl.net **Web:** http://www.matarocks.com

Type: Hotel with bar.
Clientele: Mostly hetero clientele with a gay/lesbian following
Transportation: Van. Pick up from airport US $10 round trip.
Rooms: 4 rooms, 2 suites with double, queen or king beds.
Baths: 13 private bath/shower/toilets.
Meals: Continental

breakfast.
Vegetarian: Yes.
Complimentary: Rum Punch cocktail on arrival.
Dates Open: Closed mid-Sept to mid-Oct.
High Season: Dec-Apr.
Rates: Low season: US $59-US $96; high season US $80-US $135.
Discounts: For extended stays of 7 or more days.
Credit Cards: MC, Visa,

Amex.
Rsv'tns: Required.
Reserve Thru: Travel agent or call direct.
Min. Stay: Xmas 5 days; high season inquire.
Parking: Inquire.
In-Room: AC, ceiling fans, refrigerator, maid service.
Exercise/Health: Massage. Nearby gym, weights.
Swimming: Ocean. Nearby pool.

Sunbathing: On common sun decks & at beach.
Smoking: Inquire.
Pets: Not permitted.
Children: Welcome. We don't get many children, but they're not refused.
Languages: Spanish, English.
Your Hosts: Terry & Liz.

La Plantacion Big Ruby's

Gay/Lesbian ♂
Gay-Owned & -Operated

Exclusively Big Ruby's

La Plantacion is surrounded by secondary rainforest above the Pacific Ocean. Secluded are our beautifully decorated rooms featuring luxury beds, linens and towels. A full hot breakfast is served in the morning, and wine is served each evening. Enjoy dinner at Madre's, our on-site restaurant serving international cuisine. Spend your day relaxing poolside or at secluded Playita beach. Complimentary shuttle service is provided throughout the day. Our knowledgeable staff can arrange horseback riding through the rainforest, whitewater rafting, a trip to Arenal volcano and Tabacon hot springs. Take guided tours through Manuel Antonio Park and experience world-class scuba diving... All of this and more in a beautiful setting.

Mail To: Apdo 94, Quepos Manuel Antonio, Costa Rica
Tel: (506) 777 1332, **Fax:** (506) 777 0432. In USA & Canada: (800) 477-7829, **Fax:** (305) 296-0281.
E-mail: costarica@bigrubys.com **Web:** http://www.bigrubys.com

Type: Guesthouse.
Clientele: Gay & lesbian, mostly men with some women
Transportation: Plane to Quepos, taxi from airport.
To Gay Bars: 1 block, a 2 min walk.
Rooms: 24 rooms with queen or king beds.
Baths: 24 all private baths.
Meals: Full breakfast. Dinner for most major holidays.
Vegetarian: Available on request & nearby.
Complimentary: Always coffee. Beer, wine, juice every evening "Happy Hour."
Dates Open: Closed Oct.
High Season: Nov-Apr.
Rates: Per couple +tax: off season $90, season $155.
Credit Cards: MC, Visa.
Rsv'tns: Required. Walk-ins welcome.
Reserve Thru: Travel agent or call direct.
Parking: Adequate off-street parking.
In-Room: AC, ceiling fans, color cable TV, VCR, refrigerator, maid & laundry service.
On-Premises: TV lounge, club room. Our own restaurant, Madre's, serving international cuisine.
Exercise/Health: Nearby gym, weights.
Swimming: Pool on premises. Ocean nearby.
Sunbathing: Poolside, on common sun decks, at beach.
Nudity: Permitted in pool & sunning areas only.
Smoking: Permitted on common grounds & in smoking rooms. Non-smoking rooms available.
Pets: Not permitted.
Handicap Access: Yes.
Children: No.
Languages: Spanish, English, French.
IGLTA

Hotel Colours, Guest Residence San Jose [WWW] Gay/Lesbian ♂♂

Experience Not Just a Place, But a State of Mind

Newly expanded & completely renovated resort — *Colours* is the premier gay guesthouse in Costa Rica. I features Spanish-style architecture with unique and stylish finishing touches, and all rooms feature vibrant tropical "colours" and private, tiled baths. The exciting new pool, Jacuzzi and garden areas truly make this property the BEST the capital city, San Jose, has

to offer. Total enjoyment from lounging poolside doing absolutely nothing... to lively conversation and socializing at La Esquina Bar — the in-house bar/restaurant. We're located in the clean, upscale Rohrmoser area, near the Pavas (Travelair) Airport, Plaza Mayor Mall and US Embassy and away from the noisy, congested and polluted downtown area. We're less

than a 10 minute ride to central San Jose, but only one block to pharmacies, stores, bars and restaurants. The friendly multilingual staff will advise guests of guided day excursions to attractions such as volcanoes, biological reserves, island boat cruises, whitewater river rafting, and more. From the main balcony of the poolside house, look out over the enclosed garden and pool/Jacuzzi area, with a view of the mountain ranges surrounding San Jose. *Colours* features various room types to suit your taste and budget. With San Jose's year-round spring-like weather, air conditioning is not needed. Also on property are three large social rooms, one featuring English-speaking cable and movie channels.

Call our friendly US representative at *Colours Destinations* at 1-800-ARRIVAL for details about these TWO locations with complete tour and travel planning throughout Costa Rica and to assist you in planning your entire personal holiday. Check out our extensive website with information on Costa Rica, South Beach and Key West, Florida. Our Costa Rica e-mail address is colours@sol.racsa.co.cr.

Mail To: Colours Destinations, 255 W 24th St, Miami Beach, FL 33140, USA
Tel: (800) ARRIVAL (277-4825), (305) 532-9341, **Fax:** (305) 534-0362. Local San Jose (506) 296 1880, **Fax:** (506) 296 1597.
E-mail: newcolours@aol.com **Web:** http://colours.net **IGLTA**

El Ciprés Hostel

Gay-Friendly ⚣

Your Best Choice in Quito

El Ciprés Hostel is in a safe residential area of Quito, near embassies, banks, bars, dance clubs and other entertainment venues. We offer single, double, triple and shared carpeted rooms, 24-hour hot water, color cable TV, VCR, CD player, and a pleasant outdoor area — all in a cozy environment, complete with personal service and a bilingual staff. We have a very nice, comfortable van for tours and excursions in Ecuador with an English-speaking driver at competitive prices. We provide travel information on tours to the Galapagos Islands, Indian markets, etc., and information on local gay bars.

Address: Lerida #381, at Pontevedra (La Floresta) **Mail To:** PO Box 17-03-850, Quito, Pichincha 1697, Ecuador
Tel: (593 2) 549 561, **Fax:** (593 2) 549 558.
E-mail: elcipres@hotmail.com **Web:** http://el_cipres_hostel.tripod.com/Quito/

Type: Budget hostel.
Clientele: Mostly hetero clientele with a gay/lesbian following
Transportation: Free pick up from airport if you stay at least 3 nights.
To Gay Bars: 6 block walk.
Rooms: Private & shared rooms (single-quad & larger).

Baths: Private & shared.
Meals: Continental breakfast.
Dates Open: All year.
High Season: June-Aug.
Rates: Rooms, per person: $5.00 shared, $7.00 private.
Discounts: Please inquire.
Rsv'tns: Preferred.
Reserve Thru: Call direct.
Parking: On property & on street.

In-Room: TV in private rooms.
On-Premises: Color cable TV, VCR, CD player, e-mail, public phone, laundry facilities, grill.
Exercise/Health: Weights. Nearby steam, sauna.
Swimming: Nearby pool.
Sunbathing: In backyard.

Smoking: Permitted.
Pets: Not permitted.
Children: Welcome.
Languages: Spanish, English, French.
Your Hosts: Carlos or Roberto.
IGLTA

Casa Aurora

Gay/Lesbian ⚣

Study Spanish in the City of Eternal Spring

A one hour's drive from Mexico City, on the road to Acapulco, Cuernavaca's many attractions include the Palace of Cortes, a 16th-century cathedral, the Borda Gardens, Brady Museum, San Anton waterfall, Siqueiros Workshop, and its Spanish-language schools. CETLALIC is the only gay-friendly language school. Open all year, it offers a 3-week lesbian program and a 3-week gay program each summer. Guest comment: "*Casa Aurora* is a restored Colonial home, downtown near everything. Once inside, you find an oasis where you can relax, take a siesta in one of the hammocks or listen to fascinating stories of Mexico's history told by your host..." If e-mailing, write "Attn: Antonio Ortega" in subject line.

Address: Arista No. 12, Centro, Cuernavaca, Mor. 62000, Mexico
Tel: (52-7) 3 18 63 94.
E-mail: cetlalic@mail.giga.com

Type: Bed & breakfast or guesthouse.
Clientele: Mostly gay & lesbian with some hetero clientele
Transportation: Plane or bus from Mexico City. Taxi from bus station to house.
To Gay Bars: A 10 min drive, a 5 min walk.
Rooms: 3 rooms with single, double or king bed.

Baths: Private & shared.
Meals: Continental breakfast or 3 meals.
Vegetarian: Owner only cooks vegetarian.
Dates Open: All year.
High Season: May-Aug.
Rates: B&B: US $20. Three meals: US $25.
Discounts: For 2 guests in same room: B&B US $36; Three meals: US $44.

Rsv'tns: Preferred.
Reserve Thru: Call direct.
Min. Stay: No, but prefer longer stays & students of Spanish.
Parking: Adequate pay parking, parking lot around corner.
In-Room: Terrace with hammock.
On-Premises: Small garden, laundry facilities.

Swimming: Nearby pool.
Sunbathing: In garden.
Smoking: Owner doesn't smoke, smoking permitted in terraces, garden & rooms.
Pets: Not permitted.
Languages: Spanish, English, French.
Your Hosts: Antonio Ortega.

Los Helechos Posada

WWW Gay-Friendly 50/50 ⚥

Relaxing & Informal B&B in the Center of Oaxaca

Los Helechos (The Ferns) is a small *posada* (guesthouse) where thoughtful attention to detail creates a cheerful and natural environment where visitors feel at home while on vacation. Our house is located within the historical center of Oaxaca, just ten blocks from the famous *Zócalo* (Main Square), one of the finest in Mexico. A patio and a terrace with several hammocks provide a relaxing and informal atmosphere. Oaxaca offers a world full of colors and flavors, where the blue of the sky is of an unforgettable hue, and where a smiling and hospitable people keep alive their traditions and rich cultural life.

Address: Guerrero 1029-B, Centro, Oaxaca, OAX CP 68000, Mexico
Tel: (52-9) 514 0057 (Tel/Fax).
E-mail: helechos@prodigy.net.mx **Web:** http://www.mexonline.com/helechos.htm

Type: B&B with bar.
Clientele: 50% gay & lesbian & 50% hetero
Transportation: Taxi from bus station or airport.
To Gay Bars: 5 min drive.
Rooms: 4 rooms, 1 suite with double beds.
Baths: All private bath/shower/toilets.
Meals: Full breakfast.
Vegetarian: Vegetarian

breakfast available. Veg. restaurants nearby.
Complimentary: Coffee, tea, soda.
Dates Open: All year.
High Season: Jul 15-31, Oct 26-Nov 5, Dec 15-Jan 15, Easter.
Rates: Per person (in Mexican Pesos): low $230-$430, high $290-$540.
Discounts: Inquire.

Rsv'tns: Required.
Reserve Thru: Travel agent or call direct.
Parking: Limited on-street pay parking.
In-Room: Maid service.
On-Premises: Meeting rooms, TV lounge, internet.
Exercise/Health: Nearby Temazcal (native sauna), bicycle tours.
Swimming: Nearby pool.

Sunbathing: On patio & common sun decks.
Smoking: Permitted everywhere.
Pets: Not permitted.
Children: No.
Languages: Spanish, English, French.
Your Hosts: Camux, Yamil, Tensy, Rafael.

Accommodations in Puerto Vallarta

Arco Iris

WWW Gay/Lesbian ♀♂
Gay-Owned & -Operated

Feel the Breezes, Get Lost in the Views!

Located on the upscale Conchas Chinas hillside of Puerto Vallarta, this unique B&B's tranquil setting above the bay is surrounded by lush vegetation, tropical fruit trees and an abundance of flowers and herbs. Guest and gay travel professionals speak of sparkling and comfortable accommodations, perfect meals, soft Ralph Lauren linens, a pleasant staff, privacy and "the best gay views of the bay". The staff is always friendly and respectful. Guest privacy and comfort is paramount. A beautiful tropical breakfast is served daily poolside or in your dining room overlooking the bay. At day's end, guests and friends gather for complimentary sunset margaritas on the upper terrace.

Elegant private meals and professional massage available in-house. Also available: Tequila/ Guadalajara tour, gay cruises, many water sports, jungle tours, whale watching, horseback riding, hot springs, directions to many gay bars and restaurants. *Arco Iris* offers breathtaking views, television, large video and reading library, in room long-distance telephone and air conditioning. Also 3-bedroom/3-bath and 4-bedroom/4-bath casitas w/private pools, as well as 2-bedroom apartments. All within a secure and private property on the south side. Reservations advised. Visit website for easy reservations.

Address: 115 Paseo de los Delfines, Fracc. Conchas Chinas, Puerto Vallarta, JAL 48390, Mexico
Tel: (52-3) 221 5579, **Fax:** (52-3) 221 5528.
E-mail: pvViews@prodigy.net.mx **Web:** http://www.GayBnB.com

Type: Bed & breakfast with room, villa & apt. rentals.
Clientele: Gay/Lesbian, and their friends
Transportation: Taxi or airport transfer.
To Gay Bars: 10 blocks.
Rooms: 18 single or 2/2 bedroom, 3/3 BR, 1/4 BR w/ double and queen beds.
Baths: Private & shared.
Meals: Full tropical breakfast. Gourmet room

service available.
Complimentary: Sunset margaritas & beer on common terrace.
High Season: Nov 16-Apr 24.
Rates: US $50-US $145. Prices in US$, can accept pesos at current exchange rate.
Discounts: Inquire.
Credit Cards: MC, Visa.
Rsv'tns: Advised.

Reserve Thru: Website, travel agent or call direct.
Parking: Ample free on-street parking, security.
In-Room: Phone, fans, kitchen, fridge, coffee, maid & laundry service (high season). Some w/ AC, TV, VCR, stereo.
On-Premises: Video, book & game library, fax, internet.
Exercise/Health: Massage. Nearby gyms.

Swimming: Private pools.
Sunbathing: Poolside, private & common sun decks, beach.
Nudity: Permitted.
Smoking: Permitted.
Children: Inquire.
Languages: Spanish, English.
Your Hosts: Thom & Ran.

Boana Torre Malibu

WWW Gay/Lesbian ♂♂
Gay-Owned & -Operated

With forty-seven units on ten floors, *Boana Torre Malibu* is Puerto Vallarta's largest straight-friendly basic, modern condo-hotel. We're located, quite conveniently for access to swimming and sunbathing, just one block directly behind the blue-green chairs at Los Muertos Beach. Just a short walk away from the hotel, you'll find a large variety of popular gay lounges and dance bars, an incredible array of restaurants serving excellent cuisine at low-prices

Because they are condos, all units have one bedroom, two separate bathrooms, a kitchenette, a living room, air conditioning, and a comfortable balcony with scenic views of Banderas Bay. An exception is unit #701, which is larger and has two separate bedrooms. A large terrace and pool, and a poolside restaurant and bar, are open to the public. We also offer tour information and a ticket office, making it possible for you to plan a host of excursions available in Puerto Vallarta. There are snorkeling excursions, sunset cruises, horseback riding excursions, and shopping. There is never a reason to be bored in Puerto Vallarta, and we can take care of all of your arrangements for you.

Address: Amapas 325, Col. Emiliano Zapata, Puerto Vallarta, JAL , Mexico
Tel: (52-3)) 222 0999, **Fax:** (52-3) 222 6695.
E-mail: boana@pvnet.com.mx **Web:** http://www.boana.net

Type: Condo/Hotel with restaurant & bar.
Clientele: Mostly gay & lesbian with some hetero
Transportation: Plane, then taxi. Hotel van pick up US $20 per person.
To Gay Bars: 6 blocks.
Rooms: 47 apartments with double or king beds.

Baths: Private shower/ toilets (2 per apartment).
High Season: Nov-Apr.
Rates: Summer: USD $35-$100; winter USD $69-$190.
Rsv'tns: Required.
Reserve Thru: Travel agent or call direct.
Parking: Ample on- & off-street parking.

In-Room: AC, ceiling fans, color cable TV, kitchen, fridge, coffee & tea-makers, maid, room & laundry svc.
Exercise/Health: Nearby gym, weights, Jacuzzi.
Swimming: Pool. Ocean nearby.
Sunbathing: Poolside.
Smoking: Permitted. No

non-smoking rooms.
Pets: Not permitted.
Handicap Access: Yes, wide doors.
Children: No.
Languages: Spanish, English, French.
Your Hosts: Suzanna.

Bugambilia Blanca

Your New Friends in Puerto Vallarta

In the heart of Puerto Vallarta's gay-friendly South Side, *Bugambilia Blanca* is a colourful Mexican colonial guesthouse providing stylish accommodations, attentive service and ocean views in a secure and relaxed environment. Our gay-owned and -operated bed and breakfast is a popular choice with gay and lesbian visitors and their straight friends. *Bugambilia Blanca* is a 6-minute walk away from the gay beach, gay bars, clubs, restaurants and shops.

Stylishly furnished guestrooms and suites with Mexican Jalisco furnishings, new orthopaedic mattresses, pillows, luxury sheets and towels. The Penthouse suite provides spacious accommodation over two levels with a king bed loft above and open plan living, dining and kitchen areas below. Junior suites provide versatile living in open plan accommodation with queen bed, living, dining and kitchen areas. Comfortable master guestrooms with king beds have small balconies with ocean or tropical views. Sit and relax on our open breezeways and enjoy the refreshing breezes that continuously flow through the guesthouse, or experience the tranquility of spectacular sunset views across the Bay. *Bugambilia Blanca* provides wonderful hospitality and a friendly environment in which to relax, unwind and enjoy all that gay Puerto Vallarta has to offer.

Address: Carretera Barra de Navidad #602, Colonia Emiliano Zapata, Puerto Vallarta, Jalisco C.P. 48380, Mexico
Tel: (52 3) 222 1152 (Tel/Fax).
E-mail: arcadia@pvnet.com.mx **Web:** http://www.bestinns.net/mexico/bb.html

Type: Bed & breakfast, guesthouse, inn.
Clientele: Mostly men with women welcome
Transportation: Taxi from airport.
To Gay Bars: 1 block, 1/6 of a mile, a 5 min walk, a 1 min drive. Nearest gay bars: Paco's Sunset Bar & Olas Altas, Apaches, Kit Kat.
Rooms: 6 rooms & 3 suites with queen or king beds.
Baths: 10 private shower/toilets.
Meals: Continental breakfast.

Vegetarian: Vegetarian breakfast items. Some local vegetarian restaurants. Vegetarian food shopping nearby.
Complimentary: Welcome refreshments served on arrival. Purified bottled water always provided.
Dates Open: All year.
High Season: Nov-Apr.
Rates: Winter (Nov-Apr): US $70-$125; Summer (May-Oct): US $60-$90. Taxes included.
Discounts: Varies throughout season. Inquire

direct for discounts of 5 to 20%
Rsv'tns: Recommended.
Reserve Thru: Call direct or travel agent.
Parking: Adequate free off-street parking.
In-Room: All rooms: ceiling fans, clock radios, full daily maid svc, laundry svc. Some rooms: AC. Suites also: kitchens, fridges, toasters, blenders. Suites & Master Guestrms: tea & coffee makers.
On-Premises: Selected gay tours available.

Exercise/Health: Massage. Nearby gyms & weights.
Swimming: Nearby pool & ocean.
Sunbathing: At nearby pool & beach.
Smoking: Permitted throughout. No non-smoking rooms available.
Pets: Not permitted.
Handicap Access: No.
Children: No.
Languages: English, Spanish.
Your Hosts: From England, Clive & Simon.

Casa de Los Arcos

WWW Gay/Lesbian ⚥

Your Piece of Paradise Starts Here

Wake up each morning to a panoramic vista of Banderas Bay at *Casa de Los Arcos,* beautifully situated on the hillside overlooking old town Puerto Vallarta and the Pacific Ocean. All of our living areas have ocean and jungle views, and we have maintained the integrity of the Spanish Colonial architecture while giving you all the modern amenities that you are accustomed to. Three sumptuous suites accommodate a single group of up to ten people, or each suite may be rented separately. All bedrooms are air-conditioned, and have king-sized beds and face the ocean. Each casa has its own living room, dining room, kitchen and terrace. The "Main Casa" is a two-bedroom suite of about 1,600 square feet. The style is colonial, and the views never stop. Our "Casa Palapa" is pure tropics. A magnificent traditional palapa roof covers this suite. "La Casita" is the perfect retreat, with a view that takes your breath away.

Your holiday begins the moment you step off the plane and we meet you at the airport. Once home, the blender starts going and margaritas and tasty Mexican snacks are on the way. Whether you want a registered massage therapist to be waiting when you arrive, or restaurant recommendations or reservations, we're here to guarantee that your time is worry free. The beach, restaurants, and bars are just a short walk down the hill, but you never really have to leave here. Sit poolside or relax in the shade. Our staff are trained to make you feel at home. Tired of restaurants? Come home at the end of the day to a fabulous meal prepared by our cook. Don't worry about drinking the water, we have our own purification system on the premises.

Address: Calle Hortensias 168, Puerto Vallarta, Jalisco 48300, Mexico
Tel: (52-3) 222 5990 (Tel/Fax). In USA: (800) 424-3434, ask for Ron Oyer.
E-mail: rddr@pvnet.com.mx **Web:** http://www.casadelosarcos.com

Type: Guesthouse.
Clientele: Mostly gay & lesbian, some straight
Transportation: Taxi, car. Free airport pick up.
To Gay Bars: 6 blocks.
Rooms: 3 suites with double or king beds.
Baths: 4 private shower/ toilets.
Vegetarian: Cook available at extra charge, can prepare vegetarian food.

Complimentary: Welcome cocktails & snacks. In high season, sunset & margueritas.
High Season: Dec 20-Mar 31.
Rates: $85-$400 (holidays excluded).
Rsv'tns: Required.
Reserve Thru: Travel agent or call direct.
Min. Stay: Required.
Parking: Ample free on-street parking.
In-Room: Phone, AC, ceiling fans, color cable TV (optional), kitchen, fridge, coffee & tea makers, maid svc. Extra fee for laundry svc.
Exercise/Health: Massage. Nearby gym, weights, steam.
Swimming: Pool. Ocean nearby.
Sunbathing: Poolside, on

private & common sun decks, beach.
Nudity: Permitted only where it is totally out of view of neighboring villas.
Smoking: Prefer no smoking in bedrooms.
Pets: Not permitted.
Children: No.
Languages: Spanish, English.
Your Hosts: Susan & Christopher

Casa Dos Comales

Vacation Apartments in Puerto Vallarta

Casa Dos Comales offers centrally located vacation apartments, along with a guesthouse, on a hillside overlooking the town of Puerto Vallarta. The ocean is just a few blocks away. Cable TV, sun decks, maid service and a small pool are all available. On the ground floor is the display gallery of Hugh Holland, locally known for his dreamlike color photo scenes that reveal the magic of everyday life in Vallarta. José can help you, in English or Spanish, to have the best possible time with advice and directions for dining and other pleasures.

Address: Calle Aldama 274, Puerto Vallarta, JAL , Mexico **Mail To:** 2554 Lincoln Bl. #378, Marina del Rey, CA 90291, USA
Tel: (52-3) 223 2042 (Tel/Fax). Toll-free in USA: (888) 881-1822 (Tel/Fax).
E-mail: comales2@casadoscomales.com **Web:** http:// www.casadoscomales.com

Type: Apartments.
Clientele: Mostly gay & lesbian with some straight clientele
Transportation: Free pick up from airport.
To Gay Bars: 2 blocks, 1/2 mile, a 5 min walk, a 2 min drive.
Rooms: 8 rooms, 1 suite with double beds.
Baths: 9 private bath/shower/toilets.
Meals: Continental breakfast.
Dates Open: All year.
High Season: Nov 2-Apr 30.
Rates: May 1-Nov 1: US $35-US $75, Nov 2-Apr 30: US $70-US $125. Rates are per room + 15% tax.
Discounts: 15 days 10% off.
Credit Cards: MC, Visa, Discover.
Rsv'tns: Required with 50% deposit.

Reserve Thru: Travel agent or call direct.
Min. Stay: 2 nights.
Parking: Adequate on-street parking.
In-Room: AC, color cable TV, kitchen, refrigerator, coffee & tea-making facilities, maid & laundry service.
On-Premises: Laundry facilities.
Exercise/Health: Nearby gym.

Swimming: Pool on premises, ocean nearby.
Sunbathing: On roof, patio & at beach.
Smoking: Non-smoking rooms.
Pets: Permitted.
Handicap Access: No.
Children: Welcome.
Languages: Spanish, English.
Your Hosts: José.

Color Photo on Page 10

Casa Dos Comales

Vacation Apartments in Puerto Vallarta

Casa Palapa

Between the Mountains and the Moon

At *Casa Palapa* we have tried to create an exceptional Vallarta experience. Guests are immersed in a contemporary architectural masterpiece filled with original artwork. From our Grand Palapa living room, look across our secluded Infinity Pool to the tropical valley below as it disappears into the sea. From our large suites, through expansive folding glass walls opening onto a breath-taking view of the setting sun, guests enjoy a complimentary drink and hors d'oeuvres. After an evening of dining and dancing in Old Vallarta, return to a cool, candle-lit room with a turned down king-sized tropical canopy bed. For those who prefer to sleep in a more natural setting, the window walls can be left open to enjoy the soft sea breeze that flows through the room.

Our home is located just minutes from the highlights of the Old Town/ Southside. By day, enjoy shopping, sailing, the beach, diving, wonderful restaurants — or choose to stay at home by our sparkling blue pool. For those who choose to stay home, a light lunch is available upon request. Because we have only three guest suites, we view each guest as very special. We welcome you to experience *Casa Palapa* and Puerto Vallarta at its finest.

Address: #107 Paseo de Conchas Chinas, Col. Conchas Chinas, Puerto Vallarta, JAL 44380, Mexico
Tel: (52-3) 221 5561 (Tel/Fax).
E-mail: CasaPalapa@pvnet.com.mx **Web:** http://www.casapalapa.com

Type: Bed & breakfast.
Clientele: Mostly gay & lesbian with some hetero clientele
Transportation: Transportation provided to & from airport.
To Gay Bars: 3 miles, a 5 min drive.
Rooms: 3 suites with king beds.
Baths: 3 private bath/ shower/toilets.
Meals: Full breakfast.

Vegetarian: Always available.
Complimentary: Sunset hors d'oeuvres & cocktails (1 cocktail daily), tea & coffee, mints on pillows.
Dates Open: All year.
High Season: Nov-May.
Rates: US $150-US $175.
Discounts: Stay 7 days, 8th comp.
Credit Cards: MC, Visa.
Rsv'tns: Required.
Reserve Thru: Travel agent

or call direct.
Min. Stay: 3 days.
Parking: Limited, free on-street parking.
In-Room: AC, color TV, VCR, coffee & tea-making facilities, maid service.
On-Premises: TV lounge, video tape library, internet access, laundry facilities.
Exercise/Health: Jacuzzi, massage. Nearby gym, weights.
Swimming: Pool. Ocean

nearby.
Sunbathing: Poolside, on roof, at beach.
Nudity: Clothing optional sun deck.
Smoking: Non-smoking business. Non-smoking rooms available.
Pets: Not permitted.
Children: No.
Languages: Spanish, English.
Your Hosts: Shannon.

Color Photo on Page 9

Quinta Maria Cortez

WWW Gay-Friendly 50/50 ⚤

Sumptuously Romantic — Beautifully Baroque

Quinta Maria Cortez is a beautiful beachfront retreat in Puerto Vallarta, complemented by sunny terraces and spectacular views of the ocean. This "Mexaterranean Villa" is especially appealing for those who appreciate a unique ambiance along with a bit of whimsical antiquity by the sea.

The INN consists of seven suites on seven levels, rising above the white-sand beach. The large-suite/junior-suite accommodations feature eclectic European-style decor with private bath and phone. Most include a kitchenette and balcony. Mid-level at the inn is a common area with a sitting room, fireplace, terrace and palapa-roofed dining area — all with gorgeous ocean views. One level down is the swimming pool and sun terrace.

Address: 132 Calle Sagitario, Playa Conchas Chinas **Mail To:** PO Box 1799, Salt Lake City, UT 84110, USA
Tel: in USA: (801) 531-8100, (888) 640-8100, **Fax:** (801) 531-1633.
E-mail: qmc@travel-zone.com **Web:** http://www.quinta-maria.com

Type: Inn.
Clientele: 50% gay & lesbian & 50% straight clientele
Transportation: Taxi is best, or airport transfer.
To Gay Bars: 1 1/2 miles.
Rooms: 3 rooms, 4 suites with single, double, queen or king beds.
Baths: All private.
Meals: Full breakfast.

Vegetarian: Stores nearby.
Dates Open: All year.
High Season: Dec-Apr.
Rates: US $165-US $240.
Discounts: Off-season discounts, subject to availability.
Credit Cards: MC, Visa, Amex.
Rsv'tns: Required.
Reserve Thru: Travel agent or call direct.

Min. Stay: 3 nights.
Parking: Limited on-street parking.
In-Room: Telephone, ceiling fans, kitchen, refrigerator, coffee & tea-making facilities, maid service, robes, hair dryers.
Exercise/Health: Nearby gym, weights, massage.
Swimming: Pool & ocean on premises.

Sunbathing: Poolside, on roof, common sun decks & at beach.
Smoking: Permitted. Open-air hotel & rooms.
Pets: Not permitted.
Handicap Access: No.
Children: No.
Languages: Spanish, English.
Your Hosts: Jose.

Discovery Vallarta

Contact Us for the Best Selection in Puerto Vallarta — Gay Hotel, B&B & Guest House Reservations

Discovery Vallarta is Puerto Vallarta's first and foremost gay accommodations expert. It is the only free gay reservation service which books all the gay accommodations in town at no extra charge to you. We also specialize in condos, ocean view luxurious villas and apartment vacation rentals, as well as promoting and reserving all local gay and lesbian activities, cruises and tours.

Charming Puerto Vallarta is nestled between brilliant Banderas Bay and the lush tropical forests of the Sierra Madre mountains on Mexico's west coast. It is known for its handsome men, long sandy beaches, beautiful ocean and mountain views, and many fine restaurants. The South Side of Vallarta is particularly gay-friendly and is home to the majority of gay-owned establishments, the gay beach, and nightlife. I can find just about everything from a fully furnished 1-BR condo, to a luxurious gay B&B with pool, courtyard and hacienda-style décor, to select private villas with ocean and mountain views. Visit our website for complete, up-to-date information on gay Puerto Vallarta. Let *Discovery Vallarta* find the right gay-owned or gay-friendly accommodation for you.

Address: Carretera a Mismaloya 101 Esq. Abedul, Costa Linda #11, Puerto Vallarta, Jalisco 48380, Mexico
Tel: (52-3) 222 6918, **Fax:** (52-3) 222 3520.
E-mail: michaelmayo@pvnet.com.mx **Web:** http:// www.discoveryvallarta.com/guide.html **IGLTA**

Doin It Right in Puerto Vallarta

Vallarta — The Hottest, Fastest-Growing, Gay-Friendly Tropical Paradise

Vallarta is tropical, affordable, gay-friendly and CLOSE! MAGICAL Puerto Vallarta is at the same latitude as Hawaii, but 1-1/2 hours closer and more affordable. There are 1-1/2 gay beaches, 9 clubs, gay hotels/B&Bs, excursions (hot springs, snorkeling cruises), restaurants rivaling NY and SF at much lower prices, friendly locals, cobblestone streets, shopping. *Doin' It Right* is the only "family" agency with its own legit "family" land operator, Boana, for airport greets, mini-tours, air tickets, realty, etc. We have over 210 villas and condos (from moderate to the BEST), and gay-friendly hotels & B&Bs. We work ONLY with honestly gay-friendly businesses.

Mail To: 1010 University Ave C-113-741, San Diego, CA 92103
Tel: (619) 297-3642 (Tel/Fax), (800) 936-3646.
E-mail: gaypvr@aol.com **Web:** http://www.doinitright.com

Mission San Francisco Rental Homes

WWW Gay-Friendly ⚤

Your Private Casa Overlooking the Bay

Allow yourself to experience the extraordinary *Mission San Francisco* and its panoramic bay view. From your private luxurious home, you'll view the bay, tropical hillsides, margarita sunsets, nighttime city lights and palm studded village. Relax under the dome of the master bedroom suite or sun yourself on the very private rooftop terrace. *Mission San Francisco* is in the heart of the village, within walking distance of the gay beach, Mexican bazaar, supermarket, bars and restaurants. Eight luxurious homes, from two to five bedrooms each, at just $195-$580 per home, per week (4th week is free) NOTE: Also available in Mexico City, in the very heart of the Zona Rosa, is our one-bedroom rooftop apartment "Casita del Cielo," renting at only $500 per month (3 month minimum stay).

Tel: In Mexico: (52-3) 222 0651 (Tel/Fax). In USA: (916) 933-0370 (Tel/Fax).
E-mail: mpizza@madre.com **Web:** http://www.VallartaMexico.com

Type: 8 rental homes.
Clientele: Mostly hetero with a gay & lesbian following
Transportation: Airport taxi to home approximately $5.
To Gay Bars: 6 blocks or a 10-minute walk.
Rooms: 8 different homes with single, double & king beds.

Baths: Private bath/toilets.
Complimentary: Refrigerator stocked with beer & soft drinks upon arrival.
Dates Open: All year.
Rates: $195-$495 per week, per home (not per person).
Discounts: 4th week free.
Rsv'tns: Required.

Reserve Thru: Call direct.
Min. Stay: Rates are by the week.
Parking: Ample on-street parking.
In-Room: Completely furnished homes with ceiling fans, color cable TV & full kitchens.
Exercise/Health: Nearby gym.

Swimming: 6 block walk to gay beach.
Sunbathing: On private sun decks or nearby beach.
Smoking: Permitted.
Pets: Not permitted.
Handicap Access: No.
Children: Welcome.
Languages: Spanish, English.
Your Hosts: Mike.

Casa Schuck Bed & Breakfast

Mexican Highland Retreat, Just North of Mexico City

This 10,000-square-foot Spanish colonial villa, once built as a private family compound with old-world style and sophistication, is now a luxury B&B. Minutes from the village jardin and the famous Parrochia cathedral, it's a perfect resting spot convenient to horseback riding, hiking in the cactus preserve, soaking in the nearby natural hot springs, golf, shopping, galleries, and the famous Insituto Allende. Guests can live like a king — or queen — right in the middle of town and enjoy the local cafe and art-world culture that has made San Miguel a popular destination for the smart set since the 1960s.

You may not want to leave the house much though, as the rooftop deck may beckon, or you might find a cozy spot to relax in the shaded, landscaped courtyard or the heated pool. Easy access from the U.S. and Europe; fly into Bajio de Leon International airport just an hour away and *Casa Schuck* will have a car waiting to take you into town. Fax service, purified water, and deluxe private bathrooms with deluxe robes and slippers are standard. This inn is perfect for group retreats or special events (weddings) for up to 175 guests and comfortably sleeps 12 people.

Address: Garita #3, APDO #180, San Miguel de Allende, GTO CP-37700, Mexico
Tel: (52-415) 20657 (Tel/Fax) in Mexico (Mary), e-mail: casaschuck@yahoo.com. In USA: Susan, (212) 362-0561
E-mail: scordelli@yahoo.com **Web:** http://www.casaschuck.com

Type: Bed & breakfast inn.
Clientele: Mostly straight, with a gay/lesbian following
Transportation: Airport pickup with our private driver (about US $50, price varies w/ price of peso).
To Gay Bars: 10 blocks.
Rooms: 6 suites with single or king beds.
Baths: All private.
Meals: Full Mexican- or American-style breakfast.
Vegetarian: Vegetarian

restaurants in town.
Complimentary: Refreshment bar from 5pm.
Dates Open: All year.
High Season: Dec-Mar.
Rates: $98-$150 per night.
Discounts: Rental of entire property (a 6 suites) for 1 week minimum.
Rsv'tns: Required.
Reserve Thru: Travel agent or call direct.
Min. Stay: 3 days.
Parking: Adequate on-

street parking.
In-Room: Fans, electric blankets, robes/slippers, gas heaters for cold weather, maid service.
On-Premises: TV lounge, book library, board games, fax, access to computer e-mail.
Exercise/Health: Massage, facials, scrubs. Nearby gym, weights, Jacuzzi, massage, facials, scrubs.
Swimming: Pool. Nearby

pool & hot spring with naturally hot water.
Sunbathing: Poolside, on roof & private sun decks.
Smoking: Permitted only in outdoor patio areas. Rooms are ALL non-smoking.
Pets: Not permitted.
Children: Only if older than 17 yrs & with adults.
Languages: Spanish only, some limited English.
Your Hosts: Mary.

Foxwood Bed & Breakfast, The

WWW Gay/Lesbian ♂♀
Gay-Operated

Calgary's Perfect Place to Stay

Beautifully restored *Foxwood* is a charming 1910 Edwardian home in the heart of Calgary. Each sleeping room has its own style, with antique decor, plush pillow-top queen beds, fine linens, down duvets and feather pillows. Explore the city, mountain parks, or unwind in our indoor "Spa Room" — with deluxe aromatherapy Jacuzzi and large glass block shower, or treat yourself to an on-site relaxation massage. In the historic "Uptown 17 District," we're near shopping, fine dining, galleries and local nightlife.

Address: 1725-12 Street SW, Calgary, AB T2T 3N1, Canada
Tel: (403) 244-6693, **Fax:** (403) 244-4098.
E-mail: foxwoodbandb@home.com **Web:** http://www.thefoxwood.com

Type: Bed & breakfast.
Clientele: Mostly gay & lesbian with some cool straight clientele
Transportation: Car, taxi.
To Gay Bars: 10 blocks, 15 min walk, 5 min drive.
Rooms: 3 rooms w/ queen beds. 1 suite w/ queen & sofa beds.
Baths: Private & shared.
Meals: Expanded continental breakfast, hot breakfast available.

Vegetarian: On advance notice, when making reservation.
Complimentary: Coffee, tea, ice, bottled water.
Dates Open: All year.
High Season: Jun-Sept.
Rates: Low: CDN $65-$100; High: CDN $75-$145.
Credit Cards: MC, Visa.
Rsv'tns: Required.
Reserve Thru: Call direct, fax, e-mail.
Min. Stay: Holiday wknds: 2

nts. Gay Rodeo & Calgary Stampede: 3 nts, rooms billed at dble occ.
Parking: Adequate free on-street parking. Winter plug-ins.
In-Room: Color cable TV, VCR, robes, blow dryers, slippers, alarm clock.
On-Premises: TV lounge, video tape library, verandah, deck, garden, free local calls.
Exercise/Health: Jacuzzi,

relaxation massage. Bike paths, nearby gym.
Swimming: Nearby pool & river.
Sunbathing: 1 room w/ private deck.
Nudity: In hot tub area.
Smoking: Permitted on outside patio & porches only.
Pets: Not permitted.
Children: No.
Languages: English.
Your Hosts: Brent & Wayne.

Stonewall Guest House

WWW Gay/Lesbian ♂♀
Lesbian-Operated

Peace by the Pacific Forest

Let the stresses and worries of everyday life slip away in our quiet rural setting on Vancouver Island, near major recreational and tourist areas. *Stonewall Guest House's* comfortable and thoughtfully appointed guestrooms offer a range of accommodation: the Iris room has private deck and ensuite double Jacuzzi overlooking the mountains and valley meadows. The Rose Room is wheelchair accessible with private bathroom; The Lily Suite has two rooms and a soaker tub with a view and sleeps four. Our outdoor hot tub invites relaxation in the fresh country air. Horse and buggy rides are available from our door. We're 1-1/2 hours from Victoria, BC and Long Beach, a national park on miles of ocean beach.

Address: 4171 Stonewall Dr, RR 3, Ladysmith, BC , Canada
Tel: (250) 245-3346.
E-mail: relax@stonewallinn.bc.ca **Web:** http://www.stonewallinn.bc.ca

Type: Bed & breakfast 20 min outside Nanaimo.
Clientele: Gay & lesbian with 20% straight clientele
Transportation: Car best. Free pick up from airport, bus, ferry dock.
To Gay Bars: 10-16 km.
Rooms: 2 rooms, 1 suite with single or queen beds.
Baths: All private.
Meals: Full breakfast.

Vegetarian: On request & 10-20 min away.
Complimentary: Tea, coffee, arrival & pm snack.
High Season: May 1-Oct 31.
Rates: CDN $85-$150. Winter: CDN $75-$135.
Discounts: Inquire.
Credit Cards: Visa, MC.
Rsv'tns: Encouraged.
Reserve Thru: Travel agent

or call direct.
Parking: Ample free parking.
On-Premises: Meeting rms, laundry, lounge.
Exercise/Health: Jacuzzi. Nearby gym, weights, massage, hiking trails, horseback & bicycle riding.
Swimming: Nearby ocean, river, lake.
Sunbathing: On private &

common sun decks, by spa.
Nudity: Permitted by Jacuzzi/spa.
Smoking: Outside. All rooms non-smoking.
Pets: Negotiable.
Handicap Access: Yes.
Children: Welcome.
Languages: English, French, German, ASL.
Your Hosts: Connie.

IGLTA

West Wind Guest House

Gay/Lesbian ♀♂
Gay-Owned & -Operated

A Fine West Coast Experience in Any Season!

In this area of pounding surf and windswept shores is *West Wind.* Situated on two acres, enjoy the privacy of our property surrounded by lush, temperate rainforest. Our West Coast ambiance includes luxuriously appointed accommodation featuring beds with goose-down duvets, fireplaces, pine vaulted ceilings, skylights, ceiling fans and private decks, antiques and local native artworks. Boardwalks along forested paths lead to private gardens or the glass-roofed outdoor hot tub. A year-round destination, Tofino offers whale watching, kayaking, hiking, endless beaches and ancient rainforest. The area boasts fine restaurants, coffee bars and galleries to explore.

Minutes from Pacific Rim National Park and ocean beaches, it is no mystery that Tofino has magnetic appeal for nature lovers from all over the world. Here, ancient giant trees in moss-draped forests stand watch over one of the planet's last great wild areas amongst lush temperate rainforest. Situated on a major flyway for Canada geese and home to bald eagles, Tofino is a birdwatcher's paradise. We invite you to explore this majestic paradise and to capture its serenity, seclusion and solitude.

Address: 1321 Pacific Rim Hwy, Mail: Box 436, Tofino, BC V0R 2Z0, Canada
Tel: (250) 725-2224, **Fax:** (250) 725-2212.
E-mail: westwind@island.net **Web:** http://www.island.net/~westwind

Type: Private accommodations.
Clientele: Good mix of gays & lesbians
Transportation: Car is best. Complimentary aiport or bus pick up/drop off.
Rooms: 1 cottage, 1 suite, 1 oceanfront studio, queen or king beds.
Baths: Private baths.
Meals: Deluxe breakfast tray served to suite.
Vegetarian: Available on request.
Complimentary: Coffee,

teas, fruit basket, snacks. National Park passes.
Dates Open: All year.
High Season: May-Sept.
Rates: Winter from CDN $75 double, summer from CDN $85 dbl (addt'l person CDN $20).
Discounts: On extended stays in low season, inquire.
Credit Cards: MC, Visa, Amex.
Rsv'tns: Recommended.
Reserve Thru: Call direct or e-mail us.
Parking: Of course!

In-Room: VCR, video tape library, refrigerator, coffee/tea-making facilities, terry robes, hairdryer, ceiling fans. Kitchen in cottage, fireplace.
On-Premises: Video library, laundry facilities, phone.
Exercise/Health: Outdoor, glass-roofed hot tub, gym w/ weight system, hiking, beachcombing, kayaking, canoeing, golfing, surfing.
Swimming: 5 min walk to ocean & beaches. 10 min drive to nude beach (but

why leave the back deck?).
Sunbathing: On private sun decks, private garden & at nude beach.
Nudity: Clothing optional with discretion. Nude sunbathing in private garden, sun decks & hot tub.
Smoking: Permitted on outdoor deck areas only.
Pets: Sorry, not permitted. Cats in residence.
Handicap Access: No.
Children: Inquire.
Your Hosts: Dale or Jim.

Nelson House B & B

WWW Gay/Lesbian ⚢

An "Oasis" in the City

Set in a garden, **Nelson House** is a handsome, 1907 Edwardian on a quiet, residential street, only minutes' walk from the business district, clubs, shopping, Stanley Park and the beaches. Guestroom decor playfully suggests travel destinations. Will it be Bombay, Sailor's, Vienna, Hollywood or the Cabin? Our top-floor suite, with an Asian ambiance, a fireplace, deck, kitchen and Jacuzzi ensuite, is especially appealing. We are complimented on our fine breakfasts. We are remembered for fun, conversation and camaraderie. Visit awhile. Vancouver is right at your doorstep.

Address: 977 Broughton St, Vancouver, BC V6G 2A4, Canada
Tel: (604) 684-9793.
E-mail: bestinvan@lightspeed.bc.ca **Web:** http://www.bbcanada.com/ nelsonhousebnb

Type: Bed & breakfast.
Clientele: Mostly gay & lesbian with some hetero clientele
Transportation: By car or airport bus to Landmark Hotel, walk or taxi remaining 2 blocks.
To Gay Bars: Four blocks.
Rooms: 5 rooms & 1 suite with double or queen beds.
Baths: 4 private (1 with Jacuzzi), 1 shared. Guestrooms sharing bath have wash basins.
Meals: Full breakfast.
Vegetarian: Available upon request, prior notice

appreciated. Plenty of veggies nearby.
Complimentary: 2 kitchenettes stocked with tea & coffee.
Dates Open: All year, except Christmas thru New Year.
High Season: May thru mid-Oct.
Rates: Low season CDN $58-$120, high season CDN $88-$175.
Discounts: Available by week in low season.
Credit Cards: MC, Visa.
Rsv'tns: Required.
Reserve Thru: IGLTA travel

agent or call direct.
Min. Stay: 2 nights on holiday weekends only.
Parking: Ample free off-street parking.
In-Room: Maid service, some rooms with kitchens, some refrigerators. Studio has cable colour TV.
On-Premises: TV lounge, VCR, stereo, house telephone, complimentary storage of bicycles & bags.
Exercise/Health: Massage. Nearby gym, weights, Jacuzzi, sauna, steam & massage.
Swimming: Five- to ten-

minute walk to ocean beach.
Sunbathing: On beach or private sun decks.
Nudity: Directions available to excellent clothing-optional beaches.
Smoking: Permitted on front porch or in garden.
Pets: Not permitted.
Handicap Access: No.
Children: Permitted by prior arrangement, 12 or older only.
Languages: English & French.
Your Hosts: David & O'Neal.
IGLTA

O Canada House

The Home of Canada's National Anthem

"O Canada" House offers old-world charm in a beautifully restored 1897 Victorian home. Its spacious main floor contains a large entry hall with open staircase, front and rear parlors, and a large dining room. The Common Room is furnished with museum-quality lighting, furniture and artwork from the Victorian and Edwardian eras. Our five large bedrooms have comfortable sitting areas, designer linens, television, VCR, refrigerator and telephone. We're a short walking distance to bars, restaurants and shopping. Your hosts invite you to this historic home, where our national anthem, "O Canada" was written in 1909.

Address: 1114 Barclay St, Vancouver, BC V6E 1H1, Canada
Tel: (604) 688-0555, **Fax:** (604) 488-0556.
Web: http://www.ocanadahouse.com

Type: Bed & breakfast.
Clientele: Mostly straight with a gay & lesbian following
Transportation: Car is best, taxi, airport shuttle bus.
To Gay Bars: 3 blocks, 5 min walk, 3 min drive.
Rooms: 5 rooms with king or queen beds.
Baths: Private: 4 shower/toilets, 1 bath/toilet/shower.
Meals: Full breakfast.
Vegetarian: Nearby.

Complimentary: Late afternoon sherry in front parlor. Mints on pillows, cookies in room. 24 hrs: snacks, fruit juices, pop, coffee, tea.
Dates Open: All year.
High Season: May-Oct.
Rates: High: CDN $150-$220. Low CDN $125-$160.
Discounts: Extended stays, singles, AAA.
Credit Cards: MC, Visa.
Rsv'tns: Required.

Reserve Thru: Travel agent or call direct.
Min. Stay: 2 days on weekends.
Parking: Adequate free off-street parking.
In-Room: Color cable TV, VCR, telephone, refrigerator, maid service.
On-Premises: Meeting rooms, TV lounge, video tape library, fax. Front & rear parlors have fireplaces.
Exercise/Health: Nearby

gym, weights, Jacuzzi, sauna, steam, massage.
Swimming: Nearby pool, ocean, short walk to beaches.
Sunbathing: At beach.
Smoking: Permitted on front porch.
Pets: Not permitted.
Children: Children ages 12 & over welcome.
Languages: English.
Your Hosts: Mike & Jim.

Claddagh House Bed & Breakfast

Savor the Comfort, Diversity & Joy

A warm welcome and genuine hospitality await you in our 1913 heritage home. At *Claddagh House B&B,* you can step back from the pressures of everyday life and give yourself up to the relaxation and charm of an authentic Irish B&B experience. Our elegant bedrooms feature ensuite baths and Jacuzzi, and each morning we serve breakfasts to remember from homemade & homegrown foods. Centrally located, we're also near the ocean. Enjoy a quiet time or conversation with new friends on the front porch or balcony, or perhaps an evening in front of a fire. Relax in our garden or let us arrange an escape for you.

Address: 1761 Lee Ave, Victoria, BC V8R 4W7, Canada
Tel: (250) 370-2816, **Toll-free:** (877) 377-2816, **Fax:** (250) 592-0228.
E-mail: laserbrown@home.com **Web:** http://www.claddaghhouse.com

Type: Bed & breakfast.
Clientele: Mostly gay & lesbian, some hetero
Transportation: Easy access to city by car, bus, bicycle, taxi, tour companies.
To Gay Bars: 8 min drive.
Rooms: 4 rooms with double, queen or king beds.
Baths: Private bath/toilets. 2 rooms with Jacuzzi.
Meals: Hearty breakfast.

Vegetarian: Fully available.
Complimentary: Tea, coffee, fresh flowers, Belgian chocolates.
High Season: May-Sept.
Rates: CDN $99-$249.
Discounts: For groups & off-season bookings.
Credit Cards: MC, Visa, Amex.
Rsv'tns: Recommended & preferred.
Reserve Thru: E-mail or

call toll-free.
Min. Stay: 2 nights on holiday weekends.
Parking: Ample free on-street parking.
In-Room: Coffee & tea-making facilities.
On-Premises: TV lounge, front porch, garden & fireplace.
Exercise/Health: Health & recreation centre & bicycle rental 1 block. Massage,

reflexology & aromatherapy with advance notice.
Swimming: Pool 1 block, ocean beach 5-min drive.
Sunbathing: At ocean beach or in garden.
Smoking: Outdoors only.
Pets: No.
Children: Welcome.
Your Hosts: Elaine & Ken.

Oak Bay Guest House

WWW Gay-Friendly ♂♀

Our gracious old Tudor-style home, located one block from the Pacific Ocean in genteel Oak Bay, not far from the Inner Harbour, has been happily looking after generations of travelers since 1922. *Oak Bay Guest House* is easily the oldest operating B&B in Victoria. Our 11 rooms are newly decorated and have private ensuite bathrooms, and our famous 4-course breakfast is served in our dining room which seats 22 guests at seven separate tables. Relax in our Fireplace Lounge or the upper floor Sun Lounge which has a lovely aspect out onto the gardens and surrounding neighbourhood. Within easy walking distance one can golf, go whale watching, fishing, go to a sandy beach, catch a double decker bus to town, or go by yacht, stroll to the Village (a little bit of England) to nearby tea rooms or the Marina restaurant (the best!). Or, the charm of Oak Bay with its lovely gingerbread houses and leafy streets could encourage you to relax and do nothing at all. You'll love Oak Bay — we guarantee it.

Address: 1052 Newport Ave, Victoria, BC V8S 5E3, Canada
Tel: (250) 598-3812, (800) 575-3812, **Fax:** (250) 598-0369.
E-mail: OakBay@beds-breakfasts.com **Web:** http://beds-breakfasts.com

Type: Inn.
Clientele: Mostly straight clientele with a gay & lesbian following
Transportation: Car is best. Bus stop right outside.
To Gay Bars: 2 miles, 10 min drive.
Rooms: 11 rooms with single or queen beds.

Baths: All private bath/toilets.
Meals: Full breakfast.
Vegetarian: On request.
Complimentary: Tea & coffee.
Dates Open: All year.
High Season: Jun-Sept.
Rates: CDN $65-$120 winter, CDN $120-$165

summer.
Credit Cards: MC, Visa, Amex.
Rsv'tns: Required.
Reserve Thru: Call direct.
Parking: Ample free off-street & on-street parking.
On-Premises: TV lounge, coffee & tea-making facilities in guest lounge.

Swimming: Nearby pool, lake, ocean beach.
Sunbathing: At beach.
Smoking: Non-smoking guesthouse.
Pets: Not permitted.
Children: Not permitted.
Languages: English, French, Czech, German.

Ocean Wilderness

WWW Gay-Friendly ♂♀

An Elegant Jewel in a Wilderness Setting

Ocean Wilderness is set on five forested acres of oceanfront with breathtaking view of forests, the Straits of Juan de Fuca and the Olympic Mountains. Guestrooms are large and beautifully decorated, with private baths and bed canopies. A silver service of coffee is delivered to your door, and home baking makes breakfast a special treat. The hot tub (filled with ocean water), in a Japanese gazebo, is popular with weary vacationers. Book your time for a private soak. Several rooms have private soak tubs for two, overlooking the ocean. Massage, mud facials and seaweed wraps are available to rejuvenate and revitalize!

Address: 109 West Coast Rd RR#2, Sooke, BC V0S 1N0, Canada
Tel: (250) 646-2116, (800) 323-2116, **Fax:** (250) 646-2317.
E-mail: ocean@sookenet.com **Web:** http://www.sookenet.com/ocean

Type: Bed & breakfast inn with gift shop.
Clientele: Mostly straight with gay/lesbian following
Transportation: Car is best.
To Gay Bars: 30 miles.
Rooms: 9 rooms with single, queen or king beds.
Baths: All private.
Meals: Full breakfast.
Vegetarian: On prior notice or on arrival.

Complimentary: Wake up coffee, 24-hr beverage station.
Dates Open: All year.
High Season: May-Oct.
Rates: June 1-Sept 30: CDN $85-$175; Oct 1-May 30: CDN $85-$130.
Discounts: Winter: + 3 nights for cost of 2.
Credit Cards: MC, Visa.
Rsv'tns: Required in season.

Reserve Thru: Travel agent or call direct.
Parking: Off-street parking.
In-Room: Refrigerator, room & maid service.
On-Premises: Wilderness, wildlife, gardens, telephone.
Exercise/Health: Gazebo hot tub, massage, mud treatment, seaweed wraps.
Swimming: Ocean, river.
Sunbathing: On beach, patio, private sun decks.

Nudity: Permitted on private sun decks.
Smoking: Permitted outdoors only, all rooms non-smoking.
Pets: Permitted by prior arrangement.
Handicap Access: Yes, 1 room.
Children: Inquire, must be adult oriented.
Languages: English.

Free Spirits

WWW Gay/Lesbian ♀♂
Gay-Owned & -Operated

Serge and Alex invite and welcome you into the warmth colour, artistry and aroma of their "yellow house," *Free Spirits*. For your comfort, our 1904 character home includes spacious bedrooms, bath, and gourmet French breakfast. The Exotic Room features a queen-sized bed with canopy, bathroom with shower and bath-tub, TV, electric fireplace, sun deck access from your room and private entrance. La Parisienne Room has a queen-sized bed, private bathroom with shower and tub, TV, private kitchen and private entrance. La Provencale Room with single bed, has a bathroom with shower and bath-tub, TV, sun deck access from your room and private entrance. Guests' options include free hot tub access, in-house professional massage, facials, meditation room, and more.

Address: 827 Grosvenor, Winnipeg, MB R3M 0M3, Canada
Tel: (204) 475-7603 (Tel/Fax).
E-mail: sergealex@hotmail.com **Web:** http://www.aromansse.com/free-spirits.html

Type: Bed & breakfast with restaurant, bar & disco.
Clientele: Mostly gay & lesbian with some hetero clientele
Transportation: Car, bus, taxi. Pick up from airport, train.
To Gay Bars: 5 min drive, 15 min walk.
Rooms: 3 rooms with single or queen beds.
Baths: Private & shared.
Meals: Continental breakfast.
Vegetarian: Available.
Complimentary: Coffee, tea, juice.
Dates Open: All year.
Rates: CDN $65-CDN $70.
Credit Cards: MC, Visa, Amex, Eurocard.
Rsv'tns: Required.
Reserve Thru: Call direct.
Parking: Free private parking.
In-Room: Color cable TV, kitchen. Suite has refrigerator.
On-Premises: Laundry facilities.
Exercise/Health: Massage. Nearby gym, weights.
Swimming: Pool nearby.
Sunbathing: On common sun decks.
Smoking: Inquire.
Pets: Not permitted.
Children: No.
Languages: English, French.
Your Hosts: Serge & Alex.

Barrens at Bay Coastal Cottages

WWW Gay-Friendly 50/50 ♀♂
Gay-Owned & -Operated

Where Subtle Beauty Helps Restore Balance & Tranquility

Barrens at Bay Coastal Cottages are three secluded oceanfront houses on Chedabucto Bay. This very rural setting is ideal for those wanting to enjoy the outdoors, peace and quiet. The "Old House" (circa 1810) and the two newer houses reflect the traditional architecture and style of the area. All have full, equipped kitchens and are furnished with an eclectic blend of modern and antique furniture, original artwork, woodstoves, down duvets, and whirlpool bathtubs. They are privately situated on a 200-acre property with gardens, barn, hiking trails and cross-country skiing, perfect for kayaking, cycling and just relaxing.

Address: 6870 Highway #16, Halfway Cove, Guysborough County, NS , Canada
Tel: (902) 358-2157, **Fax:** (902) 358-2097.
E-mail: barrensatbay@ns.sympatico.ca **Web:** http://www3.ns.sympatico.ca/barrensatbay

Type: Cottages.
Clientele: 50% gay & lesbian & 50% hetero clientele
Transportation: Car is best.
Rooms: 3 cottages with queen beds.
Baths: All private.
Vegetarian: In some restaurants & shops.
Dates Open: All year.
High Season: Summer, fall.
Rates: $175-$190/night, $1,100-$1,300/weekly.
Credit Cards: MC, Visa.
Rsv'tns: Required.
Reserve Thru: Call direct.
Min. Stay: 2 nights.
Parking: Ample, off-street.
In-Room: Phone, ceiling fans, color TV, VCR, kitchen,
refrigerator, coffee & tea-making facilities.
On-Premises: Video tape library, books.
Exercise/Health: Hiking trails, etc.
Swimming: Ocean & lake.
Sunbathing: On private sun decks & at beach.
Smoking: Permitted outside only. Non-smoking
rooms.
Pets: Friendly dogs welcome.
Handicap Access: Yes, ramps, wide doors, rails in bathroom.
Children: Welcome.
Languages: English.
Your Hosts: Stephen, Gary.

Cedars Tent & Trailer Park

Gay/Lesbian ⚥

Experience The Cedars

Cedars Tent & Trailer Park is the only mixed campground in Ontario. We are located on 130 acres of unspoiled land between Hamilton and Guelph. Here, you will be welcomed by the friendly staff and relaxed atmosphere. The Park also offers both seasonal and overnight camping. Also, you will find an in-ground pool, laundry room, showers, games room, licensed pool bar, clubhouse and restaurant. During your stay, take advantage of our exercise room and participate in tennis, 18-hole miniature golf, baseball and volleyball.

Address: Millgrove, ON **Mail To:** PO Box 195, Millgrove, ON L0R 1V0, Canada
Tel: (905) 659-7342 or 659-3655, **Fax:** (905) 659-3316.
E-mail: cedars15@aol.com

Type: Campground with rental trailers, clubhouse, restaurant & pool bar.
Clientele: Good mix of gay men & women
Transportation: Car is best.
To Gay Bars: 15 miles to gay bars.
Baths: Shower & toilet building plus outhouses throughout.
Camping: 600 campsites with shared shower facilities.
Meals: Full-service restaurant on premises.
Dates Open: May 1-Sept 30.
Rates: CDN $14 per person per day.
Credit Cards: Visa, MC.
Reserve Thru: Call direct.
Parking: Ample free parking.
On-Premises: Clubhouse, bar, dance floor & game rooms. Dances Fri & Sat during season.
Exercise/Health: Recreational area.
Swimming: Pool.
Sunbathing: At poolside.
Smoking: Permitted in designated areas.
Pets: Permitted. Must be on leash.
Handicap Access: Yes.
Children: Welcome. Children under 12 free, parent responsible.
Languages: English & French.

Burnside

Gay-Friendly 50/50 ⚥

Burnside is an ancestral, turn-of-the-century home featuring many family heirlooms and antiques, redecorated in light, airy colors. Our host is a horticultural instructor and an authority on local and Canadian geneology. Relax amid flowers and herbs in the gardens overlooking Lake Victoria. We are a mere 12 minutes' walk from the Stratford, Avon and Tom Patterson theatres and a short walk from interesting shops and good restaurants. Nearby is the Avon Trail, part of a network of trails enabling one to walk from London, Ontario to Niagara Falls. We will pick up guests at the train or bus stations.

Address: 139 William St, Stratford, ON N5A 4X9, Canada
Tel: (519) 271-7076, **Fax:** (519) 271-0265
E-mail: lwilker@burnside.on.ca **Web:** http://www.burnside.on.ca

Type: Bed & breakfast.
Clientele: 50% gay & lesbian & 50% hetero clientele
Transportation: Car is best. Free pick up from train & bus station. Use Stratford Airporter from airport to our front door.
To Gay Bars: 5-minute walk to gay/lesbian bar (Down the Street Bar & Cafe).
Rooms: 4 rooms with single/twin, double or king beds.
Baths: Shared: 1 full bath, 2 bathtubs, 2 showers & 1 toilet room.
Meals: Full or expanded continental breakfast.
Vegetarian: Cater to special diets.
Complimentary: Ice provided.
Dates Open: All year.
High Season: July & Aug.
Rates: Student CDN $25, single CDN $50, twin & double CDN $70, king CDN $80.
Discounts: For stays of over 3 nights.
Rsv'tns: Preferred.
Reserve Thru: Call direct.
Min. Stay: 2 nights on July & Aug weekends.
Parking: Adequate free off-street parking.
In-Room: Central AC/heat, refrigerator.
On-Premises: Private dining room, TV lounge with color cable TV, spacious gardens.
Swimming: Lions Club pool 1/2 block, YMCA pool 3 blocks.
Sunbathing: At Grand Bend Beach & Shakespeare Conservation Park.
Smoking: Permitted outside.
Pets: Not permitted.
Handicap Access: No.
Children: Permitted but not encouraged during festival season (May-Oct).
Languages: English.
Your Hosts: Les.

Cawthra Square B & B Inns

Living in Style

Edwardian elegance or Victorian splendor, you choose. Two magnificent historic retreats in the heart of Toronto's vibrant gay village. Relax in an elegant parlour. Enjoy the fireplace, grand piano and views that look onto a quiet, tree-shaded street or into our carefully tended gardens. *Cawthra Square B&B Inns (Great Inns of Toronto)* offer spacious, traditionally furnished guest rooms with such amenities as private terraces, fireplaces and writing desks, cotton bedding and down duvets. An expanded continental breakfast is served in our beautiful breakfast room.

The entire city and all of its attractions are quickly and easily accessible via the nearby subway. A few steps across the adjacent park you will find the most inviting array of shops, restaurants, cafes & nightclubs that Toronto has to offer. The city's theatres, museums and galleries are almost at your doorstep. No matter what you do, you are certain to enjoy yourself in this enchanting atmosphere with all the comforts of home. We invite you to compare!

Address: 10 Cawthra Square, (& 512 Jarvis Street), Toronto, ON M4Y 1K8, Canada
Tel: (416) 966-3074, (800) 259-5474, **Fax:** (416) 966-4494.
E-mail: host@cawthra.com **Web:** http://www.cawthra.com

Type: B&B & inn.
Clientele: Gay & lesbian business traveler focused, with some straight clientele
Transportation: Airport bus to subway. Readily accessible by all means of transport. Reduced rate limo available.
To Gay Bars: 2 blocks.
Rooms: 18 rooms & suites, single, twin, queen beds.
Baths: Some shared; mostly ensuites.
Meals: Expanded continental.
Vegetarian: Excellent vegetarian restaurants &

supplies within 2 blocks.
Complimentary: Tea & coffee, juices & snacks all day.
High Season: May-Jan.
Rates: CDN $79-CDN $358.
Discounts: Weekly, monthly & frequent-visitor discounts.
Credit Cards: MC, Visa, Amex, Diners Club.
Rsv'tns: Credit card required for confirmed reservation.
Reserve Thru: Prefer call direct, or will work with your travel agent. Book on-line

secure server.
Min. Stay: 2-3 days on weekends.
Parking: Ample underground parking available.
In-Room: Color TV, VCR, telephones with voice mail & data-port, writing desk, ceiling fans, AC.
On-Premises: Meeting rooms, business service (complete home office: access to Internet, fax, PC, copier, etc.), laundry facilities.
Exercise/Health: Jacuzzi & massage services. Access

to nearby gym with weights, sauna, steam, massage, bike & running trails.
Swimming: Nearby pools & lake.
Sunbathing: On private & common sun decks, patio, garden.
Smoking: Strictly non-smoking inside. Permitted outdoors (w/ doors closed).
Pets: Kennel nearby. Resident dogs. Not in rooms.
Children: No.
Languages: English, ASL.
Your Hosts: Christopher, Frank, Ric.

Chicago House Bed & Breakfast

WWW Gay/Lesbian ⚥
Gay-Owned & -Operated

Your Tranquil Refuge in the Heart of Downtown Toronto!

Your hosts Riko and Dennis invite you to share the pleasure of living in *Chicago House Bed & Breakfast*, a restored Edwardian house, with charming decor and luxurious up-to-date amenities. The home features original leaded glass windows, ornamental plasterwork, fireplaces and other graces of period homes. Many of the furnishings are fine antiques. The amenities, including the cheerful modern kitchen, are all up-to-date and provide you with the best of modern conveniences.

Our city is safe and pleasant to stroll through night and day. We are within walking distance of excellent dining, fine shopping, two universities, museums and galleries, the financial district and the theatre district. Timely and frequent public transit runs 24 hours a day, stopping within a block of the house. We are half an hour from the airport by limousine.

Address: 37 Dundonald St., Toronto, ON M4Y 1K3, Canada
Tel: (416) 944-2919, **Fax:** (416) 922-0495.
E-mail: guningle@chicagohousetoronto.com **Web:** http://www.chicagohousetoronto.com

Type: Bed & breakfast.
Clientele: Mostly gay & lesbian with some hetero clientele
Transportation: Taxi, limo.
To Gay Bars: 1 block.
Rooms: 3 rooms, 1 suite with queen beds.
Baths: 1 private & 2 shared bath/shower/toilets.
Meals: Expanded

continental breakfast.
Complimentary: Coffee, tea, juices, soda.
Dates Open: All year.
High Season: Apr-Oct.
Rates: High: 100-140; low: 75-95.
Credit Cards: MC, Visa.
Rsv'tns: Required.
Reserve Thru: Travel agent or call direct.

Min. Stay: 2 nights.
Parking: Ample, pay parking.
In-Room: AC, color cable TV, VCR.
On-Premises: Meeting rooms, video tape library.
Exercise/Health: Nearby gym, weights, Jacuzzi, massage.
Swimming: Nearby pool,

lake.
Sunbathing: On common sun decks, at beach.
Smoking: Non-smoking house.
Pets: Not permitted.
Handicap Access: Wide doors.
Children: No.
Languages: English.
Your Hosts: Dennis, Riko.

Aberdeen Guest House

Ideal for Couples

In the heart of Toronto's Cabbage Town, in a neighborhood of parks and tree-lined streets, is *Aberdeen House*. Our spacious rooms contain queen-sized beds, television, ceiling fans, central air-conditioning and bathrobes, and a beautifully appointed, spacious bath is shared. Continental breakfast is served weekdays, and weekends a full, hot breakfast is served in the dining room. Our "Secret Garden" with its bright blossoms, patio table and glowing lanterns makes warm city nights and hot afternoons peaceful and enjoyable. Cafes and restaurants are just around the corner and Yonge St. is within easy walking distance.

Address: 52 Aberdeen Ave, Toronto, ON M4X 1A2, Canada
Tel: (416) 922-8697, **Fax:** (416) 922-5011.
E-mail: aberinn@interlog.com **Web:** http://www.interlog.com/~aberinn

Type: Bed & breakfast guesthouse.
Clientele: 50% gay & lesbian & 50% hetero clientele
To Gay Bars: 5-min walk to Gay Village.
Rooms: 4 rooms with twin or queen beds.

Baths: Shared.
Meals: Breakfast.
Vegetarian: Available on request.
Dates Open: All year.
High Season: Jun-Oct.
Rates: Single $70-$90, double $90-$225 (includes parking, breakfast, taxes).

Credit Cards: MC, Visa, Amex.
Rsv'tns: Requested.
Min. Stay: 2 nights in high season & holidays.
Parking: Included.
In-Room: AC, ceiling fans, TV, keyed security.
Smoking: Permitted in

designated areas.
Languages: English, Japanese, some French & Spanish.
Your Hosts: Gary & Richard.

Amazing Space B&B

Location, Location, Location!

Our home, located right downtown, is the oldest Toronto gay and lesbian guesthouse. Newly renovated, each room at *Amazing Space B&B* has a different personality, and all are cozy, comfortable and non-smoking, with air conditioning, television, and new quality beds. A full breakfast is also included. Relax in a casual, informal atmosphere just steps from all Toronto has to offer...theatre, nightlife, shopping, world-famous tourist attractions. For your convenience, we're close to 24-hour public transportation.

Address: 246 Sherbourne St, Toronto, ON M5A 2S1, Canada
Tel: (416) 968-2323, Reservations: (800) 205-3694, **Fax:** (416) 968-7194.
E-mail: mhughes@istar.ca

Type: Bed & breakfast guesthouse.
Clientele: Good mix of gay men & women
To Gay Bars: 2 blocks or 1/4 mile. 5 minutes by foot.
Rooms: 9 rooms.
Baths: 1 private bath only, 3 shared bath/shower/toilets.
Meals: Full breakfast.
Vegetarian: Readily available.
Dates Open: All year.

High Season: May-Sept (Victoria Day - Labour Day).
Rates: Rooms CDN $75-$110.
Credit Cards: Visa.
Rsv'tns: Recommended.
Reserve Thru: Call direct, e-mail, fax.
Min. Stay: 2 nights.
Parking: Adequate off-street parking, CDN $5 per night.
In-Room: Color cable TV,

AC, clock radios, ceiling fans & maid service.
On-Premises: Kitchen, tourist information, courtesy phone.
Exercise/Health: Gym, weights, sauna, steam, massage & Jacuzzi nearby.
Swimming: Lake Ontario (Toronto Islands), YMCA & other clubs nearby.
Sunbathing: On beach at Toronto Islands and on

house sun decks (private & common).
Nudity: Permitted on decks.
Smoking: No.
Pets: By permission.
Handicap Access: No.
Children: Not recommended.
Languages: English, French & German.

Banting House

WWW Gay/Lesbian ♀♂
Gay-Owned & -Operated

A Welcome Respite from the Urban Bustle

A gracious 1900s Edwardian house, **Banting House** is named after its most famous inhabitant, the co-developer of insulin, Frederick Grant Banting. Carefully restored to its original splendour, the home features a winding three-story oak staircase and stained-glass windows. The spacious, secluded garden with century-old trees and fountains is a welcome respite from the urban bustle. Guests will appreciate the dozens of restaurants, bars and dance clubs to be found in the gay and lesbian village, just two blocks away, as well as the many museums and theatres also within walking distance.

Address: 73 Homewood Ave, Toronto, ON M4Y 2K1, Canada
Tel: (416) 924-1458 (Tel/Fax).
E-mail: bantinghs@aol.com **Web:** http://www.bantinghouse.com

Type: Bed & breakfast. **Clientele:** Mostly gay & lesbian with some hetero clientele **Transportation:** Airport bus drops you off 2 blocks from house. **To Gay Bars:** 2 blocks, a 5 min walk. **Rooms:** 9 rooms with double or queen beds. **Baths:** 1 room ensuite. 2 shared bath/shower/toilets.

Meals: Extended continental breakfast. **Vegetarian:** Available upon request & at most local restaurants. **Complimentary:** Tea & coffee all day. **Dates Open:** All year. **High Season:** May-Sept. **Rates:** CDN $85 & up. **Discounts:** Inquire about group rates, cash & time of stay discounts.

Credit Cards: MC, Visa, debit. **Rsv'tns:** Required. **Reserve Thru:** Travel agents or call direct. **Min. Stay:** Usually required in high season. **Parking:** Ample free off-street parking. **In-Room:** AC, color cable TV, towels, soap, shampoo & conditioners, maid service. **Sunbathing:** On patio.

Smoking: No, outside sheltered areas provided. **Pets:** Notice must be provided upon reservation. Pet may not be left unattended. **Handicap Access:** No. **Children:** Welcome under parental supervision. **Languages:** English, French. **Your Hosts:** Maurice & Paul.

SOURIS • PRINCE EDWARD ISLAND

Johnson Shore Inn

WWW Gay-Friendly 50/50 ♀♂
Lesbian-Owned & -Operated

Overlooking the Gulf of St. Lawrence

A charming country inn built on a high, rocky red cliff, the **Johnson Shore Inn** offers spectacular ocean views from every window. The inn features twelve spacious guest rooms, a sitting area and private baths. Fireside meals, paired with antique and island-made furnishings create a casual elegance and a cozy appeal. Experience beautiful sunsets, hike miles of secluded walking trails, and enjoy nearby sand dunes and white sandy beaches. We're on 50 acres of ocean shoreline just off Route 16 between St. Pete's Bay and Eastpoint. We offer easy access to many island attractions, but are removed from the heavily visited tourist areas.

Address: RR #3, Route 16, Souris, PEI C0A 2B0, Canada
Tel: (902) 687-1340, (877) 510-9669, **Fax:** (902) 687-1853.
E-mail: johnsonshore@aol.com **Web:** http://www.johnsonshoreinn.com

Type: Inn with restaurant. **Clientele:** 50% gay & lesbian & 50% straight **Transportation:** Car. Pick up from airport US $25. **To Gay Bars:** 45 miles. **Rooms:** 12 rooms with single or queen beds. **Baths:** Private. **Meals:** Full breakfast. **Complimentary:** Mints on

pillow, tea & coffee, local wine for afternoon wine tasting. **High Season:** June-Sept. **Rates:** High: $195-$250. **Discounts:** Inquire. **Credit Cards:** MC, Visa. **Rsv'tns:** Strongly recommended. **Reserve Thru:** Travel agent or call direct.

Min. Stay: 2 nights in high season. **Parking:** Ample parking. **In-Room:** Phone, AC, ceiling fans, color cable TV, VCR, maid svc, computer & fax lines. **On-Premises:** Meeting rooms, video tape library. **Swimming:** Ocean. Nearby ocean, river, lake.

Sunbathing: On the grounds. **Smoking:** Inn is non-smoking. OK outside. **Pets:** Not permitted. **Handicap Access:** Yes, ramps, rails in bathroom, wide doors, low sink. **Children:** 10 years & up. **Your Hosts:** Julie & Arla.

Aux Berges

Men ♂

From the time *Aux Berges* was founded in 1967, it has acquired an atmosphere which is relatively unique among establishments having a constant flow of guests. The fact that they are from various countries and backgrounds certainly helps to make their stay with us a most pleasant and memorable experience. We regard ourselves as a large family, and would gladly welcome you to join us. Our staff are always ready to help you with any problems you might have during your stay in Montréal. The hotel went through a major renovation and redecoration in 1996-1999.

Address: 1070 rue Mackay, Montreal, QC H3G 2H1, Canada
Tel: (514) 938-9393, (800) 668-6253.
Web: http://www.auxberges.ca

Type: Hotel.
Clientele: Men only
Transportation: Shuttle bus from airport to downtown then transit to hotel, CDN $9.50. Taxi directly from airport CDN $25.
To Gay Bars: Lounge bar on premises, 1 block to gay bar.
Rooms: 42 rooms with double or queen beds.
Baths: 29 private, 13 shared.

Meals: Continental breakfast.
Dates Open: All year.
High Season: May-Oct.
Rates: CDN $85-CDN $120.
Discounts: Nov-Apr 20% off on stays of 4 nights or more.
Credit Cards: MC, Visa, Amex, Diners Club, En Route, Discover.
Rsv'tns: Recommended.
Reserve Thru: Travel agent or call direct.

Parking: Adequate on- & off-street parking.
In-Room: Color TV, in-house movies, AC, heat, telephone, laundry & maid service.
On-Premises: Kitchen facilities, TV lounge, snack bar.
Exercise/Health: Jacuzzi, dry & steam saunas.
Swimming: Pool & lake nearby.
Sunbathing: On private rooftop sun deck & garden

terrace.
Nudity: Permitted on the sun deck, terrace & sauna area.
Smoking: Non-smoking rooms available.
Pets: Small pets permitted.
Handicap Access: No.
Children: Not permitted.
Languages: French, English, Spanish.
Your Hosts: Serge.

Château Cherrier B & B

Gay/Lesbian ⚥

Experience Montreal near the Gay Village

Château Cherrier is a magnificent Tudor building decorated throughout with authentic period furniture. Large original oils of the same period adorn the sitting room and entry. Our strategic location near the gay village, restaurants, boutiques and nightlife, is further enhanced by a private parking lot, a rarity in the area. Leo and Jacques invite you to experience Montréal.

Address: 550 rue Cherrier, Montreal, QC H2L 1H3, Canada
Tel: (514) 844-0055, (800) 816-0055, **Fax:** (514) 844-8438.
E-mail: chateau.cherrier@sympatico.ca

Type: Bed & breakfast in a private home.
Clientele: Mainly gay/lesbian with some hetero clientele
Transportation: Taxi from airport 20 minutes. Limousine service (flat rate charge).
To Gay Bars: 4 blks to rue Ste-Catherine gay bars.

Rooms: 8 rooms with double & twin beds & a fourfold.
Baths: 1 private bath/toilet/shower, 2 shared showers & 4 shared toilets.
Meals: Full breakfast prepared by Chef Leo.
Complimentary: Ice cubes.
Dates Open: May-Nov.
Rates: CDN $60-$85+.

Credit Cards: MC, Visa, Amex.
Rsv'tns: Required.
Reserve Thru: Travel agent or call direct. TAC 10%.
Min. Stay: 3 nights long weekends or grand event.
Parking: Free private valet parking.
In-Room: AC, fan, color cable TV and maid service.

On-Premises: 2 living rooms, laundry service on long stays, shared refrigerator, safety box.
Smoking: Non-smoking guesthouse.
Languages: French, English, Spanish.

La Conciergerie Guest House

Your Resort in the City!

La Conciergerie is Montréal's premier guest house. Since our opening in 1985, we have gained an ever-growing popularity among travelers from Canada, the United States, Europe and Australia, winning the 1995-1999 Out & About Editor's Choice Award. The beautiful Victorian home, built in 1885, offers 17 air-conditioned rooms with queen-sized beds and duvet comforters. A complimentary European breakfast is served either in the breakfast room or on an outdoor terrace. The house is within walking distance of most major points of interest, including downtown shopping, Old Montréal, rue St.-Denis, rue Ste.-Catherine, and the East Village, with its many gay shops, restaurants and bars. We're two blocks from the Metro (subway) and there is plenty of on-street parking for those who drive.

Address: 1019 rue St.-Hubert, Montreal, QC H2L 3Y3, Canada
Tel: (514) 289-9297, **Fax:** (514) 289-0845.
Web: http://www.laconciergerie.ca

Type: Bed & breakfast.
Clientele: Mostly men with women welcome
Transportation: Airport bus to Voyageur Bus Station, then walk, or taxi directly for CDN $25. Take a cab if arriving by train.
To Gay Bars: 2 blocks to men's & women's bars.
Rooms: 17 rooms with queen beds.
Baths: 9 private. Shared: 1 bathtub, 3 showers, 3 toilets, 1 full bath.

Meals: Expanded continental breakfast.
Vegetarian: Bring your own. Vegetarian restaurants nearby.
Dates Open: All year.
High Season: Apr-Dec.
Rates: High season CDN $79-$135, low season CDN $69-$115.
Discounts: On 7-day stays in off-season.
Credit Cards: MC, Visa.
Rsv'tns: Recommended.
Reserve Thru: Call direct.

Min. Stay: 3 nights on long weekends.
Parking: Ample free on-street parking.
In-Room: Maid service & AC.
On-Premises: Meeting rooms, TV lounge, public telephone, central AC/heat, laundry facilities, private terrace, gardens, & kitchen privileges.
Exercise/Health: Jacuzzi & small gym on premises. Massage by appointment

only.
Swimming: At nearby pool.
Sunbathing: On common sun deck & roof.
Nudity: Permitted on roof & Jacuzzi.
Smoking: Permitted, except in bedrooms.
Pets: Permitted with prior notice.
Handicap Access: No.
Children: Not permitted.
Languages: French & English.
Your Hosts: Luc & Michael.

Le St. Christophe Bed & Breakfast

Men ♂

An Unexpected Canadian Treat

A Montreal-style townhouse built in 1875, *Le St-Christophe* is now fully restored to offer guests all the modern luxuries while maintaining the charm of the past. For more than ten years we have collected and filled our inn with antiques and memorabilia to enchant and delight you. There is always something new to discover at *Le St-Christophe*. We offer five spacious guest rooms: The Library, The French Canadian, The Sunrise, The Gallery and The China Room, each decorated in a different theme. Some have their own private baths, others share bathrooms, and all have color TVs and VCRs. There are two common rooms for your enjoyment. The first one is a great place for relaxing, reading or just socializing. It houses our collection of sailing ships reminiscent of the type Captain Jacques St-Pierre, the original owner of the house, once sailed. The second common room, also a nice place in which to spend some time, has a working fireplace, a small library of gay reading materials and a four-man Jacuzzi.

Full breakfast is served each morning from 9:00 am to 11:00 am in our dining room, where you can expect eggs Benedict, omelets, or Stephen's famous French toast. Guests may also use our very private clothing-optional, rooftop sun deck, with sun all day and a million stars at night. We're in the gay village, 1 block from Ste-Catharine St., where the gay bars and restaurants are situated, and walking distance to Old Montreal, rue St-Denis and China Town.

Address: 1597 St.-Christophe, Montreal, QC H2L 3W7, Canada
Tel: (514) 527-7836, **Fax:** (514) 526-6488.
Web: http://www.stchristophe.com

Type: B&B guesthouse
Clientele: Men only
Transportation: Airport bus to Central Stn bus stn. Walk 1 block. Metro to Berri if coming by train.
To Gay Bars: 1 block.
Rooms: 5 rooms with double beds.
Baths: Private & shared.
Meals: Full breakfast.
Vegetarian: Available by pre-arrangement.
Complimentary: Fruits, coffee & tea.
High Season: May-Dec.
Rates: CDN $55-$79. High season CDN $65-$95.
Discounts: On 7-day stays in off season.
Credit Cards: MC, Visa.
Rsv'tns: Required.
Reserve Thru: Call direct.
Min. Stay: 3 nights on long weekends.
Parking: Ample, free on-street parking.
In-Room: Color TV & VCR with video tapes, ceiling fans, maid service.
On-Premises: 2 lounges, private dining room, laundry service, working fireplace, breakfast deck.
Exercise/Health: Jacuzzi.
Swimming: Nearby pool.
Sunbathing: On private sun decks.
Nudity: Permitted.
Smoking: No restrictions.
Pets: No.
Children: Not permitted.
Languages: French & English.
Your Hosts: Stephen.

Chambres Au Village

Parfum d'Europe, Vie d'Amérique!

Looking for a quiet, homey and small BnB a block away from Montreal's Village? Well! You've just found it! Bruno, your host, and the two cutest cats in town, Voltaire and Bouboulle, welcome you in their home! *Chambres Au Village* puts you right in the middle of Montreal's best. We welcome travelers looking for a quiet getaway, but at the same time next door to all the action. Make reservations to visit Montreal's most intimate bed and breakfast during your next getaway! We prefer email reservations.

Address: 850 de la Gauchetière Est, Montreal, QC H2L 2N2, Canada
Tel: (514) 844-6941.
E-mail: info@chambresauvillage.com **Web:** http://
www.chambresauvillage.com

Type: Bed & breakfast.
Clientele: 50% gay & lesbian & 50% straight clientele
Transportation: Taxi from airport (flat rate).
To Gay Bars: 5 min walk.
Rooms: 2 rooms with double beds.
Baths: Shared: 1 bathtub only, 1 shower only, 2 toilets only.

Meals: Continental breakfast.
Vegetarian: Upon request.
Dates Open: All year.
High Season: Jul-Aug.
Rates: CDN $55-$75, special dates or events: CDN $80-$100.
Rsv'tns: Preferably by email.
Reserve Thru: Travel agent or call direct.

Min. Stay: 2 nights on weekends.
Parking: Adequate free on- & off-street parking.
In-Room: AC, color TV, laundry service.
On-Premises: Library, internet access, laundry facilities.
Exercise/Health: Nearby gym, weights, Jacuzzi, sauna, steam, massage.

Swimming: Pool nearby.
Smoking: Permitted in living room only.
Pets: Healthy cats only.
Handicap Access: No.
Children: No.
Languages: French, English.
Your Hosts: Bruno.

La Douillette

Women ♀

Love to Travel, but Hate to Leave Home & Cat? Borrow Mine!

La Douillette is a private home with small garden, purring cat and wonderful cuisine. The house, furnished with antiques, conveys a feeling of tranquility. Each room is supplied with local maps and information about current events, to help you enjoy this great city of Montréal to the fullest. I will also be pleased to advise you in any way that will help you enjoy your stay. In summer, relax and enjoy a home-cooked breakfast in our flower garden. Bienvenue à toutes! *Micheline*

Address: 7235 de Lorimier St, Montreal, QC H2E 2N9, Canada
Tel: (514) 376-2183.

Type: Bed & breakfast.
Clientele: Women only
Transportation: Pickup from airport when possible, CDN $20.00. Bus from airport to Bonaventure Subway Stn, then to Fabre Stn.
To Gay Bars: 15 minutes by car or metro.
Rooms: 3 rooms with

double or queen beds.
Baths: 1 shared bath/ shower/toilet.
Meals: Full breakfast.
Vegetarian: Available at all times.
Complimentary: Juices, tea, coffee.
Dates Open: All year.
High Season: Spring, summer & autumn.

Rates: CDN $40-$60.
Discounts: 5% for stays of over 4 days.
Rsv'tns: Recommended.
Reserve Thru: Call direct.
Parking: Ample on-street parking.
In-Room: Ceiling fans.
On-Premises: TV/stereo lounge, telephone, AC.
Swimming: At nearby pool

or river.
Smoking: Permitted with some restrictions.
Pets: Not permitted.
Handicap Access: No.
Children: Permitted with restrictions.
Languages: French, English, Spanish & German.
Your Hosts: Micheline.

Roy d'Carreau (King's) Guest House

WWW Gay/Lesbian ♀♂
Gay-Owned & -Operated

Your Hotel Disguised as the Comforts of Home

At the *Roy d'Carreau Guest House* you will enter into a charming, century-old row house. It's the former home of the renowned Québec artist Marcel Barbeau. Amid the comforts of each room, his prints and paintings are on display. At the advice of their clientele, the new owners, Duane and Richard, have relocated to the "Gay Village" of Montréal. They've lovingly restored their home to create an embracing, gay-positive environment. Steps away, you will discover the exciting, vibrant and sexy village. *Venez à Montréal!*

Address: 1637, rue Amherst, Montreal, QC H2L 3L4, Canada
Tel: (514) 524-2493, **Fax:** (514) 489-3148.
E-mail: kings@cam.org **Web:** http://www.cam.org/~kings

Type: Guesthouse.
Clientele: Mostly gay & lesbian, some hetero
Transportation: Taxi from Dorval Airport, or CN station.
To Gay Bars: Next door or 1 block.
Rooms: 4 rooms, 1 suite, single, queen or king beds.
Baths: Private & shared.
Meals: Expanded continental breakfast.
Vegetarian: On request.
Complimentary: Sherry in room, cocktails upon arrival, tea & coffee, truffles on pillow.
High Season: May-Oct.
Rates: Winter rates $70-$80, summer $85-$105.
Credit Cards: MC, Visa, Amex, ATM.
Rsv'tns: Required.
Reserve Thru: Travel agent or call direct.
Min. Stay: Required over major holidays only.
Parking: Ample, covered, free & pay, on- & off-street. Must reserve, $10/day.
In-Room: Telephone, AC, ceiling fans, color cable TV, VCR, kitchen, refrigerator, coffee & tea-making facilities, maid service.
On-Premises: Meeting rooms, TV lounge, laundry facilities.
Exercise/Health: Nearby gym, weights, Jacuzzi, sauna, steam, massage.
Swimming: Nearby pool.
Sunbathing: On roof.
Nudity: Permitted on rooftop terrace only.
Smoking: Permitted in back garden only. Sleeping rooms are non-smoking.
Children: Welcome.
Languages: English & French.
Your Hosts: Duane & Richard.
IGLTA

Le Coureur des Bois

WWW Gay/Lesbian ♀♂

Le Coureur des Bois is located in a historic stone house typical of the early French Canadian period. Well-maintained, the interior of the house is modern. Seven guest rooms, each with its own character, are simply furnished with emphasis on cleanliness and comfort. None of our rooms have private bath, but with 3 full baths to 7 rooms, we've yet to have anyone complain. Fresh fruit, croissants, rolls, muffins, cheeses, cereals and coffee make up the continental breakfast. What distinguishes us from the competition is our unique location within the walled city and the famous *Coureur des Bois* hospitality.

Address: 15 rue Ste.-Ursule, Quebec, QC G1R 4C7, Canada
Tel: (418) 692-1117, (800) 269-6414.

Type: Guesthouse.
Clientele: Good mix of gay men & women
Transportation: Taxi from airport or train.
To Gay Bars: 6-minute walk to gay/lesbian bars.
Rooms: 7 rooms with double or queen beds.
Baths: 3 shared.
Meals: Our continental breakfast is a hearty combination of croissants, muffins, sweet breads, fruit dishes, cereals & assorted beverages.
Vegetarian: Available with advance notice.
Dates Open: All year.
High Season: Apr-Nov.
Rates: CDN $42-$92.
Credit Cards: MC, Visa, Amex, Diners.
Rsv'tns: Recommended.
Reserve Thru: Travel agent or call direct.
Parking: 4-minute walk to underground parking for CDN $6 per day.
In-Room: Maid service.
On-Premises: TV lounge, outdoor terrace, & fridge in lounge.
Swimming: River & lake 15 minutes by car.
Sunbathing: On the terrace.
Smoking: Permitted, but not in bedrooms.
Pets: Permitted by prior arrangement.
Handicap Access: No.
Children: Not permitted.
Languages: French & English.
Your Hosts: Jean Paul & Mark.

Spring Valley Guest Ranch

www Gay-Friendly 50/50 ⚥
Gay-Owned

Enjoy bed and breakfast at the *Spring Valley Guest Ranch* in a cozy three-story, 1913-era home, or in our four-bedroom log cabin. Home-cooked evening meals are available. Outdoor showers and bathrooms are available for guests staying in the log cabin. Outdoor activities for you to enjoy include horseback riding and hiking on 1,100 acres of prairie and wooded valley. Our saloon seats 100 people and is ideal for retreats, weddings, reunions, etc. Our gay-only event, the "Ranch Rendezvous," happens annually on the August long weekend with entertainment, dances, etc. Both men and women are welcome.

Mail To: PO Box 10, Ravenscrag, SK S0N 0T0, Canada
Tel: (306) 295-4124, **Fax:** (306) 295-2611.

Type: Bed & breakfast & campground with restaurant.
Clientele: 50% gay & lesbian & 50% straight clientele
Transportation: Private auto best.
To Gay Bars: No gay bars in area.
Rooms: 4 doubles in house. 4 doubles in log cabin.
Baths: 1 shared in house. Outdoor facilities for cabin.

Camping: Unlimited space for tents, trailers, RV's but no water or electrical hook-ups.
Meals: Full breakfast for B&B guests.
Vegetarian: Fresh vegetables available, no special dishes cooked.
Dates Open: All year.
High Season: July-August.
Rates: Log cabin & house: single CDN $40, double CDN $60.

Discounts: Group discounts.
Credit Cards: MC.
Rsv'tns: Required one week in advance.
Reserve Thru: Call direct.
Parking: Ample free parking.
In-Room: Maid service, room service.
On-Premises: Laundry facilities, public telephone, TV lounge, refrigerator.
Exercise/Health:

Horseback riding on the ranch.
Sunbathing: On lawn.
Smoking: Permitted in TV lounge and veranda.
Pets: Permitted, except in restaurant & kitchen.
Handicap Access: No.
Children: Permitted but no cribs or facilities for infants.
Languages: English.
Your Hosts: Jim.

Spring Creek Campground

www Gay/Lesbian ⚥
Gay-Owned & -Operated

Meet Me in the Woods

...at *Spring Creek Campground*. Enjoy the creek and acres and acres of hiking trails. You never know when that special someone will be waiting behind one of those trees. Our camping facilities include: cabin rentals, tent sites, and RV sites with full hook-ups. Come stay with us and enjoy the in-ground pool. We also have planned activities, but don't forget our state-of-the-art sound system (BYOB) dance club. So, come as a guest and leave as a friend. Your friends, Jim & Vaughn.

Address: 163 Campground Road, Geneva, AL 36340
Tel: (334) 684-3891.
E-mail: gocamp@alaweb.com **Web:** http://www.springcreekcampground.net

Type: RV/Campground.
Clientele: Gay & lesbian. Good mix of men & women
To Gay Bars: 25 miles, a 30 minute drive.
Rooms: Cabins.
Camping: 20 sites (12 with drive-through, 18 electric, 18 water, 7 sewer). 22 tent

sites. 4 showers, 2 washrooms, dump station, on-site propane.
Dates Open: All year.
Rates: $17.50-$40.
Discounts: Weekly, monthly & seasonal rates.
Rsv'tns: Suggested on weekends.

Min. Stay: Required on holiday weekends.
Swimming: Pool & creek on premises. 1-hr drive to ocean.
Sunbathing: Poolside.
Nudity: Permitted poolside.
Smoking: No smoking in bath houses.

Pets: Permitted if leashed.
Handicap Access: Yes, ramps, wide doors, rails in bathroom.
Children: No.
Languages: English.
Your Hosts: Jim & Vaughn.

Aurora Winds B & B Resort

WWW Gay/Lesbian ⚥

Only One Thing Is Missing — YOU!

Far exceeding the standards expected by today's most discriminating traveler, the 5,200-square foot *Aurora Winds, An Exceptional B&B Resort* has five sumptuous guest suites, each with its own private bathroom on two secluded acres overlooking Anchorage. The professionally decorated and furnished B&B has an atmosphere of quiet elegance and a contemporary style with an Alaskan home ambiance. Each of the nonsmoking guest rooms is furnished with queen-sized beds, televisions, VCRs, phones, and private sitting areas. Mornings, you have your choice of breakfast selections. Either a full complement of culinary delights or an expanded continental breakfast is available in the dining room or, if you prefer, in bed.

You will be pleasantly surprised by the many amenities we offer, including a 10-person Jacuzzi where you can visit with other guests and enjoy a glass of wine following your workout in the exercise room. You might wish to relax in the sauna, play a game of billiards, watch a video on the 52-inch surround sound TV, or just curl up with your best friend in front of one of the four fireplaces.

As your hosts, we strive to provide you with all the services you may need. The *Aurora Winds* is less than 20 minutes from many local attractions. In addition to the unlimited natural wonders that you will find in Anchorage, there are also three gay bars, five bookstores, and a thriving gay community. We look forward to providing you with the special hospitality that only Alaskans can offer.

Address: 7501 Upper O'Malley, Anchorage, AK 99516
Tel: (907) 346-2533, (800) 642-9640, **Fax:** (907) 346-3192.
E-mail: awbnb@alaska.net

Type: Bed & breakfast.
Clientele: Good mix of gay men & women with some straight clientele
Transportation: Car advised. Pick up by prior arrangement.
To Gay Bars: 15 min.
Rooms: 5 suites with twin or queen beds.
Baths: All private.
Meals: Full or expanded continental breakfast.
Vegetarian: Available with advance notice.

Complimentary: Coffee, tea, sodas, mineral waters, evening nightcap.
High Season: May 15-Sept 15.
Rates: Winter $65-$125 & summer $85-$165.
Discounts: For longer stays. Inquire for others.
Credit Cards: MC, Visa, Amex.
Rsv'tns: Recommended, esp. in high season.
Reserve Thru: Travel agent or call direct.

Parking: Ample free off-street parking.
In-Room: Phone, color TV. Fireplaces in 3 rooms.
On-Premises: Meeting rms, billiards rm, TV lounge, theatre rm, laundry facilities, kitchen privileges.
Exercise/Health: Jacuzzi in 4 rms. Exercise rm, free weights, sauna, 10-person Jacuzzi.
Swimming: 3 min to Olympic indoor pool.
Sunbathing: On common

sun deck.
Nudity: Permitted in hot tub
Smoking: In designated areas only. No smoking in sleeping & common areas.
Pets: Inquire.
Handicap Access: Partial.
Children: Inquire.
Languages: English. Emergency translator available.
Your Hosts: Bill & James
IGLTA

Cheney Lake Bed & Breakfast

Gay-Friendly ♀♂

Cheney Lake Bed & Breakfast is located on Cheney Lake in a quiet residential neighborhood on the east side of Anchorage, near the Chugach Mountains. We have a great view of the mountains from the living and dining rooms, while the lake can be viewed from each bedroom and the deck. Curl up beside the fireplace, watch videos, or chat with your hosts who are long-time Alaskans and can offer numerous suggestions on how to enjoy the beauty and adventure of Anchorage and Alaska.

Address: 6333 Colgate Dr, Anchorage, AK 99504
Tel: (907) 337-4391, (888) 337-4391, **Fax:** (907) 338-1023.
E-mail: cheneybb@alaska.net **Web:** http://www.alaska.net/~cheneybb

Type: Bed & breakfast.
Clientele: Mostly straight with a 20% gay/lesbian following
Transportation: Car is best.
To Gay Bars: 10-15 minute drive to 2 bars.
Rooms: 3 rooms with king beds.
Baths: Private: 2 bath/toilet/showers, 1 shower/toilet.

Meals: Continental breakfast.
Vegetarian: Available upon request.
Complimentary: Coffee, tea, sodas, beer, wine, juice. Candy & nuts in room.
Dates Open: All year.
High Season: May 15-Sept 15.
Rates: Summer $95, winter $65.

Credit Cards: MC, Visa.
Rsv'tns: Preferred.
Reserve Thru: Call direct.
Parking: Ample free on- & off-street parking.
In-Room: Color TV, VCR, phone, ceiling fans, maid service.
On-Premises: TV lounge, video tape library, fax, copier, computer.
Exercise/Health: Nearby

gym with weights.
Smoking: Permitted on outside deck. Non-smoking home.
Pets: Not permitted.
Handicap Access: No.
Children: No.
Languages: English.
Your Hosts: Mary & Janetta.

Fairbanks Hotel

Gay-Friendly ♀♂
Woman-Owned & -Operated

The newly renovated *Fairbanks Hotel* is so charming and quaint, it feels like a bed and breakfast. Chat with the owners over your morning coffee and plan an enjoyable day of sightseeing, shopping, fishing, or just relaxing. This unique hotel is the oldest hotel in Fairbanks and has been restored in the Art Deco style. As a matter of fact, many guests say that they're reminded of South Beach when they see the hotel for the first time. Some rooms have a private bath, others share down the hall — but each room has a beautiful pedestal-style sink, brass headboard and antique dresser. Transportation to and from the airport is provided free of charge.

Address: 517 Third Ave, Fairbanks, AK
Tel: (907) 456-6411, (888) 329-4685, **Fax:** (907) 456-1792.
E-mail: fbxhotl@alaska.net **Web:** http://www.alaska.net/~fbxhotl

Type: Hotel.
Clientele: Mostly straight clientele with a gay/lesbian following
Transportation: Car, taxi or hotel suttle from airport or train station. Free pick up from airport or train.
To Gay Bars: 2 miles, a 3 min drive, a 20 min walk.
Rooms: 36 rooms with single, double or queen beds.
Baths: Private: 10 bath/

shower/toilets, 26 sinks only. Shared: 4 showers only, 7 WCs only.
Vegetarian: Walking distance to nearby restaurants & grocery store.
Complimentary: Morning coffee & tea.
Dates Open: All year.
High Season: Jun-Aug.
Rates: Summer $60-$89, winter $40-$59.
Discounts: AAA, in winter only.

Credit Cards: MC, Visa, Discover, Amex.
Rsv'tns: Highly recommended in summer season.
Reserve Thru: Travel agent or call direct.
Parking: Limited on-street pay parking.
In-Room: Free telephone, color cable TV, maid service.
On-Premises: TV lounge.
Sunbathing: Not too common in AK, but we do

have a private fenced-in area!
Smoking: Smoking & non-smoking rooms available.
Pets: Not permitted.
Handicap Access: No.
Children: No.
Languages: English, Spanish.
Your Hosts: Doris & Theresa.

Billie's Backpackers Hostel

Gay-Friendly ♂

The Great Gathering Place

Billie's Backpackers Hostel, started about ten years ago in a little tool shed in the garden, has since grown into a full-service hostel with 20 beds. But it is more than a typical hostel — here, our visitors find a relaxing, informal family-run hostel that is one of the best in Alaska. Our yard is quite small, but we can handle about 20 tents, and two or three campers. We're conveniently located on bus routes, within easy access of the airport, the University of Alaska, post office, restaurants, pubs, shops, sporting goods stores, and trails. We're also near Hot Licks Ice Cream Shop which, by the way, has run every other ice cream parlor out of town. Featuring all homemade ice cream, it was founded by a professor who got so dang busy he had to retire just to keep running the shop!

In our small dining room (it seats about seven people) you can enjoy the best sourdough pancakes in town. There are common rooms where you can relax, read, surf the net, or meet a fellow traveler. We have several BBQs for your use and a sundeck where you can while away the warm Fairbanks evenings. Or, soak up some sun on a hammock out in the yard. The coffee pot is always on, and chances are good that you will get to try some of Billie's wonderful homemade bread. For a more complete information on what Billie's has to offer, explore our website and see for yourself what makes this a special place. You are sure to find lots of valuable information about both Fairbanks, and Alaska.

Address: 2895 Mack Road, Fairbanks, AK
Tel: (907) 479-2034, (800) 236-5350, **Fax:** (907) 457-2034.
E-mail: akbillie@aol.com **Web:** http://www.alaskahostel.com

Type: Hostel, RV/ Campground, cottage, B&B, inn.
Clientele: Mostly straight clientele with a gay male following
Transportation: City bus, Yellow Cab, or Airlink Shuttle. Ask about pick up.
To Gay Bars: 5 miles, 15 min drive.
Rooms: 5 rooms, 2 suites, 1 cottage, bunkhouse with single, double, queen or bunk beds.
Baths: Shared: 3 bath/ shower/toilets, 2 tubs only, 1 shower only.
Camping: 15 tent sites, 5 showers, 4 washrooms. No dumpstation, propane nearby.
Meals: Breakfast $5 extra, served daily.
Vegetarian: Anytime, with any meal, just ask.
Complimentary: Coffee, cocoa, tea, homemade bread, cheese.
Dates Open: All year.
High Season: Jun 1-Aug 15.

Rates: $18-$90.
Rsv'tns: Walk-ins welcome, if space available. Call ahead for large groups. Cancellation: 24-hr advance notice, please.
Min. Stay: 3-5 days.
Parking: Limited off-street parking.
In-Room: Kitchen, refrigerator, coffee & tea-making facilities.
On-Premises: Meeting rooms, TV lounge, brochure racks, video tape library, large yard, BBQs, picnic tables.
Exercise/Health: Volleyball, massage.
Swimming: Pool nearby.
Sunbathing: On common sun decks, patio.
Smoking: Permitted outside only.
Pets: Not permitted.
Handicap Access: Yes, wide doors.
Children: No.
Languages: English.
Your Hosts: Billie, Art.

Hotel Monte Vista

WWW Gay-Friendly ⚧

Experience Yesteryear

Located on what was once the well-known Route 66, the *Hotel Monte Vista* has been a social and business center for Flagstaff since its inception in 1927. Today the hotel has been restored to its original splendor with antique reproductions, ceiling fans, brass, and plush carpeting. The renovation has created a unique atmosphere designed to make your stay a pleasant one. Notables including Clark Gable, John Wayne, Walter Brennan, Jane Russell, Spencer Tracey, Carol Lombard and Gary Cooper have, in years gone by, enjoyed the ambiance and comforts of Flagstaff's finest full-service hotel.

Address: 100 North San Francisco St, Flagstaff, AZ 86001
Tel: (520) 779-6971, (800) 545-3068, **Fax:** (520) 779-2904.
Web: http://www.hotelmontevista.com

Type: Hotel with restaurant, bar & shops.
Clientele: Mostly straight clientele with a gay & lesbian following
Transportation: Car is best. Free pick up from train. 2 blocks from Amtrak, 1 mile from Greyhound & 3 miles from airport.
To Gay Bars: 2 blocks.
Rooms: 50 rooms with single, double, queen, king or bunk beds.
Baths: Private & shared.
Meals: Many restaurants walking distance of hotel.
Dates Open: All year.
High Season: May-Oct.
Rates: $40-$120.
Discounts: AAA, AARP.
Credit Cards: MC, Visa, Amex, Discover.
Rsv'tns: Required, if possible. Walk-ins are welcome.

Reserve Thru: Travel agent or call direct.
Parking: Adequate free off-street & on-street parking. We have our own lot, pass required.
In-Room: Color cable TV, telephone, ceiling fans & maid service.
On-Premises: Fax, copier, laundry facilities, cocktail lounge with music.
Exercise/Health: Body wrap spa services.
Swimming: 15 miles to Oak Creek.
Smoking: Permitted inside some of the rooms.
Pets: Permitted. Pet deposit required.
Handicap Access: No.
Children: Welcome.
Languages: English, Spanish.

Casa De Mis Padres

WWW Men ♂
Gay-Owned & -Operated

Your Oasis in the Desert

A private and exclusive resort-like retreat, *Casa De Mis Padres* is an oasis in the Arizona Desert. This 8,000 square foot Santa Barbara-style home is surrounded by mature palm trees, fragrant citrus and lawn areas. The pool garden features an outdoor fireplace and shower, Mexican paver patios, and manicured lawn areas. The pool is heated in cooler months for evening swims by firelight.

The Pool Casita includes two king suites, full kitchen with separate dining and living rooms that open to the pool patio, barbeques and outside wet bar. The two-room Library Suite features a home theatre system, extensive video library (available to all guests), book and magazine collection. *Casa De Mis Padres* is just two miles from Old Town Scottsdale. The business traveler is provided all the services of a hotel resort, yet our relaxed atmosphere lets you be *who you are* as if you were at home.

Address: 5965 E Orange Blossom Lane, Phoenix, AZ 85018
Tel: (480) 675-0247, **Fax:** (480) 675-9476.
E-mail: info@casadmp.com **Web:** http://www.casadmp.com

Type: Bed & breakfast in a private home.
Clientele: Men only
Transportation: Car or a short taxi drive.
To Gay Bars: 2 miles.
Rooms: 2 suites, plus casita with king beds.
Baths: All private: 2 bath/shower/toilets, 2 shower/toilets.
Meals: Expanded continental breakfast.
Complimentary: In-room tea, coffees & cold beverages.
Dates Open: All year.
High Season: Late Oct-May.
Rates: $150-$300, double occupancy.
Discounts: 5+ nts 10% off, corp. rate.
Credit Cards: MC, Visa, Amex, Discover.
Rsv'tns: Preferred.
Reserve Thru: Travel agent or call direct.
Min. Stay: 2 nights. 3 nights on holiday weekends.
Parking: Ample free off-street parking.
In-Room: Private telephones, AC, ceiling fans, color cable TV, VCR, coffee & tea-making facilities, maid service. Casita has kitchen. Library suite has refrigerator/freezer.
On-Premises: Video tape library, pool shower.
Swimming: Pool on premises, heated in cooler months.
Sunbathing: Poolside & in garden patios.
Smoking: Permitted outside. All non-smoking rooms.
Pets: Not permitted.
Children: No.
Languages: English.
Your Hosts: Brian & Vic.

Color Photo on Page 12

Arizona Royal Villa

Men ♂

Enjoy Palm Springs-style accommodations in downtown Phoenix. Accommodations are available for long or short stays, ranging from one day to several months. The walled complex is totally private, with keyed entry. Rooms range from small hotel rooms to furnished one-bedroom apartments. The pool and Jacuzzi are open year-round. *The Arizona Royal Villa* is popular, because of the amenities, competitive rates and strategic location to all the bars. Book early to avoid disappointment! Day passes available for $10.

Address: 1110 E Turney Ave, Phoenix, AZ 85014
Tel: (602) 266-6883 (Tel/Fax), toll free: (888) 266-6884.
E-mail: azroyalvil@aol.com **Web:** http://www.royalvilla.com

Type: Bed & breakfast motel.
Clientele: Men only
Transportation: Car is best. $10 for pick up from airport.
To Gay Bars: Walking distance to 1 local gay bar & restaurant, others 1 mile away.
Rooms: 3 rooms, 3 suites & 3 apartments with queen beds.

Baths: All private.
Meals: Continental breakfast.
Dates Open: All year.
High Season: Oct-May.
Rates: High season (Oct-May) from $59.95. Low season (Jun-Sep) from $45.95.
Credit Cards: MC, Visa, Amex.
Rsv'tns: Recommended.
Reserve Thru: Travel agent

or call direct.
Min. Stay: Two nights on holiday weekends.
Parking: Adequate free parking.
In-Room: Color cable TV, AC, coffee & tea-making facilities, kitchen, refrigerator.
On-Premises: Laundry facilities.
Exercise/Health: Jacuzzi, weights.

Swimming: Heated pool on premises (in season only).
Sunbathing: At poolside.
Nudity: Permitted.
Smoking: Permitted.
Pets: Not permitted.
Handicap Access: No.
Children: Not permitted.
Languages: English, some French, Italian, Spanish.

Larry's B & B

WWW Gay/Lesbian ♂

A Gay Place to Stay

At *Larry's B & B*, our large private home offers three guest rooms, with shared bath or private bath, living and family rooms, all at economical rates. Guests enjoy the beauty of Phoenix's weather in the privacy of our pool area, surrounded by walls and tropical vegetation. We are near both golf and tennis facilities. Full breakfast is provided; Lunch and dinner available by arrangement at additional cost.

Address: 502 W Claremont Ave, Phoenix, AZ 85013-1309
Tel: (602) 249-2974.

Type: A true bed & breakfast in our home.
Clientele: Mostly gay men with women welcome. Some straight clientele such as relatives or friends
To Gay Bars: 5 minutes to gay/lesbian bars.
Rooms: 3 rooms with queen or king beds.
Baths: 3/4 private bath, 1 shared full bath.
Meals: Full breakfast.

Lunch & dinner by arrangement with charge.
Vegetarian: Upon request.
Complimentary: Tea, coffee & soft drinks.
Dates Open: All year.
High Season: Jan-Apr.
Rates: Singles $50-$60 daily, $305-$370 weekly. Doubles $60-$70 daily, $370-$435 weekly. No seasonal rate change.
Discounts: $5 off 3rd to 6th

day per room on daily rate.
Rsv'tns: Preferred.
Reserve Thru: Call direct.
Parking: Ample free off-street parking.
In-Room: Telephone, color TV & ceiling fans, AC.
On-Premises: Central AC/ heat, laundry facilities & use of refrigerators.
Exercise/Health: Jacuzzi.
Swimming: Pool, solar heated.

Sunbathing: At poolside, on patio & common sun decks.
Nudity: Permitted.
Smoking: Permitted on outside patio only.
Pets: Yes, $5 charge per night.
Handicap Access: Yes.
Children: Permitted.
Languages: English, some Spanish.
Your Hosts: Larry & Ken.

Yum Yum Tree Guest House

Gay/Lesbian ⚥
Gay-Owned & -Operated

Secluded Intimacy in Historic Central Phoenix

The **Yum Yum Tree Guest House,** located in the historic Willo neighborhood, provides a relaxing environment and luxury accommodations within a quiet residential setting. Originally built as the historic Fairhope School in the 1920's, the building was purchased by a prominent Phoenix philanthropist who remodeled and expanded the property for residential use during the 1940's. Its Spanish Mission design provides spacious covered patios surrounding a lush courtyard featuring fruit trees and a barbecue for our guests' enjoyment. Relax by our heated pool and enjoy complimentary continental breakfast in the Cabana. Whatever your desire, be it relaxing by the fountains, strolling through the historic neighborhoods, or just enjoying intimate privacy, your stay promises to be a pleasant one.

Address: 90 W Virginia Ave, Phoenix, AZ 85003
Tel: (602) 265-2590.

Type: Guesthouse.
Clientele: Mostly gay & lesbian with some straight clientele
Transportation: Car is best.
To Gay Bars: 1-2 mi, 5 min drive.
Rooms: 5 suites with queen beds.

Baths: 5 private shower/toilets.
Meals: Continental breakfast.
Dates Open: All year.
High Season: Oct-May.
Rates: In-season $109-$129, off-season $99-$119.
Discounts: Weekly, monthly, corporate.

Credit Cards: MC, Visa, Amex.
Rsv'tns: Required.
Reserve Thru: Call direct.
Min. Stay: 2 nights on weekends.
Parking: Ample free off-street parking.
In-Room: Phone, AC, color TV, fridge, coffee & tea-

making facilities, maid svc.
Swimming: Pool.
Sunbathing: Poolside.
Smoking: Smoking outside. All non-smoking rooms.
Pets: Not permitted.
Children: No.
Languages: English.
Your Hosts: Tracy & Tom.

CASA TiiGAVA B&B, Sedona Experience

Gay/Lesbian ⚥
Gay-Owned & -Operated

Opening Soon: Bed, Breakfast & Sedona Experience

Experience Sedona's magnificent red rock formations from the enchanted environment of *CASA TiiGAVA*. Derived from the Native American Yavapai and Havasupai languages, our name translates as *"house to gather,"* and that's exactly what we invite you to do in this newly constructed luxury six-room bed and breakfast. "Casual yet chic" describes the eclectic Southwest decor, as the comforting hues of Sedona wilderness are captured indoors in each individually decorated room. Rest and rejuvenate in style with features such as Jacuzzi tubs, showers, dual sinks, fireplaces, hand-crafted beds, TV/VCRs, refrigerators, personal bathrobes and exquisite views. In-room or creekside massages are available on site, and day spa activities are nearby. Gourmet breakfasts are served daily.

Address: 840 Jordan Rd, Sedona, AZ 86339
Tel: (520) 203-0102, (888) Tii-GAVA (844-4282), **Fax:** (520) 204-1075.
E-mail: tiigava@sedona.net

Type: Bed & breakfast inn with boutique & restaurant.
Clientele: Mainly gay & lesbian clientele, straight-friendly.
Transportation: Car is best. Sedona shuttle from Phoenix airport approx $35.

To Gay Bars: 2 hours to Phoenix gay bars.
Rooms: 6 rooms with queen or king beds.
Baths: 6 private bath/shower/toilets.
Meals: Full breakfast.
Vegetarian: Available on

request at time of reservation. Restaurants nearby.
Complimentary: Soft drinks, coffee, tea, afternoon snack.
Dates Open: All year.
Rates: $135-$250.

Credit Cards: Visa, MC.
Min. Stay: 2 nights with a Saturday stayover.
Parking: Free/handicap.
Smoking: Smoke-free environment.
Handicap Access: Yes.

Cozy Cactus Bed and Breakfast

You've Found Your High-Desert Hideaway

Just beyond your door at *Cozy Cactus Bed and Breakfast* you can hike trails winding among some of Sedona's world-famous red rock formations. World-class golf courses, excellent restaurants and outlet shopping are nearby, as are galleries, ancient Native American ruins and a thriving former ghost town. Four rooms in this ranch-style home are furnished on Southwestern themes. The fifth boasts a Victorian flair. Each pair of Southwest rooms shares a sitting room, with fireplace, TV/VCR, and a kitchen with refrigerator and microwave. Sumptuous breakfasts are served in the great room where you can watch the sun warm Bell Rock. We pride ourselves in creating home-baked goodies and delicious, healthy meals with a Southwest flair.

Address: 80 Canyon Circle Dr, Sedona, AZ 86351
Tel: (520) 284-0082, (800) 788-2082, **Fax:** (520) 284-4210.
E-mail: cozycactus@sedona.net **Web:** http://www.cozycactus.com

Type: Bed & breakfast.
Clientele: Mostly straight clientele with a gay & lesbian following
Transportation: Car is best.
Rooms: 5 rooms with single, queen or king beds.
Baths: 5 private bath/shower/toilets.
Meals: Full breakfast.

Vegetarian: On request for breakfast & at restaurants.
Dates Open: All year.
High Season: Mar-May & Sept-Oct.
Rates: Low: $85-$115, high: $ 95-$125.
Discounts: AAA & Senior discount 10%. Canadians 20%.
Credit Cards: MC, Visa,

Amex.
Reserve Thru: Travel agent or call direct.
Parking: Adequate free off-street parking.
In-Room: AC, maid service.
On-Premises: Meeting rooms, TV lounge, video tape library, fireplaces.
Exercise/Health: Nearby gym, Jacuzzi.

Swimming: Nearby pool & creek.
Smoking: Permitted outside. All rooms are non-smoking.
Pets: Not permitted.
Children: Welcome.
Languages: English, some French.
Your Hosts: Linda & Bruce.

Little Brown Cocker Cottage, The

Beautiful Sedona, known for its incomparable red rock formations, clean air, fine restaurants, great hiking, and fabulous Oak Creek is home to *The "Little Brown Cocker" Cottage.* Quiet and clean, this private, fully appointed studio/guesthouse includes features such as kitchenette, washer/dryer, fireplace, patio, queen bed, double-sized futon and full bath. Our studio is best suited for two people and is a charming and economical alternative to hotel/motel living. The washer/dryer is a definite "plus" since Sedona does not have a laundromat. We do not offer maid service or food. The owners live next door and are available to help you with your needs, and restaurants, shopping and trails are close to the studio. We offer a friendly, relaxed, open environment and would enjoy having you as our guests. There is a two-night minimum and, PLEASE, no smoking indoors.

Address: 350 Arroyo Pinon Dr, Sedona, AZ
Tel: (520) 203-0656.
E-mail: kml5@dana.ucc.nau.edu

Type: Guesthouse.
Clientele: 50% gay & lesbian & 50% straight clientele
Transportation: Car is best, or fly to Phoenix & shuttle to Sedona.
To Gay Bars: 100 miles.
Rooms: 1 studio guesthouse with double futon or queen bed.

Baths: 1 private bath/shower/toilet.
Vegetarian: At local restaurants.
Dates Open: All year.
Rates: $75/night, $450/week.
Rsv'tns: Required.
Reserve Thru: Call direct.
Min. Stay: 2 nights.
Parking: Adequate free off-

street parking.
In-Room: Telephone, AC, ceiling fans, color cable TV, VCR, kitchen, refrigerator, coffee & tea-making facilities, washer & dryer.
On-Premises: Laundry facilities.
Sunbathing: On patio.
Smoking: Permitted outside only.

Pets: Permitted. Can't be left alone, must be leashed.
Handicap Access: No.
Children: No.
Languages: English.
Your Hosts: Rick & Kristine.

Paradise by the Creek B & B

Women ♀

Serenity Awaits You at Our Red Rock Hideaway

Nestled in a green valley amidst red rock canyons, our cozy ranch home sits on a quiet lane surrounded by willows and cottonwoods. You can swim in the creek or laze on its banks and watch the sun set orange on spectacular Cathedral Rock. *Paradise by the Creek's* two guest rooms with shared bath are perfect for two couples travelling together, but if it's just a getaway for the two of you, then the whole suite is yours. Wait till you see the stars in the Sedona sky!

Address: 215 Disney Lane, Sedona, AZ 86336
Tel: (520) 282-7107, **Fax:** (520) 282-3586.
E-mail: 2suns@sedona.net

Type: Bed & breakfast. **Clientele:** Mostly women with men welcome **Transportation:** Car is best. We're 2 hours north of Phoenix. **To Gay Bars:** 120 miles. None in Sedona. **Rooms:** 2 rooms with double & queen beds. **Baths:** 1 private bath/toilet/shower, 1 shared bath/shower/toilet. **Camping:** RV parking only, electric hook up only. **Meals:** Continental breakfast. **Vegetarian:** Vegetarian restaurants in Sedona township, 3 miles away. **Complimentary:** Fresh fruit, juices, pastries, cereals, milk, tea, coffee. **Dates Open:** All year. **Rates:** $85-$135. **Credit Cards:** Not accepted. **Rsv'tns:** Required. **Reserve Thru:** Call direct. **Min. Stay:** 2 nights weekends & holidays. **Parking:** Ample free off-street parking. **In-Room:** Cooler, telephone, TV, ceiling fans, refrigerator, coffee & tea-making facilities. **Exercise/Health:** Nearby massage, floats, healings, psychic readings. **Swimming:** Creek nearby. **Sunbathing:** In private garden. **Smoking:** Permitted outside, rooms are non-smoking. **Pets:** Not permitted. **Handicap Access:** Able to accommodate special needs on individual basis. **Children:** Welcome. There are pets, farm animals, creek & trees for them to explore. **Languages:** English. **Your Hosts:** Debbie.

Armory Park Guesthouse

WWW Gay-Friendly 50/50 ♀♂
Gay-Owned & -Operated

Historic District Bed & Breakfast

Situated in Tucson's Armory Park Historic Neighborhood, the *Armory Park Bed and Breakfast* consists of the owner's residence, built in 1896, with two detached guest suites. In the garden courtyard, guests are welcome to use the Jacuzzi or sit by the koi pond to relax after the day's activites. For those who enjoy animals, the two resident dogs will be glad to relax with you and make you feel welcome. An extended continental breakfast is served each morning in the butler's pantry featuring blended coffee, tea, juice, cereal, yogurt, fresh baked pastries and fresh fruit. Walking visitors can enjoy the old homes of the neighborhood and easily reach restaurants, galleries or live theater.

Address: 219 S 5th Ave, Tucson, AZ 85701
Tel: (520) 206-9252.
E-mail: armorypark@aol.com **Web:** http://www.ns4b.com/armorypark

Type: Bed & breakfast. **Clientele:** 50% gay & lesbian & 50% straight **Transportation:** Car. 2-3 blocks to train & bus. **To Gay Bars:** 10 blocks. **Rooms:** 1 room, 1 suite with queen beds. **Baths:** Private. **Meals:** Expanded continental breakfast. **Complimentary:** Sodas & juice. **Dates Open:** All year. **High Season:** Oct-May. **Rates:** $60-$110. **Discounts:** 10% on stays of 1+ wk, 10% senior discount. **Rsv'tns:** Required. **Reserve Thru:** Travel agent or call direct. **Parking:** Adequate free off-street parking. **In-Room:** Color cable TV, VCR, kitchen, fridge, coffee & tea-makers. **On-Premises:** Video tape library, laundry facilities. **Exercise/Health:** Jacuzzi. **Sunbathing:** On patio. **Nudity:** Permitted. **Smoking:** On patio. **Pets:** Not permitted. **Handicap Access:** Yes, rails in bathroom. **Children:** No. **Languages:** English, Spanish. **Your Hosts:** Jim.

Adobe Desert Vacation Rentals

WWW Gay-Friendly ♀♂

In the Heart of the Sonoran Desert

Morning in the desert... As the sun rises over the Tucson Mountains, the coyote howls, mourning doves call, quail venture out of the brush and the giant saguaro cacti loom above the desert floor. Experience such moments in the privacy of a custom-built house in the heart of the Sonoran desert. *Adobe Desert Vacation Rentals* offers unique accommodations in spectacular desert settings a short drive from Tucson... a great place for hiking, birding and viewing sunsets. Near the Arizona-Sonora Desert Museum, Old Tucson Studios and Saguaro National Park.

Mail To: PO Box 85456, Tucson, AZ 85754-5465
Tel: (520) 578-3998, **Fax:** (520) 578-1493.
E-mail: adobedes@azstarnet.com **Web:** http://www.adobedesert.com

Type: Guesthouses & rental houses.
Clientele: Mostly straight clientele with a gay/lesbian following
Transportation: Car is needed.
To Gay Bars: 18 miles, a 30 min drive.
Rooms: 2 houses with double or queen beds.
Baths: All private.
Dates Open: All year.
High Season: Dec-Apr.
Rates: Weekly $600-$1400.
Rsv'tns: Required.
Reserve Thru: Call direct.
Min. Stay: 7 days.
Parking: Ample, covered off-street parking.
In-Room: Telephone, AC, ceiling fans, kitchen, refrigerator, coffee & tea-making facilities.
On-Premises: Laundry facilities.
Exercise/Health: Jacuzzi.
Swimming: Pool.
Sunbathing: Poolside, on patio.
Nudity: Depends on property.
Smoking: No.
Pets: Depends on property.
Handicap Access: No.
Children: Welcome.
Languages: English.

Hills of Gold Bed & Breakfast

WWW Women ♀
Lesbian-Owned & -Operated

We are the Gold at the End of the Rainbow

Experience the Southwest at *Hills of Gold* in a single private suite on four acres of Sonoran desert, only 10 minutes from downtown Tucson. Hike Sabino Canyon, visit the Desert Museum, explore Kitt Peak Observatory, or relax right here. Your suite has a bedroom, sitting area, bath and private deck with mountain views. Enjoy the shared areas of our home — covered porches, hot tub, pool, gas grill and library. A hearty Southwestern or expanded continental breakfast is included, and box lunches and dinners can be arranged.

Sunsets where the mountains turn pink... Giant soldier-like Saguaro cactus... Mexican food to die for... Tucson is in a desert valley, surrounded by five mountain ranges. Its year-around sunny climate is perfect for outdoor activities like hiking, biking, golf, tennis and swimming.

Address: 3650 W. Hills of Gold, Tucson, AZ 85745
Tel: (520) 743-4229 (Tel/Fax).
E-mail: hillsgold@theriver.com

Type: Bed & breakfast.
Clientele: Women only
Transportation: Car is best.
To Gay Bars: 15 min drive.
Rooms: 1 suite with queen & sofa bed, can accommodate 4 people.
Baths: Private shower/toilet.
Meals: Full breakfast.
Vegetarian: Available by arrangement & nearby.
Complimentary: Tea, coffee, bottled water.
Dates Open: All year.
Rates: $80. 3 or more - $10 extra person fee.
Discounts: 10% discount for 5 or more nights.
Rsv'tns: Required.
Reserve Thru: Travel agent or call direct.
Min. Stay: $10 premium for single night.
Parking: Ample off-street parking.
In-Room: AC, ceiling fans, color cable TV, VCR, CD/stereo, toaster, refrigerator, coffee & tea-making facilities, microwave. Laundry service by arrangement.
On-Premises: Video tape & book libraries.
Exercise/Health: Jacuzzi, treadmill, hand weights. Massage by arrangement.
Swimming: Pool on premises.
Sunbathing: Poolside.
Nudity: Permitted poolside.
Smoking: Permitted only on private deck. Room is non-smoking.
Pets: Not permitted.
Handicap Access: No.
Children: All ages welcome, have pool toys & books for children.
Languages: English, some ASL.
Your Hosts: Terry & Melissa.

Tortuga Roja Bed & Breakfast

WWW Men ♂
Gay-Operated

Come, Share Our Mountain Views

For men only, the *Tortuga Roja Bed & Breakfast* is a 4-acre cozy retreat at the base of the Santa Catalinas, whose windows look out on an open landscape of natural high-desert vegetation. Some accommodations have fireplaces and kitchens. A bicycle and running path along the Rillito River behind our house can be followed for four miles on either side.

Near upscale shopping, dining, and hiking trails, it's also an easy drive to the university, bars and tourist attractions. Tucson has a wealth of things to do and see. The newest attraction is the nearby Kartchner Caverns, a stunning limestone cave system boasting many world-class features. Closer to central Tucson is Old Tucson Studios, the old western town that you may recognize from cowboy movies you've seen, over the years. If you visit at the right time, you may be involved in a wild west shoot-out. Catalina State Park is a scenic desert park with hiking, camping and equestrian trails. Biosphere 2, in the Santa Catalina Mountains, blends science exhibits, a college campus, a research center, restaurant, and hotel. Tours and educational programs there offer a unique experience. San Xavier Mission, built in the late 18th century, exhibits beautiful Spanish colonial architecture and colorful art in its interior. You'll find this church, also known as the "White Dove of the Desert," on the Tohono O'dham Indian Reservation.

Address: 2800 E River Rd, Tucson, AZ 85718
Tel: (520) 577-6822, (800) 467-6822.
E-mail: redtrtl@goodnet.com **Web:** http://www.goodnet.com/~redtrtl

Type: Bed & breakfast.
Clientele: Gay men only
Transportation: Car is best.
To Gay Bars: 10-minute drive.
Rooms: 2 rooms & 1 cottage with queen beds.
Baths: All private.
Meals: Expanded continental breakfast.
Dates Open: All year.

High Season: Sept-May.
Rates: $75-$105.
Discounts: For weekly & monthly stays.
Credit Cards: Discover, MC, Visa, Amex.
Rsv'tns: Often essential.
Reserve Thru: Travel agent or call direct.
Min. Stay: 2 nights on holiday weekends.
Parking: Ample free off-

street parking.
In-Room: Color cable TV, VCR, AC, ceiling fan, radio & telephone. Cottage has kitchen.
On-Premises: Video library, gas BBQ, laundry facilities, kitchen privileges.
Swimming: Pool & hot tub on premises.
Sunbathing: At poolside & on the patio.

Nudity: Permitted.
Smoking: Permitted outdoors only.
Pets: Not permitted.
Handicap Access: Limited. Not wheelchair accessible.
Children: Please inquire.
Languages: English.
Your Hosts: Carl.
IGLTA

Color Photo on Page 13

Casa Alegre Bed & Breakfast Inn

WWW Gay-Friendly ♀♂

Warmth & Happiness of a Bygone Era

Our charming, 1915 craftsman-style bungalow is just minutes from the University of Arizona and downtown Tucson. At *Casa Alegre,* each guest room has private bath and TV, and its decor reflects an aspect of Tucson's history, such as the mining industry or the Indian Nation. The Arizona sitting room opens onto the inn's serene patio and pool area. A scrumptious full breakfast is served in the sun room, formal dining room or outside on the patio. Shopping, dining and entertainment are all within walking distance.

Address: 316 East Speedway Blvd, Tucson, AZ 85705
Tel: (520) 628-1800, (800) 628-5654, **Fax:** (520) 792-1880.
E-mail: alegre123@aol.com **Web:** http://www.bbonline.com/az/alegre

Type: Bed & breakfast.
Clientele: Mostly straight with a gay & lesbian following
Transportation: Car is best. Shuttle service from airport $15 maximum.
To Gay Bars: 3 blocks.
Rooms: 5 rooms with queen or king beds.
Baths: All private bath/ toilets.
Meals: Full breakfast.
Vegetarian: Available upon request.

Complimentary: Cool soft drinks & snacks by pool in summer, tea & goodies in front of fireplace in winter.
Dates Open: All year.
High Season: Sept 1-May 31.
Rates: Summer $60-$75, rest of year $80-$125.
Discounts: 10% senior, corporate, week or longer stays.
Credit Cards: MC, Visa, Discover.
Rsv'tns: Preferred.

Reserve Thru: Travel agent or call direct.
Parking: Ample free on-street & off-street covered parking.
In-Room: AC, ceiling fans, maid service.
On-Premises: Meeting rooms, guests' refrigerator on covered patio.
Exercise/Health: Spa on premises. Nearby gym, weights, sauna, steam & massage.
Swimming: Pool on premises.
Sunbathing: At poolside or on patio.
Smoking: Permitted outside only.
Pets: No facilities available for pets.
Handicap Access: No.
Children: Permitted under close supervision of parents because of antiques & pool.
Languages: English.

Milagras B & B

WWW Gay-Friendly 50/50 ♀♂
Lesbian-Owned & -Operated

A Beautiful B&B in the Heart of the Sonoran Desert

Come to *Milagras B&B,* a lovely two-room, natural adobe guesthouse with private bath. One side of this oasis opens to a beautiful, interior, arched courtyard filled with native plants, where you will enjoy breakfast next to a calming, bubbling fountain. The other side provides a private patio with spectacular mountain views. Our guest suite contains two rooms, one with a queen bed, the other with a futon couch that opens to another double bed. On over six acres of pristine, Sonoran Desert wilderness, we're surrounded by stately saguaro cacti, prickly pear, mesquite and palo verde trees. Nights, coyotes serenade you as you sit in the hot tub, looking at a sky full of stars.

Address: 11185 W. Calle Pima, Tucson, AZ 85743
Tel: (520) 578-8577.
E-mail: milagras@sprintmail.com **Web:** http://home.sprintmail.com/ ~milagras/

Type: Guesthouse.
Clientele: 50% gay & lesbian & 50% straight
Transportation: Car.
To Gay Bars: 20 miles.
Rooms: 2 rooms w/ 2 beds.
Baths: 1 private.
Meals: Expanded continental breakfast.
Complimentary: Coffee

beans, grinder, pot. Teas, fruit basket, snacks, micro popcorn. Soda & herb tea w/ juice in fridge.
High Season: Oct-Apr.
Rates: $75-$100/night.
Discounts: 7th night free.
Rsv'tns: Required.
Reserve Thru: Call direct.
Min. Stay: 2 nights.

Parking: Ample free parking on property.
In-Room: Phone, AC, ceiling fans, color cable TV, VCR, kitchenette.
On-Premises: Laundry facilites, video tape library (not X-rated), BBQ grill.
Exercise/Health: Hot tub, rowing machine, exercise

bike, bicycle.
Sunbathing: On patio.
Nudity: In hot tub only.
Smoking: Permitted only on guest patio with doors to guesthouse closed.
Pets: Not permitted.
Handicap Access: Yes.
Your Hosts: Helen & Vivian.

Montecito House

Mom, I'm Home!

Experience the friendly, relaxed atmosphere of *Montecito House,* my home, not a business. My B & B is a hobby, a way to meet people from around the world. Discussions at breakfast over fresh grapefruit juice from the tree in my yard are usual. Many guests meet here once and establish friendships that grow each year. Returning guests often mention the feeling of coming home again.

Mail To: PO Box 42352, Tucson, AZ 85733
Tel: (520) 795-7592.

Type: Bed & breakfast. **Clientele:** Mostly lesbian with men welcome. Some straight clientele. **Transportation:** Car is best, pick up from airport or bus available, prices vary. **To Gay Bars:** 2 miles. **Rooms:** 2 rooms with double beds. **Baths:** 1 private bath/toilet & 1 shared bath/shower/ toilet. **Camping:** RV parking with electric only, share inside bathroom. **Meals:** Continental breakfast. **Vegetarian:** Available upon prior arrangement. **Complimentary:** Tea, soda, coffee, juices, fresh fruit, nuts, crackers. **Dates Open:** All year. **High Season:** February. **Rates:** Summer $35-$40, winter $40-$45. **Discounts:** On weekly rates with reservation. **Rsv'tns:** Recommended. **Reserve Thru:** Call direct. **Min. Stay:** $10 surcharge for 1-night stay. **Parking:** Ample, free off-street & on-street parking. **In-Room:** Color TV, AC, telephone, maid service. **On-Premises:** TV lounge, pinball, laundry facilities, use of kitchen if pre-arranged. **Exercise/Health:** Nearby Jacuzzi/spa, massage, golf, tennis. **Swimming:** In nearby pool. **Sunbathing:** At poolside or on patio. **Nudity:** Permitted in the house with consent of other guests. **Smoking:** Permitted on outside front porch only. **Pets:** Not permitted, cat & dog in residence. **Handicap Access:** Baths not accessible. **Children:** Not encouraged, call to discuss. **Languages:** English. **Your Hosts:** Fran.

A Cliff Cottage & The Place Next Door [WWW] Gay-Friendly 50/50 ♀♂

The Only B&B in the Heart of Historic Downtown Eureka

A Cliff Cottage, built in 1892 and lovingly restored and refurbished, is a magical place. It is filled with eclectic Victoriana and tastefully designed to satisfy your every wish for a relaxing getaway, romantic honeymoon or rare special moment. Home of the first mayor of Eureka, the cottage is nestled against a timeless bluff surrounded by award-winning gardens in the heart of the Village's quaint downtown, just 17 steps from all the area's neat shops and restaurants. We also do vow commitments and holy unions.

Address: 42 Armstrong St, Eureka Springs, AR 72632
Tel: (501) 253-7409, (800) 799-7409.
E-mail: cliffctg@aol.com **Web:** http://www.cliffcottage.com

Type: Bed & breakfast inn. **Clientele:** 50% gay & lesbian, 50% straight **Transportation:** Pick up from Fayetteville, AR, airport $50 r/t. **To Gay Bars:** 1/4 block. **Rooms:** 2 rooms, 2 suites, 1 cottage with queen or king beds. **Baths:** All private with Jacuzzi whirlpool tubs. **Meals:** Full breakfast. **Vegetarian:** Available, inform when reserving. 5 min walk to veggie restaurants. **Complimentary:** Champagne or white wine, sodas, spring water, imported teas & coffees, hot chocolate, hot cider, chocolates, candies, homemade cookies. **High Season:** May-Oct. **Rates:** $120-$195. **Credit Cards:** MC, Visa. **Rsv'tns:** Preferred, walk-ins welcome. **Reserve Thru:** Travel agent or call direct. **Min. Stay:** Required. **Parking:** Ample off-street parking. **In-Room:** AC, ceiling fans, color cable TV, refrigerator, coffee & tea-making facilities. 1 room has kitchen, some rooms have VCR. **On-Premises:** Meeting rooms, piano. **Exercise/Health:** Jacuzzi, massage. **Swimming:** Nearby river & lake. **Sunbathing:** At beach. **Smoking:** Smoke-free inn, no smoking on property. **Pets:** Call for details. **Languages:** English, French, Spanish, German.

ARIZONA • TUCSON

ARKANSAS • EUREKA SPRINGS

Arbour Glen B&B Victorian Inn

WWW Gay-Friendly 50/50 ♀♂

Kindle Your Romance in Old-World Elegance!

The Arbour Glen, circa 1896, sits on a hillside overlooking the Eureka Springs historical district. Our tree-covered hollow is the perfect picturesque setting for relaxation and enjoyment and is home to hummingbirds, deer, and rare birds. *The Arbour Glen* has been completely restored with comfort in mind but retains its old world charm and elegance. Each guest room is decorated with antiques, handmade quilts, and brass and iron bedsteads. We serve a full gourmet breakfast, with china, silver and fanciful linen, on the veranda overlooking the hollow. Our guests enjoy sipping coffee, while watching the deer and the birds. Spacious, shady verandas with swings overlook the rock and flower garden, complete with fish pond and fountain. There is a nearby nature trail for walking. Accommodations have hardwood floors with hand-hooked area rugs; clawfoot tubs; deluxe, in-bath, brass-trimmed Jacuzzis for two; and color cable TV with remote and VCR, all hidden in armoires. The house has heirloom antiques throughout and queen-sized Victorian beds. At Christmas, we feature a Victorian Christmas display.

Located on the Historic Loop and Trolley Route, *The Arbour Glen White Street Guesthouse* is adjacent to Ermillio's Fine Italian Restaurant, with art galleries, coffee shop, bookstore and horse-drawn carriage rides only steps away. Adding to the luxury are country club privileges at nearby Holiday Island. Eureka Springs is a real Victorian village whose narrow, winding streets, hand-cut limestone walls and hillside parks and homes take advantage of the natural Ozark Mountain setting. Your stay here will definitely be an unforgettable experience. Always a special occasion!

Address: 7 Lema, Eureka Springs, AR 72632
Tel: (501) 253-9010, (800) 515-GLEN(4536).
E-mail: arbglen@ipa.net **Web:** http://www.arbourglen.com

Type: Bed & breakfast.
Clientele: 50% gay & lesbian & 50% straight.
Transportation: Car is best. Pick up from airport.
To Gay Bars: 5 blocks.
Rooms: 5 suites with double or queen beds.
Baths: All private.
Meals: Full gourmet breakfast.
Complimentary: Mints, tea, coffee, soft drinks, afternoon desserts on request.
High Season: Apr-Oct & holidays.
Rates: Low $65-$115, high $75-$125.
Discounts: On reservations for 3+ nights. Honeymoon packages.
Credit Cards: MC, Discover, Visa, Amex.
Rsv'tns: Highly recommended.
Reserve Thru: Travel agent or call direct.
Min. Stay: 2 nights on weekends, 3 nights on holiday & festival weekends.
Parking: Ample free off-street parking.
In-Room: Color cable TV, VCR, AC, ceiling fans, refrigerator, coffee & tea-making facilities, fireplaces, Jacuzzis for two & maid service.
Exercise/Health: Jacuzzi & nature trail on premises.
Swimming: In nearby river, lake & country club.
Sunbathing: On premises or nearby lakes.
Smoking: Permitted outside on verandas only.
Pets: Not permitted.
Children: Not especially welcome.
Languages: English.
Your Hosts: Jeffrey.

Pond Mountain Lodge: B&B Inn & Resort

Relax, Rejuvenate, Reawaken Romance...

Mountain breezes, panoramic views, and thoughtful hospitality await at historic Eureka Springs' *Pond Mountain Lodge & Resort.* Both a bed & breakfast inn with large suites and resort with housekeeping cabins with full kitchens... all on 150 private acres — complete with horseback riding, game room with billiards, and hiking with the native wildlife. *Pond Mountain* is conveniently located just two miles south of Eureka Springs at the county's highest elevation.

Enjoy your choice of distinctively styled suites and cabins, all with king or queen beds, furnished with your comfort in mind. Amenities such as personal in-room Jacuzzi, TV/VCR, refrigerator, microwave, gourmet coffee service, and complimentary beverages, as well as lots of little loving touches enhance your enjoyment and satisfy your search for serenity and comfort. Suite guests also relax to hearty breakfasts each morning; all guests enjoy warm and unintrusive hosting, and the natural beauty of 150 acres of mountain wonder and luxuriate for the moment in this ideal respite. *Pond Mountain* is ideally suited for those romantic escapes (what a natural setting for a holy union!), or for reunions seeking accommodations for the diversity of family interests! Give us a call for special information on groups. "Family-"owned and -operated.

Address: 1218 Hwy 23 South, Eureka Springs, AR 72632
Tel: (501) 253-5877, (800) 583-8043, **Fax:** (501) 253-9087.
Web: http://www.eureka-usa.com/pondmtn/

Type: B&B resort with riding stables. Cabins with spa room.
Clientele: 50% gay & lesbian & 50% straight.
Transportation: Car is best.
To Gay Bars: 5 min or 1hr.
Rooms: 5 suites with queen or king beds. 1- & 2-BR cabins.
Baths: All private.
Meals: Full buffet breakfast (except cabin).
Vegetarian: Breakfast on request. Several excellent restaurants nearby.
Complimentary: Beverages, non-alcoholic

sparkling cider, popcorn. Gourmet coffee, candy in room. Winter: sherry.
Dates Open: Cabins: all year. B&B: Feb-Dec.
High Season: Apr 15-Nov 5.
Rates: Dbl occ: high $110-$160, winter $95-$140. Cabin $140 all year.
Discounts: 10% on stays of 3+ days, rental of 3+ units, or "family" AARP. 5% AARP.
Credit Cards: MC, Visa, Discover.
Rsv'tns: Recommended wknds for Jacuzzi suites & cabins.
Reserve Thru: Travel agent

or call direct.
Min. Stay: 2 nights for special events.
Parking: Ample free off-street parking.
In-Room: Color TV, VCR, video tape library, AC, coffee/tea makers, fridge, kichen. Some ceiling fans, most have fireplace. Phone in guest house.
On-Premises: Meeting room.
Exercise/Health: Jacuzzi in suites, massage by appt. Hiking on 150 acres, fishing in private ponds. Horseback riding add'l fee.
Swimming: Heated pool.

Nearby river, lake.
Sunbathing: At poolside & on common sun decks.
Smoking: Permitted on outside covered verandah only. All rooms non-smoking.
Pets: Inquire, limited availability.
Handicap Access: Yes, cabin.
Children: Welcome. Separate building has family units which accommodate children.
Languages: English.
Your Hosts: Judy.

Edgewater Resort & RV Park

WWW Gay-Friendly ⚥
Gay-Owned & -Operated

The Only Thing We Overlook is the Lake!

Guaranteed the best full-service campground in the 100-mile shoreline of Clear Lake in Northern California. Exclusive gay/lesbian events include Valentine's, Wild Women's, and Battle of the Homosexual Weekends. *Edgewater Resort & RV Park's* beautiful, park-like setting with sun and shade offers RV, camping and cabins with 600' of lakefront, 230-foot fishing pier, a 300' beach and pool, volleyball, ping pong, a boat launch, docks and rentals.

Address: 6420 Soda Bay Rd, Kelseyville, CA 95451
Tel: (707) 279-0208, (800) 396-6224, **Fax:** (707) 279-0138.
E-mail: business@edgewaterresort.net **Web:** http://www.edgewaterresort.net

Type: RV campground with cabins & clubhouse.
Clientele: 25% gay & lesbian following. 4 gay & lesbian wknds per year
Transportation: Car best.
Rooms: 8 cabins w/ single-king beds.
Baths: Cabins: 2 private bath/shower/toilets, 6 private shower/toilets.
Camping: 61 RV & camping sites. RV: 8 drive-thru, 59 electric, water & sewer. Tent sites: 59 electric & water. 8 showers &

washrooms. No dumpstation (all 59 sites have sewer), propane nearby.
Meals: Special events only
Vegetarian: Special events only & nearby.
Complimentary: Coffee in cabins.
Dates Open: All year.
High Season: May-Oct.
Rates: $25-$250.
Discounts: Good Sam & AAA in RV, camping sites.
Credit Cards: MC, Visa, Amex, Discover.
Rsv'tns: Required.

Reserve Thru: Travel agent or call direct.
Min. Stay: Cabins: 2 nights.
Parking: Ample free parking.
In-Room: AC, color cable TV, kitchen, refrigerator, coffee & tea-making facilities.
On-Premises: Meeting rooms, laundry facilities, TV lounge, business services, modem/fax.
Exercise/Health: Nearby gym, weights, Jacuzzi, sauna, steam.

Swimming: Pool & lake.
Sunbathing: Poolside, patio, at beach.
Smoking: Permitted outside only.
Pets: Must have current shots, be friendly, can't be unattended.
Children: Welcome (not on gay & lesbian wknds).
Languages: English.
Your Hosts: Sandra & Lora.

Sea Breeze Resort

Gay-Friendly ⚥

Glistening Water, Tree-Covered Mountains, Clear Blue Skies

Sea Breeze is a lakefront resort on California's largest natural lake. Enjoy swimming, boating and fishing just steps away from your tastefully-decorated, impeccably-clean cottage with fully-equipped kitchen. Relax and enjoy our beautifully-landscaped grounds, and picturesque lake and mountain views. Exclusively for our guests are a covered lighted pier, boat slips/mooring, launching ramp, beach, swim float, picnic tables, chaise lounges and Weber barbecues. For those seeking more arduous activities, boat and jet ski rentals, parasailing, glider rides and top name entertainment are a short distance away.

Address: 9595 Harbor Dr, Glenhaven **Mail To:** PO Box 653, Glenhaven, CA 95443
Tel: (707) 998-3327.

Type: Resort with cottages.
Clientele: Mostly straight clientele with a gay & lesbian following.
Transportation: Car is best.
Rooms: 6 cottages with full kitchens, 1 room with refrigerator. Single, double, queen or king beds.
Baths: All private bath/toilet/showers.

Vegetarian: Available at nearby restaurants.
Complimentary: Coffee, tea, hot cocoa & ice.
Dates Open: Apr 1-Oct 31.
High Season: June-Sep.
Rates: $60-$90.
Credit Cards: MC, Visa.
Reserve Thru: Call direct.
Min. Stay: 3-night minimum on holidays.
Parking: Ample free off-

street parking. Ample parking for boat trailers on-site
In-Room: Color cable TV, AC, ceiling fans, coffee/tea-making facilities, kitchen & refrigerator.
On-Premises: Large enclosed rumpus/club room.
Swimming: Lake on premises.
Sunbathing: At the beach &

on the lawns.
Smoking: Smoking outdoors only.
Pets: Not permitted.
Handicap Access: No.
Children: Well-disciplined children welcome.
Languages: English.
Your Hosts: Phil & Steve.

Rancho Cicada

Gay/Lesbian ♂

Get Back to Nature in the Heart of the Gold Country

Rancho Cicada retreat is located on a beautiful, isolated and private stretch of the Cosumnes River, in the Gold Country of the Sierra foothills, about 50 miles east of Sacramento. Peacocks stroll through rock gardens and lawns in our natural riverside setting. Private groups often rent the entire facility and enjoy swimming, sunbathing, hot tubbing, croquet, volleyball, Native American sweat lodge, floating on air mattresses, and nature hikes led by the owner/naturalist. We're not in any telephone directory, and are only discreetly advertised. **Guest comment:** *"Rancho Cicada is a terrific alternative to the B&B circuit." —Ernie, SF CA*

Address: Plymouth **Mail To:** PO Box 225, Plymouth, CA 95669
Tel: (209) 245-4841, **Fax:** (209) 245-3347.
Web: http://www.ranchocicadaretreat.com

Type: Camping retreat with platform tents & cabins.
Clientele: Mostly men with women welcome
Transportation: Car.
To Gay Bars: 1 hour by car.
Rooms: 2 cabins with queen beds.
Baths: 2 private in cabins, shared at campsites.
Camping: 25 tents on platforms w/ queen, double or single mattress. Hot

showers, wash basins & flush toilets in separate men/women facilities.
Meals: On weekends.
Complimentary: Coffee available in cabins.
Dates Open: Cabins, all year. Tents, May 1-Oct 15.
High Season: June-Aug.
Rates: Tents $100 per person entire wknd. Cabins $200 entire wknd, $350/wk.
Discounts: Inquire.

Rsv'tns: Required.
Reserve Thru: Call direct.
Min. Stay: 2 nts wknds.
Parking: Ample, free.
In-Room: Color TV, VCR, ceiling fans, refrigerator & coffee/tea-making facilities in cabins only.
On-Premises: Fully furnished kitchen with fridge & BBQ. 900 sq. ft. deck.
Exercise/Health: 2 Jacuzzis.

Swimming: River, nearby swimming holes.
Sunbathing: Private cabin sun decks, common sun decks, large lawn.
Nudity: Clothing optional.
Smoking: Permitted in designated areas. Non-smoking rooms available.
Pets: Not permitted.
Children: Not permitted.
Languages: English.
Your Hosts: David & Mark.

Pine Cove Inn, The

Gay-Friendly ⚥

Picture yourself in one of the nine A-frame chalet units at *The Pine Cove Inn*, surrounded by natural landscaping and enjoying the clear, crisp mountain air. You're up at 6,200 feet, and the views are nothing less than incredible. Your individually-decorated room has private bath, fridge and microwave oven. Each of our seven rooms has a fireplace, one unit has a full kitchen and a television, and three have larger private decks with magnificent mountain views. In winter, our toboggan run will carry you down a mountain of fun.

Address: 23481 Hwy 243, Idyllwild, CA 92549
Tel: (909) 659-5033, toll-free (888) 659-5033, **Fax:** (909) 659-5034.

Type: Bed & breakfast & conference center.
Clientele: 25% gay & lesbian & 75% straight clientele.
Transportation: Car is best.
To Gay Bars: 1 hour to Palm Springs' gay/lesbian bars.
Rooms: 10 units (1 apartment unit is above the lodge).
Baths: All private.

Meals: Full breakfast.
Vegetarian: Just let us know when you make your reservation.
Complimentary: Tea & coffee in room.
Dates Open: All year.
Rates: $70-$100 plus 10% tax.
Discounts: On mid-week stays (Sun-Thurs).
Credit Cards: MC, Visa, Amex, Discover.
Rsv'tns: Recommended.

Reserve Thru: Travel agent or call direct.
Min. Stay: 2 nights on weekends, 3 nights on holiday weekends.
Parking: Ample, free, off-street parking.
In-Room: Fridge, microwave oven. 1 unit has full kitchen & TV.
On-Premises: TV lounge, meeting rooms, lodge with fireplace, books, games, puzzles.

Sunbathing: On private sun decks.
Smoking: Some rooms non-smoking. Smoking permitted outdoors, in TV lounge & lodge.
Pets: Not permitted.
Handicap Access: Limited accessibility.
Children: Permitted, $10 extra 12 years and older.
Languages: English.
Your Hosts: Bob & Michelle.

Coast Inn

The *Coast Inn* is the oldest and most popular gay resort in America, providing year-round fun right on the Pacific Ocean, with the world's most beautiful beaches. All rooms have color TV, phones, private baths, and a sun deck or balcony overlooking the bathing beach. We are also home to the world famous "Boom Boom Room," with dancing to the hottest and latest music til 2 am. We are 2 minutes from the West Street gay beach and 15 minutes from San Onofre nude beach. Dana Point Harbor is only five miles away and provides some of the finest surfing, windsurfing, sailing, fishing, snorkling, and scuba diving in Southern California. Disneyland is 30 miles away. Laguna Beach itself has an abundance of fine shopping and dining and is home of The Pageant of the Masters.

Address: 1401 S Coast Hwy, Laguna Beach, CA 92651
Tel: (949) 494-7588, (800) 653-2697, **Fax:** (949) 494-1735.
E-mail: coastinn@boomboomroom.com **Web:** http://
www.boomboomroom.com

Type: Resort hotel with restaurant & "Boom Boom Room" bar & disco.
Clientele: Mostly men with women welcome.
Transportation: Rental car from LAX or San Diego Airport or John Wayne Airport, 12 mi north.
To Gay Bars: World famous "Boom Boom Room" on the premises. 3 other bars in walking distance.

Rooms: 23 rooms
Baths: Each room has a private bath & sun deck or balcony.
Vegetarian: We have a full menu in the restaurant with some vegetarian food available.
Dates Open: All year.
High Season: Apr-Oct.
Rates: $59-$199.
Discounts: Stay 6 nights & get the 7th night free.

Credit Cards: MC, Visa, Amex, Diners, Discover.
Rsv'tns: Strongly suggested.
Reserve Thru: Travel agent or call direct.
Min. Stay: 1-night on weekends.
Parking: Limited free off-street parking.
In-Room: Color cable TV, telephone, maid service, & room service.

Swimming: In the ocean.
Sunbathing: On the beach & on private common sun decks.
Nudity: Limited.
Smoking: No smoking in bar & restaurant.
Pets: Yes, with $100 deposit.
Handicap Access: No.
Languages: English.

Black Bear Inn

WWW Gay/Lesbian ⚤

A Luxury Lodge with Three Cabins

Amidst the pristine beauty of the Sierra Nevada sits **Black Bear Inn,** a spacious luxury lodge and three cabins on a wooded acre near the south shore of Lake Tahoe. The lake, several restaurants, shops and ski rentals are within easy walking distances and shuttles for nearby ski resorts and casinos stop in front of the lodge. In summer, enjoy hiking, biking, swimming, horseback riding, or exploring the exquisite granite peaks, lakes, and forestland. Return to the lodge and take in the cool pine-scented mountain air while lounging on the grounds. Winter is the time for skiing (Tahoe's largest ski resort is one mile away), where you can enjoy snowmobiling, horse-drawn sleigh rides, roaring fires, and watching the snow quietly fall while soaking in the hot tub.

Black Bear Inn's main lodge has five generous guest rooms, each with private bath, king bed, fireplace, TV/VCR, telephone and dataport. Rates include daily maid service, a hearty breakfast and use of the lodge facilities, including the great room with its two-story, river rock fireplace and vaulted ceiling with open log trusses. The grounds house three spacious cabins: One duplex cabin and two with two bedrooms/one bath. Each has a fireplace, kitchenette, king beds, TV/VCR, telephone and dataport. Continental breakfast is delivered to the cabins. Operated by the former owners of the Bavarian House, members of Gay Innkeepers of Tahoe. Please visit our website or e-mail us.

Address: 1202 Ski Run Blvd, South Lake Tahoe, CA 96150
Tel: (530) 544-4411, (800) 431-4411.
E-mail: info@TahoeBlackBear.com **Web:** http://www.TahoeBlackBear.com

Type: Bed & breakfast.	**Vegetarian:** Available with	**Reserve Thru:** Call direct.	**Nudity:** 30-minute drive to
Clientele: A good mix of	advance notice.	**Min. Stay:** 2 night	nude beach.
straight and gay.	**Complimentary:** Wine &	minimum, seasonally.	**Smoking:** Permitted
Transportation: Shuttle or	cheese upon arrival. Setups,	**Parking:** Adequate free off-	outside.
rental car from Reno airport	coffee, tea & juices.	street parking.	**Pets:** Not permitted.
(1 hr).	**Dates Open:** All year.	**In-Room:** Color cable TV,	**Handicap Access:** Fully
To Gay Bars: 5 minutes by	**High Season:** Dec-Mar &	VCR, video tape library,	ADA-compliant.
car.	Jul-Aug.	robes, soap, shampoo, hair	**Children:** Not permitted.
Rooms: 7 rooms with king	**Rates:** $150-$225.	dryers, fireplaces, maid	**Languages:** English.
beds.	**Discounts:** During off	service.	**Your Hosts:** Jerry & Kevin.
Baths: All private bath/	season.	**Swimming:** At nearby lake.	
toilets.	**Credit Cards:** Visa, MC.	**Sunbathing:** On grounds or	
Meals: Full breakfast.	**Rsv'tns:** Required.	nearby beach.	

Holly's Place

A Special Vacation Place for Women

What do you call a place where you can get away from it all, smell the fresh pine air, be with friends or alone, where you can cook your own meals or go out on the town? It's called *Holly's Place* at beautiful Lake Tahoe! We're 2 blocks from the beach, near shopping, casinos, and hiking and biking trails. In winter, the skiing is great! We're 2 miles from Heavenly Valley and near many other downhill ski areas. Snowmobiling, snowboarding and x-country trails are also in the vicinity.

Our main desire is to provide a place where women can be themselves in an environment that is safe, supportive, relaxed and fun! Our grounds are on 2 woodsy acres near downtown. For privacy, we've surrounded the property with 110 cords of split firewood stacked 7 feet high. Many guests have called *Holly's* "a wonderful oasis in the middle of South Lake Tahoe, two blocks from the lake."

We want women to feel at home. Our cozy, clean cabins and rooms are decorated in rustic elegance, and allow for privacy as well as group interaction. This is a special place for all open and accepting women to vacation or celebrate special occassions. We welcome well-behaved boys and girls and well-behaved, non-aggressive, loving dogs. They'll love it here as much as their moms. Almost everyone comes back time and time again, so we invite you to come find out for yourself. Member: Gay Innkeepers of Tahoe.

Address: South Lake Tahoe **Mail To:** PO Box 13197, South Lake Tahoe, CA 96151
Tel: (530) 544-7040, (800) 745-7041.
E-mail: hollys@oakweb.com **Web:** http://www.hollysplace.com

Type: Cabins, guest rooms, group accommodations.
Clientele: Women only
Transportation: Car.
Rooms: 3 rooms & 9 cabins with queen beds.
Baths: Mostly private baths.
Meals: Continental breakfast.
Complimentary: Tea, coffee & muffins in cabins.
Dates Open: All year.
High Season: Major holidays, Dec-Mar, June-Sept.
Rates: $100-$300.
Discounts: Cabins only: off-season 20% off midweek, 7th night free. In season, 8th night free.
Credit Cards: MC, Visa, Discover, Debit (ATM).
Rsv'tns: Required.
Reserve Thru: Call direct.
Min. Stay: Yes.
Parking: Ample off-street.
In-Room: Color cable TV, VCR, stereos, ceiling fans, fully equipped kitchen, coffee/tea-making facilities & fireplaces.
On-Premises: Laundry, bikes, video library, ping pong, volleyball, badminton, recreation & conference room.
Exercise/Health: Hot tub. Nearby: gym, sauna, steam, massage, hiking, golf, mountain bike trails, water sports & skiing.
Swimming: 2 blocks from lake, pool nearby.
Sunbathing: Decks, lawn and nearby lakeside beach.
Nudity: In hot tub only.
Smoking: Permitted outside only. All cabins & rooms are non-smoking.
Pets: Well-behaved dogs with prior approval only.
Children: Well-behaved boys & girls.
Languages: English.
IGLTA

Sierrawood Guest House

The Privacy Is a Luxury in Itself

SierraWood is a romantic, cozy chalet in the woods, where you've dreamed of taking a special friend for an exciting vacation together or getting away by yourself for relaxation and renewal. Here, beside a rippling stream, we're surrounded by U.S. Forest preserve. For those who want to balance the peace and privacy of the wooded chalet, the glittering allure of Lake Tahoe's gaming casinos, superstar entertainers, clubs, restaurants and nightlife is only a few miles away. In summer, you can charter *SierraWood's* own 25-foot *Lancer* for an exciting day on the waters of Lake Tahoe. Your hosts will serve cocktails and lunch, while you soak in the sun and the sights. On another day, try hiking through flowering meadows to the pristine alpine lakes nearby. The winter delight is downhill and cross-country skiing at one of three major ski resorts.

The chalet is an inviting, 6-bedroom, 4-bath home whose unique architecture incorporates open-beam cathedral ceilings, pine paneling and both a rock fireplace and an antique potbelly stove. There are bay windows, floor-to-ceiling windows, and skylights, plus an outdoor redwood hot tub with a view of the river, white fir and aspen woods. Our convivial cocktail hour begins with a soak in the hot tub. Then we join in the warm glow of a sumptuous dining table, sparkling with candlelight, Waterford crystal and the laughter and good conversation of happy company. A healthy breakfast is also included in the daily fare.

Mail To: PO Box 11194, Tahoe Paradise, CA 96155-0194
Tel: (530) 577-6073, (800) 700-3802, **Fax:** (530) 577-4739.
E-mail: Swooddave@aol.com **Web:** http://www.q-net.com/sierrawood

Type: Bed & breakfast guesthouse with dinner included.
Clientele: Good mix of gay men & women
Transportation: Car is best. Free pick up from airport & bus.
To Gay Bars: 12 miles to gay/lesbian bar & the casinos.
Rooms: 4 rooms with double, queen or king beds.
Baths: 1 private bath, 2 private sinks, 2 shared bath/shower/toilets.

Meals: Full breakfast & dinner.
Vegetarian: Available with 3 days' notice.
Complimentary: BYOB, setups provided, tea & coffee, beverages, mints on pillow, wine with dinner.
Dates Open: All year.
Rates: Single $85, double $120-$140. Holidays $100-$150.
Rsv'tns: Preferred 2 days in advance.
Reserve Thru: Travel agent or call direct.

Min. Stay: 2 days on holidays.
Parking: Ample free parking.
In-Room: Telephone, VCR, maid, room & laundry service.
On-Premises: Fireplace, lounge with color TV, laundry facilities.
Exercise/Health: Weights & hot tub with Jacuzzi. Free snowmobiling on premises & adjacent forest. Sailing charters piloted by your hosts.

Swimming: River on premises, lake nearby, nude beach 45 min.
Sunbathing: On beach or common sun decks.
Nudity: On decks & in hot tub.
Smoking: Permitted without restrictions.
Pets: None.
Handicap Access: No.
Children: OK.
Languages: English.
Your Hosts: David & LeRoy.

Spruce Grove Cabins & Cottages

WWW Gay/Lesbian ⚤
Gay-Owned & -Operated

A New Alternative Resort for ALL People

Situated in a woodsy one-acre grove, *Spruce Grove* puts you amidst a private, quiet, secluded mountain resort off Ski Run Blvd., at the foot of Heavenly Ski Area and walking distance from Lake Tahoe at the new Marina Village. *Spruce Grove* offers private cabins and cottages, a hospitality room and shady grounds for relaxing or having BBQs. We're close to shopping, restaurants, the beach, entertainment and casinos.

Smell the fresh pine air and soak in the beauty of nature in Lake Tahoe, CA, where you are close to all hiking and bicycling trails. In winter, the skiing is great! Ski packages, coupons and ski shuttles are available. We're located on Spruce Avenue off of Ski Run Blvd, at the base of Heavenly Ski area, and are close to many other downhill ski areas. Snowmobiling, snowboarding and cross-country trails are also in the vicinity. Whether you're looking for fun in the snow or summer sun, there is something here for everyone in every season.

Our main desire is to provide a place where all gays and lesbians can be themselves in an environment that is safe, supportive, relaxed and, most of all, fun! We want gays, lesbians and their families to feel at home together. Our cozy, clean cabins and cottages are decorated in a vintage Tahoe charm, and accommodations allow for privacy as well as group interaction. If this is something you're looking for, we think you'll enjoy our cabins and cottages. We also welcome well-behaved dogs (leashes optional).

Address: South Lake Tahoe **Mail To:** PO Box 16390, South Lake Tahoe, CA 96151
Tel: (530) 544-0549, (800) 777-0914, **Fax:** (530) 544-3937.
E-mail: info@sprucegrovetahoe.com **Web:** http://www.sprucegrovetahoe.com

Type: Cabins & cottages.
Clientele: Mostly gay & lesbian, some straights
Transportation: Car.
To Gay Bars: 5 min drive.
Rooms: 3 cottages, 4 cabins with queen beds.
Baths: All private.
Meals: Fresh-ground gourmet coffee & O. Spunkmeyer muffins.
Vegetarian: Nearby.
Complimentary: Wine &

Cheese Welcome every Fri night 5-8pm. Potluck BBQ every Sat night in summer.
High Season: June-Sept & holidays.
Rates: $120-$195, holidays 15% more.
Discounts: Inquire.
Credit Cards: Visa.
Rsv'tns: Required.
Reserve Thru: Travel agent or call direct.
Parking: Ample parking.

In-Room: Ceiling fans, color cable TV, VCR, kitchen, refrigerator, coffee & tea-making facilities.
On-Premises: TV lounge, laundry facilities, video tape library, hospitality room, BBQ grills.
Exercise/Health: Jacuzzi, massage. Nearby gym, weights, sauna, steam.
Sunbathing: At beach, on patio.

Nudity: Nude beach on east shore of Lake Tahoe.
Smoking: Permitted outside only.
Pets: Dogs permitted. Leash optional if well behaved.
Children: Welcome.
Languages: English, Spanish.
Your Hosts: Holly, Linda & Kerry.

Grove Guest House, The

Luxury and Privacy — Perfect Central Location!

The unique *Grove Guest House* provides you with your own very private, luxurious villa with a separate bedroom, kitchen and spacious high-ceiling living room. Located in a beautiful historical district, it's a walk to nearby clubs and restaurants, or a short drive to Beverly Hills. A glamorous pool and spa amidst lush tropical landscaping are featured. Suntan nude, if you like. Leather furniture, VCR, CD, cable, private phone (free local calls) and a refrigerator stocked with goodies. Everything you need to relax, or to party West Hollywood style!

Address: 1325 N Orange Grove Ave, Los Angeles, West Hollywood, CA 90046
Tel: (323) 876-8887, **Fax:** (323) 876-0890. Toll-free reservations: (888) L.A.-GROVE (524-7683).
E-mail: GroveLA@aol.com **Web:** http://www.groveguesthouse.com

Type: Guesthouse.
Clientele: Gay & lesbian
Transportation: Car is best, taxi or LAX super shuttle.
To Gay Bars: 1 block.
Rooms: Private guest villa with 1 bedroom.
Baths: Private shower/toilet.
Meals: Continental breakfast & snacks.
Vegetarian: Lots of vegetarian food nearby.
Complimentary: Kitchen is well stocked with a range of food & goodies.
Dates Open: All year.
Rates: $169/day, 1-2 people. Add'l people & selected dates slightly higher.
Discounts: On extended stays.
Rsv'tns: Required.
Reserve Thru: Travel agent or call direct.
Parking: Ample free parking.
In-Room: Color cable TV, HBO, VCR, CD, video tape & book library, AC, ceiling fans, phone, kitchen, microwave, blender, coffee & tea-makers.
Exercise/Health: Jacuzzi. Nearby gyms offer discounts to our guests.
Swimming: Tropical pool.
Nearby pool & ocean.
Sunbathing: Poolside.
Nudity: By pool & spa.
Smoking: Permitted, but not in bedroom, please.
Pets: Not permitted.
Children: Not especially welcome.
Languages: English, French.
Your Hosts: Oliver.

Saharan Motor Hotel

An Oasis in Los Angeles

The *Saharan Motor Hotel* is conveniently located in the heart of Hollywood. We're surrounded by famous restaurants, night clubs, theaters and shopping centers, not to mention many of the most popular gay night spots. Minutes from downtown LA, Universal Studios, Dodger Stadium, the Hollywood Bowl, the Chinese Theater and the Farmers' Market, the *Saharan* is equally convenient for both the business and the vacation traveler.

Address: 7212 Sunset Blvd, Los Angeles, CA 90046
Tel: (323) 874-6700, **Fax:** (323) 874-5163.
E-mail: sahara-jaco@worldnetatt.net

Type: Motel.
Clientele: Mostly straight clientele with a 20%-30% gay male following.
Transportation: Super shuttle from LAX.
To Gay Bars: 4 blocks to men's bars.
Rooms: 54 rooms & 8 suites with double, queen or king beds.
Baths: All private.
Complimentary: Coffee all day.
Dates Open: All year.
High Season: May-Sept.
Rates: Summer $45-$80, rest of year $40-$70.
Credit Cards: MC, Visa, Amex, Diners.
Rsv'tns: Recommended.
Reserve Thru: Travel agent or call direct.
Parking: Adequate free parking.
In-Room: Maid service, satellite color TV, telephones & AC.
Swimming: Pool on premises or 20 minutes to ocean beach.
Sunbathing: At poolside or on beach.
Smoking: Permitted without restrictions.
Pets: Not permitted.
Handicap Access: No.
Children: Permitted.
Languages: English, Spanish, Japanese & Chinese.

San Vicente Inn & Resort

WWW Gay/Lesbian ♂
Gay-Owned & -Operated

The Only Gay Resort in Los Angeles & West Hollywood

With the careful attention of an inn and the superior amenities of a resort, the San Vicente Inn & Resort is the only gay resort in West Hollywood. Accommodations range from self-contained cottages, to suites and rooms with both private and shared baths. Clothing is optional on the sun deck, and the large solar-heated pool is surrounded by sprays of colorful tropical flowers. The comfortable, intimate atmosphere is reflected in the friendly, helpful management and staff. Monthly rentals available.

Address: 845 San Vicente Blvd, West Hollywood, CA 90069
Tel: (310) 854-6915, **Fax:** (310) 289-5929.
E-mail: info@gayresort.com **Web:** http://www.gayresort.com

Type: Bed & breakfast guesthouse resort, executive suites for extended stays.
Clientele: Mostly men with women welcome
Transportation: Airport shuttle, rental car.
To Gay Bars: 1/2 block.
Rooms: 2 penthouse, 2 sr executive, 10 jr suites, 4 BR & bath, 12 shared bath BR, 3 cottages, 12 units. Executive suites for extended stays.
Baths: Private & shared.

Some with Jacuzzi tubs.
Meals: Expanded continental breakfast.
Vegetarian: 5 min walk.
Complimentary: Tea, coffee, juice.
Dates Open: All year.
High Season: Year round.
Rates: $69-$199 +tax. Monthly from $1600/mo.
Discounts: Students under 25.
Credit Cards: MC, Visa, Amex, Diners, Discover.
Rsv'tns: Required, but

walk-ins OK.
Reserve Thru: Travel agent or call direct.
Parking: Parking on property & on street. Semi-valet.
In-Room: Color TV, phones, kitchen, fridge, coffee/tea-making facilities, maid service. Most w/ AC
On-Premises: Gardens, guest BBQs.
Exercise/Health: Jacuzzi, mini-gym, steamroom.
Swimming: Pool.

Sunbathing: At poolside or on common sun decks.
Nudity: Permitted poolside, decks & hot tub.
Smoking: Permitted.
Pets: Permitted with prior arrangement.
Handicap Access: No.
Children: Not especially welcome.
Languages: English & Spanish.
Your Hosts: Terry & Rocky.

Inn at Schoolhouse Creek, The

WWW Gay-Friendly ♀♂

This Country Environment is Relaxation at its Best

Facing the Pacific Ocean like a small, rural community, The Inn at Schoolhouse Creek has offered lodging to coastal visitors since the 1930's. Separate cottages and rooms in small lodges all have private baths, fireplaces, and most have ocean views. The inn offers a relaxed and comfortable atmosphere where you can enjoy your vacation on your own schedule. The charming, historic village of Mendocino with its many fine galleries and shops is only three miles away. The surrounding area offers rivers, harbors, beaches and spectacular state parks, as well as wine tasting in the nearby Anderson valley.

Address: 7051 N Highway One, Mendocino **Mail To:** PO Box 1637, Mendocino, CA 95460
Tel: (707) 937-5525, (800) 731-5525, **Fax:** (707) 937-2012.
E-mail: innkeeper@schoolhousecreek.com **Web:** http://www.schoolhousecreek.com

Type: Cottage inn.
Clientele: Mostly straight clientele with a gay & lesbian following
Transportation: Car is best.
Rooms: 7 rooms & 6 cottages with double or queen beds.
Baths: Private.
Meals: Enhanced

continental breakfast.
Complimentary: Tea & coffee in rooms. Wine & hors d'oeuvres in ranch house
High Season: May-Sept.
Rates: Summer $110-$195, winter $95-$195.
Credit Cards: MC, Visa, Amex, Discover.
Rsv'tns: Suggested.
Reserve Thru: Call direct.

Min. Stay: Required.
Parking: Ample off-street parking.
In-Room: Kitchen, refrigerator, coffee & tea-making facilities.
On-Premises: Lounge.
Exercise/Health: Hot tub. Nearby canoe, sea kayak, mountain bikes.
Swimming: Ocean nearby.

Sunbathing: At beach, private sun decks, hot tub deck.
Smoking: Permitted outside only.
Pets: Limited.
Children: Yes.
Languages: English.
Your Hosts: Al & Penny.

Sallie & Eileen's Place

Sallie & Eileen's Place offers a safe and comfortable place for women near Mendocino, state parks, beaches, hiking, biking, horseback riding, river canoeing and a large women's community. The A-frame is a studio with fireplace and rockers, double bed and a large private bathroom with sunken tub. The cabin has lots of windows, and is wonderful in the rain. It also has a private yard and deck, a woodburning stove, and a loft bedroom with queen bed.

Address: Mendocino **Mail To:** PO Box 409, Mendocino, CA 95460
Tel: (707) 937-2028
E-mail: werwolfe@mcn.org **Web:** http://www.q-net.com/
sallieandeileensplace

Type: Studio cottage and a guesthouse.
Clientele: Women only
Transportation: Car.
To Gay Bars: 3 1/2 hours by car.
Rooms: 2 cottages with double or queen beds.
Baths: All private bath/ toilets.
Complimentary: Mints, special blend of coffee, regular & decaf.
Dates Open: All year.

High Season: Spring break, summer & Christmas.
Rates: A-frame $72.50, cabin $90 for 1-2, $15 each add'l woman, plus county tax.
Discounts: Weekly rates, mid-week specials during fall & winter.
Rsv'tns: Required.
Reserve Thru: Call direct.
Min. Stay: 2 nights, 3-4 on holiday weekends.
Parking: Ample free off-street parking.
In-Room: Kitchen, refrigerator & coffee/tea-makers. Fireplace in A-frame. Ceiling fans in cabin.
Exercise/Health: Hot tub $5 a day per person.
Swimming: 3 miles to ocean and river beaches.
Sunbathing: A-frame has private sun deck. Cabin has sun deck and its own yard.
Nudity: Permitted anywhere on the land.

Smoking: Not permitted in A-frame, permitted in cabin.
Pets: Dogs in cabin only, $5 per day per dog.
Handicap Access: No.
Children: Permitted in cabin only. $10 to age 12. No boy children over 10.
Languages: English, Spanish & French.
Your Hosts: Sallie & Eileen.

Accommodations in Palm Springs

CALIFORNIA • MENDOCINO COUNTY

CALIFORNIA • PALM SPRINGS

Bee Charmer Inn

WWW **Women** ♀
Women-Owned & -Operated

A Private Hotel For Women, in the Quiet Paradise of Palm Springs

Retreat to the desert and enjoy the comfort and privacy of the *Bee Charmer Inn,* Palm Springs' long-established women's hotel. Southwestern tones accent your room, while deep colors of the desert landscape surround you at poolside. Our inn is the perfect place to rekindle romance, renew the spirit, meet new friends, and swim under the stars. Our mature, landscaped grounds provide a tranquil setting for reading, relaxing, or working on your tan year round. The pool is heated in the winter and the misting system cools the warm desert air in the summer. The private courtyard and patio provide an intimate setting for union ceremonies, and birthday or retirement celebrations. Choose from king or queen accommodations, all with full private baths. A complimentary expanded continental breakfast is served each day.

Discover the beauty of the historic Indian Canyons, venture to the top of the San Jacinto Mountains by way of the Palm Springs Aerial Tramway, or explore the treasures of the Living Desert. The Palm Springs village atmosphere provides an opportunity for visitors to stroll along Palm Canyon Drive, sample the fare of the sidewalk cafes, and browse through art galleries and boutiques. Our staff is "at your service," ready to make your stay relaxing and enjoyable. It's *your* vacation, let *us* do the work! We'll make dinner reservations and schedule your tee-times at the golf course. We can also arrange in-room special requests such as flowers or massage.

Address: 1600 E Palm Canyon Dr, Palm Springs, CA 92264
Tel: (760) 778-5883, (888) 321-5699, **Fax:** (760) 416-2200.
E-mail: BeeCharmPS@aol.com **Web:** http://www.beecharmer.com

Type: Private women's resort.
Clientele: Women only
Transportation: Rental car from Palm Springs Regional Airport (about 3 mi), taxi, bus.
To Gay Bars: 1 1/2 miles to 10 min drive.
Rooms: 13 rooms, queen or king beds, sleeper sofas.
Baths: Private full baths.
Meals: Expanded continental breakfast served poolside each morning.
Vegetarian: 2 natural food restaurants nearby.
Dates Open: All year.
High Season: Sept 1-July 10.
Rates: High $95-$125, low $85-$115.
Discounts: 7 days or longer, call for midweek specials.
Credit Cards: All major credit cards accepted.
Rsv'tns: Recommended.
Reserve Thru: Travel agent or call direct.
Min. Stay: During holidays & special events.
Parking: Ample, free on-site parking.
In-Room: Color cable TV, telephone, AC, refrigerator with honor bar, microwave, maid service.
On-Premises: Gas BBQ, book/game library.
Exercise/Health: Massage therapist available by appointment.
Swimming: Large, heated pool on premises.
Sunbathing: Poolside.
Nudity: Tops optional.
Smoking: Permitted outside only.
Languages: English.
Your Hosts: Denise.
IGLTA

Chestnutz

The Best Place to be Pampered in Palm Springs

Each morning begins with a full breakfast made to order which you may enjoy either poolside, in the privacy of your patio, or even in bed! Later, you can choose to nude sunbathe beneath our cooling outdoor mist, take a refreshing swim, enjoy a video, book or magazine from our private library, or engage a new friend in a board or card game. If a home-cooked meal is in your plans, you will appreciate our fully appointed gas kitchen units with microwaves or BBQ grills — and you can dine in your suite or out on your private patio in the shadow of the spectacular mountain sunset.

Centrally located in the heart of the "HOT" San Lorenzo district, *Chestnutz* is a short walk to downtown Palm Springs where famous restaurants and shopping await you. Stroll through an array of antique shops, sip espresso at a sidewalk cafe, or try your luck at the new Spa Casino. If it's a more high-energy workout you're looking for, grab a pass to Golds Gym, or bike or roller-blade down the newly completed bike path to Cathedral City. A five-minute drive will take you to the gay nightlife in Palm Springs, or to the hiking and exploring adventures found in the historical Indian Canyons. And what better way to top off a long day than in our large tiled Jacuzzi under the bright desert stars, comparing notes with other guests. As the newest and finest in private resorts, we offer guests all of the amenities and comforts you have come to expect.

Address: 641 San Lorenzo Rd, Palm Springs, CA 92264
Tel: (760) 325-5269, (800) 621-6973, **Fax:** (760) 320-9535.
E-mail: chestnutz@email.msn.com **Web:** http://www.chestnutz.com

Type: Resort.
Clientele: Men only
Transportation: Car is best. Free pick up at airport or bus.
To Gay Bars: 6 blocks to 1 mile, a 15-min walk.
Rooms: 6 queen & 6 king rooms, 2-BR suites.
Baths: All private.
Meals: Full breakfast. Sunday brunch.
Vegetarian: On request.

Complimentary: Morning newspaper, passes to associated resorts, evening hors d'oeuvres
Dates Open: Year round.
High Season: Nov-May.
Rates: $89-$149. Ask for summer specials.
Discounts: 7 days or longer & VIP guests.
Credit Cards: MC, Visa, Amex, Discover.
Rsv'tns: Preferred.

Reserve Thru: Travel agent or direct.
Min. Stay: 2 nts wknds & 3-5 nts on holidays.
Parking: Ample off-street parking.
In-Room: Color cable TV, VCR, AC, telephone, ceiling fans, refrigerator, maid service. King rooms & 2-BR suites have kitchens.
On-Premises: Video/book/game library.

Exercise/Health: Large Jacuzzi & indoor gym.
Swimming: Large heated pool on premises.
Sunbathing: Everywhere.
Nudity: Clothing tolerated.
Smoking: Permitted.
Pets: By pre-arrangement, pet-rent applies per visit.
Handicap Access: Access limited in bathrooms.
Children: Not permitted.
Languages: English.
Your Hosts: Paul & Jim.

Desert Paradise Resort Hotel

WWW Men ♂
Gay-Owned & -Operated

It's Time to Come to Paradise...

Lush garden settings and majestic mountain views create the mood at *Desert Paradise Resort Hotel,* Palm Springs' most intimate getaway for gay male travelers. Our convenient Warm Sands location is just moments away from world-class shopping, restaurants and a large variety of exciting night spots.

Stylish accommodations surround the large heated pool and spa and include private bath, telephone, color TV, VCR with a large video library, air conditioning and complete kitchens with microwaves. A complimentary continental breakfast and refreshments during the day are served daily. A fax machine is available for guests. With cool mist, refreshing fountains, and clothing always optional, your comfort is ensured. Exotic grounds, a poolside mix of music and laughter, and proximity to the excitement of Palm Springs combine to meet your every expectation. Remember, when it's time for a break from the ordinary, it's time to come to Paradise. This gentleman's resort of the highest caliber represents the best the desert has to offer!

Address: 615 Warm Sands Dr, Palm Springs, CA 92264
Tel: (760) 320-5650, (800) 342-7635, **Fax:** (760) 320-0273.
E-mail: dparadise9@aol.com **Web:** http://www.desertparadise.com

Type: B&B, guesthouse, inn & hotel.
Clientele: Men only
Transportation: Car or taxi.
To Gay Bars: 8 blocks.
Rooms: 12 suites with queen or king beds.
Baths: All private.
Meals: Continental breakfast.

Vegetarian: Nearby.
High Season: All year.
Rates: $89-$199.
Credit Cards: MC, Visa, Amex, Discover.
Rsv'tns: Required.
Min. Stay: Required.
Parking: Ample off-street parking.
In-Room: Phone, AC,

ceiling fans, color cable TV, kitchen, fridge, coffee & tea-makers, maid & laundry svc.
On-Premises: TV lounge, video tape library, in-house adult TV channels.
Exercise/Health: Jacuzzi.
Swimming: Pool with misting system.
Sunbathing: Poolside & on

patio.
Nudity: Permitted.
Smoking: Permitted outside only.
Pets: Small pet dogs.
Children: No. Pool not fenced in.
Your Hosts: Dale & Bill.

INNdulge Palm Springs

For Adventurous Gay Men!

Pamper, pleasure, and gratify yourself at *the* Warm Sands resort for adventurous gay men, *INNdulge Palm Springs.* Located in Palm Springs' premier gay area of 15 gay resorts, *INNdulge* has 20 large rooms surrounding a secluded, private courtyard with a large 24-hour pool and 10-man Jacuzzi. CLOTHING IS FOREVER OPTIONAL! Spoil yourself with an expanded continental breakfast served poolside. Mingle with other guests at the daily afternoon "happy hour" hosted by the owners. Rated "four-palms" by *Out & About!* Inquire about the weekday specials and summer rates, which can be up to 50% off!

Address: 601 Grenfall Rd, Palm Springs, CA 92264
Tel: (760) 327-1408, Reservations: (800) 833-5675, **Fax:** (760) 327-7273.
E-mail: inndulge@ix.netcom.com **Web:** http://www.inndulge.com

Type: Inn.
Clientele: Men only
Transportation: Car is best. Free pick up from airport (5 blocks away).
To Gay Bars: 5 blocks, a 10-minute walk, a 3-minute drive.
Rooms: 18 rooms & 2 suites with king beds.
Baths: 20 private shower/toilets.
Meals: Continental breakfast.

Vegetarian: None available.
Complimentary: Afternoon poolside wine & cheese service 5:00pm-7:00pm.
Dates Open: All year.
High Season: Jan-May.
Rates: Winter $89-$135, summer $79-$115.
Discounts: Summer discounts up to 50%.
Credit Cards: MC, Visa, Amex, Discover.
Reserve Thru: Travel agent

or call direct.
Parking: Ample free off-street parking.
In-Room: Color cable TV, VCR, AC, coffee/tea-making facilities, telephone, refrigerator, maid & laundry service. Some rooms with kitchen.
On-Premises: Video tape library, laundry facilities.
Exercise/Health: Gym on site.
Swimming: Pool on

premises.
Sunbathing: At poolside.
Nudity: Permitted throughout pool area & courtyard.
Smoking: Permitted.
Pets: No pets.
Handicap Access: No.
Children: No.
Languages: English, French.
Your Hosts: John & Jean-Guy.
IGLTA

InnTrigue

Men ♂

The Two Worlds of InnTrigue Await You

You'll be intrigued by these two deluxe adjoining properties in the heart of Palm Springs. They have spacious, colorfully landscaped courtyards and magnificent mountain vistas. Relax around the totally private, CLOTHING OPTIONAL sparkling pools and secluded spas of *InnTrigue*. The poolside one- and two-bedroom suites have private patios, fully equipped kitchens, king-sized beds, remote cable TV with VCR, and an extensive video library. Out & About Editor's Choice Award.

Address: 526 Warm Sands Dr, Palm Springs, CA 92264
Tel: (760) 323-7505, (800) 798-8781, **Fax:** (760) 323-1055.
E-mail: inntrigue@earthlink.net **Web:** http://www.gaytraveling.com/inntrigue

Type: Private male resort.
Clientele: Men only
Transportation: Car is best. Free pick up from the airport or bus station.
To Gay Bars: Within walking distance of gay bars & restaurants.
Rooms: 28 rooms.
Baths: All private.
Meals: Continental breakfast & evening social gathering.
Complimentary: Coffee &

tea. Occasional cookouts, large cocktail parties & holiday dinners.
Dates Open: All year.
Rates: $75-$175.
Discounts: For extended stays. Please inquire.
Credit Cards: All major credit cards.
Rsv'tns: Recommended.
Reserve Thru: Travel agent or call direct.
Min. Stay: 2 nights on weekends, 3 nights on

holidays.
Parking: Adequate free off-street parking.
In-Room: Color cable TV, VCR, male video tape library, AC, phone, kitchen, refrigerator, coffee/tea-makers, houseman service.
On-Premises: Laundry facilities, cool-mist system, security access gate.
Exercise/Health: 2 Jacuzzis, massage by appt.
Swimming: 2 pools on

premises.
Sunbathing: At poolside & on patios.
Nudity: Permitted everywhere.
Smoking: Permitted without restrictions.
Pets: No pets allowed.
Handicap Access: Yes.
Children: Not permitted.
Languages: English.
Your Hosts: Denny, Randy & Jerry.
IGLTA

Queen of Hearts Resort

WWW Women ♀
Lesbian-Owned & -Operated

Palm Springs' Newest Resort — Exclusively for Women

Formerly known as The Desert Knight, this beautiful resort has now been entirely renovated exclusively for women! The *Queen of Hearts Resort* has nine designer furnished rooms, all enclosing the sparkling, heated pool. The secluded patio, surrounded by luscious fruit trees, boasts striking views of the beautiful Santa Rosa Mountains. You'll be pampered in our luxuriously appointed queen bedrooms, as you relax listening to music of your choice from the stereo system in your room. Or watch your favorite show or movie on cable TV or VCR as you prepare a romantic dinner in the fully equipped kitchen.

We're walking distance to some of the finest dinner houses in Palm Springs with gay nightlife only minutes away. We provide hair dryers, terrycloth robes, and irons in each room; with a guest laundry for your convenience. Complimentary continental breakfast served poolside daily completes your getaway to Paradise.

Address: 435 E. Avenida Olancha, Palm Springs, CA
Tel: (760) 322-5793, (888) 275-9903, **Fax:** (760) 322-5795.
E-mail: kathleen@queenofheartsps.com **Web:** http://www.queenofheartsps.com

Type: B&B hotel.
Clientele: Women only
Transportation: Rental car from airport or taxi.
Rooms: 9 rooms with double or queen beds.
Baths: All private.
Meals: Expanded continental breakfast.
Vegetarian: Nearby.
Complimentary: Tea &

coffee in rooms.
High Season: Oct-June.
Rates: Fall/winter: $95-$125 + tax.
Discounts: 7+ days 10% in winter.
Credit Cards: MC, Visa, Amex, Discover.
Rsv'tns: Required.
Reserve Thru: Travel agent or call direct.

Parking: Ample free off-street parking.
In-Room: Phone, AC, color cable TV, VCR, kitchen, fridge, coffee & tea makers, maid svc.
On-Premises: Laundry facilities, video tape library, BBQ on patio.
Exercise/Health: Massage. Nearby gym, weights,

Jacuzzi, sauna, steam.
Swimming: Heated pool.
Sunbathing: Poolside & on patio.
Nudity: Topless only poolside.
Smoking: Outside only.
Pets: Not permitted.
Children: No.

Sago Palms

Men ♂

Your Home in the Desert

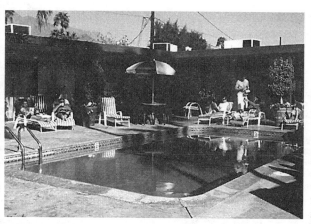

A private, clothing-optional resort in the Warm Sands area, the *Sago Palms* offers peaceful and secluded surroundings for total relaxation. Step through our gates and find lush tropical gardens with statuary and beautiful flowering plants shaded by tall palm trees. Our units surround a rectangular full-sized swimming pool with a misting system to lower temperatures on those really hot days. Off to the side in its own shaded tropical setting is our Jacuzzi/spa where you can relax and enjoy the heated and soothing bubbling waters. Choose from either our one-bedroom batchelor unit, studios, or suites. Our two-bedroom unit is perfect for couples travelling together who might want to share a bath to save on expenses. Our rooms have all the amenities of home — king-sized beds, TV/VCRs, telephones and full baths. The studios come with a full kitchen and the suites have separate bedrooms and living rooms with fireplaces. Each unit is equipped with its own air conditioning and heating, and most units have semi-private rear patios.

The complex includes a weight/workout area and we have available day passes to the local gym. Bicycles are also available for exploring Palm Springs. An extensive continental breakfast is provided each morning by the pool. Our tremendous library of movies is here for your enjoyment, including many of classics, new releases and, of course, an extensive library of adult movies, as well. Unique among the Palm Springs resorts, we are small enough to get to know our guests and we have many repeat customers. Many of them tell us that they consider this their "home in the desert."

Address: 595 Thornhill Rd, Palm Springs, CA 92264
Tel: (800) 626-SAGO (7246), (760) 323-0224, **Fax:** (760) 320-3200.
E-mail: sagopalmca@aol.com **Web:** http://www.webworksps.com/sago/

Type: Guesthouse.
Clientele: Men only
Transportation: Car is best. Free pickup from airport or bus.
To Gay Bars: 10 min walk.
Rooms: 6 suites with king beds.
Baths: All private bath/toilets.
Meals: Continental breakfast.
Vegetarian: 2 natural food restaurants nearby. We have had vegan couples stay here with no problem.
Complimentary: Small chocolates or treats in rooms occasionally.
High Season: Oct-May.
Rates: High season $79-$149, low season $59-$109.
Discounts: Midweek & on extended stays.
Credit Cards: MC, Visa, Amex, Bancard, Discover.
Rsv'tns: Required.
Reserve Thru: Call direct.
Min. Stay: 2 nights, 4 nights on holidays.
Parking: Ample off-street parking.
In-Room: Phone, color cable TV, VCR, AC, ceiling fans, refrigerator, coffee/tea-making facilities & maid service. 5 suites have kitchens, 1 suite has microwave & small fridge.
On-Premises: Laundry facilities, video tape library.
Exercise/Health: Gym, weights, Jacuzzi.
Swimming: Pool.
Sunbathing: At poolside.
Nudity: Permitted in the compound.
Smoking: Permitted anywhere outside. All rooms are non-smoking.
Pets: Inquire.
Handicap Access: Yes.
Children: No.
Languages: English.
Your Hosts: David.

PALM SPRINGS • CALIFORNIA

Santiago Resort

Palm Springs' Most Spectacular Private Men's Resort

We're winner's of Out & About's 1997 Editor's Choice Award for "exceptionally notable & distinctive gay lodging...a men's guesthouse that reflects stylish sophistication," and *Genre Magazine* says we're "...one of Palm Spring's most refined gay resorts," voting us "the most elegant men's guesthouse." Exotically landscaped, secluded grounds provide a peaceful enclave for the discriminating traveller. Enjoy magnificent mountain views from our terrace level, while an oversized diving pool, a 12-man spa and an outdoor cooling mist system complete the setting.

Our poolside, courtyard or terrace suites and studios, featuring king-sized beds with feather duvet covers, superior quality towels and linens and shower massages, set the *Santiago's* standard of excellence and luxury.

And clothing is forever optional...

Address: 650 San Lorenzo Rd, Palm Springs, CA 92264-8108
Tel: (760) 322-1300, (800) 710-7729, **Fax:** (760) 416-0347.
E-mail: santiagops@earthlink.net **Web:** http://www.santiagoresort.com

Type: Hotel resort.
Clientele: Men only
Transportation: Car is best. Free pick up from airport or bus.
To Gay Bars: A 10-minute walk or a 3-minute drive.
Rooms: 10 rooms, 13 suites with king beds.
Baths: Private: 19 shower/toilets, 4 bath/toilet/showers.
Meals: Expanded continental breakfast, lunch.

Vegetarian: Available.
Complimentary: Courtyard luncheon, Gold's gym passes.
Dates Open: All year.
High Season: Jan-May.
Rates: $99-$129.
Discounts: On extended stays.
Credit Cards: MC, Visa, Amex, Discover.
Rsv'tns: Recommended.
Reserve Thru: Travel agent

or call direct.
Min. Stay: Required at times, please inquire.
Parking: Ample free off-street parking.
In-Room: Color cable TV, VCR, AC, telephone, refrigerator, microwave, houseman service.
On-Premises: Video tape library, fax, photocopier, laundry facilities.
Exercise/Health: Jacuzzi,

nearby gym.
Swimming: Diving pool on premises.
Sunbathing: At poolside.
Nudity: Permitted without restriction.
Smoking: Permitted without restriction.
Pets: Not permitted.
Handicap Access: Yes.
Children: No.
Languages: English, French.

Color Photo on Page 13

Triangle Inn Palm Springs

WWW Men ♂

Clothing Always Optional! Always Warm & Inviting!

The *Triangle Inn,* described by *Genre* magazine as "Palm Springs' most romantic gay men's resort," is also its most warm and inviting. Escape to the secluded privacy of our unique enclosed compound where clothing is always optional. Once inside, discover lush tropical gardens, a sparkling swimming pool, soothing Jacuzzi, large sun deck, and spectacular mountain views. Nine elegantly appointed suites have been furnished with all the comforts of home, and include a choice of central air or evaporative cooling systems, fully equipped kitchens or kitchenettes, large baths with hair dryers and top-quality linens, plenty of closet space, a private reading library, and TVs, VCRs and stereos.

A generous breakfast is served poolside each morning, and afternoon mixers provide the perfect setting for meeting fellow guests and making new friends. Bicycles are available for use by guests, as are gas barbecue facilities and a large video collection. Digital music is provided throughout the pool and breakfast areas, and a Micro-Cool® outdoor cooling system runs throughout the property. The inn is conveniently located, and is within walking distance of downtown Palm Springs, many popular gay bars, restaurants and shops, and a number of area attractions.

Address: 555 San Lorenzo Road, Palm Springs, CA 92264
Tel: (760) 322-7993, (800) 732-7555.

Type: Inn.
Clientele: Gay men
Transportation: Rental car suggested.
To Gay Bars: 5 min drive, walk to others.
Rooms: 9 suites with queen or king beds.
Baths: All private baths.
Meals: Expanded continental breakfast.
Dates Open: All year.
High Season: Oct 1-May 31.

Rates: $95-$205.
Discounts: Special summer rates 6/1-9/30 (excluding holidays).
Credit Cards: Visa, MC, Amex, Discover.
Rsv'tns: Recommended.
Reserve Thru: Call direct or travel agent.
Min. Stay: Varies.
Parking: Ample free off-street parking.
In-Room: AC, kitchen or kitchenette, TV/VCRs,

stereos, hair dryers, telephones, alarm clocks, daily maid service.
On-Premises: Large video library, reading library.
Exercise/Health: Jacuzzi, bicycles, massage (by appointment), yoga.
Swimming: Pool on premises.
Sunbathing: Two large decks (1 poolside) with outdoor mist system.
Nudity: Permitted

throughout property.
Smoking: Permitted without restrictions.
Pets: Not permitted.
Handicap Access: Inquire.
Children: Not permitted.
Languages: English, some French.
Your Hosts: Michael & Stephen.
IGLTA

Villa — Palm Springs, The

Gay/Lesbian ♂

An Oasis of Indulgence

As one of Palm Springs' largest full-service resorts, *The Villa — Palm Springs* is truly an oasis of indulgence. Stroll the 2-1/2 acres of lush gardens and historic date palms. Relax, enjoy the sun, or take advantage of one of the desert's favorite culinary experiences, as you enjoy the day poolside at Dates Bar & Café, or dine fireside or under the stars at the famous Adobe Restaurant.

Address: 67-670 Carey Rd, Cathedral City, CA 92234
Tel: (760) 328-7211. Reservations (877) PS VILLA, **Fax:** (760) 321-1463.
E-mail: thevillaps@aol.com **Web:** http://www.thevilla.com

Type: Resort with full-service bar & restaurant.
Clientele: Predominantly men
Transportation: Car or cab.
To Gay Bars: 1/2 mile by car to men's bars.
Rooms: 45 rooms with double, queen or king beds.
Baths: All private.
Meals: Full-service restaurant.
Vegetarian: Please inquire.
Dates Open: All year.

High Season: Jan-July 4.
Rates: $59-$119; holidays $109-$139.
Discounts: Please inquire.
Credit Cards: MC, Visa, Amex, Diners, Carte Blanche (all).
Rsv'tns: Recommended.
Reserve Thru: Travel agent or call direct.
Min. Stay: 2-4 days on holidays.
Parking: Ample off-street parking.

In-Room: Separate entrances, remote control color TV/radio, direct-dial phone, maid services, refrigerators, microwaves, coffeemakers, hair dryers, AC.
On-Premises: Meeting room, fireplace dining room, public telephone.
Exercise/Health: Sauna, Jacuzzi.
Swimming: Pool on premises.

Sunbathing: At poolside or on lawn.
Nudity: Permitted in some private patios.
Smoking: Permitted. Non-smoking rooms available.
Pets: Not permitted.
Handicap Access: Please inquire.
Children: Not permitted.
Languages: English, limited Spanish.
Your Hosts: Shawnen.

CCBC Resort Hotel & Campgrounds

WWW Men ♂
Gay-Owned & -Operated

The Most Talked-About Gay Resort in the World

Nestled in the foothills of the Santa Rosa Mountains is the largest and friskiest gay resort and campground in Palm Springs, *CCBC Resort Hotel*. Forty-eight rooms and a dozen RV spaces are spread out over a two-and-a-half-acre oasis in the desert, ideal for those who enjoy swimming, sunbathing and playing in the nude. Volleyball, steam room, sauna, pool, spa, and our famous 500-foot walks are open 24 hours a day. Free shuttle to and from the airport, bus station, bars and restaurants. *CCBC* is the most talked-about gay resort in the world.

Address: 68-369 Sunair Rd, Cathedral City, CA
Tel: (760) 324-1350, (800) 472-0836, **Fax:** (760) 328-0267.
E-mail: ccbc@earthlink.net **Web:** http://www.ccbc-gay-resort.com

Type: Hotel with RV campground.
Clientele: Men only
Transportation: Car, bus or plane to Palm Springs. Free pick up at bus station or airport.
To Gay Bars: 1/2 block, a 3 min walk, a 2 min drive.
Rooms: 48 rooms with queen or king beds.
Baths: All private shower & toilets.

Camping: 6 RV sites with electric, water, cable, TV hookup. 10 tent sites. 2 showers, 2 washrooms, dumpstation, nearby propane.
Meals: Continental breakfast.
Vegetarian: Available nearby.
Dates Open: All year.
High Season: Jan-May.
Rates: Summer $49-$109,

winter $69-$129.
Credit Cards: MC, Visa, Amex, Discover.
Rsv'tns: Required.
Reserve Thru: Travel agent or call direct.
Min. Stay: Required.
Parking: Ample free off-street parking.
In-Room: Telephone, AC, ceiling fans, color cable TV, kitchen, refrigerator.
On-Premises: TV lounge.

Exercise/Health: Jacuzzi, sauna, steam. Gym nearby.
Swimming: Pool on premises.
Sunbathing: Poolside & on patio.
Nudity: Permitted.
Pets: Not permitted.
Handicap Access: Yes, ramps, wide doors, rails in bathroom.
Children: No.
Languages: English, Spanish

Cobalt

WWW Men ♂
Gay-Owned & -Operated

Welcome to the World of Cobalt

Cobalt features beautiful custom-designed furnishings and the luxury of the finest linens, down comforters and other special touches. Floors are beautifully tiled, walls are custom painted cobalt blue, and windows are shaded by plantation shutters. With one of the largest pool areas in Palm Springs, our spacious grounds are surrounded by mature landscaping, picturesque palms and breathtaking mountain views. From the moment you enter, the gurgling fountain, the fragrance of blooming flowers, and the red Bougainvillea climbing the white stuccoed walls, may make you never want to leave.

Address: 526 S Camino Real, Palm Springs, CA
Tel: (760) 416-0168 (Tel/Fax), (888) 289-9555.
E-mail: cobalt@cobaltps.com **Web:** http://www.cobaltps.com

Type: Resort.
Clientele: Men only
Transportation: Car best. Free airport pick up.
To Gay Bars: 6 blocks, a 10 min walk, a 3 min drive.
Rooms: 10 suites with queen or king beds.
Baths: All private bath/shower/toilets.
Meals: Expanded continental.
Vegetarian: Nearby.

Complimentary: Starbucks coffee, turn down service, Aveda personal amenities.
Dates Open: All year.
High Season: Dec/Jan-May/Jun.
Rates: Low: $89-$139, high $109-$169.
Discounts: Extended stay.
Credit Cards: MC, Visa, Amex.
Rsv'tns: Required.
Reserve Thru: Travel agent

or call direct.
Min. Stay: Required on holidays.
Parking: Ample off-street parking.
In-Room: Telephone, AC, ceiling fans, color cable TV, VCR, refrigerator, coffee & tea-making facilities, maid service.
Exercise/Health: Gym, weights, Jacuzzi, steam, massage.

Swimming: Pool.
Sunbathing: Poolside.
Nudity: Permitted poolside.
Smoking: Permitted outside. All rooms non-smoking.
Pets: Not permitted.
Handicap Access: Yes, rails in bathroom, wide doors.
Children: No.
Languages: English.

El Mirasol Villas

Over 20 Years as One of Palm Springs' Premier Gay Resorts

Returning again and again to the villas built by Howard Hughes in the 1940s, our established multi-national clientele enjoy reserve, class, the finest service and a pleasant ambiance behind the walls and gates of *El Mirasol.*

Address: 525 Warm Sands Dr, Palm Springs, CA 92264
Tel: (760) 327-5913, (800) 327-2985, **Fax:** (760) 325-1149.
E-mail: mirasolps@aol.com **Web:** http://www.elmirasol.com

Type: Resort hotel.
Clientele: Men only
Transportation: Drive. Fly to: Palm Springs Regional Airport (free pick up), Ontario or Los Angeles airports.
To Gay Bars: A few blocks to major nightclub & neighborhood bars.
Rooms: 15 king studios, 1-bedroom bungalows.
Baths: All private.
Meals: Breakfast & lunch.
Vegetarian: By arrangement.

Complimentary: Lemonade, iced tea, bottled spring water.
Dates Open: All year.
Rates: $95-$150.
Discounts: On extended stays.
Credit Cards: All major credit cards.
Rsv'tns: Recommended.
Reserve Thru: Travel agent or direct.
Min. Stay: Required at times.
Parking: Ample, free off-street parking.

In-Room: Color cable TVs & VCRs in bed- & living rooms. AC, telephone, some kitchens (at least fridge & microwave), maid service. Bungalows have private patios.
On-Premises: Laundry facilities, video library, fax, copier, fireplace.
Exercise/Health: Eucalyptus steam room, Jacuzzi, bicycles, discounted passes to gyms. Massage by appointment.
Swimming: 2 pools on premises.
Sunbathing: At poolside, on private sun decks or on patio.
Nudity: Permitted throughout property.
Smoking: Permitted.
Pets: Welcomed, fee.
Children: Not permitted.
Languages: English, French.
Your Hosts: Hugh & Ray.
IGLTA

La Posada

The Perfect Escape

Desert home of many Hollywood stars, the Las Palmas area is also home to *La Posada,* upscale and romantic, done in the style of the area's Spanish Colonial, Mediterranean and Old California heritage. Ten studios and rooms surround a large, clothing-optional pool and Jacuzzi, and landscaped patio. Many rooms have dramatic views of nearby Mt. Jacinto. All studios and suites have direct-dial phones, color TV, coffee-makers, refrigerators and most have full kitchens. Continental breakfast is served poolside or in the comfortable reception area. We're walking distance to restaurants, bars, shopping, and the center of Palm Springs village.

Address: 120 W. Vereda Sur, Palm Springs, CA 92262
Tel: (760) 323-1402, (888) 411-4949, **Fax:** (760) 416-3842.
E-mail: laposada@laposada.com **Web:** http://www.laposada.com

Type: Hotel inn resort.
Clientele: Men only
Transportation: Car. Free airport pick up.
To Gay Bars: 9 blocks.
Rooms: 7 studios with king or queen beds & 3 rooms.
Baths: All private.
Meals: Expanded continental breakfast.
Complimentary: Bottled water, iced tea. Wknd

cocktail happy hour.
High Season: Oct-May.
Rates: High: $109-$159, low: $99-$119.
Discounts: Inquire.
Credit Cards: MC, Visa, Amex, Discover.
Rsv'tns: Suggested.
Reserve Thru: Travel agent, call or email direct.
Min. Stay: 2-3 nts. Call for single nt avail.

Parking: Ample off-street.
In-Room: Phone, AC, color cable TV, VCR, fridge, coffee & tea makers, maid & laundry svc. Most rooms have kitchen.
On-Premises: TV lounge, laundry facilities, fax.
Exercise/Health: Nearby hiking, tennis, gym, weights, Jacuzzi, massage. Gym passes at local gyms.

Swimming: Large, heated pool on premises.
Sunbathing: Poolside & Jacuzzi.
Nudity: Permitted in pool area & Jacuzzi.
Smoking: Outside. All rooms non-smoking.
Pets: Inquire.
Children: No.
Your Hosts: Thom.
IGLTA

Applewood Inn & Restaurant

Russian River's Preeminent B&B

Once a mission-style redwoods retreat, *Applewood* is now an elegant country inn and restaurant that has become the darling of food critics and editors steering their readers to romantic getaways. *Wine Spectator* calls *Applewood*, "intimate and refined," while *Condé Nast Traveler* suggests the meals at the Applewood Restaurant meet the "Burgundian ideal."

Let *Applewood* be your great place to unwind and relax. Drive down country lanes, picnic or taste wine at boutique wineries, raft or canoe the Russian River, take a short drive to the coast to kick up a little sand on the beach, or just luxuriate in bed with a mimosa and someone special. The beauty of the redwoods, apple trees and vineyards...the relaxing pool and Jacuzzi...the stylish rooms with European down comforters...the pleasure of sitting by the fire or reading in the library...the marvelous food in a firelit dining room...your willing hosts and two tail wagging dogs...all await your arrival at this contemporary Eden.

Address: 13555 Hwy 116, Guerneville, CA 95446
Tel: (707) 869-9093, (800) 555-8509, **Fax:** (707) 869-9170.
E-mail: stay@applewoodinn.com **Web:** http://www.applewoodinn.com

Type: Inn with restaurant and wine bar.
Clientele: Mostly straight clientele with a gay & lesbian following
Transportation: Car is best. Free pick up from Santa Rosa airport.
To Gay Bars: 5-minute drive to men's/women's bars.
Rooms: 9 rooms, 7 suites.
Baths: All private.
Meals: Full breakfast included, dinner offered to guests & public Tuesdays thru Saturdays.
Vegetarian: On menu.
Complimentary: Coffee & tea all day.
Dates Open: All year.
High Season: Apr-Nov.
Rates: $145-$350.
Credit Cards: MC, Visa, Amex, Discover.
Rsv'tns: Recommended.
Reserve Thru: Travel agent or call direct.
Min. Stay: 1 night midweek, 2 nights on weekends, 3 nights on holiday weekends.
Parking: Ample, free off-street parking.
In-Room: Color TV, phone & maid service. Suites also have showers for two or private patios or verandas.
On-Premises: Meeting rooms, private dining rooms, public telephone, laundry facilities & fax.
Exercise/Health: Jacuzzi, massage. Jacuzzi baths in suites.
Swimming: Heated pool on premises, river nearby. 10 minutes to ocean.
Sunbathing: At poolside & on private verandas with suites.
Smoking: Not permitted.
Pets: Not permitted.
Handicap Access: Yes, ramps, wide doors, grab bars.
Children: Not permitted.
Languages: English.
Your Hosts: Darryl & Jim.

Color Photo on Page 14

Eagle's Peak

Luxurious Amenities, Glorious Seclusion

Soaring above the Russian River, *Eagle's Peak* is a private, 1500-square-foot vacation home on 26 secluded acres, commanding majestic views of the lovely rolling hills above Forestville. Escape the city and indulge yourself in total relaxation. Enjoy a gourmet meal served as the sun sets over wooded wilderness and vineyards.

The sounds of the forest will gently lull you into a deep and restful night's sleep to awaken refreshed with the light of a new day. Our menu includes a First Course of mixed green salad or Caesar salad, a Main Course of grilled Chateaubriand, chicken or salmon with vegetables, and a Dessert that is made fresh daily. Relax in the private hot tub just off your luxurious bedroom and afterwards, melt into the hands of a skilled masseur.

Experience a unique massage experience by Michael La Count, where massage is treated not only as spiritual and physical therapy, but also as an art form. Through music and touch, your body is given complete focus which helps you receive the wonderfully meditative rest state from which your body truly heals. The massage style is a combination of strong, deep tissue work balanced by long, healing Swedish strokes. Deep, positive breathing is encouraged to help open up your body's energy and release stress.

Address: Forestville **Mail To:** PO Box 750, Forestville, CA 95436
Tel: (707) 887-9218, **Fax:** (707) 887-9219.
E-mail: info@lacount.com **Web:** http://www.eaglespeak.net

Type: 1500 sq ft vacation home.
Clientele: Mostly gay men with lesbians welcome
Transportation: Car is best.
To Gay Bars: 20 miles, 18 minute drive.
Rooms: 1 bedroom with king bed, living room with king futon.

Baths: 1 bath.
Meals: Catered dining at extra charge.
Dates Open: All year.
Rates: 2-night stays: $195. 1-night: $255. Weekly stays: $1,170.
Rsv'tns: Required.
Reserve Thru: Travel agent or call direct.
Parking: Ample free parking.

In-Room: Telephone, color TV, VCR, kitchen, refrigerator, coffee & tea-making facilities.
On-Premises: Outdoor shower on sun deck.
Exercise/Health: Indoor Jacuzzi, massage.
Swimming: Nearby pool, ocean, river.

Sunbathing: On patio & private sun decks.
Nudity: Permitted anywhere on 26 acres.
Smoking: Not permitted anywhere on property due to fire danger.
Handicap Access: No.
Children: No.
Languages: English.
Your Hosts: Michael.

> Color Photo on Page 14

Fern Falls

WWW Gay/Lesbian ♀♂

Romance Amidst the Redwoods

Fern Falls is a hillside habitat in a captivating canyon of Cazadero, whose cascading creeks merge with the languid waters of the Russian River. The custom-designed curved deck of the main house looks over the creek and ravine, and an ozonator spa sits above the waterfall on a hill nestled below a giant boulder amidst beautiful gardens. Nearby you can try wine tasting at the Korbel Winery, horseback riding, or canoeing the languid waters of the Russian River.

Relax with a soothing enzyme bath and massage at Osmosis, or go hiking in the redwood forests. We're walking distance from the Elim Grove Restaurant and within a mile of the Cazadero General Store, offering video rental, produce and munchies. The Cazadero tennis courts are nearby. Just down the road is another fun dining spot, the Cazanoma Lodge, where can catch your own trout for dinner. If you prefer, you may continue on to the coast for a picnic at sunset, or dine at Rivers End.

Address: 5701 Austin Creek Rd, Cazadero **Mail To:** PO Box 228, Cazadero, CA 95421
Tel: (707) 632-6108, **Fax:** (707) 632-6216.

Type: Guesthouse & cottages.
Clientele: Gay & lesbian. Good mix of men & women.
Transportation: Car is best.
To Gay Bars: 12 miles to bars in Guerneville.
Rooms: 3 cottages with double or queen beds.
Baths: Private.
Dates Open: All year.

High Season: May-Oct.
Rates: $135-$165.
Discounts: Weekly rates.
Rsv'tns: Required.
Reserve Thru: Travel agent or call direct.
Min. Stay: 2 nights on weekends in season.
Parking: Adequate free parking.
In-Room: Color cable TV, VCR, coffee/tea-making

facilities, kitchen, refrigerator. Cabins have fireplaces.
On-Premises: Video tape library, fax, phone, laundry facilities.
Exercise/Health: Jacuzzi, gym on premises, massage.
Swimming: Creek on premises. Nearby ocean, river & waterfall.
Sunbathing: On private &

common sun decks.
Nudity: Permitted on decks, in garden & at creek.
Smoking: Permitted outside on decks.
Pets: Permitted in cottages if well-behaved.
Handicap Access: No. Terrain is hilly & steep.
Children: Permitted, must be supervised & well-behaved.
Languages: English.

> **Color Photo on Page 15**

Highlands Resort

WWW Gay/Lesbian ♀♂

Experience the Magic of the Redwoods!

Built in the 1940s, the classic bungalows and rooms of *Highlands Resort* reflect the casual comfort of that era. The grounds of our contry resort cover three acres and are lush with mature redwood trees and gardens. The pool area has the ambiance of a private home and the spa tub sits out under the redwood trees. Both the pool and spa areas are clothing-optional. Make new friends in our lounge over breakfast, or enjoy a game of Scrabble by the pool. We are just a short walk to the bars, restaurants and shops in Guerneville, and a short drive to the area's wineries.

Address: 14000 Woodland Dr, Guerneville **Mail To:** PO Box 346, Guerneville, CA 95446
Tel: (707) 869-0333, **Fax:** (707) 869-0370.
E-mail: muffins@HighlandsResort.com **Web:** http://www.HighlandsResort.com

Type: Inn and campground.
Clientele: Good mix of gay men & women.
Transportation: Car is best.
To Gay Bars: 2 blocks to men's/women's bars. A 5-minute walk or 2-minute drive.
Rooms: 10 rooms, 1 suite & 6 cottages with double, queen or king beds.
Baths: 10 private, others share.

Camping: 20 tent sites with 3 showers & 2 restrooms.
Meals: Continental breakfast on weekends.
Dates Open: All year.
High Season: April-Oct.
Rates: Summer $45-$130, winter $40-$100.
Credit Cards: MC, Visa, Amex, Discover.
Rsv'tns: Recommended.
Reserve Thru: Travel agent or call direct.

Min. Stay: 2 nights over weekends.
Parking: Ample free parking.
In-Room: Maid service, 2 kitchens.
On-Premises: TV lounge.
Exercise/Health: Hot tub.
Swimming: Pool on premises.
Sunbathing: At poolside or on the patio.

Nudity: Permitted around pool & hot tub.
Smoking: Permitted in designated areas.
Pets: Permitted by special arrangement.
Handicap Access: No.
Children: Not especially welcome.
Languages: English.
Your Hosts: Lynette & Kenneth.
IGLTA

Jacques' Cottage

WWW Gay/Lesbian ♂

The Ultimate in Privacy

Amidst oaks, redwoods, and fruit trees, *Jacques' Cottage* is located in the heart of California wine country, only minutes from the wineries and fine restaurants that made Sonoma County famous. Many gay clubs and restaurants are 10 minutes away. Enjoy fishing and canoeing in the tranquil Russian River, five minutes from the cottage. At *Jacques' Cottage,* enjoy a hot tub under the stars, lounge by the pool, or have a glass of wine on your private deck overlooking the vineyards. The Cottage has spectacular views through every window, and a large living/dining room with a sunny deck, full bath, and a bedroom with a loft above. With the queen size bed in the loft and a sofa bed in the living room, it can sleep 4 comfortably. The kitchen is fully equipped with a stove, refrigerator and microwave. There's also a color TV, VCR, and stereo system with a tape deck and CD player. The Cottage has its own driveway and a private phone line, and is a totally private getaway, where you can enjoy all the comforts of home.

Address: 6471 Old Trenton Road, Forestville, CA 95436
Tel: (707) 575-1033, (800) 246-1033, **Fax:** (707) 573-8988.
E-mail: jacques@wco.com **Web:** http://www.wco.com/~jacques

Type: Large, private guest cottage.
Clientele: Mostly men with women welcome
Transportation: Car is best.
To Gay Bars: 8 miles to all the bars.
Rooms: 1 cottage with 2 queen beds.
Baths: Private bath/toilet/ shower.
Complimentary: Coffee &

coffee-maker in cottage.
Dates Open: All year.
High Season: May-end of Oct.
Rates: $125.
Discounts: Weekly rates available.
Rsv'tns: Required.
Reserve Thru: Travel agent or call direct.
Min. Stay: 2 nights.
Parking: Ample, free off-street parking.

In-Room: Color TV, VCR, video tape library, laundry service, private phone line, bathrobes, kitchen, refrigerator, coffee & tea-making facilities, CD.
On-Premises: Sun deck.
Exercise/Health: Free weights poolside, Jacuzzi on premises. Nearby gym, massage.
Swimming: Pool on premises. 5 miles to river

Sunbathing: At poolside or on private sun deck.
Nudity: Permitted.
Smoking: Permitted.
Pets: Permitted.
Handicap Access: No.
Children: No.
Languages: English.
Your Hosts: Jacques & Craig.

Willows, The

Gay/Lesbian ⚣

Where Tourists Are Treated Like Home Folks!

The Willows guesthouse offers a country home vacation on five spectacular acres overlooking the Russian River. In the main lodge, there are thirteen private, cozy bedrooms, some with fireplaces and color TVs, all with direct-dial telephones. Nine bedrooms have private baths. In the spacious living room is a large stone fireplace, extensive library and grand piano. A sun deck with hot tub and sauna extends the length of the lodge. On the rambling, well-tended property, ideal for tent camping, you'll find quiet, wooded seclusion and sunny, landscaped lawns, which slope down to the private dock on the river. Use of the canoes is provided free of charge. Guests are served a complimentary breakfast of fresh fruit, pastries, juice and coffee, and are welcome to use the community kitchen and outdoor BBQs. Many excellent restaurants are a short walk away. Our relaxed, friendly atmosphere lets you get away from it all, yet be in the heart of the maddening fun on the Russian River.

Address: 15905 River Rd, Guerneville, CA 95446
Tel: (707) 869-2824, (800) 953-2828, **Fax:** (707) 869-2764.
Web: http://www.willowsrussianriver.com

Type: Guesthouse, RV/ camground.
Clientele: Mostly gay & lesbian, some straights
Transportation: Car.
To Gay Bars: 2 blocks.
Rooms: 13 rooms with queen beds.
Baths: Private & shared.
Camping: 80 tent sites, dumpstation, propane nearby, 6 showers, 2 washrooms.

Meals: Expanded continental breakfast.
Vegetarian: Nearby.
Complimentary: Coffee & tea.
Dates Open: All year.
High Season: May-Sept.
Rates: Winter $59-$109, summer $79-$139.
Discounts: Inquire.
Credit Cards: MC, Visa, Amex, Discover.
Rsv'tns: Required.

Reserve Thru: Travel agent or call direct.
Min. Stay: On weekends during summer season.
Parking: Adequate free off-street parking.
In-Room: Phone, ceiling fan, color cable TV, VCR.
On-Premises: Video tape library.
Exercise/Health: Hot tub & sauna. Nearby gym, massage.

Swimming: River on premises. Nearby pool, ocean, river.
Sunbathing: On the beach, patio or common sun deck.
Nudity: Clothing optional in Jacuzzi & sauna.
Smoking: Permitted outdoors only. No non-smoking rooms available.
Pets: Not permitted.
Children: No.

Fern Grove Cottages

Gay-Friendly 50/50 ♀♂

Sonoma Wine Country, Majestic Redwoods & the Scenic Russian River

Spend the night in your own private cottage surrounded by towering redwoods. Built in the 1920s, most cottages have woodburning fireplaces, original knotty pine interiors and private decks. Each cottage is individually decorated with rustic antique-style furnishings, televisions, refrigerators and coffeemakers. A breakfast which includes Simon's homemade scones and Anne's scrumptious granola is served each morning. *Fern Grove Cottages* are three blocks from Guerneville's shops, restaurants and swimming beach. Canoe trips, Redwoods State Park and a champagne winery are within five miles.

Address: 16650 Hwy 116, Guerneville, CA 95446
Tel: (707) 869-8105, **Fax:** (707) 869-1615.
Web: http://www.ferngrove.com

Type: Cottages.
Clientele: 50% gay & lesbian & 50% straight clientele
Transportation: Car is best. Bus available from San Francisco.
To Gay Bars: 3 blocks.
Rooms: 20 cottages with queen beds.
Baths: 20 private bath/shower/toilets. Double-sized whirlpool tubs in some units.
Meals: Expanded continental breakfast.
Dates Open: All year.
High Season: June-Sept.
Rates: $69-$159.
Credit Cards: MC, Visa, Amex. Discover.
Rsv'tns: Required.
Reserve Thru: Travel agent or call direct.
Min. Stay: On holidays & summer weekends.
Parking: Ample, free off-street parking.
In-Room: Color cable TV, kitchen, refrigerator, coffee & tea-making facilities.
On-Premises: Meeting rooms.
Swimming: Pool on premises. River nearby.
Sunbathing: Poolside, on private sun decks.
Smoking: Permitted on private decks in front of each cottage.
Pets: Permitted, $10 per animal. Must not be "barkers," must be clean, leashed on property. Guests must use "pooper scooper."
Handicap Access: No.
Children: Welcome.
Languages: English.
Your Hosts: Simon & Anne.

Hartley House Inn

 Gay-Friendly 50/50 ⚥

A New Standard of Excellence

Hartley House is a stunning turn-of-the century mansion with the sophisticated elegance of a small European hotel. The home's stately character is preserved in original inlaid hardwood floors, stained woodwork, leaded and stained glass windows, and original brass light fixtures. Authentic antique furnishings, period artworks, and collectibles decorate the parlor, dining room, and guest rooms. Mornings, savor generous breakfasts of freshly baked muffins, fresh fruit, coffees, teas, and a variety of home made specialties cooked to order. The elegant decor, relaxed atmosphere and convenient location are all qualities that bring guests back time and time again.

Address: 700 Twenty-Second St, Sacramento, CA 95816-4012
Tel: (916) 447-7829, (800) 831-5806, **Fax:** (916) 447-1820.
E-mail: randy@hartleyhouse.com **Web:** http://www.hartleyhouse.com

Type: Bed & breakfast.
Clientele: 50% gay & lesbian & 50% straight clientele
Transportation: Car is best, airporter to door approx $10.
To Gay Bars: 5 blocks to gay/lesbian bars.
Rooms: 5 rooms with double, queen or king beds.
Baths: All private.
Meals: Full breakfast. Extensive menu, cooked to order.
Vegetarian: Always

available.
Complimentary: Cookies, beverages, turndown service with mints on pillow.
Dates Open: All year.
High Season: Spring through fall.
Rates: $115-$175.
Discounts: Corporate discounts available.
Credit Cards: MC, Visa, Amex, Discover, Carte Blanche, Diners.
Rsv'tns: Recommended.
Reserve Thru: Travel agent or call direct.

Min. Stay: On holiday weekends only.
Parking: Ample, free on- & off-street parking.
In-Room: Maid, room & laundry service, color cable TV, stereo/cassette clock radios, AC, ceiling fans, robes, Neutrogena products, multi-line phones & modem ports (no charge for local calls or long distance access).
On-Premises: Meeting room, dining room, library, fax & copy facilities.

Exercise/Health: Spa. Massage on premises with appointment. Discount at nearby local health club.
Swimming: In lake, river or nearby pool.
Sunbathing: On beach or courtyard.
Smoking: Permitted outdoors.
Pets: Not permitted.
Handicap Access: No.
Children: Permitted if older and by prior arrangement.
Languages: English.
Your Hosts: Randy.

Balboa Park Inn

WWW Gay/Lesbian ♂♀

More Than You'll Pay For...

    Balboa Park Inn is a collection of 26 distinctive, immaculate and beautifully-appointed suites, located in the heart of San Diego's gay community. We're just footsteps (1-1/2 blocks) from Balboa Park and the world famous San Diego Zoo. Nearby are the numerous cafes, shops, restaurants and nightclubs of Hillcrest, the city's gayest area of town. A short drive will find you at the Pacific's doorstep. Rent a car to see the sights, or use our comprehensive public transportation system. We're just minutes from the airport, train station and bus terminal downtown, and only 20 miles from Tijuana, Mexico, the world's most visited city. The *Balboa Park Inn* is your affordable, "family"-oriented destination in San Diego. Stay with us. We promise that you'll always get more than you paid for!

Address: 3402 Park Blvd, San Diego, CA 92103
Tel: (619) 298-0823, (800) 938-8181, **Fax:** (619) 294-8070.
Web: http://www.balboaparkinn.com

Type: Bed & breakfast inn.
Clientele: Good mix of gay men & women, with some straight clientele
Transportation: Car is best or taxi from airport.
To Gay Bars: 6 blocks to men's, 3 blocks to women's bar. A 15-minute walk or 5-minute drive.
Rooms: 19 suites & 7 rooms with single, queen or king beds.
Baths: All private.

Meals: Expanded continental breakfast.
Complimentary: Coffee, tea or hot chocolate in suite.
Dates Open: All year.
High Season: Summer.
Rates: $80-$200 plus tax.
Discounts: For established business accounts.
Credit Cards: MC, Visa, Amex, Diner's, Carte Blanche, Discover.
Rsv'tns: Required 3-4 wks. ahead in summer.

Reserve Thru: Travel agent or call direct.
Min. Stay: 3 days on holiday weekends.
Parking: Ample, free, on-street parking.
In-Room: Color cable TV, telephone, AC, refrigerator, coffee/tea-making facilities, maid service.
On-Premises: Maids do laundry.
Exercise/Health: Nearby in Hillcrest.

Swimming: Pool nearby, 10-15-min drive to ocean beach, 30-min drive to Black's Beach.
Sunbathing: On private and common sun decks.
Smoking: Permitted without restrictions.
Pets: Not permitted.
Handicap Access: No.
Children: Permitted.
Languages: English, Spanish.
IGLTA

Beach Place, The

Minutes from downtown, Hillcrest and most tourist attractions, the Ocean Beach section of San Diego retains the charm of a small town. No high-rise hotels block the view or prevent access to the beach. At *The Beach Place,* you enjoy the privacy of your own apartment with deck, small garden, full kitchen with microwave, bedroom with queen bed and living room with color TV and adult films. The central courtyard has a gazebo with a huge hot tub, as well as a patio for sunbathing.

Address: 2158 Sunset Cliffs Blvd, San Diego, CA 92107
Tel: (619) 225-0746.
E-mail: beachplace@webtv.net **Web:** http://www.beach.place.cc

Type: Guesthouse.
Clientele: Mostly men with women welcome
Transportation: Car is best.
To Gay Bars: 10-minute drive to numerous bars in Hillcrest, Pacific Beach & Point Loma.
Rooms: 4 suites with queen beds.
Baths: All private.

Complimentary: Tea, coffee, sugar, salt, pepper & utensils.
Dates Open: All year.
Rates: $60 per night or $350 per week for 2 people. $15 per night per additional guest.
Credit Cards: MC, Visa, Amex.
Rsv'tns: Required.
Reserve Thru: Travel agent

or call direct.
Min. Stay: 2 days.
Parking: Adequate off-street covered parking.
In-Room: Kitchen with microwave & refrigerator, color cable TV, ceiling fans & maid service.
On-Premises: Gas barbeque available in the courtyard.
Exercise/Health: Jacuzzi.

Swimming: 4 blocks to ocean beach.
Sunbathing: On the patio & private sun decks.
Nudity: Permitted.
Pets: Sometimes with prior arrangement.
Children: Permitted at times with prior arrangement.
Languages: English
IGLTA

Hillcrest Inn, The

Good Value In the Heart of Gay Hillcrest

The Hillcrest Inn is one of San Diego's newer hotels, a 45-room establishment in the midst of the city's favorite restaurant, bar and shopping neighborhood. Each room is clean and comfortable and has a private bath and telephone. The building has security gates and a beautiful new Jacuzzi and sunning patio. The downtown business district and the harbor are directly to the south. Balboa Park, with its zoo, museums, galleries and restaurants, is immediately to the east. Mission Bay, Sea World and Pacific beaches are a short drive to the north.

Address: 3754 5th Ave, San Diego, CA 92103
Tel: (619) 293-7078, (800) 258-2280, **Fax:** (619) 293-3861.
E-mail: hillcrestinn@juno.com **Web:** http://www.bryx.com/hillcrestinn

Type: Hotel.
Clientele: Mostly gay & lesbian
Transportation: Auto, city bus or taxi.
To Gay Bars: 6 bars within a 2 block radius.
Rooms: 45 rooms with queen & king beds.
Baths: All private bath/shower/toilets.
Complimentary: Coffee 8am to closing.
Dates Open: All year.

Rates: $55-$79.
Discounts: Week-long reservations, pay for 5 nights, get 2 free. Repeat customer discount.
Credit Cards: MC, Visa, Amex, Diners, Optima, Carte Blanche.
Rsv'tns: Recommended.
Reserve Thru: Travel agent or call direct.
Min. Stay: 2 nights on holidays, special events.
Parking: Paid parking in

adjacent lot.
In-Room: Color TV with remote, VCR, telephone, ceiling fans, maid service, kitchen, refrigerator, microwave, voice mail, data ports.
On-Premises: Laundry facilities, snack machines, tour desk.
Exercise/Health: Jacuzzi.
Swimming: Ocean beach 15 min by car.
Sunbathing: On private

sunning patio.
Smoking: Permitted without restrictions. Non-smoking rooms available.
Pets: Not permitted.
Handicap Access: Yes, ramps & special bathroom facilities.
Children: Not permitted.
Languages: English, some Spanish, French.
Your Hosts: Jerry.
IGLTA

Kasa Korbett

Gay/Lesbian ⚥

Where a Guest is at Home

Each room in *Kasa Korbett*, a comfortable 70-year-old craftsman-design house, is appointed in its own theme. Enjoyable breakfasts are served each morning in your room, the dining room, or on the patio deck (dinner plans are available). Relax in the living room with a video, visit the nearby beaches, Sea World, San Diego Zoo, or nap in the backyard hammock year-round. Within a few blocks' walk, you will find bars for every taste, various bookstores and coffeehouses, and gay-owned and gay-friendly restaurants and shops.

Address: 4050 Front Street, San Diego, CA 92103
Tel: (619) 291-3962, (800) 757-KASA (5272).
E-mail: kasakorbett@hotmail.com **Web:** http://www.kasakorbett.com

Type: Bed & breakfast home.
Clientele: Gay & lesbian. Good mix of men & women
Transportation: Car is best. Taxi is inexpensive. Free pick up from airport, train, bus.
To Gay Bars: 3 block walk.
Rooms: 4 rooms.
Baths: 2 private, 2 shared.
Meals: Expanded continental breakfast.
Vegetarian: By guest

request. Many restaurants, health food stores nearby.
Complimentary: Tea, coffee, juice, soda.
Dates Open: All year.
High Season: Apr-Oct.
Rates: $79, $89, $99.
Discounts: Stay 5 nights, 6th night free.
Credit Cards: Visa, MC, Amex.
Rsv'tns: Required.
Reserve Thru: Travel agent or call direct.

Min. Stay: 2 nights on holiday/event weekends.
Parking: Ample off-street parking.
In-Room: Telephone, color TV, maid & room service.
On-Premises: TV lounge, video tape library.
Exercise/Health: Massage. Nearby gym, weights, sauna, steam.
Swimming: Pool & ocean nearby.
Sunbathing: On common

sun decks.
Smoking: No smoking except in patio area.
Pets: Not permitted.
Handicap Access: Yes. Wheelchair accessibility to all rooms.
Children: No.
Languages: English.
Your Hosts: Bob.
IGLTA

Park Manor Suites Hotel

WWW Gay/Lesbian ⚥

"Old World Charm" in Gay Hillcrest

At *Park Manor Suites Hotel* we pride ourselves on our friendly staff and hospitality. Eighty elegantly appointed suites boast full kitchens, dining areas and baths, as well as cable and color TV. Enjoy incredible views while lunching at the Top of the Park Penthouse. Its Monday-Friday lunch menu consists of daily specials to please every palate at reasonable prices. Evening dining at Inn at the Park restaurant features dishes prepared by our chef who is specially trained in European-style cuisine. Located adjacent to Balboa Park at Sixth Avenue and Spruce Street, we are within walking distance to all gay restaurants and bars.

Address: 525 Spruce St, San Diego, CA 92103
Tel: (619) 291-0999, (800) 874-2649, **Fax:** (619) 291-8844.
E-mail: parkmanor@mindspring.com **Web:** http://
www.parkmanorsuites.com

Type: Hotel with restaurant & bar.
Clientele: 60% gay & lesbian & 40% straight clientele
Transportation: Car or taxi.
To Gay Bars: On premises & 1 block walking distance.
Rooms: 80 single, double & triple suites.
Baths: All private.

Meals: Continental breakfast. Optional lunch & dinner.
Dates Open: All year.
Rates: $79-$169.
Discounts: Senior citizens 10%.
Credit Cards: MC, Visa, Amex, Discover.
Reserve Thru: Travel agent or call direct.

Parking: Free parking.
In-Room: Color TV, ceiling fans, telephone, voice mail, kitchen, refrigerator, coffeemaker, maid & room service.
On-Premises: Meeting rooms, laundry facilities, catering.
Sunbathing: On rooftop sun deck or across street at

Balboa Park.
Smoking: Non-smoking suites available.
Pets: No.
Handicap Access: Yes.
Children: Permitted with no restrictions.
Languages: English, Spanish, French & German.
IGLTA

Accommodations in San Francisco

Bock's Bed & Breakfast

WWW Gay-Friendly 50/50 ♀♂

In Operation Since 1980

Bock's is a lovely 1906 Edwardian residence in the Parnassus Heights area of San Francisco with beautiful views of the city. Golden Gate Park is two blocks away and public transportation is nearby. Host, Laura Bock, has restored the original virgin redwood walls of the dining and entry rooms as well as the mahogany inlaid oak floors of the latter, and two original pocket doors on the main floor. Laura's enthusiasm and touring tips about her native city are enjoyed by an international clientele.

Address: 1448 Willard St, San Francisco, CA 94117
Tel: (415) 664-6842, **Fax:** (415) 664-1109.

Type: Bed & breakfast.
Clientele: 50% gay & lesbian & 50% straight clientele
Transportation: From airport take one of the van shuttles outside the 2nd level.
To Gay Bars: 1 mile to gay/lesbian bars.
Rooms: 3 rooms with single, double or queen beds.
Baths: 1 private, 1 private sink, others share full bath.
Meals: Expanded

continental breakfast.
Vegetarian: I can accommodate special needs & there is vegetarian food nearby.
Complimentary: Coffee, tea, hot chocolate service in rooms. Small, shared guest refrigerator & microwave.
Dates Open: All year.
High Season: May-Oct.
Rates: $50-$90 plus tax. $10 each add'l person, plus tax.
Discounts: 10% for over 1 week.

Credit Cards: None.
Rsv'tns: Recommended.
Reserve Thru: Call direct.
Min. Stay: 2 nights.
Parking: On-street parking. Inexpensive lot 2 blocks away.
In-Room: Color TV, telephone, electric hot pot, radios, coffee/tea-making facilities. Private balcony in 1 room.
On-Premises: Deck off of living room, laundry facilities, guest refrigerator & microwave.

Exercise/Health: Nearby.
Swimming: Pool nearby, ocean beach 3 miles away.
Sunbathing: On private or common sun decks.
Smoking: Non-smokers only.
Pets: Not permitted.
Handicap Access: No.
Children: Permitted. Infants must be old enough to sleep through the night.
Languages: English, smattering of French.
Your Hosts: Laura

Atherton Hotel

Gay-Friendly ⚥

European Charm in the Heart of San Francisco

Constructed in 1927, the *Atherton Hotel* was renovated in 1996 to enhance its "Old San Francisco" feel. The lobby's original marble floor, molded ceiling and etched glass project the ambiance of an intimate European inn. The Atherton Grill, serving continental cuisine, breakfast and Sunday champagne brunch, also offers dinner mid-May through October. Our English-style pub, The Abbey room, decorated with antique abbey altar panels, offers a full bar from 5 pm. The hotel is walking distance to the Cable Cars, Union Square and theaters. With intimate charm and friendly service, we have proudly served our community for over 17 years.

Address: 685 Ellis St, San Francisco, CA 94109
Tel: (415) 474-5720, (800) 474-5720, **Fax:** (415) 474-8256.
E-mail: reservations@hotelatherton.com **Web:** http://www.hotelatherton.com

Type: Hotel with restaurant and bar.
Clientele: Mostly straight clientele with a gay & lesbian following
Transportation: Shuttle from airport about $10, taxi maximum $30. All major public transportation lines nearby.
To Gay Bars: 1 block to men's bars on Polk Street, 10 min drive to Castro (3 metro stops).

Rooms: 75 rooms with twin, queen or king beds.
Baths: All private baths.
Complimentary: Coffee from 7am-11am. USA Today in lobby weekdays.
Dates Open: All year.
High Season: June-Oct.
Rates: US $89-$139.
Credit Cards: MC, Visa, Amex, Diners, Discover.
Rsv'tns: Required.
Reserve Thru: Travel agent or call direct.

Min. Stay: 2 nights during Gay Pride & Folsom St. Fair.
Parking: Valet parking $21/ day (subject to change), 2 blocks to pay lot.
In-Room: Color satellite TV, dataport telephones, maid service.
On-Premises: Private dining room & lounge. Valet $21 (subject to change).
Exercise/Health: Nearby gym.
Swimming: In nearby

ocean.
Smoking: Not permitted in lobby. Non-smoking rooms available.
Pets: Not permitted.
Handicap Access: No.
Children: Children under 12 with accompanying parents stay free.
Languages: English, German, Spanish, Italian, French, Tagalog.
Your Hosts: Ron, Diana & Todd.

Belvedere House B & B

A Place to Be and Let Be

From the quiet ridge on a tree-lined street in upper Cole Valley, *Belvedere House* joins its neighbors in enjoying a view to the north that includes the Golden Gate Bridge. Whether you would like to sit quietly in the parlor and read one of the hundreds of volumes lining the walls, listen to music, smoke in the intimate atrium or soak in the garden spa, the time you spend with us is yours, without tedious rules or limitations. Your host, Robert, has only one rule: that all his guests are allowed to be, peacefully. When you're ready to venture out, you'll find that the Golden Gate Park, shopping, clubs, galleries, the beach and San Francisco's unique neighborhoods are all only a few blocks away. Once you have visited you will agree, *Belvedere House* is a unique, warm and practical alternative.

Address: 598 Belvedere St, San Francisco, CA 94117-4364
Tel: (415) 731-6654, **Fax:** (415) 681-0719.
E-mail: belvederehouse@mindspring.com

Type: Bed & breakfast.
Clientele: Mostly gay & lesbian with some straight clientele
Transportation: Airport shuttle (door-to-door).
To Gay Bars: 12 blocks, 1 mi, a 15 min walk, a 2 min drive.
Rooms: 6 rooms with singles or queen beds.
Baths: Shared or private

baths/shower/toilet.
Meals: Expanded continental breakfast.
Vegetarian: Vegetarian breakfast. Vegetarian shops nearby.
Complimentary: Sherry in late afternoon, cheese & crackers.
Dates Open: All year.
High Season: May-Oct.
Rates: $55-$85.

Rsv'tns: Desireable during high season.
Reserve Thru: Travel agent or call direct.
Parking: Adequate on-street parking.
In-Room: Maid & laundry service.
On-Premises: Laundry facilities.
Sunbathing: Common sun deck, patio.

Nudity: Permitted on deck.
Smoking: Permitted in garden atrium. All rooms are non-smoking.
Pets: Permitted.
Handicap Access: No.
Children: Welcome.
Languages: English, German, French.
Your Hosts: Michael & Robert.

Castro Suites

Well-Furnished Executive Suites

Your suite at Sam and Joel's architecturally restored 1890's Victorian, is your home away from home in the Castro area. Our two luxuriously appointed suites provide our guests with a sophisticated yet comfortable setting, containing the best of contemporary furniture, original art, crafts and ethnic accessories. Please note, this isn't a B&B, but two self-sufficient executive apartments. One bedroom has a firm queen-sized bed, dressers and ample closet space; the living rooms have lounge chairs, sofabed, and a desk. The other has dual twins. Each has a full bath and a fully equipped, eat-in kitchen, including dishwasher, microwave and clothes washer/dryer.

Each meticulously maintained suite has two telephone lines, one for voice and a second modem port for computers, and there is a fax machine available... providing the comforts and conveniences of home for both business and vacation travelers. Hosts Joel and Sam also provide concierge service. They'll make restaurant and theater reservations and stock the refrigerator, with advance notice.

Address: 927 14th Street, San Francisco, CA
Tel: (415) 437-1783, **Fax:** (415) 437-1784.
E-mail: jmrsrc@castrosuites.com **Web:** http://www.castrosuites.com

Type: 2 executive suites.
Clientele: Anyone nice is welcome
Transportation: Super Shuttle from airport.
To Gay Bars: 3 blocks.
Rooms: 1 suite with queen bed & sofa bed. 1 with dual twins & sofa bed.
Baths: All private baths.

Vegetarian: Nearby.
Dates Open: All year.
Rates: $180 for 1 or 2 people, $195 for 3 or 4 people.
Rsv'tns: Required.
Reserve Thru: Travel agent or call direct.
Min. Stay: 3 days.
Parking: Adequate on-

street parking & commercial garage nearby.
In-Room: Telephone, color cable TV, VCR, full kitchen with laundry.
Exercise/Health: Nearby gym, weights, Jacuzzi, sauna, steam, massage.
Sunbathing: On private sun deck.

Smoking: No smoking.
Pets: Not permitted.
Children: Inquire.
Languages: English, French, Italian, Spanish.
Your Hosts: Sam & Joel.

Chateau Tivoli

WWW Gay-Friendly 50/50 ⚤

The Greatest Painted Lady In the World

Chateau Tivoli, an authentic period restoration of a Victorian mansion, was built in 1892 by renowned architect William H. Armitage for an Oregon lumber baron, and restored a century later at a cost of more than a million dollars. The book *Painted Ladies Revisited* calls it "...the greatest Painted Lady in the world."

Fully licensed as a hotel B&B, the residence features nine lavishly appointed guest bedrooms. The exterior is painted in twenty-two different colors, and highlighted with brilliant gold leafing. The interior is resplendent with hardwood floors, stately columns and numerous stained glass windows. The walls and ceilings in bedrooms and hallways are covered in Bradbury & Bradbury wallpaper and accented by gold leaf and various faux treatments.

Address: 1057 Steiner St, San Francisco, CA 94115
Tel: (415) 776-5462, (800) 228-1647, **Fax:** (415) 776-0505.
Web: http://www.chateautivoli.com

Type: Bed & breakfast.
Clientele: 50% gay & lesbian & 50% straight clientele
Transportation: Shuttle or taxi from airport.
To Gay Bars: Ten minutes to gay & lesbian bars.
Rooms: 5 doubles, 4 suites (2 with 2 bedrooms).
Baths: 7 private, others share with only one other

room.
Meals: Expanded continental breakfast Mon-Fri, champagne brunch available Sat & Sun.
Complimentary: Afternoon wine & cheese, coffee, tea, herb tea, juice, etc.
Dates Open: All year.
High Season: Mar-Oct.
Rates: $99-$250.
Discounts: For 4 or more

days.
Credit Cards: MC, Visa, Amex.
Rsv'tns: Required.
Reserve Thru: Travel agent or call direct.
Min. Stay: 2 days on weekends.
Parking: On-street parking in residential neighborhood.
In-Room: Maid service, telephone.

On-Premises: Meeting rooms.
Smoking: Limited to outside areas.
Pets: Special permission required.
Children: Always welcome if well-behaved.
Languages: English.
Your Hosts: Victoria & Soraya.

Essex Hotel, The

WWW Gay-Friendly ⚥

The Essex Hotel, totally renovated in recent years, is centrally located and within walking distance of all major points, including Cable Car line, Union Square, Chinatown, theaters and many fine restaurants. Polk Street is only a block away and gay men's bars are two blocks away. The Airporter shuttle to our front door is $12. The hotel has a European atmosphere, pleasant, comfortable double rooms with high-quality furnishings, color TV, maid service, and direct dial phones. Most rooms have private baths.

Address: 684 Ellis St, San Francisco, CA 94109
Tel: (415) 474-4664, (800) 453-7739, **Fax:** (415) 441-1800. In CA (800) 443-7739.

Type: Hotel.
Clientele: Mostly straight clientele with a gay & lesbian following
Transportation: Airporter shuttle $12.
To Gay Bars: 2 blocks to men's bars.
Rooms: 100 rooms with queen beds.

Baths: 50 private bath/ toilets, others share. 100 private sinks.
Complimentary: Coffee.
Dates Open: All year.
Rates: Single $79, double $89.
Discounts: 10% to holders of Inn Places, subject to room availability.

Credit Cards: MC, Visa, Amex.
Rsv'tns: Suggested.
Reserve Thru: Travel agent or call direct.
Parking: Adequate on-street pay parking.
In-Room: Color TV, direct dial phone, maid service.
On-Premises: Public

telephone, central heat.
Smoking: Permitted without restrictions.
Pets: Not permitted.
Handicap Access: No.
Children: Permitted.
Languages: English, French, German.
IGLTA

Hayes Valley Inn

WWW Gay-Friendly 50/50 ♀♂
Woman-Owned & -Operated

The *Hayes Valley Inn* is situated in the heart of San Francisco's "Hayes Valley," known for its up-and-coming restaurants and boutique shops. Centrally located, San Francisco's newly refurbished City Hall is just a few blocks away. In addition, it is only three block to the Opera and Davies Symphony Hall. The Bill Graham Civic Auditorium is across the street from City Hall, and draws its share of music lovers who come to the city to see their favorite artists.

Our inn has a special personality, patterned on the popular "boutique-style" hotel you find in San Francisco and New York. *Hayes Valley Inn* guests enter a homey atmosphere where they can get to know the owner, as well as the other guests. We have opened our "Ivy Room" where guests enjoy their continental breakfast, or they may choose to have it brought to their room. Some guests may elect to play cards or borrow a good book to read during their visit. Guestrooms feature a sink and vanity in each room, and they share a bath and two toilets on each floor. There is an average of only ten rooms per floor. Our guests return often and choose our inn because it is their "home away from home."

Address: 417 Gough St, San Francisco, CA
Tel: (415) 431-9131, (800) 930-7999, **Fax:** (415) 431-2585.
E-mail: hayesvalley@aol.com

Type: Bed & breakfast hotel.
Clientele: 50% gay & lesbian & 50% straight
Transportation: Taxi or Airporter from airport.
To Gay Bars: 1/2 block & many bars within 1-2 miles.
Rooms: 30 rooms.
Baths: 3 shared bath/showers, 6 WC only.
Meals: Continental breakfast.

Vegetarian: At Pendragon Cafe on the corner.
Dates Open: All year.
High Season: Jun & Sept.
Rates: $58-$99, plus 14% SF hotel tax. Group rates.
Discounts: 10% AAA, AARP.
Credit Cards: MC, Visa, Amex, Diners.
Rsv'tns: Required (48-hr cancellation policy). Walkins if rooms available.

Reserve Thru: Travel agent or call direct.
Min. Stay: Only on special weekends & holidays.
Parking: Adequate off-street pay parking nearby, reasonable rates.
In-Room: Telephone, ceiling fans, color cable TV, maid service.
On-Premises: Paperback library area, Ivy Room, laundry facilities.

Smoking: Non-smoking rooms available. CA doesn't allow smoking in common areas.
Pets: Must call in advance, $50 pet deposit. Only a couple of rooms for pets.
Children: Must behave & not disturb other guests.
Languages: English, some Spanish.

Inn 1890

A "Very San Francisco" Queen Anne Victorian

Newly refurbished, *Inn 1890* graciously blends Victorian elegance with modern conveniences for your complete comfort. Most rooms in this newly refurbished inn have expansive bay windows, twelve-foot ceilings, hardwood floors and Oriental rugs. Brass or iron queen-sized beds with plush down and feather comforters will keep you warm and rested. Our luxurious bathrobes and slippers are especially cozy when curling up in front of one of the original wood fireplaces. Your private telephone has its own telephone number and message center, and offers free unlimited local calls and free long-distance access. Also for your convenience, kitchenettes are provided in each room and are great for light cooking and warming leftovers from the many local restaurants.

Inn 1890 is in a quiet residential neighborhood in the geographic center of the city. Minutes away is Buena Vista Park and the famous and historical Castro District. One block west is Golden Gate Park, which houses a variety of museums and world-renowned gardens, including the Japanese Tea Garden and the Strybing Arboretum. Walking and biking paths throughout the park lead to the beach and stunning vistas of the Pacific coastline. Walk to the health club, University of California at San Francisco and the University of San Francisco. A variety of public transportation options are very nearby.

Address: 1890 Page St, San Francisco, CA 94117
Tel: (415) 386-0486, (888) INN-1890 (466-1890), **Fax:** (415) 386-3626.
E-mail: inn1890@worldnet.att.net **Web:** http://www.Inn1890.com

Type: Bed & breakfast inn.
Clientele: 50% gay & lesbian & 50% straight
Transportation: Airport van or shuttle to front door. Free pick up from local bus.
To Gay Bars: 4 blocks.
Rooms: 8 rooms, 2 apartments with single, double or queen beds.
Baths: 8 private, 2 shared.
Meals: Expanded continental breakfast.
Complimentary: 24-hour

cookies, nuts, mints, coffee & tea, ceareal, fruit, jam, jelly, hot chocolate, juice.
High Season: May-Oct.
Rates: Summer $79-$99 +hotel tax; Winter $79-$99 +hotel tax; Apartment $109-$119 +hotel tax.
Discounts: On stays of 1 week or more.
Credit Cards: MC, Visa.
Rsv'tns: Required.
Reserve Thru: Travel agent or call direct.

Min. Stay: 2 nights.
Parking: Limited, covered, off-street pay parking ($5/ night).
In-Room: Telephone, color TV, coffee & tea-making facilities, kitchenette with refrigerator, microwave, sink, dishes.
On-Premises: Book library, board games, fax, modem, computer, laundry facilities, garden, patio, 24-hour kitchen.

Exercise/Health: Nearby gym, weights.
Swimming: Nearby pool & ocean.
Sunbathing: On patio, at beach & Golden Gate Park.
Smoking: Permitted outside on patio. Non-smoking rooms available.
Pets: Permitted with prior permission.
Children: Welcome.

Inn on Castro

The innkeepers invite you into a colorful and comfortable environment filled with modern art and exotic plants. All rooms vary in size and have private baths. Meet fellow travelers from all over the world for a memorable breakfast. The *Inn On Castro's* location is unique, just 100 yards north of the intersection of Market and Castro, where you are in a quiet neighborhood, yet only a stone's throw away from the Castro Theater, plus dozens of bars, restaurants and shops. With the *Underground* almost virtually adjacent to the *Inn,* big-name store shopping and cable car, etc. are just a few minutes away. There is literally something for everyone.

Address: 321 Castro St, San Francisco, CA 94114
Tel: (415) 861-0321 (Tel/Fax)
Web: http://www.innoncastro2.com

Type: Bed & breakfast.
Clientele: Good mix of gay men & women
Transportation: Supershuttle from airport approx $11 per person.
To Gay Bars: Less than 1-minute walk to men's/women's bars.
Rooms: 6 rooms & 2 suites with double, queen or king beds, self-catering apartment.
Baths: All private.

Meals: Full breakfast.
Vegetarian: Available with advance notice.
Complimentary: Afternoon wine, brandy night cap, tea, coffee, juices.
Dates Open: All year.
High Season: May-Oct.
Rates: Rooms $95-$175.
Credit Cards: MC, Visa, Amex.
Rsv'tns: Recommended 1 month in advance.
Reserve Thru: Call direct.

Min. Stay: 2 days on weekends, 3 on holidays, 4 days Folsom Fair, Castro Fair & Gay Lib days.
Parking: Adequate on-street parking.
In-Room: Private, direct-dial telephone & answering machine, color TV, maid service, refrigerator.
On-Premises: Lounge & dining room.
Exercise/Health: Gym, weights, jacuzzi, sauna,

steam & massage across the street.
Swimming: Nearby pool.
Sunbathing: On private sun decks.
Smoking: Permitted on patio, front porch, rear deck.
Pets: Not permitted.
Handicap Access: Patio suite is handicap-accessible.
Children: Permitted but not encouraged.
Languages: English, French, German & Dutch.

Inn San Francisco, The

One of the Finest Bed & Breakfast Mansions in the City

Feel the years slip away, as you step through the massive, wooden doors of the *Inn San Francisco.* Tthe Inn has been lovingly and thoughtfully restored to create an inviting ambience of past splendor and elegance. Classical music, candlelight, and the fragrance of roses set a mood that takes you back in time...a time enhanced by ornate woodwork, oriental carpets and marble fireplaces, in the grand double parlors amidst the sparkle of stained and beveled glass. Each of the guest rooms is individually decorated with antique furnishings, fresh flowers, marble sinks, polished brass fixtures and exquisite finishing touches. All are extraordinarily beautiful and the feeling of classic, old-world elegance and grandeur is carried throughout.

Mornings, treat yourself to the best breakfast buffet you've ever seen in a B&B. Enjoy it in our Double Parlors, or take it to your room, or, on warm sunny days, to the rooftop sundeck or our lovely English Garden. In the garden, under the shade of an old fig tree, an enchanting gazebo shelters the inviting hot tub. Our neighborhood is between the Folsom and the Castro and just two blocks from Valencia Street.

Address: 943 S Van Ness Ave, San Francisco, CA 94110
Tel: (415) 641-0188, (800) 359-0913, **Fax:** (415) 641-1701.
E-mail: innkeeper@innsf.com **Web:** http://www.innsf.com

Type: Bed & breakfast inn.
Clientele: Mixed, straight clientele with very strong gay/lesbian following
Transportation: Airport Shuttle $10 per person.
To Gay Bars: 8 blocks.
Rooms: 13 rooms, 7 luxury suites with Jacuzzis, 1 garden cottage apt, queens & doubles.
Baths: 19 private, 2 rooms share.

Meals: Full buffet breakfast.
Vegetarian: Veg. items at breakfast.
Complimentary: Coffee, tea, sherry complimentary in parlor, truffles in room.
Dates Open: All year.
Rates: Rooms $85-$235.
Discounts: Stays of 1+ wk.
Credit Cards: Visa, MC, Amex, Diners, Carte

Blanche, Discover.
Rsv'tns: Required.
Reserve Thru: Call direct.
Min. Stay: 2 nts wknds, esp hols. We're flexible. Call.
Parking: Several covered garages w/electric door openers, parking $10/night.
In-Room: Color TV, phone, fridge, maid, laundry svc.
On-Premises: Laundry facilities.

Exercise/Health: Redwood hot tub in tropical gazebo.
Sunbathing: On private & common sun decks, patios & on rooftop.
Smoking: Not in parlor.
Pets: Not permitted.
Children: Permitted.
Languages: English, Spanish, Chinese, limited French.
IGLTA

King George Hotel

Charm, Warmth & Tradition in San Francisco

The King George Hotel, a charming English-style hotel, is very gay-friendly and well-informed about gay venues and events. Experience the pleasure of staying in any of our first-class rooms, all with baths, remote control TVs, phones with voice mail and dataports, safes, ironing equipment, hairdryers, and electronic door.

This is great home base for visitors desiring both value and convenience. Our superb location puts San Francisco at your doorstep! Just one block from the cable cars and San Francisco's famous shopping and dining district, Union Square, *The King George Hotel* is only ten minutes from the Castro district, 15 minutes from Fisherman's Wharf and under an hour and a half from the Russian River, making it ideal for both business and leisure travel. Our guest services staff is always pleased to assist with tours, airport shuttles, car rental and other concierge services.

Address: 334 Mason St, San Francisco, CA 94102
Tel: (800) 288-6005, (415) 781-5050, **Fax:** (415) 391-6976.
E-mail: KingGeorge@KingGeorge.com **Web:** http://www.kinggeorge.com

Type: Hotel.
Clientele: Mostly straight clientele with a gay/lesbian following
Transportation: Pick up from airport $10 per person each way. Shuttle from SFO airport, Coliseum BART to Powell St Sta. from Oakland.
To Gay Bars: 5 blocks or 1/2 mile. 5-minute walk or 10 minutes by car, including parking.
Rooms: 140 rooms & 2 suites with single, twin, queen or king beds.
Baths: All private bath/toilets.

Meals: Continental breakfast (not included w/ rates).
Vegetarian: Tea room menu includes meatless tea sandwiches & pastries.
Dates Open: All year.
High Season: Apr 1-Nov 14.
Rates: $145 single, $160 double. Call 800# for year-round special rates.
Discounts: Special packages, holiday specials & membership in IGTA.
Credit Cards: MC, Visa, Amex, Diners, Eurocard, Discover, Carte Blanche,

JCB.
Rsv'tns: Required, but walk-ins taken on a space-available basis.
Reserve Thru: Travel agent or call direct.
Parking: 24hr secured pay parking. $18 daily with in-out privileges.
In-Room: Color TV, telephone, safe, room service 24hrs, maid & laundry service.
On-Premises: Meeting rooms, fax, photocopying, concierge, same-day laundry.
Exercise/Health: Nearby

gym, weights, sauna, steam & massage.
Swimming: Nearby pool.
Smoking: 50% of rooms are non-smoking.
Pets: Not permitted.
Handicap Access: Yes. Race-style wheelchairs, deaf phone kit.
Children: Welcome. Roll-away beds, cribs, concierge services of things to do with kids.
Languages: English, French, Spanish, German, Russian, Pilipino.
IGLTA

Color Photo on Page 15

Parker House Guest House, The

WWW Gay/Lesbian ⚥
Gay-Owned & -Operated

San Francisco's Premier Gay Guest House

San Francisco's most beautiful gay and lesbian guesthouse, *The Parker House*, is a 6000 sq. ft. renovated mini-mansion located in the city's vibrant and historic Castro district. We offer a relaxing library with nightly fireside sherry service, large garden sun room where breakfast is served daily, beautifully landscaped gardens and sunning areas, and a new luxury steam/spa area. Most rooms have private baths and all rooms offer terry cloth robes, down comforters, cable TV, voice mail, luxury bath amenities and second line in-room modem ports. We're steps from dozens of bars, cafes, parks and restaurants. There is also easy and convenient transportation to all San Francisco area attractions and on-site parking is available. Big hotel conveniences with the comfort and warmth of a small gay-owned and -operated guesthouse make us the perfect choice for both business and leisure travelers to San Francisco. Out and About Editor's Choice award winner 1998 & 1999 — "Five Palms."

Address: 520 Church St, San Francisco, CA 94114
Tel: (415) 621-3222, toll-free: (888) 520-7275.
E-mail: info@parkerguesthouse.com **Web:** http://
www.parkerguesthouse.com

Type: Guesthouse.
Clientele: Men & women welcome
Transportation: Airport shuttle.
To Gay Bars: 2 blocks.
Rooms: 10 rooms with king or queen beds.
Baths: Private & shared.
Meals: Expanded continental breakfast.
Complimentary: Steam

room, fireside sherry svc.
High Season: All year.
Rates: $109-$189.
Credit Cards: MC, Visa, Amex, Discover.
Rsv'tns: Suggested.
Reserve Thru: Travel agent or call direct.
Min. Stay: Required on weekends.
Parking: Pay parking.
In-Room: Color cable TV,

phone, voice mail, modem ports, maid svc, robes.
On-Premises: Meeting rooms, fax, voice mail, modem ports.
Exercise/Health: Nearby gym, weights, Jacuzzi, sauna, steam, massage.
Swimming: Nearby pool & ocean.
Sunbathing: On common sun decks, in garden area,

at beach.
Nudity: Permitted in steam room only.
Smoking: Permitted in designated common areas. No smoking in rooms.
Pets: Not permitted.
Children: No.
Languages: English.
Your Hosts: Bob & Bill.
IGLTA

Personality Hotels on Union Square

WWW Gay-Friendly ⚥

Comfort & Convenience on Union Square

Personality Hotels offers four boutique properties in San Francisco, each with their own personality. Conveniently located around Union Square, known for its variety of fine dining, excellent shopping and first-class entertainment. The concierge at each hotel can assist with dinner reservations, sight seeing tours, theatre, reservations and a variety of other options. All rooms have private baths, with hairdryers; and offer daily complimentary continental breakfast service. Rooms are equipped with cable TV, including pay-per-view movies, two phone lines with data ports, same-day laundry/valet service, as well as afternoon complimentary tea or coffee service. Valet parking is available for an additional fee.

The Hotel Diva at 440 Geary Street, steps to Union Square, and directly across the street from the Curran Theatre, has 111 modern Italian-designed rooms with air conditioning. VCRs are available in all rooms and a video library is at the front desk. *The Kensington Park Hotel* offers 87 newly renovated Queen Anne-style rooms. Located at 450 Post Street, half a block to the cable car line, it shares its address with the Theatre on the Square and the city's top-rated Restaurant Farallon. *The Hotel Union Square,* on the Powell Street cable car line at 114 Powell St, has 131 spectacular new rooms in rich tones with a nostalgic feeling of San Francisco. All rooms have a mini-bar as an additional amenity already described above. *The Hotel Metropolis,* at 25 Mason Street, one block from the Powell Street cable car line, has 105 rooms in colors reflecting the natural forces... Fire, Wind, Earth and Water. Its holistic room, gym and mezzanine library provides a relaxing atmosphere. Call 1-800-553-1900 for individual reservations, or 415-202-8700 for group reservations.

Tel: (415) 202-8700, (800) 553-1900, **Fax:** (415) 885-3268.
Web: http://www.personalityhotels.com

Type: Boutique hotels.
Clientele: Gay & lesbian travelers love the comfort & convenience of these 4 mainstream hotels on Union Square
Transportation: Shuttle busses from airport available. Easy access to public transportation.
To Gay Bars: 5 blocks.
Rooms: Rooms with single, double, queen & king beds.

Baths: All private.
Meals: Continental breakfast.
Complimentary: Afternoon tea service, or wine reception.
Dates Open: All year.
Rates: $110-$205.
Discounts: Inquire.
Credit Cards: MC, Visa, Amex, Diners.
Rsv'tns: Required.
Reserve Thru: Travel agent

or call direct. Please mention that you found these hotels in the Ferrari Guides.
Parking: Ample pay parking.
In-Room: Phone, color cable TV, maid & laundry svc.
On-Premises: Meeting rooms.
Exercise/Health: Nearby gym, weights, Jacuzzi,

massage.
Smoking: Permitted in smoking guest rooms.
Pets: Not permitted.
Handicap Access: Meets all ADA requirements.
Children: Welcome.
Languages: English, Spanish & other languages.
IGLTA

Renoir Hotel

www Gay-Friendly ♂♂
Straight -& Gay-Operated

Classic European Style in the Center of Gay San Francisco

The *Renoir Hotel* is a gay-friendly and cosmopolitan boutique hotel located in the lively heart of downtown San Francisco. Originally built in 1909, the ornate interior of this triangle-shaped historical landmark building has been renovated to restore its classic European turn-of-the-century charm. Union Square and the Cable Cars are only a few steps away. The unique Civic Cen-

ter Complex, and the largest collection of Beaux Arts architecture in the United States, is literally at our doorstep. Moscone Convention Center, the Museum of Modern Art and the Yerba Buena Center for the Arts are also within walking distance.

The hotel is centrally located between the popular downtown tourist sites and the Castro, and within walk-

ing distance to the clubs on Folsom and Polk Street. It is ideally situated with rooms facing Market Street for the annual Gay Pride Parade. Theaters, Chinatown, and the San Francisco Shopping Centre are also nearby.

Address: 45 McAllister St, San Francisco, CA 94102
Tel: (415) 626-5200, Reservations: (800) 576-3388, Sales **Fax:** (415) 626-0916,
Main **Fax:** (415) 626-5581.
Web: http://www.renoirhotel.com

Type: Hotel with Brazilian restaurant.
Clientele: Mostly straight, gay/lesbian following
Transportation: BART, airport shuttle van. Near all Bay Area transport.
To Gay Bars: Folsom St: 3-5 blocks; Polk St: 7-10 blocks; Castro: 10 min by streetcar, subway.
Rooms: 135 rooms with 2 suites & 4 view rms.
Baths: All private.

Meals: Brazilian restaurant & café in hotel.
High Season: Apr 1-Nov 15.
Rates: Standard: $119-$139; View: $139-$169; Suites: $175-$250.
Discounts: Inn Places rate: $79-$99 (based on avail.).
Credit Cards: All major credit cards accepted.
Rsv'tns: Required.
Reserve Thru: Travel agent or book directly.

Min. Stay: 2 days Gay Pride Wknd, some sold out periods (Folsom St. Fair).
Parking: Valet $18/day.
In-Room: Color TV with remote, clock radio, in-room safe, hair dryer, ironing board, maid, room & laundry service.
On-Premises: Restaurant, lounge, cafe.
Exercise/Health: YMCA 1 block, $7 a day with Renoir Hotel Discount.

Swimming: YMCA.
Smoking: 3 smoking floors, 3 non-smoking floors.
Pets: Not permitted.
Handicap Access: Full wheelchair accessibility to public places, some rooms wheelchair accessible.
Children: 12 & under stay free with adult.
Languages: English, German, French, Spanish, Portuguese, Italian, Tagalog.
IGLTA

Color Photo on Page 16

Willows Inn, The

Your Haven within the Castro Since 1981

The Willows Inn is located within the Gay and Lesbian Castro neighborhood and a few steps away from the city's subway and bus lines. Housed in a 1903 Edwardian, the decor is a blend of handcrafted bentwood willow furnishings, antique dressers, armoires, and cozy comforters. *The Willows* is noted for its homey atmosphere and personal, friendly service. Each morning, we serve an expanded continental breakfast consisting of fresh fruit, yogurt, oven-baked goods, gourmet coffee, assorted teas, and fresh orange juice along with the morning newspaper. To help plan your day's activities our innkeepers are always available with helpful suggestions and directions, and will assist with choices of restaurants, nightclubs and entertainment. At midday, while you're out and about, rooms are neatened and cleaned. In the evening, you are invited to join the innkeeper and meet other guests for a complimentary cocktail in our sitting room!

The Willows is a European-style, shared bath inn. For your comfort, each of our rooms contains a vanity sink, Kimono bathrobes, fine soaps, and shampoo. Eight individual water closets and shower rooms are located off the hallway. Each bathroom is a self-contained unit for full privacy. Room amenities include direct-dial telephones, voicemail, and separate modem jacks. All rooms have individually controlled heat. Additionally, some rooms have TVs and refrigerators. Our sitting room is ideal for conversing, reading, watching television, or just relaxing, while the guest pantry is furnished with a microwave, refrigerator, icemaker, dishes, and cutlery for your convenience. Limited off-street parking is available. *The Willows* is a non-smoking inn. For more information and web specials, please visit our web site for links to California's tourist spots that you might like to visit during your trip to San Francisco. There is so much to see and do.

Address: 710 14th St, San Francisco, CA 94114
Tel: (415) 431-4770, **Fax:** (415) 431-5295.
E-mail: Vacation@WillowsSF.com **Web:** http://www.WillowsSF.com

Type: Bed & breakfast inn. **Clientele:** Gay & lesbian. Good mix of men & women **Transportation:** Airport shuttle to the inn $12. **To Gay Bars:** 1/2 block men's, 3 blocks to mixed. **Rooms:** 10 1-BR rooms, 1 2-BR room, 1 2-BR suite. **Baths:** 4 separate water closets, 4 separate showers, sinks in all rooms.

Meals: Expanded continental breakfast. **Complimentary:** Evening beverage. **Dates Open:** All year. **High Season:** June 15-Nov 15. **Rates:** $85-$125. **Discounts:** Web specials, midweek off season. **Credit Cards:** MC, Visa, Discover, Amex.

Rsv'tns: Recommended 2 weeks in advance. **Reserve Thru:** Call direct. **Min. Stay:** 2 nts wknds. **Parking:** Adequate on-street, limited off-street pay parking. **In-Room:** TV on request, direct dial phone, computer modem jacks, alarm clock radios, maid & room svc, fridge in some rooms.

On-Premises: TV lounge, fridge in pantry, iron & ironing board, beach towels. **Exercise/Health:** Co-ed gyms 1 block. **Swimming:** Nearby pool & ocean. **Smoking:** Not permitted. **Pets:** Not permitted. **Children:** Not permitted. **Your Hosts:** Friendly staff.

Castillo Inn

Gay/Lesbian ♂

Your Home Away from Home

The *Castillo Inn* is a five-minute walk to Market and Castro Streets and one block to public transportation. The inn has four very clean rooms that share a bath. Three rooms have queen beds, one has a double. A deluxe continental breakfast is included. A voice mail, a telephone and fax are available. The *Castillo Inn*, a non-smoking establishment, has rates from $55 to $75 (rates subject to change). Ask us about our two-bedroom suite.

Address: 48 Henry St, San Francisco, CA 94114
Tel: (415) 864-5111, (800) 865-5112, **Fax:** (415) 641-1321.

Type: Bed & breakfast.
Clientele: Mostly men with women welcome
Transportation: Shuttle, taxi, other public transportation.
To Gay Bars: 2 blocks, a 2-5 min walk.
Rooms: 4 rooms,

1 apartment with double or queen beds.
Meals: Expanded continental breakfast.
Vegetarian: Available nearby.
Dates Open: All year.
High Season: Jul-Oct.
Rates: $55-$75. Rates

subject to change.
Discounts: Please inquire.
Credit Cards: MC, Visa, Amex.
Rsv'tns: Required.
Reserve Thru: By travel agent Jan-Mar or direct call. Call direct other times.
Min. Stay: Sometimes

required.
Smoking: Permitted outside, non-smoking rooms available.
Pets: Not permitted.
Handicap Access: No.
Languages: English, Spanish.

Metro Hotel, The

WWW Gay-Friendly 50/50 ⚥

A Great Discovery

A small, affordable hotel with 24 rooms on two floors, *The Metro Hotel* is centrally situated in a historic district of San Francisco, walking distance to The Castro, The Haight and Golden Gate Park. We have new interiors with private baths, as well as the advantage of an adjacent cafe. Let us make your stay in San Francisco a memorable event with our friendly atmosphere, secluded enchanted garden, and cafe. Our convenient location is only minutes by bus to downtown San Francisco, and a short walk to the Castro District.

Address: 319 Divisadero St, San Francisco, CA 94117
Tel: (415) 861-5364, **Fax:** (415) 863-1970.

Type: Hotel.
Clientele: 50% gay & lesbian & 50% straight clientele.
Transportation: Accessible public transportation or cabs.
To Gay Bars: 8 blocks to men's bars.
Rooms: 24 rooms & 2 suites, double or queen beds.

Baths: All private.
Meals: Cafe on premises for breakfast or lunch. Private catering for evenings.
Vegetarian: Available at cafe on premises.
Dates Open: All year.
High Season: Summer.
Rates: $59-$109.
Discounts: Call to see what is available at the time.

Credit Cards: MC, Visa, Amex, Discover.
Rsv'tns: Required. Cancellation notice also required 48 hours.
Reserve Thru: Call direct or travel agent.
Min. Stay: 2 nights on weekends & holidays.
Parking: Free parking 6pm-9am.
In-Room: Cable color TV,

telephone, internet connection, maid service.
Sunbathing: On patio or in garden.
Smoking: Permitted.
Pets: Not permitted.
Handicap Access: No.
Children: Permitted.
Languages: International.
Your Hosts: Dean.

Gaige House Inn

Sonoma's Most Luxurious Inn

The *Gaige House Inn* is a stylish luxury inn nestled just 20 minutes from Napa in the heart of Sonoma Wine Country. *Travel & Leisure* touted the inn, in 2000, as "the best Bed & Breakfast in America." Sophisticated décor reflects West Indian, Asian and Plantation influences. *Frommers* reports, "This is the finest Bed & Breakfast in the Wine Country. First Class."

Guestrooms offer an abundance of amenities that include Calvin Klein™ linens, hand selected CDs, robes and Aveda™ toiletries. Wake each morning to breakfast prepared by a professional chef. For dinner, *San Francisco Magazine* says, "complete indulgence is only a few blocks away."

A short drive from Sonoma, Glen Ellen is a superb base for touring the wine country. More than a dozen notable wineries are within a few miles' drive. Relaxing days can be spent wine tasting and picnicking. Outdoor activities in the area include horseback riding, golfing, hiking mountain biking and ballooning. The *Gaige House Inn* is one of A&E's top-10 romantic getaways in the world.

Address: 13540 Arnold Dr, Glen Ellen, CA 95442
Tel: (707) 935-0237, (800) 935-0237, **Fax:** (707) 935-6411.
E-mail: gaige@sprynet.com **Web:** http://www.gaige.com

Type: Inn.
Clientele: Mostly straight with a gay & lesbian following
Transportation: Car is best.
To Gay Bars: 45 mins to Russian River & 25 mins to Santa Rosa gay bars.
Rooms: 12 rooms, 3 suites with king or queen beds.
Baths: 15 private baths.
Meals: Full breakfast.
Vegetarian: Available on request. Multiple restaurant offerings.
Complimentary: Premium Wine hour with light hors d'oeuvres. Free soda, juice, bottled water, 24-hr cookie supply & no attitude.
Dates Open: All year.
High Season: Apr-Nov.
Rates: $150-$495.
Credit Cards: MC, Visa, Amex, Discover.
Rsv'tns: Required.
Reserve Thru: Travel agent or call direct.
Min. Stay: 2 days on weekends & high season.
Parking: Ample free off-street parking.
In-Room: Cable TV, AC, ceiling fans, phone, reading lights with rheostats, robes, hair dryers, fireplaces & maid service. Jacuzzis in some rooms.
On-Premises: Jacuzzi, faxes, shaded hammock, picnic deck.
Exercise/Health: Heated whirlpool spa, nearby gym & jogging trails. Full time masseuse on premises.
Swimming: 20'x40' pool on premises.
Sunbathing: At poolside, on common sun decks.
Smoking: Permitted outside only.
Pets: Not permitted.
Handicap Access: No.
Children: No.
Languages: English, French, Spanish.
Your Hosts: Ken & Greg.

Color Photo on Page 17

Sonoma Chalet B & B

WWW Gay-Friendly ⚥

A Wine Country Getaway

One of the first bed and breakfast inns established in Sonoma, our Swiss-style farmhouse and country cottages are situated on three acres, blocks from Sonoma's historic square. Relax in *Sonoma Chalet's* uniquely decorated rooms with fireplace or wood-burning stove, antiques, quilts and collectibles. Cross a wooden bridge to the popular fairy-tale-like Honeymoon Cottage. Complimentary bicycles are available for the more ambitious, or simply relax in the outdoor Jacuzzi. Enjoy a delightful continental breakfast served in your cottage or on the deck overlooking a 200-acre ranch.

Address: 18935 Fifth St West, Sonoma, CA 95476
Tel: (707) 938-3129, (800) 938-3129.
E-mail: sonomachalet@cs.com **Web:** http://www.sonomachalet.com

Type: Bed & breakfast.
Clientele: Mostly straight clientele with gays & lesbians welcome
Transportation: Car is best.
To Gay Bars: 1-hour drive to San Francisco & Russian River resorts.
Rooms: 2 rooms, 1 suite & 3 cottages with double or queen beds.

Baths: 5 private & 1 shared.
Meals: Expanded continental breakfast.
Complimentary: Tea & coffee. Sherry in room.
Dates Open: All year.
High Season: Apr-Oct.
Rates: $85-$170.
Credit Cards: MC, Visa, Amex.
Rsv'tns: Required.

Reserve Thru: Travel agent or call direct.
Min. Stay: 2 nights on weekends & holidays during high season.
Parking: Ample free parking.
In-Room: Ceiling fans, refrigerator, coffee & tea-making facilities.
Exercise/Health: Free use of bicycles, Jacuzzi on

premises. Nearby gym, weights & massage.
Smoking: Permitted outside only.
Pets: Not permitted.
Handicap Access: No.
Children: By prior arrangement.
Languages: English.
Your Hosts: Joe.

Hotel Aspen

Best Way to Stay in Aspen

This striking, contemporary 45-room hotel on Main Street has large, beautifully-appointed rooms with king or queen beds, wet bars, cable TV, air conditioning, in-room safes, refrigerators, and private baths. Most rooms open onto terraces or balconies and some have private Jacuzzis, as well as fireplaces. Guests relax year-round under beautiful mountain skies on our patio courtyard with its heated swimming pool and two Jacuzzis. In the lounge, take in incredible panoramic views while enjoying a complimentary mountain breakfast or afternoon wine and cheese in the lounge.

Hotel Aspen is the perfect home base from which to enjoy what the spirited town of Aspen has to offer. In winter, there is world-class skiing. Summer sports include golf, tennis, swimming, hiking, biking, river rafting and trout fishing. For the culturally-minded, there are daily concerts, dance and theater. And whatever the season, there are numerous shops, galleries and restaurants.

From the moment you arrive, our professional staff caters to your needs, ensuring a vacation that goes beyond expectation. *Hotel Aspen* is centrally located, just a short stroll from everything, and is convenient to free public transportation. The airport is only three miles from town and the city of Denver is a scenic 3-1/2 hour drive from Aspen.

Address: 110 W Main St, Aspen, CO 81611
Tel: (970) 925-3441, (800) 527-7369, **Fax:** (970) 920-1379.
E-mail: hotlaspn@rof.net **Web:** http://www.aspen.com/ha/

Type: Hotel with breakfast & meeting room.
Clientele: Mainly straight with a gay & lesbian following
Transportation: Car. City provides shuttle transport from airport. Amtrak from Denver to Glenwood Springs.
To Gay Bars: About 3 blocks.
Rooms: 40 rooms & 5 suites with double, queen or king beds.
Baths: All private.
Meals: Expanded continental buffet breakfast. We call it a Mountain Breakfast.
Vegetarian: At almost all restaurants. Best in Aspen, Explore Booksellers & Coffeehouse is only 2 blocks away.
Complimentary: Apres-ski receptions in season.
High Season: Ski season: Xmas thru New Year, 2nd wk of Feb thru 3rd wk of Mar, July 4th.
Rates: Summer, $119-$229 per night; winter $129-$429 per night.
Discounts: Inquire. Mention Inn Places for an instant 10% discount.
Credit Cards: MC, Visa, Amex, Diners, Discover.
Rsv'tns: Strongly suggested.
Reserve Thru: Travel agent or call direct.
Min. Stay: At certain times. Inquire.
Parking: Ample on- & off-street parking, $1 per day.
In-Room: Cable color TV, AC, telephone, refrigerator, coffee/tea-maker, maid service, microwave. 4 rooms w/ Jacuzzi & 4 w/ fireplaces.
On-Premises: Meeting rooms, valet service, & helpful front desk staff.
Exercise/Health: Jacuzzi. Day passes available at the Aspen Athletic Club off premises.
Swimming: On premises large outdoor heated pool. 25 miles to Reudi Reservoir.
Sunbathing: At poolside or on private sun decks.
Smoking: Permitted in rooms. Not in common areas.
Pets: Dogs permitted in some rooms.
Handicap Access: Yes. All 1st-floor rooms.
Children: Permitted.
Languages: English, Spanish, German, French & Australian.

Victoria Oaks Inn

WWW Gay/Lesbian ⚢

Victorian Splendor at the Foot of the Rockies

The warmth and hospitality of *Victoria Oaks Inn* is apparent the moment you enter this historical, restored 1896 mansion. Elegant, original oak woodwork, tile fireplaces and dramatic hanging staircase replete with ornate brass chandelier, set the mood for a delightful visit. The nine guest rooms are finished with stylish, restored antiques from the turn-of-the-century and have panoramic views through leaded glass windows and soft colors throughout. We're conveniently located near Denver's bustling business and financial district, numerous shopping areas and varied tourist attractions.

The mansion is quietly nestled blocks from many of Denver's finest restaurants and close to major traffic arteries, providing quick access for any excursion. The historic Capitol Hill district offers special attractions, including the Unsinkable Molly Brown House, Botanic Gardens and the domed State Capitol Building. Within walking distance are the city park, the zoo, the Museum of Natural History and Imax Theatre. As a home you'd love to come home to, whether for a night or for the week, *Victoria Oaks* stands proudly apart. As a small inn, we offer personalized services not often available at larger hotels. Begin each morning with an inspiring continental breakfast, including freshly-squeezed orange juice, blended coffee and teas and a choice of fresh pastries, croissants, bagels and fresh fruits with the morning paper. Start your evening with a complimentary glass of wine from our wine cellar.

Address: 1575 Race St, Denver, CO 80206
Tel: (303) 355-1818, **Fax:** (303) 331-1095.
E-mail: vicoaksinn@aol.com

Type: Bed & breakfast.
Clientele: Mostly gay & lesbian with some straight clientele
Transportation: Taxi.
To Gay Bars: 4 blocks.
Rooms: 9 doubles.
Baths: 7 private, 2 share.
Meals: Expanded continental breakfast.

Complimentary: Tea, coffee, juices, beer, wine & sodas.
High Season: June-Aug.
Rates: $60-$95.
Discounts: Weekly and group rates.
Credit Cards: MC, Visa, Amex, Diners, Discover.
Rsv'tns: Recommended 2

weeks in advance.
Reserve Thru: Travel agent or call direct.
Parking: Adequate free off-street parking.
In-Room: Maid & laundry service & telephone.
On-Premises: Meeting rooms, private dining rooms, TV lounge & laundry

facilities.
Sunbathing: In the backyard.
Smoking: Permitted.
Pets: Not permitted.
Children: Permitted if well-behaved.
Languages: English.
Your Hosts: Clyde.

Bobby's Bed/Breakfast

Home Away from Home

Bobby's Bed/Breakfast offers contemporary lodging at reasonable rates, with king-sized bed, private bath, color TV, VCR, bar refrigerator, air-conditioning, phone, breakfast, a library, video selections, laundry facilities, massage, and discount coupons. *Bobby's* is in a lovely, centrally located, Spanish-style complex in the heart of the gay area, near Cheesman Park. It is only one block to buses. Clubs, bars, and eateries are nearby. Your host will be glad to assist you with information about places to go and things to do. Please kick off your shoes, relax, and enjoy my home, while you're away from yours! NOTE: Owner may be moving, please call B&B for updated information.

Address: Denver, CO
Tel: (303) 831-8266 or (800) 513-7827.

Type: In home stay.
Clientele: Exclusively men
To Gay Bars: 4 blocks.
Rooms: 1 room with king bed. 2nd room available, please inquire.
Baths: 1 private tub/shower/toilet.
Meals: Expanded continental breakfast. Kitchen & BBQ privileges

available.
Complimentary: Set-up service, tea, coffee, pop.
Dates Open: All year.
Rates: $50-$70, subject to change.
Discounts: Special weekly rate available.
Rsv'tns: Preferred.
Reserve Thru: Travel agent or call direct.

Parking: Ample off-street parking.
In-Room: Color TV, VCR, video tape library, telephone & refrigerator.
On-Premises: Laundry facilities.
Exercise/Health: Massage on premises. Year-round sauna & Jacuzzi.
Swimming: Pool in

summer.
Sunbathing: On the patio or poolside.
Nudity: Please inquire.
Smoking: Permitted outside only.
Pets: Not permitted.
Handicap Access: No.
Children: Not permitted.
Languages: English.
Your Hosts: Bobby.

McNamara Ranch

The Ultimate in Ranch Life & Horseback Riding in the Colorado Mountains

McNamara Ranch is a working ranch located in a valley with a magnificent view of Pikes Peak. For a real Rocky Mountain high, come ride with us on wilderness trails seldom used by humans. Climb above timberline toward snowcapped peaks 13,000 feet high. Rides are tailored to your stamina. For variety, we load the horses into the trailer and take them to spectacular trail heads. This real working ranch presents a unique vacation opportunity for those really wanting to sample ranch life.

Our hot tub is perfect for soaking under the stars after a long ride in the saddle. A rustic canvas teepee with wood stove is also available by the pond for camping. There's even a stocked pond full of rainbow trout! For those so inclined, there is a mountain gambling town nearby, called Cripple Creek, which also has a cabaret, but after a day of riding, a soak in the hot tub, and dinner, most guests turn in early for sweet dreams. The ranch can accommodate a maximum four guests at one time. Rates include lodging and horseback riding.

Address: 4620 County Rd 100, Florissant, CO 80816
Tel: (719) 748-3466

COLORADO • DENVER

COLORADO • FLORISSANT

Cornwall Inn

WWW Gay-Friendly ⚥
Gay-Owned & -Operated

The Country Getaway We All Wish We Had

Set on 3.2 acres of nicely landscaped grounds, the *Cornwall Inn* (circa 1821), is a four-season, six-room Country Inn with tavern and restaurant, and an adjacent eight-room Mountain Lodge. Recently refurbished rooms feature private baths, cable color TV, phones, data ports, and air conditioning in season. Our beds are dressed in fine cotton linens with featherbeds and down comforters. Guests are invited to enjoy our outdoor swimming pool and relax in the Jacuzzi. Casual country dining is offered in the Tavern and Restaurant.

The property is bordered by a mountain stream, the Appalachian Trail and the Housatonic River. Mohawk Mountain, Connecticut's largest and best-equipped winter sports complex, is seven minutes away offering downhill and cross-country skiing, and snowboarding. Local activities include white water rafting, fly fishing, hiking, canoeing, kayaking, and arguably the finest antiquing in New England.

Address: 270 Kent Road (Rt 7), Cornwall Bridge, CT 06754
Tel: (860) 672-6884 (Tel/Fax), (800) 786-6884.
E-mail: cornwallinn@aol.com **Web:** http://www.cornwallinn.com

Type: Inn with bar & restaurant.
Clientele: Mostly straight with a gay/lesbian following
Transportation: Car is best. Free pick up from bus.
To Gay Bars: 30 miles.
Rooms: 14 rooms, 1 suite with single, double, queen or king beds.
Baths: Private & shared.
Meals: Continental breakfast.

Vegetarian: Available.
Complimentary: Tea & coffee in room, mints on pillow.
High Season: Mid-Apr thru mid-Nov.
Rates: Low: $59-$109, high: $79-$129.
Discounts: 10% AAA.
Credit Cards: MC, Visa, Amex.
Rsv'tns: Required.
Reserve Thru: Travel agent

or call direct.
Min. Stay: Required on weekends & holidays only.
Parking: Ample off-street.
In-Room: Phone, AC, color cable TV, data ports, coffee & tea makers, maid svc. VCR rental available.
On-Premises: Meeting rooms, video tape library, fax.
Exercise/Health: Jacuzzi. Nearby massage.

Swimming: Pool. Nearby river & lake.
Sunbathing: Poolside & on 1 private sun deck.
Smoking: Permitted in tavern & some rooms. Non-smoking rooms available.
Pets: Please inquire.
Handicap Access: Yes, restaurant & 1 room. Rails in bathroom, wide doors.
Children: Welcome.
Languages: English.

Adams House, The

Gay-Friendly ⚥

"Quaint & Cozy...Friendly...Beautiful...& Relaxing"

Adams House is a 1790's-era house on a full acre of lush greenery and flower gardens, offering a homey colonial atmosphere featuring old fashioned fireplaces in the dining room and two bedrooms. Guests can choose between the main house and the *Garden Cottage,* a self-contained building just far enough away to ensure total privacy. Breakfast is a delicious medley of fresh fruit, homemade muffins and hot entrées with fabulous coffee. Guests' comments: "Quaint, cozy, fun, relaxing." "A perfect getaway." "Friendly, beautiful." "A blessing."

Address: 382 Cow Hill Rd, Mystic, CT 06355
Tel: (860) 572-9551.
Web: http://www.visitmystic.com/adamshouse

Type: Bed & Breakfast.
Clientele: Mostly straight clientele with gays & lesbians welcome
Transportation: Plane to Groton, taxi, train or ferry to New London, then taxi. Free pick up (usually) from Mystic train station.
To Gay Bars: 9 miles.
Rooms: 6 rooms with queen beds & 1 room with double sofabed & queen bed.
Baths: 7 private.

Meals: Full breakfast.
Vegetarian: Always available.
Complimentary: Hot or iced tea on arrival or request.
High Season: Memorial Day to Labor Day.
Rates: $95-$175. Off-season rates available.
Discounts: Sun-Thur nights, 3rd night half price. November through April negotiable.
Credit Cards: MC, Visa.

Rsv'tns: Recommended for weekends & Jun-Sep.
Reserve Thru: Call direct.
Min. Stay: 2 nights on weekends & holidays.
Parking: Ample free off-street parking.
In-Room: AC & maid service. Garden Cottage has color cable TV, refrigerator.
On-Premises: TV lounge.
Exercise/Health: Sauna in Garden Cottage.
Swimming: 20-30 minutes by car to several beaches, 1

nude.
Sunbathing: On the lawn or at the beaches.
Nudity: At nude beach.
Smoking: Permitted in yard only.
Pets: Not permitted.
Handicap Access: Garden Cottage accessible, 2 steps.
Children: Welcome in Garden Cottage.
Your Hosts: Mary Lou & Greg.

Inn at Oyster Point, The

WWW Gay-Friendly ♂♂
Gay-Owned & -Operated

From the Moment You Arrive, You're Home

Photo: Woody Ford USA

Your hosts, Vinny and Steve, coddle discriminating travelers of every budget with the comforts and solicitous service that make *The Inn at Oyster Point* your safe harbor in New Haven. An anchorage of civilized pleasures…the inn offers you warm personal attention and singular surroundings in the best bed and breakfast tradition, along with the luxury, amenities, and standard of service you expect from a fine small hotel.

From the rousing aroma of buttered griddle and bacon to the lull of music, wine, and lamplight, your hosts will make your stay exceptional! Unwind in a relaxing shoreline setting of historic homes and sailing ships that's surprisingly central to the city's lively arts, lesbigay nightspots, and Yale's campus. Savor bountiful breakfasts, stroll the harbor, dream by the fire, and surrender to the bubbly abandon of your whirlpool! Whether you're coming for a romantic retreat, a back roads ramble, campus events, or important business - we're home base for your Connecticut sojourn!

Address: 104 Howard Ave, New Haven, CT 06519
Tel: (203) 773-3334, **Fax:** (203) 777-4150.
E-mail: oysterpointinn@aol.com **Web:** http://www.oysterpointinn.com

Type: Bed & breakfast.
Clientele: Mostly straight clientele with a gay/lesbian following
Transportation: 1/4 mi from I-95 exits 44/45, 1 mi from Amtrak & commuter rail station.
To Gay Bars: 2 miles, a 5 min drive.
Rooms: 3 rooms, 2 suites, 1 apartment with queen beds. Roll-aways available.
Baths: Private: 3 bath/shower/toilets, 1 shower/toilet. Shared: 2 bath/shower/toilets.
Meals: Full breakfast, weekends. Expanded continental, weekdays.

Vegetarian: Always available. 2 mi to vegetarian restaurants.
Complimentary: Baked goods & seasonal refreshments.
Dates Open: Year round.
Rates: $85-$249 year round.
Discounts: 7th night free for weekly stays. Inquire for corporate bookings.
Credit Cards: MC, Visa, Amex, Discover, Diners.
Rsv'tns: Required.
Reserve Thru: Travel agent or call direct.
Min. Stay: Required on 4 Yale U. wknds: Matriculation (late Aug), Parents (mid

Oct), Graduation (late May), Reunion (early June).
Parking: Adequate free off-street parking.
In-Room: Telephone, answering machines, AC, color cable TV, whirlpool, fireplace, computer ports, maid service.
On-Premises: Business supplies, fax, copy/printing services, data ports. Sitting porch, study, guest parlor, guest kitchens.
Exercise/Health: Whirlpools, Exercycle, harborside biking/jogging trails. Nearby gym, massage.
Swimming: 2 miles to CT

Shore beaches.
Sunbathing: On patio & at beach.
Nudity: Not on premises. 90 minutes to nearest nude beach.
Smoking: Smoke-free indoors. Smoking permitted in outdoor sitting areas.
Pets: Permitted only for physically disabled guests.
Children: Welcome aged 10+, well-behaved & sharing room w/ parent or responsible adult. Inquire about younger kids.
Languages: English, some French, Italian, Spanish.
Your Hosts: Vinny & Steve.
IGLTA

Honeysuckle

Victorian Inn & Adjoining Houses near the Beaches

Come to *Honeysuckle* and enjoy the easygoing atmosphere at our popular Victorian inn and adjoining houses, Wisteria and Larkspur, near the Delaware beaches. Women feel at home in the comfortable spaces that our houses provide. Our sauna and outdoor hot tubs are year-round favorites. In summer, stroll our porches, decks and gardens to the large in-ground pool with privacy fencing. Snuggle by the fireside in winter. VCRs, stereos, games, a canoe and our library of women's books and music will keep you busy between trips to the beaches, restaurants and outlet malls.

Besides all the little things we have to offer, we have big things, too! Like the women's beach only 12 miles away, the nature preserves and parks, the sheer freedom of swimming nude in our pool, the romance of luxuriating in one of our hot tubs or whirlpool baths, the friendliness of women-only space. Imagine a gourmet dinner at the beach, maybe a leisurely moonlit walk by the water, then a good nights' sleep out here in the quiet little town of Milton.

Address: 330 Union St, Milton, DE 19968
Tel: (302) 684-3284.

Type: Inn & 2 adjoining houses.
Clientele: Women only
Transportation: Car is best.
To Gay Bars: 12 miles to Rehoboth gay/lesbian bars.
Rooms: 4 rooms & 2 private rental houses with double or queen beds. Each private house accommodates up to 6 people.
Baths: All private baths/ whirlpool tubs. Outdoor shower by pool.
Meals: Full breakfast for inn guests only.
Vegetarian: Upon request.
Complimentary: Coffee and teas.
Dates Open: All year.
High Season: Summer (Jun-Sept).
Rates: $99-$177.
Discounts: 10% for 7 days or more.
Credit Cards: MC, Visa.
Rsv'tns: Required.
Reserve Thru: Travel agent or call direct.
Min. Stay: On holiday weekends only.
Parking: Ample free off-street parking.
In-Room: Inn: self-controlled AC/heat & 2 rooms with whirlpool in bath. Houses: AC/heat, private hot tub, whirlpool/massage room.
On-Premises: TV lounge & kitchens.
Exercise/Health: Sauna, outdoor hot tub & whirlpool in private baths. Massage available.
Swimming: Pool on premises.
Sunbathing: At poolside or on the beaches.
Nudity: Permitted poolside.
Smoking: Permitted outdoors.
Pets: Not permitted, excellent kennel nearby.
Handicap Access: 1 house w/ 1st-fl BR/bath.
Children: Not permitted.
Languages: English.
Your Hosts: Mary Ann & Julie.

Cabana Gardens Bed & Breakfast

WWW Gay/Lesbian ♂♀
Gay-Owned & -Operated

Luxury Guesthouse with Spacious, Contemporary Design

Built in 1995, *Cabana Gardens Bed & Breakfast* is the newest luxury guesthouse in Rehoboth Beach. You will delight in the home's spacious, contemporary design. Featured are three levels of plant-filled decks, including decks which overlook downtown Lake Gerar and the ocean, as well as an enormous roof-top deck. The bed & breakfast has three sitting areas for socializing with other guests and our guest rooms have private baths, decks and great views! We are centrally located, only three blocks from the many shops and restaurants of Baltimore Avenue and Rehoboth Avenue.

Address: 20 Lake Avenue, Rehoboth Beach, DE 19971
Tel: (302) 227-5429, **Fax:** (302) 227-4098.
E-mail: cabanagardens@ce.net **Web:** http://www.cabanagardens.com

Type: Bed & breakfast.
Clientele: Gay & lesbian. Good mix of men & women
Transportation: Car is best, 1/2 block from bus terminal.
To Gay Bars: 1 block to Cloud Nine & Blue Moon.
Rooms: 9 rooms with double, queen or king beds (also apartments).
Baths: All private bath/ shower/toilets.
Meals: Continental

breakfast.
Dates Open: All year.
High Season: June-Sept.
Rates: Summer: weekends $145-$195, Mon-Thurs $100-$125. Winter: $70-$95.
Discounts: Stay 7 nights, get 1 weekday free.
Credit Cards: MC, Visa, Discover.
Rsv'tns: Required.
Reserve Thru: Call direct.
Min. Stay: In season. During week 2 nights,

weekends 3 or 4 nights.
Parking: Ample free off-street parking.
In-Room: AC, ceiling fans, color cable TV, kitchen, refrigerator, maid service.
On-Premises: Private decks with lake views, enormous rooftop deck, shared kitchen area & wet bar, meeting rooms, TV lounge.
Swimming: Ocean nearby.
Sunbathing: On roof,

private & common sun decks, at beach.
Smoking: Permitted in outside areas only.
Pets: Not permitted.
Handicap Access: Ground-floor rooms available with a 2-step access.
Children: No.
Languages: English.
Your Hosts: Gary.

Mallard Guest Houses, The

www Gay/Lesbian ⚥

Voted "Best at the Beach"

Just steps to the boardwalk, beaches and the Atlantic, *The Mallard Guest Houses* offer the discriminating adult a relaxing getaway with a heart-of-town location. We provide fabulous, comfortable accommodations in this quaint Atlantic seashore community nestled just south of Delaware Bay. Our in-town location is very convenient. You can walk to fine shops, restaurants and nearby hotspots. All rooms are elegantly furnished with fine antiques and all have delightful private baths, some with Jacuzzi tubs, private balconies and CATV.

Relax and unwind in the outdoor spa, enjoy our flower-filled porches or take in some sunbathing on the sun deck. We offer complimentary gourmet breakfast and free off-street parking. Spend a warm afternoon at the beach or visit our town's many attractions. Enjoy the best of Rehoboth, while staying at the best in Rehoboth. At *The Mallard* we say, "Rehoboth is more than a beach... It's a great place to stay."

Address: 60 Baltimore Ave, Rehoboth Beach, DE 19971
Tel: (302) 226-3448, (888) 872-0644.
E-mail: guest@themallard.com **Web:** http://www.themallard.com

Type: Guesthouses. Locations in Rehoboth.
Clientele: Gay & lesbian. Good mix of men & women
Transportation: Walk.
To Gay Bars: Adjacent to bars.
Rooms: 17 rooms.
Baths: All private.
Meals: Gourmet continental breakfast.

Complimentary: Coffee & tea.
Dates Open: All year.
High Season: Memorial Day-Labor Day.
Rates: $85-$195.
Discounts: Inquire for special packages.
Credit Cards: MC, Visa.
Rsv'tns: Required.
Reserve Thru: Travel agent

or call direct.
Parking: Adequate off-street parking.
In-Room: TV & Jacuzzi tubs.
On-Premises: TV lounge.
Exercise/Health: Jacuzzi tubs in some locations & outdoor spa.
Swimming: 2 blocks to ocean beach.

Sunbathing: On private sun decks & at the beach.
Smoking: Permitted in designated areas. All rooms are non-smoking.
Pets: Sometimes in off season.
Handicap Access: Not fully accessible.
Children: Inquire.
Languages: English.

Silver Lake

WWW Gay/Lesbian ⚥

"Jewel of the Delaware Shore"

Silver Lake Guest House is "one of the 10 best North American gay guesthouses" (Out & About), "the best of the bunch" (Fodor's Gay Guide), and "the jewel of the Delaware shore" (The Washington Post). Located in a tranquil waterfront setting in the midst of a waterfowl preserve on Rehoboth Beach's most scenic drive, this beautiful home offers its guests much more than a conventional bed and breakfast. It is also the resort's closest guesthouse to gay Poodle Beach.

Completely renovated in 1997, *Silver Lake* provides spectacular lake and ocean views from its sprawling columned veranda, balconies and decks. All of the bedrooms have private baths, cable TV and central air conditioning. Many of the rooms have panoramas of the lake and ocean from private balconies. Guests may enjoy breakfast quietly in their rooms, on their private balconies, in the second-floor sunroom, or on the third-floor sun deck where the lake and ocean are on full display. Breakfast includes muffins baked daily, fresh fruit, juice, tea and coffee, along with the daily newspaper.

Behind the main house is the Carriage House with its very private, large two-bedroom apartments. Each has a private entrance, living room, dining area, decks, and complete kitchen. *Silver Lake* is about quality of life. Whether for a weekend or extended vacation, guests enjoy an ambience of comfort and relaxation in the midst of nature at its best.

Address: 133 Silver Lake Dr, Rehoboth Beach, DE 19971
Tel: (302) 226-2115, (800) 842-2115.
Web: http://www.silverlakeguesthouse.com

Type: Bed & breakfast guesthouse.
Clientele: Gay & lesbian. Good mix of men & women
Transportation: Car is best.
To Gay Bars: Walking distance.
Rooms: 14 rooms & 2 two-bedroom apartments with queen or king beds.
Baths: All private.
Meals: Expanded continental breakfast.
Complimentary: Tea, coffee, juices, fruit & ice.

Dates Open: All year.
High Season: Summer.
Rates: In season $100-$300, off season from $75.
Discounts: For longer stays.
Credit Cards: MC, Visa, Amex, Discover
Rsv'tns: Required.
Reserve Thru: Call direct.
Min. Stay: 2-4 nights on summer weekends.
Parking: Ample, free off-street parking.
In-Room: Color cable TV, AC, maid service, kitchens

in apartments. Most rooms have private decks & refrigerators.
On-Premises: Meeting rooms, guest kitchen, sun room, lounge, BBQ grills, sun decks, beach chairs & towels, ice, sodas, outdoor showers, lake front lawn & gardens.
Exercise/Health: On jogging & biking course. Gym nearby.
Swimming: 10-minute walk to gay ocean beach.
Sunbathing: At beach or on

decks.
Smoking: Permitted with restrictions.
Pets: Dogs permitted in apartments only, by prior arrangement.
Handicap Access: Yes, call for details.
Children: Not permitted except by prior arrangement.
Languages: English.
Your Hosts: Joe & Mark

Chesapeake Landing

Come Share the Wonder

Nestled in a forest of pine and bamboo on the shore of Lake Comegys is *Chesapeake Landing*. Enjoy the hospitality of our Frank Lloyd Wright-inspired home, the area's only waterfront bed and breakfast resort. Awake to birds singing in the bamboo grove. Enjoy a sumptuous breakfast beside the sparkling pool, or in our dining room overlooking the lake. Spend lazy afternoons on the beach, half a block away, or soak up the sun beside our beautiful pool. We're conveniently located to the many fine shops and restaurants of Rehoboth Beach and minutes away from one of the largest outlet malls in the country.

Address: 101 Chesapeake St, Rehoboth Beach, DE 19971
Tel: (302) 227-2973, **Fax:** (302) 227-0301.
E-mail: innkeeper@chesapeakelanding.com **Web:** http://www.chesapeakelanding.com

Type: Bed & breakfast.
Clientele: Mostly gay & lesbian with some straight clientele. Popular with gay women
Transportation: Car is best.
To Gay Bars: 10 blocks, a 5 min drive.
Rooms: 4 rooms with queen beds.
Baths: Private: 2 shower/toilets, 2 bath/shower/toilets.

Meals: Full gourmet breakfast.
Vegetarian: All special needs are accommodated.
Complimentary: Complimentary drinks, cocktails always available by pool, dock or fireside.
Dates Open: All year.
High Season: Jun-Aug.
Rates: Summer $175-$250, winter $125.
Discounts: 10% on stays of 3 days or longer.

Credit Cards: MC, Visa.
Rsv'tns: Required.
Reserve Thru: Travel agent or call direct.
Min. Stay: 2 nights.
Parking: Ample free off-street parking.
In-Room: AC, ceiling fans, maid service.
On-Premises: Meeting rooms, TV lounge, video tape library, fax, copier, etc.

Swimming: Heated pool, ocean & lake on premises.
Sunbathing: Poolside, on common sun decks & at beach.
Smoking: Permitted outside on deck or balcony.
Pets: Not permitted.
Handicap Access: No.
Children: No.
Languages: English.
Your Hosts: Richard & Rocco.

Delaware Inn

Southern Hospitality with New England Charm

Since 1930, the *Delaware Inn* has welcomed and delighted guests. Located on a quiet residential street in downtown Rehoboth, you'll be steps from beaches and many fine gay restaurants, clubs and shops. The inn's common rooms are decorated in country colonial and our seven guest rooms have different motifs. For your comfort, we have central AC. Our breakfasts are well known for their homemade muffins and breads!

Address: 55 Delaware Avenue, Rehoboth Beach, DE 19971
Tel: (302) 227-6031, (800) 246-5244, **Fax:** (302) 226-1788.
E-mail: DelawareIn@aol.com **Web:** http://www.delawareinn.com

Type: Bed & breakfast.
Clientele: 50% gay & lesbian & 50% straight
Transportation: Car is best. Free pick up from bus & ferry dock.
To Gay Bars: 1 block, a 2 min walk.
Rooms: 7 rooms with single-king beds.
Baths: Bath/shower/toilets: 3 private, 4 shared.
Meals: Expanded continental. Full breakfast Sunday.
Vegetarian: Special

requests considered w/ advance notice. 1 block to vegetarian restaurant.
Complimentary: Wine & cheese in late afternoon daily during high season & on Sat during off season.
Dates Open: All year.
High Season: May-Sept.
Rates: Summer $95-$190, fall/spring $60-$150, winter $50-$100.
Discounts: 10% on stays of 7 or more nights.
Credit Cards: MC, Visa, Discover.

Rsv'tns: Recommended during high season.
Reserve Thru: Call direct.
Min. Stay: Wknds: high 2 nights, holiday 3 nights.
Parking: Adequate free off-street parking, 1 car/room. Will provide parking pass for street parking for addt'l cars.
In-Room: AC, ceiling fans, maid service.
On-Premises: TV lounge, fax, internet, board games, paperback library, fridge.
Exercise/Health: Bicycles. Nearby gym, weights,

massage, golf courses, fishing.
Swimming: Nearby ocean.
Sunbathing: At beach.
Smoking: Smoking on porch only. No smoking in guest rooms.
Pets: Not permitted.
Handicap Access: No.
Children: Permitted ages 12 years & older.
Languages: English, some Spanish.
Your Hosts: Ron & Tom.

Rehoboth Guest House

WWW Gay/Lesbian ⚥

Rehoboth's Oldest Continually Running Gay Guesthouse

Rehoboth Guest House, is a charming Victorian beach house 1-1/2 blocks from the beach on a residential street close to gay shopping & dining. Feel at home in 12 airy, white-washed rooms with large windows and painted floors. Relax over continental breakfast in the sun room or rock on the flower-lined front porch. Enjoy sun decks, gay beaches, outdoor cedar showers, Saturday evening wine and cheese, or nearby shops, restaurants and bars. Whether you are taking a long vacation or grabbing a weekend, you will always feel relaxed and welcome. Newly renovated.

Address: 40 Maryland Ave, Rehoboth Beach, DE 19971
Tel: (302) 227-4117, (800) 564-0493.
E-mail: reho@guesthse.com **Web:** http://www.guesthse.com

Type: Bed & breakfast guesthouse.
Clientele: Mostly gay & lesbian with some hetero clientele
Transportation: Car.
To Gay Bars: 1 block.
Rooms: 12 rooms, double, queen & king beds.
Baths: Private & shared.
Meals: Continental breakfast.
Complimentary: Wine & cheese in backyard or living room on Sat afternoon.
Dates Open: May-Oct.
High Season: May-Oct.
Rates: Pre/post season: $45-$80; in season: $65-$160.
Discounts: Special rates for Sun thru Thur stays.
Credit Cards: MC, Visa.
Rsv'tns: Required.
Reserve Thru: Travel agent or call direct.
Min. Stay: 2 nights weekends, holiday weekends 3 nights.
Parking: Most rooms with free off-street parking, limited free on-street parking.
In-Room: All rooms have AC & ceiling fans.
On-Premises: 2 sun decks, front porch with rockers, 2 picnic tables in backyard, 2 outdoor, enclosed showers/ dressing rooms with hot water.
Exercise/Health: Gym a few blocks away on boardwalk.
Swimming: 1-1/2 blocks to beach, short walk to gay beaches.
Sunbathing: On common sun decks or at the beach.
Smoking: Permitted on porch or decks.
Pets: Not permitted.
Children: Not permitted.
Languages: English.
Your Hosts: Jerry.

Royal Rose Inn

WWW Gay-Friendly ⚥
Gay-Owned & -Operated

Welcome to the *Royal Rose Inn.* Located one and a half blocks from the Atlantic Ocean, we're within walking distance of the many fine restaurants and unique shops that Rehoboth Beach is famous for. You will find that our hospitality is as inviting and warm as a summer's day. We offer our guests attractive, air-conditioned rooms, a large screened front porch from which to enjoy the cool ocean breeze, off-street parking, and a full continental breakfast to start off your day.

Address: 41 Baltimore Ave, Rehoboth Beach, DE
Tel: (302) 226-2535.

Type: Bed & breakfast.
Clientele: Mixed clientele
Transportation: Car is best.
To Gay Bars: 3 doors away, 1/2 min. walk.
Rooms: 7 rooms with double or queen beds.
Baths: 5 private, 2 shared bath/shower/toilets.
Meals: Expanded continental breakfast.
Vegetarian: Upon request.
Dates Open: All year.
High Season: June-Aug.
Rates: Season $75-$130, off season $35-$55.
Credit Cards: MC, Visa.
Rsv'tns: Suggested, but not required.
Reserve Thru: Call direct.
Min. Stay: Season, 2 nights on weekends.
Parking: Adequate, free off-street parking.
In-Room: AC.
On-Premises: TV lounge.
Sunbathing: At beach.
Smoking: No smoking.
Pets: Not permitted.
Handicap Access: No.
Children: Welcome ages 6 & above.
Languages: English.

Summer Place, The

In the Heart of Gay Rehoboth

Summer Place Hotel is located on the ocean block with a sun deck overlooking the Atlantic Ocean. Known for 100 years as "Yellow House," this property was recently remodeled from the foundation up. Each room has a private bath, television, air conditioning, heat and telephone. The one-bedroom condos have a kitchen that includes a dishwasher, microwave, stove and refrigerator. Comfortable, clean and quiet, our hotel is in an excellent location in the heart of gay Rehoboth is just a walk to all bars and restaurants. Open year round.

Address: 30 Olive Ave, Rehoboth Beach, DE 19971
Tel: (302) 226-0766, (800) 815-3925, **Fax:** (302) 226-3350.
E-mail: millerd@dmv.com **Web:** http://www.atbeach.com/lodging/de/hotel/summerplace/

Type: Hotel.
Clientele: Mostly gay & lesbian with some straight clientele
Transportation: Car is best.
To Gay Bars: A 1-minute walk.
Rooms: 23 rooms, 5 apartments.

Baths: All private.
Dates Open: All year.
High Season: Jun-Aug.
Rates: Rooms: $40-$165 per day. Apartments: $60-$185 per day.
Credit Cards: Visa, MC, Discover, Amex, Nexus.
Min. Stay: 1-3 nights.
Parking: Parking pass

available.
In-Room: AC, telephone, color cable TV, refrigerator, microwave. Apartments also have dishwasher, stove, microwave, refrigerator.
On-Premises: Sun deck overlooking ocean.
Swimming: 1 minute to beach.

Smoking: Smoking & non-smoking rooms available.
Pets: No.
Handicap Access: 1st floor accommodations easy to enter.
Your Hosts: Dan.

Brenton, The

Your Accommodation of Choice in Washington, DC

Dating from 1891, *The Brenton* is located in the Dupont Circle neighborhood, 12 blocks north of the White House. Rooms are spacious and well-appointed, with antiques, art and Oriental carpets on handsome wood floors. The rooms are air conditioned, have direct-dial phones with answering machines and most have ceiling fans. In the European tradition, the baths are shared, and our beds are ultra-firm. The cozy front parlor welcomes you to relax with new friends and the staff encourages questions about local sights, activities and dining. Make yourself at home, and enjoy Washington as the locals do.

Address: 1708 16th St NW, Washington, DC 20009
Tel: (202) 332-5550, (800) 673-9042, **Fax:** (202) 462-5872.

Type: Guesthouse.
Clientele: Mostly men with women welcome
Transportation: Metro to Dupont Circle, then short walk.
To Gay Bars: 1 block to gay bar.
Rooms: 8 rooms, 1 suite with queen or king beds.
Baths: 3 shared bath/

shower/toilets, 1 shared toilet. Suite has private bath.
Meals: Expanded continental breakfast.
Complimentary: Cocktail hour in evening, coffee, tea, always.
Dates Open: All year.
High Season: Mar-Oct.
Rates: $79-$99.
Credit Cards: MC, Visa,

Amex, Discover.
Rsv'tns: Recommended.
Reserve Thru: Travel agent or call direct.
Parking: Garage nearby.
In-Room: Maid service, telephone, AC, ceiling fans. Suite has kitchen, sitting area, TV/VCR.
On-Premises: Dining rooms, TV lounge.

Exercise/Health: Nearby gym.
Smoking: Permitted without restrictions.
Pets: Not permitted.
Handicap Access: No.
Children: Not permitted.
Languages: English.
Your Hosts: Steve & Ed.

B & B at The William Lewis House

Washington's Finest Bed & Breakfast

The William Lewis House, Washington's finest bed & breakfast, is conveniently located near Logan Circle, in the heart of the gay community. We are very close to 17th Street, Dupont Circle, Adams Morgan and The Mall. Three different subway lines are within walking distance of the house, the closest of which is the U Street Station on the Green Line. Many of Washington's best restaurants are within a short walk of the house.

Built 1904, this classically inspired house has been painstakingly and faithfully restored to its original grandeur. It is appointed with antiques, authentic reproduction wall papers and working gas lights. Relax in the gilded parlor or richly paneled dining room in front of one of four working fireplaces. The spacious rooms are appointed with family heirlooms and antique carpets. Beds have cotton linens, feather mattresses and pillows, and handmade chocolates are delivered to your bedside each evening by request.

We also offer direct-dial telephones with answering machines and ceiling fans in each guest room. A hot tub in the garden helps relax you after a long day of touring. Your hosts Theron, Dave and their lovable pups, Winston and Ruth, will welcome you and try to make you feel as though you are staying with friends. We will provide you with pertinent information about the things that have brought you to Washington, as well helpful suggestions about activities in the community.

Address: 1309 R St NW, Washington, DC
Tel: (202) 462-7574, (800) 465-7574, **Fax:** (202) 462-1608.
E-mail: info@wlewishous.com **Web:** http://www.wlewishous.com

Type: Bed & breakfast.
Clientele: Mostly gay men, all welcome
Transportation: Taxi. Metro to U St or Dupont Circle, then a short walk.
To Gay Bars: 1-4 blocks.
Rooms: 4 rooms with double, 1 with queen bed.
Baths: 2 shared bath/ shower/toilets. 1 shared WC/ toilet.

Meals: Expanded continental or full breakfast.
Vegetarian: Nearby vegetarian restaurants.
Complimentary: Coffee, tea & snacks always. Homemade chocolates at your bedside, by request.
Dates Open: All year.
Rates: $75-$85.
Discounts: On extended stays.

Credit Cards: Visa, MC, Discover, Amex.
Rsv'tns: Required.
Reserve Thru: Travel agent or call direct.
Parking: Adequate on-street parking.
In-Room: Ceiling fans, direct-dial phone with answering machine.
On-Premises: Laundry facilities.

Exercise/Health: Hot tub in garden. Nearby gym.
Swimming: Nearby pool.
Sunbathing: In nearby parks.
Smoking: Permitted in garden only.
Pets: Not permitted.
Languages: English.
Your Hosts: Theron & Dave.

Bull Moose B&B on Capitol Hill

Have a Bully Good Time in DC!

Welcoming gays and lesbians to Capitol Hill for a decade, friendly and affordable *Bull Moose Bed & Breakfast on Capitol Hill* is a "city inn" infused with history, wit and sophisticated charm. Handsomely restored in January, 2000, the cornerstone of this turreted Victorian townhome was laid in 1890, when the U.S. capital city was bustling with reform and Teddy Roosevelt was serving his first stint in Washington as a Civil Service Commissioner. Later, in 1912, he founded the Bull Moose Progressive Party and was its first candidate for President.

Teddy Roosevelt's larger-than-life career inspired the *Bull Moose B&B...* its name, its décor, its rooms, and its sense of delight. Along with the restoration, the name of the house changed from the Capitol Hill Guest House. Today, as the *Bull Moose B&B on Capitol Hill* it is an ideal destination, whether you come to Washington for work, play, or a delightful combination of the two. Find singles, doubles, or larger rooms, and private baths. Each morning, enjoy fresh-baked continental breakfast and gourmet coffee at a turn-of-the-century English pub table. Stay in touch with two guest phones, fax and PC with internet. Each evening, taste imported Spanish sherry in the parlor beside a 100-year-old oak mantlepiece. Then enjoy our firm, feather bedding in rooms with am/fm alarm clock/cd players. We're five blocks from the U.S. Capitol, and it's a short walk to restaurants, shops and bars, Smithsonian, monuments, Amtrak, metro, and Eastern Market. You're sure to "Have a Bully Good Time."

Address: 101 5th Street NE, Washington, DC 20002
Tel: (202) 547-1050, (800) 261-2768, **Fax:** (202) 548-9741.
E-mail: reserve@BullMoose-B-and-B.com **Web:** http://www.BullMoose-B-and-B.com

Type: Bed & breakfast.
Clientele: 50% gay & lesbian & 50% straight clientele
Transportation: Airport shuttle, bus or taxi. Amtrak, then walk or taxi 6 blocks.
To Gay Bars: 6 blocks.
Rooms: 10 rooms with single, double or queen beds.
Baths: 4 private shower/toilets, 4 shared bath/shower/toilets.
Meals: Expanded continental breakfast.
Vegetarian: Available at nearby restaurants.
Complimentary: Sherry in parlor, coffee, tea & treats.
Dates Open: All year.
Rates: $89-$209.
Credit Cards: MC, Visa, Amex, Bancard, Eurocard, Discover.
Rsv'tns: Strongly recommended.
Reserve Thru: Travel agent or call direct.
Min. Stay: 2 nights weekends (Fri & Sat, Sat & Sun).
Parking: Adequate free on-street parking (permit provided, give us licence # & state in advance).
In-Room: Central AC, ceiling fans, maid service.
On-Premises: Kitchen privileges day & night. PC, fax, internet access, local & overnight delivery.
Exercise/Health: Massage. Nearby gym, weights, steam, massage.
Swimming: Pool nearby.
Smoking: Non-smoking premises.
Pets: Not permitted.
Handicap Access: No.
Languages: English, French.

Embassy Inn

WWW Gay-Friendly ⚥
Woman-Operated

A Lovely Haven of European Charm

The Embassy Inn is a charming, gay-friendly B&B on historical 16th St. Elegantly appointed, with comfort in every detail, guestrooms offer private bathroom, direct-dial phone, digital alarm clock, cable television with complimentary HBO, and daily maid service. We offer a relaxing, friendly atmosphere and convenience to metro, shops, restaurants, grocery store and nightlife.

You'll enjoy personalized service, continental breakfast, and evening sherry, as you relax in the warm lobby with a great selection of books and magazines. Our staff is always happy to help with dining suggestions, tourist information or directions. The inn is a great value and is easily accessible to all of Washington's sights. The neighborhood is quaint and offers something for everyone.

Address: 1627 16th St NW, Washington, DC 20009
Tel: (202) 234-7800 or (800) 423-9111, **Fax:** (202) 234-3309.

Type: Hotel inn.
Clientele: Mostly straight clientele with a gay & lesbian following
Transportation: Taxi from airport. Metro Red line from Union Station to Dupont Circle, then 4-1/2 blocks to inn.
To Gay Bars: 2 blocks to men's bar, 5 blocks to Dupont Circle gay & lesbian bars.
Rooms: 38 rooms with single & double beds.

Baths: All private shower/toilets.
Meals: Expanded continental breakfast.
Complimentary: Evening sherry year-round, coffee/tea 24 hours.
Dates Open: All year.
High Season: Apr-May & Sept-Oct.
Rates: High season $89-$159, low season $79-$129.
Discounts: On extended stays, weekend rates, government (business)

travel, based on availability.
Credit Cards: MC, Visa, Amex, Carte Blanche, Diner's.
Rsv'tns: Must be guaranteed with credit card.
Reserve Thru: Travel agent or call direct.
Parking: Limited on-street parking, 24-hr pay garage 8 blocks away.
In-Room: Telephone, color cable TV, free HBO, AC, maid service, hairdryer.
Exercise/Health: 2-block

walk to facilities.
Swimming: 2-block walk to facilities.
Smoking: Not permitted in main lobby. Non-smoking rooms available. Limited smoking rooms.
Pets: Not permitted.
Handicap Access: No.
Children: Permitted.
Languages: English, Spanish, French, Arabic.

Kalorama Guest House at Kalorama Park [WWW] Gay-Friendly ⚥

Your Home in Washington, DC

The *Kalorama Guest House* is the place to call home when you are in D.C. We are located on a quiet, tree-lined street, only a short walk from two of Washington's most trendy neighborhoods, Dupont Circle and Adams Morgan. You'll be near a potpourri of bars, ethnic restaurants, nightspots, antique shops and the underground metro.

After staying in a bedroom decorated tastefully with Victorian antiques and enjoying a continental breakfast, an evening aperitif and our nationally-known hospitality, we're sure you'll make our house your home whenever you visit Washington.

If you prefer a smaller, more intimate guesthouse, please inquire about our other property, *The Kalorama Guest House at Woodley Park.*

Address: 1854 Mintwood Pl NW, Washington, DC 20009
Tel: (202) 667-6369, **Fax:** (202) 319-1262.

Type: Bed & breakfast.
Clientele: Gay-friendly establishment. Mostly straight clientele with a gay & lesbian following
Transportation: Taxi or subway are best.
To Gay Bars: 4 blocks to men's bars at Dupont Circle.
Rooms: 24 rooms & 5 suites.
Baths: 15 private, 14 shared (2-3 rooms per bath).
Meals: Continental breakfast.
Complimentary: Sherry in parlor (afternoon aperitif), lemonade in summer.
Dates Open: All year.
High Season: Mar-Jun & Sep-Nov.
Rates: Rooms $50-$95, suites $95-$145.
Discounts: AAA.
Credit Cards: MC, Visa, Amex, Diners.
Reserve Thru: Travel agent or call direct.

Min. Stay: 2 nights required occasionally.
Parking: Limited pay parking off-street & limited free on-street parking.
In-Room: AC, maid & laundry service. Some rooms with ceiling fans.
On-Premises: Meeting rooms, TV lounge, guest fridge, laundry facilities.
Exercise/Health: Gym with weights nearby.
Swimming: In nearby pool.

Sunbathing: On landscaped backyard.
Smoking: Totally non-smoking.
Pets: Not permitted.
Handicap Access: No.
Children: Prefer those over 10 years old.
Languages: English.
Your Hosts: Michael, Stephen & Karin.

Morrison House

The Romance of Old Europe, The Charm of Early America

Designed and staffed with the utmost care, *Morrison House* blends the romance of Old Europe with the charm of Early America. Elegantly decorated with authentic Federal Period reproductions, we offer gracious hospitality and uncompromising service. Designed after the grand manors of the Federal Period, our guestrooms evoke the traditional elegance of late-eighteenth century Alexandria with their four-poster mahogany beds, brass chandeliers and sconces, and decorative fireplaces. *The Morrison House* is centrally located in historic Old Town Alexandria, just minutes from Washington, DC and Ronald Reagan National Airport.

We're a Mobil four-star and AAA four-diamond hotel.

Address: 116 South Alfred Street, Alexandria, VA 22314
Tel: (703) 838-8000, (800) 367-0800, **Fax:** (703) 548-2489.
E-mail: mhresrv@morrisonhouse.com **Web:** http://www.morrisonhouse.com

Type: Inn & hotel with 4-diamond restaurant & bar.
Clientele: Mostly straight clientele with a gay male following
Transportation: Taxi from National Airport. 7 blocks from metro station.
To Gay Bars: 7 miles, a 15 min drive.
Rooms: 42 rooms, 3 suites with single, queen or king beds.
Baths: 45 private bath/shower/toilets.

Meals: Continental breakfast.
Vegetarian: Can be accommodated at all times.
Complimentary: Continental breakfast & newspaper in the parlor, turn-down "treat" (cookies).
Dates Open: All year.
High Season: Apr-Jun & Sept-Nov.
Rates: Jan-Feb & Jul-Aug: $150-$350/nt, Mar-Jun & Sept-Dec: $200-$350/nt.
Credit Cards: MC, Visa,

Amex, Diners.
Rsv'tns: Required.
Reserve Thru: Travel agent or call direct.
Parking: Ample, pay covered parking. Valet parking.
In-Room: Telephone, AC, color cable TV, maid & room service.
On-Premises: Meeting rooms, 2 award-winning restaurants.
Exercise/Health: Gym nearby.

Smoking: Permitted in the Grill & Library. Smoking & non-smoking rooms available.
Pets: Not permitted.
Handicap Access: Yes, elevator.
Children: Welcome.
Languages: English, Spanish, Japanese, Ethiopian, Arabic, Italian, French.

Color Photo on Page 18

Windsor Inn

WWW Gay-Friendly ♂♀
Woman-Operated

A Relaxing Oasis in Washington

A relaxed atmosphere and personalized service typify the *Windsor Inn*, a charming art deco-style bed and breakfast on historical 16th Street, convenient to the metro and a variety of restaurants. We're happy to help with dining suggestions, tourist information, etc. Rooms are comfortable and pleasantly decorated. Our nine suites have beautiful ceiling borders and a basket of special soaps and shampoo, extra-thick towels and small refrigerators. The *Windsor* is also close to nightlife and sights. We are a friendly and economical alternative to the larger convention hotels.

Address: 1842 16th St NW, Washington, DC 20009
Tel: (202) 667-0300, (800) 423-9111, **Fax:** (202) 667-4503.

Type: Hotel inn.
Clientele: Mostly straight clientele with a gay & lesbian following
Transportation: Taxi from airport. From Union Station take metro red line to Dupont Circle, then walk 6-1/2 blocks.
To Gay Bars: 3 blocks to men's bars & 5 blocks to gay & lesbian bars.
Rooms: 43 rooms & 2 suites with single, double or queen beds.

Baths: All private.
Meals: Expanded continental breakfast & evening sherry.
Complimentary: Sherry in lobby all year, coffee & tea 24 hours.
Dates Open: All year.
High Season: Apr-May & Sept-Oct.
Rates: High season $89-$159, low season $79-$129.
Discounts: Govt. ID, weekend rates (space-available).

Credit Cards: MC, Visa, Amex, Diners, Carte Blanche.
Rsv'tns: Must be guaranteed with a credit card.
Reserve Thru: Travel agent or call direct.
Parking: On-street parking, some limitations.
In-Room: Maid service, telephone, color cable TV, free HBO, AC, refrigerator in 2 suites & 7 rooms, hairdryer.

On-Premises: Small conference room.
Exercise/Health: Facilities within close walking distance.
Swimming: Facilities within close walking distance.
Smoking: Lobby non-smoking. Most rooms are non-smoking.
Pets: Not permitted.
Handicap Access: No.
Children: Permitted.
Languages: English, Spanish, French, Arabic.

Center City Hotel

WWW Gay-Friendly 50/50 ♀♂

Starting with our elegant entryway, you will be surrounded by lush appointments at *Center City Hotel*. Our front desk is your start into what will be a truly wonderful hotel experience. Stop by and enjoy a complimentary piece of fruit! Need a quick pick-me-up? Ask about our espresso and cappuccino service! Stop by the lobby, and relax a while with a complimentary copy of USA Today, or one of the many other magazines available. Our meeting and dining hall is perfect for business meetings, or dinners for special occasions. The hotel is conveniently located in the heart of Washington's business and tourist districts. It's only four blocks from the Metro-Rail, one mile from Union Station, ten blocks from the White House, Smithsonian Museums and MCI Arena, and six blocks from the Convention Center and shopping.

Address: 1201 13th Street NW, Washington, DC 20005
Tel: (202) 682-5300, (888) 250-5396, **Fax:** (202) 371-9624.
E-mail: info@centercity.com **Web:** http://www.centercityhotel.com

Type: Hotel with restaurant. **Clientele:** 50% gay & lesbian & 50% straight clientele **Transportation:** Taxi or metro (4 blocks). **To Gay Bars:** 10 blocks, 10 min walk. **Rooms:** 100 rooms with single, double, queen or king beds. **Baths:** All private bath/shower/toilets, shower/ toilets. **Meals:** Continental breakfast. **Vegetarian:** Upon request. **Complimentary:** Complimentary fruit 24 hrs. **Dates Open:** All year. **High Season:** Apr, May, Oct. **Rates:** Summer & spring: $89-$129; Winter & fall $69-$109. **Discounts:** AAA, AARP. **Credit Cards:** MC, Visa, Amex, Diners, Discover. **Rsv'tns:** Required. **Reserve Thru:** Travel agent or call direct. **Parking:** Adequate pay parking. **In-Room:** Telephone, AC, color cable TV, coffee & tea-making facilities, maid & laundry service. **On-Premises:** Meeting rooms, laundry facilities. **Exercise/Health:** Gym, weights, Jacuzzi, steam. **Swimming:** Pool nearby. **Smoking:** Non-smoking rooms available. **Pets:** Not permitted. **Handicap Access:** Yes, ramps, elevator. **Children:** Welcome. **Languages:** English, Russian, Indian.

Amelia Island Williams House

WWW Gay-Friendly ♀♂

A Historic Bed & Breakfast with a Heritage of Elegance

"The most exquisite B&B in Florida and one of the most exquisite B&Bs in the South...the uncontested gem of Amelia Island." "Top Inn of the Year 1995" — *Country Inns magazine* This 1856 ante-bellum mansion is the town's oldest and most historic home, featuring outstanding architectural details and antiques and art dating from the 1500s. Eight guest suites include a regal anniversary suite with original Napoleonic antiques. Breakfast is served in the opulent red and gold dining room. From *The Amelia Island Williams House* enjoy 13 miles of unspoiled beaches, horseback riding, golf, tennis, fishing, and shopping in restored historic downtown. Also visit us at www.ameliaislandflorida.com

Address: 103 S 9th St, Amelia Island, FL 32034
Tel: (904) 277-2328, **Fax:** (904) 321-1325. Reservations only: (800) 414-9257.
E-mail: topinn@aol.com **Web:** http://www.williamshouse.com

Type: Bed & Breakfast. **Clientele:** Mainly straight clientele with a gay & lesbian following. **Transportation:** Car. 30 min to Jacksonville Int'l Airport. **To Gay Bars:** 45-min drive. **Rooms:** 8 rooms with king or queen beds. **Baths:** All private. **Meals:** Full breakfast. **Vegetarian:** On request. **Complimentary:** Wine & cheese in afternoon. **High Season:** Summer. **Rates:** $145-$225. **Credit Cards:** MC, Visa. **Rsv'tns:** Required. **Reserve Thru:** Call direct. **Min. Stay:** Required during special events weekends. **Parking:** Ample off-street & on-street parking. **In-Room:** Color cable TV, video tape library, VCR, AC, ceiling fans, maid service. 6 rms: working fireplaces. **On-Premises:** Formal English walking garden. **Exercise/Health:** 2 rooms have private Jacuzzis. Massage on call. **Swimming:** Nearby ocean. **Sunbathing:** At the beach. **Smoking:** Permitted on porch & in courtyard only. **Pets:** Not permitted. Pet boarding service available at vet's or in private home. **Handicap Access:** Yes. **Children:** 12 years & up OK. **Your Hosts:** Dick & Chris.

Deauville Inn, The

Steps to the Beach...

Fort Lauderdale Beach's *Deauville Inn* offers beautiful, affordable hotel accommodations — from cozy rooms to efficiency apartments with full kitchens. Vacation within a block of the Atlantic Ocean beach and enjoy swimming in the ocean, or relax by our courtyard swimming pool. We are located near dozens of favorite Florida vacation attractions, sports activities and Fort Lauderdale's night life.

At the *Deauville Inn,* on Fort Lauderdale Beach, we will make your vacation a memorable affair. It is our goal to provide to our patrons all the comforts of their own home. As a family-owned business, our number one goal is to cater to you. Every day we try to improve our facilities, always taking into consideration your needs and desires. Your safety and peace of mind is also of great importance to the Deauville Inn family. We have taken great care to provide a clean, secure, private "home away from home."

Leave the cold weather behind and savor everything the *Deauville Inn* has to offer: Sit back and relax in our breezy and sunny courtyard. Take a refreshing dip in our pristine swimming pool, located in the center of our courtyard. Prepare that perfect barbeque on one of our pool-side barbeque grills. Swim or take a relaxing walk along our world-renowned beaches, only steps away.

Address: 2916 N. Ocean Blvd, Fort Lauderdale, FL 33308
Tel: (954) 568-5000, **Fax:** (954) 565-7797.
E-mail: info@ftlaud-deauville.com **Web:** http://www.ftlaud-deauville.com

Type: Motel, inn.
Clientele: Mostly gay & lesbian with some straight clientele
Transportation: Car or taxi. Pick up from Ft Lauderdale airport or train $25, from Miami airport $50.
To Gay Bars: 3 blocks, 1 mile, a 10 min walk, a 2 min drive.
Rooms: 4 rooms, 6 suites with double, queen or king beds.

Baths: 10 private bath/shower/toilets.
Vegetarian: Vegetarian food nearby.
Complimentary: Coffee.
Dates Open: All year.
High Season: Nov-Apr.
Rates: Summer $40-$55, winter $55-$75.
Credit Cards: MC, Visa, Amex.
Rsv'tns: Recommended.
Reserve Thru: Travel agent or call direct.

Min. Stay: Required on holidays or special events.
Parking: Ample free parking.
In-Room: Telephone, AC, color cable TV, kitchen, refrigerator, coffee & tea-making facilities, maid & laundry service.
On-Premises: Laundry facilities.
Exercise/Health: Nearby gay gym, weights, Jacuzzi, sauna, steam, massage.

Swimming: Pool on premises. Nearby ocean.
Sunbathing: Poolside, on patio & at beach.
Smoking: Inquire.
Pets: Permitted with small pet deposit (non-refundable).
Handicap Access: No.
Children: No.
Languages: English, Spanish.
Your Hosts: Amy, Wally, Bonnie, Sonia.

Color Photo on Page 19

J P's Beach Villas

Your Vacation Paradise Awaits...

JP's Beach Villas is an all-suites private resort with luxurious one- and two-bedroom apartments. We're proud of our unsurpassed attention to detail, friendly staff, and relaxed atmosphere. We invite you to be our guest — whether you visit Ft. Lauderdale for relaxation, a romantic getaway, or business. The azure-blue Atlantic is just steps from our Lauderdale-by-the-Sea paradise, and the varied attractions of gay Ft. Lauderdale are just minutes away. Our tastefully furnished one- and two-bedroom suites have equipped kitchens, phone, TV/VCR, air conditioning, tennis, as well as a heated pool. We're the heart of an area which features fine shopping, excellent restaurants and clubs, churches, and a nearby fishing pier.

Bienvenue Francais et Canadiens! Benvenuti gli Italiani! Wilkommen Deutsch! Bienvenidos Amigos! *JP's Beach Villas* are perfect for the foreign traveler. We will treat you as our guest and not as a mere tourist. Lauderdale-by-the-Sea is in Northern Fort Lauderdale just south of Pompano Beach, bordered by the exclusive enclave of Sea Ranch Lakes. A quiet, friendly beachside location like ours sounds far away from South Florida's diverse urban scene. But we're just minutes from major attractions, clubs, shopping, and corporate offices. Ft. Lauderdale makes a convenient stop for visitors going from Key West to Orlando (Disneyworld).

Address: 4621 N Ocean Drive, Fort Lauderdale, FL 33308
Tel: (954) 772-3672, (888) 992-3224, **Fax:** (954) 776-0889.
E-mail: jpsvillas@aol.com **Web:** http://www.jpsbeachvillas.com

Type: Hotel & suites.
Clientele: Mostly men with women welcome
Transportation: Car.
To Gay Bars: 2 miles, a 6 min drive.
Rooms: 1 suite, 9 apartments with queen or king beds.
Baths: 10 private bath/shower/toilets.
Complimentary: Season (Dec 15-Apr 15): open bar Fri & Sat 5-7pm.
Dates Open: All year.

High Season: Jan-May.
Rates: Summer $60-$125, winter $90-$175.
Credit Cards: MC, Visa, Amex, Diners, Discover.
Rsv'tns: Required.
Reserve Thru: Travel agent or call direct.
Min. Stay: Required on holiday weekends.
Parking: Ample free parking (overnight guest must register car).
In-Room: Telephones, AC, ceiling fans, color cable TV,

VCR, kitchen, refrigerator, coffee & tea-making facilities, maid service.
On-Premises: Laundry facilities, video tape library, fax, modem.
Exercise/Health: Massage, free tennis. Nearby gym, sauna, steam,.
Swimming: Pool. 1/2 block to ocean.
Sunbathing: Poolside & at beach.
Smoking: Permitted.
Pets: Dog or cat under

30lbs. $50 damage deposit, $25 non-refundable cleaning deposit.
Handicap Access: Yes, 1 room.
Children: Welcome, but rarely do gay guests bring them.
Languages: English, French, some Spanish.
Your Hosts: JP & Larry.
IGLTA

Bahama Hotel, The

In the Center of Fort Lauderdale Beach

Comfortable furnished rooms, overlooking the center of Fort Lauderdale Beach and the Atlantic Ocean, will put you in a vacation frame of mind. At *Bahama Hotel*, let yourself relax in a large, heated, fresh-water pool and stretch out for tanning on our patio which gets the warm Florida sun all day long. Refreshments are always close by in our tropical patio bar. Enjoy fine cuisine morning, noon, and evening in our Deck Restaurant overlooking the bright blue waters of the Atlantic.

Address: 401 N Ft. Lauderdale Beach Blvd (A1A), Fort Lauderdale, FL 33304
Tel: (954) 467-7315, (800) 622-9995, **Fax:** (954) 467-7319.
E-mail: bahama@bahamahotel.com **Web:** http://www.bahamahotel.com

Type: Hotel with restaurant & bar.
Clientele: Mixture of gay & straight clientele
Transportation: Car or taxi from airport.
To Gay Bars: 2 miles or 5-min drive.
Rooms: 43 rooms & 23 efficiencies all with double or king beds.
Baths: Private baths.
Meals: Full breakfast.
Vegetarian: Available upon request.
Complimentary: Coffee in lobby. Pool & beach towels.
Dates Open: All year.
High Season: Dec-Apr.
Rates: Low season $69-$159, high season $95-$275.
Credit Cards: MC, Visa, Amex, Diners, Discover.
Rsv'tns: Required.
Reserve Thru: Travel agent or call direct.
Min. Stay: Required during holidays & special events.
Parking: Adequate free off-street parking.
In-Room: Color cable TV, AC, telephone, kitchen, refrigerator, maid & room service.
On-Premises: Laundry facilities.
Exercise/Health: Massage & gym with exercise equipment & personal trainer on premises.
Swimming: Pool on premises. Ocean across the street.
Sunbathing: At poolside, on common sun decks, on ocean beach.
Smoking: Permitted. Non-smoking rooms available.
Pets: Permitted. Dogs under 10 lbs.
Handicap Access: Yes.
Children: Welcome.
Languages: English, French, Spanish, Portuguese.
IGLTA

Flamingo Resort

In the Gay Lodging District on Ft. Lauderdale Beach

The Flamingo Resort, a beautiful Art Deco resort, is ablaze in pinks and teals, highlighted with soft neon lighting accents. The lush tropical landscaping throughout is accented by our bubbling Flamingo fountain. Spacious rooms, studios or suites all overlook a private, fully enclosed courtyard. Continental breakfast is served poolside daily, and guests are sure to enjoy our private, clothing-optional, heated pool. We're steps to the gay beach and minutes from shopping, cultural attractions and nightlife.

Address: 2727 Terramar St, Fort Lauderdale, FL 33304
Tel: (954) 561-4658, (800) 283-4786, **Fax:** (954) 568-2688.
E-mail: flamingors@aol.com **Web:** http://www.theflamingoresort.com

Type: Guesthouse.
Clientele: Mostly men with women welcome
Transportation: Car or taxi. A short drive from airport.
To Gay Bars: 1 mile, a 20 min walk, a 10 min drive.
Rooms: 5 rooms, 6 suites with queen or king beds.
Baths: 11 private bath/shower/toilets.
Meals: Continental breakfast.
Complimentary: Afternoon refreshments.
Dates Open: All year.
High Season: Dec-Apr.
Rates: Low: $68-$115; High: $87-$149.
Discounts: Extended stays, early bookings.
Credit Cards: MC, Visa, Amex, Discover.
Rsv'tns: Required.
Reserve Thru: Travel agent or call direct.
Min. Stay: 3 days in high season.
Parking: Adequate free off-street parking.
In-Room: Telephone, AC, ceiling fans, color cable TV, VCR, kitchen, refrigerator, coffee & tea-making facilities, maid & laundry service.
On-Premises: TV lounge, laundry facilities, fax, internet, video tape library.
Exercise/Health: Weights, massage. Nearby gym.
Swimming: Pool. Nearby ocean.
Sunbathing: Poolside, on common sun decks, at beach.
Nudity: Permitted poolside.
Smoking: Permitted in courtyard & in some rooms.
Pets: Not permitted.
Handicap Access: No.
Children: No.
Languages: English.
Your Hosts: John, Steve, Scotty.
IGLTA

Gemini House

Men ♂

This is THE Place to Get Naked & Relax!

Three houses (we live in one) on an enclosed half acre offer gay male naturist vacation rentals in the B&B tradition. Each house has two individually decorated guestrooms which share one bath. Breakfast doesn't consist of donuts and bottled juice, but a full meal with fresh-squeezed juice and Starbuck's coffee. The enclosed yard is a tropical paradise, where you can enjoy our oversized heated swimming pool, hot tub, or nap in a hammock under towering palm trees! Member: GNI, IMEN, Naturist Society.

Address: Fort Lauderdale, FL 33334
Tel: (954) 568-9791, **Fax:** (954) 568-0617.
E-mail: GeminiHse@aol.com **Web:** http://www.geminihse.com

Type: Vacation rental, guesthouse.
Clientele: Men only
Transportation: Car is best.
To Gay Bars: 3 blocks to gay bars.
Rooms: 4 rooms with single, queen & king beds.
Baths: 2 shared bath/shower/toilets.
Meals: Full breakfast.
Vegetarian: Available if requested in advance.

Complimentary: Fresh-baked cookies every night in room.
Dates Open: All year.
High Season: All year.
Rates: $90 single, $100 double.
Discounts: Students & on extended stays.
Rsv'tns: Required. 50% deposit, balance due at check-in.
Reserve Thru: Call direct or e-mail.

Min. Stay: 2 nights.
Parking: Ample off-street parking.
In-Room: AC, color cable TV, VCR, ceiling fans, maid service, all-cotton linens, oversized towels.
On-Premises: Laundry facilities, book & video tape libraries, full kitchen. Car rental discounts.
Exercise/Health: Gym, Jacuzzi, massage, outdoor tropical shower, bicycles.

Swimming: Pool on premises. Ocean nearby.
Sunbathing: Poolside.
Nudity: Enitre property is a "no clothing zone."
Smoking: Permitted outside only.
Pets: Not permitted.
Handicap Access: No.
Children: No.
Languages: English.
Your Hosts: John & Rick.
IGLTA

King Henry Arms

Men ♂

The Best Is Yet to Come: YOU!

King Henry Arms, with its friendly, home-like atmosphere and squeaky-clean accommodations, is just the place for that romantic getaway. Spend your days relaxing amidst the tropical foliage by our pool, or at the ocean beach, just 300 feet away. Enjoy your evenings at the many restaurants and clubs, before returning to the quiet comfort of your accommodations. Truly a jewel by the sea.

Address: 543 Breakers Ave, Fort Lauderdale, FL 33304-4129
Tel: (954) 561-0039 or (800) 205-KING (5464).

Type: Motel.
Clientele: Men only
Transportation: Car or taxi from Ft. Lauderdale airport.
To Gay Bars: 2 miles to gay/lesbian bars.
Rooms: 4 rooms, 5 suites & 3 apartments with double, queen or king beds.
Baths: All private bath/toilet/showers.
Meals: Continental breakfast.
Vegetarian: Restaurants & stores nearby.

Dates Open: All year.
High Season: Winter months.
Rates: Spring thru fall $67-$85, winter $101-$125.
Discounts: 10% on 8-30 nights, 15% on 31-60 nights and 20% on 61 nights or more, plus summer specials.
Credit Cards: MC, Visa, Amex, Discover, Novus.
Rsv'tns: Prefer 1 month in advance, earlier in season.
Reserve Thru: Travel agent or call direct.

Min. Stay: 7 nights in high season.
Parking: Adequate free off-street parking.
In-Room: Maid service, color cable TV, telephone, AC, safe & refrigerator. Apartments & suites have kitchens.
On-Premises: Laundry facilities.
Exercise/Health: Gym nearby.
Swimming: Pool on premises, ocean beach

nearby.
Sunbathing: At poolside, on beach or patio.
Smoking: Permitted without restrictions.
Pets: Not permitted.
Handicap Access: No.
Children: Not especially welcomed.
Languages: English.
Your Hosts: Don & Roy.
IGLTA

Orton Terrace

The INN Place for the IN Men

Orton Terrace is located in the Central Beach area only steps from the beach. We offer a quiet, relaxing and friendly atmosphere with the largest apartment accommodations found in the area. The one- and two-bedroom apartments have full-sized kitchens and 27" TVs. All rooms feature phones, cable TVs, VCRs, safes, refrigerators and microwaves. Videos are also available. Our grounds feature a pool, BBQ and a quiet tropical courtyard setting.

Address: 606 Orton Ave, Fort Lauderdale, FL 33304
Tel: (954) 566-5068, **Fax:** (954) 564-8646. Toll-free in USA, Canada & Caribbean: (800) 323-1142.
E-mail: orton@ortonterrace.com **Web:** http://www.ortonterrace.com

Type: Motel.
Clientele: Men only
Transportation: Taxi.
To Gay Bars: 3 miles, a 6-min drive, a 45-min walk.
Rooms: 7 guestrooms, some king rooms, 7 2-BR apartments with single, double or queen beds & 7 1-BR apartments.
Baths: All private.
Meals: Continental

breakfast.
Dates Open: All year.
High Season: Dec-Feb & Apr.
Rates: Dec-May: $79-$218, May-Dec: $54-$158.
Credit Cards: MC, Visa, Amex, Discover.
Rsv'tns: Not required, but strongly suggested.
Reserve Thru: Travel agent or call direct.

Min. Stay: Please inquire.
Parking: Adequate free off-street parking.
In-Room: AC, ceiling fan, color cable TV, VCR, stereo, video tape library, phone, coffee/tea making facilities, kitchen, refrigerator, microwave, maid service.
On-Premises: Laundry facilities, internet access.
Swimming: Pool on

premises. Ocean nearby.
Sunbathing: Poolside, on patio, at beach.
Nudity: Clothing optional.
Smoking: Permitted.
Pets: Not permitted.
Handicap Access: No.
Children: Please inquire.
Languages: English.
IGLTA

Palms on Las Olas, The

Fort Lauderdale's Finest Guest Suites

Affordable luxury in classic fifties style awaits at *The Palms on Las Olas.* Spacious accommodations, ranging from efficiencies to one-bedroom suites, include AC, remote control cable TV, telephones with voice mail and, in season, a full continental breakfast. We're in the heart of "chic" Las Olas Boulevard, one mile from the beach, and close to shops, restaurants and bars. This is the most central and safe location. Relax by the pool, or take a water taxi from our private dock and explore the canals and waterways of Old Fort Lauderdale.

Address: 1760 E Las Olas Blvd, Fort Lauderdale, FL 33301
Tel: (954) 462-4178, (800) 550-POLO (7656), **Fax:** (954) 463-8544.
Web: http://www.palmsonlasolas.com

Type: Guesthouse motel.
Clientele: Gay men only
Transportation: Car is best.
To Gay Bars: 5 blocks or 1/2 mile. An 8-minute walk or 2-minute drive.
Rooms: 4 suites, 6 efficiencies with full-sized, queen or king beds.
Baths: All private.
Meals: Expanded continental breakfast, high

season only.
Dates Open: All year.
High Season: Dec-Apr.
Rates: Summer $60-$85, winter $89-$125.
Credit Cards: MC, Visa, Amex, Discover.
Rsv'tns: Strongly recommended.
Reserve Thru: Travel agent or call direct.
Min. Stay: 3 days during high season, public

holidays.
Parking: Ample free off-street parking.
In-Room: Color cable TV, AC, telephones with voice mail, coffee/tea-making facilities, maid & room service. Efficiencies & apartments w/ full kitchens & microwave.
On-Premises: Fax & dedicated computer modem line.

Exercise/Health: Nearby gym.
Swimming: Heated pool on premises, ocean nearby.
Sunbathing: At poolside & on common sun decks.
Nudity: Permitted poolside.
Smoking: Permitted.
Pets: Not permitted.
Handicap Access: No.
Children: No.
Languages: English.

Worthington Guest House, The

WWW Men ♂
Gay-Owned & -Operated

Ft. Lauderdale's All-Season Gay Resort

This enticing resort is just steps to the ocean in the heart of Ft. Lauderdale's gay beach district. Lush tropical gardens provide an intimate atmosphere, and the large, sunny poolside courtyard provides the privacy for that all-over tan. *The Worthington's* spacious one-bedroom suites, efficiencies and guest rooms feature pool views, private full bath, refrigerators, TV/VCR, cable and AC. After your expanded continental breakfast enjoy a fabulous day of shopping and beautiful Florida sunshine. We're minutes from the Galleria Mall, trendy Las Olas Blvd., and a short walk to Sebastian Beach.

Address: 543 N. Birch Rd, Fort Lauderdale, FL
Tel: (954) 563-6819, (800) 445-7036, **Fax:** (954) 563-4313.
E-mail: worthingtonhotel@aol.com **Web:** http://www.worthguesthouse.com

Type: Guesthouse, hotel.
Clientele: Men only
Transportation: Car, taxi.
To Gay Bars: 5 miles, a 5 min drive.
Rooms: 12 rooms, 4 suites with king or queen beds.
Baths: All private bath/shower/toilets.
Meals: Expanded continental breakfast.
Complimentary: Cocktails during social hour.

Dates Open: All year.
High Season: Dec-May.
Rates: Jun-Nov $75-$100, Dec-May $99-$150.
Discounts: Repeat clients, referrals & off-season specials.
Credit Cards: MC, Visa, Amex, Discover.
Rsv'tns: Required.
Reserve Thru: Travel agent or call direct.
Min. Stay: 3 days on holidays.

Parking: Adequate off-street parking.
In-Room: Phone, AC, ceiling fans, color cable TV, VCR, kitchen, fridge, coffee & tea-making facilities, maid & laundry service.
On-Premises: Laundry facilities, video tape library.
Exercise/Health: Nearby gym.
Swimming: Pool. Nearby ocean.

Sunbathing: Poolside & on patio.
Nudity: Permitted.
Smoking: Rooms are non-smoking. Smoking outside room is appreciated.
Pets: OK under 20 lbs.
Children: No.
Languages: English.
Your Hosts: Jim & Jason.
IGLTA

Resort on Carefree Boulevard, The

Affordable Luxury Especially For You

Private and secluded, *Resort on Carefree Boulevard* is set on 50 acres of pine land on Florida's beautiful Gulf Coast, between Sarasota and Naples. The resort offers a full-service rental program with resort or manufactured homes available for weekly or monthly rental, accommodating two to eight people. All resort and manufactured homes in our rental program are furnished and equipped with a household package, including linens, dishes, pots and pans. Rental rates also include electric, water, sewer, local telephone and basic cable. RV and manufactured homesites offer a variety of affordable home options. Homesites are fully developed, including roads, city water and sewer, electric, telephone and cable TV. RV sites are complete with compact service pedestals for convenient hookup and concrete pad.

Our plush, private, clubhouse complex has an activities director and features a main gathering room, a library, and billiard, arts & craft, card & games, exercise, and big-screen TV rooms. There are also a 1,600 square foot swimming pool, spa, tennis and shuffleboard courts and putting green. The clubhouse facilities are operated under private club memberships. There are no signs or outdoor billboards to guide you to the resort. The main entrance is on Carefree Boulevard.

Address: 3000 Carefree Blvd, Fort Myers, FL 33917-7135
Tel: (941) 731-3000, (800) 326-0364, **Fax:** (941) 731-3519.
E-mail: cg@resortoncb.com **Web:** http://www.resortoncb.com

Type: Manufactured homes & RV rental sites, resort community, sports club & clubhouse.
Clientele: Women only
Transportation: Car or SW International Airport.
To Gay Bars: 10 miles.
Rooms: 1- thru 4-BR manufactured homes with double, queen or king beds.
Baths: 1 or 2 bath units.
Camping: RV site rentals. Electric, water, sewer, basic cable TV hookups.

Vegetarian: 1 mile.
Complimentary: Tea & coffee.
High Season: Nov 1-Apr 30.
Rates: 1-BR: summer $45-$66, winter $64-$94. 2-BR: summer $70-$91, winter $100-$130. RV: off $17-$23, on $24-$32.
Discounts: Inquire.
Credit Cards: MC, Visa.
Rsv'tns: Required.
Reserve Thru: Call direct.
Min. Stay: 3 days.

Parking: Adequate covered free off-street parking.
In-Room: Phone, AC, ceiling fans, color cable TV, kitchen, fridge, coffee & tea makers. VCR in most units. Maid & laundry svc avail.
On-Premises: 10,000-sq-ft clubhouse, meeting rms, TV lounge, fax, copier, video tape library, laundry, billiard rm, arts & crafts rm.
Exercise/Health: Gym, weights, Jacuzzi, putting green, shuffleboard, tennis

cts. Clubhouse: private club membership.
Swimming: 1,600-sq-ft pool. Nearby ocean.
Sunbathing: Poolside.
Smoking: Permitted in designated areas.
Pets: Permitted, must be leashed.
Handicap Access: Yes, ramps.
Children: No.
Languages: English, Spanish.
IGLTA

Accommodations in Key West

Coconut Grove for Men   WWW Men ♂

Enjoy unparalleled views of Old Town and the Gulf of Mexico from our roof-top decks at *Coconut Grove Guest House*. The widow's walk provides a private spot to tan, take in the ocean air or experience Key West's sunsets. Friendliest service and largest, best suites in town.

Address: 817 Fleming St, Key West, FL 33040
Tel: (305) 296-5107, (800) 262-6055, **Fax:** (305) 296-1584.

Type: Guesthouse.
Clientele: Men only
Transportation: Taxi.
To Gay Bars: 3 blocks to men's bars.
Rooms: 5 singles, 11 doubles, 2 suites, 4 1-bedroom apartments in annex across the street.
Baths: 20 private, 2 shared.
Meals: Continental breakfast.

Dates Open: All year.
High Season: December 20th-April 15th.
Rates: High season, $85-$200. Low season, $55-$100.
Credit Cards: MC, Visa.
Reserve Thru: Travel agent or call direct.
Min. Stay: Required at certain times.
Parking: On-street parking.

In-Room: Maid service, color TV, kitchen, refrigerator & AC.
On-Premises: Meeting rooms, telephone.
Exercise/Health: Gym, weights.
Swimming: Pool.
Sunbathing: At poolside & on common sun decks, or roof.
Nudity: Permitted at the

pool & sun decks.
Smoking: Permitted without restrictions.
Pets: Not permitted.
Handicap Access: No.
Children: Not permitted.
Languages: English, German, French, Swedish.
IGLTA

Alexander's Guesthouse

We Are Key West!

From the moment you arrive at *Alexander's*, you will appreciate our thoughtful service and our attention to detail. Built as a private residence in 1910 in what is now known as Old Town, *Alexander's* was established as a guesthouse in 1981. Our lovely common living areas set the mood. Handsome quarters await you, each one unique and with amenities chosen to anticipate your needs. Our bright, comfortable rooms all have bahama fans, AC, TV, VCRs, phone and refrigerators.

The secluded grounds, radiant throughout the day, are a haven for sun-worshippers. Guests can soak up the sun all day on our multi-level decks, or stroll through the lush, sunny tropical garden surrounding the heated pool. Sunbathe poolside or revel in your sense of freedom on one of our private sun decks above the gardens. If you're in the mood for a swim, frolic in the pool beneath cascading bougainvillaea. Evenings, gather by the pool with fellow guests for the complimentary evening cocktail hour.

Truly representative of Key West at its finest, Fleming Street is replete with classic Conch houses, antique stores, food markets, a ship chandlery, the public library and more. Key West is legendary for its incomparable weather and liberal attitudes. Favored daytime activities range from watersports to gallery hopping. A short walk away is Duval Street, where clubs, restaurants and bars offer fun and entertainment lasting until the early morning.

Address: 1118 Fleming St, Key West, FL 33040
Tel: (305) 294-9919 or (800) 654-9919.
E-mail: alexghouse@aol.com **Web:** http://www.alexghouse.com

Type: Guesthouse.
Clientele: 75% gay, 25% lesbian
Transportation: Taxi from the airport.
To Gay Bars: 6-7 blocks.
Rooms: 14 doubles, 3 quads
Baths: 17 private.
Meals: Expanded continental breakfast.
Complimentary: Daily

happy hour.
High Season: Dec 22-Apr 16.
Rates: Winter $145-$300, summer $80-$180.
Credit Cards: MC, Visa, Amex, Discover.
Rsv'tns: Recommended.
Reserve Thru: Travel agent or call direct.
Min. Stay:
For most holidays, special

events, high season.
Parking: Adequate free on-street parking.
In-Room: AC, VCRs, color cable TV, remote, phone, hair dryers, maid svc, fridge, ceiling fans, iron, ironing board.
Exercise/Health: Spa.
Swimming: In heated pool or at nearby ocean beach.
Sunbathing: On private &

common sun decks, on the beach & at poolside.
Nudity: Permitted for sunbathers on 2nd & 3rd floor sun decks.
Smoking: Permitted.
Pets: Not permitted.
Children: Not permitted.
Languages: English, French.

Atlantic Shores Resort

WWW Gay/Lesbian ⚢
Gay-Owned

Oceanfront — In the Heart of Old Town

The friendly, casual and qualified staff at *Atlantic Shores Resort* eagerly await to assist you on your fantasy vacation. The grounds of this tropical Art Deco-style hotel are luxurious and manicured, and our oceanfront, clothing-optional pool is a favorite with tourists and locals alike, as are a clothing-required pool and beautiful sandy beach. The popular Pool Bar and Grill boasts a stairway to the sea, water sports accessibility and the legendary "Tea by the Sea." Diner Shores Restaurant offers breakfast and lunch overlooking South Street, with frequent live entertainment. We're on the sunrise side of Key West, minutes from bars, shops and restaurants.

Address: 510 South St, Key West, FL 33040-3118
Tel: (305) 296-2491, U.S. toll-free (888) 324-8742, **Fax:** (305) 294-2753.
E-mail: info@atlanticshoresresort.com **Web:** http://
www.atlanticshoresresort.com

Type: Hotel with restaurant, pool bar & grill.
Clientele: Gays, lesbians & enlightened straights
Transportation: Airport taxi or car is best.
To Gay Bars: On premises & nearby.
Rooms: 72 with queen, king or 2 doubles. Efficiencies available.
Baths: All private.
Meals: "Two for Breakfast" plans, some restrictions.
Vegetarian: On premises.

Dates Open: All year.
High Season: Dec 23-Apr 30.
Rates: Summer $80-$125, winter $130-$250.
Discounts: Please inquire, group rates.
Credit Cards: MC, Visa, Amex, Diners, Discover, Carte Blanche, Eurocard, Bancard.
Rsv'tns: Highly recommended.
Reserve Thru: Website, call direct, internet travel

sites or travel agent.
Min. Stay: On holidays & special events.
Parking: Free parking based on availability.
In-Room: Color cable TV, AC, telephone, maid service. Efficiencies have refrigerator, microwave, coffee maker.
On-Premises: Fax, copy machine, internet access, laundry facilities, safe deposit boxes.
Exercise/Health: Nearby

gym, weights & massage.
Swimming: Pool on premises, also on ocean front, natural sandy beach.
Sunbathing: At poolside & pier.
Nudity: Permitted in pool area.
Smoking: Permitted.
Pets: Permitted.
Children: Inquire.
Languages: English, Spanish.
IGLTA

Big Ruby's Guesthouse

Gay/Lesbian ♂
Gay-Owned & -Operated

Peace & Privacy in the Heart of Old Town

On our quiet little lane, in peace and privacy, our three guesthouses, each in traditional historic design, stand secluded behind a tall fence. Inside *Big Ruby's*, luxury touches are everywhere. Immaculate rooms have sumptuous beds with four king-sized pillows and superthick bath sheets for towels. Awaiting you outside are a beautiful lagoon pool, spacious decks and lounge areas in a completely private tropical garden. Full breakfast is served at poolside. Evenings, we gather by the pool for wine and the easy companionability of good conversation. You'll never feel so welcome, so comfortable, so at home.

Address: 409 Appelrouth Lane, Key West, FL 33040
Tel: (305) 296-2323, (800) 477-7829, **Fax:** (305) 296-0281.
E-mail: keywest@bigrubys.com **Web:** http://www.BigRubys.com

Type: Guesthouse.
Clientele: Mostly men with women welcome
Transportation: Taxi from airport.
To Gay Bars: 1/2 block, a 5 min walk.
Rooms: 17 rooms with queen or king beds.
Baths: 15 private shower/toilets. 2 shared bath/shower/toilets.
Meals: Full breakfast. Dinners on most major holidays.
Vegetarian: Available upon request & nearby.

Complimentary: Coffee always. Beer, wine, juice each evening.
Dates Open: All year.
High Season: Dec-Jun.
Rates: Per evening: off season $85-$245; season $145-$345.
Credit Cards: MC, Visa, Amex, Diners, Discover, Carte Blanche.
Rsv'tns: To be safe: season 4 months in advance, off season 3 mo. in advance.
Reserve Thru: Travel agent or call direct.
Min. Stay: 4 nights in season, 3 nights off season.
Parking: Ample free off-street parking.
In-Room: AC, ceiling fans, color cable TV, VCR, refrigerator, maid & laundry service.
On-Premises: TV lounge, video tape library, TTY phone system for hearing impaired.
Exercise/Health: Jacuzzi, outdoor shower "The Rainforest." Nearby gym.
Swimming: Pool. Ocean nearby.
Sunbathing: At poolside, on common sun decks, at beach.
Nudity: Permitted in pool & sunning yard only.
Smoking: Permitted in rooms & common areas. Non-smoking rooms available.
Pets: Not permitted.
Handicap Access: Yes, ramps, rails in bathroom.
Children: No.
Languages: English.
IGLTA

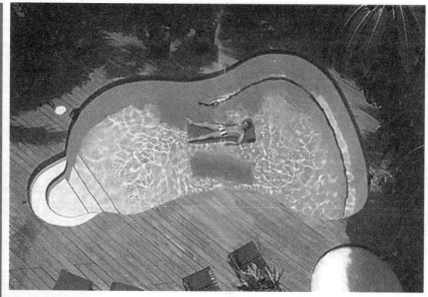

Curry House   Men ♂

Key West's Premiere Guest House for Men

If you find that many of your new friends speak with an intriguing accent, it is because the *Curry House* is internationally popular. With only nine rooms, getting to know your fellow guests happens naturally while lounging by our black lagoon pool or at our daily happy hour. As your hosts, we are wholeheartedly at your service. Your room will be immaculate, your bed as comfortable as any you have ever slept in. *Curry House* is a short three-block stroll from Duval Street, Key West's lively mainstream.

Address: 806 Fleming St, Key West, FL 33040
Tel: (305) 294-6777, (800) 633-7439, **Fax:** (305) 294-5322.
Web: http://www.gaytraveling.com/curryhouse

Type: B&B guesthouse.
Clientele: Men only
Transportation: Airport taxi, approx. $8.
To Gay Bars: 4 blocks to men's bars.
Rooms: 9 rooms with double & queen beds.
Baths: 7 private.
Meals: Full breakfast.
Vegetarian: Available nearby.

Complimentary: Free cocktail hour from 4-6 PM.
Dates Open: All year.
High Season: Dec-Apr 30.
Rates: Summer $75-$120, winter $140-$190.
Credit Cards: MC, Visa, Amex.
Rsv'tns: Recommended during in-season (3-6 months in advance).
Reserve Thru: Call direct

or travel agent.
Min. Stay: Holidays only.
Parking: Ample free on-street parking.
In-Room: Refrigerator, maid service, AC, ceiling fans, telephone, TV.
Exercise/Health: Jacuzzi.
Swimming: Pool or ocean beach.
Sunbathing: At poolside or on private or common sun

decks.
Nudity: Permitted at poolside and on balconies.
Smoking: No smoking in common areas indoors.
Pets: Not permitted.
Handicap Access: No.
Children: Not permitted.
Languages: English.

Equator

Men ♂

The Next Generation of Male Accommodation

Equator ushers in a new millennium in Key West men's resorts. Deluxe suites, rooms with private decks, rooms with pocket kitchens and bungalow rooms create a world of whimsy and comfort unlike any other. Our spacious accommodations feature specialty lighting, Italian tile floors, climate control and Florida tropical interiors. Luxuriate in our tropical setting with a black lagoon pool, sunning decks, fountain pond and monsoon outdoor shower. *Equator,* a place where time stands still... poised on the edge of the 21st century.

Address: 818 Fleming St, Key West, FL 33040
Tel: (305) 294-7775, (800) 278-4552, **Fax:** (305) 296-5765.
Web: http://www.gaytraveling.com/equator

Type: Guesthouse.
Clientele: Men only.
Transportation: Taxi from airport.
To Gay Bars: 4 blocks to gay bars.
Rooms: 14 rooms, 1-2 room suite, 3 addt'l suites. King or queen beds, 2 rooms with x-long full beds.
Baths: All private baths.
Meals: Full breakfast.
Vegetarian: Available across the street.

Complimentary: Cocktails, room snacks.
Dates Open: All year.
High Season: Mid-Dec thru Apr.
Rates: High season $140-$195, mid-season $110-$150, summer $90-$125.
Credit Cards: MC, Visa, Amex.
Rsv'tns: Required.
Reserve Thru: Travel agent or call direct.
Min. Stay: Required.

Parking: Car not necessary, but on-street parking available.
In-Room: AC, ceiling fans, color cable TV, VCR available, video tape library, phone, refrigerator, maid service. Some rooms have pocket kitchen, 3 have private decks, 4 have street-side balcony.
Exercise/Health: Whirlpool.
Swimming: Pool on premises, ocean nearby.

Sunbathing: Poolside, on private sun deck, at beach.
Nudity: Permitted poolside.
Smoking: All rooms non-smoking.
Pets: Sorry, no pets.
Handicap Access: Yes.
Children: No.
Languages: English.
Your Hosts: John & Bill.
IGLTA

Fleur de Key Guesthouse

The Only Thing Missing is You!

Key West's premier gay and lesbian guesthouse offers attentive service and luxury accommodations in a traditional Conch-style setting of wide verandas, louvered plantation shutters and ceiling fans. Expansive sun decks, a sparkling heated pool and a whirlpool spa glisten within the private, hedged compound with hibiscus, bouganvillaea, jasmine and exotic palms.

On a quiet street in the heart of Old Town's finest neighborhood, the *Fleur de Key* is surrounded by restored homes, galleries, restaurants and shops and is minutes from the nightlife of Duval Street. The harborfront is two blocks away, offering casual waterside restaurants, salty bars, gay sailing excursions and seaplane adventures.

The sixteen guest rooms and one-bedroom suites are light and airy, featuring handcrafted furniture and traditional antiques, tropical fabrics and local artworks. Each offers king/queen bed, air-conditioning, telephone with voicemail, color television with VCR and videocassette library, hair dryer, deluxe toiletries, refrigerator and nightly turndown. Our amenities and service are first-class, and the atmosphere is always friendly and laid-back. For the energetic, we can also arrange group charters for an afternoon snorkel cruise or sunset champagne sail. We've been featured by *The Advocate, Conde Nast Traveler, Genre,* and has consistently been awarded *Out & About's* highest rating "Five Stars - Exceptional."

Address: 412 Frances St, Key West, FL 33040
Tel: (305) 296-4719, (800) 932-9119, **Fax:** (305) 296-1994.
E-mail: keywest@brasskey.com **Web:** http://www.brasskey.com

Type: B&B guesthouse.
Clientele: Mostly men with women very welcome
Transportation: Airport pick up $15.
To Gay Bars: 5-7 blocks.
Rooms: 14 rooms & 2 suites with queen or king beds.
Baths: All private.
Meals: Expanded continental breakfast.
Complimentary: Afternoon cocktails.
High Season: Late Dec to early Apr.
Rates: Winter $170-$305. Summer $85-$190.
Credit Cards: Amex, Discover, MC, Visa.
Rsv'tns: Highly recommended.
Reserve Thru: Travel agent or call direct.
Min. Stay: Required holidays, special events.
Parking: On-street parking.
In-Room: AC, ceiling fan, phone w/ voicemail, color cable TV, VCR, videocassette library, hair dryer, fridge, robes, laundry, maid & turndown svc.
On-Premises: Living room & breakfast area.
Exercise/Health: Whirlpool spa, bikes. Gym nearby.
Swimming: Heated pool. Nearby ocean beaches.
Sunbathing: Poolside & on sun decks.
Nudity: Permitted on rooftop sun deck.
Smoking: Non-smoking rooms available.
Pets: Not permitted.
Handicap Access: Yes. Wheelchair ramp. 1 guestroom/bath.
Children: Not permitted.
Languages: English.
IGLTA

Harbor Inn

Gay-Friendly ⚥
Gay-Owned & -Operated

The Real Key West Experience!

Discover all the lively extras that bring so many people back to the *Harbor Inn*... the special comforts, uncommon conveniences and personalized touches that can make this your most wonderful vacation ever. Our extra-spacious rooms overlook the historic Key West Seaport on one side and our own lush tropical gardens on the other. Complimentary continental breakfast is served every morning and our complimentary evening Happy Hour features a full open bar and gourmet hors d'oeuvres. We're here to serve you. Our friendly and thoughtful staff can arrange for fishing, diving or sailing activities, make a reservation or a recommendation, solve a problem or just to share a moment with you during the best vacation of your life! Winner of the coveted "Superior Florida Keys Lodging Award."

Address: 219 Elizabeth St, Key West, FL 33040
Tel: (305) 296-2978, toll-free in US: (800) 374-4242, **Fax:** (305) 294-5858.
E-mail: kwharborinn@yahoo.com **Web:** http://www.keywestharborinn.com

Type: Guesthouse inn.
Clientele: All welcome
Transportation: Taxi.
To Gay Bars: 4 blocks, a 10 min walk.
Rooms: 14 rooms, 3 suites with king or queen beds.
Baths: Private & shared.
Meals: Expanded continental breakfast.
Vegetarian: Vegetarian market around corner.

Complimentary: Happy Hour 6-7pm Mon-Sat (full bar).
Dates Open: All year.
High Season: Jan-Apr.
Rates: Low $75-$125, high $125-$200, shoulder $105-$165.
Discounts: 10% 7+ days
Credit Cards: MC, Visa, Amex, Discover.
Rsv'tns: Required.

Reserve Thru: Travel agent or call direct.
Min. Stay: 2 nts wknds, 3 nts hol. wknds, 5 nts Fantasy Fest & New Years.
Parking: Adequate on-street parking.
In-Room: Phone, AC, ceiling fans, color cable TV, fridge, coffee & tea-makers, maid svc.
Exercise/Health: Jacuzzi.

Swimming: Pool.
Sunbathing: Poolside.
Pets: Not permitted.
Handicap Access: Yes, ramps, rails in bathroom.
Children: No.
Languages: English, Spanish.
Your Hosts: Alexis & Steve.

Heron House

Feel Free...Feel Relaxed...Feel Welcomed

Amidst orchids, bougainvillaea, jasmine and palms, a secluded tropical garden fantasy awaits you. This warm and friendly place is *Heron House* — meticulously designed by Key West's most gifted artists and craftsmen. Lacking pretense, this style has been inspired by the informality of the Florida Keys' natural environment, free of rigid architectural conformities,

lending itself to a casually elegant style in which you will feel totally free, welcome and relaxed. Thus, with generous private decks and balconies, your private room merges with private gardens. Luxurious tropical gardens, draped around our rich complex of luxurious tropical homes, seem to penetrate every room as if to share themselves with you.

Many rooms feature "signature walls" in teak, oak or cedar. Granite baths are elegantly understated. Tile floors are cool and tropical. Our shady Chicago brick patios are reminiscent of old English gardens. Stained-glass transoms above French doors capture the warmth of natural sunlight and filter it through sparkling colors. Interiors feature rich, original commissioned watercolors of the Keys created by local artisans. We even have our own Heron House vintage champagne ready to put on ice. In 1998 we were awarded the AAA 4-Diamond rating and 4-Crowns by the American Bed & Breakfast Association.

Address: 512 Simonton St, Key West, FL 33040
Tel: (305) 294-9227, (888) 676-8654, **Fax:** (305) 294-5692.
E-mail: HeronKYW@aol.com **Web:** http://www.heronhouse.com

Type: Guesthouse.
Clientele: Mostly straight with a gay & lesbian following
Transportation: Car or airport, then taxi.
To Gay Bars: 1 block.
Rooms: 21 rooms with double, queen or king beds.
Baths: All private.
Meals: Deluxe continental breakfast.

High Season: Dec 20-Apr 30.
Rates: Dec 20-Apr 30: $179-$349; May 1-30 & Oct 20-Dec 19: $139-$299; Jun 1-Oct 19: $109-$229.
Credit Cards: MC, Visa, Amex, Diners.
Rsv'tns: Recommended.
Reserve Thru: Travel agent or call direct.
Min. Stay: During holidays

and special events.
Parking: Ample on-street.
In-Room: Maid svc, ceiling fans, AC, color TV, fridges, phones, private entrances.
Exercise/Health: Some rooms have Jacuzzis.
Swimming: Pool, ocean beach.
Sunbathing: At poolside, on roof or on private or common sun decks.

Nudity: Permitted on sun deck.
Smoking: Restricted.
Pets: Not permitted.
Handicap Access: Yes. Ramps.
Children: Not permitted.
Languages: English.

Color Photo on Page 20

Island House

WWW Men ♂
Gay-Owned & -Managed

A Tropical Resort for Men

Newly renovated this year, *Island House* is an exclusively gay resort in Old Town, Key West. This private, clothing-optional compound with large swimming pool also offers guests its own Health Club, featuring workout room with machines and free weights, sauna, steam room, Jacuzzi and massage. The Island House Café serves breakfast and lunch at poolside, and the Garden Bar has a daily free full-bar happy hour. There is also an erotic video room which is open 24 hours. Our concierge will assist you in discovering gay Key West. Gay-owned & -managed.

Address: 1129 Fleming St, Key West, FL 33040
Tel: (305) 294-6284, (800) 890-6284, **Fax:** (305) 292-0051.
E-mail: ihkeywest@aol.com **Web:** http://www.islandhousekeywest.com

Type: Guest house with restaurant, bar & health club.
Clientele: Men only
Transportation: Taxi from Key West airport.
To Gay Bars: 7 blocks, a 15 min walk, a 5 min drive.
Rooms: 34 rooms with double, queen or king beds.
Baths: Shower/toilets: 25 private, 9 shared.
Meals: Breakfast & lunch served in poolside cafe.
Vegetarian: Salads/fruit only, no special menu. 4 blocks to vegetarian restaurant (delivery

available).
Complimentary: Full bar happy hour every day.
Dates Open: All year.
High Season: Dec 25-Apr 20.
Rates: Summer $64-$114, winter $83-$169, holidays slightly higher.
Credit Cards: MC, Visa, Amex, Discover.
Rsv'tns: Recommended during season.
Reserve Thru: Travel agent or call direct.
Min. Stay: Required during holiday periods only.
Parking: Adequate on- &

off-street parking.
In-Room: Color cable TV/ VCR, video library, AC & heat with individual room controls, ceiling fans, direct-dial phones with voice mail & data ports, security safes, daily maid service (all-male staff).
On-Premises: Laundry facilities.
Exercise/Health: Jacuzzi, sauna, gym, weights, steam, massage (on-call service).
Swimming: Pool on premises, ocean nearby.
Sunbathing: At poolside & on private sun decks.

Nudity: Permitted anywhere.
Smoking: Permitted in all areas, except sauna. No non-smoking rooms.
Pets: Small or medium dogs only. Must be controlled at all times & comfortable w/ strangers & strange places.
Handicap Access: Yes, all public areas & 1 guestroom accessible.
Children: No children permitted.
Languages: English.
IGLTA

Lavadia

Gay-Friendly 50/50 ♀♂
Gay-Owned & -Operated

Distinctive Lodging in Paradise

Legend of the island claims that *Lavadia* (view of the sea) was built in 1890 by a Russian sea captain. City records indicate that the estate was occupied by Frank J. Roberts in 1906, an accountant for Richard Peacon, Jr., the vice president of Tropical Building Investments, who resided in the substantial home until 1923. Today, it is a private retreat, enjoyed by families from around the world. Another home of Southernmost Hospitality, it is located on William Street in Old Town Key West, and is within walking distance of local attractions. Boasting typical gingerbread trim on the wrap-around veranda, the home's two-thousand-square-feet of exquisitely appointed furnishings and antiques await the most discriminating tastes.

Within the stately three-story traditional home, the first floor offers a formal parlor, romantic dining room for candle-lit dinners, a gourmet kitchen and a large Florida room with additional bath. The second level features three bedrooms and two bathrooms, all uniquely appointed. Executives will appreciate the writing table with two-line telephone, fax and answering machine. French doors lead you to the heated swimming pool and outdoor deck area with mini bar, barbecue grill and ice maker. A privacy fence ensures all the ingredients for a magical vacation. The third-floor attic apartment has a private entrance from the main home, is ideal for servants' quarters, and can sleep six teenagers. The 700-square-foot apartment is air-conditioned and has skylights, a queen-sized bed and two futons in the living area, a fully equipped kitchen, and a private Jacuzzi in the bathroom. The apartment is not available separately and will only be rented to ensure privacy.

Address: Old Town Key West, Key West, FL
Tel: (305) 294-3800, (800) 352-4974, **Fax:** (305) 294-9298.
E-mail: VIPVillas@aol.com **Web:** http://www.InnCentral.com

Type: Seasonal private rental home.
Clientele: 50% gay & lesbian & 50% straight clientele
Transportation: Taxi from airport.
To Gay Bars: 4 blocks.
Rooms: 3 rooms, 1 apartment with single, queen & king beds.
Baths: Private & shared bath/shower/toilets.
Vegetarian: Several gourmet markets .
Dates Open: All year.
High Season: Dec 15-Apr 15.
Rates: $325-$500 per night.
Rsv'tns: Required.
Reserve Thru: Travel agent or call direct.
Min. Stay: 7 nights.
Parking: Limited on-street parking.
In-Room: Telephone, AC, ceiling fans, color cable TV, VCR, kitchen, refrigerator, coffee & tea-making facilities, maid service.
On-Premises: TV lounge, laundry facilities, fax.
Exercise/Health: Jacuzzi.
Swimming: Pool on premises. Ocean nearby.
Sunbathing: Poolside & on common sun decks.
Nudity: Permitted anywhere except the front porch.
Smoking: Permitted outside.
Pets: Not permitted.
Handicap Access: No.
Children: No.
Languages: English.

Newton Street Station

Men ♂
Gay-Operated

Join Us in Our Corner of Paradise

Newton Street Station, formerly the home of the stationmaster of the Florida East Coast Railway, is an intimate guesthouse in a quiet, residential section of Old Town Key West. Rooms are individually-decorated and breakfast is served on the tropical sun deck. Lounge by the pool, nude, if you like, enjoy the tropical gardens, or work out on the exercise deck. Visit shops and galleries, or enjoy some of the finest water sports in the country. *Newton Street Station* is one of the friendliest, all-men's guesthouses in Key West, where our goal is to make you feel welcome.

Address: 1414 Newton St, Key West, FL 33040
Tel: (305) 294-4288, (800) 248-2457, **Fax:** (305) 292-5062.
E-mail: JohnNSS@aol.com **Web:** http://www.newton-street-station.com

Type: Guesthouse.
Clientele: Men only
Transportation: Inexpensive taxi ride from airport.
To Gay Bars: 5 minutes by car to men's bars.
Rooms: 6 rooms & 1 suite with double beds.
Baths: 4 private, 2 shared & 1 half-bath.
Meals: Continental breakfast.
Dates Open: All year.

High Season: Dec 15-Apr 30.
Rates: Winter $80-$150, summer $60-$100.
Discounts: 10% for a week or more, or for members of nudist/naturist groups.
Credit Cards: MC, Visa, Amex.
Rsv'tns: Highly recommended.
Reserve Thru: Travel agent or call direct.
Min. Stay: During holidays

& special events.
Parking: Ample free on-street parking.
In-Room: Maid service, color cable TVs, AC, refrigerator, phone, some ceiling fans.
On-Premises: TV lounge & free local phone calls.
Exercise/Health: Weights & bicycles
Swimming: Pool or nearby ocean.
Sunbathing: At poolside,

on private & common sun decks, or patio.
Nudity: Permitted anywhere on premises.
Smoking: Permitted without restrictions.
Pets: Not permitted.
Handicap Access: No.
Children: Not permitted.
Languages: English, limited French & limited German.
Your Hosts: John.
IGLTA

Pilot House

Your Key to Paradise

Gay-Friendly 50/50 ♀♂
Gay-Owned & -Operated

Pilot House is a grand two-story Victorian mansion built, circa 1900. Today, standing proudly in the center of the Key West's historical Old Town district, it boasts verandas and porches with hand-milled spindels and gingerbread trim. After the labored restoration in 1990, receiving the prestigious "Excellence Award for Preservation" by the Florida Keys Preservation Board, we opened the mansion's doors as a guest residence. The careful blend of antiques and tropical furnishings, accommodates the discriminating tastes of experienced travelers. We offer unique lodging accommodations with eight guest rooms to choose from, all with private bath, color cable TV, phone, air conditioning and paddle fans. Our brand-new poolside cabana suites feature in-room Jacuzzis, mini-bars and modern tropical decor. Each has its own outside entrance and selected "smoking-allowed" suites are also available.

Address: 414 Simonton St, Key West, FL 33040
Tel: (305) 293-6600, (877) 809-4237, **Fax:** (305) 294-9298.
E-mail: PilotKW@aol.com **Web:** http://www.PilotHouseKeyWest.com

Type: Guesthouse.
Clientele: 50% gay & lesbian & 50% straight clientele
Transportation: Taxi from airport.
To Gay Bars: 2 blocks, a 3 min walk.
Rooms: 12 rooms, 2 suites with double, queen or king beds.
Baths: All private.

Dates Open: All year.
High Season: Dec 15-Apr 15.
Rates: Summer $100, winter $300.
Credit Cards: MC, Visa, Amex, Diners, Bancard, Eurocard, Discover.
Reserve Thru: Travel agent or call direct.
Min. Stay: 3 nights.
Parking: Limited off-street

pay parking.
In-Room: Telephone, AC, ceiling fans, color cable TV, kitchen, refrigerator, coffee & tea-making facilities, maid service.
Exercise/Health: Hot tub.
Swimming: Pool. Ocean nearby.
Sunbathing: Poolside, on private sun decks, at beach.
Nudity: Permitted in pool &

hot tub.
Smoking: Permitted in cabana rooms.
Pets: Not permitted.
Handicap Access: Yes, ramps, rails in bathroom, wide doors.
Children: No.
Languages: English, Spanish, French.

Colours Destinations in Key West

Step into this elegant Victorian mansion, recently renovated and maintaining its original architectural detail. Built in 1889 by Francisco Marrero, a prominent cigarmaker, for his wife, she promised to come back when she was evicted after his death. Some believe she still moves through "her" house, keeping a benevolent eye on things. Located in the heart of Old Town, *Marrero's Guest Mansion* (formerly known as Colours) is literally steps from everything that attracts you to Key West. It's only half a block to Duval Street's great restaurants, shopping, art galleries, famous clubs and pubs. Water sports, beaches, snorkeling, sailing, fishing, diving and sunset cruises are all close at hand.

Accommodations range from spacious guestrooms to large suites with private verandahs. Rooms are beautifully decorated with antiques and unique period furnishings, refrigerators, cable TV and air conditioning. You will discover a lush tropical courtyard where you can enjoy a dip in a large heated pool and relax in the bubbling hot tub. In the morning, follow the wonderful aromas of a full continental breakfast. Rates: Season (Dec 14-Apr 30) $115-$190. Off Season (May 1-Dec 14) $85-$160.

Mail To: Colours Destinations, 255 W 24 Street, Miami Beach, FL 33140
Tel: (305) 532-9341, (800) 277-4825, **Fax:** (305) 534-0362.
E-mail: NEWCOLOURS@AOL.COM **Web:** http://www.colours.net

Coral Tree Inn

Coral Tree Inn is a newly renovated resort in the heart of Old Town, across the street from The Oasis, our mother house. Eleven rooms open onto balconies, with multi-level sun decks cascading from the 3rd level down to the pool, courtyard and whirlpool under the trellis and the coral tree. Tastefully decorated rooms have AC, color cable TV & VCR, Bahama fans, refrigerators, hair dryers, coffeemakers, and robes to wear during your visit. Clothes are optional and complete concierge services are available. You will find our award-winning hospitality genuine and generous.

Address: 822 Fleming St, Key West, FL
Tel: (305) 296-2131 or (800) 362-7477, **Fax:** (305) 296-9171.
E-mail: oasisct@aol.com **Web:** http://www.coraltreeinn.com

Type: Guesthouse.
Clientele: Men only
Transportation: Taxi from airport.
To Gay Bars: 3-1/2 blocks.
Rooms: 11 rooms with queen beds.
Baths: All private.
Meals: Expanded continental breakfast.
Complimentary: Wine & hors d'oeuvres at sunset for an hour by the pool.

Dates Open: All year.
High Season: Dec 16-May1.
Rates: Summer $99-$155, winter $159-$199.
Discounts: Airline flight service.
Credit Cards: MC, Visa, Amex.
Rsv'tns: Strongly advised.
Reserve Thru: Travel agent or call direct.
Min. Stay: Required on holidays & special events.

Parking: Limited free on-street parking. Car is not really needed.
In-Room: Color TV, VCR, AC, ceiling fans, refrigerator, maid service.
Exercise/Health: Jacuzzi & use of 2 Jacuzzis at The Oasis.
Swimming: Pool & nearby ocean beach. Use of 2 pools at The Oasis.

Sunbathing: At poolside or on common sun decks.
Nudity: Permitted in public areas.
Smoking: Permitted.
Pets: Not permitted.
Handicap Access: Yes.
Children: Not permitted.
Languages: English, Spanish.

Cypress House

WWW Gay-Friendly ⚦
Gay-Operated

We Offer the Amenities You Want... and the Luxury You Deserve

Cypress House is a luxury guesthouse for those who wish to reside in an atmosphere of style and comfort. A congenial staff awaits to show you to your spacious, air conditioned bedroom in a grand, 1887 Conch mansion. Whether you feel like partying and sleeping late, or rising early for a dip in our long pool, you'll enjoy the mind-soothing experience...sunny days, exciting nights!

Address: 601 Caroline St, Key West, FL 33040
Tel: (305) 294-6969 or (800) 525-2488, **Fax:** (305) 296-1174.
E-mail: CypressKW@aol.com **Web:** http://www.cypresshousekw.com

Type: Guesthouse.
Clientele: 70% straight, 30% gay adults
Transportation: Taxi from airport.
To Gay Bars: 4 blocks to men's bars.
Rooms: 14 rooms & 1 suite with double, queen or king beds.
Baths: 10 private bath/toilets, others share.
Meals: Expanded continental breakfast.

Complimentary: Daily cocktail hour.
Dates Open: All year.
High Season: Dec 20-May 1.
Rates: Summer $109-$198, winter $130-$270.
Discounts: 7 nights or more 10%.
Credit Cards: MC, Visa, Amex, Discover, Eurocard, Bancard.
Rsv'tns: Recommended 1-2 months in advance.

Reserve Thru: Travel agent or call direct.
Min. Stay: Required for some holidays and weekends.
Parking: Adequate on- and off-street parking.
In-Room: Self-controlled AC/heat, refrigerator, color TV w/cable, direct-dial phone, maid service.
Swimming: 40-foot heated pool or ocean beach.
Sunbathing: On beach,

common sun decks or at poolside.
Nudity: Permitted on roof terrace.
Smoking: Permitted outdoors only.
Pets: Not permitted.
Handicap Access: Partially, call for details.
Children: Not permitted.
Languages: English.
Your Hosts: Dave.

Lighthouse Court

Men ♂

Lighthouse Court is Key West's largest, most private guest compound. A variety of restored conch houses connected by decking, nestled in lush tropical foliage, it combines the charm of days past with contemporary taste and design. Accommodations include rooms, apartments and suites. Rooms have TV, air conditioning and/or Bahama fans, refrigerators, and many have kitchen facilities. Located one block from historic Duval Street, *Lighthouse Court* is a short stroll from shops, galleries, beaches, sailing & snorkeling as well as Key West's famous nite life.

Address: 902 Whitehead St, Key West, FL 33040
Tel: (305) 294-9588.

Type: Guesthouse with restaurant, bar & health club.
Clientele: Men only
Transportation: Taxi from airport.
To Gay Bars: 1 block to Duval St bars.
Rooms: 4 singles, 30 doubles, 4 suites & 4 efficiencies.
Baths: 38 private, 4 shared.

Vegetarian: Breakfast & lunch.
Dates Open: All year.
High Season: Jan 20 - Easter, Fantasy Fest - late Oct, New Years' Eve.
Rates: $60-$235.
Credit Cards: MC, Visa.
Rsv'tns: Preferred.
Reserve Thru: Call direct.
Min. Stay: Required on holidays.

Parking: Ample free on-street parking.
In-Room: Maid & room service, AC, ceiling fans, fridge, telephone, TV.
On-Premises: Meeting rooms, TV lounge, beer & wine bar.
Exercise/Health: Jacuzzi, health club, gym, weights, massage.
Swimming: Pool on

premises, ocean beach nearby.
Sunbathing: At poolside, on roof, common sun decks. Beach nearby.
Nudity: Permitted.
Smoking: Permitted without restrictions.
Pets: Not permitted.
Handicap Access: Inquire.
Children: Not permitted.
Languages: English, French.

Oasis, A Guest House

Oasis, A Guest House is Key West's most elegant guesthouse, a magnificently restored 1895 mansion in the historic district, where you capture the true charm and excitement of this idyllic isle. Multi-level sun decks allow secluded sunbathing. Tastefully appointed rooms have AC, private bath, color TV, Bahama fans and robes to wear during your visit. We have two of the island's largest private pools (one heated) and Florida's largest private Jacuzzi. The sun decks and pools are open 24 hours a day, clothes optional. Share the tranquil beauty of our home and experience our genuine and generous hospitality.

Address: 823 Fleming St, Key West, FL 33040
Tel: (305) 296-2131 or (800) 362-7477, **Fax:** (305) 296-9171.
E-mail: oasisct@aol.com **Web:** http://www.oasiskeywest.com

Type: Guesthouse with beer & wine bar.
Clientele: Men only
Transportation: Taxi from airport.
To Gay Bars: 4 blocks to men's/women's bars.
Rooms: 20 rooms with queen beds.
Baths: 20 private bath/ toilets.
Meals: Expanded continental breakfast.

Complimentary: Wine party every evening with hors d'oeuvres by the main pool.
Dates Open: All year.
High Season: Jan-May.
Rates: Summer $99-$155, winter $159-$199.
Discounts: 10% airline travel agents.
Credit Cards: MC, Visa, Amex, Discover.
Rsv'tns: Preferred.

Reserve Thru: Travel agent or call direct.
Min. Stay: During holidays & special events.
Parking: Plenty of on-street parking.
In-Room: Maid service, color TV, VCR, refrigerator, AC & ceiling fans.
Exercise/Health: Jacuzzi.
Swimming: 2 large pools on premises.
Sunbathing: At poolside or

on private sun decks.
Nudity: Permitted.
Smoking: Permitted without restrictions.
Pets: Not permitted.
Handicap Access: Yes.
Children: Not permitted.
Languages: English.
Your Hosts: Gerry.
IGLTA

Colours Destinations in South Beach

Experience Not Just a Place, But a State of Mind

Colours Destinations is affiliated with the best lodgings to accommodate all your needs. For the best location on Ocean Drive, right across from the beach, *The Penguin Hotel,* directly across from the "hot gay beach" or the sister property *The Presidential Hotel* on Collins Ave. These historic Art Deco hotels have been renovated to become the New Penguin Resort, featuring varied rooms with rates ranging from low single of $78 to high double of $215.

Next, we have three beautiful little Art Deco hotels, also in the heart of South Beach. *The Nassau Suite* on Collins Ave. features exquisite studios and one-bedroom units with rates from low $100 to high $170. *The Beachcomber,* also on Collins Ave. with bar and bistro, is another Art Deco gem with rooms from low $65 to high $145. *The Bayliss Guesthouse* offers hotel rooms, efficiencies and one-bedroom apartments with rates from low $45 to high $110. They also offer very affordable weekly rates.

Additionally, we have *The Mantell Plaza* for those who prefer to swim in a secluded tropical pool surrounded by beautiful landscaping, only a block from the ocean, at the north end of South Beach. This hideaway offers renovated studios with kitchen and rates from low $79 to high $159. **Call our reservation line at 1-800-ARRIVAL and let us help you make your stay in South Beach a memorable one. Please visit our extended website for more information on our two other exciting destinations: Costa Rica and Key West.**

Tel: (800) ARRIVAL (277-4825), (305) 532-9341, **Fax:** (305) 534-0362.
E-mail: Newcolours@aol.com **Web:** http://www.colours.net **IGLTA**

Abbey Hotel, The

WWW Gay-Friendly ♂

One of the original 1940 Art Deco hotels, the *Abbey Hotel* is located in the South Beach section of Miami Beach. This fifty-room designer boutique hotel was splendidly restored in 1999. Designer Harry Schnaper transformed this once sleepy hotel into a tranquil retreat to soothe the senses...a fabulously chic enclave in the Deco District's serene north end; a sublime environment to retreat to at the end of a full day in Miami. We're 1-1/2 blocks from the beach, two blocks from the Miami Beach Convention Center (where many of the gay events take place), four blocks from Lincoln Road, and a short walking distance to the fabulous South Beach gay life and magnificent restaurants. In December, 2000, we will open our rooftop solarium and bar and grill, with nude sunbathing, water walls, and a great ocean view. The *Abbey* is across from the Bass Art Museum and the Miami City Ballet, and is close to the Jackie Gleason Theatre, but just a few blocks away from the revelry.

Address: 300 21st Street, Miami Beach, FL 33139
Tel: (305) 531-0031, (888) 61 ABBEY (888-612-2239), **Fax:** (305) 672-1663.
E-mail: abbeysales@aol.com **Web:** http://www.abbeyhotel.com

Type: Designer boutique hotel with restaurant & bar.
Clientele: 50% straight clientele with a mostly gay male following
Transportation: Rental car, Super Shuttle ($12 per person), taxi ($24 flat fee).
To Gay Bars: A 10-15 min walk.
Rooms: 40 rooms with queen, king, dbl/dbl; 10 suites with king bed & king sofa bed.
Baths: All private.
Meals: Breakfast, lunch, dinner & room service available.
Vegetarian: Available at restaurant.
Dates Open: All year.
High Season: Dec 24-Apr 2.
Rates: Dec 24-Apr 2: $175-$225; Apr 3-May 31 & Oct 1-Dec 23: $150-$175; Jun 1-Sep 30: $115-$155.
Discounts: Groups: depends on length, # persons, etc. Separate corp. accounts available & are based on yearly volume.
Credit Cards: MC, Visa, Amex, Diners.
Rsv'tns: Required.
Reserve Thru: Travel agent, web or call direct.
Min. Stay: Required during some high volume periods (White & Winter parties, New Year, Convention period).
Parking: Adequate, pay on- & off-street parking. Metered parking or use of lot w/ full in/out privileges for addt'l charge.
In-Room: AC, stereo/CD player, TV w/ VCR & cable, telephones w/ 2 lines & computer data port, mini-bar, in-room safe, hair dryer, iron & ironing board.
On-Premises: Meeting rooms, business services, lobby bar.
Exercise/Health: Exercise room.
Swimming: 1 1/2 block to beach.
Sunbathing: At beach, rooftop solarium & bar.
Smoking: Permitted throughout public spaces, lobby & bar. Non-smoking rooms available.
Pets: Inquire. Not usually permitted, but exceptions have been made.
Handicap Access: No.
Children: Welcome. We have cribs for guest use.
Languages: English, Spanish, Italian, German, Portuguese.
IGLTA

Bohemia, The

The Enchantment of a Bohemian Getaway

When the architect Henry Hohauser designed *The Bohemia* in the 1930s, he never knew what an enchanting getaway he was creating. Situated in the Miami Beach Art Deco Preservation District, it has been recently renovated and is listed on the National Registry of Historic Places. The property is within walking distance of all major areas of Miami Beach. You can shop and dine on fashionable Lincoln Road, stop at a hot spot for happy hour, then go dancing. By walking five blocks east, you will reach the exciting Ocean Drive area of South Beach, where beautiful people, buildings and beaches await you.

Upon returning, you can relax in the Jacuzzi area where clothing is an option. Your relaxation will be heightened by the lush tropical vegetation that surrounds the property. You will be shaded by palm trees, bougainvillea, hibiscus, and bird of paradise in full bloom.

Upon awakening, enjoy breakfast in the midst of a lush tropical garden. For those interested in working out, there are guest passes available for The Ironworks Gym compliments of *The Bohemia*. For male travelers who enjoy a change of pace, and are looking for a truly bohemian experience, we'll be sure to please.

Address: 825 Michigan Avenue, Miami Beach, FL
Tel: (305) 534-1322, Toll-free: (888) 883-4565.
E-mail: BohemiaHouse@aol.com **Web:** http://www.bohemia825.com

Type: Vacation rentals.
Clientele: Men only
Transportation: Car, taxi, shuttle, bus.
To Gay Bars: Short walk to all restaurants & bars.
Rooms: Rooms & apartments with king & queen beds (hideaway bed in living rooms).
Baths: All private bath/shower/toilets.
Meals: Expanded continental breakfast.
Vegetarian: 2 blocks to

vegetarian food store & restaurants.
Dates Open: All year.
High Season: Nov-Apr.
Rates: High season $100-$130, low $70-$110.
Discounts: 10% on extended stays over 1 week.
Credit Cards: MC, Visa, Amex.
Rsv'tns: Required.
Reserve Thru: Travel agent or call direct.
Min. Stay: Varies with season & holidays.

Parking: Ample off-street parking.
In-Room: Telephone, AC, ceiling fans, color cable TV, VCR, kitchen, refrigerator, coffee & tea-making facilities, maid service.
Exercise/Health: Hot tub with outdoor shower. Complimentary guest passes to Ironworks Gym.
Swimming: Nearby ocean, nude beach & gay beach.
Sunbathing: On patio, in yard area & at beach.

Nudity: Permitted in hot tub, outdoor shower area & secluded gardens.
Smoking: Non-smoking property.
Pets: Not permitted.
Handicap Access: No.
Children: No.
Languages: English.
Your Hosts: John & Steve.
IGLTA

Island House: South Beach

WWW Men ♂

South Beach's Biggest All-Gay Guesthouse

Award-winning *Island House,* a fully restored historic Art Deco guesthouse, offers comfortably furnished accommodations for men, ranging from rooms to studios and suites. This well-appointed guesthouse with its tropical, eclectic flavor and casual flair is South Beach's biggest all-gay guesthouse. Onehundred percent gay-owned, *Island House* and its friendly staff will make you feel right at home. Start the morning off by enjoying a complimentary full breakfast buffet with your new neighbors, served upstairs in the breakfast room overlooking Collins Avenue. After the beach or before dinner, enjoy complimentary beer and wine for happy hour on the front porch with old and new friends.

Centrally located in the heart of South Beach, we're walking distance to hot sizzling nightlife, cruisy bars, and a variety of restaurants — from outdoor cafes and neighborhood diners, to trendy bistros and elegant restaurants with world-famous cuisine. South Beach serves up what you're hungry for... The fabulous white sandy beaches, the tropical ocean breezes, the swaying coconut palms and the clear, blue ocean water and warm rays from the sun all create a steamy romantic setting. And beaches full of hot, sexy, sweaty men create bountiful social opportunities...

Our original location at 715 82nd Street in Miami Beach is off the beaten track, yet only five minutes to the gay nude beach and 15 minutes to South Beach. Enjoy our lushly landscaped tropical patio area, or unwind in the Jacuzzi. Nude sunbathing is always permitted at this more intimate location.

Address: 1428 Collins Avenue, Miami Beach, FL 33139
Tel: (305) 864-2422, (800) 382-2422, **Fax:** (305) 865-2220.
E-mail: ihsobe@bellsouth.net **Web:** http://www.q-net.com/islandhouse

Type: Guesthouse.
Clientele: Gay men
Transportation: From airport: taxi, Supershuttle. A car is not needed.
To Gay Bars: Walking distance to all bars & restaurants.
Rooms: 20: rooms, standard rooms, deluxe rooms & studios.
Baths: Private.
Meals: Full breakfast buffet.
Complimentary: Beer & wine for Happy Hour (weekends & holidays).
Dates Open: All year.
High Season: Thanksgiving-Apr 30.
Rates: Off season: $59-$99. Season: $79-$149. Student/military (under 24 w/ valid ID): $39-$54.
Discounts: For extended stays & airline employees, subject to availability.
Credit Cards: MC, Amex, Visa, Discover, Diners Club.
Rsv'tns: Recommended. However, we will try to accommodate your last minute plans, subject to room availability.
Reserve Thru: Call direct.
Min. Stay: Required during holiday periods & special events.
Parking: 1-1/2 blocks to municipal garage. Limited street parking.
In-Room: Color satellite TV, room phones, AC, ceiling fans, refrigerator, wet bar/ kitchenette, maid service.
Exercise/Health: Masseur on call. Discount gym passes.
Swimming: 1 block to gay beach.
Sunbathing: 1 block to gay beach.
Nudity: 10 min to gay nude beach.
Smoking: Permitted.
Pets: No.
Handicap Access: No.
Languages: English, Spanish, French.
IGLTA

Miami River Inn

Enjoy the Charm of the Past Complemented by the Technology of Today

Miami River Inn is located in the ethnically diverse Miami River Neighborhood of East Little Havana. Centrally located across the Miami River from downtown, the inn is an oasis in the heart of Miami. The "compound" consists of four wooden cottages surrounding a pool and Jacuzzi in a lush tropical setting full of flowers, soaring palms and other native greenery. South Beach, Coconut Grove, Key Biscayne and Coral Gables are all within a 15-minute drive. Downtown & Little Havana are within walking distance.

Address: 118 SW South River Dr, Miami, FL 33130
Tel: (305) 325-0045, (800) HOTEL 89 (468-3589), **Fax:** (305) 325-9227.
E-mail: miamihotel@aol.com **Web:** http://www.miamiriverinn.com

Type: Bed & breakfast with furnished apartments.
Clientele: Mostly straight clientele with a gay & lesbian following
Transportation: Car is best. Taxi or SuperShuttle from airport. Pick up for large parties can be arranged for a fee.
To Gay Bars: 5 miles or a 10-minute drive.
Rooms: 40 rooms & 14 apartments with single, double, queen or king beds.
Baths: All private.
Meals: Expanded continental breakfast.

Vegetarian: Available at nearby restaurants.
Complimentary: Glass of wine at check-in.
Dates Open: All year.
High Season: Nov-Apr.
Rates: Nov 1-Apr 30 $89-$199, May 1-Oct 31 $59-$109.
Discounts: Gov't rate $79, AAA 10%, AARP 10%, Airline & travel 25%.
Credit Cards: MC, Visa, Amex, Diners, Discover, Carte Blanche.
Rsv'tns: Preferred. Necessary during high season.

Reserve Thru: Call direct.
Parking: Ample free parking in enclosed lot. Locked at night with guest access.
In-Room: Color cable TV, AC, ceiling fans, telephone & maid service.
On-Premises: Lounge, meeting rooms, fax, copier, conference call & laundry facilities (coin operated).
Exercise/Health: Jacuzzi on premises. Nearby gym, Jacuzzi, sauna, steam, massage, walking/running path, tennis & golf.
Swimming: Pool on premises.

Sunbathing: At poolside.
Smoking: Prohibited in rooms & closed public spaces.
Pets: Permitted with reservation.
Handicap Access: Yes. General access & rooms.
Children: Welcome.
Languages: English, Spanish.
Your Hosts: Sallye, Jane & Debbie.
IGLTA

Normandy South

www Men ♂

If Gauguin Had Stopped Here, He May Never Have Made it to Tahiti!

On a palm-lined street in a quiet, safe, residential neighborhood near the convention center, *Normandy South* is a Mediterranean revival home among similar architectural gems dating from Art Deco's heyday, the Roaring 20s. Within easy walking distance of South Beach's superb choice of gay clubs, trendy restaurants and chic shops, we welcome the sophisticated male traveler who demands a prime location, luxury and elegance without formality and stuffiness.

Guest accommodations are generous, each with a new marble and tile bath en suite, and are poshly furnished with queen- and king-sized beds, exciting, original art and colorful dhurries. In addition to three doubles and three suites (one with its own terrace) in the main house, there are two doubles in the carriage house at the opposite end of the spectacular "Miami Vice" pool.

When not out dancing, shopping or cruising the gay beaches, guests are encouraged to lounge poolside, perfecting a no-tan-line tan, socialize in the Jacuzzi or work off those extra piña coladas in the 44-foot lap lane. For a change of pace, one can slip off to the shaded grotto and luxuriate in the hot tub beneath a thatched chickee, or snooze in the oversized hammock. Clothing is optional both inside and outside — a freshly-plucked hibiscus or jasmine tucked behind one's ear is raiment enough. What is not optional is smoking. Guests are strictly limited to non-smokers, no exceptions. Enjoy, without interference, the freshly-scented ocean breezes and fragrant blossoms that abound.

Address: Miami Beach, FL
Tel: (305) 674-1197, **Fax:** (305) 532-9771.
E-mail: normandyso@aol.com **Web:** http://www.normandysouth.com

Type: Guesthouse.
Clientele: Men only
Transportation: Super Shuttle or taxi direct from airport to guesthouse.
To Gay Bars: 10 minutes.
Rooms: 5 rooms & 3 suites with queen or king beds.
Baths: All private.
Meals: Tropical continental breakfast.
Dates Open: Oct–May.
High Season: Christmas to Easter

Rates: Nov-Xmas & Easter-May $110-$165; Xmas-Easter $120-$175; May, Oct $80-$120.
Credit Cards: MC, Visa, Amex.
Rsv'tns: Recommended.
Reserve Thru: Travel agent or call direct.
Min. Stay: Varies with season & holiday.
Parking: Ample, free off-street parking.
In-Room: Full-range cable

TV, central air, maid & complimentary laundry service, refrigerator, VCR w/ fun flics, ceiling fans.
Exercise/Health: Gym & Jacuzzi with massage by appointment.
Swimming: Heated pool w/ lap lane on premises. 10 min to gay beach.
Sunbathing: At poolside, on private or common sun decks & at public beaches.
Nudity: Clothing optional

inside, poolside, on sun decks, in grotto, at nude gay beach.
Smoking: Accommodations are for non-smokers only.
Pets: Permitted with prior arrangement.
Handicap Access: No.
Children: Not permitted.
Your Hosts: Hank & Bruce.
IGLTA

Richmond Hotel

A Truly Distinctive South Beach Experience

The Richmond represents a return to a gentler era when Miami Beach was the winter capital of North America. Launched prior to the outbreak of World War II, it was the creation of a modern-day Marco Polo whose travels took him from the capitals of Europe to the trade routes of Asia and, finally, to the warm sands of South Florida. **The Richmond** was designed by Miami Beach's most famous Art Deco architect, L. Murray Dixon, and was one of the first oceanfront hotels on Collins Avenue. Its restoration has resulted in a small luxury hotel offering beautiful accommodation in a fabulous location. Its service is reminiscent of the days when our guests were picked up by our Woody station wagon at Miami's old FEC railway station and were greeted personally by our parents and grandparents.

The Verandah dining terrace offers fantastic creations combining the savory tastes of the Old South with great American favorites, all served in South Beach's most romantic setting. Mornings, guests enjoy deluxe continental breakfast as the sun begins to rise over the sparkling blue waters of the Atlantic. Its perfect location is a short walk to the gay beach, the pulsating night clubs and world-famous Ocean Drive and Lincoln Road. "Four Palms, highly recommended," Out & About, November, '97.

Address: 1757 Collins Ave, Miami Beach, FL 33139
Tel: (305) 538-2331, (800) 327-3163, **Fax:** (305) 531-9021.
E-mail: richmondmb@aol.com **Web:** http://www.richmondhotel.com

Type: Hotel with restaurant. **Clientele:** Mostly straight with a gay male following **Transportation:** From airport: taxi $23 or Super Shuttle $10 per person. **To Gay Bars:** 5 blocks. **Rooms:** 99 rooms with queen beds. **Baths:** All private. **Meals:** Continental breakfast. Restaurant with lunch menu & specials. **High Season:** Dec-Apr.

Rates: Winter $220-$400; Summer $125-$225. **Discounts:** Corporate rates. Mention Inn Places get 10% off. **Credit Cards:** MC, Visa, Diners, Amex. **Rsv'tns:** Required. **Reserve Thru:** Travel agent or call direct. **Min. Stay:** 3 nts some holiday periods. **Parking:** Adequate off-street pay parking. Valet only: $14.91 overnight, unlimited in/out. **In-Room:** AC, color cable TV, telephone with voice mail capability, maid, room & laundry service. **On-Premises:** Meeting rooms, business services. **Exercise/Health:** Gym & Jacuzzi on premises. Nearby weights, sauna, steam, massage. **Swimming:** Pool, ocean. **Sunbathing:** Poolside, on private sun decks, at beach. **Smoking:** Permitted in common areas, guest rooms. Non-smoking rooms avail. **Pets:** Not permitted. **Handicap Access:** Yes. **Children:** No. **Languages:** English, Portuguese, Spanish, French, Creole. **Your Hosts:** Pat, Allan & friendly staff.

South Beach Villas

An Intimate Bed & Breakfast

WWW Gay/Lesbian ♂
Gay-Owned & -Operated

South Beach Villas is a renovated 16-unit Art Deco building within walking distance of all the magic that makes South Beach infamous! The private courtyard with lush foliage, heated pool and secluded Jacuzzi offers many opportunities to socialize with guests from all over the globe. Experience all the comforts of home at this luxury gay guesthouse on Miami Beach. Our charming accommodations are furnished with contemporary solid wood furniture with private baths, color cable TV, refrigerators, coffeemakers and microwaves. Choose from a huge one-bedroom suite with full kitchens, a two-room poolside bungalow, or a quaint single studio. We offer free parking, free local calls and a delicious poolside continental breakfast and daily maid service by a gracious and courteous staff. Our office can receive and send faxes and e-mails, and dedicated phone lines in each room allow internet access for your laptop.

For keeping in shape, we're steps from health clubs or popular Flamingo Park. Stroll through South Beach photographing the historic Art Deco districts and palm-lined streets. Walk to Lincoln Road a few short blocks away, renowned for people-watching and a pulsating gay experience. The 12th Street gay beach is world-reknowned. Be a real local and rent a bike or a pair of roller blades, or just laze around our dazzling pool and relax.

Address: 1201 West Avenue, at 12th Street between Alton & West Avenue, Miami Beach, FL 33139
Tel: Toll-free: (888) GAY SOBE (429-7623), Local: (305) 673-9600, **Fax:** (305) 532-6200.
E-mail: sobevillas@aol.com **Web:** http://www.beachvillasfla.com

Type: Accommodations, guesthouse, B&B.
Clientele: 80% gay men, 20% lesbian, family & friends
Transportation: Car, taxi, bus. Super Shuttle approx $10 from Miami airport.
To Gay Bars: 5 min walk.
Rooms: 16 rooms with queen or king beds.
Baths: All private.
Meals: Deluxe continental breakfast.
Complimentary: Setup service.
Dates Open: All year. Office hours 8am-midnight.
High Season: Nov 15-Apr 1 & holidays.
Rates: $100-$195. Holiday rates add $25 nightly.
Credit Cards: MC, Visa, Amex.
Rsv'tns: Recommended. Necessary high season.
Reserve Thru: Travel agent or call direct.
Min. Stay: 2 nts wknds.
Parking: 18 free off-street parking spaces.
In-Room: Phone w/ internet access (free local calls), AC, ceiling fans, color cable TV, kitchen, fridger, coffee & tea makers, maid svc. 12 rooms have full kitchens.
On-Premises: Manager, tropical courtyard, laundry facilities.
Exercise/Health: Jacuzzi. Special rates at nearby gym with weights, tennis, track. Nearby Jacuzzi, sauna, steam, massage.
Swimming: Heated pool on premises. Ocean nearby.
Sunbathing: Poolside, on patio or at beach.
Smoking: Non-smoking accommodations. Permitted on porch areas only.
Pets: Not permitted.
Children: Not especially permitted.
Languages: English, Spanish.
Your Hosts: Joe.
IGLTA

Rick's Bed and Breakfast

WWW Gay/Lesbian ♂
Gay-Owned & -Operated

Concierge Accommodations at a B&B Rate

Experience Walt Disney World "Family Style"at *Rick's Bed and Breakfast*, gay-owned and -operated since 1988. We're ideally located adjacent to Disney World, Lake Buena Vista and Downtown Disney, and minutes from the Orlando Convention Center, Universal Studios, Sea World, Splendid China, Cypress Gardens, and Wet and Wild Water Park. Accommodations are casual and relaxed. Special features include a complete recreational facility with outdoor pool, tennis, basketball courts, a baseball diamond and exercise trail. Concierge services and a Florida Licensed massage therapist are available by appointment at an additional cost. To make a reservation, please send a check payable to **Rick Borucki** as a deposit. Deposits will be refunded if cancellations are received two weeks prior to arrival and if no other requests for reservations have been received.

Address: Lake Buena Vista **Mail To:** PO Box 22318, Lake Buena Vista, FL 32830
Tel: (407) 396-7751, Cell phone: (407) 414-7751. Both answer 24 hrs.
E-mail: RICKsBnB@aol.com **Web:** http://members.aol.com/rickb7751/home/index.htm

Type: Bed & breakfast.
Clientele: Mostly men with women welcome
Transportation: Car.
To Gay Bars: 15 miles.
Rooms: 2 rooms (1 with king, 1 with queen bed).

Baths: Bath/shower/toilet: 1 private & 1 shared with Rick.
Meals: Full breakfast.
Dates Open: All year.
High Season: All year.
Rates: $85-$100.
Parking: Adequate, free off-street parking.

In-Room: AC, ceiling fans, color cable TV, VCR, maid service.
On-Premises: TV lounge, laundry, video tapes.
Exercise/Health: Massage.

Nudity: Permitted in house & on patio.
Smoking: Permitted outside.
Your Hosts: Rick.

Things Worth Remembering

Gay/Lesbian ⚥

Movie, Television, Broadway & Sports Memorabilia

Dustin Hoffman's bust from the movie "Hook," autographed photos, costumes and props are among the items for you to view at *Things Worth Remembering*, a B&B decorated with collectibles, memorabilia and autographs. Whether you choose to relax among the collectibles, or simply watch the birds in flight, this will be a vacation you will never forget. Your hosts are business professionals with many interesting inside stories from their years as theme park employees.

Address: 2603 Coventry Ln, Orlando, FL 34761
Tel: (407) 291-2127, (800) 484-3585 (code 6908), **Fax:** (407) 291-7725.
E-mail: orlandob2b@aol.com

Type: Bed & breakfast.
Clientele: Mostly gay & lesbian with some straight clientele
Transportation: Car is best.
To Gay Bars: A 15 min drive to gay bars.
Rooms: 2 rooms with queen bed.
Baths: Private & shared.
Meals: Continental breakfast buffet.

Vegetarian: Full access to kitchen. Special requests OK.
Complimentary: Guest fridge with drinks, water, snacks.
Dates Open: All year.
High Season: Summer & holidays.
Rates: $65-$80.
Discounts: 10% discount if you mention Inn Places ad, or stay 1 wk, 7th day free.

Rsv'tns: Required.
Reserve Thru: Travel agent or call direct.
Parking: Adequate free off-street parking.
In-Room: AC, ceiling fans, telephone, color cable TV, VCR.
On-Premises: Video tape library.
Exercise/Health: Nearby gym, weights, Jacuzzi, sauna, steam, massage.

Swimming: Screened-in pool. Ocean, river, lake & water parks.
Sunbathing: On patio.
Smoking: Permitted outside only.
Pets: Not permitted.
Handicap Access: No.
Languages: English.
Your Hosts: James & Lindsey.

INN PLACES® 2001

USA 271

Mill House Inn

WWW Gay/Lesbian ♂

Exclusively Yours on Scenic Perdido Bay

The Mill House on Perdido Bay was built in the 1870s to serve as housing for local mill workers. After Hurricane Erin in 1995, the house underwent major renovation and now boasts a new upper-level secluded back porch, as well as private entrances to all rooms. There are first- and second-story verandas equipped with ceiling fans, sound system and a magnificent view of Perdido Bay. Rooms are large and have either queen or king bed, ceiling fan, TV, refrigerator and a wonderful view of the bay. We're 10 minutes from Johnson Beach on Perdido Key.

Address: 9603 Lillian Highway, Pensacola, FL 32506
Tel: (850) 455-3400, toll-free: (888) 999-4575, **Fax:** (850) 458-6397.
E-mail: TMHBB@aol.com

Type: Bed & breakfast guesthouse.
Clientele: Mostly men with women welcome
Transportation: Car.
To Gay Bars: 15 min drive to men's & 5 min drive to women's bars.
Rooms: 3 rooms with king or queen beds.
Baths: Private & shared.
Meals: Full breakfast.
Vegetarian: If requested at time of reservation.
Complimentary: Iced tea always, coffee mornings, mint/candy on pillow. Welcome basket w/ chips, soda, bottled water, etc.
Dates Open: All year.
High Season: Apr 1-Oct 31.
Rates: Winter $55-$75, summer $65-$89.
Discounts: Stay 5 nights, 6th free.
Credit Cards: MC, Visa.
Rsv'tns: Required.
Reserve Thru: Travel agent or call direct.
Min. Stay: Required on holidays only.
Parking: Ample off-street parking.
In-Room: AC, color TV, ceiling fans, VCR, fridge, maid & laundry service.
On-Premises: TV room.
Exercise/Health: Large hot tub. Massage can be brought on to premises.
Swimming: Nearby Gulf of Mexico.
Sunbathing: On patio & at beach.
Nudity: Permitted in house, on upstairs sun deck & in spa.
Smoking: Permitted outside only. All rooms are non-smoking.
Pets: Not permitted.
Handicap Access: Downstairs king room with private bath is accessible.
Children: No.
Languages: English.
Your Hosts: Scott.

Midtown Manor

WWW Gay/Lesbian ⚥
Gay-Operated

Midtown Manor is a group of turn-of-the-century homes nestled in the shadow of downtown Atlanta's skyline, in the heart of Atlanta's gay and lesbian community. Whether you are travelling for business or pleasure, our guesthouses are convenient and relaxing. Many wonderful historic sites, parks, shops and restaurants are only a stroll away down one of the many tree-lined streets around us. For nightlife, we are close to the symphony, theater, clubs and dancing. Our helpful staff goes out of its way to make your trip to Atlanta as pleasant as possible.

Address: 811 Piedmont Ave NE, Atlanta, GA 30308
Tel: (404) 872-5846, (800) 724-4381, **Fax:** (404) 875-3018.
E-mail: MidtownMoe@aol.com **Web:** http://www.gayinnatlanta.com

Type: Nightly & extended stay guesthouses.
Clientele: Mostly gay & lesbian clientele
Transportation: MARTA bus & rail, taxi & on foot.
To Gay Bars: Walk to 6 area gay & lesbian bars.
Rooms: 60 rooms.
Baths: Private & shared.
Meals: Nice continental breakfast.
Complimentary: Coffee & donuts.
Dates Open: Year round.
High Season: Late June -- Atlanta Pride Week.
Rates: $85-$45, weekly rates available.
Discounts: Pay full month in advance & receive 5% discount.
Credit Cards: MC, Amex, Visa, Discover.
Rsv'tns: Recommended.
Reserve Thru: Travel agent or call direct.
Parking: Free off-street parking.
In-Room: Color TV, AC, refrigerator, answering machine & maid service.
On-Premises: Soda machines, laundry, ice, microwaves.
Exercise/Health: 3 private gyms in area, tennis at public park.
Swimming: At public park (within walking distance, 6 blocks).
Sunbathing: At public park (within walking distance, 6 blocks).
Smoking: Permitted without restrictions.
Pets: None.
Handicap Access: No.
Children: OK with supervision.
Languages: English.
Your Hosts: Quinn & Steve.

Abbett Inn

WWW Gay-Friendly 50/50 ⚥
Gay-Owned & -Operated

The *Abbett Inn* is a historic bed and breakfast located ten minutes from downtown Atlanta. The inn, a landmark in historic downtown College Park, was built in the 1880's and was the home of H.M. Abbett, secretary and treasurer of the Atlanta and West Point Railroad. The home was later passed down to his granddaughter, Miss Frances Mason. This 4,000-plus-square-

foot Victorian house is situated on a triple wooded lot in a quiet neighborhood, creating an inviting park-like setting. Amenities include six guest rooms (four with private bath), private room phones with answering machine, and cable television in all guest rooms. Fully equipped modern kitchens are located on each floor exclusively for guest use. There is 24-hour security and free off-street parking. Banquet facilities and laundry facilities, fax and internet access are also available. Located nearby are Hartsfield International Airport and MARTA (rapid rail) with convenient complimentary shuttle service to and from both destinations.

Directions to the Inn: From the airport, take I-85 North to exit 19B (Virginia Ave. westbound), go 0.7 mile, the inn is on the left. If you are coming from downtown Atlanta, take I-85 South approximately 10 miles to exit 19 (Virginia Avenue Exit), go right 0.7 mile to the inn on the left. If using public transportation from the airport, take MARTA to the College Park Rail Station (1 stop), proceed north out of the station (turn right) on East Main Street 4 blocks to Virginia Ave., turn right 1/2 block to the inn at 1746 Virginia Avenue.

Address: 1746 Virginia Ave, College Park, Atlanta, GA 30337
Tel: (404) 767-3708, **Fax:** (404) 767-1626.
E-mail: abbettinn@bellsouth.net **Web:** http://www.abbettinn.com

Type: Bed & breakfast.	**Baths:** Bath/shower/toilets:	Amex, Diners.	**Exercise/Health:** Nearby
Clientele: 50% gay &	4 private, 2 shared.	**Rsv'tns:** Required.	gym, weights, massage.
lesbian & 50% straight	**Meals:** Expanded or	**Reserve Thru:** Travel agent	**Swimming:** Nearby pool.
clientele	continental breakfast.	or call direct.	**Smoking:** Not permitted.
Transportation: Car or	**Complimentary:** Afternoon	**Parking:** Adequate free off-	**Pets:** Not permitted.
MARTA. Free pick up from	tea.	street parking.	**Handicap Access:** No.
airport.	**Dates Open:** All year.	**In-Room:** Telephone, AC,	**Children:** Welcome over 12
To Gay Bars: 8 miles, a 10	**Rates:** $79-$149.	ceiling fans, color cable TV,	years of age.
min drive.	**Discounts:** 10% on stays	maid service.	**Your Hosts:** Donald &
Rooms: 6 rooms, 1 suite	longer than 5 days.	**On-Premises:** TV lounge,	John.
with queen beds.	**Credit Cards:** MC, Visa,	laundry facilities.	

Nine Twelve Barnard Bed & Breakfast   WWW Gay/Lesbian ♀♂

A Victorian B&B in the Hostess City of the South

We warmly welcome you to *912 Barnard*, Savannah's only exclusively gay and lesbian bed and breakfast. A restored double house in the heart of Savannah's Victorian district, our home is within walking distance of shops, restaurants, museums and beautiful Forsyth Park, the crown-jewel of Savannah's historic squares. Antique furnishings and four original fireplaces set the decor. On the first floor is the double parlor living room-dining room, full kitchen and laundry facilities. Upstairs, two graciously appointed guest rooms await. We serve continental breakfast, complimentary beverages and, of course, plenty of assistance for sightseeing, shopping or dining.

Address: 912 Barnard St, Savannah, GA 31401
Tel: (912) 234-9121.
E-mail: 912barnard@msn.com **Web:** http://www.912barnard.com

Type: Bed & breakfast.
Clientele: Exclusively gay & lesbian
Transportation: Car, bus or taxi.
To Gay Bars: 12 blocks, a 5-minute drive.
Rooms: 2 rooms.
Baths: Shared bath/shower/toilet & 1 half bath.
Meals: Expanded continental breakfast.
Vegetarian: Available upon prior request & at nearby deli.
Complimentary: Coffee, tea, soft drinks, alcoholic beverages.
Dates Open: All year.
High Season: Mar-Aug.
Rates: $99 per night, year-round.
Discounts: $5 for cash payment.
Rsv'tns: Required.
Reserve Thru: Call direct.

Min. Stay: 2 nights on weekends.
Parking: Adequate free on-street parking.
In-Room: Color cable TV with HBO, VCR, phone, ceiling fans, fireplaces, AC, maid service.
On-Premises: Laundry facilities, video tape library.
Exercise/Health: 1 block to tennis courts, walking & running paths.

Swimming: 15 minutes to ocean & Tybee Beach, gay beach nearby.
Sunbathing: On common sundecks, at beach.
Nudity: Inquire.
Smoking: Permitted outside only, rooms are non-smoking.
Pets: Not permitted.
Handicap Access: No.
Children: No.
Languages: English.
Your Hosts: Don.

Paradise Inn

WWW Gay-Friendly ♂♂
Gay-Owned & -Operated

A Welcome Retreat

Paradise Inn is friendly, relaxed and unpretentious, with a congenial staff dedicated to providing the highest level of guest service. Our newly restored 1866 townhouse has five comfortable guestrooms, three with working fireplaces and one with its own private deck. We are located in Savannah's famed Historic District within walking distance of shops, great restaurants and friendly bars. Whether relaxing in the pool or socializing with other guests during our afternoon cocktail hour, you'll find our inn, and Savannah, a welcome retreat.

Address: 512 Tattnall St, Savannah, GA 31401
Tel: (912) 443-0200, (888) 846-5093, **Fax:** (912) 443-9295.
E-mail: info@link2paradise.com **Web:** http://www.link2paradise.com

Type: Bed & breakfast inn.
Clientele: 50% gay & lesbian & 50% straight clientele
Transportation: Car is best, or airport (15 min away). Free pick up from airport or train with advance notice.
To Gay Bars: 4 blocks, a 10 min walk.
Rooms: 5 rooms with queen beds.

Baths: 5 private shower/toilets.
Meals: Expanded continental or buffet breakfast.
Vegetarian: 3 blocks to healthfood store.
Complimentary: Afternoon cocktails.
Dates Open: All year.
High Season: Mid-Mar thru Jul 4 & Oct.
Rates: $99-$139.

Credit Cards: MC, Visa, Amex.
Rsv'tns: Recommended.
Reserve Thru: Inquire.
Parking: Adequate free on-street parking.
In-Room: Telephone, AC, ceiling fans, color cable TV, VCR, hair dryer, refrigerator with ice-maker, coffee & tea-making facilities, maid service.
On-Premises: Video tape

library.
Exercise/Health: Nearby full-service health facility.
Swimming: Pool. Ocean nearby.
Sunbathing: On common sun decks.
Smoking: Permitted outside only.
Pets: Not permitted.
Handicap Access: No.
Children: No.
Languages: English.

Park Avenue Manor B & B

Gay/Lesbian ♂♂
Gay-Owned & -Operated

Retaining the True Ambiance of Graceful Southern Living

Our pristine inn with its lace-upon-lace draperies, fine furnishings, angel ceiling borders and double staircases, greets you with charm upon entering our two formal parlors. *Park Avenue Manor B&B's* five suites feature four-poster beds, antique furniture, silk carpets, period prints, porcelains, working fireplaces and private baths (some with original claw-foot tubs). The Dining Room for your full, formal breakfast, has the air of the Old South, with its stately portraits, stained glass and working fireplace. We offer a full breakfast, televisions, and more.

Address: 107-109 West Park Avenue, Savannah, GA
Tel: (912) 233-0352.
E-mail: pkavemanor@aol.com **Web:** http://www.bbonline.com/ga/parkavenue

Type: Bed & breakfast.
Clientele: Mostly gay & lesbian with some gay-friendly straight clientele
Transportation: Car is best.
To Gay Bars: 1 mile to gay bar owned by B&B, a 12 min walk, a 1 min drive.
Rooms: 5 rooms with single or queen beds.
Baths: 5 private bath/shower/toilets.

Meals: Full breakfast.
Vegetarian: 1 block to restaurant.
Complimentary: Set ups, sherry in parlors, tea & coffee.
Dates Open: All year.
High Season: Apr-May.
Rates: $85-$110.
Discounts: ARRP 10%. Ask about special rates.
Credit Cards: MC, Visa, Amex.

Rsv'tns: Required.
Reserve Thru: Call direct.
Parking: Ample, free off-street parking.
In-Room: Telephone, AC, color cable TV, maid, room & laundry service.
On-Premises: Laundry facilities, private phone jacks for business computers.
Swimming: 20 min to ocean.
Sunbathing: On patio &

private sun decks, at beach.
Smoking: Permitted on enclosed decks. No non-smoking rooms available.
Pets: Not permitted.
Handicap Access: No.
Children: No.
Languages: English.
Your Hosts: Jonathan.

Hale Aloha Guest Ranch

WWW Gay/Lesbian ⚥
Gay-Operated

Find the Real Spirit of Aloha at a Luxurious Hillside Hideaway

Discover the "house of welcome and love" with its spacious lanais and spectacular ocean views. *Hale Aloha* is nestled at 1,500 feet in the lush South Kona hillside. Guests will enjoy the peace and tranquillity of the five-acre park-like citrus and macadamia nut plantation which borders a state forest preserve. Stroll, get a massage, relax in the Jacuzzi, sunbathe, or be more adventurous and bike and snorkel. The City of Refuge and Kealakekua Bay (famous for its tropical fish, sea turtles and often-present dolphins) are right down below, and Volcano National Park is a scenic 68 miles away.

Address: 84-4780 Mamalahoa Hwy, Captain Cook, HI 96704
Tel: (808) 328-8955 (Tel/Fax), (800) 897-3188.
E-mail: vacation@halealoha.com **Web:** http://www.halealoha.com

Type: Bed & breakfast.
Clientele: Gay & lesbian
Transportation: Car is best.
To Gay Bars: A 25-minute drive to Kona gay bar.
Rooms: 4 rooms, 1 suite, 1 studio apartment with king, queen or double beds.
Baths: Master suite: private double shower/Jacuzzi, bath/toilet. Apartment: private shower/toilet. 3 rooms share bath/toilet.
Meals: Full breakfast.

Vegetarian: Available at breakfast & at local stores & restaurants.
Complimentary: Refreshments on arrival, Kona coffee, iced tea.
Dates Open: All year.
High Season: Holidays.
Rates: $60-$140.
Discounts: 10% on stays of 4 nights.
Rsv'tns: Required.
Reserve Thru: Travel agent or call direct.
Min. Stay: 2 nights on

weekends & holidays.
Parking: Ample free off-street parking.
In-Room: Maid service, 3 rooms share kitchen. Master suite uses main kitchen.
On-Premises: Video tape library, kitchenette, color TV & VCR, coffee & tea-making facilities.
Exercise/Health: Jacuzzi, massage, mountain bikes, snorkel gear, boogie boards.
Swimming: Nearby ocean.
Sunbathing: On common

sun decks, on private areas throughout 5-acre property, at beach.
Nudity: Permitted while sunbathing, in Jacuzzi & at nude beach near Kona.
Smoking: Permitted outside. All rooms are non-smoking.
Pets: Not permitted.
Children: Please inquire.
Languages: English, German, French.
Your Hosts: Johann & Chuck.

Hale Kipa 'O Pele

Romance Flows Where Lava Glows!

Hale Kipa 'O Pele B&B is named for the sacred spirit, Madam Pele, goddess of fire, ruler of Hawaii's volcanoes and protector of the forest. It is believed that Pele's spirit guards the property even today! Situated on the volcanic slopes of Mt. Hualalai, above the sunny southern Kona coast, the tropical estate and plantation-style home are unique. A majestic volcanic dome graces the entrance drive. The house surrounds an open-air atrium with lava rock waterfall, koi pond and a tiled walkway providing a private entrance to each room-suite.

The *Maile* is a corner room with spacious sitting area, private bath and intimate covered patio. The *Ginger* has a large walk-in closet, private bath with sunken tub and sliding glass doors that access the wooden deck and provide garden views. The expansive *Pele Bungalow* has a cozy bedroom, full bath, living room, mini-kitchen and a large private covered patio overlooking the fruit tree grove. A covered wooden lanai wraps around the entire front of the home, providing full panoramic views. Enjoy a buffet-style tropical continental breakfast at YOUR leisure on the lanai or in the dining room. After a day of activities, relax in the garden Jacuzzi or enjoy movies on the Pro-Logic Surround Sound(tm) system. Massage therapy is available on-site.

Eight miles to beach and all activities, guests enjoy scuba diving, para-sailing, deep sea fishing, helicopter tours, or walks along the scenic shores and quaint village-style shops of old Kona Town. We can pre-arrange tours, activities and commitment ceremonies. We cater to singles and couples seeking the true "ALOHA" spirit and a serene, romantic atmosphere that only a tropical-style B&B can offer!

Address: Kailua Kona **Mail To:** PO Box 5252, Kailua Kona, HI 96745
Tel: (800) LAVAGLO, (808) 329-8676.
E-mail: halekipa@gte.net. **Web:** http://www.gaystayhawaii.com

Type: B&B & bungalow.	Refreshments on arrival,	**Min. Stay:** 2 nights.	**Swimming:** Nearby ocean.
Clientele: Good mix of gays & lesbians	wine & cheese at sunset.	**Parking:** Adequate free off-street parking.	**Sunbathing:** Jacuzzi sun deck, beach, lawn.
Transportation: Rental car.	**Dates Open:** All year.	**In-Room:** Ceiling fans,	**Nudity:** In Jacuzzi.
To Gay Bars: 6 miles.	**Rates:** $85-$115 + room & state taxes.	maid svc. Bungalow: mini-kitchen, cable TV, VCR.	**Smoking:** Permitted outside & on covered decks.
Rooms: 2 suites with queen beds, 1 bungalow with 1 queen bed.	**Discounts:** 10% for 7 nights.	**On-Premises:** TV lounge with theatre sound & video tape library. Expansive	**Pets:** Not permitted.
Baths: All private.	**Credit Cards:** MC, Visa, Amex.	covered decks.	**Children:** Not especially welcome.
Meals: Tropical island-style continental breakfast.	**Rsv'tns:** Required.	**Exercise/Health:** Jacuzzi.	**Languages:** English.
Complimentary:	**Reserve Thru:** Travel agent or call direct.	Gym, racquetball nearby.	**IGLTA**

Kalani Oceanside Eco-Resort

WWW Gay/Lesbian ♀♂
Gay- & Lesbian-Owned & -Operated

Soulful, Sensual & Natural Hawaii

Kalani Oceanside Eco-Resort is the only coastal lodging facility within Hawaii's largest conservation area. Here, you are treated to Hawaii's real aloha comfort, traditional culture, healthful cuisine and a rainbow of seminars. Among the many extraordinary adventures guests can experience here are: thermal springs, a swimsuit-optional dolphin beach, snorkel tidal pools, steam bathing, kayaking, waterfalls, orchid farms, botanical gardens, historic villages and spectacular Volcanoes National Park.

Come for an anytime getaway or for one of several annual week-long events: Gay Spirit, Pacific Men, Hula Heritage, Adventure Hawaii, Body Electric, Dance & Music Festivals and spa weeks. Our cuisine is a heavenly experience, to *live* for! In addition to our alfresco dining lanai, lawn and oceanside settings grace special occasions. Vegetarian and vegan options are always available. Relish our locally grown organic produce and fresh catch from the sea. Our international, native, gay and lesbian staff welcome you!

Address: RR2, Beach Road, Pahoa **Mail To:** Box 4500-IP, Pahoa, HI 96778-9724
Tel: (800) 800-6886, (808) 965-7828, **Fax:** (808) 965-0527.
E-mail: kalani@kalani.com **Web:** http://www.kalani.com

Type: Eco-resort with restaurant & native gift shops.
Clientele: 70% gay & lesbian & 30% straight clientele.
Transportation: Rental car is best, taxi & Kalani shuttle services.
To Gay Bars: 15-min drive.
Rooms: 35 lodge rooms & 8 cottage units with single, double, queen or king beds.
Baths: Private & shared.
Camping: 20 tent sites with convenient hot showers & restrooms.
Meals: Breakfast, lunch,

dinner served daily.
Vegetarian: Available.
Complimentary: Tea, coffee, juices.
Dates Open: All year.
Rates: Rooms $45-$120, cottages $90-$145. With $27/day meal plan. Campsites $20-$30 per person. Week-long adventures & events $570-$1,240.
Discounts: 10-20% week & vacation (long-term), rentals, etc.
Credit Cards: MC, Visa, Amex, Discover, Diners.
Rsv'tns: Preferred.

Reserve Thru: Travel agent or call direct.
Parking: Ample, free off-street parking.
In-Room: Cottages with fridge, partial maid service, rattan furnishings, heritage books, fans.
On-Premises: Meeting rooms, kitchens, dance & yoga studios, 113 acres of tropical beauty.
Exercise/Health: Yoga, weights, Jacuzzis, sauna & massage options.
Swimming: Olympic pool on premises. Ocean beach, river, lake, snorkel tidal

pools & waterfalls nearby.
Sunbathing: At poolside, oceanfront & on beach.
Nudity: Permitted anytime oceanfront, at ocean beach, or after 7pm at pool & spa.
Smoking: Permitted outdoors.
Pets: Not permitted.
Handicap Access: Yes.
Children: Permitted.
Languages: English, Spanish, French, German & Japanese.
Your Hosts: Richard, Howie, Dotty, Donna.
IGLTA

E Walea by the Sea

The Most Hawaiian B&B on the Island of Hawai'i

Aloha e komo mai i ko makou hale! (Aloha and welcome to our home!). Let us make you feel at home at *E Walea by the Sea,* a modest island beach home on the sunny Kohala coast in one of Hawai'i's oldest beach communities. We offer three guestrooms, each with either a mountain or ocean view. A Hawaiian continental breakfast is served daily, featuring fresh island-grown fruits, papayas, local baked goods, Guava, Liliko'i and Poha or 'Ohelo preserves, island juices and 100% Kona coffee. We're across from the ocean and near some of the island's best beaches, golf courses, luxury resorts and fine restaurants. We invite you to experience Hawai'i, its many diverse cultures, rich history and scenic beauty.

Address: 25 Puako Beach Drive, Kamuela, HI 96743
Tel: (808) 882-1331.
E-mail: ewalea@gte.net **Web:** http://www.ewaleabythesea.com/

Type: Bed & breakfast.
Clientele: Mostly straight clientele with a gay/lesbian following
Transportation: Rental car, taxi.
To Gay Bars: 30 mi to Kailua Town (Kona, HI).
Rooms: 2 rooms, 1 suite w/ double, queen, king beds.
Baths: 1 private bath/ shower/toilet, 2 shared

bathtubs only.
Meals: Expanded continental or full breakfast.
Vegetarian: Available.
Complimentary: Pupu party for groups of 6.
Dates Open: All year.
High Season: Dec-Apr.
Rates: $85-$65, all year (2000).
Discounts: 7th night free program.

Credit Cards: MC, Visa.
Rsv'tns: Required.
Reserve Thru: Call direct.
Min. Stay: 2 nights.
Parking: Free parking.
In-Room: Ceiling fans, color cable TV, VCR, maid & laundry service.
On-Premises: Laundry facilities, video tape library.
Swimming: Ocean nearby.
Sunbathing: At beach.

Nudity: Permitted in home & nearby nude beach.
Smoking: Permitted outside.
Pets: Not permitted.
Children: Welcome.
Languages: English, Hawaiian.
Your Hosts: Punahele & Kelly.

Ho'onanea

Aloha — E Komo Mai

Ho'onanea means "go with the flow of life and the wind." This Big Island — Hawaii bed and breakfast offers a unique, year-round Hawaiian romantic and separate space for women only. We are 10-15 minutes from Hawaii's most beautiful beaches, with full views of both Mauna Kea and Mauna Loa mountains. Our quiet, back-to-nature surroundings offer outdoor hot tub, lap pool, and access to mountain bikes and snorkeling equipment. We guarantee that you will leave relaxed, refreshed and energized. With its exquisite restaurants and stores, the very Hawaiian Kamuela Town is only 10 miles away.

Address: Kamuela **Mail To:** PO Box 6450, Kamuela, HI 96743
Tel: (808) 882-1177, **Fax:** (808) 882-1505.
E-mail: barshay@aloha.net **Web:** http://www.kamuela.com/lodgings/ hoonanea

Type: Bed & breakfast.
Clientele: Women only
Transportation: Car is a must.
To Gay Bars: 40 miles to gay bars in Kona, a 40 min drive.
Rooms: 1 cottage with queen beds.
Baths: Private bath/shower/ toilet.
Meals: Continental

breakfast.
Vegetarian: Available nearby.
Complimentary: Tea, coffee, fruit basket.
Dates Open: All year.
Rates: Daily per-night rate: single $60, double $75. Weekly per-night rate: single $55, double $70.
Rsv'tns: Required.
Reserve Thru: Call direct.

Min. Stay: 2 nights.
Parking: Ample free parking.
In-Room: Telephone, ceiling fans, color TV, VCR, kitchen, refrigerator, coffee & tea-making facilities.
Exercise/Health: Hot tub. Nearby golf & tennis, hiking, star gazing.
Swimming: 8'x50' lap pool on premises. Ocean nearby.

Sunbathing: Poolside & at beach.
Nudity: Permitted.
Smoking: No smoking.
Pets: Not permitted.
Handicap Access: Yes, wide doors.
Children: Welcome if coming with parents.
Languages: English.
Your Hosts: Barbara & Shay.

Pamalu

WWW Gay/Lesbian ⚦
Gay-Owned

An Island Within an Island

"A home away from home. I feel like I've been in a different world," is how one guest described the Hawaiian country house *Pamalu* (in Hawaiian: "a peaceful enclosure"), situated on five private acres in sunny Kapoho, 10 minutes from Pahoa Town. The screened lanai with vaulted ceiling overlooks palms, plumeria, bougainvillea and lawns surrounding a 40-foot pool and pavilion with BBQ. Background music is provided by birds and fresh tradewinds. It's an easy walk to snorkeling with colorful reef fish among underwater coral gardens. Nearby is a lagoon warmed by volcanic vents, a surfing area, and a black sand, clothing-optional beach. Volcano National Park with many hiking trails is an hour's drive.

Address: RR 2, Pahoa **Mail To:** Box 4023, Pahoa, HI
Tel: (808) 965-0830, **Fax:** (808) 965-6198.

Type: Country retreat.
Clientele: Mostly gay & lesbian with some straight clientele
Transportation: Car rental from airport.
Rooms: 3 rooms & 1 suite, all with queen beds
Baths: All private, tiled.
Meals: Continental breakfast, tropical fruits.

Complimentary: Tea, coffee, juice.
Dates Open: All year.
Rates: $60-$100.
Discounts: 10% for stay of 1 week.
Rsv'tns: Required.
Reserve Thru: Travel agent or call direct.
Min. Stay: 2 nights.
Parking: Ample free off-

street parking.
In-Room: Ceiling fans.
On-Premises: Video tape library, computer phone jack.
Exercise/Health: Massage on premises by appointment. Gym nearby.
Swimming: Pool on premises, warm springs lagoon nearby, black sand beach (clothing opt'l) 20-min

drive, walk to snorkeling.
Sunbathing: Poolside, on patio, at beach.
Nudity: Permitted IN pool, beach (20 min away).
Smoking: Permitted outside & at poolside pavilion.
Pets: Not permitted.
Children: Inquire.
Languages: English.

Steamvent Guesthouse

Men ♂

The Big Island ~ So Hot, Even the Ground Steams

This modern, spacious, guesthouse was built in 1995 and features soaring ceilings, tile floors, rooms with ocean or garden views, and a huge sundeck with panoramic ocean views. The home sits on 20 acres of rainforest with natural steamvents, tropical flowers and fruit trees, trails, and a sunken garden. Amenities include a natural steam bathhouse, geothermal hot pool, and Jacuzzi. Guests can also use the adjacent property which contains natural steam caves and is open to the general public. These caves are an attraction unto themselves and you should visit them even if you can't get a room in the guesthouse. The guesthouse is a short drive to many Big Island attractions.

Address: 13-3775 Kalapana Hwy, (Hwy #130 Mi. Marker 15), Pahoa, HI 96778
Tel: (808) 965-8800 (Tel/Fax).
E-mail: info@steamventguesthouse.com **Web:** http:// www.steamventguesthouse.com

Type: Private guesthouse.
Clientele: Men only
Transportation: Car rental. Hilo Airport pick up $25 sngl, or $15 ea.
Rooms: 2 private, 5 shared.
Baths: 4 full baths with geothermal heated water.
Meals: Tropical continental breakfast.

Dates Open: All year.
Rates: $100-$160, + tax.
Discounts: Inquire.
Credit Cards: MC, Visa, Discover, Paypal.
Rsv'tns: Recommended, 50% deposit. Cancellation policy.
Reserve Thru: Call, fax, email, web, travel agent.

Parking: Ample parking.
In-Room: Cleaning service.
On-Premises: Eco-tour, computer, phone, TV, video, gay books.
Exercise/Health: Hiking trails. Steam room & shower.
Swimming: Nearby nude beach.
Sunbathing: Decks,

grounds, beach.
Nudity: On sun deck, pool, steam areas 24 hrs.
Smoking: Outside.
Handicap Access: Partial.
Languages: English & French.
Your Hosts: Didier & Phil.
IGLTA

Mohala Ke Ola B & B Retreat

Escape to Paradise

Imagine yourself waking to the sounds of the breeze and birds. Then you'll breakfast on fresh island fruit on a private terrace. Swim in the pool. Relax in the Jacuzzi. Leave the cares and stresses of civilization behind. Enjoy a Hawaiian lomi-lomi massage or rejuvenate with one of the other body treatments available, including shiatsu, acupuncture and Reiki.

Mohala Ke Ola B&B Retreat is situated high above the lush Wailua River Valley and is surrounded by magical mountain and waterfall views. It provides an ideal location from which to explore the island. We'll gladly share our insights on the best hikes, scenic lookouts, secret beaches, tropical gardens, helicopter and boat tours. We hope you accept our invitation to relax, play and rejuvenate, and we look forward to having you as a guest.

Address: 5663 Ohelo Rd, Kauai, Kapaa, HI 96746
Tel: (808) 823-6398 (Tel/Fax), toll-free (888) GO-KAUAI (465-2824).
E-mail: kauaibb@aloha.net **Web:** http://www.waterfallbnb.com

Type: Bed & breakfast.
Clientele: Mostly straight clientele with a gay & lesbian following
Transportation: Car is best.
To Gay Bars: 5 miles or a 10-minute drive to Sideout.
Rooms: 3 rooms with queen beds. 1 room with king bed.
Baths: 3 private, 1 shared.
Meals: Continental breakfast.

Vegetarian: Local Thai & health food store deli.
Complimentary: Coffee & tea.
Dates Open: All year.
High Season: Nov-May.
Rates: $65-$95.
Discounts: Weekly rate 10%.
Rsv'tns: Required.
Reserve Thru: Travel agent or call direct.
Min. Stay: Prefer 3 nights minimum.

Parking: Ample free off-street parking.
In-Room: Ceiling fans.
On-Premises: TV lounge, meeting rooms & laundry facilities.
Exercise/Health: Jacuzzi, massage, acupuncture, lomi lomi, shiatsu, Reiki on premises.
Swimming: Pool on premises. Ocean & river nearby.
Sunbathing: At poolside or

on the beach.
Nudity: Permitted in hot tub & pool at discretion of other guests. 15 min to nude beach.
Smoking: Permitted outside only. This is a non-smoking environment.
Pets: Not permitted.
Handicap Access: No.
Children: Not especially welcome.
Languages: English, Japanese & German.

Aloha Kauai Bed & Breakfast

WWW Gay/Lesbian ⚥

Seclusion and Hawaiian Hospitality

Above the lazy Wailua River in a quiet garden surrounding, there is a place called *Aloha Kauai*. Here, Hawaii speaks in the soft murmur of wind chimes, the sweet smell of tropical flowers, and the shimmery water of the pool. Five minutes from Kapaa town beaches and 15 minutes to Donkey Beach, this is not only a B&B alternative to hotel accommodations, it is a hideaway conveniently located within minutes of shops and scenic attractions. It is close to spectacular Opaekaa Falls, hiking trails in the forests of Sleeping Giant, and freshwater spots at the Wailua Reservoir. Choose from four rooms: the Hibiscus Room, the Bamboo Room, the Orchid Suite, or the Pool House.

Address: 156 Lihau St, Kapaa, HI 96746
Tel: (808) 822-6966, (800) 262-4652.
E-mail: alohabb@aloha.net **Web:** http://www.aloha.net/~alohabb

Type: Bed & breakfast.
Clientele: Gay & lesbian. Good mix of men & women.
Transportation: Car is best.
To Gay Bars: 5 miles or a 5-minute drive.
Rooms: 4 rooms with single, queen or king beds.
Baths: Private & shared.
Meals: Full breakfast.
Vegetarian: Available upon request.
Complimentary: Sunset refreshments (cocktails, sodas, etc.).
Dates Open: All year.
Rates: $65-$90.
Rsv'tns: Required.
Reserve Thru: Travel agent or call direct.
Parking: Ample off-street parking.
In-Room: Color cable TV, VCR, ceiling fans, maid service.
On-Premises: Meeting rooms, TV lounge.
Exercise/Health: Nearby gym with weights, Jacuzzi, sauna, steam, massage.
Swimming: Pool on premises. Nearby pool, ocean, river.
Sunbathing: At poolside, on patio & at beach.
Nudity: At poolside.
Smoking: Permitted on patios & other outside areas.
Pets: Not permitted.
Handicap Access: Yes.
Children: No.
Languages: English.
Your Hosts: Dan & Charlie.
IGLTA

Anuenue Plantation B & B and Cottage

WWW Gay/Lesbian ♂
Gay-Owned & -Operated

Your Rainbow Plantation

Above Kauai's Coconut Coast and midway between awesome Waimea Canyon and the famous Na Pali Coast, is *Anuenue Plantation*. In the quiet of this modern estate, surrounded by ocean and mountain views, you'll relax while watching the ever-changing rainbows, clouds, waterfalls, sunsets and stars. Explore surrounding beaches, jungle trails, galleries, restaurants, gardens and shops. Mornings, you will be treated to a buffet tropical breakfast. At the end of the day, visit on the lanais and, occasionally, there are dances, concerts and seminars on-site in the ballroom.

Mail To: PO Box 226, Kapaa, HI 96746-0226
Tel: (808) 823-8335, toll-free (888) 371-7716, **Fax:** (808) 821-0390.
E-mail: BnB@anuenue.com **Web:** http://www.anuenue.com

Type: Bed & breakfast & 3-room cottage.
Clientele: Mostly men with women welcome
Transportation: Car rental necessary.
Rooms: 3 rooms & 1 cottage; each with private bath, king or queen bed.
Baths: 3 private bath/shower/toilet, 1 private shower/toilet.
Meals: Buffet tropical breakfast.
Vegetarian: Vegetarian breakfast served, also available island-wide.
Dates Open: All year.
Rates: $70-$95.
Discounts: 10% weekly.
Rsv'tns: Required.
Reserve Thru: Travel agent or call direct.
Parking: Ample off-street parking.
In-Room: Telephone, ceiling fans. Cottage has full kitchen & laundry.
On-Premises: TV lounge, DVD films.
Exercise/Health: Weights, massage, sauna, hot tub.
Swimming: Nearby pool (at Princeville Spa), ocean.
Sunbathing: At beach, in gardens.
Nudity: At nearby beach.
Smoking: Permitted outdoors only.
Pets: Not permitted.
Handicap Access: No.
Children: No.
Languages: English.
Your Hosts: Fred & Harry.

Hale Kahawai

Don't Settle for Straight Imitations!

Across Kuamoo Road from Opaekaa Falls, *Hale Kahawai* overlooks the Wailua River gorge, near one of Kauai's largest sacred temples. A serene garden surrounds the guestrooms and studio, with cable TV, bath, kitchenettte and ceiling fans. Enjoy tropical breakfasts in the dining lounge or on the lanai, overlooking the bamboo-shaded sun deck, koi and waterlily pond, and Mounts Waialeale and Kawaikini. Evenings, relax in the garden hot tub, illuminated by Tiki torches. Outdoor activities include helicopter tours, horseback riding, golf and snorkeling. Secluded beaches, fine dining and shopping are close by.

Address: 185 Kahawai Place, Kapaa, HI 96746
Tel: (808) 822-1031, **Fax:** (808) 823-8220.
E-mail: BandBKauai@aol.com **Web:** http://members.aol.com/BandBKauai

Type: Bed & breakfast.
Clientele: Gay & lesbian. Good mix of men & women
Transportation: Rental car from airport.
To Gay Bars: 5 mi, 10 min drive.
Rooms: 3 rooms, 1 apt w/ queen or king beds.
Baths: 2 private, 2 shared bath/shower/toilets.
Meals: Expanded continental breakfast.

Vegetarian: On request.
Complimentary: Tea, coffee, juice.
Dates Open: All year.
High Season: Dec-Mar.
Rates: Rooms $60-$80, Apt. $90. Plus 10% tax.
Discounts: On stays of 7 nights or longer.
Rsv'tns: Required.
Reserve Thru: Travel agent or call direct.
Min. Stay: 2 nights.

Parking: Ample free off-street parking.
In-Room: Apt: kitchen, coffee & tea-making facilities, color cable TV, refrigerator. All rooms have ceiling fans.
On-Premises: TV lounge & video tape library.
Exercise/Health: Jacuzzi, massage. Nearby gym.
Swimming: Nearby ocean & river.

Sunbathing: On private sun decks, at beach.
Smoking: Permitted on lanai or in garden.
Pets: Not permitted.
Handicap Access: No.
Children: No.
Languages: English.
Your Hosts: Arthur & Thomas.

Ku'oko'a at Plumeria Moon

"Dreams Really Do Come True"

Imagine your own Hawaiian hideaway, nestled on a bluff overlooking the Pacific Ocean. Tranquility surrounds you on three acres of tropical flowers, fruit trees and lava rock gardens. *Ku' oko' a*, the Garden Island's treasure, is a meticulously maintained, comfortable, one-bedroom cottage, decorated in a tropical decor. Perfect for romance, this Hawaiian hideaway comes completely furnished and features an outdoor Jacuzzi and shower overlooking the ocean. A private path leads you to one of the most secluded beaches on the island.

Mail To: PO Box 385, Kauai, Kilauea, HI 96754
Tel: (808) 828-0228 (Tel/Fax), (888) 8-KUOKOA (586562).
E-mail: kuokoa@gte.net **Web:** http://home1.gte.net/kuokoa

Type: Cottage.
Clientele: 25% gay & lesbian & 75% straight
Transportation: Car is best.
To Gay Bars: 12 miles.
Rooms: 1 bedroom with queen bed.
Baths: Private. Outdoor shower.
Vegetarian: Restaurants, food stores nearby.
Complimentary: Fresh fruit & flowers, Hawaiian coffee,

condiments.
Rates: $1700/wk, $250/day. Ask about "specials."
Discounts: To educators, community college staff members.
Rsv'tns: Required.
Reserve Thru: Call direct or e-mail.
Min. Stay: 4 days.
Parking: Ample parking beside cottage.
In-Room: Telephone, ceiling fans, color satellite

TVs, VCR, full kitchen, stereo, video tape & CD/ cassette library, cleaning service available.
On-Premises: Entry gate, security system, laundry facilities, BBQ grill.
Exercise/Health: Weights, thigh & ab equip., cadio-glide, Jacuzzi, massage. Nearby gym, weights, Jacuzzi, sauna, steam, massage, golf, tennis, horse ride, kayak, snorkel, scuba

dive.
Swimming: Pool. Nearby ocean, river, pool.
Sunbathing: Poolside, on patio, beach, private deck, 3 acres.
Nudity: Permitted.
Smoking: Permitted outdoors only.
Pets: Not permitted.
Children: Teenager okay.
Languages: English.

Pali Kai

Gay/Lesbian ♂♀

Where Mountains Greet the Sea

Kauai's spectacular North Shore surrounds you at *Pali Kai,* on a hilltop with panoramic views of mountains, the Kalihiwai valley and the ocean. All bedrooms in this beautiful home have queen beds, private baths, TV/VCR, literature about the island, and sweeping ocean views. An inviting hot tub and swimming pool which overlook the ocean are also available for your relaxation. A luxurious lawn and lush gardens surround the house and a private hiking trail leads to the Kalihiwai River and beach. Swimming and snorkeling beaches, hiking trails and rivers for kayaking are nearby.

Address: Kilauea **Mail To:** PO Box 450, Kauai, Kilauea, HI 96754
Tel: (808) 828-6691, toll-free: (800) 335-6968.
E-mail: palikai@aloha.net **Web:** http://www.palikai.com

Type: Bed & breakfast.
Clientele: Gay & lesbian. Good mix of men & women
Transportation: Car is essential, rent at airport.
To Gay Bars: 20 minutes by car.
Rooms: 1-bdrm suite, studio, cottage.
Baths: All private.

Meals: Self-catering island-style breakfast.
Dates Open: All year.
Rates: Start at $80.
Rsv'tns: Required.
Reserve Thru: Travel agent or call direct.
Parking: Ample off-street parking.
In-Room: Telephone, TV,

VCR, CD/cassette player, refrigerator, microwave, ceiling fan, coffee/tea-making facilities & maid service.
On-Premises: BBQ.
Exercise/Health: Hot tub on premises. Jogging path to river & beach. Spa, tennis & golf nearby.

Swimming: In pool on premises & at nearby ocean beaches.
Sunbathing: At beach & in front yard.
Nudity: In hot tub & at some nearby beaches.
Smoking: Permitted outdoors only.
Languages: English.

Royal Drive Cottages

WWW Gay-Lesbian ♂♀
Gay Man- & Lesbian-Owned & -Operated

An Enchanted Tropical Hideaway

Centrally located on the gorgeous island of Kauai, nestled in the lush green hills of Wailua, down a private road, is our tropical hideaway. Three separate units at *Royal Drive Cottages* open onto lovely gardens and are surrounded by spectacular mountains. A brief walk finds you at the hiking trail to Sleeping Giant Mountain and its glorious vistas. A five-minute drive takes you to local beaches or to a generous sampling of shops and restaurants. As a recent visitor noted in the guest book, "Such a wonderful place to rest and heal from life's realities."

Address: 147 Royal Drive, Kauai, Wailua, HI 96746
Tel: (808) 822-2321, **Fax:** (808) 822-3528.
E-mail: sand@aloha.net **Web:** http://www.royaldrive.com

Type: 2 private cottages & 1-BR house.
Clientele: Mainly gay/lesbian with some straight clientele
Transportation: Car essential, discount Avis rentals thru host.
To Gay Bars: 10 min drive.
Rooms: 2 cottages with king or twin beds, 1-BR house with 2 baths.
Baths: All private.
Meals: Near restaurants.

Vegetarian: Healthfood store, farmers' markets.
Complimentary: Concierge svc, snorkeling & beach gear. Tropical fruit trees for guests' picking in season.
Dates Open: All year.
Rates: Cottages: $80; House $120.
Rsv'tns: Suggested.
Reserve Thru: Travel agent, call, e-mail direct.
Parking: Ample free off-street parking.

In-Room: Well-equipped kitchenette in cottages, phone, TV, VCR, fans. 1-BR house: living & dining rooms, private lanai.
On-Premises: Laundry facilities, BBQs.
Exercise/Health: Massage on premises. Nearby gym, hiking, tennis, golf, beach & river water activities.
Swimming: Ocean, river nearby, gay nude beach 15 min.

Sunbathing: On sun deck, lawn, beaches.
Nudity: On sun deck & some beaches.
Smoking: Permitted outdoors.
Pets: Not permitted.
Handicap Access: 3 stairs up to one cottage, 1 step to the other cottage & house.
Languages: English.
Your Hosts: Sandy & Bob.

Cliff's Edge Oceanfront Estate, The

www Gay-Friendly 50/50 ⚥

Private, Private, Private...

The Cliff's Edge Oceanfront Estate is just that. This two-acre estate, perched at the edge of a 300-foot cliff overlooking Waipio Bay, is situated in the middle of the Pacific Ocean; at the end of the road; at the edge of a cliff; at the end of the world. Accommodations offer spectacular views of the turquoise bay, surrounding lava cliffs and Maui's dormant volcano, Haleakala. Relax, read, romanticize and realize that you have found paradise. Let the waves crashing against the rocks below sing you to sleep at night. Visit the natural pools of Twin Falls, just minutes away, or watch the whales and dolphins from your private hot tub just feet from the cliff's edge. We are only 30 minutes from the airport, yet close to natural pools and waterfalls. Perfect for private getaways or secret rendezvous. Private, Private, Private...

Address: Maui's North Shore, Huelo, HI
Tel: (808) 572-4530.
E-mail: clifedge@maui.net **Web:** http://www.cliffsedge.com

Type: Bed & breakfast cottage.
Clientele: 50% gay & lesbian & 50% straight clientele
Transportation: Car is best.
To Gay Bars: 20 miles.
Rooms: 2 rooms, 1 cottage with double, queen or king beds.
Baths: Private: 3 bath/

shower/toilets, 3 shower/ toilets.
Meals: Continental breakfast.
Dates Open: All year.
Rates: $125-$250.
Discounts: Weekly.
Rsv'tns: Required.
Reserve Thru: Travel agent or call direct.
Min. Stay: Required.
Parking: Ample, free

parking.
In-Room: Telephone, ceiling fans, color cable TV, VCR, kitchen, refrigerator, coffee & tea-making facilities, laundry service.
On-Premises: Laundry facilities.
Exercise/Health: Jacuzzi. Nearby massage.
Swimming: Pool. Nearby ocean, river & natural pools.

Sunbathing: Poolside, on private sun decks & patio.
Nudity: Permitted.
Smoking: All rooms & cottage are non-smoking. Permitted outside.
Pets: Not permitted.
Handicap Access: No.
Children: No.
Languages: English, German.

Color Photo on Page 21

MAUI • HAWAII

Hale Huelo

Gay-Friendly 50/50 ⚥
Gay-Owned

Azure Ocean, Misty Volcano, Verdant Rainforest — Heavenly Hale Huelo

To enter *Hale Huelo* is to truly surround yourself in "Maui Time." The magnificent vistas of craggy volcano and blue Pacific excite the senses, yet somehow soothe the mind. Unwinding is our specialty! Whether swimming in the main pool or relaxing in the secluded hot tub, the tensions of the world seem to drift off into the rainforest below, often startling the rosy cheek parrots living there to take to the air. Our very private and quiet setting is situated in a tropical rainforest valley. Here at *Hale Huelo* you will find beautiful white water, as well as panoramic ocean and thrilling volcano views. There is even whale watching from the house. The dark, starry nights are ideal for stargazing.

A variety of activities and sights are nearby, including swimming at white sand beaches and natural waterfall ponds, surfing, wind surfing, snorkeling and scuba diving. Also nearby are opportunities for both personal and commercial island tours, geological explorations and whale watching boat tours. The local plantation villages offer antiques, Hawaiian crafts and art for sale. Dine at great restaurants and enjoy the local nightlife. Indulge yourself in this special place in the Hawaiian jungle paradise.

Address: Haiku **Mail To:** PO Box 1237, Haiku, HI 96708
Tel: (808) 572-8669, **Fax:** (808) 573-8403.
E-mail: halehuel@maui.net

Type: Bed & breakfast.
Clientele: 50% gay & lesbian & 50% straight
Transportation: Car. Pick up from airport $20.
To Gay Bars: 25 miles.
Rooms: 3 rooms with queen beds.
Baths: All private.
Meals: Expanded continental breakfast.

High Season: Nov-Mar.
Rates: Summer $110; Winter $125; Whole house $2400/week all year.
Discounts: 7+ days 10%.
Rsv'tns: Required.
Reserve Thru: Travel agent or call direct.
Min. Stay: 2 nights.
Parking: Ample, free off-street parking.

In-Room: Ceiling fans, color TV, VCR, tea & coffee-maker, fridge, micro.
On-Premises: Phone, fax, IBM computer, book & video tape libraries, laundry.
Exercise/Health: Jacuzzi, massage. Nearby gym, weights, massage.
Swimming: Pool. River, ocean nearby.

Sunbathing: Poolside, on patio, common sun decks, at beach.
Nudity: Permitted with discretion at pool, on decks & in Jacuzzi.
Smoking: Outside only.
Pets: Not permitted.
Children: No.
Your Hosts: Doug.

Huelo Point Flower Farm

A Romantic & Magical Oceanfront Hideaway

Imagine yourself staying at an exquisitely beautiful, private oceanfront estate tucked away from the crowds in a lush, tropical valley, reminiscent of old Hawaii. Perched at the edge of a 300-foot sea cliff, this magical North Shore Maui hideaway offers spectacular views of crashing surf, plus dolphins and whales, in Waipio Bay. *Huelo Point Flower Farm Vacation Rent-*

als' elegant and tasteful accommodations range from the studio Gazebo Cottage to the 1-bedroom plus den Carriage House, the 2-bedroom Guest House, or the 3-bedroom plus den Main House. You can take a swim in the 50-foot pool with waterfall, take a dip in one of three hot tubs, or pick organic fruits and vegetables right from the gardens. We have been warmly welcoming

guests here for more than 10 years, and were pleased to be named by *Travel and Leisure* magazine as one of "Hawaii's Top Ten." Aloha!

Address: Paia **Mail To:** PO Box 1195, Maui, Paia, HI 96779
Tel: (808) 572-1850.
E-mail: huelopt@maui.net **Web:** http://www.mauiflowerfarm.com

Type: Vacation rental homes & cottage.
Clientele: 50% gay & lesbian & 50% straight clientele
Transportation: Rental car, 1/2 hour from airport.
To Gay Bars: 45 min drive, in Kihei.
Rooms: Main house for 8: 1 king, 2 queens, 1 double; Cottage for 2: 1 queen; Carriage house for 6: 2 queens, 1 double; Guest house for 4: 1 king, 1 double.
Baths: All private.

Complimentary: Tea, coffee, farm-fresh fruits & vegetables.
Dates Open: All year.
High Season: Dec 15-Jan 15, rates 25% higher.
Rates: Cottage $135/night, Carriage House $150/night. Guest House $275/night, Main House $350/night. All rates dbl. occ. + tax & extra person charges.
Discounts: Weekly discount.
Rsv'tns: Required. Walkins welcome if space is available.

Reserve Thru: Call direct.
Min. Stay: 2 days.
Parking: Ample off-street parking on gated estate.
In-Room: Private phones, color TV/VCR, stero receiver, CD player, kitchen, refrigerator, hair dryers.
On-Premises: Laundry facilities.
Exercise/Health: 3 hot tubs, massage.
Swimming: Pool on premises. 20 min drive to ocean beach. 10 min drive to waterfalls & natural pools.
Sunbathing: At poolside &

on the patio.
Nudity: Permitted on private patios.
Smoking: Permitted.
Pets: Cats & dog on premises.
Handicap Access: Minimal.
Children: Small children could be a problem because of 300 foot cliff.
Languages: English, French, & Russian.
Your Hosts: Guy & Doug.

Iao Valley Gardens

WWW Gay/Lesbian ♀♂
Gay-Owned & -Operated

This is Maui ~ Iao Valley ~ Heaven on Earth

Iao Valley Gardens — a million-dollar house, three private suites with their own separate entrances, and a fabulous garden-cottage deep in the heart of Iao (ee-ow) Valley — "The most spectacular valley in all of Hawaii." Many of the most famous events in Hawaiian history took place in Iao Valley — and it still retains the majesty and mystery which have drawn people here through the centuries. Soaring up to virtually 6,000 feet, the near-vertical valley walls are covered with lush vegetation — pale-leaved "Kukui" trees, orange-bloomed "African Tulips," mango and guava trees in a riot of green and yellow — and through it all runs the Iao River, patient architect of its beautiful surroundings.

Iao Valley is wonderfully convenient, too. Quiet and private, yet only 15 minutes from the airport, shopping malls and beautiful beaches. There are nearby award-winning restaurants, fantastic scenic drives, a huge variety of sea-sports and (in season) spectacular hump-back whale watching trips, too. We're 45 minutes from Lahaina and Hana, at the other end of the island, is a spectacular two-hour drive along the Hana Highway. The crater rim of mighty Haleakala (the world's largest dormant volcano) is a 1-1/2 hour drive.

Address: 585, Iao Valley Road, Wailuku, HI 96793
Tel: (808) 242-8760, (888) 558-8760, **Fax:** (808) 242-2886.
E-mail: iao2000@maui.net **Web:** http://www.ThisisMaui.com

Type: Guesthouse.
Clientele: Mostly gay & lesbian with some straight clientele
Transportation: Car is best.
To Gay Bars: 20 min drive.
Rooms: 3 suites, 1 cottage, 1 deluxe house with queen or king beds.
Baths: Private: 1 bath/shower/toilet, 3 shower/toilets.
Vegetarian: Vegetarian

restaurant nearby.
Complimentary: Tea, coffee in rooms.
Dates Open: All year.
High Season: Same all year.
Rates: $55-$260.
Discounts: Long-stay discounts can be discussed.
Credit Cards: MC, Visa.
Rsv'tns: Required.
Reserve Thru: Travel agent or call direct.
Min. Stay: 2 nights.

Parking: Ample off-street parking.
In-Room: Telephone, ceiling fans, color cable TV, VCR, kitchen, refrigerator, coffee & tea-making facilities.
On-Premises: TV lounge, laundry facilities.
Exercise/Health: Jacuzzi. Nearby gym, weights, massage.
Swimming: Ocean nearby.
Sunbathing: On private &

common sun decks, beach.
Nudity: Permitted in/near outdoor shared hot tub.
Smoking: Permitted outside.
Pets: Not permitted.
Handicap Access: Yes, wide doors, ramps, rails in bathroom.
Children: No.
Languages: English.
Your Hosts: John, Gary.

Jack & Tom's Maui Condos

Tropical Sun, Sandy Beaches, Gentle Trade Winds...
Maui No Ka Oi (is the best)

Explore the island, play a little tennis, relax by the pools or enjoy the sand and surf of the finest beaches on Maui, including the nude beach at Makena (only minutes away). At the end of your day, return to your private one- or two-bedroom condominium to freshen up for a night out. Or, if you prefer, prepare dinner in your own fully-equipped kitchen and enjoy a quiet

evening at home. All units at *Jack & Tom's Maui Condos* have either ocean or garden views, are clean, comfortable and are equipped to make you want to stay a lifetime.

For those who wish the privacy of their own cottage, come stay with us at the Pualani Island Cottage here in sunny Kihei. All the convenience of the above, plus the use of our very private back

yard and 20X40 pool. Still just minutes from the beaches of Kihei or Little Beach, but with the privacy for nude swimming and sun bathing just outside your back door. Contact Jack or Tom for more information on any of the properties, or visit our website.

Address: Maui Suncoast Realty, 3134 Hoomua Drive, Kihei, HI 96753-9443
Tel: (800) 800-8608, (808) 874-1048, **Fax:** (808) 879-6932.
E-mail: mauijack@aol.com **Web:** http://www.mauisuncoast.com

Type: Private condominiums within larger complexes & private cottage.
Clientele: Mostly straight clientele with a gay & lesbian following
Transportation: Car is a must on Maui. We can arrange car rental.
To Gay Bars: 5 miles.
Rooms: 45 condos with queen or king beds & private

cottage.
Baths: All private.
Dates Open: All year.
High Season: Dec 15-Apr 15.
Rates: Summer $45-$125, winter $45-$165.
Rsv'tns: Required.
Reserve Thru: Travel agent or call direct.
Min. Stay: 4 days.
Parking: Ample off-street

parking.
In-Room: Color cable TV, AC, ceiling fans, telephone, kitchen & laundry facilities. Most units have VCRs, stereos.
Exercise/Health: Nearby gym.
Swimming: Pool on premises. Ocean beach across the street.
Sunbathing: At poolside or

on the beach.
Nudity: Permitted at cottage pool.
Smoking: Permitted. Non-smoking units available.
Pets: Not permitted.
Handicap Access: Yes.
Languages: English.
Your Hosts: Jack & Tom.

Kailua Maui Gardens

WWW Gay-Friendly 50/50 ♀♂

"A Lush & Lovely Resort" ~ Out & About Award Winner '99

Kailua Maui Gardens is a two-acre, private estate located at the start of the most picturesque section of Maui's Hana Highway — "one of the most beautiful drives in the world." Enchanting pathways and bridges wind through two acres of fabulous gardens — "possibly the best private gardens on the island." The gardens sit at the edge of Maui's vast rainforest and, within this lush, tropical tapestry sit our well-appointed accommodations — most of which have ocean views. Our guests have discovered the "real" Hawaii.

We have four romantic and secluded cottages, an impressive three-bedroom house and an additional garden apartment — altogether providing extensive facilities for up to eighteen guests. All (except the garden apartment) have vaulted wooden ceilings with fans, large picture windows, and all have private bathrooms — some even have outside showers for that special, tropical feel! A shared swimming pool provides recreation by day and our fabulous garden spa, surrounded by stands of exotic helliconia and scented, yellow ginger encourages lazy star-gazing by night.

A great base for day excursions, too — like to the famous Hana Highway, hugging the coastline like a roller coaster; or the huge Haleakala volcano with its crater hikes and fantastic views; or browse the art galleries of Lahaina for a special memento of your trip. Maui is a fantastic island and we're sure you'll agree that *Kailua Maui Gardens* is THE place to enjoy it!

Address: SR 1 Box 9 (Hana Hwy), Maui, Haiku, HI 96708
Tel: (800) 258-8588, (808) 572-9726, **Fax:** (808) 572-5934.
E-mail: kmg@maui.net **Web:** http://www.ThisisMaui.com

Type: Studios, cottages & house rentals.
Clientele: 50% gay & lesbian & 50% straight
Transportation: Rental car. $30 airport pickup.
To Gay Bars: 40 min.
Rooms: 4 cottages, 1 3-BR house, 1 1-BR apt w/ queen or king beds.
Baths: All private.
Vegetarian: With prior

notice.
Complimentary: Fresh fruit, tea, coffee & tropical flowers from estate gardens.
High Season: June-Sept & Dec-Mar.
Rates: $65-$200 plus tax.
Discounts: 4+ days.
Credit Cards: Visa, MC.
Rsv'tns: Required.
Reserve Thru: Travel agent or call direct.

Min. Stay: 2 nights.
Parking: Ample, free off-street parking.
In-Room: Color TV, VCR, stereo/CD player, kitchen, phone, ceiling fans.
On-Premises: 2 BBQs, covered lanais.
Exercise/Health: Private & garden spas.
Swimming: Pool. Beach 8 mi, natural pools, waterfall 1/

4 mi.
Sunbathing: Poolside, on private patios.
Nudity: Permitted in pool area & around spas.
Smoking: Outdoors.
Handicap Access: Main house is accessible.
Children: Over 12+ years.
Your Hosts: Tom, Marty & John.

IGLTA

Anfora's Dreams

Maui Condos with Your Lifestyle in Mind

Like a jewel piercing the Pacific Ocean, lush, tropical Maui and her magnificent volcanoes rise out of the sea to warmly caress your soul. *Anfora's Dreams*, with both one- and two-bedroom condos, are located in sunny Kihei. Both ocean and park are just across the road. Units are completely furnished in deluxe style, with total comfort in mind, and rooms have beach or ocean views. Take a walk along the beach or a refreshing dip in the pool or Jacuzzi. Here, on Maui, you will learn the true meaning of "Maui No Ka Oi." Maui is the best!

Mail To: Attn: Dale Jones, PO Box 74030, Los Angeles, CA 90004
Tel: (323) 467-2991, Reservations: (800) 788-5046, **Fax:** (323) 461-8467.
E-mail: mauicondo@earthlink.net **Web:** http://home.earthlink.net/ ~mauicondo/

Type: Condo.
Clientele: 50% gay & lesbian & 50% straight clientele.
Transportation: Car is best.
To Gay Bars: 15 miles or 20 minutes by car.
Rooms: Singles to suites with queen beds.
Baths: All private bath/ toilets.
Vegetarian: Complete kitchens in condos.
Dates Open: All year.
High Season: Nov 15-Feb 15.
Rates: $79-$139.
Credit Cards: MC, Visa.
Rsv'tns: Required, but can do spot bookings on available basis.
Reserve Thru: Call direct or travel agent.
Min. Stay: 4 nights.
Parking: Ample free off-street parking. Assigned space with guest spaces available.
In-Room: Color cable TV, telephone, kitchen, ceiling fans, coffee & tea-making facilities. Some with AC.
On-Premises: Laundry facilities. 2-bedroom, 2-bath has washer/dryer in unit.
Exercise/Health: Jacuzzi, nearby gym.
Swimming: Pool on premises, ocean across the road.
Sunbathing: At poolside, on patio & nearby beach.
Nudity: Nude beach 10 minutes away.
Smoking: Permitted.
Pets: Not permitted on Maui.
Handicap Access: Yes.
Children: We welcome all guests with open arms.
Languages: English.

A Tropic Paradise

WWW Gay-Friendly 50/50 ♀♂
Gay-Owned

The Heart of Aloha

We look forward to hosting your stay in what we feel is one of this Earth's most serene and beautiful places. *A Tropic Paradise,* our elegant Hawaiian home in the friendly town of Kailua, has large, beautiful rooms with private baths, in-room refrigerator, television and cable. A waterfall whispers beside the tropical pool and spa, and the island's most beautiful beach is steps from your home. We provide beach mats, towels and coolers for guests to use when touring the area's many grottos and waterfalls. Walk our beach at sunrise, or on a moonlit night and touch the Soul of Aloha. Whether it's shopping, Oahu's nightlife, a luau, or Hawaii's thrilling water sports, it's all here for you.

Address: 43 Laiki Place, Kailua, HI
Tel: (808) 261-2299, (888) 362-4488, **Fax:** (808) 263-0795.
E-mail: darreld@gte.net **Web:** http://home1.gte.net/darreld/gay.htm

Type: Bed & breakfast vacation homes.
Clientele: 50% gay & lesbian & 50% straight clientele
Transportation: Car is best. Airport pick up $20.
To Gay Bars: 8 miles, a 20 min drive.
Rooms: 5 rooms, 1 suite, 1 apartment, 2- & 3-BR home with single, queen or king beds.
Baths: 4 private & 4 shared bath/shower/toilets.

Meals: Expanded continental breakfast.
Vegetarian: Available as requested.
Complimentary: Tea & coffee.
Dates Open: All year.
Rates: B&B rooms $70-$85, weekly rates available. Suites $125-$250/day. 2-3BR homes $200-$400.
Discounts: Weekly & monthly rates available.
Rsv'tns: Required.
Reserve Thru: Call direct.

Min. Stay: 3 days.
Parking: Ample free off-street parking.
In-Room: Fans, color cable TV, refrigerator, maid service.
On-Premises: TV lounge, laundry facilities.
Exercise/Health: Jacuzzi, massage. Nearby gym, weights, Jacuzzi, sauna, steam, massage.
Swimming: Pool & ocean on premises.
Sunbathing: Poolside, on

patio & at beach.
Smoking: Non-smoking home. Permitted in outdoor smoking area.
Pets: Not permitted.
Handicap Access: Yes, ramps.
Children: Welcome. Pool toys for children with parental supervision.
Languages: English, Spanish.
Your Hosts: Ken & Alex.

Cabana at Waikiki, The

WWW Gay/Lesbian ♂
Gay-Owned & -Operated

Waikiki's Hot Gay Getaway

Sun-drenched beaches... towering palm trees... blue skies and beautiful bronzed bodies as far as the eye can see... welcome to *The Cabana at Waikiki!* Friendly and exclusively gay, this is "the gay place to stay" in Waikiki. Located off the beaten path yet close to it all, this four-story, fifteen-unit upscale property is perfectly situated on Cartwright Street (a quiet respite off Kapahulu Avenue), one block from world-famous Waikiki Beach. Suites feature custom furniture, queen-sized bed and pull-out sofa, entertainment center with TV, VCR, stereo with CD player, equipped kitchen, and individual private lanai.

Bathed in sun and drenched by Hawaii's clear, blue skies, we're just a short stroll from Queen's Surf Beach, Waikiki's gay beach. Other local and tantalizing treats include Kapiolani Park, Hula's Bar, a gym, unique shops and the best restaurants in Waikiki. Such tropical delights make this the ideal choice for your next vacation. Honolulu's proximity to the neighbor islands of Maui, Kaua'i, Moloka'i, and The Big Island make us part of the perfect island-hopping vacation. And since Waikiki is the "gay crossroads of the Pacific," we're an ideal stop-over for the Asia-bound traveller, or for a long weekend in the sun with the "in" crowd.

Address: 2551 Cartwright Rd, Honolulu, HI 96815
Tel: (808) 926-5555, toll-free: (877) 902-2121, **Fax:** (808) 926-5566.
E-mail: infocabana@cabana-waikiki.com **Web:** http://www.cabana-waikiki.com

Type: Guesthouse.
Clientele: Mostly men with women welcome
Transportation: Rental car or taxi from airport.
To Gay Bars: 1 block.
Rooms: 15 suites with queen & queen sofa beds.
Baths: All private.
Meals: Expanded continental breakfast.

Complimentary: Bi-weekly Mai Tai parties.
Dates Open: All year.
Rates: $99-$175 per night.
Credit Cards: MC, Visa, Amex.
Rsv'tns: Recommended.
Reserve Thru: Travel agent or call direct.
Parking: Adequate covered off-street pay parking.

In-Room: Phone, AC, ceiling fans, color cable TV, VCR, stereo w/ CD, kitchen, fridge, coffee & tea makers, maid svc.
On-Premises: Laundry facilities.
Exercise/Health: Jacuzzi. Nearby gym, weights, sauna, steam, massage.
Swimming: Ocean nearby.

Sunbathing: At beach.
Smoking: Permitted on each private lanai.
Pets: Not permitted.
Children: No.
Languages: English, Chinese.
IGLTA

Color Photo on Page 22

Little House On The Prairie, The

WWW Gay-Friendly ⚥

Home of the Stars

The **Little House On The Prairie** is a Queen Anne Victorian homestead surrounded by acres of woodlands, gardens, swimming pool and pond. "It is a showpiece of a home, full of turn-of-the-century Victorian antiques, wooden parquet floors and theater memorabilia...and it is anything but little." (Mike Monson, *Champaign-Urbana News-Gazette*) Guests at **The Little House On The Prairie** have included many stars who performed at the The Little Theatre On The Square in Sullivan druing the 60s, 70s and 80s. It is in the heart of Amish country, yet only 3 hours from Chicago and 2 hours from St. Louis.

Address: Sullivan **Mail To:** PO Box 525, Sullivan, IL 61951
Tel: (217) 728-4727.
E-mail: gsljr@juno.com **Web:** http://www.bbonline.com/il/littlehouse/

Type: Bed & breakfast.
Clientele: Mostly straight clientele with a gay & lesbian following
Transportation: Car is best.
To Gay Bars: 60 miles to Champaign, IL.
Rooms: 4 rooms with single, double & queen beds. 1-BR suite with king bed.
Baths: 3 private shower/

toilets, 2 private bath/shower/toilets.
Meals: Full breakfast.
Vegetarian: Available if asked for in advance.
Complimentary: Wine, tea, cheese, crackers & fruit.
Dates Open: April 1-Jan 1.
High Season: Jun-Aug.
Rates: $55-$125.
Rsv'tns: Required.
Reserve Thru: Call direct.
Parking: Ample free

parking.
In-Room: AC, maid service & video tape library. 2 rooms with color TV & VCR. Fireplace in suite.
On-Premises: Meeting rooms & TV lounge.
Exercise/Health: Jacuzzi in suite & sunroom. Nearby gym, weights, sauna & massage.
Swimming: Pool on premises. Nearby lake.

Sunbathing: At poolside.
Nudity: Permitted in the wooded area.
Smoking: Permitted in sun room & outdoor areas.
Pets: Not permitted.
Handicap Access: No.
Children: Not especially welcome.
Languages: English, French & Italian.
Your Hosts: Guy & Kirk.

Flemish House of Chicago

WWW Gay-Friendly ⚥
Gay-Owned & -Operated

Flemish House of Chicago offers comfortably furnished studio and one-bedroom apartments in an 1890s greystone rowhouse. As our renovation progresses, we're keeping the best of the old and updating kitchens and baths for modern-day living. Two studio units and one one-bedroom suite are now available. The apartments are available for short-term stays (two-night minimum may apply) or as furnished corporate units (by the week or month). Apartments feature some combination of wood-paneled rooms, fireplaces, in-laid wood floors, high ceilings and decorative moldings. We're in downtown Chicago's Gold Coast neighborhood, minutes from North Michigan Avenue, Water Tower Place, the lakefront and Oak Street Beach.

Address: 68 E. Cedar Street, Chicago, IL 60611
Tel: (312) 664-9981 (Tel/Fax).
E-mail: mmaczka@21stcentury.net

Type: Bed & breakfast, furnished apartments.
Clientele: Mostly straight clientele with a gay/lesbian following
Transportation: Subway or airport van from O'Hare to downtown Chicago.
To Gay Bars: 6 blocks, a 15 min walk, a 5 min drive.
Rooms: 3 apartments with queen beds.
Baths: Private bath/shower/

toilet.
Meals: Continental breakfast.
Complimentary: Apartment kitchen stocked with coffee, tea, milk, juice all day long.
Dates Open: All year.
Rates: $135-$175.
Discounts: On weekly stays.
Credit Cards: MC, Visa, Amex.
Rsv'tns: Required.

Reserve Thru: Travel agent or call direct.
Min. Stay: Required.
Parking: Limited pay parking in nearby lots & garages.
In-Room: Telephone, AC, ceiling fans, color TV, VCR, kitchen, refrigerator, coffee & tea-making facilities.
On-Premises: Laundry facilities.
Exercise/Health: Nearby

gym, weights, Jacuzzi, sauna, steam.
Swimming: Nearby lake.
Smoking: Smoking not permitted on premises. Permitted outdoors only.
Pets: Not permitted.
Handicap Access: No.
Children: No.
Languages: English.
Your Hosts: Mike & Tom.

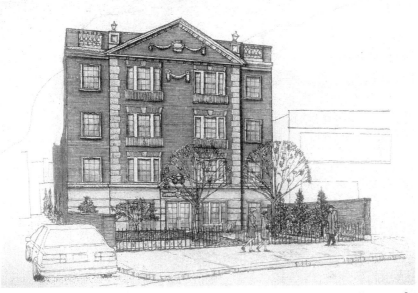

Best Western Hawthorne Terrace

Gay-Friendly 50/50 ⚥

In the tradition of fine old Colonial manors, *Best Western Hawthorne Terrace* offers charming accommodations set in picturesque period architecture, fully restored to modern convenience. Steps away from Lincoln Park and Lake Michigan, *Hawthorne Terrace* is right in the heart of Chicago's gay community, where fine dining, eclectic nightlife, shopping and theatres abound. Wrigley Field, Halsted Street, Lincoln Park Zoo and Chicago's great lakefront beaches are all close by, and it is only ten minutes from downtown along scenic Lake Shore Drive.

Address: 3434 N Broadway, Chicago, IL 60657
Tel: (773) 244-3434, (888) 675-BEST (2378), **Fax:** (773) 244-3435.

Type: Hotel with exercise facility.
Clientele: 50% gay & lesbian & 50% straight clientele
Transportation: Taxi is best.
To Gay Bars: Across the street.
Rooms: 44 rooms, 15 suites with double or queen beds.
Baths: 59 private bath/shower/toilets.
Meals: Continental breakfast.
Vegetarian: Not available

on premises, numerous vegetarian restaurants nearby.
Dates Open: All year.
High Season: May-Oct.
Rates: $119-$149.
Discounts: AAA, AARP, airline, government, corporate (15%) available all year, must mention affiliation at time of reservation to apply.
Credit Cards: MC, Visa, Amex, Diners, Discover.
Rsv'tns: Strongly recommended.
Reserve Thru: Travel agent

or call direct.
Parking: Ample covered, off-street pay parking.
In-Room: 2-line speakerphone with data jack, AC, color satellite TV, modem hookups, refrigerator, microwave, maid & room service.
On-Premises: Laundry facilities, fax (free incoming, charge for outgoing), copier.
Exercise/Health: Jacuzzi, sauna, cardio-vascular exercise equipment. Nearby gym.
Swimming: Pool at nearby

healthclub. Lake nearby.
Sunbathing: On roof & at beach.
Smoking: Permitted, except in non-smoking rooms. Non-smoking rooms available.
Pets: $250 addt'l deposit, small pets in carriers.
Handicap Access: Yes, ramps, CC TVs. Limited wide doors, rails in bathrooms, smoke detectors for the hearing impaired.
Children: Welcome. Under age 12 are free.
Languages: English, Spanish.

City Suites — Neighborhood Inns of Chicago Gay-Friendly ♀♂

City Suites Hotel offers a stunning Art Deco style reminiscent of the fine residential buildings of the 30's and 40's. Located on Chicago's dynamic near north side, close to famous Halsted St., Wrigley Field and the eclectic Sheffield/Belmont area, we're in the heart of Chicago's gay community. Only steps from our door, you'll find the city's finest dining, shopping, theatres and exciting nightlife. The *City Suites* is truly Chicago's best value!

Address: 933 West Belmont, Chicago, IL 60657
Tel: (773) 404-3400, **Fax:** (773) 404-3405. Reservations: (800) CITY-108.

Type: Hotel.
Clientele: Mostly straight, with a gay & lesbian following
Transportation: Taxi. Subways 1/2 block west. Limousine service available.
To Gay Bars: 1 block to gay/lesbian bar.
Rooms: 16 guest rooms & 29 suites.
Baths: All private.

Meals: Continental breakfast.
Vegetarian: Nearby.
Complimentary: Newspaper.
Dates Open: All year.
Rates: $99-$159, rates based on single occupancy & availability.
Discounts: Group.
Credit Cards: MC, Visa, Amex, Discover, Diners.

Rsv'tns: Recommended.
Reserve Thru: Travel agent or call direct.
Parking: Ample, off-street, pay parking.
In-Room: Maid & full room service, 2-line speakerphones with data jack, AC, color cable TV, robe, hairdryer, makeup mirror, honor bar, refrigerator.
Exercise/Health:

Discounted daily rates at nearby health club with gym & weights.
Swimming: Lake Michigan nearby.
Sunbathing: At the lake.
Smoking: No restrictions.
Pets: No pets.
Handicap Access: No.
Children: Permitted.
Languages: English, French, Spanish.

Majestic — Neighborhood Inns of Chicago Gay-Friendly ⚥

French Elegance with the Flair of Chicago Style

The *Majestic* offers a romantic getaway. Steps away from the park and Lake Michigan, and only ten minutes from downtown via scenic Lake Shore Drive, the *Majestic* is located in Chicago's largest gay district, where fine dining, shopping and theatres abound. Wrigley Field, Halsted Street, Lincoln Park Zoo and a beautiful lakefront are nearby.

Address: 528 W Brompton, Chicago, IL 60657
Tel: (773) 404-3499, **Fax:** (773) 404-3495. Reservations: (800) 727-5108.

Type: Inn.
Clientele: Mostly straight clientele with a gay/lesbian following
Transportation: Taxi & public transportation. Private cars available.
To Gay Bars: 1 block to gay/lesbian bars.
Rooms: 23 suites, 31 singles.
Baths: All private.
Meals: Continental breakfast.
Vegetarian: Several restaurants nearby.
Complimentary: Newspaper.
Dates Open: All year.
Rates: $99-$159, based on single occupancy & availability.
Discounts: Group.
Credit Cards: MC, Visa, Amex, Discover, Diners.
Rsv'tns: Recommended.
Reserve Thru: Travel agent or call direct.
Parking: Ample off-street pay parking nearby.
In-Room: Maid & full room service, 2-line speakerphone with data jack, AC, color cable TV, robe, honor bar, hair dryer, makeup mirror.
Exercise/Health: Discounted daily rates at nearby health club with gym & weights.
Swimming: Lake Michigan across the street.
Sunbathing: At the lake, Belmont Rocks.
Smoking: No restrictions.
Pets: No pets.
Handicap Access: No.
Children: Permitted.
Languages: English, French, Spanish.

ILLINOIS · CHICAGO

Old Town Bed & Breakfast

WWW Gay/Lesbian ⚤

Old Town Bed & Breakfast rests in an Art Deco mansion in a leafy Lincoln Park neighborhood adjacent to the Gold Coast, North Michigan Avenue shopping, restaurants, museums, theaters, art galleries, coffeehouses and world-famous boutiques. The neighborhood is a mixture of the hip and the chic. It is highly diverse, relaxed, vibrant and always lively.

There are four suites in the main house. A separate and private guesthouse has three bedrooms, private gardens, roof decks and a playroom. It is just steps away from the main house. The main house has a fifty-foot drawing room with a grand piano and black marble fireplace, a dining room, a chef's kitchen, a gymnasium, a conference room, and a penthouse sitting area. Both the main house and the guesthouse have laundry facilities available to guests. Public transportation is a half block away. Both airports and all five train stations are short rides from us.

Guests can sun and relax in the rooftop gardens whose city views take in a dramatic part of Chicago's skyline, including the Sears Tower and the John Hancock Building.

Address: 1442 N North Park Ave, Chicago, IL 60610
Tel: (312) 440-9268, **Fax:** (312) 440-2378.
Web: htto://www.oldtownbandbchicago.com

Type: Bed & breakfast.
Clientele: Mixed
Transportation: 1/2 block to bus.
To Gay Bars: A short walk.
Rooms: 4 suites, 1 private guesthouse.
Baths: All private.
Meals: Continental

breakfast and snacks at all times.
Vegetarian: Always available.
Complimentary: Coffee, teas, juices, yogurt, popcorn, cookies.
Dates Open: All year.
Rates: $139 to $189.

Discounts: Negotiated.
Credit Cards: MC, Visa, Amex.
Rsv'tns: Required.
Reserve Thru: Call direct.
Parking: Ample.
In-Room: TV, phone.
On-Premises: Sitting rooms, private gardens.

Exercise/Health: Gym.
Sunbathing: Roof, gardens, decks, and walled garden.
Smoking: Not permitted.
Pets: Not permitted.
Handicap Access: No.
Your Hosts: Michael & Elizabeth.

Color Photo on Page 23

Willows — Neighborhood Inns of Chicago
Gay-Friendly ⚥

In the Heart of Chicago's Gay Community

On a quiet, tree-lined street in Lincoln Park, and just 10 minutes from downtown Chicago via scenic Lake Shore Drive, *The Willows* combines atmosphere with accessibility. This intimate, Parisian-style hotel is steps away from Chicago's beautiful lakefront, the park, the zoo, the city's finest restaurants and Chicago's version of the Off-Broadway theatre district. Built in 1920, the *The Willows* offers tastefully appointed rooms and is a truly affordable alternative for discriminating guests who prefer personality and ambiance when choosing lodgings.

Address: 555 W Surf, Chicago, IL 60657
Tel: (773) 528-8400, **Fax:** (773) 528-8483. Reservations: (800) 787-3108.

Type: Hotel.
Clientele: Mainly straight clientele with a gay/lesbian following
Transportation: Taxi & public transportation. Private cars available.
To Gay Bars: 1 block to gay & lesbian bars.
Rooms: 20 singles, 31 doubles & 4 suites.
Baths: All private.
Meals: Continental breakfast.
Vegetarian: Available nearby.
Complimentary: Newspaper.
Dates Open: All year.
Rates: $99-$159, based on single occupancy & availability.
Discounts: Group.
Credit Cards: MC, Visa, Amex, Discover, Diners.
Rsv'tns: Recommended.
Reserve Thru: Travel agent or call direct.
Parking: Ample, off-street pay parking nearby.
In-Room: Color cable TV, AC, 2-line speakerphone with data jack, robe, honor bar, hair dryer, makeup mirror, maid & full room service.
On-Premises: Laundry facilities.
Exercise/Health: Discounted daily rates at nearby health club with gym & weights.
Swimming: Lake Michigan & health club pool nearby.
Sunbathing: At the lake, Belmont Rocks.
Smoking: No restrictions.
Pets: No pets.
Handicap Access: No.
Children: Permitted.
Languages: English, French, Spanish.

La Corsette Maison Inn & The Sister Inn

Gay-Friendly ⚨

Two Historical Properties

La Corsette Maison Inn, a Mission-style mansion built in 1909, is acclaimed by historians as one of the finest examples of Arts and Crafts architecture in the Midwest. The original mission oak woodwork, art nouveau windows, and brass light fixtures highlight the decor. Guest rooms are furnished in French country decor, with goose down comforters and pillows. Enjoy a gourmet dinner in the 4-1/2 star restaurant preceded by a history and tour of the inn. *The Sister Inn*, a 140-year-old Federal-style building, features two luxurious bed chambers, both lavishly furnished and designed with privacy in mind. We're a 25-minute drive from Des Moines.

Address: 629 1st Ave E, Newton, IA 50208
Tel: (515) 792-6833, **Fax:** (515) 792-6597.
Web: http://www.innbook.com/inns/LaCor

Type: Two inns, one with restaurant.
Clientele: Mainly straight clientele with a gay & lesbian following.
Transportation: Car. Free airport pick up.
To Gay Bars: 25 min.
Rooms: 5 doubles, 2 suites with double, queen & king beds.
Baths: All private.

Meals: Full breakfast.
Vegetarian: By prior arrangement.
Complimentary: Tea, coffee, pop & snacks.
Dates Open: All year.
High Season: May-Aug, Dec.
Rates: $70-$185.
Discounts: Corporate discount with corporate number.

Credit Cards: MC, Visa, Amex.
Reserve Thru: Call direct or travel agent.
Min. Stay: Required at certain peak times.
Parking: Ample off-street parking.
In-Room: Ceiling fans, AC, double whirlpools, fireplaces. Phones & color TV upon request.

On-Premises: Meeting rooms & laundry facilities.
Swimming: At nearby pool.
Smoking: Outside only, all rooms non-smoking.
Pets: OK by prior arrangement, but not in rooms.
Children: Permitted by pre-arrangement.
Your Hosts: Kay.

Bed & Breakfast at Sills Inn

Southern Hospitality ~ 10 Minutes from Lexington

Enjoy the ambiance of Southern Hospitality as you step into *Bed & Breakfast at Sills Inn*, a 1911, three-storied restored Victorian inn. The nearly 9000 square feet are highly decorated and filled with Kentucky antiques. The B&B is located in historic downtown Versailles and the hub of activity in the Bluegrass Horse farm region.

You are invited to relax on the wrap-around porch in a wicker swing or rocking chair, or step inside to enjoy a book from the library. Later, when you retire to one of the distinctive guestrooms, each with their own private bath, you may want to enjoy a complimentary snack or newspaper.

The staff at the *Bed & Breakfast at Sills Inn* will be at your beck and call to help with travel plans, restaurant reservations and any other needs. But, don't eat too much — you will definitely want to save room for the full gourmet breakfast served on fine china, crystal and linen in the Sun Porch Breakfast Room. We're a short drive from Pleasant Hill (Shakertown), the Kentucky state capital, Keeneland Race Course, Kentucky Horse Park and antiquing.

Address: 270 Montgomery Ave, Versailles, Lexington, KY 40383
Tel: (606) 873-4478, (800) 526-9801, **Fax:** (606) 873-7099.
E-mail: sillsinn@aol.com **Web:** http://www.SillsInn.com

Type: Bed & breakfast inn.
Clientele: Mostly straight clientele with a gay/lesbian following
Transportation: Car is best. Free pick up from airport or bus.
To Gay Bars: 10 min drive.
Rooms: 3 rooms, 9 suites with queen or king beds.
Baths: 12 private bath/shower/toilets.
Meals: Full breakfast.
Vegetarian: Breakfast

made to order. 10 mins to vegetarian restaurant.
Complimentary: Turndown service, soda, coffee, tea, popcorn, chocolate chip cookies.
Dates Open: All year.
High Season: Mar-Oct.
Rates: $89-$179.
Discounts: AAA discount.
Credit Cards: MC, Visa, Amex, Diners, Discover.
Rsv'tns: Required.
Reserve Thru: Travel agent

or call direct.
Min. Stay: 2 nights in Apr & Oct.
Parking: Ample free off-street parking.
In-Room: Telephone, AC, color cable TV, VCR, stereo, coffee & tea-making facilities, maid service.
On-Premises: Meeting rooms, TV lounge, business services.
Exercise/Health: Jacuzzi, Nearby gym, weights,

sauna, steam, massage.
Swimming: Pool nearby.
Smoking: Permitted on outside porches only. All rooms non-smoking.
Pets: Not permitted.
Handicap Access: No.
Children: No.
Languages: English, Spanish.
Your Hosts: Tony & Glen.
IGLTA

Color Photo on Page 24

Accommodations in New Orleans

Bourgoyne Guest House

Gay/Lesbian ♀♂

A Courtyard Retreat on Bourbon Street

The excitement of Bourbon Street, coupled with a courtyard retreat from the hullabaloo, is what *Bourgoyne Guest House* offers visitors to the fabled French Quarter. Fine restaurants, museums, bars, discos...everything you'd want to see in the old section of the city is an easy walk from our central location. Guest accommodations range from cozy studios to spacious one- and two-bedroom suites of unusual style and elegance. All are furnished with antiques and all have private baths, kitchens, air conditioning and telephones.

Address: 839 rue Bourbon, New Orleans, LA 70116
Tel: (504) 524-3621 or (504) 525-3983.

Type: Guesthouse.
Clientele: Mostly gay & lesbian with some straight clientele.
Transportation: Taxi or airport shuttle.
To Gay Bars: 1 block to men's bar, 7 blocks to women's bars.

Rooms: 3 rooms & 2 suites.
Baths: All private.
Dates Open: All year.
Rates: $80-$170.
Credit Cards: MC, Visa.
Rsv'tns: Recommended.
Reserve Thru: Travel agent or call direct.
Parking: Off-street pay

parking nearby.
In-Room: AC, telephones, complete kitchens, maid & laundry service. TV in suites.
On-Premises: Meeting rooms, laundry facilities, kitchen.
Sunbathing: On the patio.
Smoking: Permitted without

restrictions.
Pets: Not permitted.
Handicap Access: No.
Children: Permitted.
Languages: English & French.

Green House Inn, The

A New Orleans Tropical Guesthouse

The Green House Inn is a beautiful 1840's New Orleans grand home which has been converted into a guesthouse. Surrounded by tropical plants, and conveniently located in the Lower Garden District, it is near to all New Orleans has to offer. Each of the six guestrooms features king-sized beds with deluxe mattresses, linens, towels and extra pillows. All rooms have private baths with showers (one has a tub), color TV with cable, VCRs, mini-refrigerators, clock radios, ceiling fans, central air conditioning and heat, hardwood floors and direct dial phones with modem jacks. Three are on the first floor and three are on the second floor (there is no elevator).

The Green House Inn is only 12 walkable blocks from the French Quarter, three blocks from the St. Charles Avenue streetcar and five blocks from the Convention Center. Also nearby are antique shops, art galleries and many fine New Orleans restaurants. In addition, free secured parking, complimentary continental breakfast and daily maid service are all reasons for staying at *The Green House Inn*. Lifelong resident of the area, your host Jesse will help you enjoy New Orleans to its fullest.

Address: 1212 Magazine St, New Orleans, LA 70130
Tel: (504) 525-1333, (800) 966-1303, **Fax:** (504) 525-1383.
E-mail: greeninn@aol.com **Web:** http://www.greeninn.com

Type: Bed & breakfast guesthouse.
Clientele: Mostly gay & lesbian with some straight clientele
Transportation: Airport shuttle van or taxi.
To Gay Bars: 12 blocks, 20-min walk or 5-min drive.
Rooms: 6 rooms with king beds.
Baths: Private: 5 shower/toilets, 1 bath/shower/toilet.
Meals: Continental breakfast.
Vegetarian: 14 blocks to vegetarian restaurant.
Complimentary: Mints on pillow, morning coffee.
Dates Open: All year.
High Season: Fall & spring.
Rates: Low season (summer) $68, high season (fall, winter, spring) $88, special events $128.
Discounts: Weekly rate 10% off, monthly rate 25% off. Student discounts available.
Credit Cards: Amex, Visa, MC, Discover.
Rsv'tns: Required.

Reserve Thru: Travel agent or call direct.
Min. Stay: Required only on special events (Mardi Gras, Jazz Fest, etc.)
Parking: Ample free, fenced off-street parking.
In-Room: AC, color cable TV, ceiling fans, refrigerator, maid service.
On-Premises: TV lounge, laundry facilities, copier, fax.
Exercise/Health: Weights. Nearby gym, weights, Jacuzzi, sauna, steam, massage.

Swimming: Heated pool with hot tub, waterfalls, tree-shaped fiber-optic lights.
Sunbathing: On patio.
Nudity: OK by pool.
Smoking: Permitted only in rooms or outside. No non-smoking rooms available.
Pets: On request.
Handicap Access: No.
Children: No one under 16.
Languages: English, Spanish.
Your Hosts: Jesse.
IGLTA

Lafitte Guest House

WWW Gay-Friendly 50/50

The French Quarter's Premier Guest House For Over 40 Years

Rob Ambelang, Photographer

This elegant French manor house, meticulously restored to its original splendor and furnished in fine antiques and reproductions, has all the comforts of home, including air conditioning and cable TV. Located in the quiet, residential section of famous Bourbon St., *Lafitte Guest House* is just steps from the French Quarter's attractions.

Continental breakfast is served in your room or in our tropical courtyard. Wine and hors d'oeuvres are served each evening at cocktail hour.

Get to know us — we're as New Orleans as streetcars, jazz musicians and voodoo queens. *Lafitte Guest House* offers easy access to antique shops, museums and world-famous restaurants. We are only steps away from quiet strolls through rows of colorful Creole and Spanish cottages, or the lively action of the 24-hour nightclub scene on Bourbon Street. The atmosphere of our guesthouse is tranquil and pleasant. We have a warm, friendly staff which is qualified and willing to help you with side tours, restaurant reservations, or whatever extra accommodations you may be seeking. Parking is available on the premises.

Address: 1003 Bourbon St, New Orleans, LA 70116
Tel: (504) 581-2678, (800) 331-7971, **Fax:** (504) 581-2677.
E-mail: lafitte@travelbase.com **Web:** http://www.lafitteguesthouse.com

Type: Bed & breakfast guesthouse.
Clientele: 50% gay & lesbian & 50% straight clientele
Transportation: Limo from airport, $65 for 2. Pick up from airport or train, $21 taxi, airport shuttle $10/ person.
To Gay Bars: 1 block.
Rooms: 12 rooms, 2 suites with queen or king beds.
Baths: 7 private bath/toilets

& 7 private shower/toilets.
Meals: Continental breakfast.
Vegetarian: Vegetarian food nearby.
Complimentary: Wine & hors d'oeuvres.
Dates Open: All year.
High Season: Sept 1-Dec 1, Jan 1-May 31.
Rates: $109-$209.
Discounts: AAA 10%.
Credit Cards: MC, Visa, Amex, Discover, Diners

Club.
Rsv'tns: Required with deposit.
Reserve Thru: Call 800 number direct.
Min. Stay: 2 days on weekends. Inquire for special events.
Parking: Paid off-street parking.
In-Room: Color cable TV, AC, telephone, sound machines, down comforters, maid service & many more

unique amenities.
On-Premises: Victorian parlor & courtyard.
Exercise/Health: Nearby gym, weights, Jacuzzi/spa, sauna, steam & massage.
Smoking: Not permitted in house.
Pets: Not permitted.
Handicap Access: No.
Children: Permitted.
Languages: English.
Your Hosts: Ed & Andy.

Color Photo on Page 24

Macarty Park Guest House

WWW Gay/Lesbian ⚥

A Tropical Paradise in the City

Enjoy beautiful, private poolside cottages, spacious suites and rooms in this Eastlake Victorian guesthouse. Step out of your room into lush, tropical gardens and jump into the sparkling heated pool and hot tub. Enjoy the tranquility of the cool water on moonlit nights. Rooms are tastefully decorated primarily in antique and reproduction furnishings, and are impeccably clean, each with a private bath. Located in a national historical district, *Macarty Park's* staff is eager to make your stay enjoyable and fun. All this for a fraction of what you would pay elsewhere!

Address: 3820 Burgundy St, New Orleans, LA 70117-5708
Tel: (504) 943-4994, (800) 521-2790, **Fax:** (504) 943-4999.
E-mail: faxmehard@aol.com **Web:** http://www.macartypark.com

Type: Bed & breakfast guesthouse with cottages, condos.
Clientele: Mostly gay & lesbian with some straight clientele
Transportation: Cab from airport.
To Gay Bars: 5 minutes.
Rooms: 6 rooms & 2 cottages & 6 condos with king, queen, full or twin beds.
Baths: All private.
Meals: Expanded

continental breakfast in guesthouse.
Complimentary: Brewed coffee & tea in guesthouse.
Dates Open: All year.
Rates: Off season $59-$160, In season $59-$160 (except special events).
Credit Cards: MC, Visa, Amex, Discover.
Rsv'tns: Required with deposit.
Reserve Thru: Travel agent or call direct.
Min. Stay: 2 days on most

weekends.
Parking: Ample free off-street parking at guesthouse.
In-Room: Color cable TV, AC, telephone & maid service. Some accommodations have kitchen, refrigerator, ceiling fans, coffee & tea-making facilities.
Exercise/Health: Hot tub.
Swimming: In-ground heated pool on premises.
Sunbathing: At poolside,

on common sun decks & on patio.
Nudity: Permitted around pool.
Smoking: Permitted without restrictions.
Pets: Not permitted.
Handicap Access: No.
Children: Not welcomed.
Languages: English & French.
Your Hosts: John.

Rober House

Welcome to America's most fascinating city! New Orleans is a city with a unique personality that is a blend of many cultures. New Orleans is a place of fun, music, excitement and delicious foods, and the greatest party on earth: Mardi Gras is an unforgettable experience that is simply not to be missed. The French Quarter turns into a continuous party. People throw beads and trinkets from their balconies to the revelers below. Everyone tries to outdo everyone else by wearing the most fantastic costume.

Come, experience and capture the charm of the French Quarter at *Rober House.* Here, in a quiet, residential location, our one-bedroom, living, kitchen, and full-bath condos are fully furnished and have all the amenities, plus courtyard and swimming pool. Three of the apartments can sleep up to four people. The *Rober House* provides quality lodgings and great savings only minutes from fabulous restaurants and tourist attractions.

Address: 820 Ursulines St, New Orleans, LA 70116-2422
Tel: (504) 529-4663 or 523-1246, (800) 523-9091.
Web: http://www.neworleansgay.com

Type: Guesthouse.
Clientele: Mostly gay & lesbian with some straight clientele
Transportation: Taxi from airport $21. Shuttle bus, $11 per person, stops across street at #827.
To Gay Bars: Two blocks to 1 bar & three blocks to 4 other bars, all in the same direction.
Rooms: 5 apartments (3 apts. sleep up to 4 people

each) with queen beds & queen sofa beds.
Baths: All private.
Vegetarian: Health restaurant nearby.
Complimentary: Coffee, OJ.
Dates Open: All year.
High Season: Special events weeks & weekends.
Rates: July 1-Aug 27, $89. Rest of year, $90-$125, except special events periods (call for rates).

Discounts: Weekly rates.
Credit Cards: All accepted, except Diners.
Rsv'tns: Required.
Reserve Thru: Travel agent or call direct.
Min. Stay: 3 days in summer & 2 days rest of year.
Parking: On-street parking & plenty of parking garages near Canal St.
In-Room: Color TV, AC, ceiling fans, telephone &

kitchen with refrigerator.
Swimming: Pool.
Sunbathing: At poolside.
Nudity: Permitted poolside if no one else objects.
Smoking: Preferably outside the apartments.
Pets: Not permitted.
Handicap Access: 1 unit is accessible with help.
Children: Welcomed.
Languages: English, German & Danish.

Boys On Burgundy

Boys on Burgundy is located in the heart of the French Quarter, only steps from the bars and famous New Orleans sights and restaurants. This spacious, quiet B&B with friendly, courteous hosts, offers reasonable rates, cable TV, unlimited local calls and large, comfortable rooms that make you feel at home. Everyone is invited to enjoy our large, well-landscaped patio. No standard institutional hotel stay here! Members of Gala Choruses and NOGMC.

Address: 1030 Burgundy St, New Orleans, LA 70116
Tel: (504) 524-2987, (800) 487-8731.

Type: Bed & breakfast.
Clientele: Men
Transportation: Airport shuttle service.
To Gay Bars: 3 blocks.
Rooms: 3 rooms with king beds.
Baths: 1 private bath/shower/toilet, 1 shared bath/shower/toilet.
Meals: Continental

breakfast.
Vegetarian: Available nearby.
Dates Open: All year.
High Season: Sept-May.
Rates: Call for rates.
Credit Cards: MC, Visa.
Rsv'tns: Required.
Reserve Thru: Call direct.
Min. Stay: 2 nights, except for certain holidays.

Parking: On-street parking.
In-Room: Color cable TV, AC, telephone.
On-Premises: Kitchen, refrigerator, coffee/tea-making facilities, large, well-landscaped patio.
Exercise/Health: Nearby gym, weights, spa, sauna, steam & massage.
Swimming: Nearby pool.

Sunbathing: On the patio & at private clubs.
Smoking: Permitted on patio only.
Pets: Not permitted.
Handicap Access: No.
Children: Not especially welcome.
Languages: English.

Bywater Bed & Breakfast

A Folk Art Feast for the Eyes

Bywater Bed & Breakfast is a late Victorian "double shot-gun" cottage in the Bywater neighborhood, a short distance from Faubourg Marigny and the French Quarter and close to tourist attractions. Decorated with contemporary Southern folk art, guest space includes living room, library, dining room, kitchen and enclosed backyard patio. Groups can be accommodated with special prior arrangement. This is a women-owned B&B.

Address: 1026 Clouet St, New Orleans, LA 70117
Tel: (504) 944-8438, **Fax:** (504) 947-2795.
E-mail: bywaterbnb@juno.com **Web:** http://www.bywaterbnb.com

Type: Bed & breakfast.
Clientele: Mostly gay & lesbian with some straight clientele
Transportation: Car or taxi.
To Gay Bars: 1 mile or a 5-minute drive.
Rooms: 3 rooms with king or twin beds.
Baths: 1 private bath/shower/toilet, 3 private sinks, 2 shared bath/shower/

toilets.
Meals: Expanded continental breakfast.
Vegetarian: Request in advance. Vegetarian restaurants nearby.
Complimentary: Coffee & tea.
Dates Open: All year.
High Season: Mardi Gras, Jazz Fest.
Rates: $65-$80. No

increase for special events.
Credit Cards: MC, Visa.
Rsv'tns: Required.
Reserve Thru: Call direct.
Min. Stay: 2 nights on weekends, longer during Jazz Fest & Mardi Gras.
Parking: Ample on-street parking.
In-Room: AC, ceiling fans.
On-Premises: TV lounge, laundry facilities, video tape

library.
Sunbathing: On the patio.
Smoking: Permitted only outdoors & on rear patio.
Pets: Permitted with advance arrangements.
Handicap Access: No.
Children: Welcome with advance arrangements.
Languages: English.
Your Hosts: Betty-Carol.

Crescent City Guest House

WWW Gay/Lesbian ⚥
Gay-Owned & -Operated

Enjoy the Excitement & Charm of New Orleans

Crescent City Guest House is located in the historic Faubourg Marigny, just three short blocks from the French Quarter and the Riverfront streetcar line. Many of the city's most popular restaurants and nightclubs are within walking distance of our doorstep. Your room is complete wtih a large private bath, hair dryer, iron and ironing board, telephone with voice mail and television. Daily maid service and continental breakfast are included. Our large common room is a great place to spend time with friends. Join in the fun and festivities of the city or relax in our yard while listening to the sounds of steamboat calliopes on the nearby Mississippi River.

Address: 612 Marigny St, New Orleans, LA 70116
Tel: (504) 944-8722, **Toll-free:** (877) 203-2140, **Fax:** (504) 945-0904.
E-mail: matlynccgh@msn.com

Type: Guesthouse.
Clientele: Mostly gay & lesbian with some straight clientele
Transportation: Taxi from airport is best.
To Gay Bars: 1/2 block.
Rooms: 2 standard, 2 deluxe with queen-sized beds.
Baths: 4 private bath/ shower/toilets.

Meals: Continental breakfast.
Vegetarian: Vegetarian restaurant nearby.
Dates Open: All year.
High Season: Sept-May.
Rates: Jun-Aug $59-$79, Sept-May $69-$139.
Discounts: Long term & summer rates.
Credit Cards: Visa, MC, Amex, Discover, Novus.

Rsv'tns: Recommended.
Min. Stay: During special events.
Parking: Adequate free off-street parking.
In-Room: Telephone, AC, ceiling fans, color cable TV, refrigerator, coffee & tea-making facilities, maid service, iron & ironing board.
Exercise/Health: Hot tub on premises. Gym nearby.

Sunbathing: On patio.
Nudity: Permitted.
Smoking: Unrestricted.
Pets: Permitted without restrictions.
Handicap Access: No.
Children: No.
Languages: English.
Your Hosts: Matthew.

Fourteen Twelve Thalia, A B&B

WWW Gay/Lesbian ⚥

A Quiet Retreat in the "Big Easy"

Brant-lee and Terry wish to welcome you into their home, *Fourteen Twelve Thalia, A Bed & Breakfast.* Your spacious, bright and comfortable one-bedroom apartment in this renovated Victorian house has a king-sized bed, private bath, kitchen with microwave, a large living room with queen-sized sofa sleeper, access to laundry facilities, color cable TV and a private entrance. The patio is available for sunbathing and relaxing among the flowers. Our location in the lower Garden District is convenient to the French Quarter, downtown and the art and warehouse districts, the convention center and Super Dome.

Address: 1412 Thalia, New Orleans, LA 70130
Tel: (504) 522-0453, **Fax:** (504) 523-3912.
E-mail: grisgris@ix.netcom.com

Type: Bed & breakfast.
Clientele: Mostly gay & lesbian with some straight clientele.
Transportation: Car, streetcar or taxi.
To Gay Bars: 14 blocks to French Quarter bars. From 5-20 minutes by car, taxi or streetcar.
Rooms: Self-contained apartment with king bed, queen sleeper sofa & private entrance. For 2-4 people.

Baths: Private.
Meals: Breakfast furnishings supplied for self-catering kitchen.
Vegetarian: Available with advance notice.
Complimentary: Tea, coffee, juices & fresh fruit.
Dates Open: All year.
High Season: Mardi Gras, Jazz Fest, Sugar Bowl/New Years.
Rates: $85-$95 or $150-$200 during special events.

Discounts: For stays of more than 5 nights.
Rsv'tns: Required.
Reserve Thru: Call direct.
Min. Stay: 2 nights. Mardi Gras 4 nights, other special events 3 nights.
Parking: Ample on-street parking.
In-Room: Color cable TV, AC, telephone, ceiling fans, kitchen & refrigerator. Washer/dryer available.
On-Premises: Laundry

facilities.
Sunbathing: On the patio.
Smoking: Not permitted in the apartment. Permitted on deck or patio.
Pets: Small pets that are crate trained.
Handicap Access: Yes. Low steps, wide doors, accessible bath.
Children: Welcomed but limited to 2.
Languages: English.

French Quarter Reservation Service

You'll Love New Orleans — and She'll Love You Right Back

The **French Quarter Reservation Service** specializes in locating accommodations in small inns and condo apartments in the historic French Quarter, adjacent to the Faubourg Marigny and the famous Garden District of southern mansions, just ten minutes by streetcar from downtown Canal Street. We have over 75 listings, including historic inns, bed and breakfasts, fully furnished private condos (some with swimming pool) and much more. Make just one call to book marvelous accommodations in the Vieux Carré. If you stay in the French Quarter (which we recommend), you won't need a car as you can walk or take a streetcar everywhere.

New Orleans, America's most fascinating city, has a unique personality, a result of the blending of many cultures. Her dramatic and sometime glamorous history has been preserved for us by her strong traditions, language, cuisine, music and architecture. New Orleans offers you fun, music excitement, delicious foods, beauty and history. You'll love New Orleans — and she'll love you right back! Come, experience the charm and culture of the French Quarter. Plan to visit New Orleans for at least a few days. A two- or three-day stay simply isn't enough! *Laissez les bon temps rouler!*

Address: 1000 Bourbon Street **Mail To:** PM Box 263, New Orleans, LA 70116
Tel: (504) 523-1246, (800) 523-9091, **Fax:** (504) 527-6327.
E-mail: fqrsinc@Bellsouth.net **Web:** http://www.neworleansgay.com **IGLTA**

Glimmer Inn

WWW Gay-Friendly ♀♂
Woman-Owned & -Operated

A Gay-Friendly Place To Come Home To

We invite you to experience New Orleans by staying in our home, the *Glimmer Inn*. This 1891 Victorian features grand period elements such as a cypress and mahogany staircase, 13-foot cove ceilings, pocket doors, stained glass and ceiling medallions with crystal chandeliers. A New Orleans theme is carried throughout the inn, with poster art, music, books and memorabilia. Each guestroom is unique and individually appointed with custom fabrics. We're located on the St. Charles streetcar line, across from the Garden District, 15 minutes via streetcar to the French Quarter or uptown attractions.

Address: 1631 7th St, New Orleans, LA 70115
Tel: (504) 897-1895.

Type: Bed & breakfast & cottage.
Clientele: Mostly straight clientele with a gay/lesbian following
Transportation: Taxi from airport (1/2 hour, $21 flat rate for 2).
To Gay Bars: 3 miles, a 45 min walk, a 10 min drive.
Rooms: 5 rooms, 1 cottage with single, double, queen or king beds.
Baths: Private: 1 shower/ toilet. Shared: 3 bath/ shower/toilets.
Meals: Expanded continental breakfast.
Vegetarian: Vegetarian restaurants are up- & downtown from us.
Dates Open: All year.
High Season: Oct-Nov & Mar-May.
Rates: $60-$85; summer $55-$80; special events (Jazzfest, Mardi Gras) $100-$145.
Rsv'tns: Required.
Reserve Thru: Travel agent or call direct.
Min. Stay: 2 nights.
Parking: Ample free on-street parking.
In-Room: AC, ceiling fans, color TV, B/W TV, maid service.
On-Premises: TV lounge, video tape library.
Smoking: Permitted everywhere, except in dining room. Sleeping rooms aired between guests, but not restricted.
Pets: Cats allowed in main house & cottage. Dogs in cottage only. Must be quiet & well-behaved.
Handicap Access: No.
Children: Must be well-behaved.
Languages: English.
Your Hosts: Sharon & Cathy.

Ingram Haus

WWW Gay/Lesbian ♀♂

Accommodations in the Heart of the Gay Area

Located in historic Faubourg Marigny, that more Bohemian extension of the French Quarter, *Ingram Haus* is a half block from the The Mint, the Phoenix and New Orleans Eagle. Access to the street is through security gates with your own key — no doorman, no lobby, no hassle. Each comfortable, air-conditioned two-bedroom suite has big queen-sized beds, private bath, phone, color cable TV and a full kitchen for self-catered snacks, coffee or breakfast. Two courtyards offer a place to relax over cocktails or morning coffee. Bars and restaurants are within easy walking distance.

Address: 1012 Elysian Fields, New Orleans, LA 70117
Tel: (504) 949-3110.
E-mail: ingramhaus@yahoo.com **Web:** http://sites.netscape.net/ingramhaus/flag

Type: Guesthouse. **Clientele:** Mostly gay & lesbian with some straight clientele **Transportation:** Taxi from airport ($24 flat rate). **To Gay Bars:** 1/2 block. **Rooms:** Two 2-BR apartments with queen beds. **Baths:** 2 private shower/toilets. **Vegetarian:** 1/2 block to a small supermarket. **Complimentary:** Coffee, tea. **Dates Open:** All year. **High Season:** Oct-Nov, Mardi Gras, Mar-May. **Rates:** Jun 1-Aug 15 $65/night, Aug 16-May 31 $85/night, +$10/person over 2. Special events $100-$150/night. **Discounts:** Weekly rates (except during special events): Jun 1-Aug 15 $300/wk, Aug 16-May 31 $420/wk. Summer & extended stay rates available. **Reserve Thru:** Call direct. **Min. Stay:** 2 nights (5 nights for some events). **Parking:** Adequate on-street parking. **In-Room:** Telephone, AC, ceiling fans, color cable TV, kitchen, refrigerator, coffee & tea-making facility, microwave & toaster. **On-Premises:** Guest laundry facilities. **Swimming:** 12 blocks to Country Club (bar) pool. **Sunbathing:** In courtyard. **Smoking:** Permitted, no non-smoking rooms available. **Pets:** Not permitted. **Children:** Please inquire. **Languages:** English. **Your Hosts:** Scott.

La Dauphine, Residence des Artistes

WWW Gay/Lesbian ♀♂
Gay-Owned & -Operated

Relaxed, Quiet, Unpretentious

Located in the artsy, bohemian Faubourg Marigny gay area, just four blocks from the French Quarter, *La Dauphine* is a hundred-year-old charmingly renovated Victorian — a mellow and relaxing, non-smoking retreat. *La Dauphine* offers large, quiet rooms with queen-sized, four-poster beds. Each room has a private bath, either within the room or just outside, ceiling fans, cable TV/VCR and phone. Bicycles are provided free of charge to guests. Your host, Ray Ruiz, is a native writer/photographer, specializing in gay travel.

Address: 2316 Dauphine St., New Orleans, LA 70117
Tel: (504) 948-2217, **Fax:** (504) 948-3420.
E-mail: LaDauphine@aol.com **Web:** http://www.ladauphine.com

Type: Bed & breakfast. **Clientele:** Mostly gay & lesbian with some straight clientele **Transportation:** $21 taxi from airport. Free pick up from airport, train or bus on stays over 1 week. **To Gay Bars:** 2 blocks, a 4 min walk, a 1 min drive. **Rooms:** 4 rooms with queen beds. **Baths:** All private. **Meals:** Continental breakfast. **Complimentary:** Coffee & tea. **High Season:** Sep 1-Jul 4. **Rates:** $65-$125 per night, $400/wk 1 person, $500/wk 2 persons. **Discounts:** Call for special event rates. **Credit Cards:** MC, Visa, Discover, Eurocard, Amex, Diners. **Rsv'tns:** Required. **Reserve Thru:** Travel agent or call direct. **Min. Stay:** 3 nights. **Parking:** Ample, on-street parking. **In-Room:** Telephone, AC, ceiling fans, color cable TV, VCR. **On-Premises:** TV lounge, laundry facilities, fax, computer (PC), video tape library. **Exercise/Health:** Weights. **Swimming:** Nearby pool, ocean, lake. **Sunbathing:** On patio & common sun decks. **Smoking:** All non-smoking. Permitted outside only. **Pets:** Not permitted, dog on premises. **Children:** No. **Languages:** English, French, German, Danish. **Your Hosts:** Ray & Kim. **IGLTA**

Royal Barracks Guest House

A World of Your Own

In a newly-renovated Victorian home located in a quiet, residential neighborhood of the French Quarter, this gay-owned & -operated guesthouse will offer you the hospitality of historical New Orleans. Within a few blocks are 24-hour restaurants, bars and delicatessens. Rooms at *Royal Barracks* are individually decorated, have private entrances and have all modern conveniences. All open onto our high-walled, private patio with wet bar, refrigerator, ice maker and hot tub. Our avid return customers, many of whom often book a year in advance, consider their accommodations here their own secluded, private hideaway.

Address: 717 Barracks St, New Orleans, LA 70116
Tel: (504) 529-7269, (888) 255-7269, **Fax:** (504) 529-7298.

Type: Guesthouse.
Clientele: Mostly gay
Transportation: $15 per person airport shuttle, taxi $21 flat fee.
To Gay Bars: 1/2 block to men's & 3 blocks to women's bars.
Rooms: 5 rooms & 1 suite

with double & queen beds.
Baths: All private.
Meals: Coffee bar.
Dates Open: All year.
High Season: Oct-May.
Rates: Jun 15-Sep 15, $65-$100. Winter, $85-$135.
Credit Cards: MC, Visa.
Rsv'tns: Required.

Reserve Thru: Call direct.
Parking: On-street parking, numerous parking lots.
In-Room: Color TV, VCR, telephone, ceiling fans, AC & maid service.
On-Premises: Ice machine & refrigerator in the courtyard.

Exercise/Health: Jacuzzi.
Nudity: Permitted.
Smoking: Permitted without restrictions.
Pets: Not permitted.
Handicap Access: No.
Children: No.
Languages: English.
Your Hosts: Blake & Tim.

Maple Hill Farm B & B Inn

Gay-Friendly 50/50 ⚢
Gay-Owned & -Operated

Get Away From It All, Yet Be Near It All...

Maple Hill Farm B & B Inn was rated "Best bed & breakfast hands down" by a statewide poll. Escape the tourist crowds at this Augusta-area inn and relax on 130 serene acres of unspoiled rural beauty. Our rolling fields and woods with trails and secluded clothing-optional swimming hole give you a taste of the "real Maine." Our farm is adjacent to a 550-acre wildlife preserve with pristine pond for swimming, canoeing, and more trails for hiking. Yet just minutes from eclectic and ethnic dining and antique shops in the National Historic District of gay-friendly Hallowell, on the banks of the Kennebec River.

From here you can easily see the rest of Maine, with many coastal, lakes or mountain trips (even Freeport shopping) an easy hour's drive. Take a bike ride on our rural roads, relax on the front porch with a Maine microbrew or cocktail from our lounge, visit our barnyard menagerie, sun by the swimming hole, or curl up by the fireplace with a cup of herbal tea and a homemade cookie. Our spacious rooms are furnished with antiques, have air conditioning, TVs, and phones. One suite has a two-person whirlpool tub, and renovations, due for completion in 2000, will add two additional whirlpool suites! Our own fresh eggs are featured in full menu choice breakfast included in the room rate.

Address: Outlet Rd, RR1, Hallowell **Mail To:** Box 1145, Hallowell, ME 04347
Tel: (207) 622-2708, (800) 622-2708, **Fax:** (207) 622-0655.
E-mail: stay@MapleBB.com **Web:** http://www.MapleBB.com

Type: B&B with gallery.
Clientele: Mixed gay/lesbian & straight (50/50) at B&B. Camping exclusively gay/lesbian.
Transportation: Car is best.
To Gay Bars: 5 mi to Augusta, 1 hr to Portland.
Rooms: 6 rooms & 1 suite with double or queen beds.
Baths: Private & shared.
Camping: Primitive camping adjacent to small spring-fed pond in woods. Very private. RV parking nearby at edge of woods.
Meals: Full breakfast

cooked to order from menu. Liquor service.
Vegetarian: Breakfast, nearby restaurants.
Complimentary: Evening tea or coffee. Mints in room. Bathroom amenities.
High Season: Jul-Oct (summer & fall foliage).
Rates: Summer $55-$145 winter $45-$125. Camping $15-$25.
Discounts: Government rates available midweek.
Credit Cards: MC, Visa, Amex, Diners, Discover.
Rsv'tns: Recommended.
Reserve Thru: Travel agent

or call direct.
Min. Stay: Required some peak summer & fall wknds.
Parking: Ample free off-street parking.
In-Room: AC, telephone, color TV, clock radio & maid service. 1 room with whirlpool bath.
On-Premises: TV lounge, meeting rooms, fax.
Exercise/Health: Whirlpool in 1 guest room. Nearby gym & massage.
Swimming: Swimming hole in the woods. 1 mile to lake.
Sunbathing: Common sun decks, swimming hole.

Nudity: Permitted at swimming hole.
Smoking: Permitted outside or on covered porch only, not inside building or rooms.
Pets: Not permitted.
Handicap Access: Yes. Ramp to 1st floor guest room & fully accessible bathroom.
Children: Well-behaved children over 8 are welcome. Younger children by permission only.
Languages: English, some French.
Your Hosts: Scott & Vince.

Devilstone Oceanfront Inn

Gay/Lesbian ⚲

On the Famous Bar Harbor Shorepath, Yet Only a Block from Town

An early neighbor of the Rockefellers and Pulitzers, *Devilstone* was one of the original estates built on the shorepath in 1885, with unusual romantic gardens flowing to the ocean's edge on nearly two acres. Located on Mt. Desert Island, Bar Harbor and Acadia National Park (ANP is five minutes from us) offer biking, golfing, kayaking, sailing, hiking, climbing, whalewatching cruises, etc. Movies and nearly 75 restaurants are all a short walk from the inn. Very quiet, peaceful and beautifully designed, *Devilstone* is the perfect place to relax.

Mail To: PO Box 801, Bar Harbor, ME 04609
Tel: (207) 288-2933.
E-mail: devilrock@aol.com

Type: Inn.
Clientele: Mostly gay & lesbian, some straights
Transportation: Car is best.
Rooms: 6 rooms with queen or king beds. Also separate 3-BR Carriage Gatehouse.
Baths: 6 private bath/toilet or shower/toilet. Carriage Gatehouse: 4 baths.
Meals: Expanded

continental breakfast.
Vegetarian: Nearby.
Complimentary: Afternoon tea, coffee, cocktail set ups, munchies, mints on pillows.
Dates Open: May 15-Oct 15.
High Season: Summer.
Rates: $150-$350 per night. Carriage Gatehse: $2,450/wk (min 1 wk).
Discounts: On stays of 1 week or more.

Credit Cards: MC, Visa.
Rsv'tns: Required.
Reserve Thru: Call direct.
Min. Stay: Please inquire.
Parking: Ample free off-street parking.
In-Room: Sitting areas, maid service. AC in some rooms. Carriage Gatehouse: full kitchen, living/dining room, den.
On-Premises: Shorepath & ponds.

Exercise/Health: Horseshoes, Jacuzzi. Nearby gym, weights.
Swimming: Ocean on premises. Nearby lake.
Sunbathing: On common sun decks, beach, patio.
Smoking: No smoking.
Pets: Not permitted.
Children: No.
Your Hosts: John.
IGLTA

Alden House Bed & Breakfast

WWW Gay-Friendly 50/50 ⚲

One of the Top Five Culturally Cool Towns in the U.S.

Come to the coast and enjoy an authentic, affordable New England community. *The Alden House* (c. 1840), located in the heart of the historic district, is graced with a hand-carved cherry staircase and mantel, several marble fireplaces, German silver hardware, a curved pocket door, formal parlors and library. The town has lovely shops, art galleries and restaurants and was named by *USA Today* as one of the top five "culturally cool" towns in the U.S. Activities abound, including antiquing, skiing, biking, hiking, kayaking, the theatre, cruises and train excursions.

Address: 63 Church St, Belfast, ME 04915
Tel: (207) 338-2151, (877) 337-8151.
E-mail: innkeeper@thealdenhouse.com **Web:** http://www.TheAldenHouse.com

Type: Bed & breakfast.
Clientele: 50% gay & lesbian & 50% straight clientele
Transportation: Car, or air to Bangor or Portland, ME.
Rooms: 7 rooms with single, double or queen beds.
Baths: 5 private shower/toilets, 2 shared bath/shower/toilets.

Meals: Full breakfast.
Vegetarian: Available upon request, with notice.
Complimentary: Coffee, tea, lemonade, mid-afternoon snack.
Dates Open: All year.
Rates: $86-$120.
Discounts: Extended stay discounts.
Credit Cards: MC, Visa, Discover.

Reserve Thru: Call direct.
Parking: Ample off-street parking.
In-Room: VCR.
On-Premises: Video tape library.
Exercise/Health: Massage. Nearby gym, weights, Jacuzzi, sauna.
Swimming: Nearby pool & ocean.
Smoking: Permitted on

outside porches only.
Pets: Not permitted.
Handicap Access: No. First-floor room has some accessibility.
Children: No.
Languages: English.
Your Hosts: Bruce & Sue.

Bay Meadows Inn, Country Inn by the Sea WWW Gay-Friendly ♂♂

Just 350 yards from its own private beach, *Bay Meadows Inn, Country Inn by the Sea* overlooks one of Maine's most beautiful bays. Complementing the Victorian atmosphere are original paintings, Persian carpets, fine porcelains and sculptures. The bright and airy guestrooms in the main house and the completely renovated barn combine old-fashioned atmosphere with today's conveniences. Breakfast features a lobster omelet entrée with many options, and we're known for Patty's incredible muffins and baked goodies. Belfast has beautiful sea captains' homes, antiques shops, galleries, restaurants, boutiques, many year-round activities, and decisively supported Maine's gay rights initiative.

Address: 192 Northport Ave, Belfast, ME
Tel: (207) 338-5715, (800) 335-2370.
E-mail: bbmi@ctel.net **Web:** http://www.baymeadowsinn.com

Type: Bed & breakfast.
Clientele: Mostly straight w/ a gay/lesbian following
Transportation: Car is best.
Rooms: 20 rooms with single, queen or king beds.
Baths: Private: 14 bath/ shower/toilets, 6 shower/ toilets.
Meals: Full breakfast.
Vegetarian: Breakfast & at local restaurant.
Complimentary: Tea & coffee on request.

Dates Open: All year.
High Season: Jun 15-Oct 31.
Rates: High: $85-$165, low: $65-$105.
Discounts: Inquire.
Credit Cards: MC, Visa, Discover.
Rsv'tns: Highly recommended in high season.
Reserve Thru: Travel agent or call direct.
Min. Stay: 2 days high season wknds.

Parking: Ample free off-street parking.
In-Room: Telephone, AC, color cable TV, maid service. Ceiling fans in 7 rooms, 4 refrigerators on request.
On-Premises: VCR, limited video tape library, fax, e-mail.
Exercise/Health: Nearby gym, weights, sauna, massage.
Swimming: Penobscot Bay. Nearby pool, ocean, lake.
Sunbathing: On common

sun decks, beach.
Smoking: Permitted outside off deck. All rooms non-smoking.
Pets: 14 rooms OK for supervised pets.
Handicap Access: Yes, ramps, wide doors.
Children: 14 rooms for children.
Languages: English.
Your Hosts: Patty & John.

Welch House Inn

Built in 1873 by a family of seafarers, *Welch House Inn* was one of the first residences built atop McKown Hill. The serene hilltop setting provides an unsurpassed view of town and Boothbay Harbor. Restaurants, shops, galleries and all the harbor activities are but a two-minute walk down the hill. Breathtaking is only one word describing the 180-degree view from our third-floor deck. In the crisp, clear light of early morning or the mellow glow of late afternoon sun, the scene is an ever-changing one, as pleasure craft and fishing boats sail in and out of the harbor. At night, the inner shoreline twinkles with lights and the darkness of outer harbor is accentuated by blinking lighthouses and winking stars. Savor a sunset, relish a rainbow or feel the fog creep in from an extraordinary vantage point above it all.

Our spacious, airy and smoke-free guestrooms offer a pleasant mix of the old and new, and each room projects its unique personality... a canopy four-poster here, a hooked Oriental rug there, antique prints and hand-crafted needlework on the walls. Most rooms provide a water view and all have private baths. Buffet breakfast, served in our glass-enclosed breakfast room, includes banana pancakes or cinnamon French toast, home-baked muffins and granola, cereals, fresh fruit, juices and coffee or tea. Because we're centrally located, guests may leave their cars in our parking area and walk to the charming shops, galleries and restaurants that line the streets of Boothbay Harbor. Boat docks are also just down the hill from the inn and visitors may take select from a one-hour harbor tour to a full-day outing to Monhegan Island, all of which provide a most enjoyable method of observing the rock-bound coast and islands for which the area is famous.

Address: 56 McKown St, Boothbay Harbor, ME
Tel: (207) 633-3431, (800) 279-7313.
E-mail: welchhouse@wiscasset.net **Web:** http://www.welchhouse.com

Type: Bed & breakfast.
Clientele: Mostly straight clientele
To Gay Bars: 35 miles, a 45 min drive.
Rooms: 16 rooms with double, queen or king beds.
Baths: 16 private bath/ shower/toilets.
Meals: Full breakfast.
Vegetarian: 2 blocks.
Complimentary: Tea & coffee.

Dates Open: Apr 1-Dec 10.
High Season: Jun 1-Oct 10.
Rates: Summer: $85-$165, winter: $65-$95.
Discounts: 10% 7 days, 10% AAA & AARP.
Credit Cards: MC, Visa, Amex.
Rsv'tns: Required, but we do accept walk-ins.

Reserve Thru: Travel agent or call direct.
Parking: Ample free off-street parking.
In-Room: AC, color cable TV, refrigerator, maid service.
Exercise/Health: Nearby gym, weights, sauna, massage.
Swimming: Nearby pool, ocean.

Sunbathing: On common sun decks.
Smoking: Inn is non-smoking. Smoking permitted on decks.
Pets: Permitted. Limited rooms, under 30 lbs.
Handicap Access: No.
Children: Welcome if 12 or older.
Languages: English.

Black Duck Inn On Corea Harbor, The

WWW **Gay-Friendly** ⚥

Explore the Real Downeast!

Retreat from the hassles of daily city life on 12 acres in a tranquil, Downeast fishing village. The land is full of rock outcrops (to sit, read, paint, or birdwatch), wild berries, hidden tidal bays, and salt marshes. From *The Black Duck Inn*, enjoy the sight of one of the most picturesque harbors in Maine. The inn is only a few miles from the Schoodic section of Acadia National Park and is close to other wildlife sanctuaries, a fresh water pond, sand beaches, public golf courses, antique shops, and restaurants.

Address: Crowley Island Rd **Mail To:** PO Box 39, Corea, ME 04624
Tel: (207) 963-2689, **Fax:** (207) 963-7495.
E-mail: bduck@acadia.net **Web:** http://www.blackduck.com

Type: Bed & breakfast.
Clientele: Mostly straight clientele with a gay/lesbian following.
Transportation: Car is best. Free pick up from boat into harbor.
To Gay Bars: 50 miles.
Rooms: 3 rooms, 1 suite, 2 cottages with single, double or queen beds.
Baths: Private: 3 shower/toilets, 1 bath/shower/toilet. 1 shared bath/shower/toilet.

Meals: Full breakfast.
Vegetarian: Vegan by advance request, otherwise fully available. Restaurants nearby in season.
Complimentary: Early coffee (6:30 am).
Dates Open: All year.
High Season: July-Sept.
Rates: Winter $70-$110, summer $80-$150.
Discounts: On weekly & monthly cottage rentals, without breakfast.

Credit Cards: MC, Visa, Discover.
Reserve Thru: Travel agent or call direct.
Min. Stay: 3 nights to 1 week in cottages.
Parking: Ample free off-street parking.
In-Room: Maid service.
On-Premises: Meeting rooms, TV lounge, VCR, library, fireplaces, fax.
Exercise/Health: Walking trails on premises & in

nearby national park.
Swimming: Ocean, nearby lake.
Sunbathing: On patio, at beach.
Smoking: No smoking in house or cottages.
Pets: Not permitted.
Handicap Access: No.
Children: Please inquire.
Languages: English, Danish.
Your Hosts: Barry & Bob.

Arundel Meadows Inn

Gay-Friendly ⚥

A Relaxing Getaway With a Four-Star Breakfast!

Small and personal, this nineteenth-century farmhouse has rooms and suites decorated in art and antiques, with private bathrooms and summer air conditioning. Three rooms have working fireplaces and all have comfortable sitting areas for reading and relaxing. Nearby Kennebunkport has antiques, artists' studios and excellent restaurants. Golf, tennis, fishing and cross-country skiing are readily accessible. At *Arundel Meadows Inn*, guests enjoy spring picnic meadows, summer flower gardens, fall foliage and winter fires in the living room.

Mail To: PO Box 1129, Kennebunk, ME 04043-1129
Tel: (207) 985-3770.
Web: http://www.gwi.net/arundel_meadows_inn

Type: Bed & breakfast.
Clientele: Mostly straight clientele, with gays & lesbians welcome.
Transportation: Car is best.
To Gay Bars: 10 miles to Ogunquit, ME, 25 miles to Portland, ME gay bars.
Rooms: Five rooms and two suites with single, double, queen and king beds.

Baths: All private.
Meals: Full breakfast.
Vegetarian: Available upon request.
Complimentary: Afternoon tea.
Dates Open: All year (subject to change).
High Season: Memorial Day through Columbus Day.
Rates: Summer $75-$135, winter $55-$95.
Discounts: 10% on 5

nights or more.
Credit Cards: MC, Visa.
Rsv'tns: Required.
Reserve Thru: Call direct.
Min. Stay: 2 days on weekends Memorial Day through Columbus Day.
Parking: Adequate free off-street parking.
In-Room: AC & maid service. 3 rooms have color TV.
Swimming: Ocean beach is

nearby.
Sunbathing: At the beach, on the patio, 2 rooms with private sun decks.
Smoking: Not permitted.
Pets: Not permitted.
Handicap Access: Yes.
Children: Not permitted under 12 years of age.
Languages: English.

Lamb's Mill Inn

WWW Gay-Friendly ⚤

Ewe Hike, Ewe Bike, Ewe Ski, Ewe ZZzzz...

Lamb's Mill Inn is a small country inn nestled among the foothills of the White Mountains in the picturesque village of Naples. Surrounded by two of Maine's largest lakes, Sebago and Long Lake, Naples is the hub of summertime water activities in this area. Winter brings cross-country and alpine skiers, snowmobilers and ice fishermen. The spectacular fall foliage invites hikers and bikers to hit the trails. In spring, canoeing the Saco River and nearby ponds is a popular pastime.

The inn is a 19th-century farmhouse, newly renovated and abounding with country charm. Our six rooms offer a romantic atmosphere and feature private baths. You will awaken to the aroma of a full country breakfast served in our two gracious dining rooms. Enjoy the privacy and scenic beauty of twenty acres of field and woods, or a leisurely stroll to the charming village. Browse along the causeway and discover parasailing, aerial sightseeing, watercycling, windsurfing and tours on the Songo River Queen. Play golf and tennis, or visit the many country fairs and flea markets. Dine in gourmet restaurants, or sample local Yankee recipes in small cafes and diners. To end an exciting day, unwind in our hot tub. All this and more is yours at *Lamb's Mill Inn*, an inn for all seasons.

Address: Lamb's Mill Rd **Mail To:** PO Box 676, Naples, ME 04055
Tel: (207) 693-6253.
E-mail: lambsmil@pivot.net

Type: Bed & breakfast inn.
Clientele: Large gay & lesbian clientele
Transportation: Car from Portland airport 25 miles away.
To Gay Bars: 25 miles to Portland gay/lesbian bars.
Rooms: 6 rooms with 1 king, 4 queens, 1 full bed.
Baths: All private.
Meals: Full gourmet breakfast.
Vegetarian: Yes.
Complimentary: Ice & munchies available in afternoon as well as tea & coffee.
Dates Open: All year.
High Season: Summer & for fall foliage.
Rates: High peak (May 1- Dec 31) $90-$120; Low (Jan 1-Apr 30) $70-$100.
Discounts: Sixth consecutive night free. 15% midweek (Mon-Thurs) for 3 night stay.
Credit Cards: MC, Visa.
Rsv'tns: Recommended.
Reserve Thru: Travel agent or call direct.
Min. Stay: Two nights on weekends in high season.
Parking: Ample free off-street parking.
In-Room: AC, color cable TV, maid service, refrigerators.
On-Premises: 2 private dining rooms, 2 TV lounges, stereo, BBQ's, 1 reading & game lounge.
Exercise/Health: Hot tub, treadmill, canoeing, windsurfing, parasailing, boat rides, water cycling, trails, downhill skiing, bicycling.
Swimming: Town beach is at the bottom of our hill on Long Lake.
Sunbathing: On patio, private sun decks or anywhere on 20 acres.
Smoking: Permitted outside.
Pets: Not permitted.
Handicap Access: No.
Children: Not permitted.
Languages: English.
IGLTA

Admiral's Inn & Guesthouse & Hotel

WWW Gay/Lesbian ♂
Gay-Owned & -Operated

Unique in Ogunquit...

The Admiral's Inn is located 65 miles north of Boston in Ogunquit, Maine. Our spacious grounds are within walking distance of the beach and all other village pleasures, and the privacy of our backyard pool is perfect for enjoying a morning or late-night swim, or a quiet afternoon retreat. Guests are also invited to enjoy our six-man hot tub, enclosed deck and clothing-optional area.

We are unique in that we offer not only traditional guesthouse accommodations, but also efficiency and hotel rooms with refrigerators, and most have private baths. All rooms have individually controlled air-conditioning, as well as television. Most rooms have telephones. The rooms in the guesthouse have access to telephone in the common areas. Enjoy casual fine dining in one of our full-service dining rooms, featuring fresh Maine seafood and an assortment of other professionally prepared dishes by our internationally renowned chef. We also offer the relaxing atmosphere of our intimate cocktail lounge for your enjoyment. *Admiral's Inn* is gay-owned and -operated.

Address: #79 US Rte. 1 South **Mail To:** PO Box 2241, Ogunquit, ME 03907
Tel: (207) 646-7093, **Toll-free:** (888) 263-6318, **Fax:** (207) 646-5341.
E-mail: Office@theadmiralsinn.com **Web:** http://www.theadmiralsinn.com

Type: Bed & breakfast, guesthouse, hotel.
Clientele: Mostly gay men
Transportation: Car is best.
To Gay Bars: On-site cocktail lounge, dance floor. 1/4 mile (5 min walk) to men's/women's bars.
Rooms: 16 rooms, 1 apartment, w/ double, queen or king beds.
Baths: 10 private, 2 rooms w/ private sink & toilets w/ full shared bath at end of hall, 4 rooms w/ full shared bath.
Meals: Continental breakfast. On-site full-service dining facilities w/ full liquor license, serving full breakfast & dinner.
Vegetarian: On-site.
Dates Open: All year.
High Season: Late June thru Labor Day.
Rates: In season $105-$125, spring & fall $55-$75.
Credit Cards: MC, Visa, Amex, Discover.
Rsv'tns: Strongly recommended during high season.
Reserve Thru: Call toll-free or e-mail direct.
Min. Stay: 2 nights weekends, 3 nights on holidays.
Parking: Ample, free parking, 2 lots on property.
In-Room: Color TV, AC, maid service, some w/ kitchen, refrigerator, some w/ ceiling fans.
On-Premises: TV lounge, intimate cocktail lounge, dance floor.
Exercise/Health: Hot tub. Nearby gym, weights, Jacuzzi, sauna, massage.
Swimming: Outdoor 20x40 pool on premises. 10 min walk to ocean beach w/ gay section.
Sunbathing: Poolside, hot tub area on back deck.
Nudity: Permitted poolside, in hot tub area on rear deck. Some units have clothing optional private deck areas. discretion in more public areas.
Smoking: Permitted outside only.
Pets: Not permitted. Boarding facilities nearby.
Handicap Access: No.
Children: No.
Languages: English.
Your Hosts: Garry John & David.

Color Photo on Page 25

Inn at Two Village Square, The

Ogunquit, Maine —The Quiet Alternative

Overlooking Ogunquit Square and the Atlantic Ocean, *THE INN* is an 1886 Victorian home perched on a hillside amidst towering trees. Our heated pool, hot tub and extensive decks provide views far to sea. Our atmosphere is congenial and relaxed. Deluxe continental breakfast is served in our wicker-filled dining room, and guest rooms have color TV, ceiling fans and air conditioning.

The original double parlor offers a color TV and cozy fireplace, and a white-wicker-filled dining room invites guests to partake of our expanded continental breakfast. Refreshments and snacks can be prepared in the butlers pantry, which we call our guest kitchen, with its refrigerator, ice, glasses, plates and other amenities conveniently located only steps from the pool. Our home is a warm place in which to enjoy annual summer vacations, to celebrate anniversaries and birthdays, to strengthen and renew relationships and to relax among old friends and new acquaintances. Innkeepers and staff invite you to join our Saturday "get acquainted" party, Tuesday poolside barbeque and reserved seating at Ogunquit's Playhouse. We cordially invite you to make our "home on the hill" YOUR home in Ogunquit.

Address: 135 US Rte 1 **Mail To:** PO Box 864, Ogunquit, ME 03907
Tel: (207) 646-5779, **Fax:** (207) 646-6797.
E-mail: reservations@theinn.tv **Web:** http://www.theinn.tv

Type: Bed & breakfast inn.
Clientele: Primarily gay & lesbian couples
Transportation: Car. Free pick up from airport limo or bus in Portsmouth NH.
To Gay Bars: 2-minute walk to gay & lesbian dance bar & piano bar.
Rooms: 18 rooms with double, queen or king beds.
Baths: Private: 14 full baths, 3 sinks. Shared: 1 full bath, 2 toilets.
Meals: Expanded continental breakfast.

Complimentary: Tea/coffee in guest kitchen. In season: Tues pm BBQ; Sat nite get-acquainted party (also holidays).
Dates Open: Mostly year round.
High Season: Late June-Labor Day.
Rates: In season $75-$130. Spring & fall $50-$75.
Discounts: Ask about spring & fall specials.
Credit Cards: MC, Visa, Amex, Discover.
Rsv'tns: Strongly

recommended in season.
Reserve Thru: Call direct.
Min. Stay: On holidays and in season. Short stays as space permits.
Parking: Ample free off-street parking.
In-Room: Color TV, AC, ceiling fans & maid service.
On-Premises: Common sitting rooms, TV lounge, public telephone, & piano. Shared guest kitchen with refrigerator & microwave.
Exercise/Health: Hot tub. Massage nearby. Free guest

membership in local gym.
Swimming: Heated pool on premises. Gay section of beach a short walk away.
Sunbathing: On poolside deck, sun deck, or nearby public beach.
Smoking: Permitted in outdoor areas.
Pets: Not permitted (facilities for cats & dogs nearby).
Handicap Access: Minimal accessibility.
Languages: English.
Your Hosts: Bob & Jeff.

Color Photo on Page 25

Moon Over Maine

Gay/Lesbian ⚥

Tranquility and Romance Await You

Moon Over Maine, built in 1839, has been beautifully restored. Many rooms feature original New England pine floors and gabled ceilings and most have direct access to the multilevel deck, overlooking a wooded yard. It will take you two minutes to walk to Ogunquit's gay nightlife and five minutes to walk to the beach. Spend a relaxing day at the beach and a quiet evening with us. Gaze at the moon as you sit in the hot tub or simply relax with someone you love.

Address: 6 Berwick Rd **Mail To:** PO Box 1478, Ogunquit, ME 03907
Tel: (207) 646-MOON (6666), (800) 851-6837.
E-mail: MoonMaine@aol.com **Web:** http://www.moonovermaine.com

Type: Bed & breakfast.
Clientele: Mostly gay & lesbian with some straight clientele.
Transportation: Car is best.
To Gay Bars: 1 block to The Club or The Front Porch.
Rooms: 9 rooms with queen beds.
Baths: All private shower/toilets.

Meals: Expanded continental breakfast.
Vegetarian: Breakfast is vegetarian. Most local restaurants have vegetarian entrees.
Complimentary: Soft drinks, candy.
Dates Open: All year.
High Season: Jun-Aug.
Rates: Summer $69-$120, winter $49-$79.
Discounts: Discounts on

weekly stays.
Credit Cards: MC, Visa, Discover.
Reserve Thru: Travel agent or call direct.
Min. Stay: July-August: 2 nights on weekends.
Parking: Adequate free off-street parking.
In-Room: Color cable TV, AC, maid service.
Exercise/Health: Jacuzzi. Nearby gym, weights,

massage.
Swimming: Ocean nearby.
Sunbathing: On common sun decks & at beach.
Smoking: Permitted outside only.
Pets: Not permitted.
Handicap Access: No.
Children: No.
Languages: English.
Your Hosts: John.

Ogunquit Beach Inn & MainEscape

WWW Gay/Lesbian ⚥
Gay-Owned & -Operated

Ogunquit's Favorite Gay Guesthouse

Located in the village, only a 5-minute walk to the beach, *Ogunquit Beach Inn* is close to everything special! Feel at home in our uniquely decorated guestrooms, all of which feature color cable TV. Enjoy an expanded continental breakfast buffet in the breakfast porch. Stroll along the Marginal Way (an ocean cliff walk along the jagged coast), or simply relax on the white sands of the gay beach. The inn is near gay bars and world-famous restaurants. Ask about our four-bedroom *MainEscape* house, rented Saturday to Saturday. We are only 1.15 hours from Boston and 4.5 hours from New York City.

Address: 8 School St **Mail To:** Box 1803, Ogunquit, ME 03907
Tel: Toll-free (888) 976-2463 or (207) 646-1112, **Fax:** (207) 646-8858.
E-mail: ogtbeachin@aol.com **Web:** http://www.ogunquitbeachinn.com

Type: Bed & breakfast, guesthouse, cottage, inn.
Clientele: Gay & lesbian. Good mix of men & women
Transportation: Car is best.
To Gay Bars: 2 blocks, a 3 min walk. Near Front Porch.
Rooms: 7 rooms with queen & doubles. 1 4-BR cottage.
Baths: 5 private bath/shower/toilets, 3 shared

bath/shower/toilets.
Meals: Expanded continental breakfast.
Vegetarian: Available at 3 nearby restaurants.
Complimentary: Soft drinks, soda, fruit & treats.
Dates Open: Mar 15-New Years.
High Season: Jun-Aug (Memorial Day-Labor Day).
Rates: $65-$140.
Discounts: Call on weekly

stays & mid-week specials.
Credit Cards: MC, Visa.
Rsv'tns: Required.
Min. Stay: 2 nts wknds, 3 nts holidays.
Parking: Adequate free off-street parking.
In-Room: Color cable TV, maid service.
On-Premises: TV lounge, video tape library. Outside beach shower, patio.
Exercise/Health: Nearby

gym, weights, massage.
Swimming: Ocean nearby.
Sunbathing: Patio, beach.
Smoking: Permitted outside.
Pets: Facility nearby for dogs & cats.
Children: Welcome in cottage.
Languages: English, French, Pilipino.
Your Hosts: Mike & Greg.

Ogunquit House

WWW Gay/Lesbian ⚥

Originally a schoolhouse in 1880, *Ogunquit House* is now a tastefully-restored bed and breakfast in a country setting at the edge of town. We offer a clean, comfortable, reasonably-priced vacation spot. Guest rooms are spacious, with both private and shared baths. Beach, restaurants, shops, movies and art galleries are all within walking distance. Ogunquit's trolley stops almost at your door to bring you to the Marginal Way, Perkins Cove and The Playhouse.

Address: 3 Glen Ave **Mail To:** Box 1883, Ogunquit, ME 03907
Tel: (207) 646-2967.
E-mail: OgunquitHs@aol.com

Type: Bed & breakfast & cottages.
Clientele: Mostly gay & lesbian with some straight clientele
Transportation: Car is best.
To Gay Bars: 2 blocks to men's/women's bars.
Rooms: 6 rooms & 4 cottages with single, double, queen or king beds.
Baths: 8 private, others share.
Meals: Continental breakfast.
Vegetarian: Three nearby restaurants offer vegetarian food.
Dates Open: Mar 15-Jan 2.
High Season: Jul-Aug.
Rates: $65-$135 summer, $45-$70 winter.
Credit Cards: MC, Visa, Discover.
Rsv'tns: Recommended.
Reserve Thru: Call direct.
Min. Stay: Summer 2 nights, holidays 3 nights.
Parking: Ample free off-street parking.
In-Room: Maid service, AC, some have kitchen or refrigerator and color cable TV.
On-Premises: TV lounge.
Swimming: 5-minute walk to ocean beach.
Sunbathing: On beach,
patio, or private sun decks.
Smoking: Permitted with restrictions.
Pets: Permitted with restrictions in the cottages.
Handicap Access: No.
Children: Permitted in cottages, over 12 only in the inn.
Languages: English.
Your Hosts: Tom.

Parkside Parrot Inn

WWW Gay-Friendly 50/50 ⚥
Lesbian-Owned & -Operated

Portland's Affordable Bed & Breakfast

One block from Portland's most beautiful park and four blocks from the edge of the downtown district, the *Parkside Parrot Inn* offers gay and lesbian travelers a comfortable place to stay in the heart of Portland's most diverse neighborhood. Our 100-year-old home is furnished with country antiques and retains many of its original features. Expanded continental breakfast is served in our beautiful common room, with abundant natural light streaming through the front bay window. It's easy walking distance to L.L. Bean's Factory Store, quaint waterfront shops, fine restaurants, gay/lesbian bars and gay/lesbian gift- & bookstore.

Address: 273 State Street, Portland, ME 04101
Tel: (207) 775-0224, **Fax:** (207) 871-8216.
E-mail: parpar1@maine.rr.com **Web:** http://home.maine.rr.com/pparrot

Type: Bed & breakfast.
Clientele: 50% gay/lesbian & 50% straight
Transportation: Car is best, 5 mi from airport. Free pickup from airport (wknds only) or bus.
To Gay Bars: 4 blocks, 1/4 mi, 5 min walk, 1 min drive.
Rooms: 7 rooms (4 queens, 3 doubles).
Baths: 5 private & 2 shared baths.
Meals: Expanded continental breakfast.
Vegetarian: Breakfast, nearby restaurants.
Complimentary: Fruit basket in afternoon in common room.
Dates Open: All year.
High Season: May-Oct.
Rates: $65-$85.
Discounts: Weekly & for single travelers.
Credit Cards: MC, Visa.
Rsv'tns: Required.
Reserve Thru: Call direct.
Min. Stay: 2 nights on holiday weekends.
Parking: Some off-street parking available.
In-Room: Maid service, if requested.
On-Premises: TV lounge, video tape library, backyard patio & garden.
Exercise/Health: Jacuzzi (small fee). Nearby gym,
weights, Jacuzzi .
Swimming: Nearby ocean & lake.
Sunbathing: On patio.
Smoking: In outside designated areas only.
Pets: Not permitted.
Children: No.
Languages: English.
Your Hosts: Julie & Joan.

William Page Inn

WWW **Gay-Friendly** ♀♂

B&B Inn Close to Annapolis Naval Academy

    The William Page Bed & Breakfast Inn offers distinctively appointed guestrooms in a handsomely renovated Historic District turn-of-the-century home with Victorian and traditional charm. Accommodations may include semi-private or private baths, whirlpools and suite. All accommodations include daily chambermaid service, full breakfast and onsite off-street parking. Area interest includes easy walking access to all historic sights as well as the city waterfront district, restaurants, retail shops, and the United States Naval Academy. Mobil and AAA rated and approved establishment.

Address: 8 Martin St, Annapolis, MD 21401
Tel: (410) 626-1506 ext. 7, (800) 364-4160 ext. 7, **Fax:** (410) 263-4841.
E-mail: williampageinn@aol.com **Web:** http://www.williampageinn.com

Type: Bed & breakfast.
Clientele: Mainly straight with gay & lesbian following
Transportation: Car is best.
To Gay Bars: 40 minutes to DC bars/Baltimore bars.
Rooms: 4 rooms & 1 suite with queen beds.
Baths: Private & shared. Some rooms with whirlpools.
Meals: Full breakfast.

Vegetarian: Available upon request.
Complimentary: Wet bar set-up w/ coffee, tea, sodas, juice, water & ice.
Dates Open: All year.
High Season: Mar-Nov.
Rates: $125-$225.
Discounts: Mid week, stays of 5 or more days, winter rates.
Credit Cards: MC, Visa.

Rsv'tns: Required, but walk-ins welcome.
Reserve Thru: Travel agent or call direct.
Min. Stay: For special events & high season weekends.
Parking: Limited free off-street parking.
In-Room: AC, maid service. Color cable TV in suite.
Swimming: Nearby state

park beach, 2 hrs to ocean beach.
Sunbathing: At nearby state park beach.
Smoking: Permitted outdoors.
Pets: Not permitted.
Handicap Access: No.
Children: Permitted if 12 yrs, or older.
Languages: English.
Your Hosts: Robert.

Abacrombie Badger Bed & Breakfast

Gay-Friendly 50/50 ♀♂

Elegant Lodgings in Baltimore's Cultural Center

    Across the street from the Meyerhoff Symphony Hall and two blocks from the Lyric Opera House, the Theater Project, and the beginning of Baltimore's Antique Row sits *Abacrombie Badger*. Music lovers, business people, visitors, and Baltimoreans will find the 12 individually-decorated rooms in this renovated 1880's townhouse a delight. Guests are welcome to relax in the parlor or enjoy a meal at the restaurant. The B&B subscribes to the highest standards of service, comfort, and cleanliness.

Address: 58 W Biddle St, Baltimore, MD 21201
Tel: (410) 244-7227, (888) 9BADGER (922-3437), **Fax:** (410) 244-8415.
E-mail: ABadger722@aol.com **Web:** http://www.badger-inn.com

Type: Bed & breakfast with restaurant & bar.
Clientele: 50% gay & lesbian & 50% straight clientele
Transportation: Car or taxi. Light rail from airport to Cultural Center stop.
To Gay Bars: 1 block, a 1 minute walk.
Rooms: 12 rooms with single & queen beds.

Baths: All private.
Meals: Expanded continental breakfast.
Vegetarian: Fresh fruit & homemade bread with breakfast. Six blocks to vegetarian restaurants.
Complimentary: Chocolates.
Dates Open: All year.
High Season: Mar-Nov.
Rates: $79-$165.

Credit Cards: MC, Visa, Amex, Diners, Discover.
Rsv'tns: Required.
Reserve Thru: Travel agent or call direct.
Min. Stay: 2 nights on weekends during high season.
Parking: Ample free off-street parking. Parking lot adjoins B&B.
In-Room: Color cable TV,

AC, telephone, maid service.
Smoking: Permitted outdoors only.
Pets: Not permitted.
Handicap Access: No.
Children: Well-mannered children over 10 years of age welcome.
Languages: English, French, German, Dutch.
Your Hosts: Paul & Collin.

Mr. Mole Bed & Breakfast

Maryland's Only Four-Star Award B&B
(1995-1999 Mobil Travel Guide)

Mr. Mole has renovated his grand 1870 Baltimore row house on historic Bolton Hill, close to downtown, Inner Harbor, the Symphony and Antique Row, to provide gracious accommodations for discriminating guests. The comfortable, English-style decor, with 18th- and 19th-century antiques, adorns five spacious suites with private phones and full baths. Two suites offer a private sitting room and two bedrooms. Garage parking, with automatic door opener, is included, as is a hearty Dutch-style breakfast of homemade bread, cake, meat, cheese and fruit.

Address: 1601 Bolton St, Baltimore, MD 21217
Tel: (410) 728-1179 or **Fax:** (410) 728-3379.
E-mail: MrMoleBB@aol.com **Web:** http://www.MrMoleBB.com

Type: Bed & breakfast.
Clientele: Mostly straight clientele with a gay & lesbian following.
Transportation: Car or taxi.
To Gay Bars: Five minutes by car to gay/lesbian bars.
Rooms: 3 rooms & 2 suites with queen beds.
Baths: All private bath/ toilets.
Meals: Expanded continental breakfast.
Complimentary: Chocolates.
Dates Open: All year.
High Season: Feb-Dec.
Rates: $105-$165.
Credit Cards: MC, Visa, Discover, Amex, Diners Club.
Rsv'tns: Required.
Reserve Thru: Travel agent or call direct.
Min. Stay: 2 nights on weekends.
Parking: Free parking in garage with automatic opener.
In-Room: Maid service, AC, telephone & clock radio.
Smoking: Permitted outdoors only.
Pets: Not permitted.
Children: Well-mannered children over 10 years welcome.
Languages: English.

Creekside B & B

An Art-Lover's, Book-Lover's, Cat-Lover's Feast...

Creekside B&B is located in a private home in Deale, Maryland on the western shore of Chesapeake Bay, about 20 miles south of Annapolis. Tastefully furnished in a blend of old oak and contemporary furniture, it houses a large collection of 20th century American visionary, folk, and outsider art. There is no smoking anywhere in the house, including your own guest room. Guest facilities include two bedrooms, each with private bath. Guests are welcome to use the living room and library. The owners prepare a full breakfast each morning, and can recommend local places in all price ranges for other meals.

Address: 6036 Parkers Creek Dr, Deale, MD 20751
Tel: (301) 261-9438, **Fax:** (410) 867-1253.
E-mail: mburt@ui.urban.org

Type: Bed & breakfast.
Clientele: Mostly women with men welcome.
Transportation: Car.
To Gay Bars: 35 miles, a 50-min drive to DC or Baltimore bars.
Rooms: 2 rooms with double or queen beds.
Baths: 2 private bath/toilet/ showers.
Meals: Full breakfast.
Vegetarian: By prior arrangement & at local restaurants.
Complimentary: Tea, coffee.
Dates Open: All year.
High Season: Busier in summer.
Rates: $75.
Rsv'tns: Required.
Reserve Thru: Call direct.
Min. Stay: 2 nights on weekends.
Parking: Ample, off-street parking.
In-Room: AC, telephone, ceiling fans. One room also has color cable TV & VCR.
On-Premises: Video tape library.
Exercise/Health: Hot tub, canoe, row boat, croquet.
Swimming: Pool on premises. Nearby river & bay.
Sunbathing: Poolside, on common & private sun decks & on patio.
Smoking: Permitted outdoors only.
Pets: No. Cats on premises.
Handicap Access: Pool, deck & first floor accessible, but guest rooms are up a flight of stairs.
Children: 12 & older welcome with prior arrangement.
Languages: English.

Tallulah's on Main, Ltd.

Tallulah's Tonight? Why Not.

Tallulah's well-appointed in-town and bayfront efficiency apartments allow couples, families and friends to be together in an uncrowded homelike setting. Each suite is equipped with air conditioning, ceiling fans, central heat, TV, full baths, kitchens, blinds and drapes. Bay Side accommodations are at the BayView Beach House, across from the public beach on Beach Road. We're steps from fine dining, antique, crafts shops, etc. You'll also want to check out boat and bicycle rentals, charter fishing and boat sightseeing trips. For a weekend, a week, or longer yet — Barry & Jim welcome you to stay as long as you like.

Address: 5750 Main St., Rock Hall, MD 21661
Tel: (410) 639-2596.
E-mail: tallulah@intercom.net **Web:** http://www.rockhallmd.com/tallulahs/

Type: Apartment suites with gallery gifts shop.
Clientele: Mostly straight clientele with a gay/lesbian following
Transportation: Car is best.
To Gay Bars: 30 miles, a 45 min drive.
Rooms: 5 suites with single or queen beds.
Baths: 5 private bath/ shower/toilets.
Vegetarian: Nearby.
Complimentary: Coffee/tea, fruit & pastries.
Dates Open: All year.
High Season: May-Sept.
Rates: $125-$185 double occupancy.
Discounts: Special weekly & discounted extended stay.
Credit Cards: MC, Visa.
Rsv'tns: Preferred in season.
Reserve Thru: Call direct.
Min. Stay: 2 nights. 3 nights for special events.
Parking: Adequate gated, off-street parking.
In-Room: AC, ceiling fans, color TV, VCR, kitchen, refrigerator, coffee & tea-making facilities.
Swimming: Nearby beach.
Sunbathing: On common sun decks, patio & at beach.
Smoking: Permitted outside. MD law prohibits smoking in rooms.
Pets: No. Kennel nearby.
Handicap Access: Ramps.
Children: Yes, if properly supervised & well-behaved at all times.
Languages: English & German.
Your Hosts: Barry & Jim.

B & B at Howden Farm, The

The Home of the Howden Pumpkin

Howden Farm is a working farm in the Berkshire Hills of Western Massachusetts. Our primary crop is pumpkins, specifically two varieties — the Howden Pumpkin and the Howden Biggie, species developed by Bruce's father. We also have a pick-your-own berry operation. This Greek Revival farmhouse (c. 1830) has three rooms with shared bath, AC and fans in season. Located three miles from the center of town on a road with little traffic, you can sleep with the window open, hike in the fields and woods, ride bikes, canoe the Housatonic River, or just unwind from the stresses of the world. Nearby are the Tanglewood Music and Berkshire Theater Festivals, and the Norman Rockwell Museum.

Address: 303 Rannapo Rd, Sheffield, MA
Tel: (413) 229-8481, **Fax:** (413) 229-0443.
E-mail: bhowden@rnetworx.com

Type: Bed & breakfast.
Clientele: Mostly gay & lesbian with some straight clientele
Transportation: Car is best. Pick up from bus.
To Gay Bars: 60 miles, a 1 hr drive.
Rooms: 3 rooms with single, double or queen beds.
Baths: 2 shared.
Meals: Full breakfast.
Vegetarian: Available on request & nearby.
Complimentary: Cocktail set-up on request, coffee & tea.
Dates Open: All year.
High Season: Jul 1-Oct 31.
Rates: Please inquire.
Discounts: 3-, 5- & 7-day packages.
Credit Cards: Visa.
Rsv'tns: Required.
Reserve Thru: Call direct.
Min. Stay: 2 nights during high season.
Parking: Ample off-street parking.
In-Room: AC, ceiling fans, color cable TV, coffee & tea-making facilities.
Exercise/Health: Nearby gym, weights, Jacuzzi, sauna, steam, massage.
Swimming: Nearby river & lake.
Smoking: This is a smoke-free environment.
Pets: Not permitted.
Handicap Access: No.
Children: No.
Languages: English.
Your Hosts: Bruce & David.

Summer Hill Farm

Berkshire Arts and a Country Setting

Enjoy the beauty and culture of the Berkshires at *Summer Hill Farm,* a 200-year-old colonial farmhouse on a 20-acre horse farm. Rooms are pleasantly furnished with English family antiques. Delicious country breakfasts are served family-style in the dining room or on the sunporch. A haybarn has been converted to a delightful, spacious, 2-room, all-season guest cottage. We're minutes from Tanglewood, Jacob's Pillow Dance, theatres, galleries, restaurants and shops. We also have a 3-bed, 2-bath farmhouse apartment with its own deck and great views.

Address: 950 East St, Lenox, MA 01240
Tel: (413) 442-2057, (800) 442-2059.
E-mail: innkeeper@summerhillfarm.com **Web:** http://www.summerhillfarm.com

Type: Bed & breakfast.
Clientele: Mostly straight clientele with a gay & lesbian following
Transportation: Car is best. Free local bus pick up.
Rooms: 6 rooms with single thru king beds.
Baths: All private.
Meals: Full home-cooked breakfast. Continental breakfast in cottage.
Vegetarian: Special request.

Dates Open: All year.
High Season: Mid June-Labor Day & Oct.
Rates: $65-$195.
Discounts: Inquire.
Credit Cards: Visa, MC, Amex.
Rsv'tns: Required.
Reserve Thru: Call direct.
Min. Stay: On Jul, Aug, Oct & holiday weekends.
Parking: Ample free off-street parking.
In-Room: Color cable TV,

AC, maid svc. 2 rooms w/ fireplaces, 1 w/ fridge. Cottage: coffee/tea facilities, fridge, TV, AC, microwave, toaster.
Exercise/Health: Riding by arrangement. Nearby gym, sauna, massage, hiking, biking, canoeing, skiing, tennis, horseback riding.
Swimming: 5 miles to lake.
Sunbathing: On sun decks & lawns.
Smoking: No smoking

indoors.
Pets: Not permitted.
Handicap Access: Yes. Cottage only.
Children: Infants, & children 5 & over. Must be well-behaved & closely supervised.
Languages: English.
Your Hosts: Michael & Sonya.

Walker House

A Most Harmonious Place to Visit

Walker House, is an 1804-era federal manor, furnished in antiques, on 3 acres of gardens and woods near the center of the picturesque village of Lenox. Rooms, decorated with a musical theme honoring composers, such as Beethoven and Mozart, have private baths, some with claw-foot tubs and fireplaces. Our library theatre features a large-screen video projection system. Walk to galleries, shops and good restaurants. Tanglewood, Jacob's Pillow and summer theatres are only a short drive.

Address: 64 Walker St, Lenox, MA 01240
Tel: (413) 637-1271, (800) 235-3098, **Fax:** (413) 637-2387.
E-mail: phoudek@vgernet.net **Web:** http://www.walkerhouse.com

Type: Bed & breakfast inn.
Clientele: Mainly straight with a gay & lesbian following
Transportation: Car is best. 1 block from New York & Boston buses.
To Gay Bars: 35 miles to Albany & Northampton.
Rooms: 8 rooms with double, queen or king beds.
Baths: All private.
Meals: Expanded continental breakfast.
Vegetarian: Breakfasts

have no meat; other vegetarian meals available at restaurants within walking distance.
Complimentary: Bottle of wine in room, afternoon tea or lemonade daily.
Dates Open: All year.
High Season: Jul-Aug & Oct.
Rates: Summer $80-$200, Oct $90-$160, Sept & Nov-Jun $80-$160.
Discounts: 10% off for single persons in rooms

depending on availability.
Rsv'tns: Advisable during busy periods.
Reserve Thru: Call direct.
Min. Stay: On holidays & summer weekends.
Parking: Ample free on- & off-street parking.
In-Room: AC, maid service.
On-Premises: Meeting rooms, library theatre with large-screen video projection system.
Exercise/Health: Nearby gym, massage.

Swimming: Nearby river & lake.
Sunbathing: On the patio, lawns & garden, at the beach.
Smoking: Non-smoking property.
Pets: Permitted by prior approval at reservation time.
Handicap Access: Yes. 3 1st-floor rooms accessible.
Children: 12 years of age & older welcome.
Languages: English, Spanish, French.

Chandler Inn

WWW Gay-Friendly 50/50 ♀♂

Location, Location, Location!

On the edge of historic Back Bay and the wonderfully eclectic South End, *The Chandler Inn,* Boston's most exciting small hotel, offers visitors myriad fringe benefits, great rates and a location just two blocks from the train and bus stations. Our 56 clean, comfortable guest rooms all have private bath, color television and direct-dial phone. The inn is nestled within the diverse neighborhood of the South End with its lively restaurants, shops and a wide spectrum of social life.

All this is a short walk from fashionable Newbury St., Copley Place, Theater district and convention center. Our bar, Fritz, serves brunch Saturday and Sunday.

Address: 26 Chandler St, Boston, MA 02116
Tel: (617) 482-3450, (800) 842-3450, **Fax:** (617) 542-3428.
E-mail: inn3450@ix.netcom.com **Web:** http://www.chandlerinn-fritz.com

Type: Bed & breakfast hotel with gay bar on premises.
Clientele: 50% gay & lesbian & 50% straight clientele
Transportation: Taxi from airport $17+. 2 block walk from Back Bay Amtrak/subway station.
To Gay Bars: Gay/lesbian bar inside building.
Rooms: 56 rooms with double, queen & twin beds.

Renovated in 2000.
Baths: All private.
Meals: Continental breakfast.
Dates Open: All year.
High Season: Apr-Nov.
Rates: Singles $135. Doubles $145.
Discounts: AARP, off-season.
Credit Cards: All credit cards.
Rsv'tns: Required.

Reserve Thru: Travel agent or call direct.
Min. Stay: 2 nights on weekends in season.
Parking: Limited on-street parking. Municipal lots 2 blocks away.
In-Room: Private direct-dial telephone, color Direct TV & AC.
On-Premises: Gay bar.
Exercise/Health: Discount at Metropolitan Health Club

1 block away.
Sunbathing: On Boston's Esplanade, a 10 min. walk.
Smoking: Permitted. 32 non-smoking rooms, no smoking in common areas.
Pets: No.
Handicap Access: No.
Children: Permitted.
Languages: English & Spanish.

Greater Boston Hospitality

An Uncommonly Civilized Way to Travel

Greater Boston Hospitality offers superb accommodations in the Boston area in hundreds of friendly, private homes and inns, all of which are carefully screened for comfort, cleanliness and congeniality of hosts. Bed and breakfasts range from Federal to Colonial to Georgian, from cozy to luxury, from city to suburb to country. Neighborhoods throughout Boston are included. Many of our accommodations include parking. All include breakfast and knowledgeable, friendly hosts. Be it for business or pleasure, we'll help you to have a welcoming and wonderful time.

Address: Brookline **Mail To:** PO Box 1142, Brookline, MA 02146
Tel: (617) 277-5430, **Fax:** (617) 277-7170.
E-mail: kelly@bostonbedandbreakfast.com **Web:** http://www.bostonbedandbreakfast.com

Type: Reservation service for B&Bs, guesthouses & inns.
Clientele: Very gay-friendly
To Gay Bars: 10 blocks to 1/2 mile, varies
Rooms: 180 rooms, 10 suites w/ singles-kings.
Baths: 160 private. Shared 10 bath/shower/toilets & 18 showers only.
Meals: Expanded continental, continental, or full breakfast.
Vegetarian: Local vegetarian restaurants.
Complimentary: Varies by location.
Dates Open: All year.
High Season: Apr 1-Dec 1.
Rates: $70-$150. Luxury suites up to $280.
Discounts: Inquire.
Credit Cards: MC, Visa, Amex (depends on location).
Rsv'tns: Required.
Reserve Thru: Travel agent or call direct.
Parking: Adequate parking: free, pay, off- & on-street.
In-Room: Varies by location.
On-Premises: Varies by location.
Exercise/Health: Gym, sauna, etc, varies by location.
Swimming: On premises or nearby.
Sunbathing: On patios.
Smoking: Inquire.
Pets: Not permitted.
Handicap Access: Some.
Children: Inquire.
Languages: English, French, Italian, Spanish, German.
Your Hosts: Kelly, Lauren & Jack.

Victorian Bed & Breakfast

TLC in Massive Doses

Our guests say: "Thanks for such friendly hospitality, helpful Boston hints and great food. You two are a delight!" "We feel like we've found a home in the big city." "The best place, the best hosts!" *Victorian Bed & Breakfast* offers elegant and comfortable accommodations just 5 minutes from Boston's Copley Place. All the tourist attractions of the city, plus gay and lesbian bars are nearby. We're sure you'll find your accommodations feel just like home...only better!

Tel: (617) 536-3285.

Type: Bed & breakfast.
Clientele: Women only.
Transportation: Car or taxi from airport, easy subway trip from airport.
To Gay Bars: Close to all gay/lesbian bars.
Rooms: 1 room accommodates up to 4 women with king-sized bed
& double couch.
Baths: Private bath/toilet.
Meals: Full breakfast.
Vegetarian: Food to please all tastes and needs.
Complimentary: Soft drinks.
Dates Open: All year.
High Season: All year.
Rates: $65 for 1, $80 for 2,
$90 for 3 & $100 for 4.
Rsv'tns: Required.
Reserve Thru: Call direct.
Min. Stay: 2 nights.
Parking: Free off-street parking.
In-Room: Large living room, easy chairs, black & white TV, AC, laundry done by hostess, if stay longer
than 4 nights, maid service.
Smoking: Not permitted.
Pets: Not permitted. We have 3 cats in residence.
Handicap Access: No.
Children: Not permitted.
Languages: English.
Your Hosts: Claire & Lois.

Shiverick Inn, The

WWW Gay-Friendly ⚥
Gay-Owned & -Operated

Grandly Romantic

Standing guard at the entrance to historic Edgartown, *The Shiverick Inn* welcomes you to this seaside village of 19th century mansions, built during the town's heyday as a whaling port. White picket fences, manicured gardens and linden trees are the hallmarks of this peaceful town. The Inn has meticulously preserved the graceful formalities of this distinctive period, blending American, French and English 18th and 19th century antiques with rich fabrics, fine wallpapers, Oriental rugs and vivid colors. The Inn is embellished with nine working fireplaces, a beautiful grand piano, private bathrooms, central air, garden room, drawing room, library, terraces and formal garden. Rooms are graced with canopy and four-poster beds, finely pressed linens, down comforters and French milled-soaps. Restaurants, boutiques, antique shops, art galleries, sunny beaches and local historical museums are all within walking distance.

Address: 5 Pease's Point Way, Edgartown **Mail To:** PO Box 640, Edgartown, MA 02539
Tel: (508) 627-3797, (800) 723-4292, **Fax:** (508) 627-8441.
E-mail: shiverickinn@vineyard.net **Web:** http://www.mvweb.com/shiv

Type: Inn.
Clientele: Mostly straight clientele with a gay/lesbian following
Transportation: Plane or ferry to Martha's Vineyard, then taxi or public transport to inn.
Rooms: 10 rooms, 2 suites with queen or king beds.
Baths: All private.
Meals: Full gourmet breakfast, afternoon tea.
Complimentary: Afternoon tea (baked goods, tea, coffee).
High Season: June-Sept.
Rates: High $245-$360, low $145-$225.
Credit Cards: MC, Visa, Amex, Discover.
Rsv'tns: Required.
Reserve Thru: Travel agent or call direct.
Min. Stay: Required.
Parking: Ample free off-street parking.
In-Room: AC, ceiling fans, maid service.
On-Premises: TV lounge.
Exercise/Health: Nearby gym, weights.
Sunbathing: On common sun decks, at beach.
Smoking: Permitted outside in courtyard.
Pets: Not permitted.
Children: Inquire.
Languages: English, Spanish, French, some Portuguese.

Martha's Place

WWW Gay-Friendly 60/40 ♀♂
Gay-Owned & -Operated

Come Pamper Yourself in Style

Martha's Place is a stately Greek Revival overlooking Vineyard Haven Harbor, two blocks from the ferry, village shops, restaurants and the beach. Harbor view rooms are beautifully decorated with fine antiques, oriental carpets and crystal chandeliers. Breakfast in bed is available and the pampering continues at night with turndown service in beds with fine Egyptian cotton linens. Your host's previous experience as an employee of Ritz Carlton hotels is evident in the style of hospitality. As our guest, your stay at the Vineyard will be a memorable one.

Address: 114 Main St, Vineyard Haven **Mail To:** PO Box 1182, Vineyard Haven, MA 02568
Tel: (508) 693-0253.
E-mail: info@marthasplace.com **Web:** http://www.marthasplace.com

Type: Inn.
Clientele: 60% gay & lesbian & 40% straight clientele
Transportation: Ferry. Taxi max $10 about anywhere on island.
To Gay Bars: 1-1/2 hrs to Boston, P'town.
Rooms: 6 rooms with double or queen beds.
Baths: 2 rooms with shower/toilet/sink, 4 rooms with tub/shower/toilet/sink.

Meals: Expanded continental breakfast.
Vegetarian: Nearby.
Dates Open: All year.
High Season: Jun-Oct.
Rates: In-season $175-$395; Off-season $125-$275.
Credit Cards: MC, Visa.
Rsv'tns: Required.
Reserve Thru: Travel agent or call direct.
Min. Stay: 3 nights on holiday weekends.

Parking: Ample free off-street parking.
In-Room: AC, color cable TV, VCR, room, laundry & maid service.
On-Premises: Meeting rooms, TV lounge, fax, copier.
Exercise/Health: Jacuzzi. Nearby gym, weights, sauna, Jacuzzi, steam, massage.
Swimming: Nearby pool, ocean, lake.

Sunbathing: At beach & in side yard.
Nudity: Permitted at beach.
Smoking: Outside only. All rooms non-smoking.
Pets: Not permitted.
Handicap Access: Limited.
Children: No.
Languages: English.
Your Hosts: Richard & Martin.
IGLTA

Missed the Boat Guest House

WWW Gay-Friendly ♀♂

See You on the Vineyard

Located in the town of Vineyard Haven, *Missed the Boat Guest House* is a four-bedroom Cape home with two bedrooms on the first floor, and two others on the second floor for guests. The larger room has a king-sized bed, a TV/VCR combination, and three large windows for enjoying a nice summer's breeze. The other room is a bit smaller, with a double bed, a TV/VCR combination, and two large windows. Both rooms share a full bath. There is also an outside shower that you can use when you return from the beach, or as a fun place to take a shower with your buddy. There is also a large backyard and a sunbathing area for naturalists. The house is within walking distance of town and boats. Public transportation is just a stone's throw from the dwelling. This is your basic no frills place. Coffee is made in the morning and guests are welcome to keep provisions in the main refrigerator. The owner is a single male and welcomes gay clientele. Rent is $85.00 for the larger room and $70.00 for the smaller one. Available on the weekends and possibly during the week. Give me a call or zap an e-mail (when e-mailing, please be discreet). See you on the Vineyard!

Address: 123 Edgartown Rd, Vineyard Haven **Mail To:** RR2 Box 43-T, Vineyard Haven, MA 02568
Tel: (508) 693-1260 (evenings & weekends).
E-mail: jas7@gis.net

Tin Roof Bed & Breakfast

WWW Women ♀

Visit Lesbianville, USA

Tin Roof is a turn-of-the-century farmhouse in the scenic Connecticut River Valley, five minutes from Northampton. Our peaceful backyard has panoramic views of the Berkshire Hills and gardens galore. Breakfast features home-baked muffins, fruit, yogurt, granola, juice and hot beverage of choice. There's color TV, a lesbian video library and a front porch with porch swing. Whether you're considering moving to the area or just visiting, your long-time resident hosts will give you lots of local information and acclimate you to the area. Friendly felines in residence.

Address: Hadley **Mail To:** PO Box 296, Hadley, MA 01035
Tel: (413) 586-8665.

Type: Bed & breakfast.
Clientele: A women's space where lesbian-friendly men are welcome.
Transportation: From Hartford airport, rent a car or take a bus to Northampton.
To Gay Bars: 10 minutes to gay/lesbian bars.
Rooms: 3 rooms with double beds.
Baths: 1 shared bath/shower/toilet, 1 shared toilet, sink.
Meals: Expanded continental breakfast.
Vegetarian: Upon request.
Dates Open: All year.
Rates: Single $60, $65 for two people.
Discounts: 7th night free.
Rsv'tns: Required.
Reserve Thru: Call direct.
Min. Stay: 2 nights on weekends & holidays.
Parking: Ample off-street parking.
On-Premises: Laundry facilities, TV in living room.
Exercise/Health: Nearby health club.
Swimming: In nearby river.
Sunbathing: In the garden.
Smoking: Permitted outside.
Pets: Not permitted.
Handicap Access: No.
Languages: English.
Your Hosts: Jane & Diane.

Accommodations in Provincetown

Ampersand Guesthouse

 Gay/Lesbian ♂

A Delightful Home Base in Provincetown

Ampersand Guesthouse is a fine example of mid-nineteenth century Greek Revival architecture located in the neighborly west end of Provincetown, just a short walk from town center. Each of the bedrooms is unique in its layout, creating a range of accommodations from suites of two to three rooms, to shared baths, to private baths. All are furnished in a careful blend of contemporary appointments and restored antiques, many original to the house. There is also a studio apartment that looks out on both the water and the yard.

Continental breakfast is served daily in the large, gracious living room, a gathering place for guests throughout the day & evening. It has a fireplace seating arrangement, a gaming table and a dining area for relaxing and socializing. And guests have use of the yard as well as a second-story sun deck which commands a view of the harbor and Commercial Street. You may be looking for a quiet, restful time for meeting new friends, walking or sunbathing on the nearby beaches, and enjoying the singular views of nature around Provincetown. Or you may be seeking the bustle of a resort town famous for its shops, restaurants, and active social life. In either case, *Ampersand Guesthouse* provides a delightful home base both in season and off.

Address: 6 Cottage St **Mail To:** PO Box 832, Provincetown, MA 02657
Tel: (508) 487-0959, (800) 574-9645, **Fax:** (508) 487-4365.
E-mail: ampersand@capecod.net **Web:** http://www.capecod.net/ampersand

Type: Guesthouse.
Clientele: Mostly men with women welcome.
Transportation: Take taxi from the airport or walk from town center.
To Gay Bars: 6 blocks to men's bars.
Rooms: 11 rooms & 1 apartment with double or queen beds.

Baths: 9 private bath/toilets & 2 shared bath/shower/toilets.
Meals: Continental breakfast.
Dates Open: All year.
High Season: Memorial Day-Labor Day week.
Rates: $65-$90 off season, $80-$130 high season.
Credit Cards: MC, Visa, Amex.

Rsv'tns: Required.
Reserve Thru: Call direct.
Min. Stay: 7 nts over July 4th, 5 nts rest of Jul, Aug & thru Labor Day. 2 nts May-Jun, Sept & Oct wknds & off-season holidays.
Parking: Limited free off-street parking.
In-Room: TV/VCR, maid service.

On-Premises: TV lounge.
Swimming: Ocean beach nearby.
Sunbathing: Sun decks.
Smoking: Permitted in rooms. Living room smoke-free.
Pets: Not permitted.
Children: Not permitted.
Languages: English.
Your Hosts: Robert & Ken.

Archer Inn

 WWW Gay/Lesbian ♂

Gentle Sea Breezes and the Charm of Yesteryear

This is the perfect place to escape from the hectic world. We've recaptured the grace of yesteryear with Art Deco furnishings and artwork creating an elegant, comfortable atmosphere. Modern conveniences haven't been overlooked; all of our rooms have cable TV, VCR's, in-room phones with voice mail and air conditioning. Most rooms have refrigerators and we also have an ice machine for your convenience.

Our hilltop location offers spectacular views of Provincetown, Cape Cod Bay and the dunes. The rooftop deck is one of the highest in town and a popular place to sunbathe or enjoy a glass of wine at sunset. Beautifully manicured gardens surrounding the house provide places to sit, relax and watch the passing parade on the way to the beach. We serve a leisurely breakfast in our large garden patio during warmer months with specially roasted coffee and healthy foods to start your day. The *Archer Inn* is conveniently located in the West End, minutes away from town activities and the beaches. Open year-round. Ample parking and free shuttle service to the airport and ferry.

Address: 26 Bradford St, Provincetown, MA 02657
Tel: (508) 487-2529, (800) 263-6574, **Fax:** (508) 487-0079.
E-mail: archerinn@capecod.net **Web:** http://www.archerinn.com

Type: Bed & breakfast guesthouse & cottage.
Clientele: Mostly men with women welcome
Transportation: Car, bus. Ferry or Cape Air from Boston. Free pick up from airport, bus, ferry dock.
To Gay Bars: 3 blocks or 1/8 mile, a 5 minute walk.
Rooms: 7 rooms, 2 suites & 1 cottage with double, queen or king beds.
Baths: 8 private baths, 2 semi-private baths.
Meals: Expanded continental breakfast.

Vegetarian: Available at local restaurants, delis & grocery stores. 5-minute walk to A&P.
Complimentary: Ice.
Dates Open: All year.
High Season: Mid-June through mid-Sept.
Rates: Winter $39-$79, spring & fall $59-$129, summer $89-$189.
Discounts: Off-season specials & discounts on longer stays.
Credit Cards: MC, Visa, Amex.
Rsv'tns: Highly

recommended during peak season, holidays & special events.
Reserve Thru: Call direct or travel agent.
Min. Stay: 5 nights during high season.
Parking: Free off-street parking, 1 car per room.
In-Room: Color cable TV, VCR, AC, phones with voice mail, ceiling fans, maid service, robes, fridge.
On-Premises: Roof-top sun deck, bicycle rack, patios, BBQ grill, video library, fax machine, ice machine

Exercise/Health: Local gym nearby. Weights, massage.
Swimming: At nearby pool, ocean, lake or bay.
Sunbathing: On private roof-top sun deck.
Smoking: Non-smoking rooms. Permitted on sun deck and in outdoor areas.
Pets: Not permitted.
Handicap Access: No.
Children: Not especially welcomed.
Languages: English, French.
Your Hosts: Rick & John.

Beaconlight Guest House, The

WWW Gay/Lesbian ⚥

"The Kind of House We Wished We Lived In"

Beaconlight's exceptional reputation for comfort and service has grown by the word of mouth of our many returning guests. Awaken to the aroma of freshly brewed coffee and home-baked cakes and breads. Relax in the English country house charm of elegant bedrooms and spacious drawing rooms.

The *Beaconlight* features one of the largest roof decks in Provincetown built high above the rooftops where you can enjoy stunning views of the town, the ocean, and the very tip of the Cape. Or you can simply pull up a sun lounger and flop! For the more energetic, take a bike ride through the many miles of cycle paths that snake through the Province Lands and the sea shore. After a day taken at your own pace, let us continue to pamper you with a complimentary glass of sherry and let us help you choose your dinner restaurant and nightclub entertainment. We relish the opportunity to share our knowledge about Provincetown with you. We'll give you an inside track on what's going on, where and when. We invite you to delight in the "home away from home" comfort and service upon which our reputation is built. "The kind of house we wished we lived in. Editor's Choice & 5-Palms Award," Out & About 1999.

Address: 12 Winthrop St, Provincetown, MA 02657
Tel: (508) 487-9603 (Tel/Fax), (800) 696-9603.
E-mail: beaconlite@capecod.net **Web:** http://www.capecod.net/beaconlight/

Type: Guesthouse.
Clientele: Mostly men in high season. Good mix of men & women at other times
Transportation: Car, ferry or air from Boston. Free airport/ferry pick up provided if arranged.
To Gay Bars: 2 minutes' walk to gay bars, 1/2 block to tea dance.
Rooms: 10 rooms, 2 suites with double, queen or king beds.
Baths: All private baths.
Meals: Gourmet continental breakfast.
Vegetarian: Available in local restaurants.
Complimentary: Coffee & tea.
Dates Open: All year.
High Season: Mid June to mid Oct.
Rates: High season $110-$225, off-season $55-$145.
Discounts: Off season: 10% for returning guests.
Credit Cards: MC, Visa, Amex, Discover.
Rsv'tns: Required.
Reserve Thru: Call direct or travel agent.
Min. Stay: 5 to 7 days during high season.
Parking: Free off-street parking, 1 car per room.
In-Room: Color cable TV, VCR, AC, ceiling fan, telephone with voice mail & data port, refrigerator, daily laundry & maid serice.
On-Premises: TV lounge, grand piano, fireplace, fax & internet services, cycle storage, video library.
Exercise/Health: Heated spa. Nearby gym, bike hire.
Swimming: Nearby pool & ocean.
Sunbathing: On private sun decks.
Smoking: A non-smoking guesthouse, except on outside decks.
Pets: Not permitted.
Handicap Access: No.
Children: Not permitted.
Languages: English.
Your Hosts: Trevor & Stephen.
IGLTA

Color Photo on Page 27

Bradford - Carver House, The

WWW Gay/Lesbian ♂

Your Home away from Home — Where There Are No Strangers, Only Friends You Haven't Met!

The Bradford-Carver House was built in the mid-nineteenth century and is conveniently located in the heart of Provincetown. Experience our warm hospitality and cozy accommodations in a friendly and relaxed atmosphere. Our graciously appointed rooms, all with private baths, furnished with period pieces of antiques, and equipped with the most modern conveniences to make you feel at home, are perfect for those who seek the charm of a guesthouse.

"A wonderful, intimate bed and breakfast, retaining all the classic New England charms. Lovingly appointed, spacious rooms. Plus the largest video selection we've ever seen. Highly Recommended." — *Out & About* "This relatively new guesthouse, close to nightlife, is one of the best private-bath budget properties, with clean rooms, homey public areas, in-room AC, refrigerator, and VCRs, use of substantial video collection and congenial, laid-back hosts, some rooms have private entrance." — *Fodors 1998* Want to experience it for yourself? Then, come join us in historic Provincetown. No matter what you plan to do, sightseeing, sunbathing, or nothing at all, we are here to make your visit a memorable one. We are looking forward to your staying with us.

Address: 70 Bradford St, Provincetown, MA 02657
Tel: (508) 487-4966, (800) 826-9083, **Fax:** (508) 487-7213. Guest Tel: (508) 487-5699.
E-mail: bradcarver@capecod.net **Web:** http://www.capecod.net/bradfordcarver

Type: Guesthouse.
Clientele: Mostly men with women welcome
Transportation: Bus, car, ferry or plane.
To Gay Bars: Across street, others 1 or 2 blocks.
Rooms: 5 rooms with queen & king beds.
Baths: All private.
Meals: Expanded continental breakfast.
Vegetarian: In nearby restaurants.
Dates Open: All year.

High Season: Mid-June thru mid-Sept, Memorial Day weekend.
Rates: Winter $49-$109, spring $59-$119, summer $109-$199, fall $69-$129.
Credit Cards: MC, Visa, Discover, Amex.
Rsv'tns: Highly recommended in season.
Reserve Thru: Call direct or travel agent.
Min. Stay: Required, varies with dates.
Parking: Free off street parking.

In-Room: AC, ceiling fans, color cable TV, VCR, phone with voicemail & data port, CD/AM/FM clock radio, refrigerator, maid service, fireplaces, period pieces of antiques.
On-Premises: TV lounge, large video collection, common patio.
Exercise/Health: Local gym nearby.
Swimming: Nearby pool, bay & ocean.

Sunbathing: On patio.
Smoking: We're a non-smoking guesthouse. Smoking permitted on our outside patios.
Pets: No.
Handicap Access: No.
Children: No.
Languages: English, Tagalog (Pilipino).
Your Hosts: Bill & José.

Brass Key Guesthouse, The

Unique in Provincetown

The Brass Key Guesthouse is renowned for providing gay and lesbian travelers with the finest in luxury accommodations, attentive service and meticulous housekeeping. In concert with numerous accolades from its guests and from travel writers of the gay media, *The Brass Key* is one of five lodgings throughout the United States to consistently have received *Out & About's* coveted Editor's Choice award (1994-1999).

Located on a quiet side street in the heart of town, 33 guest rooms in a collection of restored 19th-century homes and charming private cottages overlook the heated dip pool, whirlpool spa and landscaped courtyards. All accommodations offer traditional New England architecture enhanced by English and American Country antiques. Yet no two rooms are alike: each presents its own special warmth and personality with details such as a vaulted skylit ceiling, a teddy bear loft, framed antique quilts or courtyard views. Guests are offered every amenity: individually-controlled heating and air-conditioning, twin-line telephone with voice mail, color cable televisions with VCR and videocassette library, refrigerator, hair dryer, luxury bath toiletries; some deluxe rooms further feature fireplaces, king beds and oversized whirlpool baths. The staff of *The Brass Key* looks forward to the pleasure of your company.

Address: 67 Bradford St, Provincetown, MA 02657
Tel: (508) 487-9005, (800) 842-9858, **Fax:** (508) 487-9020.
E-mail: ptown@brasskey.com **Web:** http://www.brasskey.com

Type: Bed & breakfast guesthouse.
Clientele: Mostly men with women very welcome.
Transportation: Ferry, auto, or plane from Boston. Provincetown airport taxi $5.
To Gay Bars: 2 blocks to gay & lesbian bars.
Rooms: 33 rooms & cottages with queen or king beds.
Baths: All private.
Meals: Expanded continental breakfast.
Complimentary: Afternoon cocktails.
Dates Open: Apr-early Nov.
High Season: Mid-Jun to mid-Sept, also holidays, special weekends.
Rates: In season $210-$395, off season from $100.
Credit Cards: Amex, Discover, MC, Visa.
Rsv'tns: Highly recommended.
Reserve Thru: Travel agent or call direct.
Min. Stay: Required in season, during holidays & special events.
Parking: Free off-street parking.
In-Room: Color cable TV, VCR, Bose stereo, video tape library, AC, telephone, electronic safe, refrigerator, fireplace, whirlpool bath, hair dryer, bathrobes. Laundry, maid & turndown service.
On-Premises: Spacious living rooms with breakfast area, fireplaces.
Exercise/Health: Whirlpool spa & nearby gym.
Swimming: Heated pool on the premises; also nearby ocean beaches.
Sunbathing: Poolside courtyard & sun decks.
Smoking: Not permitted inside. Permitted on decks, balconies & in courtyards.
Pets: Not permitted.
Handicap Access: Yes. Wheelchair parking & ramp. 2 guestroom/baths for the physically challenged.
Children: Not permitted.
Languages: English.
IGLTA

Coat of Arms

WWW Gay/Lesbian ♂

Coat of Arms is a vintage, 1810-era, New England Colonial home. In the year 1886, the house was converted into the Victorian structure that it is today. Our location in central Provincetown, at the very tip of Cape Cod, gives our guests ready access to all that Provincetown has to offer. Our rooms are comfortable and cozy, and, like many guest houses in Provincetown, they have shared baths. You may entertain your personal guests in the lounge, which has a large private bar where you can keep your own bottles.

Everything is close by — the beach is a short walk away... great restaurants serving all manner of cuisines are all around us... and close at hand is the great variety of gay and lesbian dance bars and cocktail bars that make up Provincetown's vibrant gay nightlife... And *Coat of Arms* is within strolling distance of gift shops, art galleries, theaters, artists' studios, and a variety of interesting and eclectic bookshops, as well. And yet, our location on a quiet, residential, tree-lined street makes this a great place for a good night's sleep, and to enjoy the rest and relaxation that drew you to Provincetown for your vacation.

Address: 7 Johnson St, Provincetown, MA 02657
Tel: (508) 487-0816, (800) 224-8230.

Type: Guesthouse.
Clientele: Mostly men with women welcome
Transportation: Taxi from airport 10 min or less, 10 min walk from ferry & bus.
To Gay Bars: 1-2 minutes to closest bar, 5-10 min to others.
Rooms: 10 rooms with single, double, queen or king beds.
Baths: 4 shared showers.

Meals: Coffee & pastries in the morning only.
Complimentary: Ice, set-ups at bar, safe sex supplies.
Dates Open: Mar 15-Nov 10.
High Season: Jun-Sept, also holidays & special weekends
Rates: $60-$100 season, $50-$75 off season.
Credit Cards: Visa, MC.

Rsv'tns: Recommended.
Reserve Thru: Call direct.
Min. Stay: 4 days in summer, 7 for Carnival week, 4th of July, Labor Day.
Parking: Limited free off-street parking.
In-Room: Maid service, ceiling fans. Some rooms with AC.
On-Premises: TV lounge, VCR, piano, stereo.
Exercise/Health: Local

gyms.
Swimming: Ocean beach 100 yards.
Sunbathing: On the beach, patio or common sun decks.
Smoking: Not permitted in home.
Pets: Not permitted.
Handicap Access: No.
Children: Not permitted.
Languages: English.
Your Hosts: Skip & Arpina.

Dexter's Inn

WWW Gay/Lesbian ⚥

Come Out to Provincetown & Feel at Home With Us

The experience of a lifetime awaits you in Provincetown. Steeped in history, in the early1800's the site of Dexter's was part of a farm that supplied draft horses for local work. Because of its proximity to the Provincetown Harbor, it was later converted into a fish salting and drying compound, explaining the high content of salt scattered throughout the property to this day.

Located in the heart of downtown Provincetown, *Dexter's Inn* is just a short walk to Commercial Street, shops, restaurants, art galleries and clubs. Our unique cluster of rooms allows for private entrance from deck or patio. In-season, enjoy homemade muffins or breads, juice, and coffee each morning on the garden patio or in our cozy Keeping Room. Our spacious sun deck and patio are the perfect places to relax and meet new friends.

Address: 6 Conwell St, Provincetown, MA 02657
Tel: (508) 487-1911 (Tel/Fax), toll-free: (888) 521-1999.
E-mail: dextersinn@aol.com **Web:** http://www.ptowndextersinn.com

Type: Bed & breakfast guesthouse.
Clientele: Gay & lesbian. Good mix of men & women
Transportation: Car, air, bus & ferry. Free airport pick up available with 1 week's notice.
To Gay Bars: 5-min walk.
Rooms: 15 rooms with queen, double beds, some twins for 3 people.
Baths: 12 private, 3 rooms share 1 bath.
Meals: Expanded continental breakfast, in-season & holidays.
Dates Open: All year.
High Season: Jun 15-Sept 15 & holidays.
Rates: $75-$103 in-season & holidays, $50-$65 off-season.
Discounts: Special off-season rates for long stays.
Credit Cards: MC, Visa.

Rsv'tns: Required.
Reserve Thru: Call direct.
Min. Stay: Required in-season & holidays.
Parking: Ample on-premises free parking, 1 car per room.
In-Room: Maid service, color cable TV, AC, telephone.
On-Premises: Sun deck, patio, refrigerator.
Swimming: Ocean beach nearby.
Sunbathing: On ocean beach & sun deck.
Smoking: Non-smoking house. Smoking permitted outdoors.
Pets: Not permitted.
Handicap Access: Limited.
Children: Permitted over 14 years of age.
Languages: English.

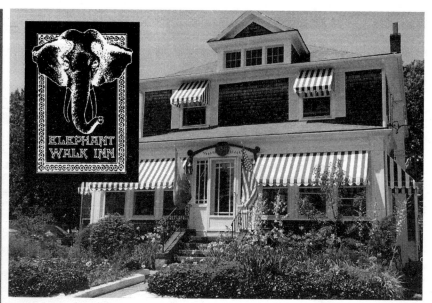

Elephant Walk Inn

WWW Gay/Lesbian ⚣

Elephant Walk "Unforgettable"

Elephant Walk Inn was built as a private country home in 1917. The large mission-style house was converted to an inn some years later. The inn's decor recalls the romantic feeling of an Edwardian house of the past. Many of the rooms are decorated with original paintings, prints and antiques. One room has a canopy bed, another a four-poster, while brass and enamel beds grace two others. Old captain's bureaus, antique tables and Oriental carpets are scattered about. Each guest room has its own private bath as well as a remote cable color TV, a small refrigerator, phone and a ceiling fan. Air-conditioning is also available as an option.

Continental breakfast is served each morning on the glass-enclosed front porch, or guests may enjoy their coffee on the large second floor sun deck overlooking the landscaped garden. Free parking is provided on the premises. While a car is not necessary for seeing Provincetown with its myriad shops, restaurants and clubs, it is convenient to have one for exploring and finding a secluded beach with windswept dunes. Please call or write for a free brochure, or visit our website.

Address: 156 Bradford St, Provincetown, MA 02657
Tel: (508) 487-2543 or (800) 889-WALK (9255). Guest phone: (508) 487-2195.
E-mail: elephant@capecod.net **Web:** http://www.elephantwalkinn.com

Type: Bed & breakfast.
Clientele: Good mix of gay men & women.
Transportation: Pick up from airport, ferry or bus available.
To Gay Bars: 5 min walk.
Rooms: 8 rooms with double, queen or king beds.
Baths: All private.
Meals: Continental breakfast.
Dates Open: Apr 20-Sept 7.
High Season: June 23-Sept 5.
Rates: In season $104-$135, off season $49-$90.
Discounts: Inquire.
Credit Cards: MC, Visa, Amex, Diners, Discover.
Rsv'tns: Required 4-8 wks in advance in high season.
Reserve Thru: Call direct.
Min. Stay: 3 nights in season, more on weekends, holidays.
Parking: Ample free off-street parking.
In-Room: Maid service, color TV, VCR, refrigerator, ceiling fans, phones, AC.
On-Premises: Lounge, sun deck, video library. Guest phone in lounge.
Swimming: Ocean beach 1-1/2 blocks.
Sunbathing: On beach or common sun deck.
Smoking: Not in the inn. Out on the deck.
Pets: Not permitted.
Children: Please inquire.
Languages: English.
Your Hosts: Len.

Four Gables, The

Enjoy P'town Like a Native

WWW Gay/Lesbian ♂
Gay-Owned & -Operated

Mona Anderson Photography

In Provincetown's quiet west end, *The Four Gables* is a group of cottages, apartments and guestrooms just a five-minute walk to downtown, the bars, the beach and National Seashore. Cottages are rented on a weekly basis from May thru October and on weekends the rest of the year. Guestrooms in the main house are rented nightly throughout the year. Each unit is a traditional Cape Cod cottage, newly remodeled and complete with a fully equipped kitchen including gas stove, refrigerator, microwave, coffeemaker and toaster; cable TV and VCR; CD player and stereo; telephone; fireplace and private bath. Linens and towels are provided. Our two guestrooms share a bath and enjoy a full breakfast in the main house. In the cottages we start your week with a welcome basket of coffee, tea, cheese, fresh fruit and pastry. Just a five-minute walk to the local supermarket, you're only steps from all the supplies you need for your stay in Provincetown. If you're driving, there is plenty of off-street parking, or we'll gladly meet your plane, bus or ferry. Bicycle rentals are two blocks away.

Experience Provincetown like a native. We'll show you where to get the best lobster and, if need be, how to cook it. We can recommend the best restaurant for a good dinner or make reservations for a special evening. Join us for a weekly BBQ with local friends or on the veranda for a surprise of homemade ice cream, cookies, pies or cakes. Our slower pace lets you relax, explore and enjoy one of the finest vacation destinations in the country.

Address: 15 Race Rd, Provincetown, MA 02657
Tel: (508) 487-2427.
E-mail: Gary@Delius.com **Web:** http://www.Fourgables.com

Type: Cottage, guesthouse & apartments.
Clientele: Mostly men with women welcome
Transportation: Drive, air or ferry from Boston. Free pick-up & drop-off from airport, bus, ferry dock.
To Gay Bars: A 5 min walk.
Rooms: 2 rooms, 2 apartments, 3 cottages with double or queen beds.
Baths: Private: 5 shower/ toilets; Shared: 2 bath/ shower/toilets.
Vegetarian: Nearby.

Complimentary: Welcome basket of coffee, tea, fruit, cheese, pastry, etc. upon arrival. A special surprise (homemade ice cream, cookies, pies) each afternoon.
Dates Open: All year.
High Season: Jun-Oct.
Rates: Low: $59-$100/ night, high: $150/night, $1,200/week.
Discounts: Frequent customer 10%. Stay 2 wks, get 10% off.
Credit Cards: MC, Visa,

Bancard, Eurocard.
Rsv'tns: Required.
Reserve Thru: Call direct.
Min. Stay: In season: 1 week for cottages.
Parking: Adequate off-street parking.
In-Room: Telephone, fans, color cable TV, VCR, kitchen, refrigerator, coffee & tea-making facilities, stereo/ CD, fireplaces. Cottages have kitchens.
On-Premises: Video tape library.
Exercise/Health: Nearby

gym, weights.
Swimming: Nearby pool, ocean.
Sunbathing: On private sun decks.
Nudity: Permitted on main deck.
Smoking: Smoking outside. All rooms non-smoking.
Pets: Permitted, must be on a leash outside.
Children: Welcome.
Languages: English, French, German, Spanish, Italian.
Your Hosts: Gary & Bob.

Gabriel's Apartments & Guest Rooms

WWW Gay/Lesbian ⚥

Perhaps There Really are Small Corners of This Earth That Come Close to Heaven

Come close to heaven.

Fine Accommodations Since 1979 — Always Open & In the Heart of Provincetown — One Block from the Beach — Breakfast — Fireplaces — Hot Tubs — Steam Room — Sauna — Massage — In-Room Phones & Refrigerators — All Private Baths — Gardens — Sun Decks — Air-Conditioned — Color Cable TV — VCRs — Private Parking — Bicycles — Bar-b-que — Exercise Equipment — Business Services — Internet Access & Computer Facilities — Group Rates Available

Since 1979, *Gabriel's* has welcomed our friends to two beautiful old homes graced by antique furnishings, patios and gardens. Each guestroom and suite, decorated differently, often with fireplaces, is distinguished by its own personality. We also offer modern conveniences such as fax, e-mail and copy services; cable TV, VCRs, in-room phones and fully-equipped kitchens.

Whether you take a soothing soak in one of our two hot tubs, unwind in our steam room or sauna, lounge on the sun decks, work out in our exercise area, relax in our lovely sky-lit common room around a fire, or set out at twilight towards the bright lights of Commercial Street, or the last, purple light of day fading over Herring Cove, you're certain to experience the unique character of Provincetown and the cozy hospitality of *Gabriel's*. Come close to heaven and accept our invitation to join us anytime in the comfortable, safe and heavenly setting of *Gabriel's*. Warmly, *Gabriel Brooke, Innkeeper*

Address: 104 Bradford St, Provincetown, MA
Tel: (800) 9MY-ANGEL, (508) 487-3232, **Fax:** (508) 487-1605.
E-mail: gabrielsMA@aol.com **Web:** http://www.gabriels.com

Type: Bed & breakfast guestrooms & apartments.
Clientele: Mostly gay women and men
Transportation: Free pick up: airport, bus, ferry dock.
To Gay Bars: 1 block.
Rooms: 10 rooms & 10 apartments with mostly queen beds, some doubles.
Baths: All private.
Meals: Homemade breakfast.
Complimentary: Coffee, tea, juice, fruit, muffins, cereal, chocolates on pillow.
Dates Open: All year.

High Season: Memorial Day to Labor Day week.
Rates: Winter $65-$125, Border season $80-$150, high season $90-$200.
Discounts: Nov 1-Apr 1, 3rd night free with coupon or mention this ad, coupons for repeat guests.
Credit Cards: MC, Visa, Discover, Amex.
Rsv'tns: Recommended.
Reserve Thru: Travel agent or call direct.
Min. Stay: 2 nts in season, wknds off season.
Parking: Reserved parking

in a private nearby lot for $5 per night.
In-Room: Color cable TV, VCRs, video tape library, AC, phones, fridges, housekeeping svc, fully equipped kitchens (in apts). Some ceiling fans, fireplaces, whirlpool baths.
On-Premises: Skylight common room with fireplace, music system, library & games. 2 garden courtyards.
Exercise/Health: 2 outdoor hot tubs, sauna, steam room, exercise area.
Swimming: Nearby beach.

Sunbathing: On beach and common sun decks.
Nudity: Permitted on patio in our enclosed yard.
Smoking: Smoke-free.
Pets: Companion animals welcome in most rooms.
Children: Permitted.
Languages: English, French.
Your Hosts: Gabriel Brooke.
IGLTA

A. Blake Gardner, Photographer

Land's End Inn

www Gay/Friendly 50/50 ♀♂

Relax in Victorian Comfort

Land's End Inn commands a splendid windswept location with breathtaking views of Provincetown Harbor and the whole of Cape Cod from on high. Built in the late Victorian period, the inn still houses part of the original owner's collection of oriental wood carvings and stained glass. Spacious rooms furnished with antiques provide a lived-in atmosphere where the modern world has not entered. Here in the quiet west end, we're close to ocean beaches, restaurants and nightlife.

Address: 22 Commercial St, Provincetown, MA 02657
Tel: (508) 487-0706, (800) 276-7088.

Type: Bed & breakfast guesthouse.
Clientele: 50% gay & lesbian & 50% straight clientele
Transportation: Car is best or fly via Provincetown Airport. Bus & ferry runs from Boston Memorial Day-Labor Day.
To Gay Bars: 15-min walk to men's/women's bars.
Rooms: 13 rooms, 1 suite

& 2 apartments with double or queen beds.
Baths: 16 private bath/toilets.
Meals: Continental breakfast.
Dates Open: All year.
High Season: Memorial Day Weekend-Sept 30.
Rates: $90-$295.
Credit Cards: MC, Visa.
Rsv'tns: Recommended.
Reserve Thru: Call direct.

Min. Stay: Summer 5-7 days, off-season weekends and some holidays have minimums.
Parking: Ample free off- & on-street parking.
In-Room: Maid service. Some units with kitchens & ceiling fans.
On-Premises: Public telephone, refrigerator, living rooms.
Swimming: Nearby ocean.

Sunbathing: On private sun decks, lawn or nearby beach.
Smoking: Not permitted inside. Permitted on decks, porches & in garden.
Pets: Not permitted.
Handicap Access: No.
Children: Permitted if under 1 year or over 12.
Languages: English.
Your Hosts: Ron.

Lotus Guest House

A Provincetown Getaway with Central Convenience

PROVINCETOWN • MASSACHUSETTS

Lotus Guest House is situated in a beautiful Victorian building in the heart of town, half a block from beaches, bus, and ferry. The guesthouse has large, spacious air-conditioned rooms decorated in a blend of antique and traditional style furnishings that reflect the charm of New England's past. Rooms have either a private or a shared bath. The bathrooms are newly renovated and have all the comforts of home. The best place to people watch is from the private balcony of the beautiful 2-bedroom suite overlooking Commercial Street. There is a charming common deck and a beautiful garden where you can enjoy your morning coffee or just relax and socialize.

The centralized location of the *Lotus Guest House* enables you to walk to every restaurant, nightclub, shop, and gallery in town. Provincetown is world renowned for its whale watching cruises with research scientists on board. Sail the waters of Cape Cod Bay at sunset, cruise the harbor, take a deep-sea fishing trip or rent your own power or sail boat. Experience Provincetown's miles of bicycle, nature and hiking trails. Go for a horseback or dune buggy ride. Enjoy swimming and sunbathing on the beautiful town beaches, or find your private spot along miles of magnificent beaches in the Cape Cod National Seashore.

Address: 296 Commercial St, Provincetown, MA 02657
Tel: (508) 487-4644.
E-mail: lotusgh@mediaone.net **Web:** http://www.provincetown.com/lotus

Type: Guesthouse with boutique.
Clientele: Mostly gay/lesbian
Transportation: Taxi from airport, Boston Ferry & bus lines 1/2 block.
To Gay Bars: 1 block.
Rooms: 12 rooms & 1 suite with double beds.
Baths: 3 private bath/toilets

& 2 shared bath/shower/toilets.
Complimentary: Morning coffee.
Dates Open: May-Oct.
High Season: July-Aug.
Rates: In season $60-$130, off season $40-$100.
Discounts: Call about weekly specials.
Credit Cards: MC, Visa,

Amex.
Rsv'tns: Recommended.
Reserve Thru: Travel agent or call direct.
Min. Stay: 3 nights weekends, 3-7 nights holidays, call.
Parking: Limited on-street parking, Municipal & private lots 1/2 block away.
In-Room: AC, ceiling fans,

maid service.
On-Premises: Large common deck, landscaped garden.
Swimming: Ocean beach.
Sunbathing: On beach & patio.
Smoking: Permitted.
Pets: Not permitted.
Handicap Access: No.
Languages: English.

Prince Albert Guest House, The

Fine Lodging on Cape Cod Bay

Built in 1870 for a wealthy Provincetown family, *The Prince Albert Guest House* was constructed during the reign of Queen Victoria and named for her husband, Prince Albert. The home, formerly known as the Casablanca Guesthouse and, most recently as the Four Bay Guesthouse, was entirely renovated, inside and out, during the spring of 1997. This renovation resulted in the addition of three new guestrooms, five new private baths and new brick patios in both the front of the guesthouse and in the fenced-in rear gardens. The guesthouse offers ten guestrooms, eight private baths and two hall baths. All rooms have telephones, air conditioning, ceiling fans, color cable televisions, VCRs and small refrigerators. Throughout the home, the *Prince Albert's* heritage is reflected in the Victorian period furnishings, antiques and the plush Oriental rugs.

The Prince Albert is an ideal spot for your summer vacation. Situated across from Cape Cod Bay, step outside and walk over to Provincetown Harbor, or stroll down Commercial Street — we're just a short walk to Provincetown's renowned restaurants, art galleries, shops and clubs, including the A-House and the Pied Piper. With all of the clubs in town, there is no lack of live shows and entertainment. The Cape Cod National Seashore is a quick bike ride from our front door and Herring Cove Beach is easily accessible by foot, bicycle or town loop bus. With miles of beach and forest cycling trails, there is ample opportunity to visit this beautiful seaside area. If your interests lean more toward water activities, Provincetown offers whale watching tours, fishing and wind surfing, as well as jet skiing, speed boating and sailing. Many annual events take place here, including Women's Week in October, Men's Singles Week in November and Carnival Week filled with parades, costume balls and contests.

Address: 166 Commercial St, Provincetown, MA 02657
Tel: (508) 487-0859, (800) 992-0859.
E-mail: princealbert@mediaone.net **Web:** http://www.princealbertguesthouse.net

Type: Guesthouse.
Clientele: Mostly gay
Transportation: Air direct to P'town, or air to Boston then ferry to P'town.
To Gay Bars: 1 block.
Rooms: 10 rooms with double, queen or king beds.
Baths: 8 private, 2 shared.

Meals: Coffee & tea only.
Complimentary: Tea & coffee.
Dates Open: All year.
High Season: June-Sept.
Rates: Summer $90-$170, winter $70-$105.
Credit Cards: MC, Visa.
Rsv'tns: Required.

Reserve Thru: Call direct.
Min. Stay: Required.
Parking: Limited pay parking. 5 spaces off-site.
In-Room: Phone, AC, ceiling fans, color cable TV, VCR, fridge, maid svc.
Sunbathing: On patio.
Smoking: Permitted

outside on patios. All guest rooms are non-smoking.
Pets: Not permitted.
Handicap Access: No.
Children: No.
Languages: English.

Ravenwood Guestrooms & Apartments

Excellent Accommodation in the Gallery District on Famous Commercial St.

Originally a sea captain's home, *Ravenwood* offers comfortable and inviting guest accommodations for the discriminating traveler. Visitors to Provincetown can select from among our guestrooms, efficiencies, penthouse apartments and an enchanting "Cape Cod Cottage." Some accommodations have ocean views, others garden views. These very private accommodations feature complete housekeeping accoutrements, beamed ceilings, skylights, flower gardens, fountains, and a private deck or picnic area. Our cottage with white picket fence comes complete with vaulted ceilings, skylights, Casa Blanca fans and plenty of charm. All accommodations are beautifully decorated with Provincetown art and have color cable VCR. Some have air conditioning.

While staying here you'll be right across the street from the water's edge — sit on our park benches and watch the sailboats round Long Point. We're on famous Commercial Street, a 5-minute stroll to the center of town. We've been the choice of guides and boast many letters of recognition.

Address: 462 Commercial St, Provincetown, MA 02657
Tel: (508) 487-3203 (Tel/Fax).
E-mail: ravenwood8@juno.com **Web:** http://www.provincetown.com/ravenwood

Type: Guest room & year-round apartments, condo & year-round cottage.
Clientele: Mostly women, men welcome
Transportation: Plane, bus, ferry, car from Boston.
To Gay Bars: 5 blocks.
Rooms: 1 room, 3 apartments & 1 cottage.
Baths: All private.
Vegetarian: Nearby.
Complimentary: Mints on pillows, fruit & cheese, flowers, juices & champagne can be arranged.
Dates Open: All year.

High Season: Whale Watching, Blessing of the Fleet, Women's Wk, Men's Wknd, Holly Folly winter fest.
Rates: Summer $80-$125, winter $60-$110.
Discounts: Off season 3rd consec nt free. Better price on 2+ wks.
Credit Cards: All major cards for deposit only.
Rsv'tns: Recommended.
Reserve Thru: Call direct, internet, travel agent.
Min. Stay: 3 nights holiday wknds, 7 nights July-Aug &

Oct Women's Week. Inquire about shorter stays.
Parking: Ample off-street. 1 private spot per rm. Other parking avail.
In-Room: Color cable TV, VCRs, ceiling fans, fridges. Apts: fully equipped kitchens.
On-Premises: Email, fax, patio, BBQ, private fenced-in yards or private decks. Special arrangements available for commitment ceremonies or domestic partner registration.
Exercise/Health: Free

passes to nearby gym & Jacuzzi. Massage avail.
Swimming: At beach.
Sunbathing: On ocean beach, private sun decks & in private garden.
Smoking: Permitted on outdoor decks only.
Pets: Not permitted.
Handicap Access: Studios are accessible.
Children: Inquire.
Your Hosts: Valerie.

Revere House

WWW Gay/Lesbian

Home Sweet Home

The *Revere House* is noted on local maps as early as 1836. This restored captain's home of the Federal period was erected at the height of Provincetown's reign as a thriving fishing port. The charm and ambiance of this bygone era still prevails throughout the ten antique-filled rooms, which include a comfortable studio with a kitchenette and a private bath. In season, coffee, tea, juice and home-made muffins and breads are served in the common room, which overlooks the garden. It's a short walk to shops, galleries, restaurants and nightclubs, and for those desiring some solitude and solace, Mother Nature has blessed Provincetown with a majestic ocean which is only minutes away. Free parking is available.

Address: 14 Court St, Provincetown, MA 02657
Tel: (508) 487-2292, (800) 487-2292.
E-mail: reveregh@tiac.net **Web:** http://www.provincetown.com/revere

Type: Guesthouse.
Clientele: Mostly gay & lesbian
Transportation: Car, bus, boat or plane.
To Gay Bars: 1 block to gay/lesbian bars.
Rooms: 7 rooms & 1 efficiency apartment with double or queen beds.
Baths: 2 private shower/toilet, 2 shared bath/shower/toilet & 1 toilet only.
Meals: Continental

breakfast.
Vegetarian: Restaurants within 2 blocks.
Complimentary: Chocolates on pillow, toiletries.
Dates Open: Apr-Nov.
High Season: June-Sept.
Rates: Summer $65-$145, Spring/Fall $35-$85.
Credit Cards: MC, Visa, Amex, Discover.
Rsv'tns: Suggested.
Reserve Thru: Call or e-

mail direct.
Min. Stay: Holidays 4-7 days, Jul-Aug 4 days on weekends.
Parking: Ample free parking on premises.
In-Room: Maid service. Some rooms have color cable TV, 4 have AC.
On-Premises: Antique-filled common lounge with fireplace. Refrigerator & microwave.
Exercise/Health: 2 blocks

to gym.
Swimming: Ocean beach.
Sunbathing: On beach or in yard.
Smoking: Permitted outside on patios & common room. All guestrooms are non-smoking.
Pets: Not permitted.
Handicap Access: No.
Children: Not permitted.
Languages: English.
Your Hosts: Gary & Kevin.
IGLTA

Somerset House — Accommodations

Service Without the Attitude

New owners have turned the *Somerset House* into Provincetown's year-round service-oriented guesthouse — service without the attitude. Upgraded services include: Land Rover airport/ferry shuttle, experienced Concierge, expanded Morning Reception, Summer evening reception, Summer Automatic Evening Turn-down service, and Guest Reception availability from 8am to 10pm. Morning/evening receptions will be served in our restored and expanded Guest Reception Lounge — during warm weather, French doors open from the lounge out onto the front deck/patio with a view of Cape Cod Bay. This historical Italianate Victorian with water views, is situated in the center of town, across the street from Cape Cod Bay.

Address: 378 Commercial St, Provincetown, MA 02657
Tel: (508) 487-0383, (800) 575-1850, **Fax:** (508) 487-4237.
E-mail: getserviced@somersethouseinn.com **Web:** http://www.somersethouseinn.com

Type: Bed & breakfast, guesthouse, inn.
Clientele: Gay & lesbian. Good mix of men & women
Transportation: Free pick up/Land Rover shuttle service from airport, bus, ferry dock.
To Gay Bars: 1 block.
Rooms: 13 rooms, 1 apartment with double, queen or king beds.
Baths: Private & shared.
Meals: Expanded continental breakfast.
Vegetarian: 1 block.
Complimentary: Evening reception: wines, beer, spring water, bries/cheese, breads, crackers. Automatic evening turndown service (condom & mint on pillow).
Dates Open: All year.
High Season: May-Sept.
Rates: Fall/winter: $75-$140; spring/summer $95-$195.
Discounts: Jan-Mar: 50% off 2nd night. Winter Get Away special.
Credit Cards: MC, Visa, Amex.
Rsv'tns: Recommended.
Reserve Thru: Call direct.
Min. Stay: Required during high season & holidays.
Parking: Ample free parking (1 car per room).
In-Room: Telephone, ceiling fans, color cable TV, refrigerator, maid service.
On-Premises: TV lounge, business & concierge svc.
Exercise/Health: Nearby gym, weights, Jacuzzi, sauna, steam, massage.
Swimming: Ocean nearby.
Sunbathing: On patio, deck & at beach.
Smoking: Non-smoking property.
Pets: Not permitted.
Children: Inquire.
Languages: English, very little Spanish & Japanese.

PROVINCETOWN • MASSACHUSETTS

Sunset Inn

You'll Love the Sunsets from The Sunset

The *Sunset Inn* is one of Provincetown's oldest guesthouses. Built in the mid-nineteenth century as a private home, it has been a guesthouse welcoming visitors for more than half a century. If the *Sunset Inn* looks familiar, it may be that you've seen one of the many paintings or photographs depicting the building. Scores of artists have been attracted by the stately elegance and beauty of the inn. Among them renowned local artist Robert Kennedy, whose paintings of the inn can be found in art galleries throughout the country, and American artist Edward Hopper, whose famous painting of the inn entitled *Rooms for Tourist* hangs in the permanent collection at the Yale University Art Gallery in New Haven.

We're just one block from the center of town and the beach. Stroll down Commercial Street and browse the unique shops and galleries that have made Provincetown famous. Enjoy dinner at one of the many fine local restaurants; from hot dogs to haute cuisine, you're sure to find what you crave. And, of course, there is the legendary excitement of the Provincetown nightlife with cabarets, comedy shows, dance clubs and nightclubs — all within walking distance of the inn. For the outdoor types, we're near the National Seashore bike trails, whale watching, fishing boats, dune rides and airplane sightseeing. We offer spacious, comfortable guest rooms, each distinct in its decor. You'll find all the modern conveniences, yet we've retained the cozy warmth of a Cape Cod inn. Our sun decks and porches afford spectacular views of Provincetown Harbor and are a perfect vantage point from which to view Provincetown's sunsets.

Address: 142 Bradford St, Provincetown, MA 02657
Tel: (508) 487-9810, (800) 965-1801.
E-mail: sunset1@capecod.net **Web:** http://www.ptown.com/sunsetinn

Type: Guesthouse.
Clientele: Mostly gay & lesbian with some straight clientele
Transportation: Car, airplane, ferry from Boston. Free pick up from Provincetown airport.
To Gay Bars: 3 blocks.
Rooms: 20 rooms with single, double or queen beds.
Baths: 14 private shower/ toilets, 6 shared bath/ shower/toilets.
Meals: Continental breakfast.
Vegetarian: Nearby.
Dates Open: Apr 15-Nov 1.
High Season: Mid-Jun to mid-Sept.
Rates: Off season (spring & fall): $46-$75; high season (summer): $64-$125.
Credit Cards: MC, Visa, Discover.
Rsv'tns: Highly suggested.
Reserve Thru: Travel agent or call direct.
Min. Stay: 4 nts wknds & Memorial Day, 5 nts July 4th & Labor Day.
Parking: Ample free off-street parking.
In-Room: Maid service, color TV, telephone. Deluxe rooms have AC, VCR, fridge.
On-Premises: Lounge.
Exercise/Health: Nearby
gym, weights, massage.
Swimming: In nearby ocean & bay.
Sunbathing: On common sun decks, at beach.
Nudity: Permitted on top deck.
Smoking: Permitted on outside decks & patio.
Pets: Not permitted.
Children: No.
Languages: English.

White Wind Inn

WWW Gay/Lesbian ⚥
Gay-Owned & -Operated

"A Provincetown Landmark — Come Make Your Own History..."

The *White Wind Inn*, "A Provincetown Landmark," is a gracious New England mansion built in the mid 1800s. Today, guests enjoy its well-appointed accommodations that feature high ceilings, antiques, chandeliers, four-poster and brass beds. Several rooms have private decks, some with water views, so that you can enjoy your own unique perspective on Provincetown from the comfort of your room. Fireplace rooms provide that extra romantic touch for visits throughout the year.

The *White Wind's* veranda that overlooks Commercial Street, across from Provincetown Bay, is a favorite — whether it's starting the day with breakfast, catching some afternoon rays, enjoying a drink in the evening while watching "The Tea Dance parade" or relaxing with friends, old and new. There is no better place to take in the sights that give Provincetown so much character.

Address: 174 Commercial St, Provincetown, MA 02657
Tel: (508) 487-1526, (888) 449-WIND (9463), **Fax:** (508) 487-4792.
E-mail: wwinn@capecod.net

Type: Bed & breakfast.
Clientele: Gay & lesbian. More men in season, good mix of men & women other times
Transportation: Car, plane, bus & ferry. Free pick up from airport & ferry dock.
To Gay Bars: 1/2 block, a 2 min walk.
Rooms: 11 rooms, 1 suite with double or queen beds.
Baths: All private bath/shower/toilets.
Meals: Expanded continental breakfast.

Complimentary: Weekly social on porch - cocktails, snacks.
Dates Open: All year.
High Season: Memorial Day weekend thru 2nd weekend in Sept.
Rates: Off season $75-$145, season $120-$225.
Credit Cards: MC, Visa, Amex, Discover.
Rsv'tns: Required.
Reserve Thru: Travel agent or call direct.
Min. Stay: Required in season & on certain holiday/

events.
Parking: Ample, free off-street parking.
In-Room: Color cable TV, VCR, refrigerator, maid service. AC (most rooms) or ceiling fans, phones, voicemail, data ports.
On-Premises: Video tape library.
Exercise/Health: Nearby gym, weights, massage.
Swimming: Nearby pool, ocean.
Sunbathing: On private sun decks, common front porch

sun deck, or at beach.
Smoking: All rooms & inside common areas are non-smoking. Smoking on outdoor decks/patio areas only.
Pets: Permitted. Limited rooms, with prior approval, additional charge.
Handicap Access: No.
Children: No.
Your Hosts: Michael & Rob.

Color Photo on Page 26

Admiral's Landing Guest House

WWW Gay/Lesbian ⚥

Accommodations in the Heart of Provincetown

Admiral's Landing Guest House offers spacious rooms with private baths, parking and a friendly social atmosphere. Located one block from the bay beach, shops and restaurants, you'll be close to everything that Provincetown has to offer. Our variety of distinctively decorated rooms have amenities that include TVs, VCRs, refrigerators, ceiling fans and outgoing phones. Freshly baked pastries, fruit, coffee, tea and juice are served each morning in our comfortable common rooms or outside on the patio. This is the perfect place to truly relax and be yourself. Call or write for photo brochure, or visit our web site.

Address: 158 Bradford St, Provincetown, MA 02657
Tel: (800) 934-0925, (508) 487-9665, **Fax:** (508) 487-4437.
E-mail: admiral@capecod.net **Web:** http://www.admiralslanding.com

Type: Guesthouse & efficiency studios.
Clientele: Gay men & women
Transportation: Courtesy transportation from airport & ferry with prior arrangement.
To Gay Bars: 3 blocks to men's bar. 5-minutes' walk to women's bar.
Rooms: 6 doubles & 2 efficiencies.
Baths: 6 private. Studio efficiencies have private baths.
Meals: Continental breakfast, afternoon snacks.
Dates Open: All year. Studios May 15-Nov 10.
High Season: May-Sept.
Rates: Summer & holidays: $95-$115; winter: $55-$85 spring/fall $65-$95.
Discounts: Group rates.
Credit Cards: MC, Visa.
Rsv'tns: Strongly recommended.
Reserve Thru: Travel agent or call direct.
Min. Stay: Holiday weekends & Jul-Aug.
Parking: Free off-street parking.
In-Room: TV, VCR, phone, ceiling fans, AC, fireplaces, refrigerator, maid service.
On-Premises: Patio, video library.
Exercise/Health: Gym nearby.
Swimming: Harbor beach nearby.
Sunbathing: On ocean beach or patio.
Smoking: No.
Pets: Permitted in studios only.
Handicap Access: Studios have limited accessibility.
Children: Not permitted.
Languages: English.
Your Hosts: Chuck & Peter

Captain's House

WWW Gay/Lesbian ♂

The Simple Elegance of a Bygone Era

The Captain's House is one of the oldest guesthouses of Provincetown. Built more than a century ago, it represents the typical architecture and simple elegance of a bygone era. Though on busy Commercial St., we're located up a secluded little alley where there is an absence of noise and a lot of unexpected privacy. Our charming little patio is great for morning coffee, cook-outs or sun tanning, and you will find the common room to be most comfortable. Our rooms are charming, immaculate and comfortable, with reasonable rates.

Address: 350-A Commercial St, Provincetown, MA 02657
Tel: (508) 487-9353, Reservations: (800) 457-8885.
E-mail: dbrennan@cape.com **Web:** http://www.captainshouseptown.com

Type: Guesthouse.
Clientele: Mostly men with women welcome.
Transportation: Taxi from airport 5 min. 2-min. walk from bus, ferry.
To Gay Bars: 5-10 minutes' walk to everything.
Rooms: 1 small single, 8 doubles & 1 room with 2 beds, 1 room with queen.
Baths: 3 private & 2 shared. All rooms have sinks.
Meals: Expanded continental breakfast.
Dates Open: All year.
High Season: Memorial Day-Labor Day.
Rates: $50-$100.
Discounts: By request on stays of 7 days or more.
Credit Cards: MC, Visa, Amex, Discover.
Rsv'tns: Necessary, as soon as possible.
Reserve Thru: Call direct.
Min. Stay: On holidays, special events
Parking: Free parking.
In-Room: Color TV, VCR, maid service, refrigerator, & ceiling or window fans.
On-Premises: TV lounge, central heat, private patio.
Swimming: Ocean beach nearby.
Sunbathing: On beach or private patio.
Smoking: Outside only.
Pets: Not permitted.
Handicap Access: No.
Children: Please inquire.
Languages: English.
Your Hosts: David & Bob.

Carl's Guest House

WWW Men ♂

Where Strangers Become Friends

An excellent alternative to higher-priced establishments, our house is decorated in the clean, simple manner most suited to a beach vacation. Friendly, decent guys come from around the world to enjoy sea, sun and sand. At *Carl's Guest House,* all guest rooms are private, clean, comfortable and fairly priced. You can kick off your shoes and relax in an inviting living room with stereo, cable TV and a selection of video tapes of all ratings. We have been catering to the *gentler gay visitor* since 1975.

Address: 68 Bradford St, Provincetown, MA 02657
Tel: (508) 487-1650, brochure/rates tape: (800) 348-CARL.
E-mail: info@carlsguesthouse.com **Web:** http://www.CarlsGuestHouse.com

Type: Guesthouse.
Clientele: Men
Transportation: $1 bus, $5 taxi from airport; short walk from bus stn & boat dock.
Rooms: 14 rooms with single, double or queen beds.
Baths: Private & semi-private.
Meals: Complimentary coffee, tea, soups and ice in lounge service area.

Complimentary: Coffee, tea, etc.
Dates Open: All year.
High Season: Mid-June to mid-Sept.
Rates: Summer (high season) $59-$129, off season $29-$69.
Discounts: For groups, gay business organizations during off season.
Credit Cards: MC, Visa.
Reserve Thru: Call direct.

Parking: Limited off-street & adequate on-street parking.
In-Room: Color TV, private sun decks, patios, AC, fridge, ceiling fans.
On-Premises: TV lounge with color cable TV & VCR.
Exercise/Health: Nearby gym.
Swimming: One block to ocean beach.
Sunbathing: On beach,

private or common sun deck.
Nudity: Permitted on sun decks, in shower rooms.
Smoking: Smoking areas are limited.
Pets: Not permitted.
Handicap Access: No.
Children: Not permitted.
Languages: English.

Grand View Inn, The

WWW Gay/Lesbian ♂
Gay-Owned & -Operated

Grand View Inn, a wonderful Victorian Captain's house built just after the Civil War period, is quietly tucked just one house away from the pulse of busy Commercial Street's restaurants, galleries, shops and entertainment. Located in Provincetown's beautiful, historic West End, the inn offers some of the best harbor views in town. There are marvelous vistas from several rooms and, especially, our two decks, where you can enjoy panoramic views of Provincetown Harbor, Lands End Lighthouse and the hilly West End. When you see the gentle English-style gardens, you'll feel the inn's special energy. We're situated conveniently between the popular Boatslip Tea Dance and Mussel Beach Health Club.

Address: No. 4 Conant St, Provincetown, MA 02657
Tel: (508) 487-9193, Toll-free: (888) 268-9169.
E-mail: grandviewinn@mediaone.net **Web:** http://www.ptownguide.com/grandviewinn

Type: Guesthouse.
Clientele: 70% men, 30% women
Transportation: Plane from Boston to P'town airport, taxi to inn. Boat 9:30am from Boston, walk to inn.
To Gay Bars: 1 block. 1 min walk to tea dance.
Rooms: 12 rooms double, queen & king beds.
Baths: Private, semi-private & shared.

Meals: Expanded continental breakfast.
Vegetarian: Health food restaurants nearby.
Complimentary: Coffee & juices available in common room daily in season.
Dates Open: All year.
High Season: June 15-Sept 15.
Rates: High: $65-$135, mid: $55-$100, off: $45-$90.
Credit Cards: MC, Visa.

Rsv'tns: Required in season.
Reserve Thru: Call or e-mail direct.
Min. Stay: 4 nights during high season.
Parking: Inquire.
In-Room: Maid service.
On-Premises: TV lounge, common rooms, kitchen.
Exercise/Health: High-tech gym 3 doors away.
Swimming: Within walking

distance.
Sunbathing: Common sun decks, nearby beaches.
Smoking: Permitted in designated outside areas.
Pets: Sep 15-Jun 16 only.
Children: No.
Languages: English.
Your Hosts: Tom & Michael.

Heritage House

WWW Gay/Lesbian ⚥

Having a Wonderful Time...Wish You Were Here!

Our house, with seven guestrooms and a spacious living room, is located next door to the Heritage Museum between Commercial Street and Bradford Street. The veranda on our second floor is a breezy, relaxing spot where you can enjoy a view of the harbor and passersby. Shops, the bay beach and many fine restaurants are just a short walk from our door. Our fluffy towels, fresh and crisp linens, sparkling clean bathrooms, delicious coffee, homemade muffins and a friendly, comfortable atmosphere will help make your stay at *Heritage House* a pleasant one. As your hosts, we'd like to help you enjoy the magic of Provincetown.

Address: 7 Center St, Provincetown, MA 02657
Tel: (508) 487-3692.
E-mail: heritageh@capecod.net **Web:** http://www.heritageh.com

Type: Guesthouse.
Clientele: Mostly gay & lesbian with some straight clientele
Transportation: Car or fly into P'town Airport from Boston's Logan Airport. Free pick up from airport & ferry wharf.
To Gay Bars: 5-min walk to women's & men's bars.
Rooms: 7 rooms & 1-bedroom condo with single, double or king beds.

Baths: 3 shared bath/shower/toilets. Condo with private bath.
Meals: Buffet breakfast.
Vegetarian: Breakfast is mostly vegetarian & restaurants featuring vegetarian selections are only a 5-minute walk.
Complimentary: Ice available. Refrigerator on each floor.
Dates Open: All year.
High Season: Jun-Sept & holiday weekends.
Rates: In season $50-$115, off season $40-$90.
Discounts: Off-season group rates available.
Credit Cards: MC, Visa, Amex.
Rsv'tns: Preferred.
Reserve Thru: Call direct.
Min. Stay: 3 nights on holiday weekends.
Parking: Free off-street parking.
In-Room: Maid service.

On-Premises: Living room has color cable TV & VCR.
Exercise/Health: Gym, weights & massage nearby.
Swimming: In nearby ocean.
Sunbathing: At the beach.
Smoking: Not permitted.
Pets: Not permitted.
Handicap Access: No.
Children: Not especially welcomed.
Languages: English, French.

Romeo's Holiday

WWW Gay/Lesbian ⚥

Let Passion Prevail

Romeo's Holiday is a Victorian-era gem in the very center of Provincetown. Recent remodeling has restored the charm of this circa 1870, nine-guestroom home. You will enjoy our new hot tub (8am-10pm) and large sun deck which, in season, is festooned with flowers and comfortable furnishings. Many nice amenities and a friendly, helpful staff is here year round to ensure a memorable stay.

Address: 97 Bradford St, Provincetown, MA 02657
Tel: (508) 487-6636, **Toll free:** (877) MY ROMEO (697-6636), **Fax/Guestline:** (508) 487-3082.
E-mail: freenite@romeosholiday.com **Web:** http://www.romeosholiday.com

Type: Guesthouse.
Clientele: Good mix of gay men & women
Transportation: Bus & ferry (in season) 3 blocks.
To Gay Bars: 1/2 block to major discos.
Rooms: 5 doubles, 1 triple, 3 quads.
Baths: 4 private, 4 shared.
Meals: Continental breakfast.
Complimentary: Beach towels, toiletries, safer-sex supplies.
Dates Open: All year.
High Season: June-Aug.
Rates: High $69-$129, low-mid $39-$89.
Discounts: 10% on stays of 5 or more days low & mid season.
Credit Cards: MC, Visa.
Rsv'tns: Required with 1/2 deposit within 5 days of booking.
Reserve Thru: Call direct.
Min. Stay: 4-7 nights high, 2-3 mid.
Parking: Free off-site parking.
In-Room: Maid service, color TV, radio alarm clock, many with AC.
On-Premises: TV/VCR, guest phone/fax, iron & board, hairdryers.
Exercise/Health: Hot tub on premises. Health clubs 1/2 mile away.
Swimming: Ocean beach nearby.
Sunbathing: On the beach or deck.
Nudity: Herring Cove Beach (at your own risk).
Smoking: Permitted outside only.
Pets: Not permitted.
Handicap Access: No.
Children: Over 6 years old.
Languages: English.
Your Hosts: Stan.

Roomers

WWW Gay/Lesbian ♂

Cozy and Intimate...

Provincetown...the name alone evokes thoughts of a quaint fishing village surrounded by beautiful beaches and untamed sand dunes, fine restaurants and a shopper's paradise. *Roomers* guesthouse maintains the charms of the past, but has the crisp, clean, contemporary feel of today. Each room is decorated with quality antiques and has private bath, queen-sized bed, ceiling fan, TV and refrigerator. We're on a quiet side street, but very centrally located in the heart of the West End. Cozy and intimate...that's *Roomers'* style. Come celebrate our 20th year in business in 2001.

Address: 8 Carver St, Provincetown, MA 02657
Tel: (508) 487-3532.

Type: Guesthouse.
Clientele: Mostly men with women welcome
Transportation: Free pickup from airport or ferry.
To Gay Bars: Gay bar across the street, others 1-3 blocks.
Rooms: 9 rooms with twin or queen beds.

Baths: All private.
Meals: Continental breakfast.
Dates Open: Apr-Dec.
High Season: Memorial Day wknd, Jul, Aug, Labor Day wknd.
Rates: In-season $90-$150, off-season $65-$120.
Credit Cards: Visa, Amex,

MC.
Rsv'tns: Required.
Reserve Thru: Call direct.
Min. Stay: 5 days in-season.
Parking: Free off-street parking, 1 space per room.
In-Room: Refrigerator, maid service, color cable TV with VCR.

On-Premises: 2 common rooms.
Sunbathing: In side yard.
Smoking: Permitted without restrictions.
Children: Not permitted.
Languages: English.
Your Hosts: Andrew.

Newnham Suncatcher Inn

Gay/Lesbian ♀♀
Women-Owned & -Operated

Country Charm and a Touch of Elegance

Newnham SunCatcher Inn is on a secluded lot in the heart of Saugatuck's business district, close to shops, restaurants, recreation and the lake beaches. The turn-of-the-century home with wraparound porch, complete with gingerbread carvings, has been carefully restored to the grandeur of its day. Period furniture once again graces its 5 bedrooms. Behind the main house, a two-cottage suite provides more private accommodations. Features are a large sun deck, hot tub and swimming pool.

Address: 131 Griffith **Mail To:** Box 1106, Saugatuck, MI 49453
Tel: (616) 857-4249.
Web: http://www.bbonline.com/mi/suncatcher/index.html

Type: Bed & breakfast.
Clientele: Mostly gay & lesbian with some straight clientele.
Transportation: Free pick up from airport, train.
To Gay Bars: 3-minute drive to gay/lesbian bars.
Rooms: 5 doubles, 2-cottage suite (cottage is a guest house with complete facilities).
Baths: 3 private, others share.

Meals: Full breakfast.
Vegetarian: Available on request.
Complimentary: Tea, coffee, juices, mints on pillow.
Dates Open: All year.
High Season: May-Oct.
Rates: Rooms $65-$120 weekdays & off-season weekends, $75-$120 summer weekends.
Discounts: During off-season.

Credit Cards: MC, Visa.
Rsv'tns: Required.
Reserve Thru: Call direct.
Min. Stay: 2 nights on weekends.
Parking: Ample free off-street parking.
In-Room: AC.
On-Premises: Common room, meeting room, fireplace, TV lounge, telephone, kitchen available.
Exercise/Health: Jacuzzi.
Swimming: In-ground

heated swimming pool.
Sunbathing: At poolside or on private sun decks.
Nudity: 3 mi to nude beach.
Smoking: Permitted on outside deck only.
Pets: Not permitted.
Handicap Access: No.
Children: Permitted weekdays only.
Languages: English.
Your Hosts: Barb & Nancy.

Kirby House, The

Across the Bridge from the Heart of Saugatuck

A beautifully-restored 110-year-old Queen Anne Victorian manor on the state historical registry, *The Kirby House* is known for its comfortable elegance, warm hospitality and sumptuous breakfast/brunch buffets. The home is graced with quarter-sawn oak woodwork and panels, prismed windows, tall ceilings with gently curved moldings, a six sided tower, wrap-around front porch and beautiful gardens. The establishment also offers a beautiful, secluded pool, Jacuzzi and sunning decks overlooking acres of woodland. Over the bridge and around the corner is the heart of Saugatuck with its unique shops and art galleries. Our serene surroundings will refresh your senses. This is more than a place to stay, it's a place to linger.

Mail To: PO Box 1174, Saugatuck, MI 49453
Tel: (616) 857-2904 (Tel/Fax), (800) 521-6473.
E-mail: kirbyinn@aol.com **Web:** http://www.bbonline.com/mi/kirby

Type: Bed & breakfast.
Clientele: Mostly gay & lesbian with some straight clientele
Transportation: Car is best.
To Gay Bars: 4 blocks.
Rooms: 8 rooms with single, double or queen beds.
Baths: 6 private & 2 share.
Meals: Full breakfast buffet.
Vegetarian: Available upon request.
Dates Open: All year.
High Season: Jun-Oct.
Rates: $90-$135.
Credit Cards: MC, Visa, Amex, Discover.
Rsv'tns: Required.
Reserve Thru: Travel agent or call direct.
Min. Stay: 3 nights July & August weekends. 2 nights other weekends.
Parking: Ample off-street parking.
In-Room: Maid service, ceiling fans, AC.
On-Premises: Courtesy telephone, kitchen privileges, ice, gas BBQ.
Exercise/Health: Bicycles, Jacuzzi.
Swimming: Pool or lake.
Sunbathing: Poolside, lakeside or on common sun decks.
Nudity: 2 miles to nude beach.
Smoking: Permitted outside.
Pets: No.
Handicap Access: No.
Children: Permitted weekdays with prior arrangement.
Languages: English.
Your Hosts: Ray & Jim.

Hallett House Bed & Breakfast

WWW Gay-Friendly 50/50 ♀♂
Gay-Owned & -Operated

The Midwest's Premier Bed & Breakfast

Built in 1920, *Hallett House,* a beautiful deco-style home rests on eleven acres of mature white pine, Norway, and oak. Significantly redesigned and expanded in 1936, it maintains its original elegance to this day. The B&B is furnished with period pieces, and accented throughout with oriental carpets and original Art Deco lighting. The dining room, living room, front hall and library are all on the first floor and are common areas for you to browse and enjoy. A hot, sumptuous (translated: pretty darn good) breakfast is served in a bright, semiformal dining room surrounded with windows and nature.

We feature the artwork of Lou Roman and Susan Amidon, both of whom share strong Minnesota ties. The well-stocked sunken library, our signature room, which dictates a literary theme. All rooms are named after famous authors and literary figures, and all are tastefully decorated, comfortable, and quiet.

Address: 12131 Hwy 6 N, Deerwood, MN 56444
Tel: (218) 546-5433, **Toll-Free:** (877) 546-5433, **Fax:** (218) 546-5933.
E-mail: minnboyz@aol.com **Web:** http://www.halletthouse.com

Type: Bed & breakfast.
Clientele: 50% gay & lesbian & 50% straight
Transportation: Car. Free airport pick up, arrange in advance.
To Gay Bars: 100 miles.
Rooms: 3 rooms, 2 suites with double or queen beds.
Baths: All private.
Meals: Full breakfast.
Vegetarian: Upon request.

Complimentary: Bottle of wine in room.
Dates Open: All year.
Rates: $70-$115.
Discounts: Inquire.
Credit Cards: MC, Visa, Amex, Diners, Discover.
Rsv'tns: Required. Cancellations: at least 7 days in advance full refund; less than 7 days 50% refund; no-shows & same-

day cancellations charged full rate.
Reserve Thru: Call direct.
Parking: Ample free off-street parking.
In-Room: Ceiling fans, color cable TV, VCR.
On-Premises: TV lounge, library, parlour.
Swimming: Nearby pool, lake.
Sunbathing: On grounds.

Smoking: Permitted outside, covered area. All rooms are non-smoking.
Pets: Not permitted.
Handicap Access: Yes, electric lift chair for inside stairs.
Children: No.
Languages: English, fair Russian, German, Spanish.
Your Hosts: Bob & Scott.

Stanford Inn

WWW Gay/Lesbian ⚥

The *Stanford Inn* is Minnesota's first gay-owned bed & breakfast. This elegant Victorian home was built in 1886 and features natural woodwork and hardwood floors throughout, as well as an entrance is graced by a hand-carved oak staircase and an eight-foot stained glass window. The 4 bedrooms are all charmingly decorated with period antiques, the suite has a private bath, and all accommodations include complete gourmet breakfast and room service coffee. We are located two blocks from Leif Erickson Park, the Rose Garden, Lake Superior, and within walking distance of shops and restaurants.

Address: 1415 E Superior St, Duluth, MN 55805
Tel: (218) 724-3044.
E-mail: stanford_inn@hotmail.com **Web:** http://www.visitduluth.com/stanford

Type: Bed & breakfast.
Clientele: Mostly gay & lesbian with a following of straight clientele
Transportation: Car is best.
Rooms: 3 rooms & 1 suite.
Baths: 1 private & 2 shared.
Meals: Full gourmet breakfast & room service coffee.

Vegetarian: Available upon request.
Complimentary: Coffee, tea, & juices.
Dates Open: All year.
High Season: May-Oct.
Rates: $75-$115.
Discounts: For weekdays (Sun-Thur), groups, also corporate & single rates.
Credit Cards: MC, Visa, Amex, Discover.

Rsv'tns: Required.
Reserve Thru: Call direct.
Parking: Adequate off-street & on-street parking.
In-Room: Room service.
On-Premises: TV lounge.
Exercise/Health: Sauna.
Swimming: Lake 2 blocks. Creek 1 mile.
Sunbathing: On the beach.
Nudity: Permitted at creek, 1 mile away. Directions on

request.
Smoking: Permitted on the porch.
Pets: Permitted with restrictions.
Handicap Access: No.
Children: OK with prior arrangement.
Languages: English.

A St. Louis Guesthouse In Historic Soulard

WWW Gay/Lesbian ♂

Come Home to St. Louis

A St. Louis Guesthouse, in historical Soulard, is tucked between downtown, Busch Stadium, the Anheuser Busch Brewery and the Farmers Market. A gay bar and restaurant are next door. Of the eight apartments in the building, five are available as guest suites. Each has two large rooms, phone, a private bath, AC, wet bar with refrigerator and a private entrance opening onto a pleasant courtyard with hot tub. If your visit to St. Louis is for business or pleasure, please consider *A St. Louis Guesthouse* your home away from home. Cancellation policy: 48 hours in advance.

Address: 1032-38 Allen Ave, Saint Louis, MO 63104
Tel: (314) 773-1016.

Type: Guesthouse.
Clientele: Mostly men with women welcome
Transportation: Car is best. Metro link from airport, bus or train.
To Gay Bars: Next door.
Rooms: 5 suites with queen beds.
Baths: All private shower/ toilets.
Complimentary: Coffee,

tea & hot chocolate always available.
Dates Open: All year.
Rates: $75-$110.
Discounts: Weekly rate (pay for 5, get 7).
Credit Cards: Amex, Discover, Visa, MC, Diners.
Rsv'tns: Required (48 hours cancellation).
Reserve Thru: Call direct.
Min. Stay: 2 nights on

weekends, 3 nights holiday weekends.
Parking: Ample free off-street & on-street parking.
In-Room: Color cable TV, ceiling fans, refrigerator, coffee/tea-maker, telephone (free local calls), maid service & laundry service, AC.
On-Premises: Laundry facilities, BBQ, hot tub in

courtyard.
Sunbathing: In courtyard.
Nudity: In hot tub & courtyard.
Smoking: Only in courtyard.
Pets: Not permitted.
Handicap Access: No.
Children: Not permitted.
Languages: English.
Your Hosts: Garry & Billy.

Brewers House Bed & Breakfast

WWW Gay/Lesbian ♀♂

Brewers House is a Civil War-vintage home, whose location amidst several breweries, is minutes from downtown and only blocks from bars, restaurants and shops. Some rooms feature fireplaces and unusual items. The hot tub in the intimate garden area offers total privacy. Enjoy a view of downtown from the deck. Visit the Soulard Market, a colorful open-air market established in 1790, or Anheuser-Busch, home of the world's largest brewery (free tours include the Clydesdales and beer tasting), or take a ride to the top of the Gateway Arch.

Address: 1829 Lami Street, Saint Louis, MO 63104
Tel: (314) 771-1542, reservations: (888) 767-4665.
E-mail: Brewerhse@aol.com

Type: Bed & breakfast.
Clientele: Good mix of gays & lesbians.
Transportation: Car is best or cab from Transit Station. Free pick up from train.
To Gay Bars: 7 blocks or 1/2 mile. 15 minutes by foot, 5 minutes by car.
Rooms: 3 with double or king beds.
Baths: 1 private bath/toilet, 1 private sink & 1 shared bath/shower/toilet.
Meals: Expanded continental breakfast.
Vegetarian: Available upon request. Restaurant nearby.
Complimentary: Coffee always available.
Dates Open: All year.
Rates: $70-$75.
Discounts: 7th day free.
Credit Cards: MC, Visa, Amex.
Rsv'tns: Recommended.
Reserve Thru: Travel agent or call direct.
Parking: Ample parking.
In-Room: Color cable TV, AC, ceiling fans, maid service & laundry service.
On-Premises: TV lounge.
Exercise/Health: Jacuzzi.
Sunbathing: On common sun decks.
Nudity: Permitted in Jacuzzi in secluded garden.
Smoking: No.
Pets: Permitted, but call ahead.
Handicap Access: No.
Children: Permitted.
Languages: English.
Your Hosts: Rick & Bob.

Lehrkind Mansion Bed & Breakfast

WWW Gay-Friendly ♀♂

Not Just a Room For the Night — An Experience

Listed in the National Register of Historic Places, the *Lehrkind Mansion* reflects the ambiance of Montana's Victorian past. Built in 1897, this Queen Anne home's spectacular features include gables, overhangs, porches, bays and a large corner tower. Relax in overstuffed chairs and enjoy the unique, rare period antiques and original woodwork. The mansion is known for its music parlor and library, with its rare, seven-foot-tall 1897 Regina music box — Montana's largest. From our filling gourmet breakfasts to beds smothered in thick down comforters, at *Lehrkind Mansion* quality is of the highest concern.

Address: 719 North Wallace Ave, Bozeman, MT 59715
Tel: (406) 585-6932, (800) 992-6932.
E-mail: lehrkindmansion@imt.net **Web:** http://www.bozemanbedandbreakfast.com

Type: Bed & breakfast.
Clientele: Mostly straight, gay/lesbian following
Transportation: Car is best, taxi from airport.
Rooms: 4 rooms, 1 suite with double or queen beds.
Baths: Private & shared.
Meals: Full breakfast.
Vegetarian: Vegetarian & vegan breakfasts available.
Complimentary: Lemonade & cookies, evening tea.
High Season: June 1-Oct 1 & Dec 15-Apr 1.
Rates: $78-$168 all year.
Credit Cards: MC, Visa, Amex.
Rsv'tns: Required.
Reserve Thru: Travel agent or call direct.
Min. Stay: 2 nts wknds.
Parking: Ample free on- & off-street parking.
In-Room: Maid service.
On-Premises: Meeting rooms, video tape library.
Exercise/Health: Large therapeutic hot tub, massage, mountain bikes. Nearby gym.
Swimming: At nearby pool.
Sunbathing: On patio & common sun decks.
Nudity: In hot tub w/ discretion & other's OK.
Smoking: Not inside. OK outside, save butts!
Pets: Not permitted.
Handicap Access: Lower floor only, wide doors.
Children: If well-behaved, watched by parents.
Languages: English & German.
Your Hosts: Jon & Christopher.

Viva Las Vegas Villas

WWW **Gay-Friendly** ⚥
Gay-Owned & -Operated

A Stone's Throw from the Bustle of the Las Vegas Strip!

Imagine spending a night in the Elvis and Priscilla Suite with decor that's been all shook up in gold lamé and splashes of hot pink, surrounded by memorabilia from the King's early career. You're sure to love the one-of-a-kind pink Cadillac bed. And the wrought-iron headboard is a replica of the gates of Graceland, with an incredible painting of the mansion in the distance behind it. Sure, it will be hard to check out in the morning, but you'll hardly be able to wait to tell your friends about your night with Elvis and Priscilla. Want something a bit more laid-back? We think newlyweds who've just thrilled to our most popular Elvis Blue Hawaii wedding will go coconuts over the tropical Blue Hawaii Room, complete with tiki hut bath, island scenery and palm-tree bed posts. You'll feel like you're sleeping right on the beach, but no sand in your shoes the next morning.

Our Camelot Room features a drawbridge bed across a painted moat, a dragon-slaying knight on horseback, and lots of medieval touches. Only Merlin knows where the magical television screen will be found. You'll revel in the storybook atmosphere of an English castle during the days of the Knights of the Round Table. Maybe you'd prefer our Austin Powers Suite, complete with beaded doorways, lava lamps and "groovy, baby" green shag carpet! Or an exotically different Egyptian Room gilded with decorative artifacts? A night in any of the rooms at *Viva Las Vegas Villas* will be one long-remembered and one never duplicated elsewhere!

Address: 1205 Las Vegas Blvd South, Las Vegas, NV 89104
Tel: (702) 384-0771, (800) 574-4450, **Fax:** (702) 384-0190.
E-mail: info@vivalasvegasvillas.com **Web:** http://
www.vivalasvegasvillas.com

Type: B&B themed rooms.
Clientele: Straight, gay & lesbian clientele
Transportation: Cab or limo.
To Gay Bars: 1 mile or less.
Rooms: 36 with doubles, queens, kings, suites.

Baths: All private, some with Jacuzzi.
Meals: Continental breakfast.
Dates Open: All year.
High Season: Feb-Oct.
Rates: $75-$175.
Discounts: 3+ nites.
Rsv'tns: Preferred.

Reserve Thru: Phone or website.
Parking: Ample, free.
In-Room: VCR, AC, heat, some fridges.
On-Premises: Diner, florist, chapel, disco, private parties, reception & catering facilities.

Exercise/Health: Gym, free weights, massage therapy.
Smoking: On balcony or outside rooms.
Pets: No.
Handicap Access: Limited.
Languages: English, German, Spanish.

Color Photo on Page 28

Las Vegas Private Bed & Breakfast

Lucky You!

Two blocks off the strip, my home, *Las Vegas Private Bed & Breakfast*, features a unique, European decor with lots of amenities. Tropical plants and trees surround the pool area. Further back are the aviaries, with tropical birds and parrots. Las Vegas has 24-hour entertainment. Other activities: desert sightseeing, Lake Mead water sports, Grand Canyon private plane tours, Laughlin excursions, alpine mountain tours, winter skiing, and hikes to Colorado River hot springs. The use of the facilities at my home is reserved for registered guests only.

Address: Las Vegas, NV
Tel: (702) 384-1129 (Tel/Fax).
E-mail: haven00069@aol.com **Web:** http://members.aol.com/haven00069/index.html

Type: Bed & breakfast.
Clientele: Mostly men with women welcome
Transportation: Pick up from airport minimal fee.
To Gay Bars: 5-block walk.
Rooms: 4 doubles with queen or king beds.
Baths: 2 shared full baths, 1 w/ whirlpool. Outside hot/cold shower.
Camping: Tent camping for large parties.
Meals: Full breakfast &
evening snack, other meals by request.
Vegetarian: On request.
Complimentary: Cocktail.
Dates Open: All year.
High Season: Spring, late summer, holidays.
Rates: 1 person $59, double $65-$79, triple $12 add'l.
Discounts: 25% after 7-day stay.
Rsv'tns: Required. Cancel policy: 1 wk in advance, fee
of 50% of deposit.
Reserve Thru: Travel agent or call direct.
Min. Stay: Wknd 2 nights, Sat arrival OK.
Parking: On-street parking.
In-Room: Color cable TV, VCR, AC, ceiling fans, room & laundry service.
On-Premises: Meeting rooms, laundry facilities.
Exercise/Health: Jacuzzi, sauna, hot tub.
Swimming: Pool.
Sunbathing: Poolside, on patio.
Nudity: Permitted without restrictions.
Smoking: Permitted outdoors in most areas.
Pets: Permitted with prearrangement.
Children: Not permitted.
Languages: English, German, French, Danish, Swedish. Norwegian.
Your Hosts: Ole.

Highlands Inn, The

A Lesbian Paradise!

Surrounded by 100 scenic mountain acres, *The Highlands Inn* is a 200-year-old lovingly restored farmhouse that has operated as a country inn for more than 100 years. Fifteen miles of trails, for walking hand-in-hand or cross-country skiing in winter, grace the property. An enormous heated pool with sun deck is a gathering place for swimmers and sunworshippers alike. Sunsets at the inn are spectacular.

Our 20 rooms are individually decorated in comfortable antiques, with lots of special touches. All have good views and most have private baths. Spacious, comfortable common areas include: an enormous fireplaced living room, a library, a tremendous, sunny breakfast room, TV/VCRs with an excellent gay & lesbian video collection, an enclosed wicker-filled sunporch, and a private whirlpool spa. Commitment ceremonies, honeymoon packages and special events are available. Join us for spectacular fall colors, super winter skiing, lush mountain springtime and all summer sports. We're here for you year round — a lesbian paradise! We're just 2-1/2 hours from Boston and the Maine coast, 4-1/2 hours from Provincetown, and three hours from Montreal. Winner of Out & About Editor's Choice Award annually since its inception (1995-2000).

Address: Valley View Lane **Mail To:** PO Box 118, Bethlehem, NH 03574
Tel: (603) 869-3978, Toll-free: (877) LES-B-INN (537-2466).
E-mail: vacation@highlandsinn-nh.com **Web:** http://www.highlandsinn-nh.com

Type: Bed & breakfast inn.
Clientele: A women-only lesbian paradise
Transportation: Car is best. Closest major airport: Manchester, NH 1-1/2 hrs. Free pick up from bus.
To Gay Bars: 1-1/2 hrs.
Rooms: 18 rooms & 1 cottage with double, queen or king beds.
Baths: 17 private, 1 shared.
Meals: Full breakfast.
Vegetarian: Breakfasts & at most local restaurants.
Complimentary: Lemonade, cider, popcorn, pretzels, coffee & tea.

High Season: Summer, fall & winter weekends.
Rates: $75-$230 per night, double occupancy..
Discounts: For longer stays varying seasonally (ex. 10-15% off 7-night stay year-round, except holidays).
Credit Cards: MC, Visa.
Rsv'tns: Recommended. (For added privacy our sign always says No Vacancy, so ignore it if driving by without reservations).
Reserve Thru: Call direct or travel agent.
Min. Stay: On in-season weekends 2 nights. Longer on holidays.
Parking: Ample free parking.
In-Room: Self-controlled heat, maid svc. Some rms w/ kitchens, some w/ TVs/ VCRs. Video tape library, fridge, coffee & tea makers, microwaves.
On-Premises: TV lounge, VCRs, use of farmhouse's full kitchen, library, piano, BBQs, stereo, boardgames.
Exercise/Health: Hot tub, Jacuzzi, lawn games, snowshoes. 15 mi of hiking & skiing trails. Massage can be arranged.

Swimming: Heated pool, nearby rivers & lakes.
Sunbathing: On common sun deck or at poolside.
Nudity: Topless sunbathing fine.
Smoking: Permitted in smoking area. Most areas & all rooms are smoke-free.
Pets: Permitted in certain rooms, with prior arrangement.
Handicap Access: Partial.
Children: Permitted with a gay parent.
Languages: English.
Your Hosts: Grace.
IGLTA

White Rabbit Inn & Catering

WWW Gay-Friendly 50/50 ⚥
Gay-Owned

Personally Exquisite

The stately, circa 1760 *White Rabbit Inn*, provides true privacy, complemented by attentive hospitality. Delicious aromas wafting from the huge, modern and immaculate kitchen remind you that your host, Executive Chef Gregory Martin, has an exclusive, first-class international culinary background. This classic brick mansion offers several formal conference rooms, dining rooms, an atrium and patio, and six very private guestrooms in over 6,000-square-feet. Its solid brick, marble and hardwood construction, tall ceilings and spacious hallways, beautiful ornate wood paneling, extravagant fireplaces and lavish moldings contribute to the serene atmosphere. The lovely, sunny Victorian Bridal Suite overlooks expansive landscape and features a classic marble bath. Private in-room sinks, lighted walk-in closets and tasteful antiquarian decor add to the pampering.

Exquisite, personalized customized catering is available by prearrangement for private dinner parties and other events. Gregory Martin's experience as Catering Services Manager with Playboy Resorts of New Jersey, his education in food service management, and his degree in culinary arts amply complement his life's ambition — to be the best in "personally exquisite" hospitality. Whether you are planning a shopping trip, an outing to your favorite ski resort, or just want to get away for a couple of days, you'll love your time with us. Tax-free outlet shopping is nearby.

Directions: From the Portsmouth/Seacoast/Boston area, I-93, Rte 101 East, to Exit 1, follow Rte 28 Bypass North 8 mi., bear left on Pleasant St., follow 1 mi. to 62 Main St. The inn is on the left, at the end of a long, climbing brick wall.

Address: 62 Main St, Suncook Village, Allenstown, NH 03275
Tel: (603) 485-9494, (888) 216-9485, **Fax:** (603) 485-9522.
E-mail: info@whiterabbitinncatering.com **Web:** http://www.whiterabbitinncatering.com

Type: Bed & breakfast inn.
Clientele: 50% gay & lesbian & 50% straight
Transportation: Car is best.
To Gay Bars: 9 miles.
Rooms: 6 sleeping rooms.
Baths: 2 private, others share.
Meals: Continental or country breakfast (addt'l charge for Sunday brunch).
Vegetarian: Available.
Complimentary: Tea & coffee.
Dates Open: All year.
High Season: Summer, autumn, Oct fall foliage.
Rates: $90-$105.
Discounts: Wkday stays.
Credit Cards: All major credit cards, except Diners.
Rsv'tns: Inquire.
Reserve Thru: Travel agent or call direct.
Parking: Ample free off-street parking.
In-Room: Color cable TV optional, maid service.
On-Premises: Meeting rooms, business services.
Exercise/Health: 7-person Thermo Spa Park Avenue hot tub.
Swimming: Nearby river & lake. Pool planned for 2000.
Pets: Not permitted.
Children: No.
Your Hosts: Gregory.

Bungay Jar

Conducive to Romance & Quiet Pleasures

Built from an 18th-century barn, the *Bungay Jar* and its exuberant gardens have been featured on the covers of national magazines. The seven large guest rooms and suites with mountain or woodland views include such welcoming touches as lavish linens, handmade quilts, ornate beds, and comfortable chairs or a desk. Breakfast specialties include oatmeal pancakes, popovers, and fresh fruit salads. Stroll through an enchanted wood to a hidden river, star gaze on a private balcony, enjoy a fireside chat, garden teas and workshops, and awaken to mountain air, and wild blueberry pancakes.

Address: Easton Valley Rd **Mail To:** PO Box 15, Franconia, NH 03580
Tel: (603) 823-7775, (800) 421-0701.
E-mail: info@bungayjar.com **Web:** http://www.bungayjar.com

Type: Bed & breakfast.
Clientele: Mostly straight. Strong lesbian following, especially in winter, men always welcome
Transportation: Car is best.
To Gay Bars: 15 min from Highland Inn.
Rooms: 6 rooms, double, queen or king beds. 1 cottage.
Baths: All private: 3 bath/ toilets, 3 shower/toilets. 2 baths with Jacuzzis.
Meals: Full breakfast & afternoon tea & snacks.
Vegetarian: All breakfasts (meat served separately). Please inform us of dairy product intolerance.
Complimentary: Afternoon snack with tea.
Dates Open: All year.
High Season: Jul-Oct.
Rates: $105-$225.
Discounts: Inquire.
Credit Cards: MC, Visa, Discover, Amex.
Rsv'tns: Advised.
Reserve Thru: Call direct.
Min. Stay: 2 nights some weekends & foliage season.
Parking: Ample, off-street parking (15 acres).
In-Room: Maid service. Cottage has full kitchen.
On-Premises: Fireplaces, common area, telephone.
Exercise/Health: Sauna, hiking trails. Massage by appointment.
Swimming: At nearby pool, river, lake, swimming hole.
Sunbathing: On many porches & hammock.
Nudity: Permitted in private, 2-person sauna.
Smoking: Not permitted.
Pets: Not permitted.
Handicap Access: No.
Children: Permitted over age 6.
Languages: English.

Horse & Hound Inn, The

Off the beaten path at the base of Franconia's Cannon Mountain and adjacent to White Mountains National Forest and the Franconia Notch State Park is one of New England's finest traditional inns. Visitors to *The Horse & Hound Inn* are treated to a quiet, relaxed atmosphere of pine paneling, three cozy fireplaces and comfortable guest rooms. The area supports plenty of activities such as hiking, boating, cross-country skiing, antiquing, and sightseeing. There are also bluegrass festivals, chamber music concerts, craft demonstrations, and museums.

Address: 205 Wells Rd, Franconia, NH 03580
Tel: (603) 823-5501 (Tel/Fax), (800) 450-5501.

Type: Bed & breakfast inn with restaurant & lounge.
Clientele: Mostly straight clientele with a gay male following
Transportation: Car is best.
To Gay Bars: 1-1/2 hrs to Manchester, NH, 2-1/2 hrs to Boston, MA.
Rooms: 8 rooms & 1 suite with double, queen or king beds.
Baths: Private: 7 bath/ toilets, 1 shower/toilet.
Meals: Full breakfast & dinner with map.
Vegetarian: Always available.
Dates Open: Closed April-early May & Nov-Thanksgiving.
High Season: Fall foliage Sep 15-Oct 15 & ski time Dec 26-Mar 31.
Rates: $86.10 double, $73.80 single. Fall foliage: $100.85 dbl, $88.55 sgl.
Discounts: Mention Inn Places for 20% discount Sun-Thur, 10% Fri-Sat.
Credit Cards: MC, Visa, Amex, Diners, Discover.
Rsv'tns: Preferred.
Reserve Thru: Travel agent or call direct.
Parking: Ample free off-street parking.
In-Room: Window fans & maid service.
On-Premises: TV lounge, VCR in lobby.
Exercise/Health: Gym with nautilus 12 miles.
Swimming: 1-1/2 mi to lake.
Sunbathing: On grassy backyard.
Smoking: Permitted except in dining room & lobby.
Pets: Permitted, $8.50.
Handicap Access: No.
Children: Permitted, additional charge.
Languages: English.
Your Hosts: Bill & Jim.

NEW HAMPSHIRE • FRANCONIA

NEW HAMPSHIRE • FRANCONIA

Notchland Inn, The

Gay-Friendly ⚥
Gay-Owned

A Magical Location...Naturally Secluded

Get away from it all, relax and rejuvenate at our comfortable 1862 granite mansion located on 100 acres in the midst of beautiful mountain vistas. *The Notchland Inn* rests atop a knoll at the base of Mount Bemis and looks out upon Mounts Hope and Crawford. Experience the comforts and pleasures of attentive and friendly hospitality! Settle in to one of our seven guest rooms or five spacious suites, each individually appointed and all with woodburning fireplaces and private baths, several with Jacuzzis. The front parlor is a perfect place to sit by the fire and read or to visit with other guests. The music room draws guests to the piano, or to the stereo to listen to music they personally select. The sun room offers a great place to sip your coffee and read a novel or just enjoy the great views.

In the evening, a wonderful 5-course dinner is served in a romantic, fireplaced dining room looking out to the gazebo by our pond. Our Chef creates a new menu daily, his elegant flair respecting the traditional while exploring the excitement of international cuisines. Morning brings a bountiful country breakfast to fuel you for the adventures of the day. Nature's wonders include 8,000 feet of Saco River frontage, two swimming holes, and the Davis Path hiking trail. Other activities to enjoy are mountain biking, cross-country skiing, snowshoeing, or soaking in the wood-fired hot tub. For animal lovers there are two Bernese Mountain dogs, a Belgian draft horse, miniature horses and two llamas. Nearby attractions include: Crawford Notch, ski areas and factory outlet stores.

Address: Harts Location, NH 03812-9999
Tel: Reservations: (800) 866-6131 or (603) 374-6131, **Fax:** (603) 374-6168.
E-mail: notchland@aol.com **Web:** http://www.notchland.com

Type: Inn with restaurant with full liquor license.
Clientele: Mostly straight clientele with a gay & lesbian following
Transportation: Car is best. Free pick up from bus.
To Gay Bars: 2 hours.
Rooms: 7 rooms, 5 suites, single, queen, king beds.
Baths: All private.
Meals: Full breakfast & dinner.
Vegetarian: Inquire.

Complimentary: Various treats at various times.
High Season: Foliage (Sep 15-Oct 20) & Christmas to New Year (Dec 23-Jan 1).
Rates: Per person per night MAP double occupancy: $112.50-$142.50, Holiday & foliage $137.50-$167.50. B&B rates on request.
Discounts: Inquire.
Credit Cards: MC, Visa, Amex, Discover.
Rsv'tns: Subject to prior

booking.
Reserve Thru: Travel agent or call direct.
Min. Stay: Required at times.
Parking: Ample free off-street parking.
In-Room: Maid service, ceiling fans, some rooms have AC.
On-Premises: Meeting rooms.
Exercise/Health: Spa, massage by appointment.

Nearby gym, weights, Jacuzzi, steam, massage, skiing, sleigh & carriage rides.
Swimming: River. Nearby pool, river & lake.
Sunbathing: On patio, lawns or at the beach.
Smoking: No smoking.
Pets: Not permitted.
Children: Mature children over 12.
Languages: English.
Your Hosts: Les & Ed.

Color Photo on Page 29

Post and Beam Bed & Breakfast

WWW Gay-Friendly 50/50 ♀♂
Gay-Owned & -Operated

"There Are No Strangers — Only Friends We Haven't Met"

The Post and Beam Bed & Breakfast overlooks the peaceful countryside of southwest New Hampshire known as the Monadnock Region. In 1797, Nathaniel Mason built the ell of the house and 8 years later completed the adjoining two story home which now houses the B&B with its wide pine floors, braided rugs, charming rooms and lovely grounds. In warmer months, relax on the patio, a trellis with a wooden swing, or the gazebo with a superb 4-person, 4-season hot-tub. In winter, guests are served hot tea or mulled cider with homemade butterscotch bars, fudge brownies, or ginger chews in the living room with its fireplace, beehive oven, and exposed hand-hewn beams. Rooms offer comfortable beds with firm mattresses, country quilts, matching comforters, cotton sheets, loads of pillows, good lighting, and an abundance of thick towels.

Address: HCR 33, Centre St, Sullivan **Mail To:** Box 380, Sullivan, NH 03445
Tel: (603) 847-3330, (888) 3 ROMANCE, **Fax:** (603) 847-3306.
E-mail: postandbeam@top.monad.net **Web:** http://www.postandbeambb.com

Type: Bed & breakfast.
Clientele: 50% gay & lesbian & 50% straight
Transportation: Car is best. Closest major airport: Manchester, NH (1 hr). Free pick up from bus in Keene.
To Gay Bars: 1 hr drive to Manchester, 2 hrs to Boston, MA.
Rooms: 7 rooms with single, queen or king beds.
Baths: Private: 2 shower/toilets, 1 WC only. 5 shared bath/shower/toilets.
Meals: Full or continental breakfast.
Vegetarian: Vegetarian breakfast available. Please inform us of dairy product intolerance.
Complimentary: Afternoon tea, cookies, snacks, apples.
Dates Open: All year.
High Season: Mid-June thru Nov 1.
Rates: High season $79-$109, low season $59-$95.
Discounts: Mention Inn Places for 10% discount. Seniors 10% discount.
Credit Cards: MC, Visa, Discover, Amex.
Rsv'tns: Preferred.
Reserve Thru: Call direct.
Min. Stay: 2 nights during fall foliage & holiday weekends.
Parking: Ample free off-street parking.
In-Room: Window fans. Some rooms have AC, gas fireplaces.
On-Premises: TV lounge, video tape & book libraries, telephone. Flower & herb gardens, apple trees, arbor with swing, large gazebo.
Exercise/Health: Nearby gym, massage.
Swimming: Nearby river, lake.
Sunbathing: On grounds.
Smoking: Permitted only in designated areas. No smoking in bedrooms.
Pets: Not permitted.
Handicap Access: Yes.
Children: Must be at least 5 years old.
Languages: English, French.
Your Hosts: Darcy & Priscilla.

Inn on Newfound Lake, The

WWW Gay-Friendly ♂

Welcoming Guests Since 1840

The Inn on Newfound Lake, a beautiful 31-room Victorian inn, is appointed in fine European antiques and paintings, and overlooks one of the most pristine lakes in the country. Nestled on eight acres, the inn has its own private beach and boat dock, and is host to all of the wonderful outdoor activities for which this historic part of New England is famous. There is antiquing, sightseeing, or something New Hampshire is known for, some of the best tax-free outlet shopping in the country! We boast one of the finest restaurants in the area. Dine overlooking the lake, or al fresco on the patio during the summer.

Address: Rt 3A, Bridgewater, NH 03222
Tel: (603) 744-9111, (800) 745-7990, **Fax:** (603) 744-3894.
E-mail: inonlk@cyberportal.net **Web:** http://www.newfoundlake.com

Type: Inn with renowned restaurant & tavern.
Clientele: Mostly straight with a gay male following
Transportation: Car is best.
To Gay Bars: 1 hr drive.
Rooms: 29 rooms & 2 suites with single or queen beds.
Baths: Private: 21 shower/toilets, 3 bath/toilets. Shared: 3 shower/toilets.
Meals: Continental

breakfast.
Vegetarian: Some selections on dinner menu.
Dates Open: All year.
High Season: Jun-Oct.
Rates: Summer $105-$245, Winter $75-$105.
Discounts: Specials when mentioning this ad.
Credit Cards: MC, Visa, Amex, Discover.
Rsv'tns: Required.
Reserve Thru: Travel agent or call direct.

Min. Stay: 2 nights on weekends in summer.
Parking: Ample free parking.
In-Room: Ceiling fans, maid service.
On-Premises: TV lounge with cable TV/VCR, meeting rooms.
Exercise/Health: Weights, Jacuzzi.
Swimming: Lake on premises.
Sunbathing: At beach.

Smoking: All non-smoking, except in tavern & on porch.
Pets: Not permitted.
Handicap Access: Ramp up porch, but a few stairs to rooms.
Children: No.
Languages: English.
Your Hosts: Phelps, Larry & Beverly.
IGLTA

Inn at Bowman a B & B, The

WWW Gay-Friendly 50/50 ⚥
Gay-Owned

Gracing the White Mountains

Tall columns, reminiscent of a Southern-style plantation, grace the front porch of *The Inn at Bowman*. Originally built in 1948 as a private summer residence, the inn has been completely renovated, graciously combining twentieth-century comfort with luxury, charm and a friendly ambience. Rooms and suites feature fresh flowers, flannel sheets in winter, plush towels and either private or shared baths. A bountiful continental breakfast is served in the dining room where guests meet to socialize. This area is a traveler's dream with inspiring mountain views and a wide variety of outdoor activities. Many parks are within an hour's drive, and tax-free shopping is six miles away in the town of Gorham.

Address: Rte 2, Randolph, NH 03570
Tel: (603) 466-5006, (888) 919-8500, **Fax:** (603) 752-6172.
Web: http://www.innatbowman.com

Type: Bed & breakfast guesthouse inn.
Clientele: 50% gay & lesbian & 50% straight clientele
Transportation: Car. Free pick up from bus.
To Gay Bars: 20 miles, a 25 min drive.
Rooms: 5 rooms & suites with single, double or queen beds.
Baths: 2 private bath/shower/toilets & sinks only. 3 shared bath/shower/toilet.
Meals: Expanded

continental or buffet breakfast.
Vegetarian: Available nearby.
Complimentary: Tea & coffee, mints on pillow, set up service, soft drinks.
Dates Open: All year.
High Season: Fall foliage, winter skiing, spring hiking, summer mtn. biking.
Rates: Off season: $79-$149; Holidays & Ski Week: $99-$179.
Discounts: Stay 3 nights, 4th night free.

Credit Cards: MC, Visa, Amex, Diners, Bancard, Discover.
Rsv'tns: Recommended.
Reserve Thru: Call direct.
Min. Stay: 2 nights on holiday weekends.
Parking: Ample free off-street parking.
In-Room: Some rooms have color cable TV w/ satellite, AC, ceiling fans, kitchen, maid & room service.
On-Premises: 2 pianos, TV lounge, sun room.

Exercise/Health: Jacuzzi (104 degrees). 8 miles to gym.
Swimming: Pool on premises (heated to 90 degrees, summer only).
Sunbathing: Poolside & on private sun decks.
Smoking: Permitted on porches & in pool area.
Pets: Not permitted.
Handicap Access: One step up to facility.
Children: No.
Languages: English & French.
Your Hosts: Jerry & Rich.

Abbott House, The

WWW Gay-Friendly 50/50
Woman-Owned & -Operated

Escape the Present While Relaxing in Our Romantic Surroundings

This Victorian-style mansion, built in the 1860s, offers visitors a quiet respite reminiscent of a forgotten age. Relax on the bluff overlooking the Great Egg Harbor River, read on the second-floor veranda with its intricate fretwork, or take afternoon tea in the belvedere with its breathtaking views of historic Mays Landing. *The Abbott House* offers five guest rooms, each individually decorated with wicker, handmade quilts, and many special touches. Historic sites, wineries, golf courses and bike trails are nearby, as are the glitter of Atlantic City and other South Jersey Beach resorts.

Address: 6056 Main Street, Mays Landing, NJ 08330
Tel: (609) 625-4400.
E-mail: theabbotthouse@email.msn.com **Web:** http://www.bbianj.com/abbott

Type: Bed & breakfast.
Clientele: A mix of gay, lesbian & straight clientele
Transportation: Car is best. Free pick up available from NC Int'l Airport or AC train station.
To Gay Bars: 12 miles, a 20 min drive.
Rooms: 3 rooms, 2 suites with queen beds.

Baths: Private bath/shower/ toilets.
Meals: Full breakfast.
Vegetarian: Available.
Complimentary: Afternoon tea.
Dates Open: All year.
High Season: Summer.
Rates: Summer $89-$129, winter $75-$95.
Credit Cards: MC, Visa,

Discover, Amex.
Rsv'tns: Preferred.
Reserve Thru: Inquire.
Min. Stay: 2 nights on weekends July-Labor Day.
Parking: Ample off-street parking.
In-Room: AC, maid service.
Exercise/Health: Nearby gym.
Swimming: Pool on

premises. Nearby ocean & lake.
Sunbathing: Poolside.
Smoking: Permitted outside. All rooms non-smoking.
Pets: Not permitted.
Handicap Access: No.
Children: No.
Languages: English.
Your Hosts: Linda & Cathy.

Pillars of Plainfield Bed & Breakfast WWW Gay-Friendly 50/50 ♀♂

Sylvan Seclusion With Easy Access to Manhattan

The Pillars is a lovingly-restored Victorian/Georgian mansion. Relax by the Music Room fire, read a book from the living room library, play the organ, listen to the stereo. Swedish breakfast at *The Pillars* is served at your convenience, but you may wish to cook your own in the huge kitchen. We have over 30 years' experience in the hospitality industry and are eager to offer a quality experience to our guests. Plainfield is a beautiful town with easy access to Manhattan by commuter train. It's a town where rainbow flags and windsocks can be seen on local houses and is fast becoming the "Gay Capital of New Jersey."

Address: 922 Central Ave, Plainfield, NJ 07060-2311
Tel: (908) 753-0922 (Tel/Fax), (888) PILLARS (745-5277).
E-mail: Pillars2@juno.com **Web:** http://www.pillars2.com

Type: Bed & breakfast.
Clientele: 50% gay & lesbian & 50% straight clientele
Transportation: Train or bus to Plainfield, walk 6 blocks to house.
To Gay Bars: 1/2 mile. 8 miles to the famous "Den" at Rutgers University.
Rooms: 7 suites with twin or queen beds.
Baths: All private bath/shower/toilets.
Camping: Parking for self-contained RV with electric & water hookup.

Meals: Full Swedish breakfast.
Vegetarian: On request.
Complimentary: Coffee, tea. Beverages afternoon & evening.
Dates Open: All year.
Rates: $89-$115.
Discounts: Call for discounts.
Credit Cards: Visa, MC, Amex.
Rsv'tns: Required.
Reserve Thru: Travel agent, call direct, or our home page.
Parking: Ample off-street

parking.
In-Room: AC, HBO, private phone with voice mail & data ports, ceiling fans, coffee service, maid & turn-down.
On-Premises: Meeting rooms, stereo, organ, laundry & kitchen facilities, library & fireplaces.
Exercise/Health: Health clubs in the area.
Swimming: Outstanding gay nude beach at nearby Sandy Hook.
Sunbathing: In secluded backyard.
Smoking: Permitted only

on the sun porch in inclement weather.
Pets: Well-behaved dogs permitted with prior arrangement. We have a Cairn Terrier.
Handicap Access: No.
Children: Welcome under 2 years old & over 12 years old. Crib, playpen & cots available.
Languages: English.
Your Hosts: Chuck & Tom.
IGLTA

Brittania & W. E. Mauger Estate B&B WWW Gay-Friendly 50/50 ⚢

Linda Ronstadt Slept Here!

Upon entering *Brittania and W.E. Mauger Estate B&B,* you'll welcome the unique and graceful atmosphere that fills this grand old home. The inn features a cozy parlor, a stunning suite with a fireplace, finely restored woodwork, and a breakfast room in what was once the home's sleeping porch. This 1897 restored Victorian B&B on the National Register of Historic Places has three floors with eight elegant rooms, all complete with private baths. Guests enjoy a full gourmet breakfast, evening treats, complimentary beverages and ample parking. From this great inn in the heart of Albuquerque you can walk to the convention center, historic Old Town, museums, the BioPark, shops and restaurants. The inn boasts a three-star rating by Mobil and a three-diamond rating by AAA.

Address: 701 Roma Ave NW, Albuquerque, NM 87102
Tel: (505) 242-8755, (800) 719-9189, **Fax:** (505) 842-8835.
E-mail: maugerbb@aol.com **Web:** http://www.maugerbb.com

Type: Bed & breakfast.
Clientele: 50% gay & lesbian & 50% straight clientele
Transportation: Car is best or taxi.
To Gay Bars: 3 miles by car.
Rooms: 7 rooms & 1 suite with single, double, queen or king beds.
Baths: All private baths with showers.

Meals: Full breakfast.
Vegetarian: Available if pre ordered.
Complimentary: Wine, cheese, juice, cookies, brownies, chips, fruit, candy & coffee.
Dates Open: All year.
High Season: Mar-Oct.
Rates: $79-$179.
Discounts: AAA.
Credit Cards: MC, Visa, Amex, Diners, Discover.

Reserve Thru: Call direct or travel agent.
Min. Stay: 2 nights for special events.
Parking: Ample, free, off-street parking, private lot, will accept RV.
In-Room: Color TV, maid & room service, AC, ceiling fans, coffee/tea-making facilities & refrigerator.
On-Premises: TV lounge, meeting rooms, catering for

special occasions.
Exercise/Health: Walking distance to downtown fitness center.
Sunbathing: On patio.
Smoking: Permitted in designated outside areas.
Pets: Small dogs permitted.
Handicap Access: No.
Children: OK.
Languages: English.
Your Hosts: Mark & Keith.
IGLTA

Hacienda Antigua Bed And Breakfast

WWW Gay-Friendly ⚧

Secluded, Serene and Romantic — Featured on TLC's "Great Country Inns"

Walk through the massive carved gates of *Hacienda Antigua* and step back in time. The gentle courtyard with its big cottonwood tree and abundance of flowers is the heart of this 200-year-old adobe hacienda. The inn has a fascinating past. It was built on the famous El Camino Real (the trade route between Mexico City & Santa Fe) and was a busy trading post & community hub. The B&B is built around an extensive courtyard, creating an enchanting, private outdoor space. In summer, relax on the peaceful portal or bask in the sun by the large swimming pool. In winter enjoy a crackling piñon fire in your own kiva fireplace. Enjoy the outdoor Jacuzzi year-round.

Visitors linger, not wanting to leave the warm Southwestern hospitality and splendid rooms comfortably furnished with antiques. A full breakfast of specialty dishes, fresh fruits and steaming coffee or tea is presented each morning. (We've shared our recipes with a gourmet food magazine — we'll share them with you, too!) The dining area adjoins the main common room, a wonderful space filled with light, art, antiques and books. Member New Mexico & Albuquerque B&B Associations and P.A.I.I.

Address: 6708 Tierra Dr NW, Albuquerque, NM 87107
Tel: (505) 345-5399, (800) 201-2986.
E-mail: info@haciendantigua.com **Web:** http://www.haciendantigua.com

Type: Bed & breakfast.
Clientele: Mostly straight clientele with gays & lesbians welcome
Transportation: Car is best.
To Gay Bars: 1-5 miles.
Rooms: 4 rooms & 2 suites with single, queen or king beds.
Baths: All private.
Meals: Full breakfast.
Vegetarian: Served upon request. Our breakfasts are ample & we will accommodate any dietary request.
Complimentary: Glass of wine. Chocolates in the room. afternoon treats, tea.
Dates Open: All year.
High Season: Aug-Oct.
Rates: $85-$150.
Credit Cards: MC, Visa, Amex, Discover.
Rsv'tns: Required.

Reserve Thru: Travel agent or call direct.
Parking: Ample free off-street parking.
In-Room: AC, ceiling fans, fireplaces, Jacuzzi tub.
On-Premises: TV lounge.
Exercise/Health: Outdoor Jacuzzi.
Swimming: Pool on premises.
Sunbathing: At poolside or on the patio.

Smoking: Permitted outside.
Pets: Not permitted.
Handicap Access: No.
Children: Limited acceptance.
Languages: English, Italian, Spanish.
Your Hosts: Melinda & Ann.

Casitas at Old Town, The

WWW Gay/Lesbian ⚣⚢

A Glimpse of the Past Beneath a Sea of Sky

Enjoy the hospitable warmth and comfort of New Mexico's classic adobe dwellings on the secluded edge of Albuquerque's oldest historical area. *Casitas at Old Town* are early dwellings restored to modern comfort with fireplace, kitchen area, bedroom, bath and patio, all furnished with authentic New Mexico pieces. Stroll into the plaza of nearby Old Town with its adjacent museums, drive an hour to Santa Fe, or just relax in absolute privacy...with one foot in the past.

Address: 1604 Old Town Rd NW, Albuquerque, NM
Tel: (505) 843-7479.

Type: Suites with private entrances.
Clientele: Mostly gay & lesbian with some straight clientele
Transportation: Car is best.
To Gay Bars: A 15-minute drive to men's & women's bars.
Rooms: 2 suites with double or queen bed.
Baths: 2 private shower/ toilets.
Complimentary: Tea & coffee makings in each suite.
Dates Open: All year.
Rates: $85 all year.
Discounts: On extended stays.
Rsv'tns: Preferred.
Reserve Thru: Travel agent or call direct.
Parking: Ample off-street parking.
In-Room: AC, kitchen, refrigerator, coffee & tea-making facilities.
Exercise/Health: 5 minutes to gay gym.
Sunbathing: On the patio.
Nudity: Permitted on patios.
Smoking: Not permitted.
Pets: Not permitted.
Handicap Access: No.
Children: Not especially welcome.
Languages: English, minimal Spanish.

Golden Guesthouses

WWW Gay/Lesbian ⚣⚢

Peace, Privacy & Southwestern Flair

Come to the *Golden Guesthouses* where we offer that "country-in-the-city" feeling. Our charming, spacious one- and two-bedroom casitas will make you feel right at home. Each house offers a front porch, private patio, living room, kitchen area and private bath. The guesthouses are located in the North Valley near the Rio Grande River, a quick block from the Rio Grande Nature Center and minutes from museums, restaurants, bars and Old Town Plaza. We are happy to offer directions, make suggestions, or leave you absolutely alone with the hope that your stay with us will be a memorable experience.

Address: 2645 Decker NW, Albuquerque, NM 87107
Tel: (888) 513-GOLD (513-4653), (505) 344-9205, **Fax:** (505) 344-3434.
E-mail: GoldenGH@aol.com **Web:** http://www.highfiber.com/~goldengh/

Type: 2 guesthouses.
Clientele: Mostly gay & lesbian with some straight clientele
Transportation: Car is best.
To Gay Bars: 3 miles to gay bars.
Rooms: 1 house w/ with queen bed, 1 house sleeps up to 6 people.
Baths: Private shower/ toilet.
Complimentary: Coffee.
Dates Open: All year.
Rates: $100 one night, $90 two or more nights, $500 per week, all double occupancy.
Rsv'tns: Recommended or take a chance.
Parking: Ample free off-street parking.
In-Room: AC, ceiling fans, coffee & tea-making facilities, refrigerator, kitchen area.
Exercise/Health: Hot tub available. Nearby gym, massage, mountain bicycle rental (will deliver).
Sunbathing: On patio.
Nudity: Permitted on private patio.
Smoking: No cigarette smoking.
Pets: Well-behaved pets permitted.
Handicap Access: No.
Children: Welcome.
Languages: English.
Your Hosts: Debbie.

Saltamontes Retreat — Grasshopper Hill

Country Lodging One Half Hour NE of Santa Fe

Geared towards writers, artists and explorers, this practical, low-budget lodging offers tranquility and inspiration. Soak in the hot tub under a starry sky, or taking in the mountain vistas of Pecos and Santa Fe National Wilderness. Local activities include ruins, fishing, hiking and swimming, photography, painting, mountain biking, cross-country skiing and backpacking along the creeks and tributaries of the Pecos River Basin. Guests at *Saltamontes Retreat — Grasshopper Hill* must not be allergic to pets as there are resident dogs, cats, ducks and geese. The lodge owner lives on premises. Brochure map needed, no street signs.

Address: Old Colonias Rd, 2 Llanitos Ln, East Pecos **Mail To:** PO Box 374, Pecos, NM 87552
Tel: (505) 757-2528.

Type: Rural residence with guest lodgings in home.	**Vegetarian:** Summer garden produce.	**Min. Stay:** 3 nights preferred, weekend OK.	**Nudity:** Permitted in hot tub, deck.
Clientele: Mostly women, some men (both welcome)	**Complimentary:** Garden produce, fresh eggs.	**Parking:** Ample, free.	**Smoking:** Permitted outside only.
Transportation: Car. In winter, front- or 4-WD vehicle only if recent snow.	**High Season:** Apr-Nov. **Rates:** $52-$75. Per month, 1 person: $500-$575.	**On-Premises:** Modern amenities, meeting room, TV lounge, wood stove, central heat, laundry, study, phone svc w/ credit card.	**Pets:** No. Many in residence.
To Gay Bars: 26 miles.	**Discounts:** Inquire.		**Children:** Permitted.
Rooms: 3 rooms.	**Credit Cards:** No cards.	**Exercise/Health:** Jacuzzi, spa, hiking, x-country skiing.	**Languages:** English, Spanish.
Baths: 2 shared baths.	**Rsv'tns:** Required. 1/2 balance holds room(s).	**Swimming:** River nearby.	**Your Hosts:** Pamela.
Meals: Fully equipped kitchen use. Meals w/ special arrangement.	**Reserve Thru:** Phone or mail.	**Sunbathing:** On patio & common sun decks.	

Four Kachinas Inn Bed & Breakfast

Our Breakfasts Will Win Your Acclaim

On a quiet street, built around a private courtyard, *Four Kachinas Inn* is a short walk from the historic Santa Fe Plaza via the Old Santa Fe Trail. Rooms have private baths, private entrances and southwestern furnishings including antique Navajo rugs, Hopi kachina dolls, handcrafted wooden furniture and saltillo tile floors. A continental-plus breakfast, prepared by our award-winning baker, is served in your room. Rated 3 diamonds by AAA. **Guest Comments:** *"I was born in New Mexico, and this B&B felt like home....Great breakfasts here, too."* -Felix, Berkeley, CA

Address: 512 Webber St, Santa Fe, NM 87501
Tel: (505) 982-2550, (800) 397-2564, **Fax:** (505) 989-1323.
E-mail: info@fourkachinas.com **Web:** http://www.fourkachinas.com

Type: Bed & breakfast.	**Vegetarian:** Available.	or call direct.	**Swimming:** Nearby pool.
Clientele: Mostly straight clientele with gays & lesbians welcome	**Complimentary:** Tea, soft drinks & cookies every afternoon in guest lounge.	**Min. Stay:** 2-5 nights.	**Sunbathing:** On the patio.
Transportation: Car is best.	**Dates Open:** All year. **High Season:** Apr 1-Oct 31 & major holidays.	**Parking:** Adequate free off-street parking.	**Smoking:** Outside only, all rooms non-smoking.
To Gay Bars: 5 blocks, 15 min walk, 5 min drive.	**Rates:** High: $73-$150, Low: $60-$120.	**In-Room:** Color cable TV, ceiling fans, telephone & maid service.	**Pets:** Not permitted. **Handicap Access:** Yes. 1 room & guest lounge wheelchair accessible.
Rooms: 6 rooms with twins, queen or king.	**Credit Cards:** MC, Visa, Discover.	**On-Premises:** Guest lounge (no TV).	**Children:** Not especially welcome.
Baths: All private.	**Rsv'tns:** Recommended.	**Exercise/Health:** Nearby gym, weights, Jacuzzi, tennis, golf, steam & massage.	**Languages:** English. **Your Hosts:** Andrew & John.
Meals: Generous continental breakfast.	**Reserve Thru:** Travel agent		

Arius Compound

Experience Adobe Living...

...in your own authentic Santa Fe *Casita*, ideally located on Canyon Road, the heart of Santa Fe's historic East Side. Around the corner from fine restaurants, charming shops, boutiques and galleries, experience Santa Fe as it has always been — a place to be, a place to breathe, a place where simplicity and warmth replace luxury and pretense. Up a quiet lane, *Arius Compound* is surrounded by high adobe walls filled with gardens, patios, fruit trees and our ever-hot California redwood tub.

Each of our *Casitas* has 1 or 2 bedrooms, fully-equipped kitchen, living room with corner Kiva fireplace (ample supplies of dried Piñon wood provided), private bath or shower, private patio, tile and flagstone floors, vigas in the ceilings, and loads of Southwest style. These are authentic old adobes built in typical Santa Fe style — hand-plastered with not a straight line or right angle in sight. Each is fully equipped with cable TV, private telephones, linens, and all kitchen necessities, including coffeemakers and microwaves, in addition to full-sized ovens.

Experience Santa Fe as it has always been — a small, quiet, cozy aesthetic, a place to *be*, a place to breathe, a place to meet yourself and others — where simplicity, honesty and warmth replace luxury and pretense. Join us and let some soul of Santa Fe enter. Don't be a visitor. Live here — if only for a few days.

Address: 1018-1/2 Canyon Rd **Mail To:** PO Box 1111, Santa Fe, NM 87504-1111
Tel: Out of Town: (800) 735-8453, Local: (505) 982-2621, **Fax:** (603) 250-7873.
E-mail: len@ariuscompound.com **Web:** http://www.ariuscompound.com

Type: Cottages.
Clientele: 60% straight & 40% gay & lesbian clientele
Transportation: Car is best.
Rooms: 4 cottages (two 1-br & two 2-br) with single, double or queen beds. Futon sleepers in living rooms.
Baths: 2 private shower/toilets & 2 private bath/shower/toilets.
Dates Open: All year.
High Season: July-Oct.
Rates: 1-BR $90-$120. 2-BR $135-$180.
Credit Cards: MC, Visa, Amex, Discover.
Rsv'tns: Not required, but usually sold out without reservations.
Reserve Thru: Call direct.
Parking: Adequate off-street parking.
In-Room: Color cable TV, telephone, ceiling fans, kitchen, refrigerator, coffee & tea-making facilities.
Exercise/Health: Jacuzzi.
Swimming: Nearby pool.
Sunbathing: On private & common sun decks & patio.
Smoking: Permitted outside. All casitas non-smoking inside.
Pets: Permitted, $5 per night.
Handicap Access: No.
Children: Welcome.
Languages: English.
Your Hosts: Len & Robbie.

SANTA FE • NEW MEXICO

Inn of the Turquoise Bear B & B

WWW Gay/Lesbian ⚣
Gay-Operated

Where the Action Is... Stay Gay in Santa Fe!

This rambling adobe villa, built in Spanish-Pueblo Revival style, is one of Santa Fe's most important historic estates. With its signature portico, tall pines, magnificent rock terraces, meandering paths, and flower gardens, the *Inn of the Turquoise Bear* offers guests a romantic retreat near the center of Santa Fe. The inn occupies the home of Witter Bynner (1881-1968), a prominent gay citizen of Santa Fe, staunch advocate of human rights and a vocal opponent of censorship. Bynner and Robert Hunt, his lover of over 30 years, were famous for the riotous parties they hosted, referred to by Ansel Adams, a frequent visitor, as "Bynner's Bashes." Their home was the gathering place for the elite of Santa Fe and guests from around the world, including D.H. & Frieda Lawrence, Igor Stravinsky, Willa Cather, Errol Flynn, Martha Graham, Christopher Isherwood, Georgia O'Keeffe, Rita Hayworth, Thornton Wilder, Robert Frost — and many others.

The only gay-oriented B&B in downtown Santa Fe, it's the perfect choice for couples or those traveling alone. Owners, Ralph and Robert, reside on the property providing their guests a unique setting that captures the essence of traditional Santa Fe. Out & About Editor's Choice Award, Santa Fe Heritage Preservation Award.

Address: 342 E Buena Vista Street, Santa Fe, NM 87501
Tel: (505) 983-0798, (800) 396-4104, **Fax:** (505) 988-4225.
E-mail: bluebear@newmexico.com **Web:** http://www.turquoisebear.net

Type: Bed & breakfast inn.
Clientele: 70% gay & lesbian and 30% straight
Transportation: Car is best, shuttle bus from Albuquerque airport.
To Gay Bars: 8 blocks.
Rooms: 9 rooms, 2 suites with queen or king beds.
Baths: Private & shared.
Meals: Expanded continental breakfast.
Vegetarian: Nearby.
Complimentary: Tea, coffee & fruit all day. Wine & cheese in afternoon. Sherry & brandy in common room.
High Season: Apr-Oct & Thanksgiving to New Year.
Rates: Per room, dbl occ: high $95-$195, low $95-$175.
Discounts: 10% AAA, AARP. Wkly rate: 10% off (low season).
Credit Cards: MC, Visa, Amex, Discover.
Rsv'tns: Required, but we accept late inquiries.
Reserve Thru: Travel agent or call direct.
Min. Stay: Required during certain holidays.
Parking: Ample free, walled off-street parking.
In-Room: Color cable TV, VCR, fans, phone, maid svc. Some rooms have fridges.
On-Premises: Meeting rooms, video tape & book libraries, fax.
Exercise/Health: Jacuzzi planned. Nearby gym, weights, Jacuzzi, sauna, steam, massage.
Swimming: Pool nearby.
Sunbathing: On patios.
Nudity: Permitted in various patio areas.
Smoking: Permitted on patios, not in rooms or public rooms.
Pets: Small pets OK in some rooms.
Handicap Access: One guest room accessible.
Children: Inquire.
Languages: English, Spanish, French, Norwegian, German.
Your Hosts: Ralph & Robert.
IGLTA

Color Photo on Page 30

Open Sky B & B

Gay-Friendly 50/50 ⚥

An Endless Open Vista

Want to get away from it all? *Open Sky B&B* is a spacious and serene adobe with spectacular open views of Jemez, the Sangre de Cristo and Ortiz Mountains, and Santa Fe. Located off the historical Turquoise Trail in the countryside of Santa Fe, this B&B offers privacy and peace to enjoy the natural beauty that has made this area popular. Our four rooms are furnished in Southwest decor and have king- or queen-sized beds and private baths. All rooms also feature high viga ceilings, saltillo tile or brick floors. The two largest rooms are located in a separate building adjacent to the main hacienda, and both have their own entrances. A breakfast of fresh breads and fruit is served at individual tables outside the rooms.

Address: 134 Turquoise Trail Court, Santa Fe, NM 87505
Tel: (505) 471-3475, (800) 244-3475.
E-mail: skymiller@earthlink.net **Web:** http://www.openskynm.com

Type: Bed & breakfast.
Clientele: 50% gay & lesbian & 50% straight clientele
Transportation: Car is best, shuttlejack from airport.
To Gay Bars: 16 miles.
Rooms: 4 rooms with queen or king beds.
Baths: All private
Meals: Expanded continental breakfast.
Vegetarian: Available upon request.

Complimentary: Gourmet coffee, herbal teas, fresh flowers!
Dates Open: All year.
High Season: Summer & holidays.
Rates: $70-$140.
Discounts: 10% for over 7 nights. Off season rates.
Credit Cards: Visa, MC, Discover.
Rsv'tns: Preferred for guaranteed availability.
Reserve Thru: Call direct or travel agent.

Parking: Ample off-street SAFE parking.
In-Room: Color TV, telephone, refrigerator, microwave, fireplaces.
On-Premises: Large 600 sq. ft. living room with fireplace.
Exercise/Health: Jacuzzi, cross-country skiing, hiking, bicycling, massage, astrology & tarot.
Swimming: At nearby river & lake.
Sunbathing: On patios.

Smoking: Permitted outside only. Entire B&B is smoke-free.
Pets: Please inquire.
Handicap Access: Yes, limited.
Children: Permitted with restrictions.
Languages: English, German & Spanish.
Your Hosts: Miria & Babette.

Triangle Inn - Santa Fe, The

Internationally Acclaimed... Exclusively Lesbian & Gay

The Triangle Inn is Santa Fe's sole exclusively lesbian and gay property and is the perfect retreat from which to explore Northern New Mexico. This rustic adobe compound, dating from the turn of the century, is on an acre of pinon- and juniper-studded land. Its nine private casitas, range from studios to a two-bedroom house. Each is furnished in Southwestern style with Mexican and handmade furniture and has living and sleeping areas, kitchenettes and private baths. Most have kiva fireplaces and private patios. Rooms are appointed with TV/VCRs, stereo/CD players, AC, phones, down comforters, gourmet teas, coffees and cocoas, bath robes and spa towels. A scrumptious heavy continental breakfast is served, in your casita, each day. We boast two large courtyards. The Hacienda Courtyard boasts a stunning free-standing portal with an outdoor fireplace and guest gathering areas. Afternoon refreshments are provided in this delightful setting, which is also frequently used for commitment ceremonies and other functions. The Main Courtyard, around which most of the casitas are situated, has extensive plantings, a large hot tub, deck and sunbathing areas.

Although Santa Fe is not a gay resort, our visitors always find themselves comfortable in this small but sophisticated artist colony. The region offers world-class opera, a famed art market, 260 restaurants, miles of hiking and skiing trails, native American pueblos and ruins, Spanish and Mexican culture, and world-renowned views.

Mail To: PO Box 3235, Santa Fe, NM 87501
Tel: (505) 455-3375 (Tel/Fax).
E-mail: Stay@TriangleInn.com **Web:** http://www.triangleinn.com

Type: Bed & breakfast inn. **Clientele:** Good mix of gays & lesbians **Transportation:** Car is best. **To Gay Bars:** 12 miles. **Rooms:** 9 cottages with queen & king beds. **Baths:** All private. **Meals:** Expanded continental breakfast. **Vegetarian:** All breakfasts are vegetarian. **Complimentary:** Gourmet coffee, herbal teas, juices, snacks & afternoon cocktail gatherings, sherry. **Dates Open:** All year. **High Season:** Apr-Oct, Thanksgiving & Christmas. **Rates:** Low $70-$140. High $80-$160. **Discounts:** On weekly stays & for NM residents. **Credit Cards:** MC, Visa, Eurocard. **Rsv'tns:** Recommended. **Reserve Thru:** Travel agent or call direct. **Min. Stay:** 3 days during holidays. **Parking:** Ample, free, walled parking. **In-Room:** TV/VCR, stereo/CD player, AC, phone, ceiling fans, robes, spa towels, kitchenettes, refrigerator, coffee/tea makers, maid svc. Some rms w/ fireplaces. **On-Premises:** 2 common courtyards (1 with covered portal & outdoor fireplace, 1 with hot tub & sun deck), VCR tape library, games, fax. **Exercise/Health:** Jacuzzi. Nearby gym, weights, sauna, steam, massage. **Swimming:** Nearby pool. **Sunbathing:** On private & common sun decks. **Smoking:** Non-smoking rooms available. **Pets:** Permitted with advance notice ($5 per day). **Handicap Access:** Yes. **Children:** Welcome. **Languages:** English & Spanish. **Your Hosts:** Sarah & Karan.

Heart Seed B & B and Spa

Gay-Friendly 50/50 ♂♀

Capture the Spirit of the Land of Enchantment

Heart Seed B&B and Spa is located on 80 acres in a spectacular mountain setting 25 miles south of Santa Fe near the historic village of Los Cerrillos and the popular artist's colony of Madrid. Stay in Santa Fe-style B&B rooms or retreat rooms. Retreat rooms provide fully equipped kitchenettes to accommodate longer stays. Enjoy the common room/library, massage and full-day spa. The grounds also include a shaded deck, outdoor hot tub, meditation garden, labyrinth, and hiking and biking trails.

Mail To: PO Box 6019, Santa Fe, NM 87502-6019
Tel: (505) 471-7026.
E-mail: hrtseed@nets.com **Web:** http://www.nets.com/heartseed

Type: Bed & breakfast and spa.
Clientele: 50% gay & lesbian & 50% straight clientele
Transportation: Individual car.
To Gay Bars: 25 miles to Santa Fe bars.
Rooms: 7 guestrooms, 6 with queen beds.
Baths: Private baths.
Meals: Full gourmet breakfast (F-M, T, W, Th: breakfast baskets delivered to rooms).
Vegetarian: Generally available.
Complimentary: Tea, coffee & snacks.
Dates Open: All year.
High Season: Currently Apr-Oct.
Rates: $79-$125.
Discounts: All year for stays of 4 or more days.
Credit Cards: MC, Visa, Amex.
Rsv'tns: Required.
Reserve Thru: Call direct.
Parking: Ample free parking.
In-Room: Some fully equipped kitchenettes.
On-Premises: TV lounge, VCR, meeting rooms, library with books, tapes & CDs, huge deck, meditation garden.
Exercise/Health: Full-day spa, hot tub, massage, Thai massage, salt glows, workshops, wellness lab & hiking. Mountain biking & horseback riding nearby.
Sunbathing: On private & common sun decks.
Smoking: Permitted in designated outdoor areas only.
Pets: Not permitted.
Children: Well-behaved children welcome. No special arrangements for children.
Languages: English.
Your Hosts: Judith & Gayle Dawn.

Adobe and Stars Bed and Breakfast

Gay-Friendly ♂♀
Woman-Owned & -Operated

In Harmony with the Natural Beauty of Taos

Perfectly located between Taos Ski Valley Canyon, Carson National Forest and Taos Plaza, this spacious and contemporary, luxurious Southwestern inn was designed especially with views in mind. Big windows, decks, patios and an indoor hot tub invite star gazing and sunset viewing. Each of the eight large guestrooms has a kiva fireplace and a light-filled private bath with either a Jacuzzi tub or double shower. Days begin with fresh-brewed coffee and a full country breakfast. The hiking, biking and horseback riding trails of the National Forest are right down the road. Golf, fishing, river rafting, galleries, and fine restaurants are all minutes away. Experience *Adobe and Stars* and Taos, an unbeatable combination!

Address: 584 State Hwy 150, Taos, NM 87571
Tel: (505) 776-2776, (800) 211-7076, **Fax:** (505) 776-2872.
E-mail: stars@taosadobe.com **Web:** http://www.taosadobe.com

Type: Bed & breakfast.
Clientele: Mostly straight clientele with a gay/lesbian following
Transportation: Car, commercial shuttle service.
Rooms: 8 rooms with single, queen or king beds.
Baths: All private.
Meals: Full breakfast.
Complimentary: Afternoon wine & snack.
High Season: Mid summer, mid winter, holidays.
Rates: $70-$220.
Discounts: AAA, AARP, Mobile.
Credit Cards: MC, Visa, Amex, Discover.
Reserve Thru: Travel agent or call direct.
Min. Stay: Christmas to New Years & some holidays.
Parking: Ample off-street.
In-Room: Telephone, ceiling fans.
On-Premises: Meeting rooms, TV lounge, fax/modem access.
Exercise/Health: Jacuzzi.
Sunbathing: On private & common sun decks, patio.
Smoking: Outdoors only.
Handicap Access: Yes, ramps, wide doors, rails in bathrooms.
Children: Well-behaved children accepted.
Languages: English, Spanish.
Your Hosts: Judy.

Dreamcatcher B & B, The

WWW Gay-Friendly ⚥

A Perfect Balance of Privacy & Personal Attention

At *The Dreamcatcher B & B,* our guest rooms, individually decorated with handmade furniture, have private baths and fireplace or woodstove. Breakfast specials include scrumptious breakfast burritos, omelettes and banana pancakes. Our lovely grounds are complete with an outdoor hot tub. A vacation in Taos might include hiking, horseback riding, world-class skiing, gallery viewing, shopping or visiting Taos Pueblo. A short stroll from historic Taos Plaza, we're northern New Mexico's most popular and relaxing gay-friendly B&B.

Address: 416 La Lomita Rd **Mail To:** PO Box 2069, Taos, NM 87571
Tel: (505) 758-0613, (888) 758-0613, **Fax:** (505) 751-0115.
E-mail: dream@taosnm.com **Web:** http://dreambb.com

Type: Bed & breakfast.
Clientele: Gay, lesbian & straight clientele
Transportation: Car is best. 2-1/2 hours from Albuquerque by car. Taxi from bus stop to B&B, $5.
To Gay Bars: 1-1/4 hours to Santa Fe gay & lesbian bars.
Rooms: 7 rooms with double, queen or king beds.
Baths: All private.
Meals: Full breakfast.
Vegetarian: Available.

Complimentary: Coffee & assorted teas.
Dates Open: All year.
High Season: Summer, holidays & ski season.
Rates: $79-$114 per night for two, $94-$129 for holidays.
Discounts: On weekly stays, if booked directly. AAA, AARP.
Credit Cards: MC, Visa, Amex, Discover.
Rsv'tns: Recommended.
Reserve Thru: Travel agent

or call direct.
Min. Stay: 2-3 days on holidays, 2 days some weekends.
Parking: Adequate free off-street parking.
In-Room: Maid service, ceiling fans. All rooms have fireplace or woodstove, refrigerator & robes.
On-Premises: Telephone, common room for guests.
Exercise/Health: Hot tub on the premises, health club in town.

Swimming: 10 minutes to pool, 20 to Rio Grande.
Sunbathing: On hot tub deck or patio.
Smoking: Permitted outdoors.
Pets: Not permitted.
Handicap Access: Yes, call for details.
Children: Ages 12 and over.
Languages: English.
Your Hosts: Bob & Jill.

Jones Pond Campground

WWW Men ♂

Gay Camping at its Best!

Jones Pond Campground is an all-male, adult retreat on 119 rustic acres with large natural trails and 135 sites. All trailer and RV sites have electric & water hookups, picnic tables and fireplaces. Many tent sites have picnic tables and fireplaces, and some have water and electric. The camp store has basic supplies and grocery items. There is a two-story recreation hall, a large pond, a 65-foot swimming pool, volleyball and basketball courts. Events include variety & craft shows, Leather weekends, Christmas in July, pool/pizza parties, and block parties.

Address: 9835 Old State Rd, Angelica, NY 14709
Tel: (716) 567-8100, **Fax:** (716) 567-2524.
E-mail: info@jonespond.com **Web:** http://www.jonespond.com

Type: Campground.
Clientele: Men only
Transportation: Car is best.
To Gay Bars: 1-1/2 hr to Buffalo or Rochester.
Rooms: Trailers for rent (supply your own bedding & utensils). 3BR guesthouse (fully equipped kitchen, towels, bed linen provided).
Baths: 2 shower/toilet facilities with 4 showers each.

Camping: Tent & trailer sites, 135 with electric & water.
Dates Open: Apr 28-Oct 8. Guesthouse all year.
High Season: Jun-Aug.
Rates: Rates vary, call for brochure.
Discounts: For weekly & monthly stays.
Credit Cards: Visa, MC, Discover.

Rsv'tns: Required, with a $20 deposit.
Reserve Thru: Call direct or email.
Parking: Ample free parking.
On-Premises: TV lounge, gathering room, dance room with DJ.
Exercise/Health: Hiking in summer, cross-country skiing in winter.
Swimming: Pool on premises.
Sunbathing: At poolside.
Nudity: Permitted at the pool & in nonrestricted areas.
Smoking: Permitted.
Pets: Permitted on leash.
Handicap Access: Yes.
Children: Not permitted.
Languages: English.
Your Hosts: Alan, Carl, Michael & Roger.

Serenity Farms

Gay-Friendly 50/50 ⚥
Gay-Owned & -Operated

Where the Grass Really is Greener...

Our newly completed upscale bed and breakfast, *Serenity Farms,* is located on 100 serene acres in upstate New York. In any season, the grounds are yours to explore — in winter there is snowmobiling and crosscountry skiing. Spring and summer are perfect for hiking and exploring nature, and in autumn, watch the leaves change color. The guesthouse has eight bedrooms, some with private baths. In the rec room you can relax by the fireplace, shoot pool, play backgammon, or just enjoy surround-sound and videos.

Address: 386 Pollard Road, Greene, NY
Tel: (607) 656-4659, **Fax:** (607) 656-5306.
E-mail: NYSerenity@aol.com **Web:** http://geocities.com/WestHollywood/
6173/SERENITY/

Type: Bed & breakfast with antique shop.
Clientele: 50% gay & lesbian & 50% straight
Transportation: Car is best. Free pick up from airport or bus.
To Gay Bars: 15 mi.
Rooms: 8 rooms with double beds.
Baths: Private & shared.
Meals: Full breakfast.
Vegetarian: With prior notice.
Complimentary: Coffee. Set ups w/ prior notice.
Rates: $105-$155.
Discounts: Groups or referrals discounts negotiable.
Credit Cards: MC, Visa, Amex.
Rsv'tns: Required.
Reserve Thru: Call direct.
Parking: Ample, free off-street parking.
In-Room: AC, color TV, VCR, fridge, coffee & tea makers, maid svc.
On-Premises: Meeting rooms, TV lounge, internet access, fax, copy service.
Exercise/Health: Gym, weights, Jacuzzi.
Swimming: Pool.
Sunbathing: Poolside, on private or common sun decks, on patio.
Smoking: Permitted in common areas.
Pets: Permitted if house trained.
Handicap Access: Yes, ramps.
Children: No.
Languages: English, Russian, Polish, Ukrainian.
Your Hosts: Gregg & Jack.
IGLTA

Bradstan Country Hotel

Gay-Friendly ⚥

That Uptown Feeling in Upstate N.Y.

After a 21 month, painstaking renovation, *Bradstan Country Hotel* was awarded The First Sullivan County Board of Realtors Award for Architectural Excellence. In addition to our large comfortable rooms, the *Bradstan* also features a 70-foot private deck and a 60-foot front porch overlooking beautiful White Lake, where your favorite water activities are at your beck and call. At the end of the day, order up your favorite cocktail and enjoy the live cabaret entertainment in *Bradstan's* own piano bar lounge. All this just 2 hours from NYC. Ask us about hosting your special affair or meeting at our inn.

Address: Route 17B, White Lake **Mail To:** PO Box 312, White Lake, NY 12786
Tel: (914) 583-4114 (Tel/Fax).

Type: Bed & breakfast inn with cottages & bar.
Clientele: Mainly straight clientele with a gay & lesbian following
Transportation: Car is best, no charge for pick up, prior arrangement required.
To Gay Bars: Piano bar on premises with mixed crowd.
Rooms: 2 rooms, 3 suites & 2 cottages with queen beds.
Baths: All private.
Meals: Expanded
continental breakfast.
Vegetarian: Our breakfast is acceptable for vegetarians.
Dates Open: Open weekends all year & 7 days a week from 4/1 to 8/31.
High Season: Memorial Day to Labor Day.
Rates: $110-$120 summer, $75-$85 winter.
Discounts: Discounts available to groups & stays of 5 nights or more.
Credit Cards: MC, Visa, Discover, Amex.
Rsv'tns: Recommended.
Reserve Thru: Call direct.
Min. Stay: 2 night minimum stay on weekends from Memorial Day to 10/31.
Parking: Free adequate on-street & off-street parking.
In-Room: B&B AC, maid service, ceiling fans, hair dryers. Year-round cottages have color cable TV, full kitchens.
On-Premises: Piano lounge, meeting rooms.
Swimming: At private lake.
Sunbathing: On sun deck or private lake front.
Smoking: Permitted.
Pets: Not permitted.
Handicap Access: No.
Children: Permitted with prior arrangement, over the age of 8.
Languages: English.
Your Hosts: Scott & Edward.

Palenville House Bed & Breakfast

WWW Gay-Friendly 50/50 ♀♂
Gay-Owned

Pallenville House is a magnificent guesthouse located in the heart of New York State's Catskill Mountains, two hours north of New York City and 40 minutes south of Albany. Ideally situated for outdoor enthusiasts, we're within walking distance of hiking trails, swimming holes and golf. Hunter Mountain, Ski Windham, Cortina Valley, North Lake State Park, Woodstock, horseback riding and the Catskill Game Farm are minutes away.

Try our romantic suite featuring breathtaking mountain views, sleeping loft, wood-burning stove with open fire, deck, cable TV, VCR and Jacuzzi. Relax in our ten-person outdoor hot tub, available to all of our guests and open year-round. Our full country breakfast includes fruit, freshly baked muffins, juice, and French toast, pancakes, waffles or omelets.

Address: Jct Rts 23A & 32A, Palenville, NY **Mail To:** PO Box 465, Palenville, NY 12463-0465
Tel: (518) 678-5649, Toll-free (877) 689-5101, **Fax:** (518) 678-9038.
E-mail: palenville@aol.com **Web:** http://catskillsbb.com

Type: Bed & breakfast.
Clientele: 50% gay & lesbian & 50% hetero clientele
Transportation: Car is best. Walk from bus.
To Gay Bars: 30 miles, a 30 min drive.
Rooms: 5 rooms & 2 suites with single, double or queen beds.
Baths: Private.

Meals: Full breakfast.
Vegetarian: On request.
Complimentary: Coffee, tea, hot chocolate, soda.
Dates Open: All year.
High Season: January.
Rates: $75-$155.
Discounts: 10% discount Tues & Wed or Wed & Thurs.
Credit Cards: Discover, MC, Visa, Amex.

Rsv'tns: Suggested.
Reserve Thru: Travel agent or call direct.
Min. Stay: Required on holidays & weekends.
Parking: Ample free parking.
In-Room: Color cable TV, VCR.
On-Premises: TV lounge, fireplace.
Exercise/Health: Jacuzzi.

Swimming: Lake & creek nearby.
Sunbathing: In backyard.
Smoking: No smoking, except on enclosed porch.
Pets: Not permitted.
Handicap Access: No.
Children: No.
Languages: English & Spanish.
Your Hosts: Jim.

River Run Bed & Breakfast Inn

A Century of Welcome

Our exquisite 1887 Queen Anne "cottage" is surrounded by the Catskill Forest Preserve, with its magnificent hiking trails, splendid foliage and superb skiing. Our eclectic Victorian village features tennis, swimming, theatre, museum, antiques, a weekly country auction, walking paths, and a variety of restaurants. Rejuvenate on our delightful wraparound porch or in our book-filled parlor, complete with piano and fireplace. Step into the oak-floored dining room, bathed in the colors of the inn's signature stained-glass windows, and enjoy homemade breakfasts and refreshments. Our outdoor setting beckons you to explore its acre of backyard, which slopes gently to a private streamside picnic area. Or simply relax in an Adirondack chair on the front porch and watch the town go by. We're 35 minutes from Woodstock and 2-1/2 hours from NYC. At *River Run,* all are welcome, and all are made comfortable.

Address: Main St, Fleischmanns, NY 12430
Tel: (914) 254-4884.
E-mail: riverrun@catskill.net **Web:** http://www.catskill.net/riverrun

Type: Bed & breakfast, 35 minutes from Woodstock, NY.
Clientele: Mostly straight clientele with a significant gay & lesbian following
Transportation: Car is best. 2 1/2 hours from NYC. Trailways bus stops at our front door, direct from NYC.
To Gay Bars: 35 miles or a 50-min drive to Kingston.
Rooms: 8 rooms & 1 apartment with single, double, queen or king beds.
Baths: Private: 3 shower/toilets, 3 bath/shower/toilets. 2 shared full baths.

Meals: Full breakfast.
Vegetarian: On request. Most diets accommodated.
Complimentary: Afternoon refreshments.
Dates Open: All year.
High Season: Memorial Day-Labor Day, Sep-Oct (foliage), Dec-Mar (skiing).
Rates: $70-$120.
Discounts: Longer stays (please call).
Credit Cards: MC, Visa, Amex.
Rsv'tns: Strongly recommended. Walk-ins accommodated if space is available.

Reserve Thru: Travel agent or call direct.
Min. Stay: 2 nights weekends, 3 nights holiday weekends (rates higher).
Parking: Ample free on-street parking.
In-Room: Color & B/W TV, maid service. Kitchen in apartment.
On-Premises: TV lounge, VCR, tea-making facilities, fireplace & piano.
Exercise/Health: Massage. Nearby gym.
Swimming: Stream on premises. Nearby pool, river & lake.

Sunbathing: On private grounds & at nearby pool.
Smoking: Inn is non-smoking.
Pets: Well-behaved, fully-trained, well-socialized pets permitted.
Handicap Access: Yes. Apartment is on ground level.
Children: Welcome. Rollaway, crib available.
Languages: English, French, German.
Your Hosts: Larry.

One Thirty-Two North Main

Gay/Lesbian ♂

The Hot Place to be COOL This Summer

To make each guest feel like a personal friend visiting has been the primary objective at *One Thirty-Two North Main* for 28 summers. On two tranquil acres, just steps from quaint village shops and trendy restaurants, we offer fifteen accommodations in various locations, including the main house, the annex, the cottage and the cabana, and an unusually inviting large and secluded swimming pool surrounded by a "jungle" of trees. From *One Thirty-Two*, it's a 5-minute drive or bike ride to one of the world's most beautiful beaches.

Address: 132 N Main St, East Hampton, NY 11937
Tel: (516) 324-2246 or (516) 324-9771.

Type: Mini-resort.
Clientele: Mostly men with women welcome.
Transportation: Car, train or bus. Short walk from Long Island RR station, Hampton Jitney & Hamptons on My Mind bus stops.
To Gay Bars: 4 miles to bar, disco & restaurant.
Rooms: 13 rooms with single, double, queen or king beds, 1 apartment & 1 cottage.
Baths: 5 private shower/toilets & 8 shared bath/shower/toilets.
Meals: Continental breakfast.
Dates Open: May-Sept.
High Season: All weekends from July 4th to Labor Day.
Rates: $110-$225.
Discounts: On stays including 5 weekdays.
Credit Cards: MC, Visa, Amex.
Rsv'tns: Required.
Reserve Thru: Travel agent or call direct.
Min. Stay: 2 nights on weekends in July & August.
Parking: Ample free off-street parking.
In-Room: Maid service, refrigerator, ceiling fans. Some accommodations have AC.
On-Premises: TV lounge.
Exercise/Health: Nearby gym, weights, steam & massage.
Swimming: 20 ft by 50 ft pool on premises, 1 mile to ocean beach.
Sunbathing: At poolside, on patio or ocean beach.
Nudity: Permitted at poolside.
Smoking: Permitted outside on decks & patios only.
Pets: Permitted in cabana.
Handicap Access: Yes, very small step at back entrance.
Children: Permitted in annex or cabana.
Languages: English, Italian.
Your Hosts: Tony

Colonial House Inn

Gay/Lesbian ⚥

Being Gay Is Only Part of Our Charm

Colonial House is like a European hotel. The inn, on a quiet street in Chelsea, has 20 modern and impeccably clean rooms. All have color cable TV, radio and air conditioning, sinks and direct-dial phone. Some rooms have private baths and fireplaces. Most have refrigerators. The roof sun deck offers a relaxing environment for guests and includes a clothing-optional area. Rates include an expanded continental breakfast. But the real attraction here is service, including a 24-hour concierge. If you have any trepidation about the Big Apple, this is the place to stay. Winner of Out & About 1994-2000 Editor's Choice Award.

Address: 318 W 22nd St, New York, NY 10011
Tel: (212) 243-9669, (800) 689-3779, **Fax:** (212) 633-1612.
E-mail: houseinn@aol.com **Web:** http://www.colonialhouseinn.com

Type: Bed & breakfast inn.
Clientele: Good mix of gays & lesbians
Transportation: Airport bus to city, then taxi. Self-pay car service. Will arrange pick up to/from airport.
To Gay Bars: 1/2 block to 10-minute walk.
Rooms: 20 rooms.
Baths: 12 shared, 8 private. All rooms have washing facilities.
Meals: Expanded continental breakfast. Fresh-baked homemade muffins, bagels, special house-blend coffee, assorted juices daily, fresh fruit & cereal.
Complimentary: Tea, coffee & mints.
Dates Open: All year.
Rates: $80-$140.
Discounts: Weekly rates available.
Credit Cards: Visa, MC.
Rsv'tns: Recommended.
Reserve Thru: Travel agent or call direct.
Min. Stay: Varied on weekends & holidays.
Parking: On-street or 1/2 blk to off-street pay parking.
In-Room: Daily maid svc, color cable TV, AC, direct dial phones, radios, alarm clocks, some w/ fridges or fireplaces.
On-Premises: TV lounge.
Exercise/Health: Weights. Gym & massage nearby.
Sunbathing: On common sun deck or rooftop.
Nudity: OK on sun deck.
Smoking: OK in rooms.
Pets: Not permitted.
Children: Mature children.
Languages: English, Spanish, Italian, French, German.
IGLTA

A Greenwich Village Habitué

Gay-Friendly 50/50 ⚥

Your Perfect Home Away From Home

A Greenwich Village Habitué has two fully appointed private apartments available in an owner-occupied 1830's Federal brownstone building in the historic West Village. Antique filled apartments come complete with living room, sleeping alcove, dining alcove, full bath, and a small service kitchen suitable for preparing a light breakfast ONLY. The apart-

ments overlook a formal English garden. Nestled between what could be considered two of the largest cities in the United States — Midtown/Times Square and the Wall Street/Financial areas — we're conveniently located three short blocks from the heart of Chelsea, allowing easy access to all that Greenwich Village, Chelsea and Manhattan have to offer. The area contains an abundance of restaurants, theaters, clubs and shops, as well as some of New York's oldest and most charming residential blocks.

Whether you are traveling to New York for business or pleasure, you will find that our home offers a high degree of comfort, privacy and friendly service in an environment that reflects the quiet elegance of an earlier time.

As Quoted by Mimi Reed of **Food and Wine Magazine:** *"It was to our delight, an immaculate, graciously stocked and elegantly furnished apartment in a brownstone. It seemed a great bargain."*

Address: New York's West Village
Tel: (212) 243-6495, **Fax:** (212) 243-6582.
E-mail: gvhabitue@aol.com **Web:** http://www.gvhabitue.com

Type: Private, fully-equipped apartments.
Clientele: Sophisticated, well-traveled persons, some of whom are gay & lesbian
Transportation: Taxi, bus or subway.
To Gay Bars: Walking distance to most gay & lesbian bars.
Rooms: 2 fully-appointed

private apartments with queen beds.
Baths: Private full baths.
Vegetarian: Complete vegetarian/health food center nearby.
Dates Open: All year.
Rates: $165 per night.
Rsv'tns: Advance reservation required.
Reserve Thru: Call direct.

Min. Stay: 4 nights.
Parking: Limited on-street parking, or nearby garages.
In-Room: AC, color TV, phone, answering machine, small service kitchen, refrigerator, coffee & tea-making facilities. Daily maid service available for extra fee.
On-Premises: Fax facilities

available.
Exercise/Health: Nearby gym.
Smoking: Not permitted.
Pets: No.
Handicap Access: No.
Children: No.
Languages: English.
Your Hosts: Matthew & Kevin.

Abode, Ltd

Gay-Friendly ⚢

Privacy & Luxury in a NYC Brownstone or Apartment

Have your heart set on staying in one of those delightful, restored brownstones? Or how about a contemporary luxury apartment in the heart of Manhattan? All of *Abode's* homes are personally inspected to ensure the highest standards of cleanliness, attractiveness and hospitality. All the attractions of New York City — theatres, museums, galleries, restaurants, parks and shopping—are within easy reach. Select an unhosted contemporary luxury apartment or a private apartment, with country inn ambiance, in an owner-occupied brownstone.

Mail To: PO Box 20022, New York, NY 10021
Tel: (212) 472-2000, (800) 835-8880.
Web: http://www.abodenyc.com

Type: Reservation service organization.
Clientele: Mostly straight clientele with a gay/lesbian following
Transportation: Taxi or public transportation.
To Gay Bars: Within a few blocks in most Manhattan neighborhoods.
Rooms: 40 apartments. Most have queen beds, some double, some king.

Baths: All private.
Meals: Fixings for continental breakfast provided in most apartments.
Vegetarian: Nearby supermarkets.
Dates Open: All year.
Rates: $140-$400 per night.
Discounts: Special rates for extended stays of 1 month or longer.

Credit Cards: Amex.
Rsv'tns: Required.
Reserve Thru: Call direct.
Min. Stay: 4 nights.
Parking: Ample pay parking.
In-Room: Color/color cable TV, VCR, AC, telephone, answering machine, kitchen, refrigerator, coffee & tea-making facilities. Daily maid service can be arranged at guests' expense.

On-Premises: Laundry facilities at several apartments.
Smoking: We have smoking & non-smoking accommodations.
Pets: Not permitted.
Handicap Access: No.
Children: Over 12 years permitted in some apartments. Please inquire.
Languages: English.

Chelsea Mews Guesthouse
Friendly, Private & Affordable

Men ♂

At *Chelsea Mews Guesthouse,* ours is an old-fashioned atmosphere. It's a tone that is set by our lovely Victorian garden with a Magnolia tree as its centerpiece. Inside the inn, the guest rooms are furnished with antiques, continuing the old-world motif. Guests enjoy relaxing on the balcony overlooking the garden, a contrast to the hustle and bustle of the city of New York, just outside.

You'll find our location, here at Chelsea Mews, to be very convenient for your stay in New York City. Chelsea is a neighborhood that divides Greenwich Village from Midtown, so it is convenient to bars and restaurants in both areas. And Chelsea, itself, is currently a very popular area for gay nightlife. You'll find a variety of popular gay bars and great gay restaurants along 8th Avenue, in the area just above 15th Street.

As an added convenience, an indoor parking garage is located across the street from Chelsea Mews. And it is open 24 hours, making it easy for you to use your vehicle, whenever you wish. The subway, of course, is the most convenient way to get around Manhattan, and a subway station is nearby. Because New York City is such a popular gay and lesbian travel destination, advance reservations are always advised.

Address: 344 W 15th St, New York, NY 10011
Tel: (212) 255-9174.

Type: Guesthouse.
Clientele: Men only
Transportation: Any city transportation.
To Gay Bars: 1-1/2 blocks.
Rooms: 8 rooms with single or double beds.
Baths: 1 private bath/toilet, others share bath/shower/ toilet, 2 semi-private baths.
Meals: Continental breakfast of coffee. Refrigerator to store snacks.
Dates Open: All year.
Rates: $85-$165.
Rsv'tns: Required.
Reserve Thru: Call direct.
Parking: Ample on-street pay parking & an indoor garage across the street open 24hrs.
In-Room: Color TV, AC, telephone, refrigerator, coffee-making facilities & maid service.
On-Premises: Garden, rear sitting balcony overlooking the garden.
Smoking: All rooms non-smoking.
Pets: Not permitted.
Handicap Access: No.
Children: No.
Languages: English.

Chelsea Pines Inn

WWW Gay/Lesbian ♂

The Cozy Bed & Breakfast in the Heart of Gay New York

Fodor's Gay Guide USA calls us "The best-known gay accommodation in the city... equidistant from the Village and Chelsea attractions... this 1850 town house is run by a helpful staff... pleasantly furnished rooms... it's a great deal!" Bordering Greenwich Village and Chelsea, *Chelsea Pines Inn* is a short walk to restaurants, shops, clubs, bars and the famous Christopher Street area. Out & About Editor's Choice Award for Excellence in Gay Travel.

The inn has newly decorated rooms, guest areas, and hallways; new carpeting; new lighting; and new colors. Charmingly decorated with vintage movie posters, the rooms have full- or queen-sized beds, direct-dial phones with voice mail, air conditioning and central heating, color cable TVs with free HBO, refrigerators, hair dryers, irons and ironing boards, and washing facilities. Daily maid service and a fax service is also available. And, despite its recent renovation, the inn still has modest rates.

A complimentary, expanded continental breakfast includes fresh fruit, homemade bread and Krispy Kreme donuts, New York's newest sensation, delivered fresh to our door. Breakfast is available in the outdoor garden when the weather permits, or in our breakfast room or year-round greenhouse. The inn is centrally located for airline travelers — JFK Airport is 45-60 minutes away, La Guardia Airport is 25-30 minutes away, and Newark Airport is 30-45 minutes from the inn.

Address: 317 W 14th St, New York, NY 10014
Tel: (212) 929-1023, **Fax:** (212) 620-5646.
E-mail: cpiny@aol.com

Type: Bed & breakfast inn.
Clientele: Mostly men with women welcome
Transportation: Car service to inn or bus to Manhattan, then taxi or subway.
To Gay Bars: 1/2 block to men's, 5-minute walk to women's bars.
Rooms: 23 rooms w/ double or queen beds (some w/ 2 beds, request when booking).

Baths: 15 private & 8 semi-private. Sink & shower in every room.
Meals: Expanded continental breakfast with homemade bread.
Vegetarian: Vegetarian restaurant nearby.
Complimentary: Coffee, cookies & Krispy Kreme donuts all day.
Dates Open: All year.
High Season: Spring, summer & fall.

Rates: $89-$139 plus taxes.
Credit Cards: All major cards.
Rsv'tns: Recommended.
Reserve Thru: Call/fax direct, or travel agent.
Min. Stay: 3 nights on weekends, 4 nights on holidays.
Parking: Paid parking in lot or garage (1 block).
In-Room: Maid service, color cable TV with free

HBO, AC, phone with voice mail, hair dryer, refrigerator, iron & ironing board.
On-Premises: Garden.
Exercise/Health: 1 block to gym.
Smoking: Permitted.
Pets: Not permitted.
Children: Not permitted.
Languages: English.
Your Hosts: Al, Jay & Ric.
IGLTA

Color Photo on Page 31

New York Bed & Breakfast Reservation Center  WWW Gay ♂

Accommodations in New York, Paris & the Loire Valley

Having started out as the host of a Manhattan bed and breakfast, we know that potential guests appreciate getting a clear and honest description of the accommodations and of the surrounding neighborhood before they book. We know they appreciate dealing with a person who is not only interested in booking once, but looking down the road for repeat business.

The New York Bed & Breakfast Reservation Center offers a wide variety of bed and breakfast accommodations in New York City at prices under $100 per night. Several are within a few blocks of major Midtown hotels and theatres. Also available are private studios and apartments for people who wish to be on their own. Unhosted facilities start at $160 per night, some less. Apartments are also available by the month. Our clients are not only tourists, but corporations who are trying to cut down on their corporate travel expenses. Our hosts are New Yorkers who make their guest rooms or apartments available for paying guests. Our hosted accommodations include continental breakfast.

All accommodations are personally inspected. We turn down an average of seven out of ten inquiries to join our center, although many have been doing bed and breakfast for years. We prefer to turn down a property, rather than to place someone in an accommodation that is not satisfactory. We can suggest reasonably-priced airport pick up to facilitate getting into New York. Aside from finding the most appropriate accommodations for our guests, we try to enhance their stay in New York by assisting in every way possible. And you can also call us for accommodations in Paris and the Loire Valley.

Tel: (212) 977-3512, (800) 353-3727.
E-mail: smartsleep@aol.com **Web:** http://www.worldaccommodations.com

Type: B&B & apartments.
Clientele: Gay
Transportation: Taxi is best. Charge for pick up from public transportation.
To Gay Bars: Walking distance to most.
Baths: Private & shared.
Meals: Continental breakfast at hosted accommodations.
Complimentary: Tea & coffee.
Dates Open: All year.
Rsv'tns: Required.
Reserve Thru: Travel agent or call direct.
Min. Stay: 2 days.
Parking: Variety of adequate parking conditions. On-street pay parking.
In-Room: Color TV, AC, telephone, refrigerator. Kitchen in apts.
On-Premises: Doorman & concierge service with secured buildings.
Sunbathing: On private sun decks when available.
Smoking: Permitted sometimes.
Pets: Permitted sometimes.
Children: Permitted.
Languages: English, Spanish & French.
IGLTA

Three Thirty-Three West 88th Associates WWW Gay/Lesbian ♂️
Gay-Operated

Beautifully-Furnished Apartments in Manhattan

For visits to New York, consider these exceptional one- and two-bedroom apartments, or a hosted room, just restored, in an 1890's brownstone on the west side of Manhattan, directly across the park from the Metropolitan Museum of Art. Apartments are unhosted, giving guests maximum independence. Coffee and tea are provided, and nearby groceries are open 24 hours a day.

From *333 West 88th's* safe and advantageous location, it's an easy trip, via subway or bus, to the theater district, the World Trade Center and the ferry to the Statue of Liberty. You can walk to Lincoln Center. Riverside Park, whose handsome promenade overlooks the Hudson, is 200 feet from the door. Broadway, Amsterdam and Columbus Avenues' shops and dozens of restaurants of all ethnic varieties are also a convenient walk. Especially famous are the Zabars Deli and Fairway, an incredible produce market. We're four blocks from Central Park for those who want to jog the famous Resevoir.

Address: 333 West 88th St, New York, NY 10024
Tel: (212) 724-9818, (800) 724-9888, **Fax:** (212) 769-2686.
E-mail: McMeen@333w88.com **Web:** http://www.333w88.com

Type: Bed & breakfast.
Clientele: Mostly gay & lesbian with some straight clientele
Transportation: Taxi from airports. #1 subway line to 86th St Station.
To Gay Bars: 8 blocks.
Rooms: Unhosted apartments & hosted B&B room.
Baths: All private.
Complimentary: Coffee & tea set-up. Hosted: help yourself.
Dates Open: All year.
Rates: $488-$1045 weekly.
Discounts: Jan & Feb 20% off.
Credit Cards: MC, Visa up to $500.
Rsv'tns: Required with deposit.
Reserve Thru: Call direct.
Min. Stay: 2 days.
Parking: Limited free on-street parking. Nearby garages suggested.
In-Room: Color TV, AC, telephone, kitchen & HiFi.
Smoking: Permitted.
Pets: Not permitted.
Handicap Access: No.
Children: Welcome.
Languages: English.
Your Hosts: Albert & Hamza.

East Village Bed & Breakfast

Women ♀

Apartment in New York's Hottest New Neighborhood

East Village Bed & Breakfast is situated in a tasteful second-floor apartment located in an urban, multi-cultural, multi-ethnic neighborhood close to shops, galleries and affordable restaurants. Greenwich Village, SoHo, Chinatown and other areas of interest are within easy reach. The kitchen comes complete with items for preparing your own continental breakfast. You are usually on your own in your own apartment.

Address: 244 E 7th St #6, New York, NY 10009
Tel: (212) 260-1865.

Type: Bed & breakfast.
Clientele: Women only
Transportation: Airport bus to Grand Central Station or Port Authority in Manhattan. Then taxi or bus.
To Gay Bars: Twenty minute bus ride or a little longer walk.
Rooms: 2 rooms with single or double bed.
Baths: 1 shared bath/shower/toilet.
Meals: Self-service continental breakfast.
Complimentary: Coffee, tea, juices & snacks.
Dates Open: All year.
Rates: $60-$85 per day for 1 or 2 people.
Rsv'tns: Required.
Reserve Thru: Call direct.
Min. Stay: 2 nights on weekends.
Parking: Adequate free on-street parking.
In-Room: AC & telephone.
On-Premises: Guests may use kitchen, refrigerator & watch TV.
Smoking: Not permitted.
Pets: Usually permitted but call in advance.
Handicap Access: No. There are stairs.
Children: Permitted.
Languages: English.

Guion House

Gay-Friendly ♀♂

In the Heart of the Finger Lakes

The Guion House Bed & Breakfast is a beautiful 1876 Second Empire home located in the historic district of Seneca Falls. Most of the home's original wood-work and wonderful ceiling rosettes still exist. Start your day with our bountiful breakfast of Belgian waffles, assorted breads and muffins, seasonal fruit and breakfast beverages. No matter what the season, there is plenty to see and do. We are one block from downtown, shops, museums and Women's Rights National Park.

Address: 32 Cayuga St, Seneca Falls, NY 13148
Tel: (315) 568-8129, (800) 631-8919.
Web: http://www.flare.net/guionhouse

Type: Bed & breakfast.
Clientele: Mostly straight clientele with a gay/lesbian following
Transportation: Car is best.
To Gay Bars: 1 hour to Syracuse, Rochester, Ithaca gay & lesbian bars.
Rooms: 4 queens, 1 full, 1 room with 2 twin beds, rollaways available.
Baths: 4 private, 1 shared.
Meals: Full candlelight breakfast.
Vegetarian: Available upon request.
Dates Open: Year round.
High Season: May-Oct.
Rates: $70-$85.
Discounts: For 4 or more days.
Credit Cards: MC, Visa, Discover.
Rsv'tns: Suggested.
Reserve Thru: Call direct.
Parking: Free off-street parking on premises.
In-Room: AC, maid service.
On-Premises: Library, double parlor.
Exercise/Health: Hiking at state parks, 5 minutes.
Swimming: 5 minutes to state park & lake.
Smoking: Permitted outdoors.
Pets: Not permitted.
Handicap Access: No.
Languages: English.
Your Hosts: Sherry.

Camp Pleiades

WWW Women ♀

A Mountain Resort for Women

Come celebrate our fifth anniversary season at *Camp Pleiades*, a 67-acre mountain resort with stream-fed swimming pond and hiking trails leading into the Appalachian Trail. Activities include swimming, hiking, sports, arts and crafts, nature studies, bird watching, gardening, and general relaxation. Tennis, horseback riding and whitewater rafting are nearby. Special events such as festivals, foliage weekends and Family Camp, are scheduled throughout the season. Private cabins with and without bath, group cabins, and camping are available. Three family-style meals are served daily.

Address: Abby Road, Bakersville, NC 28705
Tel: Toll-free: (888) 324-3110. Summer call (828) 688-9201, **Fax:** (828) 688-3449. Winter call (904) 241-3050, **Fax:** (904) 241-3628.
E-mail: starcamp@aol.com **Web:** http://www.starcamp.com

Type: Mountain resort with clothing shop.
Clientele: Women, with men welcome for Family Camp, group bookings, Fall Foliage
Transportation: All major highway access or by air to Asheville or Tri-cities airport, TN. Fee for airport pickup.
To Gay Bars: 35 mi to Johnson City, TN, 65 mi to Asheville, NC.
Rooms: 12 cabins with single, double or queen beds.
Baths: Private: 7 with shower/toilets. 5 use shower house: 6 private showers,

flush toilets & sinks, 1 tub, hot/cold H2O.
Camping: Yes.
Meals: American Plan, picnic lunches for hikers & day trippers.
Vegetarian: Available.
Complimentary: Coffee, tea, cocoa, lemonade, snacks.
Dates Open: Memorial Day-Columbus Day.
High Season: Jul-Aug, holiday weekends.
Rates: From $40 per person for camping, to $175 per couple for private cabin (2 rooms & bath) daily. Special rates for special

events.
Discounts: 10% discount for early reservation (prior to Mar 15) & on stays of 7 days or longer.
Credit Cards: MC, Visa, Amex.
Rsv'tns: Required.
Reserve Thru: Call direct.
Min. Stay: 2-day minimum.
Parking: Ample free off-street parking.
On-Premises: Meeting space, TV lounge with VCR & videos, library, board games, hammocks.
Exercise/Health: Hiking, sports.
Swimming: Pond on

premises. Nearby pool, river & lakes.
Sunbathing: At pond & in open glens around property.
Smoking: Permitted in designated areas only. All buildings are non-smoking.
Pets: No pets.
Handicap Access: No. Sign language interpreters available with advance notice.
Children: Welcome with adult supervision & during annual Family Camp.
Languages: English.
Your Hosts: Barbara & Jacque.

Another Point Of View

Gay/Lesbian ⚣

A View to Remember

Covered decks on three sides of *Another Point of View*, a beautiful, nicely appointed guest apartment, provide spectacular, panoramic long-range views of Little Pisgah Mountain and Bearwallow Mountain. The apartment, with woodstove, is completely private with easy access to the Blue Ridge Parkway, Bat Cave, Chimney Rock, and Lake Lure. It's only minutes to downtown Asheville's dining, dancing, bars, and entertainment, and only 11 miles from the Biltmore House.

Address: 108 Weeping Cherry Forest Rd, Fairview, NC
Tel: (828) 628-0005.

Type: Guest apartment.
Clientele: Mostly gay & lesbian with some straight clientele
Transportation: Car is best.
To Gay Bars: 10-15 minutes by car.
Rooms: 1 apartment with queen bed & queen sleeper.

Baths: Private bath/shower/ toilet.
Vegetarian: Many vegetarian restaurants in town.
Complimentary: Welcome fruit & wine basket.
Dates Open: All year.
High Season: April-October.

Rates: 2 people $80/night; 3-4 people $100/night; $500 per week.
Rsv'tns: Required.
Reserve Thru: Call direct.
Min. Stay: 2 nights.
Parking: Ample free off-street parking.
In-Room: Color TV, VCR, phone, kitchen, refrigerator,

microwave, ceiling fans, AC.
On-Premises: Stove, washer/dryer. Cooking & dining supplies provided.
Sunbathing: On sun decks.
Smoking: Permitted on outside deck only.
Pets: Not permitted.
Handicap Access: No.
Children: No.

Brook ~ Haven

WWW Gay/Lesbian ⚣
Woman-Owned & -Operated

Finally, Time to Relax and Rejoice...

Awake to a babbling brook just beyond your bedroom window. Arise to the warm glow of knotty pine interiors and a large, rock fireplace. Sip your morning brew on the screened porch beside a designated, stocked trout stream. Scan the lush Beech Valley stretching before you in the heart of the Appalachians, and inhale the crisp mountain air of... *Brook ~ Haven.* This spacious cedar cabin is only 15 minutes from Asheville and the Blue Ridge Parkway, five minutes from Reems Creek Golf Course, and about 35 minutes from the Appalachian Trail, white water rafting, natural hot springs, horseback riding, and snow skiing at Wolf Laurel.

Mail To: PO Box 1388 (No. 111), Weaverville, NC 28787
Tel: (828) 649-0619.
E-mail: nkhoury@madison.main.nc.us

Type: Cedar home.
Clientele: Mostly gay & lesbian with some straight clientele
Transportation: Car is best.
To Gay Bars: 15 miles.
Rooms: 3 rooms (1 double, 2 queen beds).
Baths: Private.
Vegetarian: 10-15 min to restaurants & markets.

Complimentary: Coffee, tea & cocoa with coffeemaker in fully equipped kitchen.
Dates Open: All year.
High Season: Spring-fall.
Rates: High: $80-$120 (depends on number of guests); Low: $60-$100.
Discounts: Weekly, monthly.
Rsv'tns: Required.

Reserve Thru: Call direct.
Min. Stay: 2 nights in high season.
Parking: Ample, free off-street parking.
In-Room: Telephone, ceiling fans, color cable TV, VCR, kitchen, refrigerator, coffee & tea-making facilities.
On-Premises: Laundry facilities.

Exercise/Health: Nearby strolling, hiking, fishing.
Swimming: Small wading pool in stream.
Sunbathing: On patio.
Smoking: Outside only.
Pets: Not permitted.
Handicap Access: No.
Children: No.
Languages: English.

Corner Oak Manor

Gay-Friendly ♀

Come Nurture Your Senses

Surrounded by trees, this lovely English Tudor home is located in a quiet residential neighborhood minutes from the famed Biltmore Estate and Gardens. *Corner Oak Manor* was decorated by an interior designer, whose contributions include an oval drop ceiling in the living room, beautiful bathrooms and window treatments and coordinated wall coverings. A living room fireplace, baby grand piano and an outdoor deck with hot tub are among the gracious amenities. Karen, a gourmet cook, enjoys surprising guests with creative breakfasts which include four-cheese herb quiche, blueberry-ricotta pancakes, and Italian country omelets.

Address: 53 Saint Dunstans Rd, Asheville, NC 28803
Tel: (828) 253-3525, (888) 633-3525.
E-mail: vineguy@aol.com **Web:** http://www.bbonline.com/nc/corneroak

Type: Bed & breakfast.
Clientele: Mostly straight clientele with a mostly lesbian following
Transportation: Car is best.
To Gay Bars: 2 miles.
Rooms: 3 rooms & 1 cottage with queen beds.
Baths: 1 private shower/toilet & 3 private bath/toilet/showers.
Meals: Full breakfast.

Vegetarian: Available with 1 day's notice. Several vegetarian restaurants nearby.
Complimentary: Afternoon refreshments, chocolates in room, guest fridge with beverages.
Dates Open: All year.
High Season: Apr-Dec.
Rates: $110-$165 per night double occupancy.
Credit Cards: MC, Visa,

Amex, Discover.
Rsv'tns: Required.
Reserve Thru: Call direct.
Min. Stay: 2 nights on weekends.
Parking: Ample off-street parking.
In-Room: AC & ceiling fans. Kitchen in cottage.
On-Premises: Telephone & refrigerator.
Exercise/Health: Jacuzzi on premises. Gym &

massage nearby.
Swimming: Nearby pool.
Smoking: Permitted outside only. All rooms are non-smoking.
Pets: No.
Handicap Access: No.
Children: Welcome 12 years of age & older.
Languages: English.
Your Hosts: Karen & Andy.

Emy's Nook

Women ♀

Emy's Nook, an 90-year-old New England farmhouse-style home in the Grove Park area of Asheville, is just north of downtown in a neighborhood of lovely old homes, some of which are on the Historic Register. Our guesthouse provides a spacious, comfortable room with a queen-sized bed and a small sitting area. Cool, shady and inviting, the spacious backyard has a swing, sitting chairs and a creek. The community is an active walking, jogging and cycling area with a nearby park for rest and relaxation. Access to downtown activities, businesses and shopping is quick and easy, with many nearby shops, galleries and recreational facilities.

Address: 6 Edwin Place, Asheville, NC 28801
Tel: (828) 281-4122 (Tel/Fax).

Type: Guesthouse.
Clientele: Women only
Transportation: Car is best. We're on downtown bus line. Free pick up from bus, train. Pick up from airport $10 (pre-arranged).
To Gay Bars: Close by, a 5-min drive.
Rooms: 1 room with queen bed.
Baths: 1 private bath/

shower/toilet.
Meals: Light continental breakfast.
Vegetarian: Many vegetarian possibilities nearby.
Complimentary: Tea & coffee.
Dates Open: All year.
High Season: April-Christmas.
Rates: $55 per night, 1 or 2

people.
Discounts: 5% on stays of 4 or more nights.
Rsv'tns: Required.
Reserve Thru: Travel agent or call direct.
Min. Stay: 2 nights.
Parking: Free on- or off-street parking.
In-Room: Color TV, VCR, ceiling fans, AC.
Exercise/Health: Nearby

gym, weights, massage.
Swimming: Nearby river & lake, YWCA & YMCA.
Sunbathing: In private yard.
Smoking: Permitted on patio. All rooms are non-smoking.
Pets: Not permitted.
Handicap Access: No.
Children: No.
Languages: English.
Your Hosts: VA & Jean.

Heron Cabin

A Peaceful Cabin in the Mountains

Built by hand out of local logs in the late 1800s, *Heron Cabin* has been transformed into two charming, comfortable rentals. Each side has a functional, updated kitchen with dining area, with enough flatware, glasses, cups, plates and equipment to prepare a feast or make a sandwich. The shared bath has a tiled tub/shower and high tech electric composting toilet. Vegetarian dinners can be brought to your cabin., and you can pick veggies and flowers from our organic gardens. The Blue Ridge Mountains offer many opportunities for biking, rock climbing, hiking, whitewater rafting, kayaking, and birding. Downtown Asheville, with its many shops and restaurants, is a beautiful 12-mile drive away.

Address: Alexander, NC **Mail To:** PO Box 166, Alexander, NC
Tel: (828) 683-5463.
Web: http://www.heroncabin.com

Type: Cabin.
Clientele: Mostly women with men welcome
Transportation: Car is best.
To Gay Bars: 12 miles.
Rooms: 2 apartments with double beds.
Baths: 2 private sinks only, 1 shared bath/shower/toilet.
Vegetarian: Veg. meals w/ advance notice. Restaurants in Asheville. Organic veggies in garden.
Dates Open: All year.
High Season: Summer & fall.
Rates: Low $45-$65, high $50-$75.
Discounts: Weekly, monthly.
Rsv'tns: Required.
Reserve Thru: Call direct.
Min. Stay: 2 days.
Parking: Ample free parking.
In-Room: Telephone, fans, color TV, VCR, kitchen, refrigerator, coffee & tea-making facilities.
On-Premises: Video tape library.
Exercise/Health: Regression & Rebirthing therapy by appt. on premises.
Sunbathing: On lawns.
Smoking: Smoking outdoors only. Both apartments non-smoking.
Pets: Not permitted.
Handicap Access: No.
Children: Please call.
Languages: English.
Your Hosts: Mary Anne & Deb.

Old Mill B & B

Come, be lulled to sleep on the banks of a rushing mountain stream in spectacular Hickory Nut Gorge, approximately half an hour by car from Asheville. *Old Mill B&B* provides rustic comfort in rooms overlooking the river and hearty breakfasts of eggs benedict or soda-water pancakes with sausage and homemade apple sauce to fortify you for days of hiking, tubing, rafting, canoeing, tennis or golf. Shopping and dining are all close by, as is Asheville, Biltmore House, the Blue Ridge Parkway, Chimney Rock Park, Lake Lure, Flat Rock Playhouse, and the Carl Sandburg Home.

Address: Hwy 64/74-A/9, Lake Lure Hwy **Mail To:** Box 252, Bat Cave, NC 28710
Tel: (828) 625-4256.

Type: Bed & breakfast with gift shop.
Clientele: Mostly gay & lesbian with some straight clientele
Transportation: Car is best.
To Gay Bars: 20 miles to Asheville gay/lesbian bars.
Rooms: 6 rooms.
Baths: 5 private.
Meals: Full breakfast.
Vegetarian: Prearranged.
Complimentary: Drinks on arrival.
Dates Open: Mid-Mar thru New Year's day.
Rates: $35-$85.
Discounts: 10% for INN Places readers on request.
Credit Cards: MC, Visa, Amex, Discover.
Rsv'tns: Recommended.
Reserve Thru: Travel agent or call direct.
Min. Stay: 2 nights on weekends.
Parking: Ample free on-street parking.
In-Room: Maid service, ceiling fans, & sitting areas. 4 rooms have color TV.
On-Premises: TV lounge with VCR.
Exercise/Health: Soloflex & hot tub.
Swimming: River out back with tubing.
Sunbathing: Sun decks.
Nudity: Permitted in hot tub cottage.
Smoking: Permitted without restrictions.
Pets: Permitted with restrictions.
Handicap Access: Limited accessibility.
Children: Please call.
Languages: English & limited Spanish.
Your Hosts: Walt.

Owl's Nest Inn at Engadine

WWW Gay-Friendly ⚥
Woman-Owned & -Operated

An 1885 Victorian Bed & Breakfast

Owl's Nest Inn at Engadine is an 1885 Victorian which was originally the home of Civil War captain John Hoyt. It has been lovingly restored and is featured in the historical architecture book *Cabins and Castles*. We are situated on 4.32 acres with beautiful mountain views, yet we're only 15 minutes from Asheville and its attractions, including the Biltmore Estate and Winery, great restaurants, and the Blue Ridge Parkway. We offer large, comfortable guestrooms with gas fireplaces and one suite with a two-person Jacuzzi, all elegantly furnished. Come, relax on our porches or take a stroll in our meadow.

Address: 2630 Smokey Park Hwy, Candler, NC 28715
Tel: (828) 665-8325, (800) 665-8868, **Fax:** (828) 667-2539.
E-mail: info@engadineinn.com **Web:** http://www.engadineinn.com

Type: Inn.
Clientele: Mostly straight with a gay/lesbian following
Transportation: Car is best.
To Gay Bars: 15 miles, a 20 min drive.
Rooms: 4 rooms, 1 suite with single, queen or king beds.
Baths: Private: 2 bath/shower/toilets, 2 bath/toilets

(hand-held showers, 1 is a whirlpool bath), 1 shower/toilet.
Meals: Full breakfast.
Vegetarian: On advance notice, restaurants in Asheville.
Complimentary: Snacks & soft drinks all day. Evening wine hour.
Dates Open: All year.
High Season: July-Dec.

Rates: $110-$175.
Discounts: 10% discount for 4+ nights. Biltmore Estate pkgs available.
Credit Cards: MC, Visa, Discover, Amex.
Rsv'tns: Required.
Reserve Thru: Travel agent or call direct.
Min. Stay: 2 nts on wknds, 3 nts on holiday wknds.
Parking: Adequate free off-

street parking.
In-Room: AC, ceiling fans, color cable TV, maid service.
On-Premises: TV lounge.
Swimming: Nearby river.
Smoking: Permitted outside only, ashtrays provided on porches.
Pets: Not permitted.
Children: No.
Languages: English.
Your Hosts: Marg & Gail.

WhiteGate Inn & Cottage

WWW Gay-Friendly 50/50 ⚥
Gay-Owned & -Operated

Asheville's Only Gay-Owned Bed & Breakfast

Circa 1889, this Shingle-style house, surrounded by beautifully landscaped grounds, overlooks downtown Asheville and the Blue Ridge Mountains. The *WhiteGate Inn* offers today's comforts with yesterday's ambiance and is furnished with period antiques and collectables. Enjoy a full three-course gourmet breakfast, evening social hour with refreshments, and full concierge service. There is a separate cottage for guests wishing complete privacy. We're a four-block walk to downtown Asheville with its 100-plus art galleries, antique shops, restaurants, bookstores, sidewalk cafes and gay bars. This is the perfect place for Union Ceremonies.

Address: 173 East Chestnut Street, Asheville, NC 28801
Tel: (828) 253-2553, (800) 485-3045, **Fax:** (828) 281-1883.
E-mail: innkeeper@whitegate.net **Web:** http://www.whitegate.net

Type: Bed & breakfast.
Clientele: 50% gay & lesbian & 50% straight
Transportation: Car.
To Gay Bars: 6 blocks.
Rooms: 2 rooms, 2 suites, 1 cottage with queen beds.
Baths: Private: 2 bath/shower/toilets, 2 shower/toilets.
Meals: Full breakfast.
Vegetarian: Vegetarian

meal by request.
Complimentary: Fresh baked goods, cheese, crackers, wine, tea, coffee, soft drinks.
Dates Open: All year.
High Season: Apr-Jan.
Rates: $145-$185.
Discounts: 10% to gay clientele mentioning this ad.
Credit Cards: MC, Visa, Amex, Discover.

Rsv'tns: Required (cancellation policy).
Reserve Thru: Travel agent or call direct.
Min. Stay: 2 nights wknds.
Parking: Ample free off-street parking. Covered parking by arrangement.
In-Room: AC, ceiling fans, color cable TV, VCR, maid service. Kitchen in cottage.
On-Premises: TV lounge,

video tape library.
Exercise/Health: Health club passes available. Massage with prior notice.
Sunbathing: In yard.
Smoking: Permitted outside only.
Pets: Not permitted.
Handicap Access: No.
Children: Please inquire.
Languages: English.
Your Hosts: Frank & Ralph.

Joan's Place

Joan's Place is a B&B for women in my home, offering a rustic setting, secluded among trees, with a serene and picturesque environment. I have 2 bedrooms, one large with double bed, one smaller with double bed. There is a shared, full bath across the hall. Guests have access to my living room, with TV and stereo, ping-pong room downstairs, and large deck overlooking the trees. I am 2 miles south of Chapel Hill and UNC Campus, with easy access to Raleigh, Durham and Research Triangle Park.

Address: 1443 Poinsett Dr, c/o M. Joan Stiven, Chapel Hill, NC 27514
Tel: (919) 942-5621.
E-mail: mjoanbs@aol.com

Type: Bed & breakfast.
Clientele: Women only
Transportation: Personal car only.
To Gay Bars: About 10 miles to Durham gay bar.
Rooms: 2 rooms with double beds.
Baths: 1 shared bath/ shower/toilet.
Meals: Continental breakfast.
Vegetarian: Available upon request. 2 vegetarian stores & vegetarian restaurants nearby.
Complimentary: Tea, coffee & juices.
Dates Open: All year.
High Season: Spring, summer and fall.
Rates: $60-$55 per night.
Discounts: Weekly rates.
Rsv'tns: Preferred.
Reserve Thru: Call direct.
Parking: Ample, free off-street parking.
In-Room: AC & telephone.
On-Premises: TV lounge.
Smoking: Permitted outdoors.
Pets: Not permitted.
Handicap Access: No.
Children: Not permitted.
Languages: English.
Your Hosts: Joan.

Treetops B&B

Relax in this Serene Treetop Setting

On Laurel Hill, overlooking the treetops and the University of North Carolina skyline, is a quiet bed and breakfast called *Treetops.* Each of the three large rooms has a queen bed and shared or private bath. The Oak Suite features a Jacuzzi in the private bath, and French doors which open onto the arbor deck. Enjoy a video or a good book in the library with fireplace, or just relax on the deck, in the hot tub, or in the hammock. A full or continental breakfast awaits you, served in either the open dining room or on the private deck. Visit the University of North Carolina or Duke campus, RTP or Raleigh, all a short drive from here.

Address: at the Woods on Laurel Hill, Chapel Hill, NC
Tel: (919) 260-2288, **Fax:** (919) 942-1805.

Type: Bed & breakfast.
Clientele: Mostly straight clientele with a gay/lesbian following
Transportation: Car is best. Pick up from airport $15.
To Gay Bars: 10 min drive.
Rooms: 3 rooms, 1 suite with queen beds.
Baths: Private: 2 bath/shower/toilets; Shared: 1 bath/shower/toilet, 2 WCs only.
Meals: Full or continental breakfast.
Vegetarian: By request & nearby.
Complimentary: Tea & coffee, mint on pillow, soft drinks, snack.
Dates Open: All year.
Rates: $75-$135.
Discounts: College ID discount.
Credit Cards: MC, Visa.
Rsv'tns: Required.
Reserve Thru: Travel agent or call direct.
Parking: Ample free off-street parking.
In-Room: AC, ceiling fans, color cable TV, VCR, coffee & tea-making facilities, maid service.
On-Premises: TV lounge, video tape library, copier, fax, computer.
Exercise/Health: Jacuzzi. Nearby gym, massage, nature trail.
Swimming: Nearby lake.
Sunbathing: On common sun decks.
Nudity: Permitted in Jacuzzi.
Smoking: Permitted outside only. Non-smoking rooms only.
Pets: Check at time of reservation.
Handicap Access: No.
Children: No.
Languages: English.
Your Hosts: Bruce.

Mineral Springs Inn
Gay/Lesbian ♂

Southern Hospitality with Modern Amentities

The **Mineral Springs Inn,** located in the heart of the Raleigh/Durham/Chapel Hill triangle, offers an easygoing getaway from the business bustle of the Research Triangle Park, just ten minutes away. This authentic 1890's North Carolina farmhouse has been modernized and offers four thematically decorated guestrooms and a full Southern breakfast. We are minutes from Duke University, the University of North Carolina and North Carolina State. It is also an easy ride to the Blue Ridge Mountains and Atlantic beaches.

Address: 718 South Mineral Springs Rd, Durham, NC 27703
Tel: (919) 596-2162 (Tel/Fax).
E-mail: msinn7@earthlink.net **Web:** http://home.earthlink.net/~msinn7

Type: Inn.
Clientele: Mostly men with women welcome
Transportation: Car or taxi.
Rooms: 4 rooms with double or queen beds.
Baths: Private: 3 shower/toilets, Shared: 1 bath/shower/toilet.
Meals: Full breakfast.

Vegetarian: Available upon request. Chinese & Mexican vegetarian available nearby.
Complimentary: Coffee, tea & wine in late afternoon.
Dates Open: All year.
Rates: $89-$99.
Discounts: 10% discount on weekly rental.
Credit Cards: MC, Visa,

Amex, Discover.
Rsv'tns: Required.
Reserve Thru: Travel agent or call direct.
Parking: Limited free off-street parking.
In-Room: AC, color cable TV, telephone, maid service.
On-Premises: Fax.
Exercise/Health: Free

weights & machine.
Smoking: Permitted outside only.
Pets: Not permitted.
Handicap Access: No.
Children: No.
Languages: English.
Your Hosts: John & Mike.
IGLTA

Brewmaster's House, The
WWW Men ♂
Gay-Owned & -Operated

Where Historic Brewery District Meets German Village

The Brewmaster's House is a landmark bed & breakfast inn where historic Brewery District meets German Village. These walking neighborhoods — considered Columbus' top two tourist destinations — feature architecture, antiques, parks, restaurants, gay bars, a riverfront bike/hike trail and are adjacent to all downtown attractions. Access is easy from Routes 23, 70, 71 and the airport. Columbus is rated one of the top 10 U.S. cities for gay life. This grand 1909 house, lived in for 90 years by the builder's family, retains its original fireplaces, woodwork, gas/electric lightoliers and flooring.

Address: 1083 S High Street, Columbus, OH 43206
Tel: (614) 449-8298, **Fax:** (614) 449-8663.
E-mail: brewmastershouse@compuserve.com **Web:** http://www.ferrariguides.com/brewmastershouse

Type: Bed & breakfast.
Clientele: Men only
Transportation: Taxi from airport.
To Gay Bars: Short walk to 3 gay bars, longer walk to 4 more gay bars.
Rooms: 5 rooms with single or king beds.
Baths: 2 shared bath/

shower/toilets.
Meals: Full breakfast.
Dates Open: All year.
Rates: $50-$75.
Rsv'tns: Required.
Reserve Thru: Travel agent or call direct.
Parking: Ample, free off-street parking.
In-Room: AC, color cable

TV.
On-Premises: TV lounge, laundry facilities, fax machine, library.
Exercise/Health: Weights on premises.
Sunbathing: On patio.
Smoking: Permitted everywhere. No non-smoking rooms available.

Pets: Permitted. Friendly cat & dog on premises. Guest pets must be in room, caged, or on leashes.
Handicap Access: No.
Children: No.
Languages: English.
Your Hosts: John & Chris.

America's Crossroads

Private Homestays in Oklahoma City

America's Crossroads is the reservation service for a network of homes in the metropolitan Oklahoma City area. Since 1994, Les and Michael have offered the traditional European-style bed & breakast they love. All homestays include a full breakfast on request, and most homes in our network can accommodate up to four people at one time. We are geared to the gay traveler and provide a selection of gay-owned and -operated homes. With I-35, I-40 and I-44 all passing through the metro area, this is an ideal stopover for the cross-country traveler, putting you at *America's Crossroads.*

Mail To: PO Box 270642, Oklahoma City, OK 73137
Tel: (405) 495-1111, **Fax:** (405) 943-8289.
E-mail: acbb@iname.com **Web:** http://www.bestinns.net/usa/ok/rdac.html

Type: Private homestays.
Clientele: Men only
Transportation: Private car best.
To Gay Bars: 5-15 minutes.
Rooms: 3 homes, each with 2 rooms with queen beds.
Baths: Private & shared.
Meals: Full breakfast upon request.

Vegetarian: Available with advance notice.
Dates Open: All year.
Rates: Per night rates from $30 (single) & $35 (double).
Rsv'tns: Minimum 1 week advance.
Reserve Thru: Call direct.
Min. Stay: No minimum.
Parking: On- & off-street parking.

In-Room: Telephone, radio, AC. Some rooms with TV/VCR.
Exercise/Health: Free weights & exercise bicycle. Jacuzzi, hot tub available.
Swimming: Pool at some locations.
Sunbathing: On patios.
Nudity: Permitted in hot tubs only.

Smoking: Permitted in some locations, please inquire.
Pets: Not permitted.
Handicap Access: No.
Children: No.
Languages: English.
Your Hosts: Les & Michael.

Habana Inn

The Heart of Gay Nightlife in One Complex

The *Habana Inn* complex is the hub of gay nightlife in Oklahoma City, within walking distance of a unique gay area. This 175-room hotel has everything: two swimming pools, Jungle Red (a large pride store), three bars — The Copa (a dance bar), The Finishline (a Country/Western bar), The Ledo (a piano bar), and Gusher's Restaurant, open daily with reasonably priced, excellent food. There's something for everyone at the inn. From poolside BBQ's to special events and lots of great entertainment. There's always a party brewing and you're invited. We're minutes from downtown, Bricktown, Remington Park horse racing, the zoo, fair grounds, golf courses, museums and two major shopping centers. Plan your next convention or vacation at the *Habana Inn.*

Address: 2200 NW 39th Expwy, Oklahoma City, OK 73112
Tel: (405) 528-2221, (800) 988-2221.
Web: http://www.habanainn.com

Type: Motel, bar, restaurant & gift shop.
Clientele: Mostly men with women welcome
Transportation: Airport shuttle or car.
To Gay Bars: On premises.
Rooms: 175 singles, doubles & some suites.
Baths: All private.

Meals: Restaurant on premises.
Dates Open: All year.
High Season: Jun-Sept.
Rates: $34.95-$130.
Discounts: Weekly rates available.
Credit Cards: MC, Visa, Amex, Discover.
Rsv'tns: Recommended for

holidays & weekends.
Reserve Thru: Call direct.
Min. Stay: 3 nights on holidays.
Parking: Ample free on-site parking.
In-Room: Maid service, color cable TV, telephone, AC.
Swimming: 2 pools (1

heated).
Sunbathing: At poolside.
Smoking: Permitted without restrictions.
Pets: Permitted with prior arrangement.
Handicap Access: Yes.
Children: Permitted but not encouraged.
Languages: English.

South Coast Inn Bed & Breakfast

Gay-Friendly ⚥

Charm & Comfort on Oregon's Rugged, Unspoiled Southern Coast

Surrender yourself to turn-of-the-century hospitality. Enjoy coffee in front of the stone fireplace. Relax in the spa or sauna, or bask in the warmth of beautiful antiques. Wake up to a gourmet breakfast and a beautiful ocean view. *South Coast Inn* is centrally located in Brookings, on the southern Oregon coast. Built in 1917, and designed by Bernard Maybeck, the inn exhibits the grace and charm of a spacious craftsman-style home. AAA-approved 3-diamond, Northwest Best Places.

Address: 516 Redwood St, Brookings, OR 97415
Tel: (800) 525-9273, (541) 469-5557, **Fax:** 469-6615.
E-mail: scoastin@wave.net **Web:** http://www.virtualcities.com

Type: Bed & breakfast.
Clientele: Mostly straight clientele
Transportation: Car is best.
Rooms: 4 rooms, 1 cottage.
Baths: 2 private bath/toilets & 3 private shower/toilets.
Meals: Full breakfast. Continental breakfast in cottage.
Vegetarian: On request.

Dates Open: All year.
High Season: Memorial Day-Sep.
Rates: $84-$99.
Discounts: 10% senior.
Credit Cards: MC, Visa, Amex, Discover.
Rsv'tns: Suggested.
Reserve Thru: Travel agent or call direct.
Parking: Ample free off-street parking.

In-Room: Color cable TV, VCRs & ceiling fans. Cottage has kitchenette. 1 room with gas stove/ fireplace.
Exercise/Health: Indoor Jacuzzi & sauna, Universal gym.
Swimming: Nearby pool, river & ocean.
Sunbathing: On the patio, common sun decks & at the

beach.
Smoking: Permitted outside only.
Pets: Not permitted.
Handicap Access: No.
Children: Welcomed if 12 or over.
Languages: English.
Your Hosts: Ken & Keith.

Middle Creek Run Bed & Breakfast

WWW Gay/Lesbian ⚥
Gay-Owned

Old-World Comfort in the Heart of Oregon's Wine Country

In the rolling hills of the Oregon wine country lies *Middle Creek Run,* a rural 1902 Queen Anne Victorian. After eight years of careful renovation, the proprietors have designed their home around their collection of art and antiques. Guestrooms offer a comfortable ambiance in a period setting of antique furnishings, while perennial gardens and farmlands grace each window view. Our meals, an exuberant hodgepodge of culinary delights are prepared from recipes created in-house and collected over the years. Vineyards, antique shops, galleries, golf and the Spirit Mountain Gaming Casino are in the area.

Address: 25400 Harmony Rd, Sheridan, OR
Tel: (503) 843-7606.

Type: Bed & breakfast, 1 hr from Portland, 1/2 hr from Salem.
Clientele: Mainly gay & lesbian with straight clientele
Transportation: Car is best. About 1 hr from Portland airport.
To Gay Bars: 22 miles, a 30 min drive.
Rooms: 4 rooms, 1 suite with double beds.
Baths: 3 private & shared

bath/shower/tub/toilets.
Meals: Full breakfast.
Vegetarian: Available with 1 week's advance notice & nearby.
Complimentary: Coffee, tea, snacks, truffles on pillow.
Dates Open: All year.
Rates: $85-$125.
Rsv'tns: Required.
Reserve Thru: Call direct.
Min. Stay: 2 nights on

holiday weekends.
Parking: Ample, free off-street parking.
In-Room: Maid & turn-down service.
On-Premises: Meeting rooms, library, piano, perennial gardens.
Exercise/Health: Gym nearby.
Swimming: River on premises.
Sunbathing: On common

sun decks, at river.
Nudity: Permitted at river.
Smoking: Permitted on porches & decks. All rooms non-smoking.
Pets: Not permitted.
Handicap Access: No.
Children: No.
Languages: English, some Spanish.
Your Hosts: John & Marc.

ArtSprings

Dedicated to the Creative Power of Women!

ArtSprings is 12 acres of secluded, wooded land 37 miles SW of Portland. A great place to relax, we're geared toward creativity, bird watching or personal retreat. Float on one of our five ponds, hang out in a hammock, soak in the hot tub, enjoy the outdoor espresso bar, or sleep under the stars on the outdoor waterbed. Accommodations consist of The Sappho Sweet, May Sarton Room, a variety of camp sites, and small RV parking. The first week of August is Dyke Art Camp, devoted to Lesbian visual art and good food! Drug- and alcohol-free.

Address: 40789 SW Hummingbird Lane, Gaston, OR
Tel: (503) 985-9549.
E-mail: artsprng@transport.com

Type: Bed & breakfast, RV, Campground.
Clientele: Women born women only
Transportation: Car is best. Airport pick up $15. Light rail pick up available.
Rooms: 1 suite w/ queen, 1 rustic room w/ double. King outdoor waterbed.
Baths: 1 private, 1 shared.
Camping: 2 RV sites (under 25 feet), 8 tent sites, all primitive. 2 indoor showers,

1 outdoor shower. 2 bathrooms, 3 toilets, no dump station, propane nearby. Use of kitchen $20.
Meals: Breakfast with B&B suite. All other meals by arrangement $7.50-$25.
Vegetarian: Vegetarian & organic food available.
Complimentary: Tea & coffee in B&B suite.
Dates Open: All year.
High Season: Jul-Sept.
Rates: $15-$75.

Discounts: Some work exchange available by arrangement.
Rsv'tns: Reservations & deposit required.
Reserve Thru: Call direct.
Parking: Adequate, free.
In-Room: B&B suite: phone, color TV, VCR, kitchen, fridge, coffee & tea-making facilities. Use of kitchen in cabin.
Exercise/Health: Hot tub.
Swimming: Nearby lake,

river.
Sunbathing: Anywhere.
Nudity: Permitted outside.
Smoking: All rooms non-smoking. Permitted in designated area only.
Pets: No pets.
Handicap Access: Very limited, rugged accessibility.
Children: No.
Languages: English, Spanish (conversational).
Your Hosts: Sierra & Marj.

Sullivan's Gulch Bed & Breakfast

 Gay/Lesbian ⚥

Western Hospitality Celebrating Diversity

Sullivan's Gulch Bed & Breakfast, a lovely 1904 home, decorated with Western and Native American art & artifacts, is in the charming, quiet area of NE Portland known as Sullivan's Gulch. Near the famed Lloyd Center shopping mall and cinemas, the Convention Center and the Coliseum, we're also two blocks from NE Broadway's shops, micro-breweries and restaurants, and minutes from downtown. We serve an expanded continental breakfast that celebrates our local bakeries and the natural abundance of the Pacific Northwest.

Address: 1744 NE Clackamas Street, Portland, OR 97232
Tel: (503) 331-1104, **Fax:** (503) 331-1575.
E-mail: thegulch@teleport.com **Web:** http://www.teleport.com/~thegulch/

Type: Bed & breakfast.
Clientele: Mostly gay & lesbian with gay-friendly straight folk welcome
Transportation: Car is best. Public transportation nearby. We offer free pick up service from all terminals.
To Gay Bars: 5 blocks.
Rooms: 3 rooms with queen beds.
Baths: 2 private, 1 shared.
Meals: Expanded

continental breakfast, special requests honored.
Vegetarian: Special requests honored.
Complimentary: Coffee & tea available all day.
Dates Open: All year.
High Season: Summer.
Rates: $70-$85 plus tax, double occupancy.
Discounts: Available for extended stays.
Credit Cards: Visa, MC,

Amex.
Rsv'tns: Required.
Reserve Thru: Travel agent or call direct.
Parking: Adequate free off-street & on-street parking.
In-Room: Cable TV, ceiling fans. Breakfast served in room upon request. 2 rooms with phone/internet access.
Exercise/Health: Gyms nearby.
Sunbathing: On common

sun deck.
Nudity: 20 minutes to nude beach.
Smoking: Not permitted.
Pets: Resident dog. Well-behaved dogs permitted.
Handicap Access: No. Many steps.
Children: Lesbian & gay families welcome.
Languages: English.
Your Hosts: Skip & Jack.

Cliff House Bed & Breakfast

Gay-Friendly ⚥

Pampered Elegance By the Sea

Cliff House, a luxuriously restored older home with a spectacular ocean view, offers a peaceful atmosphere in which to refresh the spirit in a romantic setting amid shore pines. Eight miles of uninterrupted beach run in front of the house. Rooms have plush bedding, antiques, ocean or bay view, cedar bath, and balcony. Two rooms have antique parlor stoves. Lounge on a chaise, play croquet, walk, explore the beach, sail, deep-sea fish or go whalewatching. Three Stars AAA.

Address: 1450 Adahi St **Mail To:** PO Box 436, Yaquina John Pt, Waldport, OR 97394
Tel: (541) 563-2506, **Fax:** (541) 563-4393.
E-mail: clifhos@pioneer.net

Type: Bed & breakfast.
Clientele: Mostly straight w/ gay/lesbian following.
Transportation: Car is best. Will arrange for rental car or pick up from local airport or Waldport bus.
To Gay Bars: 1-3/4 hrs.
Rooms: 4 rooms & 1 suite with queen or king beds.
Baths: All private.
Meals: Mon-Fri continental breakfast, Sat-Sun gourmet.
Vegetarian: On request.
Complimentary: Port or sherry in rooms, brandy in Bridal Suite.
Dates Open: Mar-Oct or by special reservation.
High Season: July-Sept.
Rates: $120-$150. Bridal Suite $245.
Credit Cards: MC, Visa or Discover to hold room.
Rsv'tns: 14-day cancellation notice ($20 fee regardless).
Reserve Thru: Call direct.
Min. Stay: 2 days on wknds, holidays, longer in season.
Parking: Ample free parking.
In-Room: Color cable TV, VCR. 2 rooms w/ fridge.
On-Premises: Meeting room, VCR & TV, grand piano, dining room, telephone, fireplace.
Exercise/Health: Golf, horseback riding, croquet, 10-jet hot tub. Massage by appt.
Swimming: Beach, river.
Sunbathing: On beach, balconies, common sun decks.
Nudity: Permitted in hot tub or sauna steam room.
Smoking: Permitted outdoors.
Pets: No. Kennel nearby.
Children: Not permitted.
Languages: English, Spanish.
Your Hosts: Gabrielle & Master Cat, "Silverman."

Glen Isle Farm Country Inn

Historic Hospitality

Come and experience, as did George Washington on June 3, 1773, the "historic hospitality" of *Glen Isle Farm*. At that time, the farm was known as the Ship Inn. Other guests have included James Buchanan, before he became the fifteenth president of the United States, as well as the United States Continental Congress, while on its way to York. During The Civil War, *Glen Isle Farm* was a stop on the underground railroad, thus it has an important place in civil rights history. Today, the farm is a secluded 8-acre gentleman's estate. The approach is down a long, heavily-wooded drive and across a small stone bridge. The drive circles up to the imposing front entrance, leading you up granite steps and across a broad checkerboard porch of black slate, white marble and red brick, through a glass vestibule and to the wide front door. Once inside, you can feel the wonderful sense of history present in this 270-year-old home.

Enjoy a cool autumn afternoon in the upstairs sunroom, sipping a cappuccino or glass of sherry, watching the fall colors and the shadows, as they gently cross the walled garden. Play a tune on the grand piano in the music room or just curl up with a good book from the library. Visit historic Valley Forge. Take the train to Philadelphia, the nation's first capital. Go antiquing, or visit beautiful Longwood Gardens and the Brandywine River Museum, the home of the Wyeth school and collection. You may want to take a bike ride or go hiking on the many nearby roads and trails. Maybe you've come in May to attend the Devon Horse Show, or to see some of the nearby Amish country, and enjoy a slice of Shoofly Pie. Come and experience the "historic hospitality" that is *Glen Isle Farm.*

Address: 130 S Lloyd Ave, Downingtown, PA 19335-2239
Tel: (610) 269-9100, Reservations/Info: (800) 269-1730, **Fax:** (610) 269-9191.

Type: Bed & breakfast inn.
Clientele: 50% gay & lesbian & 50% straight clientele.
Transportation: Car or train. Free pick up from train or airport shuttle.
To Gay Bars: 30 miles, or 40 minutes by car, to Norristown or Philadelphia.
Rooms: 4 rooms with queen or king beds.
Baths: 2 private, 2 shared.

Meals: Full breakfast, other meals by arrangement.
Vegetarian: Available with prior arrangement.
Complimentary: Tea, coffee, soft drinks.
Dates Open: All year.
High Season: Apr-Oct.
Rates: $60-$90 + tax.
Discounts: 10% stays of 7+ nights. Seniors 10%.
Credit Cards: MC, Visa, Discover.

Rsv'tns: Required.
Reserve Thru: Travel agent or call direct.
Min. Stay: 2 nights on 3-day weekends.
Parking: Ample off-street parking.
On-Premises: TV lounge. Weddings, reunions & business meeting space.
Exercise/Health: 10-15 min to nearby gyms.
Swimming: Nearby river &

lake.
Sunbathing: On the patio or in the gardens.
Smoking: Permitted outdoors only.
Pets: Not permitted. Dogs in residence.
Handicap Access: Limited.
Children: By arrangement.
Languages: English.
Your Hosts: Glenn & Tim.

Grim's Manor

WWW Gay/Lesbian ⚥
Gay-Owned

At the Edge of Pennsylvania Dutch Country

The 200-year-old *Grim's Manor* site, at the edge of Pennsylvania Dutch country, includes a historic stone farmhouse on five secluded acres of land. Step back in time, experiencing the history of this home and its laid-back, noncommercial atmosphere, while enjoying all modern comforts. The property includes a huge restored barn, complete with hex signs. The manor is near the city of Reading (outlet capital), antique shops, Doe Mountain skiing, Hawk Mountain birdwatching, the Clover Hill Winery, Crystal Cave, Dorney Park and Wildwater Kingdom.

Address: 10 Kern Road, Kutztown, PA 19530
Tel: (610) 683-7089.

Type: Bed & breakfast in a private home.
Clientele: Mostly gay & lesbian with a straight following
Transportation: Car is best, free pick up from Bieber Bus Tours in Kutztown from NYC.
To Gay Bars: 1/2 hr to Reading/Allentown, PA, 1-1/

4 hrs to Philadelphia, 2 hrs to NYC.
Rooms: 4 rooms with queen beds (3 with fireplaces).
Baths: All private shower/toilets.
Meals: Full breakfast.
Complimentary: Light refreshments upon arrival, morning coffee tray.

Dates Open: All year.
Rates: $70.
Rsv'tns: Required.
Reserve Thru: Call direct.
Parking: Ample free off-street parking.
In-Room: Color TV, AC, ceiling fans. Some rooms with fireplaces, VCR.
On-Premises: Kitchen & indoor spa.

Swimming: At nearby pool or Dorney Park & Wildwater Kingdom.
Sunbathing: On the lawn.
Smoking: Permitted outside.
Pets: Not permitted.
Handicap Access: No.
Children: Not recommended.
Your Hosts: Dave & Dick.

Fox & Hound B&B of New Hope

Gay-Friendly 50/50 ⚥

On two beautiful acres of park-like, formal grounds stands *Fox & Hound B&B*, a fully-restored historic 1850's stone manor. Full gourmet breakfasts are served on our outside patio or in our spacious dining room. Our ample guest rooms, all with private baths and four-poster canopy beds, are furnished with a fine blend of period antiques and are air-conditioned for your comfort. Guest rooms with 2 beds are available, and some feature fireplaces and Jacuzzis. We're within walking distance of the center of New Hope. AAA 3-Diamond & Mobil Guide-approved.

Address: 246 W Bridge St, New Hope, PA 18938
Tel: (215) 862-5082 or (800) 862-5082 (outside of PA).
Web: http://www.foxhoundinn.com

Type: Bed & breakfast.
Clientele: 50% gay & lesbian & 50% straight clientele.
Transportation: Car is best. Trans Bridge Bus lines from New Jersey & Port Authority NYC. Pick up from bus.
To Gay Bars: One block walking distance (4 minutes).
Rooms: 8 rooms with twin, double, queen & king beds.
Baths: All private.

Meals: Continental breakfast Mon-Fri, full breakfast Sat & Sun.
Vegetarian: Available upon request.
Dates Open: All year.
High Season: October.
Rates: Summer, spring, fall, Sun-Thurs $70-$120, Fri, Sat, $120-$170, winter specials.
Discounts: Corporate & long term.
Credit Cards: MC, Visa, Amex.

Rsv'tns: Required, especially on weekends. In high season required 2-3 weeks in advance.
Reserve Thru: Call direct.
Min. Stay: Call for details.
Parking: Ample, free off-street parking.
In-Room: Maid service, AC, ceiling fans, fireplaces, TV upon request.
On-Premises: Use of kitchen on limited basis.
Exercise/Health: Jacuzzis. Tubing & canoeing at nearby

river, tennis & fitness passes available.
Swimming: Pool within walking distance, Delaware river 1/4 mile.
Smoking: Permitted throughout house.
Pets: Not permitted.
Handicap Access: No.
Children: Permitted if 14 or older.
Languages: English.

Cordials Bed & Breakfast

WWW Gay/Lesbian ⚣
Gay-Owned & -Operated

Our Name ~ Our Way of Life

Cordials, a 2-1/2-story bed and breakfast, lies in the heart of Bucks County near the historic Delaware River and just down the road from New Hope's dining and shopping. The inn's decor harks back to yesteryear with all the creature comforts of modern-day living. Balconies offer impressive views of surrounding hemlocks and pines. Guests enjoy sipping complimentary wine in our elegant crystal stemware. "Continental-Plus" breakfast features fresh fruit.

All guests are invited to exit through our back gate and enter into the world of the Raven, with its great restaurant, famous gay bar and pool (we supply your towels), and only a short walk away from the Cartwheel (dance bar) and several other four-star restaurants and an eclectic collection of antique shops and art galleries. Nearby wineries offer tours and wine-tasting events, and the Bucks County Playhouse offers fine entertainment. Sightseers will want to visit New Hope's Parry Mansion (1784), and the 19th-century Locktender's House. The site where George Washington and the Continental Army crossed the icy Delaware River on Christmas 1776 is nearby. Tours can be booked through the New Hope Mule Barge Company, the New Hope & Ivyland Railroad, and the Wells Ferry Boat Rides. "Ghost Tours" run June through November in nearby Westminster. The folks at the Bucks County River Country in Point Pleasant will be happy to send you down the scenic Delaware River in your choice of inner tube, raft, canoe, or kayak. They also boast the nation's largest haunted woods hayride.

Address: 143 Old York Rd, New Hope, PA 18938
Tel: (215) 862-3919, (877) 219-1009, **Fax:** (215) 862-3917.
E-mail: cordialsbb@aol.com **Web:** http://www.cordialsbb.com

Type: Bed & breakfast with restaurant & bar.
Clientele: Mostly gay & lesbian, some straight
Transportation: Car. Free pick up from bus.
To Gay Bars: Next door.
Rooms: 6 rooms with queen beds.
Baths: All private.

Meals: Expanded continental breakfast.
Complimentary: Cake, cookies, fruit, wine, cheese.
High Season: July-Aug.
Rates: $85-$130.
Credit Cards: MC, Visa, Amex.
Rsv'tns: Required.
Reserve Thru: Call direct.

Min. Stay: 2 nights on weekends.
Parking: Off-street parking.
In-Room: AC, color cable TV, VCR, refrigerator, maid service.
On-Premises: TV lounge, video tape library.
Exercise/Health: Nearby gym, massage.

Swimming: Pool nearby.
Smoking: Non-smoking house.
Pets: Small pets only.
Languages: English.
Your Hosts: Bob.

Antique Row Bed & Breakfast

Gay-Friendly ♂♀

Perfectly Positioned for the Gay/Lesbian Communities

Antique Row B&B is centrally located for business and tourism, only a few blocks from the convention center. We're a small European-style B&B with mixed clientele. Rooms in this 180-year-old townhouse are attractively furnished with comfortable beds, down comforters, designer linens and sufficient pillows for watching TV and reading in bed. The color cable TV has Bravo, CineMax and Showtime. Fully furnished flats are also available.

Address: 341 South 12th St, Philadelphia, PA 19107
Tel: (215) 592-7802, **Fax:** (215) 592-9692.

Type: Bed & breakfast & fully furnished flats.
Clientele: 30% gay & lesbian & 70% straight clientele
Transportation: Easy access for all forms of transportation.
To Gay Bars: Within a few blocks of most gay & lesbian bars.
Rooms: Rooms with queen beds.
Baths: Private & shared.
Meals: Full breakfast.
Vegetarian: Within walking distance to several vegetarian restaurants.
Dates Open: All year.
High Season: Apr-Oct.
Rates: $65-$100.
Discounts: Extended stays.
Rsv'tns: Recommended.
Reserve Thru: Call direct.
Parking: On-street parking, or in nearby paid parking.
In-Room: Color cable TV & AC. Apartment has telephone, kitchen, refrigerator & coffee & tea-making facilities.
Smoking: Permitted.
Pets: Not permitted.
Handicap Access: No.
Children: Case-by-case depending on child's age, season & available accommodations.
Languages: English, a little Spanish & a little German.

Gaskill House

WWW Gay/Lesbian ♂♀
Gay-Operated

The Comfort & Privacy of Home — The Gracious Service of a European Luxury Hotel

Gaskill House is located in the heart of Philadelphia's Society Hill Historic District, and is listed with the National Registry of Historic Homes. A private residence since 1828, the townhouse has been fully restored and furnished to reflect the graciousness of the early eighteenth century — with the comforts and modern amenities of the 1990s. With only three guestrooms, visitors receive pampering and personal attention. Your hosts live on premises and work to anticipate your needs. The large, elegantly furnished rooms, each with private bath and fireplace and/or whirlpool bath, ensure luxury and comfort.

Address: 312 Gaskill St, Philadelphia, PA 19147
Tel: (215) 413-0669.
E-mail: gaskillbnb@aol.com **Web:** http://www.gaskillhouse.com

Type: B&B guesthouse.
Clientele: Mostly gay & lesbian with some straight clientele
Transportation: Car, taxi, shuttle.
To Gay Bars: 2 blocks.
Rooms: 3 rooms with queen beds.
Baths: All private.
Meals: Full breakfast.
Vegetarian: Available upon prior request.
Complimentary: Mints on pillow.
Dates Open: All year.
High Season: All year.
Rates: $100-$175.
Discounts: Negotiable for wknts & extended stays.
Credit Cards: No.
Rsv'tns: Required.
Reserve Thru: Call direct.
Parking: Ample, covered, on- & off-street pay parking.
In-Room: AC, ceiling fans, fireplaces, color cable TV, VCR, coffee & tea-making facilities, maid & room svc.
On-Premises: TV lounge, video tape library, laundry facilities.
Exercise/Health: Nearby
gym, weights, Jacuzzi, sauna, steam, massage.
Swimming: Pool nearby.
Sunbathing: On patio.
Smoking: Permitted on garden patio.
Pets: Not permitted.
Children: Welcome.
Languages: English, Spanish.
Your Hosts: Chris & Guy.

Blueberry Ridge

Women ♀

For That Romantic Country Feeling

Pat and Greta, of *Blueberry Ridge,* offer you friendship and warmth in the company of women. In a beautiful, secluded cedar house, you'll relax in the hot tub or by the wood-burning stove while enjoying a panoramic view of the Delaware Water Gap. Stroll the woods or go out for a romantic dinner. Winter brings skiing, ice skating, sleigh riding. Summer offers canoeing, whitewater rafting, riding, hiking, golf, tennis. Year-round interests include auctions, antique & candle shopping.

Address: Scotrun **Mail To:** RR 1 Box 67, McCarrick/Moran, Scotrun, PA 18355
Tel: (570) 629-5036.

Type: Bed & breakfast guesthouse.
Clientele: Women only.
Transportation: Car is best.
To Gay Bars: 10 miles or 20 minutes by car to Rainbow Mountain Disco.
Rooms: 4 rooms with double, queen & king beds.
Baths: 1 private, others shared

Meals: Full country breakfast. Holiday weekend specials include breakfasts & 1 dinner.
Complimentary: Baked goods, tea & coffee.
Dates Open: All year.
Rates: Rooms $55-$80.
Rsv'tns: Required.
Reserve Thru: Call direct.

Parking: Ample off-street parking.
In-Room: TV, ceiling fan & VCRs.
On-Premises: TV lounge, videos, kitchen.
Exercise/Health: Outdoor hot tub.
Swimming: River is 5 miles away.
Sunbathing: On common sun decks.
Nudity: Permitted in the hot tub.
Smoking: Permitted outdoors.
Pets: Not permitted.
Handicap Access: No.
Children: Permitted.
Languages: English, Spanish.

Stoney Ridge

Gay/Lesbian ⚥
Woman-Owned

For That "Warm Country Feeling in the Poconos"

For a respite from the city, stay at *Stoney Ridge,* our charming new cedar log home in the secluded Pocono Mountains of Pennsylvania. The house is beautifully furnished with antiques to give it that warm country feeling, while providing all the modern conveniences. Within 10 miles of here, you can enjoy restaurants, skiing, canoeing, hiking, trout fishing, dancing, antiquing, etc.

Address: Scotrun **Mail To:** RR 1 Box 67, P. McCarrick, Scotrun, PA 18355
Tel: (570) 629-5036.

Type: Cedar log home with 2 bedrooms, stone fireplace.
Clientele: Gay
Transportation: Car is best.
To Gay Bars: 10-minute drive to Rainbow Mountain disco/restaurant.

Rooms: Cabin with 2 double bedrooms.
Baths: 1-1/2 baths.
Dates Open: All year.
Rates: $100/$250/$550, by mid-week night, weekend, week.
Rsv'tns: Required.

Reserve Thru: Call direct.
Parking: Ample off-street parking.
In-Room: Telephone.
On-Premises: TV lounge with VCR.
Swimming: River & lake nearby.

Smoking: Permitted without restrictions.
Pets: Permitted.
Children: Permitted.
Languages: English & Spanish.

Hydrangea House Inn

WWW Gay-Friendly 50/50 ⚢

Quiet Sophistication in the "City by the Sea"

During the "gilded" period of Newport, when America's wealthy families were building lavish summer homes and bringing with them every luxury, a little luxury found its way to the natives of Newport, themselves. Gardeners who worked on the mansion grounds, it is said, took home cuttings of the exotic plants they cared for, among them the hydrangea, and grew them in their own gardens. We have taken our name from the hydrangea, which blooms all over Newport, because we, like the gardeners, have brought a little luxury home, and we would love to share that feeling of old, luxurious Newport with you.

Built in 1876, this Victorian townhouse has been carefully transformed, and its 6 guest rooms, elegantly decorated with antiques. Plush carpeting, thick cozy towels, crystal water glasses, long-stemmed goblets for your wine setups, and afternoon refreshments all help make your stay a real luxury. Your day will start with our gratifying hot buffet breakfast served in the contemporary fine art gallery. For your enjoyment we will serve our special blend of *Hydrangea House* coffee, fresh squeezed juice, home-baked bread and granola, and perhaps raspberry pancakes or seasoned scrambled eggs. We're just 1/4 mile from the mansions and in the center of Newport's "Walking District," steps to antique shops, galleries and beaches. Your hosts will be happy to recommend restaurants and night spots. We know you'll love it here: In 1989, the **Boston Globe** said of the inn, *"In a city renowned for its lodging, the Hydrangea House is not to be missed!*

Address: 16 Bellevue Ave, Newport, RI 02840
Tel: (401) 846-4435, (800) 945-4667, **Fax:** (401) 846-6602.
E-mail: bandbinn@ids.net **Web:** http://www.hydrangeahouse.com

Type: Bed & breakfast with contemporary art gallery.
Clientele: 50% gay & lesbian & 50% straight
Transportation: Car is best. Pick up from airport by shuttle $16 per person. Bus station 5-min walk to inn. Local bus line, taxi.
To Gay Bars: 5 min walk.
Rooms: 6 rooms with double, queen, king beds.
Baths: All private.
Meals: Full breakfast.

Vegetarian: On request.
Complimentary: Homemade chocolate chip cookies, afternoon tea & lemonade.
High Season: May-Oct.
Rates: Summer $125-$225, Suite $280. Off season $100-$155, Suite $195.
Discounts: 2-4-1 second night free Nov-Apr with Sun-Wed check-in.
Credit Cards: MC, Visa, Amex.

Rsv'tns: Required, but walk-ins based on availability.
Reserve Thru: Travel agent or call direct.
Min. Stay: 2 days June-Sept & weekends all year. 3 days on holidays.
Parking: Ample free off-street parking on site.
In-Room: AC, refrigerator & maid service.
On-Premises: Meeting rooms.

Exercise/Health: Massage by appt. Gym with weights, exercise room, aerobic class, $8-$12 day 5 min away.
Swimming: 5 min walk to ocean beach.
Sunbathing: On beach or common sun decks.
Smoking: Permitted outdoors ONLY.
Pets: Not permitted.
Children: Permitted.
Languages: English.

North Fenner Lodge

WWW Gay-Friendly ⚥

North Fenner Lodge was built in the mid-19th century in the Carpenter Gothic style. Three beautifully decorated double-occupancy rooms have been totally remodeled with period antiques and original works of art. The large grounds, over half an acre, include ample on-site parking. The lodge is conveniently located with quick access to all attractions Newport has to offer. Our breakfasts include such treats as banana crepes with lime-maple sauce, Croissant L'Orange and fresh fruit with Amaretto sauce. Our five o'clock "unwinding hour" in the gazebo with wine and cheese is an excellent time to meet other guests and compare notes. Please visit our new inn, Newport Las Palmas Inn, located in downtown Newport.

Address: 209 North Fenner Ave, Middletown, RI 02842
Tel: (401) 841-0484, **Fax:** (401) 848-7886.
Web: http://www.newportlaspalmas.com

Type: Bed & breakfast.
Clientele: Mostly straight clientele with a gay/lesbian following
Transportation: Car is best.
To Gay Bars: 3/4 miles, a 5 min drive.
Rooms: 3 rooms with queen beds.
Baths: 3 private bath/ shower/toilets.
Meals: Expanded continental breakfast.
Vegetarian: Available

nearby.
Complimentary: Sat. 5pm "unwinding hour" with wine & cheese in the gazebo.
Dates Open: May 1-Oct 1.
High Season: Mid-May thru Sept 30.
Rates: $139-$165.
Discounts: 10% on 5-night stay, also mid-week rates.
Credit Cards: MC, Visa, Amex.
Rsv'tns: Required.
Reserve Thru: Travel agent or call direct.

Min. Stay: 2 nights on regular weekends, 3 nights on event weekends.
Parking: Ample, free off-street parking.
In-Room: AC, ceiling fans, color TV, refrigerator, maid service. 2 rooms with fireplaces, 1 with full kitchen, 1 with wet bar, cable.
On-Premises: Sun room for socializing, gazebo.
Exercise/Health: Nearby gym, weights, massage.
Swimming: Ocean nearby.

Sunbathing: On grounds & at beach.
Smoking: Permitted in gazebo, on patios & grounds only. All rooms are non-smoking.
Pets: Not permitted.
Handicap Access: Yes, all rooms are first level.
Children: No.
Languages: English & Spanish.
Your Hosts: Cal & Seidy.

Brinley Victorian Inn

Gay-Friendly ⚥

Romantically decorated with fine antiques, Trompe l'Oeil period wallpapers and satin-and-lace window treatments, *Brinley Victorian Inn* is a haven of peace in this city by the sea. In the heart of Newport's historic district, the *Brinley* is within walking distance of historic sites, including the oldest Episcopal church and America's first synagogue. Close by are the *gilded era* mansions of the 19th century, hundreds of 17th-century colonials, the famed America's Cup waterfront, unique shops and restaurants, magnificent beaches and two gay bars.

Address: 23 Brinley St, Newport, RI 02840
Tel: (401) 849-7645, (800) 999-8523, **Fax:** (401) 845-9634.
E-mail: sweetmans@brinleyvictorian.com **Web:** http://www.brinleyvictorian.com

Type: Bed & breakfast inn.
Clientele: Mostly straight clientele with a gay/lesbian following
Transportation: By car.
To Gay Bars: Within walking distance to gay/lesbian bars.
Rooms: 16, including 1 suite.
Baths: 14 private, 2 share 1 bathroom.
Meals: Expanded continental breakfast.

Complimentary: Bottle of champagne for special occasions.
Dates Open: All year.
High Season: May 23-Oct 1.
Rates: Please call for current rates.
Discounts: Mid-week & longer stays, multiple reservations (5 rooms).
Credit Cards: MC, Visa, Amex.
Rsv'tns: Recommended.

Reserve Thru: Travel agent or call direct.
Min. Stay: 2 nights in-season wknds, 3 on holiday wknds.
Parking: Adequate, free on- and off-street parking.
In-Room: Maid service, AC, ceiling fans, refrigerators (some rooms). Some have fireplace & whirlpool tub.
On-Premises: 2 porches, 2 parlors, library & patio courtyard.

Exercise/Health: Jacuzzi in suite.
Swimming: Ocean beach or bay.
Sunbathing: On beach and in private courtyard.
Smoking: No smoking.
Pets: Not permitted.
Handicap Access: No.
Children: 8 years & older, at owner's discretion.
Languages: English.

Captain Preston House

WWW Gay-Friendly ⚥

A Charming Victorian Inn in the Heart of Historic Newport

This delightful B&B, in a large Victorian home, includes two cozy sitting rooms, a dining room and a sunny breakfast porch. It's an easy walk to all of Newport's unique attractions — the harbor, mansions, Cliff Walk, beaches and shopping. Comfortably furnished accommodations at the *Captain Preston House* include two with a double and a single and two with a queen. The inn's namesake, Captain Preston, served in the English Navy during the 18th century. His descendent, Paul Preston, also a captain, enjoys hosting guests year round and has excellent contacts for local sporting, entertainment and outdoor activities.

Address: 378 Spring St, Newport, RI 02840
Tel: (401) 847-7077, **Fax:** (401) 847-1093.
E-mail: paul@captainpreston.com **Web:** http://www.captainpreston.com

Type: Bed & breakfast.
Clientele: Mostly straight with a gay/lesbian following
Transportation: Airport shuttle. Bus (local line) or taxi from train. Bus stn 10 min walk to inn. Ask about pick up.
To Gay Bars: 5 min walk.
Rooms: 4 rooms.
Baths: Private. 1 bath/shower, 3 have shower.
Meals: Expanded

continental.
Vegetarian: Available with prior notice.
Complimentary: Afternoon tea, on request.
Dates Open: All year.
High Season: Summer.
Rates: Summer $160-$190, winter $80-$160.
Discounts: Ask about extended stays.
Rsv'tns: Recommended.
Reserve Thru: Travel agent

or call direct.
Min. Stay: 2 nights on weekends in summer.
Parking: Ample free off-street parking.
In-Room: AC, ceiling fans, maid service.
On-Premises: TV lounge, meeting rooms, business services.
Exercise/Health: Nearby gym, tennis, kayaking, sailing.

Swimming: Nearby pool & ocean.
Sunbathing: At beach & on patio.
Smoking: Permitted on porches. All non-smoking rooms.
Pets: OK if crated.
Handicap Access: Yes.
Children: No.
Languages: English, French.
Your Hosts: Paul Preston.

Calhoun House

The Charleston Experience: Ultimate Charm and Warm Hospitality

To the residents of Charleston, life in the Historic District is like stepping back into history and sharing timeless charm and majestic beauty on a regular basis. Charleston offers us a special, serene reflection of a lifestyle that has all but vanished. From the moment you arrive, you will feel the warmth of the city's hospitality for which Charleston is renown. Your stay will be a memorable one.

The *Calhoun House* is a beautiful reminder of a bright period in Charleston's tempestuous past. Begun in 1910, the house is a relatively new structure in the Historic District, by Charleston standards. The imposing three-story Edwardian-style house was the home of the Keever family for over 70 years. In 1997, the current owners began an ambitious restoration of the house.

The *Calhoun House* is a short walking distance through picturesque Harleston Village to the city's historic sites and shopping areas. When you are ready to "do the Charleston," your hosts can help arrange a tour of Antebellum homes, a horse-drawn carriage ride around the city, a harbor tour, a guided walking tour, or even a bicycle rental. Your hosts specialize in the friendly hospitality that you would naturally expect of the "Old South." Helpful recommendations on tours, entertainment, nightlife, restaurants and shopping are always available. Charleston has been welcoming visitors for over 300 years. It is a special city of charm, culture and warm hospitality. Come see for yourself!

Address: 273 Calhoun St, Charleston, SC 29401
Tel: (843) 722-7341.
E-mail: Calhounhouse@cs.com

Type: Guesthouse.
Clientele: Good mix of gays & lesbians
Transportation: Car is best.
To Gay Bars: 6 blocks.
Rooms: 4 rooms.
Baths: 3 private, 2 share.
Meals: Continental breakfast. Gourmet coffee, tea, juices, fresh fruit, yogurt, cereals, pastries.
Dates Open: All year.
High Season: Mar-Nov.
Rates: $115-$145 (all taxes included).
Discounts: One night free for 7-night stay.

Rsv'tns: Recommended.
Reserve Thru: Travel agent or call direct.
Parking: Adequate free off-street parking.
In-Room: Color cable TV, AC, ceiling fans, maid & laundry service.
On-Premises: TV lounge, laundry facilities for guests.
Swimming: 7 miles to gay beach.
Smoking: Permitted in kitchen & on porches.
Pets: Not permitted.
Handicap Access: No.
Languages: English.
Your Hosts: Frank & Jim.

Eighteen Fifty-Four Bed & Breakfast

Gay/Lesbian ⚥

A Tropical Retreat in the Heart of Charleston

Centrally located in Harleston Village, one of the premier restored areas of Charleston's renowned National Register historical district, *1854* is sited in an unusual antebellum edifice of distinctive Italianate design. Both suites are charmingly decorated with an eclectic mix of antique and modern furnishings, original art and sculpture. They have private entrance and access to a rear garden nestled in a lush grove of banana trees and other tropical plantings. The city's best restaurants, gay bars and shopping are a short walk away.

Address: 34 Montagu Street, Charleston, SC 29401
Tel: (843) 723-4789.

Type: Bed & breakfast.
Clientele: Mostly gay & lesbian with some straight clientele
Transportation: Car is best.
To Gay Bars: Four blocks or ten minutes to all local gay bars.
Rooms: 2 full suites with double beds.
Baths: All private bath/toilets.
Meals: Continental breakfast.
Vegetarian: Available with advance notice.
Dates Open: All year.
Rates: $95-$115. Rates may vary seasonally.
Discounts: 10% discount for stays of 3 or more nights.
Rsv'tns: Required, but will accept late call-ins.
Reserve Thru: Travel agent or call direct.
Parking: Ample free on-street parking.
In-Room: Kitchen, refrigerator, AC, color TV, maid service & private outdoor garden area.
On-Premises: Lush tropical garden.
Swimming: 10-15 miles from all Charleston beaches, including Folly Beach gay area.
Smoking: Permitted.
Pets: Not permitted.
Handicap Access: No.
Children: Permitted with advance notice only. No infants.
Languages: English.

Height of Folly

[WWW] Men ♂
Gay-Owned & -Operated

A Front Beach Apartment, Steps from the Ocean

Height of Folly is located just steps from the beach in Charleston, South Carolina. This front beach apartment is for men only. Welcoming amenities in this one-bedroom efficiency apartment include double bed and sleeper couch, television, VCR and telephone. Nudity is permitted in the hot tub and deck area. *Height of Folly* is situated fifteen minutes from the city's gay bars and the Historical District.

Address: 1309 East Ashley Ave, Folly Beach, SC
Tel: (843) 588-6200.

Type: Front beach apartment.
Clientele: Men only
Transportation: Car.
To Gay Bars: 9 miles, a 15 min drive.
Rooms: 1 apartment with double bed & sleeper couch.
Baths: Private shower & toilet.
Dates Open: All year.
High Season: May-Sept.
Rates: High summer: $60-$75, low winter: $50-$60.
Credit Cards: Yes.
Rsv'tns: Required.
Reserve Thru: Call direct.
Parking: Ample, free off-street parking.
In-Room: Telephone, AC, color cable TV, VCR, kitchen, refrigerator, coffee & tea-making facilities.
On-Premises: Deck, laundry facilities.
Exercise/Health: Hot tub.
Swimming: Ocean on premises.
Sunbathing: On common sun decks, at beach.
Nudity: Permitted on sun deck.
Smoking: Inquire.
Pets: Permitted.
Handicap Access: No.
Children: No.
Languages: English.

Summit House

Best Breakfast in Texas!

Photo by: Romina Derra

Located on an old Indian campground above the Colorado River, the house and herb gardens nestled under 100-year-old oak trees give the feeling of a secluded hideaway. The guesthouse is close to the heartbeat of Austin, just minutes from downtown, quaint shopping and dining. We have a very down-home atmosphere at the *Summit House.* Your visit includes re-

freshments upon arrival and a down-home breakfast with fresh-baked whole-grain bread each morning. And you'll always find snacks on the dining room table during the rest of the day. Your host, David, will be helpful in letting you know what is going on in the Live Music Capital of the World. He also conducts shopping and gourmet tours of Austin, as well as a variety

Photo by: Romina Derra

of sightseeing tours of the city, including the gay nightlife. We want you to feel right at home, so kick off your shoes and relax. Come experience the true feeling of Texas!

Address: 1204 Summit St, Austin, TX 78741-1158
Tel: (512) 445-5304.
E-mail: summit@texas.net **Web:** http://summit.home.texas.net

Type: Guesthouse.
Clientele: Gay & lesbian, straight-friendly. Bears are especially welcome
Transportation: Car, taxi, bus.
To Gay Bars: 15 minute walk, a 5 minute drive.
Rooms: 1 private suite w/ king bed. 2 in main house w/ twin or queen beds.
Baths: 1 private, 1 shared & 1 outdoor shower garden.
Meals: Full down-home breakfast.
Vegetarian: Available.

Vegetarian markets & restaurants nearby.
Complimentary: Refreshments on arrival. Home-baked breads, pineapple upside down cake in fall, variety of beverages.
Dates Open: All year.
High Season: Oct-May. Rates change for holidays & special events.
Credit Cards: MC, Visa, Amex.
Rsv'tns: Recommended. 2 weeks cancellation.

Reserve Thru: Call direct.
Parking: Off-street parking.
In-Room: Central AC & heat, ceiling fans, sitting area, color cable TV, phone service, large windows, natural fabrics, garden flowers. Suite also has coffee, fridge, private entrance.
On-Premises: Great trees, natural garden setting, lots of birds & wildlife.
Exercise/Health: Massage, weights, nearby hike & bike trail. Hot tub coming fall

2000.
Swimming: Pool. Nearby public pools. 2 mi. to Barton Springs, one of the world's best swimming holes.
Sunbathing: On patio.
Nudity: Permitted in private sunning area.
Smoking: Permitted outside only.
Pets: Permitted.
Handicap Access: No.
Children: Over the age of 13 permitted.
Languages: English.
Your Hosts: David.

Park Lane Guesthouse

WWW Gay/Lesbian ♂♀

Discover Austin (The 3rd Coast)

Austin is your destination for pleasure. Experience our exciting city with all of its natural beauty, hot nightlife and entertainment districts. Relax in our private gardens, sunbathe by the pool, and then head downtown to explore the clubs and live music. Located in quiet, historic Travis Heights, and less than one mile from the Colorado River and State Capitol, *Park Lane* offers you casual elegance with an artistic flair. Enjoy the comfort and privacy you desire, as well as all of the amenities you deserve. More than just a place to sleep, this is a place to rest your soul.

Address: 221 Park Lane, Austin, TX 78704
Tel: (512) 447-7460, (800) 492-8827, **Fax:** (512) 444-5084.
Web: http://home.austin.rr.com/supersis/BB/BB.htm

Type: Cottages & main guesthouse.
Clientele: Mostly gay & lesbian, some straights
Transportation: Car, taxi from airport. Ask about pickup.
To Gay Bars: 5 min drive.
Rooms: 1 room, 1 main house, 1 cottage sleeps 4, 1 carriage house, queen & king beds.

Baths: All private.
Meals: Expanded continental breakfast.
Complimentary: Tea, coffee.
High Season: Feb-June, Sept-Nov.
Rates: Main house: $89-$99. Cottage: $149 dbl ($20 each addt'l person).
Poolside suite: $139.
Credit Cards: Visa, MC,

Amex.
Rsv'tns: Required. Under 7-day notice, guest pays full amt. of resv'tn unless rm. re-booked.
Reserve Thru: Call direct.
Min. Stay: 2 nts wknds.
In-Room: AC, maid svc, coffee/tea-makers, ceiling fans. Carriage Hse: Direct TV & pay per view, VCR, kitchen, fridge, micro, ceiling

fans, phone.
Exercise/Health: Massage.
Swimming: Private pool.
Sunbathing: On common sun decks & patios.
Smoking: Outside only.
Pets: Inquire.
Handicap Access: Cottage.
Children: Inquire.
Your Hosts: Shakti & Dev.

Anthony's by the Sea

WWW Gay-Friendly 50/50 ♂♀

Special Memories...No Extra Charge

A few minutes from Padre Island National Seashore, *Anthony's by the Sea* is hidden by live oaks on two thirds of an acre with pool and spacious lawn. Choose from four bedrooms (some with private baths and seating areas) or two guest cottages, which have private baths, living rooms, dining areas, and fully-equipped kitchens with dishwasher and microwave. The lanai is covered and carpeted, with chandeliers, BBQ, and fountains. Your visit to *Anthony's* includes gourmet breakfast served in a large open dining area or on the patio where guests can watch hummingbirds, butterflies, squirrels, and geckos plaing in their natural environment.

Address: 732 S Pearl, Rockport, TX 78382
Tel: (361) 729-6100, (800) 460-2557, **Fax:** (361) 729-2450.

Type: Bed & breakfast.
Clientele: 50% gay & lesbian & 50% straight clientele
Transportation: Car is best.
To Gay Bars: 30 miles to Corpus Christi bars.
Rooms: 5 rooms & 1 cottage. 1 is a 740 sq ft Spanish Suite w/wet bar, large living area & king bed.
Baths: 4 private & 1

shared.
Meals: Full gourmet breakfast.
Vegetarian: Available upon request.
Complimentary: Juices, iced tea, coffee, lemonade.
Dates Open: All year.
Rates: $70-$90.
Discounts: 7th day free.
Credit Cards: MC, Visa.
Rsv'tns: Requested.
Reserve Thru: Travel agent

or call direct.
Parking: Carports.
In-Room: Color TV, VCR, AC, ceiling fans, refrigerator & maid service.
On-Premises: TV lounge, laundry facilities, telephone & full, covered lanai with fans & chandeliers.
Swimming: Pool on premises. 5 blocks to beach.
Sunbathing: On common sun decks & at the beach 5

blocks away.
Nudity: Permitted by the pool with restrictions. Private deck available.
Smoking: Permitted with restrictions.
Pets: On approval.
Handicap Access: No.
Children: Permitted in the cottage, suites.
Languages: English.
Your Hosts: Tony & Denis

Bella Vista

Gay/Lesbian ⚥
Gay-Owned & -Operated

Let the Wimberley Way Weave its Magic & Win Your Heart

Bella Vista is a beautiful new home in the Texas hill country, 30 miles from Austin and 40 miles from San Antonio. This custom-designed home has elegantly furnished rooms that offer fantastic views of the valley and hills surrounding the artsy village of Wimberley. Enjoy the nightlife in nearby Austin or San Antonio, shop Wimberley Market Days, tube the river below or in New Braunfels, shop in Fredericksburg, or simply watch the sunsets and feed the deer from your patio. Let the Wimberley Way and the Texas hill country captivate your heart as it has many others.

Address: 2121 Hilltop, Wimberley
Tel: (512) 847-6425.
E-mail: leblancmeyer@aol.com **Web:** http://www.texhillcntry.com/bellavista

Type: Bed & breakfast.
Clientele: Mostly gay & lesbian with some straight clientele
Transportation: Car is best.
To Gay Bars: 30 mi to Austin & 40 mi to San Antonio gay bars.
Rooms: 2 rooms with queen beds.
Baths: All private.

Meals: Continental breakfast.
Vegetarian: Available nearby.
Complimentary: Set up service.
Dates Open: All year.
High Season: Gorgeous year round.
Rates: $95-$125.
Discounts: For extended stays.

Rsv'tns: Required.
Reserve Thru: Call direct.
Parking: Ample off-street parking.
In-Room: Telephone, AC, ceiling fans, color cable TV, VCR, refrigerator, microwave, coffee & tea-making facilities, maid & laundry service.
On-Premises: Laundry facilities.

Swimming: Pool on premises. River nearby.
Sunbathing: On patio.
Smoking: Non-smoking home.
Pets: No pets.
Handicap Access: Yes, wide doors.
Children: No.
Languages: English.
Your Hosts: John & Max.

Casa Peregrino

WWW Gay/Lesbian ♂
Gay-Owned & -Operated

A Little Bit of Heaven Mid-Way between Austin & San Antonio

High on a ridge overlooking the Blanco River valley stands *Casa Peregrino,* looking like a cross between a Tibetan high mountain fastness, a secluded Spanish monastery, and a Hollywood starlet's stylish mansion. We offer accommodations in three lovely rooms, each with full bath and its own separate entrance: The poolside Studio Apartment with tiled patio garden, the free-standing Guesthouse with balcony overlooking the Blanco River, and the Aerie at the top of the house with private sun deck and a spectacular view of the valley. Our crystal-blue swimming pool appears suspended in space.

The four-acre property, enclosed in a rustic privacy-fenced compound, is a short drive from the center of the little gay-popular, artist colony/river resort town of Wimberley, but is situated so that there's total privacy and country seclusion. The view opens out toward grassy green — and in the spring, bluebonneted and wild-flowered — hills, rangeland, and distant limestone cliffs. At night, while the city of Austin glows just beyond the horizon, the sky is deep and dark and full of stars.

Located right in the center of the heart of Texas, Wimberley is a cute little B&B town with an old town square ringed with shops and galleries alongside shady Cypress Creek. Close by are San Marcos and New Braunfels which offer a variety of river recreation opportunities, and just under an hour away in either direction are Austin and San Antonio.

Address: Wimberley **Mail To:** PO Box 2762, Wimberley, TX 78676
Tel: (512) 847-5269, (888) 766-1965.
E-mail: CasaPeregrinoTX@aol.com **Web:** http://hometown.aol.com/CasaPeregrinoTx

Type: Bed & breakfast.
Clientele: Mostly men with women welcome
Transportation: Car.
To Gay Bars: 1 hr to Austin or San Antonio.
Rooms: 1 room, 1 apartment, 1 cottage with double, queen or king beds.
Baths: All private.
Meals: Expanded continental breakfast.

Vegetarian: On request & at nearby restaurants.
Complimentary: Coffeemaker, tea & beverages in room. Wine & cheese served poolside.
Dates Open: All year.
High Season: Spring.
Rates: $125.
Discounts: On stays of 4+ nights.
Credit Cards: MC, Visa.

Rsv'tns: Required.
Reserve Thru: Travel agent or call direct.
Min. Stay: 2 nights on weekends & holidays.
Parking: Adequate free off-street parking.
In-Room: Telephone, AC, ceiling fans, color cable TV, VCR, refrigerator, coffee & tea-making facilities.
Swimming: Pool. River

nearby.
Sunbathing: Poolside, on private & common sun decks.
Nudity: Permitted poolside & on sun decks.
Smoking: Permitted outdoors.
Pets: By prior arrangement.
Children: Inquire.
Your Hosts: Kip & Toby.

Lovett Inn, The

You'll Love It at the Lovett!

A distinctive bed and breakfast located in Houston's Montrose/Museum district, *The Lovett Inn* was built in 1924 as the home of former mayor Judge Joseph Hutcheson, who lived here until his death in 1973. Tom Fricke, the current owner, bought the home in 1989 with the purpose of creating an inn. Located on elegant, tree-lined Lovett Boulevard, the inn is reminiscent of an earlier time and continues to be maintained in the traditional style of the era in which it was built. Many of the same amenities offered in larger hotels can be found here. Rooms are available with microwaves, wet bars and coffeemakers. And what better way to relax after a day of meetings or shopping than to enjoy the landscaped grounds, swimming pool and Jacuzzi?

Many of Houston's finest restaurants are within a short walk of *The Lovett*, while others are only a short drive away. We are situated in the heart of Houston, with easy access to downtown, the Galleria, the medical center and the museum district. Houston's theater district, home to the opera, ballet and symphony, is only ten minutes from the inn. We are also within walking distance of a number of museums, such as The Museum of Fine Arts, the Menil Collection, the Contemporary Arts Museum and the Holocaust Museum. The Imax Theater, Hermann Park, the University of St. Thomas and Rice University are equally close. Montrose is the heart of Houston's gay and lesbian community, featuring bars, coffee houses, bookstores and eclectic shops catering to the community. We look forward to having the opportunity to host you at *The Lovett Inn*. Please feel free to call our toll-free number for reservations and information.

Address: 501 Lovett Blvd, Houston, TX 77006
Tel: (713) 522-5224, **Fax:** 528-6708, (800) 779-5224.
E-mail: lovettinn@aol.com **Web:** http://www.HoustonGayLodging.com

Type: Inn.
Clientele: 75% gay & 25% straight clientele.
Transportation: Airport shuttle to downtown Hyatt, then taxi.
To Gay Bars: 1/2 block.
Rooms: 3 rooms, 3 suites, 1 apartment & 1 cottage with double, queen or king beds.
Baths: All private. 3 with whirlpool baths.
Meals: Continental

breakfast.
Complimentary: Tea, coffee, candy in rooms.
Rates: $85-$175.
Discounts: Group and long-term rates.
Credit Cards: MC, Visa, Amex, Discover.
Rsv'tns: Suggested.
Reserve Thru: Call direct.
Min. Stay: Required at peak times.
Parking: Ample, free

parking.
In-Room: Color cable TV, VCR, kitchen, coffee & tea-making facilities & laundry service.
On-Premises: Meeting rooms & TV lounge. Laundry available.
Exercise/Health: Jacuzzi. Nearby gym, weights, Jacuzzi, sauna, steam & massage.
Swimming: Pool on

premises, 30-60 minutes to ocean beach, lake.
Sunbathing: At poolside or on private sun decks.
Smoking: Permitted in public areas & in some smoke-friendly rooms.
Pets: Permitted on approval.
Children: Inquire.
Languages: English.
IGLTA

Gar-den Suites

Gay/Lesbian ♂

Quiet, Affordable Lodging In the Center of Montrose

In the center of the Montrose area, walking distance to several clubs, restaurants and shopping is the *Gar-Den Suites* bed and breakfast. Our location is close to museums, parks, the zoo, the Astrodome and theaters. Each two-room suite is adjacent to quiet, private sun decks and features a full bath, refrigerator, microwave, TV/VCR combination and a central video library. Telephone and fax are available on premises. Neighborhood travel is commonly done on foot, bicycle, taxi or metro bus, so no rental car is needed. Airport shuttles are available.

Address: 2702 Crocker St, Houston, TX 77006
Tel: (713) 528-2302, (800) 484-1036 (code 2669).
E-mail: garden2@earthlink.net **Web:** http://www.webspawner.com/users/garden2suites

Type: Bed & breakfast.
Clientele: Mostly men with women welcome
Transportation: Car. Airport, then shuttle bus, pickup from airport $20-$30.
To Gay Bars: 1 block, 1/2 mile, a 5 min. walk.
Rooms: 3 suites with double, queen or twin bed.
Baths: Private: 1 bath/toilet, 2 shower/toilet.
Meals: Continental breakfast.

Vegetarian: Available nearby.
Complimentary: Popcorn & bottled water upon arrival.
Dates Open: All year.
Rates: $65-$105.
Discounts: 5% stays of 3 days or more, with payment by cash or check.
Credit Cards: MC, Visa, Amex, Discover.
Rsv'tns: Required.
Reserve Thru: Call direct.
Parking: Adequate free off-

street parking.
In-Room: AC, color TV, VCR, video tape library, refrigerator, coffee & tea-making facilities, kitchen, maid service.
On-Premises: Laundry facilities.
Exercise/Health: Hot tub/spa. Nearby gym, weights, Jacuzzi, sauna, steam, massage.
Swimming: Pool nearby.
Sunbathing: On common

sun decks.
Nudity: Permitted on sun deck, pool, hot tub.
Smoking: Permitted outside only.
Pets: Limited, pets under 20 lbs will be considered.
Handicap Access: No.
Children: No.
Languages: English.
Your Hosts: Dennis & Gary.

Montrose Inn

Gay/Lesbian ♂
Gay-Owned & -Operated

Basic & Butch

The *Montrose Inn* is a gay and lesbian bed and breakfast situated in the middle of gay Houston, within walking distance of a dozen gay bars. Our slogan, "Basic & Butch" means just that — we have no antique furniture, no sauna and no swimming pool. What we DO have are clean, modern, private, comfortable rooms with color TV, VCR, phone and firm queen-sized beds... and the price is right. Rooms offer access to a full kitchen and free laundry. If you're a gay person   coming to Houston to party, cruise and experience local gay nightlife, then we're definitely the place to stay — right in the middle of gay Houston!

Address: 408 Avondale, Houston, TX 77006
Tel: (713) 520-0206, (800) 357-1228.

Type: Bed & breakfast.
Clientele: Mostly men with women welcome
Transportation: Airport bus to downtown, then taxi.
To Gay Bars: 3 blocks.
Rooms: 7 rooms with queen beds.
Baths: Private: 1 bath/toilet/

shower, 1 shower/toilet.
Shared: 2 bath/shower/toilets.
Meals: Full breakfast.
Complimentary: Coffee, tea & soft drinks 24 hrs.
Dates Open: All year.
Rates: $59-$99.
Credit Cards: MC, Visa,

Amex, Diners, Discover.
Reserve Thru: Travel agent or call direct.
Parking: Adequate, free off-street parking.
In-Room: Telephone, AC, color TV, VCR, maid & laundry service.
On-Premises: Laundry

facilities, video tape library.
Smoking: Smoking & non-smoking rooms available.
Pets: Permitted if well-behaved.
Handicap Access: No.
Children: No.
Languages: English.
IGLTA

Arbor House Inn & Suites

WWW Gay-Friendly ⚥
Gay-Owned

The Best-Kept Secret in Downtown San Antonio

The *Arbor House Inn* invites you to the most unique all-suites inn in San Antonio. Although it looks like a B&B, the five buildings, built in 1903, have central AC/heat, state-of-the-art phone and messaging systems, private baths and furnishings unlike any hotel you have ever visited. The location is downtown, 1-1/2 blocks to Riverwalk, but you won't have to fight the crowds to "get away from it all" — just relax in our formal gardens under the grape arbor. Come see for yourself — you will be forever grateful that you found us.

Address: 540 South St. Mary's St, San Antonio, TX 78205
Tel: (210) 472-2005, **Toll-free:** (888) 272-6700, **Fax:** (210) 472-2007.
E-mail: arborhaus@aol.com **Web:** http://www.arborhouse.com

Type: Historic inn.
Clientele: Mostly straight clientele. Looking to increase gay & lesbian clientele
Transportation: Airport limo or taxi.
To Gay Bars: 2 blocks, a 5 minute walk, a 2 minute drive.
Rooms: 18 rooms (11 suites w/ king or double beds, 7 rooms w/ queen beds).
Baths: Private: 6 shower/toilets, 12 bath/shower/ toilets.

Meals: Continental breakfast.
Vegetarian: Inquire. Available nearby.
Complimentary: Coffeemaker in all suites, some frigs, some microwaves.
Dates Open: All year.
Rates: High season (Oct-May): $140-$175; Low season (Jun-Sept): $85-$150.
Credit Cards: MC, Visa, Amex, Discover.

Rsv'tns: Required.
Reserve Thru: Travel agent or call direct.
Min. Stay: Required on holiday weekends.
Parking: Adequate free off-street parking.
In-Room: AC, color cable TV, telephone, maid service. Refrigerators in some suites. Ceiling fans in all rooms/ suites. All suites have coffeemaker.
Exercise/Health: 1 block to Riverwalk, nearby weights, Jacuzzi, sauna, massage.

Swimming: Pool nearby.
Sunbathing: Poolside & on patio.
Smoking: Permitted outside, on porch & on balcony. All rooms & suites are non-smoking.
Pets: Small-medium dogs permitted (under 25 lbs), $15 charge per night.
Handicap Access: Yes, 1 room.
Children: Welcome.
Languages: English.
Your Hosts: Reg & Dale.

New Upper Deck Hotel & Bar, The

WWW Men ♂
Gay-Owned & -Managed

An Island of Pure Fun and Relaxation

The only gay hotel and bar on South Padre Island, *The New Upper Deck* has a swimming pool, Jacuzzi, pool table, and lots of sun decking. Under new ownership, rooms have been updated and our new Bunk House is also available. Clothing is optional on the first level, except in the bar, and we're 1/2 a block from the gay beach area, which can sometimes be cruisy. This tropical island with miles of unspoiled beaches and warm water, lies beside the sparkling Gulf of Mexico. Only 30 miles from the border, you can shop in Mexico, making your visit a "two-nation" vacation. Enjoy watersports, horseback riding, bungee jumping, fine dining, and more. Whatever you choose, you'll have the time of your life!

Address: 120 E Atol St **Mail To:** P.O. Box 2309, South Padre Island, TX 78597
Tel: (956) 761-5953, **Fax:** (956) 761-4288.
E-mail: newupperdeck@travelbase.com **Web:** http://www.newupperdeck.com

Type: Hotel and bar.
Clientele: Gay men
Transportation: Airport shuttle (small fee).
To Gay Bars: In hotel & 30-35 min drive.
Rooms: 19 rooms w/ double, king, queen, bunk beds, daily locker rental.
Baths: All private, except bunkhouse.
Meals: Coffee & Danish.
High Season: Mar-Sept.
Rates: $55-$140.
Credit Cards: MC, Visa, Discover, Amex.
Rsv'tns: Recommended.
Reserve Thru: Call direct.
Min. Stay: 3 nights on holidays.
Parking: On premises.
In-Room: Color remote TV, ceiling fans, AC, maid svc.
On-Premises: TV lounge, laundry facilities, game room, kitchen.
Exercise/Health: Jacuzzi. Horseback riding, jet ski, bike rental nearby.
Swimming: Pool, ocean.
Sunbathing: On beach, common sun deck, poolside.
Nudity: In pool & Jacuzzi. Nude beach 10.6 mi.
Smoking: Non-smoking rooms available.
Children: Not permitted.
Languages: English, Spanish.

Rainbow Country B&B

WWW Gay-Friendly 50/50 ⚥

Experience this Truly Unique Area Near Four National Parks

The spectacular wilderness of the Grand Staircase Escalante National Monument surrounds you at *Rainbow Country B&B*, a hilltop B&B with views of nearby mountains and slick rock. Conveniently located near a charming rustic town and four national parks, our modern home offers spa, pool table, cable TV and full breakfast. We are open all year.

Address: 586 E 300 S, Escalante, UT 84726
Tel: (435) 826-4567, (800) 252-UTAH (8824).
E-mail: rainbow@color-country.net

Type: Bed & breakfast guesthouse with jeep tours.
Clientele: 50% gay & lesbian & 50% hetero clientele
Transportation: Car or commuter flight from Las Vegas or Salt Lake City. Free pick up from Bryce Canyon airport.
To Gay Bars: 200 miles.
Rooms: 4 rooms with single, double, queen or king beds.
Baths: All private baths.
Meals: Full breakfast.
Vegetarian: Almost always available.
Complimentary: Coffee, tea, soft drinks & munchies.
Dates Open: All year.
Rates: $55-$65.
Discounts: Group rates, travel agents 10%.
Credit Cards: MC & VISA.
Reserve Thru: Travel agent or call direct.
Parking: Ample free off-street parking.
In-Room: AC.
On-Premises: TV lounge.
Swimming: River & lake nearby.
Sunbathing: On common sun decks.
Smoking: Permitted outside.
Pets: Well-trained pets permitted.
Handicap Access: No.
Languages: English.
Your Hosts: Clark & Catherine.

Anton Boxrud B & B

Gay-Friendly ♀♂

Salt Lake's Closest Traditional B&B to Downtown

When looking for a warm homebase from which to explore Salt Lake City and the Wasatch mountains, we invite you to relax in the casual elegance of our historic home, *Anton Boxrud B&B*. We're half a block from the Governor's Mansion, and just a 15-minute walk to downtown. In the evenings, enjoy complimentary beverages and snacks. The hot tub can provide liquid refreshment of a different kind. We serve full breakfasts featuring Grandma Glady's freshly baked cinnamon buns.

Address: 57 South 600 East, Salt Lake City, UT 84102
Tel: (801) 363-8035, (800) 524-5511, **Fax:** (801) 596-1316.
E-mail: antonboxrud@inquo.net **Web:** http://www.netoriginals.com/antonboxrud/

Type: Bed & breakfast.
Clientele: Mostly straight clientele with a 30% gay & lesbian following
Transportation: Car or taxi.
To Gay Bars: 8 blocks.
Rooms: 6 rooms & 1 suite with single, queen or king beds.
Baths: 5 private, 2 share.
Meals: Full breakfast.
Vegetarian: Upon request.
Complimentary: Evening snacks, beverages, coffee & tea.
Dates Open: All year.
High Season: Jun-Oct (summer) & Jan-Mar (ski season).
Rates: $69-$140.
Credit Cards: MC, Visa, Amex, Diners, Discover.
Rsv'tns: Recommended.
Reserve Thru: Call direct.
Min. Stay: 2 nights on weekends.
Parking: Ample on-street & off-street covered parking.
In-Room: AC, mints, terrycloth robes, flowers, shampoo & soap, maid service.
On-Premises: TV lounge, meeting rooms.
Exercise/Health: Jacuzzi on premises. Nearby gym, weights, Jacuzzi, sauna, steam & massage.
Swimming: Nearby pool & lake.
Sunbathing: At the beach.
Smoking: Permitted outside only.
Pets: Not permitted.
Handicap Access: No.
Children: Welcome.
Languages: English, French.
Your Hosts: Jane & Jerome.

Red Rock Inn

Gay-Friendly ♀♂

Experience the spectacular red rock cliffs of Zion National Park in relaxed comfort at *Red Rock Inn.* Each of our five cottages is individually decorated to offer a unique flavor and ambiance. They all have patios with a view and private baths (4 rooms feature jetted tubs, suite has outdoor hot tub). Enjoy your complimentary breakfast (delivered in a basket to your door each morning) in the shade of an old pecan tree as you plan your day in one of the world's most beautiful and inspiring natural wonders.

Address: 998 Zion Park Blvd, Springdale **Mail To:** PO Box 273, Springdale, UT 84767
Tel: (435) 772-3139.
E-mail: rrinn@infowest.com **Web:** http://www.redrockinn.com

Type: Intimate bed & breakfast cottages.
Clientele: Mostly straight clientele with a gay & lesbian following
Transportation: Car is the only way.
To Gay Bars: 150 miles to Las Vegas.
Rooms: 3 rooms with queen beds, 1 with king bed, 1 2-room suite.
Baths: Private: 4 whirlpool bath/shower/toilet, 1 full bath.
Meals: Full breakfast.
Vegetarian: Available with prior arrangements.
Dates Open: All year.
High Season: May-Sept.
Rates: $65-$145.
Credit Cards: MC, Visa, Amex, Discover.
Rsv'tns: Required in high season.
Reserve Thru: Call direct.
Min. Stay: 2 nights on holidays.
Parking: Adequate free off-street parking.
In-Room: Color cable TV, AC, ceiling fans & maid service. Suite has VCR.
Exercise/Health: Massage available by appointment.
Swimming: Nearby pool & river.
Sunbathing: On private sun decks & patios, common patio & lawn.
Smoking: Not permitted.
Pets: Not permitted.
Handicap Access: Yes. One unit & garden area.
Children: Allowed with special arrangements.
Languages: English.
Your Hosts: Eileen.

Inn at Highview, The

Vermont the Way You Always Dreamed It Would Be...

Everyone who arrives at *The Inn at HighView* has the same breathless reaction to the serenity of the surrounding hills. Our hilltop location offers incredible peace, tranquility and seclusion, yet is convenient to skiing, golf, tennis and antiquing. Enjoy our gourmet dinner, relax by a blazing fire, snuggle under a down comforter in a canopy bed, or gaze 50 miles over pristine mountains.

Ski cross-country or hike our 72 acres. Our rock-lined outdoor pool provides welcomed refreshment. Secluded and with an amazing view, it is a great place to while away a summer afternoon. The romance of our white gazebo isn't reserved only for weddings. Here you can quietly sit and enjoy the views or a that book you've been wanting to read. Our country dining room is well-known for excellent, imaginative cuisine. In addition to traditional full breakfasts, we offer congenial dinners on Saturdays, often featuring delicious Italian fare. Our "guest only" dinner policy assures you attentive, personal service in elegant but comfortable surroundings. Leave the arrangements to us for an evening of memorable dining.

Address: 753 East Hill Road, Andover, VT 05143
Tel: (802) 875-2724, **Fax:** (802) 875-4021.
E-mail: hiview@aol.com **Web:** http://www.innathighview.com

Type: Inn with restaurant for Inn guests only.
Clientele: Mostly straight with a gay & lesbian following
Transportation: Car is best. Amtrak to Bellows Falls, VT (19 mi), Rutland (Killington) 30 mi. Taxi from Bellows Falls $20. Car rental from Rutland.
To Gay Bars: 40 min by car. Proximity to a bar is NOT the reason to come here!
Rooms: 6 rooms & 2 suites with single, double, queen or king beds.
Baths: All private.
Meals: Full breakfast with

dinner avail. most wknd nts at prix fixe rate.
Vegetarian: Available.
Complimentary: Sherry in room & turn-down service. Tea & coffee always. Conferences receive coffee service, snacks.
Dates Open: All year except for 2 weeks in Nov & 2 weeks in Apr.
High Season: Sep 15-Oct 25, Christmas holiday week, & all of Feb.
Rates: Fall/Winter: $115-$155 double occupancy. $20 per extra person in suite.
Discounts: 10% on stays of 4 days or longer.
Credit Cards: MC, Visa.

Rsv'tns: Required.
Reserve Thru: Travel agent or call direct.
Min. Stay: 3 nights on holiday weekends & week between Christmas & New Year.
Parking: Ample free off-street parking.
In-Room: Maid & laundry svc. 1 rm w/ fireplace, 3 w/ canopy beds, 7 w/ private balconies & entrances, 2 w/ AC.
On-Premises: Meeting rooms, TV lounge, laundry facilities, gazebo w/ view, BBQ picnic area, game room, huge fireplace w/ comfortable couches in

living room, library & CD player.
Swimming: Pool.
Sunbathing: At poolside.
Smoking: Permitted outside only.
Pets: Small pets sometimes permitted depending on how full we are. Please inquire.
Handicap Access: 1 room accessible, but doorway is narrow.
Children: Permitted in suites only except during peak season. Please inquire.
Languages: English, Italian & Spanish.
Your Hosts: Greg & Sal.

Color Photo on Page 31

Country Cousin

Experience Vermont's Gay Bed & Breakfast

Located on 15 beautifully landscaped acres, *Country Cousin* is a truly traditional bed and breakfast housed in an 1824 Greek Revival farmhouse. It is nestled in a valley between the West Mountains and the Green Mountains of Southwestern Vermont, just north of Bennington. Three major downhill ski areas are within 30 minutes and you can cross-country ski right from the front door. Enjoy biking, canoeing or horseback riding through the Green Mountains. Antiquing and sightseeing along historic Route 7A, exploring Vermont's quaint hamlets, or enjoying the outlet stores and gourmet dining of nearby Manchester are other popular activities. You may, however, just prefer to curl up next to the fireplace with a good book or relax in the sun and enjoy the company of our friendly guests and staff.

The spacious farmhouse offers two common areas for guests: a quiet antique-filled living room with views of Mt. Equinox and a magnificent post and beam music room with cathedral ceilings, stained-glass, grand piano and a 25-foot natural stone fireplace. The music room leads to a large sunning deck complete with hot tub. The rolling lawns beyond take you to a large spring-fed pond, perfect for nude swimming and sunbathing, with clothing being optional. Our inn offers four uniquely decorated guest rooms, some with feather beds, down comforters, or patchwork quilts. Warm robes are provided. A full country breakfast is served daily after morning coffee in front of the fireplace. Afternoon tea, snacks and conversation are also a part of our hospitality. We are sure you will enjoy our country retreat and return again and again, as so many of our guests have!

Address: 192 Old Depot Rd, Shaftsbury, VT 05262
Tel: (802) 375-6985 or (800) 479-6985.

Type: Bed & breakfast.
Clientele: Gay & lesbian only
To Gay Bars: 1 hr to Brattleboro, VT & 1-1/4 hours by car to Albany, NY.
Rooms: 4 rooms with double or queen beds.
Baths: All private.
Meals: Full breakfast.
Vegetarian: On request.

Complimentary: Tea, coffee, juices, snacks.
Dates Open: All year.
High Season: Fall.
Rates: $90-$100 (surcharge: $10/nt hols., $20/nt fall foliage).
Discounts: Weekly rates.
Credit Cards: MC, Visa.
Rsv'tns: Required.
Reserve Thru: Travel agent

or call direct.
Min. Stay: 2 days on weekends preferred.
Parking: Adequate off-street parking.
On-Premises: Music room with stone fireplace & great room, partial AC.
Exercise/Health: Hot tub.
Swimming: In pond.
Sunbathing: On sun deck.

Nudity: Permitted on deck, in spa & pond areas.
Smoking: Permitted outdoors.
Pets: Permitted with prearrangement.
Handicap Access: Ask.
Children: With prearrangement.
Languages: English.
Your Hosts: Dennis.

Black Bear Inn

WWW **Gay-Friendly** ♀♂
Gay-Owned & -Operated

A True Vermont Country Inn

In the Green Mountains, only 20 minutes from Burlington and Stowe, the **Black Bear Inn** offers fabulous views and the blaze of fall colors. Individually decorated rooms and suites feature handmade quilts, and many have Vermont firestoves or fireplaces. Our warm summer days and cool evenings are perfect for sightseeing, horseback riding, or enjoying our hot tubs and heated pool. Skiing, ice skating, snow boarding and night skiing are all at our doorstep. AAA Three-Diamond Rating. Civil Union ceremonies can be held at the inn.

Address: 4010 Bolton Access Rd, Bolton Valley, VT 05477
Tel: (802) 434-2126, (800) 395-6335, **Fax:** (802) 434-5161.
E-mail: blkbear@wcvt.com **Web:** http://www.blkbearinn.com

Type: Inn w/ restaurant & bar
Clientele: Mostly straight with a gay/lesbian following
Transportation: Car is best. Pick up: airport (prior arrangement) $20; bus $10.
To Gay Bars: 20 miles.
Rooms: 24 rooms, 2 suites, 1 chalet w/ dbl-king beds.
Baths: All private.
Meals: 2 plans: breakfast only, or breakfast & dinner.
Vegetarian: Inquire.

Complimentary: Tea, coffee, Vermont apple cider, snacks, popcorn.
Dates Open: All year.
High Season: Jul-Aug, 1/2 Sept & 1st 1/2 Oct.
Rates: Summer: $79-$140; fall: $135-$170.
Discounts: Mention: Inn Places 15%, AAA 10%.
Credit Cards: MC, Visa.
Rsv'tns: Advised.
Reserve Thru: Travel agent or call direct.

Parking: Ample free parking.
In-Room: Phone, ceiling fans, color cable TV, maid & room svc, VT firestoves, fireplaces, hot tubs.
On-Premises: Laundry facilities.
Exercise/Health: Nearby tennis, gym, weights, Jacuzzi, sauna, steam.
Swimming: Pool. Nearby pool, river, lake, waterfalls.
Sunbathing: Poolside & on

6000 private acres.
Nudity: Permitted at certain waterfalls & certain areas.
Smoking: Outside only, state law. Non-smoking rooms available.
Pets: 3 kennels, $15/day.
Handicap Access: Yes, ramps, wide doors.
Children: Welcome.
Languages: English, French.
Your Hosts: Ken & Chris.

Phineas Swann B & B

WWW **Gay-Friendly 50/50** ♀♂

A Light-hearted, Premier Bed & Breakfast

A beautifully appointed 1890s gingerbread Victorian with newly expanded Carriage House Suites, **Phineas Swann** has recently been written about and recommended by *Country Living Magazine, The Boston Phoenix* and *Out Magazine*. In the main house, hand-picked antiques, hardwood floors and a cozy fireplace set the relaxed mood. Our Carriage House Suites have superlative accommodations with in-room Jacuzzi whirlpool baths and fireplaces. The inn is just minutes from Jay Peak Ski Resort, hiking, mountain biking, golf, stream fishing and antiquing. Come experience gourmet breakfasts, afternoon teas and refreshing attention to detail.

Address: The Main Street **Mail To:** PO Box 43, Montgomery Center, VT 05471
Tel: (802) 326-4306.
E-mail: phineas@sover.net **Web:** http://www.pbpub.com/phineasswann

Type: Bed & breakfast.
Clientele: 50% gay & lesbian & 50% straight clientele
Transportation: Car is best. Pick up from airport.
To Gay Bars: 1 hour to gay bars in Burlington, VT & 1 hour to Montreal.
Rooms: 4 rooms with queen & double beds & a 1-BR & 2-BR suite.

Baths: 2 private baths, 1 shared full bath.
Meals: Full gourmet breakfast & afternoon tea.
Vegetarian: Available.
Complimentary: 4pm tea with home-baked surprises. Mints & chocolates in room.
Dates Open: All year.
High Season: Jul-Aug & Feb-Mar.
Rates: $79-$145.

Credit Cards: MC, Visa, Discover.
Rsv'tns: Recommended.
Reserve Thru: Call direct.
Parking: Free covered parking.
In-Room: Ceiling fans & maid service.
On-Premises: TV lounge, VCR, game boards & meeting rooms.
Exercise/Health:

Snowmobile paths, skiing, tennis, hiking, fishing & golf.
Swimming: Swimming hole with mountain waterfalls.
Smoking: Not permitted.
Pets: Not permitted.
Handicap Access: No.
Children: Not especially welcome.
Languages: English.
Your Hosts: Michael & Glen.

Fitch Hill Inn

WWW **Gay-Friendly** ♀♂
Gay-Owned & -Operated

Elegant, But Not Stuffy

Historic *Fitch Hill Inn,* c. 1797, occupies a hill overlooking the magnificent Green Mountains. Its location, central to Vermont's all-season vacation country, offers a special opportunity to enjoy the true Vermont experience. Antique-decorated guest rooms all have spectacular views. Breakfasts and, by arrangement, gourmet dinners for six or more people, are prepared by the innkeeper. The library has video tapes, books, and an atmosphere of comfort and ease. The newly-renovated 18th century living room is wonderful for music, reading, and sitting by the fireside. We're near three major downhill ski area, nine cross-country ski centers, and are a 10-minute drive from Stowe Village. Mentioned in *Bon Apetit* (1998), *Country Living* (1997), and *Yankee* (1999).

Address: 258 Fitch Hill Rd, Hyde Park, VT 05655
Tel: (802) 888-3834, (800) 639-2903, **Fax:** (802) 888-7789.
E-mail: fitchinn@aol.com **Web:** http://www.irsl.com/vermont/hydepark/bb/fitchhill/

Type: B&B inn with restaurant for guests only
Clientele: Mostly straight with a gay & lesbian following
Transportation: Car is best.
To Gay Bars: 40 miles
Rooms: 4 rooms, 1 suite, 1 efficiency apt w/ doubles, queens or full sofa beds.
Baths: All private.
Meals: Full breakfast.
Vegetarian: W/ rsvt'n & prior arrangement.
Complimentary: Tea,

coffee, sherry, bathrobes, bottled water, mints, candy.
Dates Open: All year.
High Season: Dec 25-Jan 3, Sept 15-Oct 15 & Feb.
Rates: $85-$139; suite/apt: $149-$189 (maybe higher on holidays).
Discounts: Stays of 2+ days (except in high season), 10% AAA.
Credit Cards: MC, Visa, Amex, Discover.
Rsv'tns: Suggested.
Reserve Thru: Travel agent or call direct.

Min. Stay: 2+ nights in high seasons.
Parking: Ample off-street.
In-Room: AC, maid & laundry svc, color TV, VCR, phone, ceiling fans, 300+ video library. Suite & apt: fireplaces, Jacuzzis, color cable TV, VCRs, ceiling fans, phones, AC, kitchens.
On-Premises: Meeting rooms, TV lounge, VCR library. Refrigerator privileges available.
Exercise/Health: Outdoor hot tub, skiing, hiking,

biking, horseback riding, golf & canoeing.
Swimming: Lake & river nearby.
Sunbathing: On the beach.
Smoking: Not permitted inside. Permitted on 3 outdoor porches.
Pets: Not permitted.
Handicap Access: No.
Children: Permitted over 10.
Languages: English, Spanish & some French.
Your Hosts: Richard & Stanley.

Honeywood Country Lodge & Inn

Gay-Friendly

Experience Vermont Hospitality at Its Best

Experience the ambiance and luxury of a country inn with the privacy of a motel. At *Honeywood Country Lodge & Inn* we're famous for early-morning baking and continental-plus breakfasts. Our large tastefully decorated rooms have cathedral ceilings and patio doors leading to a common balcony and our nine acres of land. The rooms feature double, queen and king

brass or canopy beds with handmade quilts. The inn also offers guests a large guest living room with fireplace, as well as a TV room with satellite TV. Enjoy mountain views or dabble your feet in the brook which runs behind our property. In winter, cross-country ski from your door. We are the closest AAA Three-Diamond lodging to the slopes at Stowe Mountain Resort. Try our new B&B on the same property — two buildings, same owners.

Address: 4527 Mountain Rd, Stowe, VT 05672
Tel: (802) 253-4124, (800) 659-6289, **Fax:** (802) 253-7050.
E-mail: honeywd@aol.com **Web:** http://www.honeywoodinn.com

Type: Choice of B&B motel or traditional bed & breakfast.
Clientele: Mostly straght clientele with a gay & lesbian following
Transportation: Pick up from airport, train, bus & ferry dock. We use a local taxi service, usually $20-$50.
To Gay Bars: 30 mi to Burlington gay bars.
Rooms: Lodge: 12 rooms, 1 suite with single, double, queen or king beds. B&B: 8 rooms & 2 suites.
Baths: All private baths, 3 with Jacuzzi tubs.
Meals: Expanded continental breakfast, or full country breakfast.
Vegetarian: Available nearby.
Complimentary: Afternoon hors d'oeuvres & refreshments.
Dates Open: All year.
High Season: Sept 15-Oct 10, Dec 24-Jan 3, Feb 18-27.
Rates: Summer $69-$149, winter $75-$179, high season $99-$279.
Discounts: Seniors & multi-day discounts 3 days or more, midweek Sun-Thurs stay 5 pay 4 days. Not available during peak periods, direct bookings only.
Credit Cards: MC, Visa, Amex, Discover.
Rsv'tns: Recommended in regular & high season.
Reserve Thru: Travel agent or call direct.
Min. Stay: 2 nights on weekends, 3-4 nights high season.
Parking: Ample free off-street parking.
In-Room: All rooms: AC, ceiling fans, maid service. Some rooms: cable TV, telephone, refrigerator, fireplace, efficiencies, Jacuzzi tubs.
On-Premises: Inn has large guest living room with fireplace & a TV room with satellite TV.
Exercise/Health: Jacuzzi.
Nearby gym, weights, Jacuzzi, sauna, steam, massage.
Swimming: Pool, river on premises. Nearby river & lake.
Sunbathing: Poolside & on grass near rooms or pool.
Smoking: Inn is totally non-smoking inside. Permitted outside or in smoking rooms. Non-smoking rooms available.
Pets: Not permitted.
Handicap Access: Yes, 1 room handicap-equipped with some restrictions.
Children: We accommodate families with 1 or 2 well-behaved children.
Languages: English.
Your Hosts: Carolyn & Bill.

Grünberg Haus Bed & Breakfast & Cabins www Gay-Friendly ⚥

Spontaneous Personal Attention in a Handbuilt Austrian Chalet

Our romantic Austrian inn, *Grünberg Haus*, rests on a quiet hillside in Vermont's Green Mountains, perfect for trips to Stowe, Montpelier, Waterbury and Burlington. Choose guest rooms with wonderful views from carved wood balconies, secluded cabins hidden along wooded trails or a spectacular carriage house with skywindows, balconies and modern kitchen. Relax by the fire or warm-weather Jacuzzi, ski or walk our cross-country trails, gather fresh eggs or enjoy the grand piano as you savor your imaginative, memorable breakfast.

Address: 94 Pine Street, Route 100 South, Waterbury, VT 05676
Tel: (802) 244-7726, (800) 800-7760.
E-mail: grunhaus@aol.com **Web:** http://www.waterbury.org/grunberg

Type: Bed & breakfast guesthouse & cabins.
Clientele: Mostly straight clientele with a gay & lesbian following
Transportation: Car is best; local taxi & car rental available; Amtrak trains & Vermont Transit bus lines stop daily in Waterbury.
To Gay Bars: 25 miles to Burlington, VT.
Rooms: 10 rooms, 1 suite & 2 cottages with single, double or queen beds.
Baths: 9 private shower/ toilets & others share

shower/toilets.
Meals: Full, imaginative breakfasts.
Vegetarian: Breakfast always vegetarian.
Complimentary: Set-ups, soft drinks, coffee & tea, cordials & snacks. BYOB OK.
Dates Open: All year.
High Season: Feb-Mar, Jul-Oct, Christmas.
Rates: $59-$145.
Discounts: 10% for seniors & stays of 4 or more days.
Credit Cards: MC, Visa, En Route, Discover.

Rsv'tns: Suggested.
Reserve Thru: Travel agent or call direct.
Min. Stay: 2 nights during foliage season.
Parking: Ample free off-street parking.
In-Room: Maid service, fans & balcony. One kitchen unit.
On-Premises: Steinway grand piano, library, fireplace, chickens, BYOB pub. Walking & xc/snowshoe trails.
Exercise/Health: Jacuzzi, sauna, 40 acres for hiking.

Swimming: Pool, river or lake nearby.
Sunbathing: At poolside, by river or lake or on common sun decks.
Nudity: Clothing-optional swimming areas nearby.
Smoking: Permitted outside.
Pets: Not permitted. Pick up & delivery of pets at registered kennel is available.
Handicap Access: No.
Children: Permitted.
Languages: English.
Your Hosts: Chris & Mark.

Photo by: Willie Docto

Moose Meadow Lodge

WWW Gay-Friendly 50/50 ⚥
Gay-Owned & -Operated

A Unique Adirondack-Style Bed & Breakfast

On 86 secluded acres in the Green Mountains, the Adirondack-style *Moose Meadow Lodge* invites you to experience a truly unique B&B. Whether you love skiing, hiking, snowmobiling, biking, hunting, fishing, antiquing, fine dining, the arts, or simply getting some rest, this a perfect location to do everything — or nothing at all. Entering its long driveway surrounded by maple, spruce, and birch trees, you know you've arrived somewhere special. The large, covered front deck allows guests to enjoy magnificent views of the meadow, woods, Hunger Mountain and the valley below. Each guestroom has a unique theme, and all feature a private bath, distinctive log walls, comfortable beddings, great views, and at least one resident teddy bear. For extra privacy and panoramic views, you'll love the Sky Loft. An invigorating 20-minute hike from the house, this glass gazebo offers a respite from phones, computers, and noise.

Address: 607 Crossett Hill, Waterbury, VT 05676
Tel: (802) 244-5378, **Fax:** (802) 244-1713.
E-mail: innkeepers@moosemeadowlodge.com **Web:** http://www.moosemeadowlodge.com

Type: Bed & breakfast.
Clientele: 50% gay & lesbian & 50% straight clientele
Transportation: Car is best. Pick up from train (Waterbury) $5, airport (BTV) $40.
To Gay Bars: 30 miles.
Rooms: 3 rooms with king or queen beds.
Baths: All private.

Meals: Full breakfast.
Vegetarian: Upon request. 20 miles to excellent health food stores & restaurants catering to vegetarians.
Dates Open: All year.
Rates: $95 year round.
Rsv'tns: Required.
Reserve Thru: Call direct.
Min. Stay: 2 nights during peak seasons & long weekends.

Parking: Ample free parking.
On-Premises: TV lounge, video tape library, fax.
Exercise/Health: Weights, Jacuzzi. Nearby gym, massage.
Swimming: Pond. Pool, river, lake nearby.
Sunbathing: On property, usually by pond.
Nudity: Permitted around

pond or other private area on the property.
Smoking: All rooms non-smoking. Smoking permitted outside only.
Pets: Not permitted.
Children: No.
Languages: English, Tagalog, limited French.
Your Hosts: Willie & Greg.

Wilson - Lee House Bed & Breakfast

Relaxation as it Should Be in the Land That Time Forgot

On Virginia's Eastern Shore in historic Cape Charles, life moves at a deliciously slower pace. The *Wilson-Lee House Bed & Breakfast*, furnished with heirloom antiques and modern classics, offers six luxurious rooms, each with private bath. The James W. Lee Room features a splendid whirlpool. Mornings, full gourmet breakfasts are served and, after dark, the nightlife in Norfolk awaits just 45 minutes across the Chesapeake Bay Bridge Tunnel. With the beach only steps away, sunset sails can be arranged at your request. Pamper yourself — you deserve it.

Address: 403 Tazewell Ave, Cape Charles, VA 23310-3217
Tel: (757) 331-1954, **Fax:** (757) 331-8133.
E-mail: WLHBnB@aol.com. **Web:** http://www.wilsonleehouse.com

Type: Bed & breakfast, 45 min from Norfolk.
Clientele: Mostly straight clientele
Transportation: Car is best, Norfolk Int'l airport.
To Gay Bars: 40 miles, a 50 minute drive.
Rooms: 6 rooms with queen beds.
Baths: All private. One with whirlpool & 1 private bath across hall.

Meals: Full breakfast.
Vegetarian: With advance notice.
Complimentary: Welcome mint on pillow, setups provided, soda, ice, BYOB.
Dates Open: All year.
High Season: Late Apr to mid-Nov.
Rates: High $85-$120, low 2nd night 1/2 price.
Credit Cards: MC, Visa, Amex.

Rsv'tns: Required.
Reserve Thru: Travel agent or call direct.
Parking: Ample free on-street parking.
In-Room: AC, AM/FM clock radio & stereo CD player. Color cable TV available.
On-Premises: Meeting rooms, video tape & CD libraries. Refrigerator for guest use.
Swimming: 5-10 min walk

to beach.
Sunbathing: At beach.
Smoking: Permitted only on NON-enclosed porch area.
Pets: Not permitted.
Handicap Access: No.
Children: Only children over 12 years of age.
Languages: English.
Your Hosts: David, Leon.

Mark Addy, The

Lodging in an Elegant Tradition

The Mark Addy is conveniently located between the beautiful Blue Ridge Mountains and Thomas Jefferson's Charlottesville. This beautifully restored and lovingly appointed country inn dates back to 1884, offering all who stay here the richness of a bygone era. The charming rooms and luxurious suites have private bathrooms with either a double whirlpool bath, double shower, or an antique claw-foot tub with shower. Much of what we know about gracious living and warm welcomes we learned from our family. It is with considerable pride and affection that this historic home bears their names.

Address: 56 Rodes Farm Dr, Nellysford, VA 22958
Tel: (804) 361-1101, (800) 278-2154.
E-mail: markaddy@symweb.com **Web:** http://www.symweb.com/rockfish/mark.html

Type: Country inn.
Clientele: Mostly straight with a gay & lesbian following
Transportation: Airport or Amtrak pick up available at extra charge.
To Gay Bars: 30 minutes to gay bar.
Rooms: Rooms & suites.
Baths: All private. Double whirlpool bath, double shower or tub with shower.
Meals: Bountiful breakfast.

Dinner. Catering available.
Vegetarian: Upon request.
Complimentary: In guest kitchen: soda, juice, iced tea, snacks, homemade cookies.
Dates Open: All year.
Rates: $90-$145.
Discounts: Some available Sun-Thurs or for extended stays.
Credit Cards: MC, Visa.
Rsv'tns: Required.
Reserve Thru: Travel agent

or call direct.
Min. Stay: 2 nights in Sept, Oct, Feb, Apr-June & holidays.
In-Room: Down comforters, liqueur decanters, local goat's milk skin products, central AC.
On-Premises: 5 porches. Catering, including commitment ceremonies.
Exercise/Health: Excercise facilities nearby.
Swimming: Swimming

nearby.
Smoking: Permitted on porches only.
Pets: Not permitted.
Handicap Access: 1 room totally wheelchair accessible.
Children: Permitted age 12 & over.
Languages: English, German.
Your Hosts: John.

Bellmont Manor Bed & Breakfast

WWW Gay-Friendly 50/50 ⚢
Gay-Owned & -Operated

Thrill Your Taste Buds and Your Appetite for History

Bellmont Manor's location provides the traveler to historic Richmond and Chesterfield County, Virginia, with a veritable treasure-trove of sites and museums. This area of Virginia is at the center of the spirit and drama of the Civil War. Bellmont Manor is also an historic property, with the original portion of the house dating back over 150 years. Several years ago, the older portion was joined with a new two-story addition, uniting the two into a highly functional house which became a home, where innkeepers Uly Gooch and Worth Kenyon welcome the travelers from around the country. True Southern and Virginia hospitality abounds at *Bellmont Manor,* a place where great food and stimulating conversation are always at hand.

Overnight lodging is accommodated within a variety of room furnishings and arrangements. Of the three bedrooms, two have private baths and one in the older portion of the house shares a bath. Two bedrooms have queen-sized beds, and one bedroom has a double bed. All of the bedrooms are tastefully decorated with antiques and Virginia heirlooms. Here, you privacy is respected and your comfort assured.

We're located outside of Richmond on five acres of countryside. A large garden provides many of the vegetables and fruits served at the bountiful table, presided over by Innkeeper Gooch, a "country gourmet" cook. Of the hundreds of B&Bs only a few can offer such "down home" informality, wonderful food, and an atmosphere that truly says, *"Welcome, we're glad you're here!"*

Address: 6600 Belmont Rd, Chesterfield, VA 23832
Tel: (804) 745-0106, **Fax:** (804) 745-0740.
E-mail: bellmont@aol.com

Type: Bed & breakfast.
Clientele: 50% gay & lesbian & 50% straight clientele
Transportation: Car is best. Pick up from airport & train station, $20 charge.
To Gay Bars: 5 miles or a 15-min drive.
Rooms: 3 rooms with double, queen beds.
Baths: 2 private, 1 shared.

Meals: Full breakfast. Other meals by prior arrangement.
Vegetarian: Available by prior arrangement.
Complimentary: Wine, tea, coffee, hors d'oeuvres.
Dates Open: All year.
Rates: $75-$125, plus tax.
Discounts: 10% on stays of 3 nights or more.
Credit Cards: MC, Visa, Discover, Amex.

Rsv'tns: Required.
Reserve Thru: Travel agent or call direct.
Min. Stay: 2 nights on weekends.
Parking: Ample free off-street parking.
In-Room: AC, TV, ceiling fans, phone.
On-Premises: TV lounge.
Exercise/Health: Gym nearby.

Swimming: Nearby pool & river.
Sunbathing: On patio.
Smoking: Permitted outside only.
Pets: Not permitted. Dogs on premises.
Handicap Access: No.
Children: No.
Languages: English.
Your Hosts: Uly & Worth.

Ruby Rose Inn, The

WWW Gay/Lesbian ⚣
Lesbian-Owned & -Operated

An Ideal Setting with a Peaceful Retreat, 2 Hours from Washington, DC

Built in 1890, *The Ruby Rose Inn* is a lovely Victorian home located on the edge of a tiny town (population 1,100) in the Shenandoah Valley. Our grounds are dotted with huge oak trees, fruit trees and colorful flower beds — relax on the patio and watch the hummingbirds zip by. Your private cottage or room bids you to relax in front of a cozy, crackling fire, or take a soothing Jacuzzi bath. Your day starts with a full breakfast, complete with fresh baked bread or coffee cake, egg specialties, Belgian waffles, or pancakes and more, served with breakfast meats. We make our own preserves from the fruits in our orchard. Every effort is made to respect vegetarian and other dietary needs.

Four seasons of activities are available here in the Valley. We are minutes from Shenandoah National Park and George Washington National Forest, both renowned for beautiful scenery, hiking and nature trails. The famed Luray Caverns is just six miles away, as is their championship golf course. Canoeing, tubing, horseback riding, and lake or river fishing are nearby. Sample a fine Virginia wine at one of the wineries in the area. Fine dining restaurants as well as "country" fare will tempt your palate around dinnertime.

Address: 275 Chapel Road, Stanley, VA 22851
Tel: (540) 778-4680, **Fax:** (540) 778-4773.
E-mail: rm4u2222@aol.com **Web:** http://www.Shenandoah-RubyRoseInn.com

Type: Bed & breakfast.
Clientele: Mostly gay & lesbian with some straight clientele
Transportation: Car is best.
To Gay Bars: 60 miles, a 90 min drive.
Rooms: 1 room, 2 cottages with queen or king beds.
Baths: 3 private bath/ shower/toilets.
Meals: Full breakfast.
Vegetarian: Innkeepers respect all dietary requirements.
Complimentary: Tea, coffee, Belgian chocolates.
Dates Open: All year.
High Season: Oct.
Rates: $115-$145.
Discounts: $75 single. Full week 20% discount (Fri-Fri, Mon-Sun).
Credit Cards: MC, Visa, Discover.
Rsv'tns: Required with credit card.
Reserve Thru: Travel agent or call direct.
Min. Stay: 2 nights on weekends & holidays required in cottages.
Parking: Ample, free off-street parking.
In-Room: AC, ceiling fans, color cable TV, refrigerator, coffee & tea-making facilities, maid service.
On-Premises: TV lounge.
Exercise/Health: Jacuzzi. Nearby gym.
Swimming: Nearby pool, river, lake.
Sunbathing: On patio & in yard.
Smoking: All buildings are smoke-free. Smoking on porches & patios.
Pets: Not permitted.
Handicap Access: No.
Children: Welcome. Carriage House has daybed, children can be accommodated.
Languages: English.
Your Hosts: Deb, Rosemary.

Mary Kay's Romantic Whaley Mansion
WWW Gay-Friendly ♀♂

Take Someone You Love to Mary Kay's

Slip off your shoes, sink into our soft carpets, snuggle into our satin sheets, sip champagne and enjoy our superb coffee and our own hand-dipped truffles. *Mary Kay's Romantic Whaley Mansion Inn* is listed by AAA as a 3-diamond B&B. We specialize in romantic rendezvous, birthdays, anniversaries, honeymoons and retreats. We have six elegant bedrooms with private baths in a historical Victorian mansion. All rooms have AC, VCR, color TV, refrigerators, and free movies. The candlelit breakfast is presented on crystal and sterling silver in the formal dining room. An early breakfast is scheduled to allow guests to take the Lady of the Lake boat trip on 55-mile-long Chelan Lake.

Address: 415 Third St, Chelan, WA 98816
Tel: (509) 682-5735, (800) 729-2408 (USA & Canada).
E-mail: whaley@televar.com **Web:** http://www.marykaysbandb.com

Type: Bed & breakfast.
Clientele: Mostly straight clientele with a gay/lesbian following
Transportation: Car is best. Free pick up from airport in Chelan.
To Gay Bars: 175 miles from Seattle gay/lesbian bars.
Rooms: 6 rooms with double, queen or king beds.
Baths: All private.
Meals: 4-course candlelight breakfast.
Vegetarian: Always

available.
Complimentary: Chocolates & truffles.
Dates Open: All year.
High Season: May 15-Sept 15
Rates: $115-$135 summer, $85-$105 winter.
Discounts: Off-season specials.
Credit Cards: MC, Visa.
Rsv'tns: Required. 72-hour cancellation policy.
Reserve Thru: Call direct or travel agent.
Min. Stay: 2 days on

weekends, 3 days on holidays (summer).
Parking: Ample off-street parking.
In-Room: Color TV, VCR, AC, ceiling fans, refrigerators, maid service & free movies.
On-Premises: Meeting rooms, TV lounge, laundry facilities, & player piano.
Exercise/Health: Nearby cross-country skiing, boating, tennis courts, hiking & walking trails, fitness center. 150 mi. of packed

snowmobile trails.
Swimming: At Lake Chelan.
Sunbathing: On common sun decks.
Smoking: Permitted outdoors.
Pets: Not permitted.
Handicap Access: No.
Children: Not permitted, unless renting whole house.
Languages: English.
Your Hosts: Mary Kay & Carol.

Wild Lily Ranch

WWW Gay/Lesbian ♀♂

A Rustic Forest Retreat under Towering Cedars & Firs

In the Cascade Mountains one hour from Seattle, near the gay-friendly town of Index, are several cozy cabins made of cedar logs and cobblestones known as *Wild Lily Ranch.* Each cabin has a woodstove or fireplace and loft with skylights. They also have large picture windows with mini-blinds, dutch doors, small rustic porches looking out over the Skykomish River, nicely-finished hardwood floors, and spectacular views from every window. Or, stay in our authentic 20-foot-wide painted Sioux tipi with full bedding (sleeps four people). Among the many local activities available to guests are whitewater rafting, horseback riding and cross-country and downhill skiing. A buffet breakfast is served in the picnic area each morning.

Mail To: PO Box 313, Index, WA 98256
Tel: (360) 793-2103.
E-mail: wildlilyranch@aol.com **Web:** http://www.wildlilyranch.com

Type: Bed & breakfast with luxury camping in 1 tipi.
Clientele: Mainly gay & lesbian with some straight clientele
To Gay Bars: Gay-friendly bars in Index.
Rooms: Small log cabins & tipi.
Baths: Modern, shared, centrally located tropical bath house with bath/shower/toilets.
Camping: Sioux tipi with full bedding, sleeps 4.
Meals: Continental breakfast.
Dates Open: All year.
High Season: June-Sept.
Rates: Single: $75 all year. $10 for each additional person.
Discounts: Stay 6 days & get the 7th free.
Credit Cards: MC, Visa, Amex.
Rsv'tns: Required.
Reserve Thru: Call direct.
Min. Stay: 2-days on weekends.
Parking: Ample free parking.
In-Room: Refrigerator, fireplaces, cable color TV in cabins.
Exercise/Health: Recreational building has Jacuzzi, sauna, Health Rider & tropical plants. Kayaking, rock climbing.
Swimming: In river on premises.
Sunbathing: On the beach.
Nudity: Permitted on the beach with discretion.
Smoking: Permitted outside only.
Pets: Permitted with $10 daily pet fee.
Handicap Access: No.
Children: Not permitted.
Languages: English.
Your Hosts: Mike.

Madrigal Inn Bed & Breakfast

WWW Gay/Lesbian ⚥

Close to the City...Yet a World Away

Escape to a quiet sanctuary in the country and experience the joy of a working gentleman's farm. The *Madrigal Inn Bed & Breakfast* is located just 35 minutes southeast of Seattle and is an excellent base from which to visit Western Washington. It's perfect for a romantic weekend get-a-way, or a retreat from the hectic work schedule of a traveling business person. Lake Madrigal offers a serene setting with waterfall and fountain. The inn offers a guest kitchen, fifty-four jet Jacuzzi, recreation room with dual pool and ping-pong table, tavern-style electronic darts, foos ball, wet bar, fireplace, card and board games. Guests may also purchase food from a nearby grocery store to prepare on the BBQ or campfire site. The three miniature cows, chickens, rabbits, cat and birds offer peaceful activity on the 2-1/2 acre farm. A 1996, 37' motor home with tip-out is available for rent to tour the Northwest. See the best of the Northwest in day trips to Mt. Rainier, Mt. St. Helen's, the Pacific Ocean and Seattle.

Address: 14421 SE 232nd St, Kent, WA 98042
Tel: (253) 638-6566, **Fax:** (253) 638-6466.
E-mail: madrigalinn@imajis.com **Web:** http://www.madrigalinn.com

Type: Bed & breakfast.
Clientele: Mostly gay with straight clientele
Transportation: Car is best. Airport pick up $20.
To Gay Bars: 10 min drive.
Rooms: 5 rooms with queen beds.
Baths: 2 private shower/toilet. Shared: 1 bath/shower/toilet, 1 shower/toilet, 1 toilet/sink.

Meals: Full breakfast or tray.
Vegetarian: On request.
Complimentary: Bottle of wine & fruit in room on arrival. Cocktail/hors d'oeuvre hour 5-6pm nightly, marshmallows for roasting over campfire on request.
Dates Open: All year.
Rates: $100 per night, $10 each addt'l guest in room.

Discounts: Variable.
Credit Cards: MC, Visa, Discover, Amex.
Reserve Thru: Call direct.
Min. Stay: 2 nights weekends.
Parking: Off-street.
On-Premises: Game room, wet bar, office, internet, fax, copier.
Exercise/Health: Jacuzzi, workout room. Hiking trails,

nearby gym.
Sunbathing: Patio, gardens.
Nudity: Permitted in private areas & Jacuzzi.
Smoking: Permitted outside only.
Pets: Inquire.
Handicap Access: Inquire.
Children: No.

Shakti Cove Cottages

Experience the Peacefulness of Shakti Cove

Though much of the Long Beach peninsula is heavily touristed, you'll find Ocean Park much quieter. *Shakti Cove Cottages* are secluded on three wooded acres. They're rustic, but have all the amenities you'll require. Don't expect chic, but DO expect quiet, privacy and the sound of the ocean. It's a five-minute walk over a footpath to the beach. Stroll in search of sand dollars, go hiking in a wildlife refuge, or browse the many antique shops nearby. An easy drive from Seattle or Portland, it's a good place to kick back and relax.

Address: 25301 Park Ave, PO Box 385, Ocean Park, WA 98640
Tel: (360) 665-4000.
E-mail: shakti@aone.com **Web:** http://www.shakticove.com

Type: Cottages.
Clientele: Mainly gay & lesbian with some straight clientele
Transportation: Car is best.
To Gay Bars: 2-1/2 hours to Portland, Oregon.
Rooms: 10 cottages with queen beds.

Baths: All private.
Dates Open: All year (except Jan).
High Season: Mar-Oct.
Rates: $65-$75.
Discounts: Nov-Feb 3 nights for 2.
Credit Cards: MC, Visa.
Rsv'tns: Suggested.
Reserve Thru: Call direct.

Min. Stay: Required during holidays & some weekends.
Parking: Ample free covered parking.
In-Room: Color TV, kitchen, refrigerator.
Swimming: Public pool nearby.
Sunbathing: On the beach or on our lawn.

Smoking: Permitted.
Pets: Permitted.
Handicap Access: No (sorry).
Children: Permitted.
Languages: English.
Your Hosts: Liz & Celia, the Covekeepers.

Oyster Bay

We Don't Mind if You're Straight, As Long As You Act Gay in Public

Parade through the tunnel of trees to *Oyster Bay,* a spectacular custom log home in serene, park-like surroundings. Our home boasts 364 feet of waterfront and overlooks Totten Inlet and the Black Hills. Built from handcrafted logs, the house also features a carved stairway, a 35-foot stone fireplace and decks galore! *Oyster Bay's* beautiful rooms are furnished with queen-sized beds and down comforters. We offer complete privacy, combined with a casual air, to ensure our guests' ultimate comfort, and we look forward to your special requests, whether it's dinner, flowers, or champagne. While relaxing in a hot bath choose from our complimentary selection of bath oils and soak and massage creams, then lounge on the private decks in our Turkish robes, followed by a wonderful gourmet meal.

Oyster Bay is great for couples or groups of friends who just want to get away. While staying at *Oyster Bay,* trail ride on our beautiful Arabian horses (weather permitting), or just visit the barn and play with the babies. Boating, kayaking, fishing, biking and hiking are all within a 20-minute drive. Many other outdoor options are available, including ocean beaches and Hood Canal (40 minutes from us by car), or exploring the beautiful Olympic Peninsula with its mountains and rainforests. The Little Creek Casino is five minutes away. We're one hour from Seattle or Portland — let us chauffer you to either city for the ultimate shopping experience. Please call us for specials and discount rates.

Address: 2830 Bloomfield Rd, Shelton, WA
Tel: (360) 427-7643.

Type: Bed & breakfast.
Clientele: Mostly gay & lesbian with some straight clientele
Transportation: Car is best.
To Gay Bars: 20 min drive.
Rooms: 3 rooms with single or queen beds.
Baths: 2 shared bath/ shower/toilets.
Meals: Expanded continental breakfast.
Vegetarian: Available upon request.
Complimentary: Sherry in room, tea, coffee, imported chocolates, bath oils, soaks, massage creams.
Dates Open: All year.
High Season: May/Sept.
Rates: $85-$140.
Discounts: Call for specials & discount rates.
Rsv'tns: Recommended.
Reserve Thru: Call direct.
Parking: Ample, free off-street parking.
In-Room: Maid service.
On-Premises: Telephone, fireplace, private decks, TV lounge w/ satellite TV, video tape, reading & music libraries, foosball table, board games, picnic area, kitchen, executive chef on premises.
Exercise/Health: Hot tub & garden room by Spring '98. Arabian horses & riding instruction.
Swimming: Puget Sound nearby.
Sunbathing: On private sun decks.
Nudity: Permitted under certain conditions, see manager.
Smoking: Permitted on decks & porches.
Pets: Not permitted.
Handicap Access: No.
Children: No.
Languages: English, Italian.
Your Hosts: Ingrid.

Ravenscroft Inn

Gay-Friendly ⚥

Take a Short Trip to Far Away...

One of the most romantic hideaways in the Pacific Northwest is located high on a bluff overlooking historic Port Townsend, the Olympic Peninsula's Victorian seaport. Noted for its colonial style, a replication of a historic Charleston single house, the inn offers a unique combination of colonial hospitality, mixed with a casual air that spells comfort to its guests. The hosts take great pleasure in looking after their guests' special requests, whether it's dinner, theatre, concert reservations, or arranging for flowers or champagne, all are carried out with ease and alacrity.

While staying at the *Ravenscroft Inn,* you can explore the Olympic National Park, walk the seven mile sand spit at Dungeness or hike through North America's only rainforest. Port Townsend and its environs meets all your vacation requirements offering scenic beauty, theatre, unparalleled dining, boating, biking, fishing, kayaking and hiking. Top this off with a delectable breakfast and fresh roasted gourmet coffee, served each morning. **Guest Comment:** "There was never a detail left unattended."

Address: 533 Quincy St, Port Townsend, WA 98368
Tel: (360) 385-2784, (800) 782-2691, **Fax:** (360) 385-6724.
E-mail: ravenscroft@olympus.net **Web:** http://www.ravenscroftinn.com

Type: Bed & breakfast.
Clientele: Mainly straight with a gay & lesbian following
Transportation: Car is best. Free pick up from Port Townsend Airport (from Seattle via Port Townsend Airways).
To Gay Bars: 2 hrs by car.
Rooms: 8 rooms & 2 suites with single, queen or king beds.
Baths: All private baths with either shower or shower/bath.
Meals: Full breakfast.
Vegetarian: Available on request. When making reservation, all dietary restrictions addressed.
Complimentary: Coffee, tea, set-up service, juices.
Dates Open: All year.
High Season: May 15-Oct 15.
Rates: $75-$175 May 15-Oct 15, $67-$175 Oct 16-May 14.
Discounts: Single discount.
Credit Cards: MC, Visa, Amex, Discover.
Rsv'tns: Required.
Reserve Thru: Call direct.
Min. Stay: Some weekends, special holidays & special events.
Parking: Ample free off-street parking.
In-Room: Color TV on request, maid service.
On-Premises: Meeting room, library, great room.
Exercise/Health: Soaking tub in suite, gym available,
weights, Jacuzzi, sauna, steam & massage at nearby Athletic Club.
Swimming: At local school pool.
Sunbathing: On common sun decks & at beach.
Smoking: Permitted on outdoor balconies only.
Pets: Not permitted.
Children: Permitted over 12 years of age.
Languages: English.

Bacon Mansion

WWW Gay-Friendly ♀♂

Seattle's Finest B&B for Sun (and Rain!) Lovers!

Shields of red and white can be seen on the round stained glass windows as you pass through the gates of *The Bacon Mansion,* an elegant English Tudor house in the Harvard-Belmont Historical District. Here in Capitol Hill, one of Seattle's most exciting neighborhoods, dining, sightseeing, nightlife and boutiques are just a few blocks away.

The main Guest House, consisting of 9,000 square feet of living space is divided among four levels. A spacious outside patio leads to the historical Carriage House. A variety of well-appointed accommodations, from moderate rooms to suites and even the carriage house, warmly welcome every guest. Nine rooms have private baths. Besides a delicious breakfast including a potpourri of cereals, muffins and delicacies, catered lunches, dinners and receptions are also available. We have immense, beautifully decorated day rooms and a large, private, partially-covered patio for sun (and rain!) lovers. Don't miss it!

Address: 959 Broadway East, Seattle, WA 98102
Tel: (206) 329-1864, (800) 240-1864, **Fax:** (206) 860-9025.
E-mail: info@baconmansion.com **Web:** http://www.baconmansion.com

Type: Bed & breakfast guesthouse.
Clientele: 30% gay & lesbian & 70% straight clientele.
Transportation: Shuttle Express from airport, taxi from train.
To Gay Bars: Two blocks to famous Elite Tavern on Broadway.
Rooms: 9 rooms & 2 suites with double or queen beds.
Baths: Private: 4 shower/ toilet, 5 full baths. 2 shared full baths.
Meals: Buffet breakfast.
Vegetarian: Always available.
Complimentary: Tea, coffee, mints on pillow.
Dates Open: All year.
High Season: May-Oct & holidays.
Rates: High: $94-$159, low: $79-$129.
Discounts: 10% on stays of over 6 nights, low only.

Credit Cards: MC, Visa, Amex, Discover.
Rsv'tns: Required.
Reserve Thru: Call direct.
Min. Stay: Required.
Parking: Ample, off-street parking.
In-Room: Color TV, telephone with voice mail & data, maid service.
On-Premises: Meeting rooms, refrigerator & fax.
Exercise/Health: Nearby gym, weights & massage.

Swimming: At nearby pool & lake.
Sunbathing: On patio & common sun deck.
Smoking: Permitted outside only.
Pets: Not permitted.
Handicap Access: One suite accessible.
Children: Permitted in some rooms only.
Languages: English.
Your Hosts: Daryl.

Bed & Breakfast on Broadway

WWW Gay-Friendly 50/50

Your Home Away From Home

Gleaming chandeliers, antiques and Oriental rugs grace the interior of *Bed & Breakfast on Broadway*. This distinctive 1901 Pacific Northwest-style house is filled with antiques and art objects. Original paintings and contemporary works of art by Northwest artists, as well as our own resident artist, Russ Lyons, are on display throughout the house. In the parlor is a grand piano, fireplace and antiques. Oriental rugs adorn polished hardwood floors. Relax in complete privacy in one of four spacious, bright and airy guestrooms with TV, queen-sized bed, goose-down comforter and private bath with lots of thick, fluffy towels. A scrumptious continental breakfast with fruits, milk, tea or fresh-brewed coffee is served in the dining room. Our quiet and intimate B&B features four charming guest rooms with private bath. We're within walking distance of the area's restaurants & shops.

Address: 722 Broadway E., Seattle, WA 98102
Tel: (206) 329-8933, **Fax:** (206) 726-0918.
E-mail: bbonbroadway@chcs.com **Web:** http://www.bbonbroadway.com

Type: Bed & breakfast.
Clientele: 50% gay & lesbian & 50% straight clientele
Transportation: Car, taxi or Super Shuttle.
To Gay Bars: 1 block.
Rooms: 4 rooms with queen beds.
Baths: 4 private bath/toilets.
Meals: Expanded continental breakfast.
Vegetarian: Available upon request.
Dates Open: All year.
High Season: May-Sept.
Rates: $99-$135.
Credit Cards: Visa, MC.
Rsv'tns: Recommended 2-3 weeks in advance.
Reserve Thru: Call direct.
Min. Stay: 2 nights on weekends, 3 nights on holidays.
Parking: Limited off-street parking.
In-Room: Color cable TV, maid service. 2 rooms with private deck.
Exercise/Health: Nearby gym, weights.
Swimming: Nearby pool, ocean, lake.
Smoking: Smoke-free.
Pets: Not permitted.
Handicap Access: No.
Children: No.
Languages: English.
Your Hosts: Don & Russ.

Gaslight Inn

WWW Gay/Lesbian ♂♂

Welcome to *Gaslight Inn*, a Seattle four-square house built in 1906. In restoring the inn, we have brought out the home's original turn-of-the-century ambiance and warmth, while keeping in mind the additional conveniences and contemporary style needed by travelers in the nineties. The interior is appointed in exacting detail, with strikingly rich, dark colors, oak paneling, and an enormous entryway and staircase.

Our comfortable and unique rooms and suites are furnished with quality double or queen-sized beds, refrigerator and television. Additional features, such as private bath and phone service, are available in some rooms. Some rooms also have decks with fabulous views or fireplaces. The living room, with its large oak fireplace, is always inviting, as is the library. Through the late spring and summer, we encourage you to unwind with a glass of wine beside our private, in-ground, heated pool with several decks and interesting plant arrangements. We're convenient to central Seattle's attractions and to a plethora of gay and lesbian bars, restaurants and shops in the Broadway district.

Address: 1727 15th Ave, Seattle, WA 98122
Tel: (206) 325-3654, **Fax:** (206) 328-4803.
E-mail: innkeepr@gaslight-inn.com **Web:** http://www.gaslight-inn.com

Type: Guesthouse.
Clientele: Mostly gay/lesbian, some straight
Transportation: Airport Shuttle Express $15, (206) 286-4800 to reserve.
To Gay Bars: 2-3 blocks.
Rooms: 9 dbls, 7 suites.
Baths: 14 private, 2 shared.
Meals: Expanded continental breakfast.

Complimentary: Coffee, tea & juices, fresh fruit, pastries.
Dates Open: All year.
High Season: Summer.
Rates: $88-$178.
Credit Cards: MC, Visa, Amex.
Rsv'tns: Recommended at least 2 weeks in advance.
Reserve Thru: Call direct.

Min. Stay: 2 days wknds, 3 days holidays.
Parking: Ample on-street & off-street parking.
In-Room: Color TV, cable, telephones, maid service.
On-Premises: Meeting rooms, living room, library.
Swimming: Seasonal heated pool.
Sunbathing: On private or

common sun decks or at poolside.
Smoking: Permitted on decks & porches only.
Pets: Not permitted.
Children: Not permitted.
Languages: English.
Your Hosts: Trevor, Stephen & John.
IGLTA

Color Photo on Page 32

Landes House

Gay/Lesbian ♀♂

Landes House is an historic turn-of-the-century home a short walk from the shops and restaurants of the popular Broadway district. It is named for Bertha Landes, Seattle's only woman mayor, who was elected in 1926. The house has a warm and inviting ambiance, large gracious day rooms, elaborate woodwork and a private garden courtyard with hot tub. Most rooms have private baths, and several have private decks with views of Seattle's skyline, Puget Sound and the Olympic Mtns.

Address: 712 11th Ave E, Seattle, WA 98102
Tel: (206) 329-8781, (888) 329-8781, **Fax:** (206) 324-0934.
Web: http://www.landeshouse.com

Type: Bed & breakfast.
Clientele: Mostly gay/lesbian with some straight clientele
Transportation: For airport shuttle, call 622-1424 or (800) 942-0711.
To Gay Bars: 2-10 blocks to most men's & women's bars.
Rooms: 10 rooms & 1 apartment with queen or king beds.
Baths: 9 private, others share.

Meals: Expanded continental breakfast.
Vegetarian: Always available, 3 blocks to The Gravity Bar.
Complimentary: Coffee, tea, summer beverages.
Dates Open: All year.
High Season: Apr-Oct.
Rates: Winter $68-$180, summer $70-$180.
Discounts: 7th night free.
Credit Cards: MC, Visa.

Rsv'tns: Strongly suggested (6-8 weeks in season).
Reserve Thru: Call direct.
Min. Stay: 2 nights on weekends, 3 on holidays.
Parking: Adequate free off-street parking.
In-Room: Color TV, telephone, maid service, ceiling fans.
On-Premises: Laundry facilities.
Exercise/Health: Hot tub.

Swimming: Lake & beach nearby.
Sunbathing: On private & common sun decks.
Nudity: Permitted in hot tub.
Smoking: Permitted (Non-smoking rooms available).
Pets: Not permitted.
Handicap Access: No.
Children: Not permitted.
Languages: English.
Your Hosts: Tom & Dave.

A Peaceful Respite

Secluded Victorian Farm cradled in the mountains of West Virginia

- Bed & Breakfast
- Cottage in The Wood
- Cellar House Suite
- Horses (Bring your own horse)
- Campsites/Trails
- 230 Acres
- Abundant wildlife
- Farm Animals
- Waterfall/Pond

Rt. 1, Box 158, Orlando, WV 26412 (I-79 near Weston)
Phone: (304) 462-7075 ⟶ Reservations/Deposit
gsc01504@mail.wvnet.edu ⟶ Fax: (304) 462-7373

FriendSheep Farm

Gay/Lesbian ⚥

A Place Less Touched by Modern Times...

FriendSheep Farm stood many years abandoned, fences gone, barns empty. Now, reestablished to its 1905 grandeur, it is again home to many farm animals and offers a peaceful respite to those seeking to step back into its timeworn ambience and just enjoy the serene beauty of its soft meadows, quiet brooks and majestic mountains.

The facilities include a *Bed and Breakfast,* where you will enjoy antiques, wonderful beds, good conversation, and a delicious gourmet breakfast offering our own eggs, fruits and vegetables (when in season). *The Cellar House Suite* is a private accommodation also furnished, with all the amenities. You can cook your own meals or prearrange for us to prepare them for you. This is a charming "little house" behind the main house. *The Cottage in the Wood* is offered for those who wish to be nestled in the forest. It, too, is completely furnished and has a complete kitchen. Both facilities can be used for intimate getaways or for small groups or gatherings.

The *Campsites* are tranquil and secure, many are primitive and allow visitors to really relax in nature and view the abundant wildlife (No Hunting). *Bring Your Own Horse (BYOH)* allows those who have an equine friend to bring him along and enjoy the many trails and unpaved back roads. Other pets are acceptable in certain situations. All animals must have a health certificate and all horses a negative coggins. *Reservations and deposit are required.*

Address: Rt #1, (near Weston I-79), Orlando **Mail To:** Box 158, Orlando, WV 26412
Tel: (304) 462-7075, **Fax:** (304) 462-7373.
E-mail: gsc01504@mail.wvnet.edu

Roseland Guest House & Campground

Kick Back & Relax in the West Virginia Mountains

In the northern panhandle, 32 miles south of Wheeling, *Roseland Guest House & Campground* is one mile off a country road at the end of a lane. Our private, secluded mountain location is on 222 clothing-optional acres, and a locked gate at the end of the property ensures your privacy. Our 19th-century guesthouse features modern conveniences as well as a 42-foot-long Great Room with cathedral ceiling, loft, dining area, kitchen and stunning mountain views. Numerous campsites are scattered throughout and are available for both tenting and campers

Address: Proctor, WV **Mail To:** RD 1, Box 185B, Proctor, WV 26055-9703
Tel: (304) 455-3838.
E-mail: roseland@rcvideo.com **Web:** http://www.rcvideo.com/roseland

Type: B&B guesthouse & campground w/ food service & theme wknds.
Clientele: Men only
Transportation: Car is best.
To Gay Bars: 32 miles.
Rooms: 8 rooms, barracks with single, double or queen beds
Baths: Shared: 5 bath/shower/toilets, 2 outdoor showers for campers.
Camping: 50 tent sites, 10 RV parking only.

Meals: Full breakfast, dinner for guesthouse & barracks only (campers w/ advance rsv'tn & charge).
Vegetarian: Upon request. Advise of any special dietary needs.
Dates Open: All year.
High Season: June-Oct with theme weekends.
Rates: $80-$150.
Discounts: 10% to groups.
Credit Cards: MC, Visa, Amex.
Rsv'tns: Preferred 1 week

in advance.
Reserve Thru: Travel agent or call direct.
Min. Stay: 2 nights on holidays.
Parking: Ample off-street parking.
In-Room: Ceiling fans.
On-Premises: Meeting rooms, kitchen, convenience store.
Exercise/Health: Jacuzzi, horseshoes, volleyball, hiking.
Swimming: Pool & pond on

premises.
Sunbathing: Poolside & in yard.
Nudity: Permitted throughout.
Smoking: Permitted outside only.
Pets: Permitted, must be good around people.
Handicap Access: No.
Children: No.
Languages: English.
Your Hosts: Daniel & Brian.

Eleven Gables Inn on the Lake

A Harbour Village Holiday on Lake Geneva

Eleven Gables Inn on the Lake is located on beautiful Lake Geneva in a quiet exclusive residential historic district, three blocks from downtown. This quaint lakeside 1847 Carpenter's Gothic inn, offers privacy in a prime resort area, a short lakefront stroll to fine dining, boutiques and entertainment. Fringed by multimillion-dollar estates, this "Newport of the Midwest" lake area is busy in all seasons. Activities include golf, tennis, equestrian activities, huntclubs and stock theatre, as well as magnificent autumn-color tours, biking, hiking, and colder sports during the pristine white snows of winter.

Breakfast is served overlooking the lake in warmer months and before the front drawing room fireplace in winter. Naturally shaded and cool in the summer, cheerily warm in the winter, this historic inn invites you to indulge in the pleasures of a lakefront lifestyle!

Address: 493 Wrigley Dr, Lake Geneva, WI 53147
Tel: (262) 248-8393.
E-mail: egi@lkgeneva.com **Web:** http://www.lkgeneva.com

Type: Bed & breakfast.
Clientele: Mostly straight with a gay/lesbian following
Transportation: Car is best. Limo charter from Milwaukee or O'Hare Airport.
To Gay Bars: 40 miles.
Rooms: 12 (bedrooms, bridal chamber and 2- & 3-bedroom country cottages).
Baths: All private.
Meals: Full or expanded continental breakfast.

Complimentary: Cocktail set ups.
High Season: June 15-Labor Day.
Rates: $95-$275 per night, per room, dble occ.
Credit Cards: MC, Visa, Amex, Diners, Discover.
Rsv'tns: Required.
Reserve Thru: Travel agent or call direct.
Min. Stay: 2-3 nts wknds & holidays.

Parking: Limited off-street parking, 1 car per unit.
In-Room: Fireplaces, down comforters, wet-bar, kitchenettes, TV/VCRs, whirlpools, AC, ceiling fans, courtyard & balcony, private entrances, Jacuzzi.
On-Premises: Meeting rooms, fax, copy machine, BBQ, bike rental, courtesy phone, private pier, boating, hiking, fishing.

Exercise/Health: Nearby gym, weights, Jacuzzi, sauna, steam, massage.
Swimming: In lake.
Sunbathing: On private & common sun decks, patio, private pier, at beach.
Smoking: Permitted in private courtyards, balconies, pier & in some rooms.
Languages: English.

Birch Creek Inn

Your Home Away From Home

The *Birch Creek Inn* whose roots date to the 1800s, is a little bit of ethnic country in an urban setting. A German farm which, over time, has evolved from farm to motor inn, is now a quirky, cozy private inn. All guestrooms have private outside entrances, private full baths, cable TV with HBO, in-room coffee, queen or two double beds. All of our suites are decorated with quilts, crochet pillows, Teddy bears, and more. We're near all local attractions, shopping, Lake Michigan, and less than an hour from Door County, Milwaukee and Green Bay. "Find unusual, but comfortable, lodgings at Birch Creek Inn,..." Mike Michaelson — *Chicago Daily Herald* "Around the Midwest," August, 1999.

Address: 4626 Calumet Avenue, Manitowoc, WI 54220
Tel: (920) 684-3374, (800) 424-6126, **Fax:** (920) 684-9464.
E-mail: info@birchcreekinn.com **Web:** http://www.birchcreekinn.com

Type: Bed & breakfast inn.
Clientele: Mostly straight clientele with a gay/lesbian following
Transportation: Car. Free ferry dock pick up (rsvt'n required).
To Gay Bars: 45 miles.
Rooms: 20 suites with queen or double beds.
Baths: 20 private bath/shower/toilets.

Meals: Breakfast basket.
Vegetarian: At Kristina's restaurant.
Complimentary: Tea & coffee, snacks.
Dates Open: All year.
High Season: Jul-Aug.
Rates: All year $40-$275 (subj. to change).
Discounts: Business, corporate, AARP, senior.
Credit Cards: MC, Visa, Amex, Discover.
Rsv'tns: Preferred.
Reserve Thru: Call direct.
Parking: Ample free parking.
In-Room: Phone, AC, ceiling fans, color cable TV, coffee & tea-making facilities, laundry service. Some have fireplaces.
On-Premises: Fax, copier, FedEx.

Exercise/Health: Nearby gym, weights, massage.
Swimming: Nearby lake.
Sunbathing: On patio.
Smoking: 6 smoking rooms or in specified outside areas.
Pets: Small dogs only.
Handicap Access: Yes, all on 1 level.
Children: Not discouraged.
Languages: English.

Chanticleer Guest House

Gay-Friendly 50/50 ♂♂

A Romantic Country Inn

Welcome to the *Chanticleer,* nestled among the orchards on 70 private acres in picturesque Door County, WI. With over 250 miles of shoreline, 12 lighthouses, 5 state parks and countless antique and gift shops, you're not far from unlimited fun and adventure. The *Chanticleer's* majestic maples and delicate fields of wild flowers are a grand sight as you stroll on our nature trail. After your walk, tour our beautiful gardens, lounge poolside or relax on your private terrace overlooking the *Chanticleer's* serene countryside. All deluxe suites include double whirlpools, fireplaces, private baths and breakfast delivered to your room. Come and enjoy the peace and serenity in one of our romantic cottages with all the same amenities, plus a full kitchen, work station and laundry.

Address: 4072 Cherry Rd (Hwy H. H.), Sturgeon Bay, WI 54235
Tel: (920) 746-0334.
E-mail: chanticleer@itol.com **Web:** http://www.chanticleerguesthouse.com

Type: Bed & breakfast.
Clientele: 50% gay & lesbian & 50% straight
Transportation: Car.
To Gay Bars: 45 mi in Green Bay.
Rooms: 8 suites (6 with queen & 2 with king beds). 2 cottages with king beds.
Baths: All private bath/ toilet/showers.
Meals: Expanded continental breakfast (except in cottages).
Vegetarian: Our breakfast is vegetarian. Vegetarian restaurants nearby.

Complimentary: Tea, coffee, juice, cookies, fresh fruit & candy.
Dates Open: All year.
High Season: Jun-Oct for summer festivals, fall & pumpkin festivals. Feb-Mar for ski season.
Rates: $120-$210.
Discounts: 10% summer 5+ days. 10% winter 3+ days (Sun-Thurs). Weekday specials.
Credit Cards: MC, Visa, Discover.
Rsv'tns: Required. Walk-ins welcome if rooms

available.
Reserve Thru: Call direct.
Min. Stay: 2 nights on weekends. Cottages 2 nights all week.
Parking: Ample free off-street parking in paved lot.
In-Room: Color TV, VCR, CD & cassette stereo, AC, coffee/tea-making facilities, ceiling fans, refrigerator, fireplace, double whirlpool tub, room & maid service.
On-Premises: Meeting rooms.
Exercise/Health: Sauna. Nearby gym & weights.

Swimming: Heated pool. Nearby lake.
Sunbathing: Poolside, on patio & private & common sun decks.
Smoking: Permitted with restrictions. Non-smoking sleeping rooms available.
Pets: Not permitted.
Handicap Access: Yes.
Children: Not especially welcome.
Languages: English.
Your Hosts: Bryon & Darrin.

...Continued from Page 1

■ Gay Orientation & Gender

At the top right corner of each listing is the answer to the perennial first question, "How gay is it and is it for men or women?" The range of possible answers, and what they mean, is given below. In describing clientele, these answers employ both words and the symbols for male and female .

Men	♂	Gay male clientele
Women	♀	Female clientele
Gay/Lesbian	♂	Mostly gay men
Gay/Lesbian	♀	Mostly gay women
Gay/Lesbian	⚥	Gay men and women about 50/50
Gay-Friendly Gay-Owned	⚥ } ⚥ }	Mostly straight (non-gay) clientele with a gay and lesbian following, or a place that welcomes gay and lesbian customers
Gay-Friendly Gay-Owned	♀ } ♀ }	Mostly straight (non-gay) clientele with a gay female following
Gay-Friendly Gay-Owned	♂ } ♂ }	Mostly straight (non-gay) clientele with a gay male following
Gay-Friendly 50/50 Gay-Owned 50/50	♂ } ♂ }	Half gay and half straight (Symbols indicate gay male or lesbian predominance)

■ WWW Logo

Placement of the WWW logo next to an entry signifies that a detailed entry with color photography appears on www.ferrariguides.com, the most searchable gay travel information site on the worldwide web.

■ Member AGLTA, IGLTA

AGLTA is the Australian Gay & Lesbian Travel Association. IGLTA is the International Gay & Lesbian Travel Association.

■ Description

A description of the inn's architecture, ambiance, decor, amenities and services helps you to decide which inn to choose. Information is frequently also given on local activities.

■ Addresses

Some businesses do not list their addresses. Others list mailing addresses only. Some have deleted their zip codes to indicate they do not wish to receive advertising solicitations from other publications using this book as a lead list.

■ Telephones

Inside the US, area codes appear within parentheses. Outside the US, both country and city codes are used. For example, "Country: Netherlands, City: Amsterdam" is expressed by "(31-20)" followed by the phone number. When calling between two cities which are both within a country's boundaries (except in the US), always drop the country code and add a zero in front of the city code (some listings already do include the zero). Some countries are now dropping the city code and enlarging phone numbers to 9 digits. This requires dialing all digits that appear, including zeros.

■ All the Facts

Up to 32 facts may be included in a given listing. Variations in the length of listings are determined by the amount of information supplied to us by each establishment.

■**Type** - Defines the kind of establishment (bed & breakfast, hotel, resort, etc.), and indicates whether restaurants, bars or shops are on the premises.

■**Clientele** - A more specific and detailed description than provided in the gay orientation & gender line.

■**Transportation** - Tells you if airport/bus pickup is provided and, if not, the best mode of transport is indicated.

■**To Gay Bars** - The distance from your lodgings to the nearest gay or lesbian bar(s).

■**Rooms** - The number and kind of accommodations provided. A cottage or cabin is an accommodation in a freestanding building. A bunkroom is a large room in which beds can be rented singly at a reduced rate. Bed sizes are also indicated.

■**Bathrooms** - The number and type of private bathrooms and shared bathrooms.

■**Campsites** - The number and kind of sites provided. Full RV hookups have both electric and sewer unless otherwise noted.

■**Meals** - Describes meals included with room rate and those available at extra charge. Full breakfast includes meat, eggs and breads with coffee, tea, etc. Continental breakfast consists of breads and jams with coffee, tea, etc.

■**Vegetarian Food** - Availability indicated.

■**Complimentary** - Any complimentary foods, beverages or amenities.

■**Dates Open** - Actual dates, if not open all year.

■**High Season** - Annual season of high occupancy rate.

■**Rates** - The range of rates, from lowest to highest, is given. Note: Rates are subject to change at any time and travelers should always request current rates when making reservations.

■**Discounts** - Amounts and conditions.

■**Credit Cards** - Lists cards accepted (MC=MasterCard, Amex=American Express). Access is MC in Europe. Bancard is British and Australian.

■**Reservations** - Tells if required and how far in advance.

■**Reserve Through** - How to make reservations.

■**Minimum Stay** - If required, indicates how long.

■**Parking** - Availability and type.

■**In-Room** - Facilities provided INSIDE your room (TV, phone, AC, etc).

■**On-Premises** - Facilities not provided inside your room, but available on the premises.

■**Exercise/Health** - Availability of facilities such as hot tub, gym, sauna, steam, massage, weights.

■**Swimming** - Availability, type, location.

■**Sunbathing** - Areas described.

■**Nudity** - Indicates if permitted and where.

■**Smoking** - Restrictions, if any, are noted and availability of non - smokers' rooms is indicated.

■**Pets** - Indicates if permitted, and restrictions are described.

■**Handicap Access** - Indicates if accessible, and limitations are described.

■**Children** - Preferences described.

■**Languages** - All languages spoken by staff.

■**Your host** - Name(s) of innkeeper(s).

■**Travel Safety** - Constantly changing political and social situations in every nation can increase or decrease the risks of visiting any given destination without warning. This book does not include specific information about health and safety risks that readers may encounter in the places described herein. Travelers should always be mindful of their health and safety when traveling or staying in unfamiliar places.

■**Advertisements** - The author, editor, and publisher of this book are not responsible for the contents of advertisements that appear in this book and make no endorsements or guarantees about their accuracy.

■**We Welcome Reader Comments** - Specific information described in the listings, articles and other materials in this book may change without the knowledge of the author, editor and publisher, and the author, editor, and publisher cannot be responsible for the accuracy of such information or advice. We welcome all information sent to us by readers. We will consider your comments and suggestions in updating the next issue. Information on new areas, not yet covered, are especially valued.

RV & CAMPING INDEX

FERRARI GUIDES™

WOMEN'S INDEX

INDEX TO ACCOMMODATIONS

DEF

GHI

JKL

MNO

XYZ

UVW

FERRARI GUIDES™